COURTS AND JUSTICE
A Reader
Second Edition

COURTS AND JUSTICE
A Reader
Second Edition

G. Larry Mays
New Mexico State University

Peter R. Gregware
New Mexico State University

WAVELAND
PRESS, INC.
Prospect Heights, Illinois

For information about this book, write or call:
  Waveland Press, Inc.
  P.O. Box 400
  Prospect Heights, Illinois 60070
  (847) 634-0081

To Otis H. Stephens—mentor and friend—
the person who first sparked my interest in the courts.

GLM

To Nancy, whose caring and ongoing support has made my life
so much better and, thus, this effort so much easier.

PRG

Preface

While continuing the central themes of the first edition, we have made numerous changes in this second edition to update the text where appropriate and to provide a clearer organization for the final two sections. We have also taken into consideration numerous responses from those who have used the text in a classroom context and hope the new text provides appropriate improvements. Twelve new articles have been included in the second edition of which five were written expressly for this text, some by instructors who use the text and felt certain additions would be desirable. We particularly draw your attention to the article by Chaires and Lentz, which may provide valuable assistance to new instructors in this subject area.

The first edition's final section on program implementation and reform has been divided into two different sections in this new edition. Section VI focuses on specialized courts, looking in turn at tribal courts, juvenile courts, drug courts and mental health courts. Section VII addresses three issues related to change: why some good ideas have gone nowhere, why some bad ideas are gaining momentum, and where we can go for new reform ideas. We believe these changes make the complex area of reform more manageable for classes covering the range of court issues, tie reform issues into the text's central themes, and provide appropriate material for classroom discussion.

Acknowledgements

The editors have a number of people to whom we owe a debt of gratitude. First, we appreciate the encouragement and support provided by L. Thomas Winfree, Jr., our department head and colleague. Second, we have benefitted greatly from our undergraduate students at New Mexico State University. They have taught us what does and doesn't work in class, what they have trouble understanding, and what they want to know more about. Third, the editors of the journals and the various authors of the articles we have used were extremely gracious in allowing us to reprint the materials included here. Fourth, the people at Waveland (Neil, Carol, Jeni, Gayle, and others) made this a reasonably painless experience. And, finally, Carlos Posadas and Annette Robinson performed good and faithful services as our graduate assistants throughout this project. Without their conscientious efforts the task would have been much more difficult.

Contents

Introduction 1
Trying to Make Sense of It All

Section I: OVERVIEW OF COURTS **5**

1 In the Eye of the Beholder 7
The Relationship Between the Public and the Courts
Frances Kahn Zemans

2 On the Myth of Written Constitutions 25
The Disappearance of Criminal Jury Trial
John H. Langbein

3 Teaching Courts 33
Some Curriculum and Pedagogy Perspectives
Robert H. Chaires and Susan A. Lentz

Questions to Consider 52

Section II: DECISION MAKING IN THE SHADOWS
Little-Understood Components and Processes in the Criminal Justice System **53**

4 From U.S. Magistrates to U.S. Magistrate Judges 55
Developments Affecting the Federal District Courts' Lower Tier of Judicial Officers
Christopher E. Smith

5 The Changing Role of the United States Courts of Appeals 69
The Flow of Litigation Revisited
Sue Davis And Donald R. Songer

x   Contents

Section III: LIMITING OR TRUSTING JURIES?   115

Section IV: PROBLEMS FOR THE JUDICIARY   205

**Section VII: THE FUTURE OF COURTS
              Thinking Outside the Lines   453**

Introduction
Trying to Make Sense of It All

It has become clear to many of us who toil in the vineyards of court-related research and academic teaching that most students (and citizens in general) do not understand much about courts, and what they do know is often based on inaccurate media representations. Many people cannot articulate basic civic theories about the role of court personnel, such as lawyers and judges, and about the role of courts in enhancing the social good. Aside from emotional responses about the adequacy of government institutions, few can discuss with any specificity how well our current legal institutions actually meet the goals of our social and political theories. When institutions fail to meet our goals, it seems to us imperative that we begin to understand the underlying stresses and conflicts that concerned citizens, both within and outside the court system, must understand if they are to keep government functions which do work and reform those which do not.

The first goal of this text is to provide information on the function of courts and on the underlying conflicts that must be resolved if we are to increase the level of justice that courts can contribute to our society. Here we seek to challenge what are often incorrect assumptions about the roles or functions of courts. Second, we seek to provide in-depth material on often overlooked areas of court study, which hopefully will ensure the clear understanding that can be gained by a multi-faceted perspective. Third, by providing an analysis of court functions and problems, we hope to provide a useful framework for class and small-group discussion. The interactive and personal dynamic provided by such discourse has continually impressed educators with its ability to break down rigid assumptions and inspire deeper levels of discernment. It is to such increasing levels of understanding and insight that we dedicate this book.

There are two major related themes which run throughout these articles. The first is the political nature of courts; courts are political institutions just as much as the legislative or executive branches of government, although the political nature of courts is usually more hidden from the public eye.

1

The second theme is really a question: In a democratic society within a constitutional framework, who owns the courts? That is, do we entrust the operation of our dispute management system to the discretion of professional legal experts, or do citizens have an ongoing and ultimate say in how this essential part of their government operates? The fact that the operation of courts is political not only helps us to answer this question but also helps to explain the ongoing conflict between citizens and professionals over control of our courts.

The first section begins by examining these themes. In the process it asks why approximately one-third of Americans report little or no confidence in our legal system and why this opinion seems to be growing (1999 University of Chicago, National Opinion Research Center).[1] The articles here locate courts in the broader social and political process, looking at the distrust professionals feel toward citizens and distrust many citizens feel toward both the legal professional and the courts.

Much of what courts do remains hidden from public view. The second section explores this shadow world, asking questions about judicial accountability, where judges preside over an institutional world with relatively little public awareness or participation. Here we begin to investigate the political culture of judicial decision making and ask who, if anyone, is responsible for making necessary choices. In the ongoing debate between the values of efficiency and justice, how are these values being balanced and who does the balancing?

Sections III and IV continue this citizen/professional debate by first focusing on citizen/juror participation in the court process: What should be the role of citizens in deciding issues of social concern? To what extent has this role been limited by professional groups wielding the power to do so? Section IV then explores the record of the legal professions' management of our courts. Is the record one of just stewardship or one of a turf battle between "insiders" and "outsiders"? Regardless of the record, how do we now resolve the conflict between the need for some level of judicial independence and the need for accountability to reduce abuses of power?

Section V directly addresses the issue of politics in the courts. Contrary to popular impressions, politics is not a dirty word. The articles in this section reiterate the fact that we cannot escape from politics in the operation of our political institutions. They challenge us not to eliminate politics but rather to seek a balance by harnessing the wisdom acquired through the political process while limiting the prejudices of our human foibles. They also suggest that the more we collectively organize our decision-making processes, the more we can provide accountability in pursuing the goal of justice.

Section VI focuses on current efforts to specialize (or generalize) courts in order to provide structural "fixes" for social problems. Many specialized courts, such as the tribal, juvenile, drug, or mental health courts mentioned in these articles, can provide both laboratories for innovation and expertise in coping with special needs. Politically, some see such courts as catering to special interests when other values, such as uniformity of punishment, are more important. Others may see them as superfluous and feel that they involve courts in areas best handled by other social institutions.

The last section looks to the future by addressing several issues: why some seemingly good ideas have gone nowhere, why some seemingly bad ideas have gained momentum, and where we can look for new ideas to address our most salient problems. Change can be for good or ill, but clearly some change is needed to address ongoing problems.

Each effort at reform must cope with a larger political context that may at times assist but more often may impede these attempts. Additionally, those who work in the court process may actively resist change because it may threaten self-interest or accepted methods of behavior. It is difficult enough to control these interacting elements without taking into consideration the variety of responses resulting from any reforming intervention. It is our hope that by expanding our understanding of both underlying problems and potential conflicts, we can not only increase our ability to formulate appropriate policy but also implement such policies successfully.

Endnote

[1] Joan Biskupic, "Veto by Jury," *Washington Post National Weekly Edition*, March 29, 1999, p. 7.

Section I
Overview of Courts

In the first selection, Frances Zemans lays the groundwork for the subsequent articles contained in this book by highlighting a variety of issues underlying the study of courts, such as the relationship of courts to the political process and the inherent conflicts in mass-production justice. We (the outsiders) gain a vital perspective on courts by attempting to understand our own view of courts and how it might differ from the views of professionals (the insiders) who work within the court system.

Citizen outsiders often have some experience with the court process but still feel less informed about the judicial system than about legislative and executive systems. In an era of growing concern about the operations of government, evidenced by anti-incumbency feelings and disillusionment with administrative operation, there is also increased criticism of judges and decreasing perceptions that courts are places to obtain justice.

While the media clearly have provided a distorted picture of court processes, some of the blame must be placed on insiders, the court personnel who have exhibited some disdain for the public's ability to participate in and understand the judicial process.

This indictment of courts is echoed by John Langbein, who describes how lawyers and judges limit public involvement in court functions by limiting jury trials. He argues that many of these limitations on juries have been (and still are) compounded by the historical decision to adopt an adversary system that gave lawyers the power to control court proceedings. Abuse of this power in turn led to demands that lawyers be controlled, resulting in more and more power being given to lawyers who have been elevated to the rank of judge. Now judges referee a clumsy and time-consuming court process that leads many to seek reductions in the use of jury trials, thus reducing the public involvement in court processes that was envisioned by constitutional framers.

If we are to have an informed citizenry that not only respects the role of courts in society but also is willing to use courts to seek justice, how can exclusion of citizens from the process improve levels of understanding and respect? What changes must be made in the way courts function and in the way court professionals view public involvement?

Finally, Chaires and Lentz provide a much-needed overview, helping us to address the seeming complexity of our court system by placing courts in a broader political and cultural context. They provide insightful categories that readers may wish to revisit as they proceed through the other selections in this text. We begin to understand why our society increasingly relies on courts to resolve our disputes, and we become amused, enlightened, and sometimes a bit depressed at the many ways courts participate in the myths and foibles of the larger political process. Yet the authors also provide the necessary tools for further inquiry, pragmatic methods to separate the ideal from the real, and give incentives to read on. Quite simply, there is power in understanding law in ways that law schools are unwilling to explore. We can begin to understand how courts really work and that they are part of the larger political process in which we all participate. Regardless of the legal jargon used by lawyers and judges, we need no longer be mystified by law.

1

In the Eye of the Beholder
The Relationship Between the Public and the Courts

FRANCES KAHN ZEMANS

Courts as Institutions of Government

In considering the courts' relationship to the public it is appropriate to view the courts as institutions of government and to consider the public's relationship to those institutions more generally. For, as viewed by political scientists, courts very much qualify as political institutions.

The relationship between courts and the public is one of dynamic equilibrium much like that between citizens and other institutions of government. As diagrammed below, the public translates its desires and wants into demands on government.

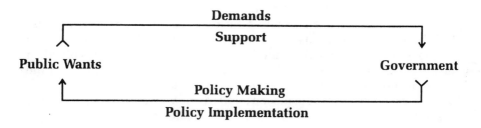

Reprinted by permission of the *Justice System Journal* from vol. 15, no. 2 (1991), pp. 722–740.

Government institutions (including courts) respond by developing policies and taking actions. Outcomes from government activity constitute the feedback to the public that they can evaluate to determine whether their demands have been satisfied. Satisfaction or lack thereof is then expressed in support for that government and/or in further demands upon it.

In practice of course, both support and demands are likely to occur simultaneously. On a day-to-day basis and under most circumstances the public is largely quiescent in relation to its government, thereby providing inactive support. As noted in a classic text on American government, "effective leadership indeed requires compliance with the leaders' decisions from the bulk of the members [of society] . . . most of the time" (Easton, 1975:185). In American society that compliance and support has generally been forthcoming. Political Scientist David Adamany has applied that concept to courts, noting that the public is generally supportive and "permissive." That is to say, the public is largely content to leave both the "agenda and initiative" for court reforms to those most involved in the daily operations of the courts (Adamany, 1978).

There have, however, been times in our history when the citizenry has become more vocal and active, demanding change to better satisfy their desires and wants. Public support for government is not a constant, but rises and falls over time, and the judiciary, as part of that government, is affected by those general shifts in public regard for political institutions. Thus, for example, in recent years we have observed a general decline of public support for government as evidenced in lower voter turnouts, a growth of ballot propositions by which citizens appropriate the legislative function, and widespread discussion of term limitations for office holders. This declining support affects the judiciary as well. For example, in 1990 Missouri's judges were retained in office by the lowest margins since merit selection was adopted in 1940 (Birkes, 1990). In other instances, public dissatisfaction has focused more specifically on the judicial arena.

One example has been society's periodic demands for greater access to justice for the legal claims of ordinary people, claims that are seen as too small to justify the time, money, and complexity involved in normal litigation. One institutional response to this demand was the creation and then national dispersion of small claims courts.[1] The growth of the legal services movement can similarly be viewed as an institutional response to demands by the public for greater access to the judicial system. The recent development of extensive alternative dispute resolution programs is another response, although it is not yet clear whether the public views this as satisfying their current demands for access to justice. (Compare this *Journal*, Volume 14, No. 2 [1990]).

By and large, however, the public has been, and continues to be, extraordinarily supportive of the judicial branch of government. An oft-cited example of this phenomenon was the Supreme Court's 8–0 decision that required then-President Nixon, despite his insistence otherwise, to cooperate in a criminal investigation by turning over his presidential tapes to prosecutors. Two messages of that decision were very clear and widely accepted. First, under a system that operates within the rule of law, even the rulers are subject to that law. Second, and more closely related to our concerns here, is that when it comes to a determination of whether the law applies even to the individual who has been elected by the people at large, it is the courts (and in this instance unelected courts) who are accepted as the appropriate decision-makers.

Courts are also significantly different from other political institutions. They are different in two very important ways that are worth addressing here. First, the courts are in many ways the institutions with which individual citizens most directly interact, or at least have the potential for interacting. Unlike other institutions of government where citizen action is most typically engaged in as a group activity (and indeed is most effective as a group activity), interaction with a court is by and large an individual enterprise. There are, of course, group actions in court and we continue to see attempts by organizations with particular interests to use the courts to achieve their goals. Still, that remains a relatively small proportion of the work of the courts. By and large the courts respond to the demands of individual citizens; it is indeed the one governmental institution for which a demand by a single individual is sufficient to evoke a full hearing. Such a hearing in some cases may even result in governmental policy-making with wide and long-term implications. The classic example is the case of Clarence Gideon whose pencil-written note to the Supreme Court complaining of a lack of a fair hearing because of his inability to pay for a lawyer resulted in a Sixth Amendment guarantee of free counsel in all felony cases (*Gideon v. Wainwright*, 372 U.S. 335 (1963)).

Second, and as we will see later, the public still considers the courts the place to go to get what is their due. In the aggregate these individual interactions with a large proportion of the citizenry provides courts with both a burden and an opportunity. Courts have an opportunity to engender a broad base of support that is necessary to the operation of governmental institutions; at the same time, that extent of interaction also opens the courts to demands for accountability and for responsiveness from a broad base of the society. We will return later to the implications of the double-edged sword of citizens' interaction with their courts.

Courts are also distinctive among the branches of government in the extent to which they are dependent on others for setting their agendas.

It is true that appellate courts by the nature and content of their decisions often send signals as to the kinds of cases and arguments that they would be receptive to hearing. Indeed even trial courts by the pattern of their decisions send signals that help generate the many settlements that occur in our legal system (see Mnookin, 1979). Still, as compared to other institutions courts are truly at the mercy of others for setting their agenda and determining their workload. One need look no further than the contemporary influx of drug cases in both state and federal courts to observe this phenomenon.

Courts are expected to continue their normal operations to satisfy demands of the populace over a wide range of issues and yet still handle the geometric growth in drug cases. Unfortunately, though perhaps predictably, political demands for the investment of more and more resources in drug enforcement almost always overlook the need to increase court resources in a like manner. Indeed, the courts are often projected in political rhetoric as part of the problem rather than part of the solution.

As Alexander Hamilton noted in *The Federalist Papers* No. 78, the courts have neither the power of the sword nor the power of the purse to enable them to address some of their most serious needs. While, according to Hamilton, that made the judiciary the least dangerous of the three branches of government, it also left it vulnerable to the support of others. It is often noted in the literature that courts must rely on general public grants of authority and legitimacy and that such grants are critical to their power and the role they play in our system of government. But relying on that kind of support can be hazardous, for unlike the other branches, the judiciary has few natural supporters. Most critically, the support the courts enjoy is diffuse support, that is, spread throughout the society as opposed to narrowly organized in the kinds of special interest groups that are so effective in generating both funding and support for particular governmental programs.

Public debate on issues like the exclusionary rule and judicial salaries is conducted largely in a substantive vacuum. Whatever one's view of the exclusionary rule, to be understood at all, it requires comprehension of the adversary system that structures our judicial process. Such understanding is clearly not widespread. The same can be said regarding the public debate over judicial salaries. The public support necessary for the courts to function is directly related to public knowledge and the level of public debate about our judicial institutions. Court personnel have a central role to play. For communication between the courts and the citizenry can help build the constituency necessary to support the courts and enhance the perceived and actual quality of justice.

Public Knowledge of the Courts

A treasury of anecdotes could be offered to make the point that this theme might well be public ignorance, not knowledge, of the courts. There is also considerable systematic documentation of the breadth of public misunderstanding of the courts. The results of a survey commissioned by the *National Law Journal* and LEXIS to mark the 200th anniversary of the establishment of the Supreme Court is a recent case in point. The survey found that less than a quarter of Americans over the age of 18 knew the number of justices on the United States Supreme Court (*National Law Journal* 1990:1). Close to two-thirds of the respondents could not name a single justice (a note of interest is that the best known justice was Sandra Day O'Connor). Such ignorance of the judicial system has been documented more than once. A 1978 survey by Yankelovich, Skelly and White revealed the public's self-perceived lack of familiarity with the federal, state, and local courts. From 63 percent to 77 percent of the respondents reported knowing very little or nothing about the courts (Yankelovich, 1978). "The American public, the Media and the Judicial System," a national survey sponsored by the Hearst Corporation in 1983, had similar results. The survey revealed that the public feels least informed about the judicial system as compared to other branches of government; responses to other questions indicate the validity of that perception. For example, 77 percent of the respondents believe that every decision by a state court can be reviewed and reversed by the U.S. Supreme Court, and less than half (44%) know that federal judges are appointed for good behavior. Unfortunately, most undergraduate curricula do little to address this problem.

Several years ago the American Judicature Society surveyed major American government textbooks and a more limited number of state government and urban politics texts and discovered that despite the co-equal formal status of the judicial branch of government, it is accorded only limited attention in the teaching of American government. Moreover, it is typically treated as a separate module without integration with other topics. The presentation goes something like this. A brief reference to Article III of the United States Constitution is followed by a short discussion of the United States Supreme Court. The Court, students are told, decided *Marbury v. Madison* and *Brown v. Board of Education*, among other cases. After the appropriate discussion of the relevance of these to judicial review and the civil rights movement respectively, little more is said about the third branch of government. The not very subliminal message conveyed by this brief coverage and quick progression to other topics is that the courts are not very important to understanding our system of government.

Some years ago A. Bartlett Giamatti, then President of Yale University, in a speech before the Second Circuit Judicial Conference expressed the need for general education in the law:

> I think America's ignorance about the law is neither inevitable nor trivial; I also think it is a scandal. And so must anyone who believes that the rule of law in a democracy must assume first comprehension on the part of the citizenry in order then to be effective on behalf of the citizenry. (Giamatti 1983:34)

What is to be done about this reality? And who is to do it? It will be a theme addressed later that it is in the self-interest of those intimately involved in the operation of the courts to attempt to fill this gap. But lest we think this job is an easy one, we need recognize not only that there has been a gap in education about the courts, but that the public is regularly exposed to misrepresentation of the judicial process that makes the job significantly more difficult.

The Courts and the Media

Media coverage of the courts takes two distinct forms, although it is not always clear which form contributes more to public misunderstanding of the courts. First, there is the entertainment side of the media, which devotes a significant amount of time to the administration of justice. Clearly, television networks and cable channels have discovered that the American public has an enormous appetite for this topic. There are the early entries like "The Defenders" and "Perry Mason," the latter of which remains popular in reruns and now is broadcast in a new and updated version. There is "Miami Vice," it too in continuous reruns in which almost every potential defendant is "taken care of" before entering the judicial process at all. There is, of course, "L.A. Law," the popular weekly night-time soap that is credited by many law school deans with having contributed significantly to the recent upsurge in law school applications. One can only wonder whether it is the intricacies of the law or the lifestyle of Arnie Becker that is the major attraction. "Equal Justice" appears to be the latest entry, modeled after "L.A. Law," but set in a metropolitan prosecutor's office.

And then there is the ubiquitous Judge Wapner who, as noted in a devastating review by D.C. circuit federal appeals court Judge Abner Mikva, may be the most troubling of all. Precisely because of the "veneer of realism" that exists in Judge Wapner's courtroom, the clear implication is that this is how the administration of justice works in this country, and how it ought to work (Mikva, 1989). The veneer of realism to which he refers and which he finds most troubling is that it "offers itself up as a slice of real law'' (at 14). It has real people with real controversies. It has a real judge—or at least a real former judge, sporting the real trappings of a judge: a high bench and a black robe. After documenting a number of legal errors in Wapner's courtroom, Judge Mikva expresses particular concern about Judge Wapner's judicial temperament or lack thereof. In one example, Wapner ends the argument between two dog owners by announcing "there will be no more testimony. I'm leaving now." Judge Mikva notes that most real trial judges would be delighted to know that they could stop testimony whenever they felt like it. He concludes with his verdict that the show "does for law what Dynasty does for monogamy" (at 14).

The media, of course, do not have to rely on dramatic representations or fictional stories to present the judicial process in a way that will be appealing to the average viewer. As noted in a recent critique of television coverage, "trials that earn the most attention from local news and magazine shows, not to speak of docudramas, have all the elements of the nation's prime-time favorites: sex and violence, conflict and commotion" (Goodman, 1990: B1 and B6). Missing from this coverage, Goodman goes on to note, are the subtleties that are also involved in such major trials. The typical report conveys very little understanding of the law or judicial process. Goodman actually asks quite a bit more when pointing out that trials, in addition to being inherently dramatic, are "tests of the society, and the way those tests are conducted can reveal its strengths and weaknesses. That aspect rarely makes it to the tube" (Goodman, 1990:B1).

With the trend toward cameras in the courtroom (44 states allow cameras in some courtrooms and an experiment is being conducted in selected federal courts), there is an opportunity to do more; whether that opportunity will be pursued is as yet an open question. It is certainly the case that the trials that have received gavel to gavel coverage have, in most instances, also been the most sensational. Still it could be argued that gavel-to-gavel coverage will in and of itself bring out some of the subtleties and complexities that are inherent in any real trial. That opportunity is now being explored by a new cable channel devoted exclusively to the judicial process and the legal system. The channel will rely heavily on coverage of actual trials. What remains to be seen is whether it will do what it promises and use coverage of the courtroom to convey a true understanding of the judicial process.

As noted by Steven Brill, publisher and editor-in-chief of *The American Lawyer Magazine* and founder and president of the new cable channel, "the irony of the debate over cameras in the courtroom is that, of the three branches of government, the judiciary's work is clearly meant to be public and is clearly the most amenable to television coverage" (1990:3). Brill goes on to point out that the clarity of the judiciary's work is in stark contrast to coverage of the floor of the United States Congress or television speeches of the President. The bulk of the work of those branches of government goes on behind closed doors. What you see is decidedly not what you get. With the judiciary, what you see is precisely what you get. ABC Network News legal affairs reporter Tim O'Brien, in a speech at the Mid-year Meeting of the American Judicature Society, stated that the best kept secret in our government is just how well the judiciary works (1990:341). Perhaps done well, day-to-day coverage of trials with appropriate commentary will make that less of a secret.

There is more to news about of the judicial system than even that revealed in the coverage of sensational trials; it has to do with coverage that seeks to contribute to public understanding of how the process works and to examine the courts as institutions of government. It may be here that the journalists' lack of understanding is perhaps the most damaging and the most subject to manipulation by interested parties. News coverage of an unpopular ruling is illustrative of the problem.

Unlike other public office-holders, judges are little known to the citizenry at-large. If a mayor, governor, or legislator does something that enrages constituents, it can be put in the context of other information that is known and other policies that are attached to that governmental actor. For judges it is typically only the individual controversial decision that is the measure of performance. The public has no broader context within which to evaluate the judge.

It is almost unheard of for news reports on these kinds of decisions to include any reference to the fact that making unpopular decisions is part of the job of being a judge. That the role of the judge is to be faithful to the Constitution and the law even if the result reached is not the one preferred by the judge. There was, for example, virtually nothing in the very extensive coverage of the flag-burning case that in any way suggested that this decision did not mean that the United States Supreme Court was condoning flag-burning. While the media certainly have no obligation to address the institutional role of the courts, the reality is that it is not done elsewhere. Public reliance on the media for such information does at a minimum provide an opportunity for them to inform the public more broadly.

This is not to suggest that if only there were better media coverage of the courts the result would be strong public support for the courts. But better coverage and more information would be beneficial by generating respect for those aspects of the system worthy of respect, and generating demands for change in those aspects of the system that clearly bear changing.

Citizens' Experience with the Courts

Public opinion on any topic is influenced both by personal experience and by what one learns from others. As has been made clear elsewhere, attitudes about personal experiences may vary significantly from views about the operation of institutions more generally. For example, Curran (1977) has documented that members of the public have much more positive attitudes toward their own lawyers based on actual experience with those lawyers than they do toward the legal profession as a whole. To the extent that the same may be true with regard to the judiciary, it is worth considering some recent studies that examine public views about the courts based on personal experience.

The first is a study conducted by psychologist Tom Tyler based on a survey of Chicago residents. Close to 1,600 respondents were first interviewed by telephone in 1984; a subsample of more than 800 respondents was subsequently reinterviewed in 1985. Focusing particularly on the courts and the police, the study examined personal contacts that citizens had with authorities where they had a "personal stake in the situation." The research indicates that the attitudes of the citizens who have participated in the judicial process is not so much a matter of whether they have won or lost, but very much a matter of how they perceive they have been treated. People seem to care most about having neutral, honest authorities who allow them to state their views and who treat them with dignity and respect. Interestingly, judgments of that fairness are independent of success in the courtroom. The study demonstrates that people comply with the law if they feel that legal authorities are legitimate, and views of that legitimacy are linked to the perceived fairness of the procedures used by those legal authorities (Tyler, 1990). The message to judges and court administrators may be that the treatment of judicial system clients will have a major impact on how those people view that system. In the aggregate those experiences may bear on the extent to which the public will grant the authority and legitimacy that the judicial system needs to fulfill its role.

Another recent study may shed some interesting light on the findings of the 1978 Yankelovich survey referred to earlier. It was found in the earlier study that courts dealing with minor criminal and juvenile matters receive more unfavorable ratings than civil and major criminal courts (Mahoney, et al., 1978:83). To some extent that may be a reflection of Tyler's findings that attitudes are particularly influenced by perceptions of fair treatment. For it is precisely in the high-volume minor criminal and juvenile courts where the formal procedures that may generate a sense of fairness are sometimes short-circuited in the interests of moving the caseload. But it also may be that those somewhat more negative views reflect a significant variance between court personnel and the public as to what it is that courts can and should achieve in dealing with what the system views as relatively minor matters.

Merry (1990) recently examined the use of courts for help with personal problems such as protection from violence, controlling neighbors and relatives, or managing rebellious teenagers. What she found was that plaintiffs come to court with a very different view from the one with which they are received. They come with a sense of entitlement and a desire to assert legal claims. They want to get the zero-sum game that they view on television dramatizations of the courtroom. They want a winner and a loser; they want an assertion of who is right and who is wrong and they want those deemed wrong to be punished. The courts, in contrast, receive these claims with great ambivalence. Court personnel try to provide help for what they see as problems rather that to focus on underlying legal claims. Many complaints are seen by the courts as frivolous, with lectures or direction to social service agencies deemed appropriate responses. Yet what the plaintiffs want is protection or punishment. The fact that many or most of these claims are interpersonal in nature does not diminish the plaintiffs' perceptions of legal entitlement.

This discontinuity between what the claimants seek and the way in which the courts respond may help explain why burgeoning alternative dispute resolution mechanisms are still a supply largely in search of a demand. For there remains an enormous reservoir of public trust in the courts and a belief that the courts are responsible to citizens as Americans to protect their rights to property and their safety (Merry, 1990:2). These claimants over so-called minor issues find it easy to get into court, but much more difficult to get a hearing before a judge; and they find it even more difficult to get punishment for an adversary or an abusive spouse (Merry, 1990:3).

It is in this context that nonjudicial court personnel exert great influence on public perceptions of the courts. According to Merry, the courts these people get are not those of elaborate procedures and complex rules. Rather they are exposed to informality and the attention of lesser court actors. Yet the working poor she studied "share the common American understanding that all members of society are entitled to ask the courts for help in protecting their fundamental rights" (Merry, 1990:17).

Whose Courts Are They Anyway?

In 1979 the Wingspread Conference on Contemporary and Future Issues in the Field of Court Management was held in Racine, Wisconsin. The goal was to review developments in court administration and to consider contemporary and future issues in the field. According to the conference reporters, one conferee characterized the public view of the courts as "a private game preserve in which judges, lawyers and frequent litigants romp playfully while those who foot much of the bill watch from over the fence" (Nejelski and Wheeler, 1979:10). There are many who would suggest that little has changed since then.

The *Report of the Federal Courts Study Committee* unfortunately reflects the same reality. The report proposed an extraordinary number of substantive changes in the operation of the courts that were clearly designed to enhance the administration of justice in the United States. Yet the work of the Committee as reflected in the report looked inward. The Committee gave little cognizance to the important link between the courts and the public they were created to serve. The suggested designation of a media contact person for each of the federal circuits (*Report*, 1990:164) does not serve this purpose, for it focuses on improving the image of the courts rather than enhancing public understanding. In reflecting upon its burdensome caseload the *Report* goes on to comment that "many . . . people do not realize, however—or do not care—that the demands they place on the system make it less able to serve the needs of other groups, or even their own needs in the long run" (*Report*, 1990:4). At the same time, however, the Committee fails to acknowledge that the taxpayers are unlikely to foot the bill for a system they do not see as closely tied to their own lives.

Another recent example of a similar attitude toward the public is found in *The Report of the Twentieth Century Fund Task Force on Judicial Selection* (1989), which made a number of suggestions to enhance our system of selecting federal judges. The attitude toward the public is expressed in two ways in the report. First, and to its credit, the task force recommends the following: bipartisan nominating commissions to screen and recommend nominees, advance announcement of confirmation hearings on nominees, and open Senate subcommittee hearings in the locale of the vacancy (*Report*, 1989). Unfortunately, the task force fails to mention any role that the public could appropriately play in this process. Instead they emphasize the importance of participation by leaders of state and local bar associations and of announcing the upcoming confirmation hearings in legal newspapers and periodicals. While that is certainly proper, the report would have done well to consider the role that non-lawyer members of the general public should play in the selection of federal judges and how notice of hearings for that consideration might be communicated to them.

When it came to Supreme Court nominations, the task force, (although with some dissent) suggested that to depoliticize the process nominees should no longer appear before the Senate Judiciary Committee. While depoliticization of that process may be a worthy goal, Senate confirmation is intended to be a democratic check on a non-democratic branch of government. To exclude the populace from that process smacks of an elitism that is untenable in a democratic society.

There are a whole host of other examples that reflect a disdain for the public and their ability to participate in and understand the judicial process. These include objections to juror participation in complex trials, a hesitancy (if not outright objection) to allowing cameras into public courtrooms, and a hesitancy (if not outright objection) to more active juror participation in trials through both note-taking or jurors asking questions of witnesses. It should be noted that judicial experience with cameras in the courtroom, juror note-taking, and juror question-asking tends to make judges more positive toward these mechanisms. Still, they are resisted in a way that the public can certainly interpret as a closing of ranks and containment of the judicial process for professionals only.

Language in the courtroom continues to be a problem both for jurors and litigants. The oft-quoted Will Rogers observation makes the point: "the minute you read something that you can't understand, you can almost be sure it was drawn up by a lawyer" (Wilde, 1987). A humorous example of this phenomenon in operation is quoted by 2nd Circuit federal appeals court Judge Roger Miner in a recent law review article. The courtroom exchange goes something like this:

Q. Mrs. Jones, is your appearance pursuant to a deposition notice which I sent to your attorney?

A. No, this is how I dress when I go to work. (Miner, 1989:6 quoting Lederer, 1987:33).

In addition, despite the yeoman efforts of many, by and large jury instructions continue to be written for appellate courts and not for jurors.

Closing out the public in the long run will not enhance the status of the judiciary or its capacity to make its unique contribution to our system of government. Public frustration is high, and we are seeing some of its results in efforts to limit the powers and prerogatives of the courts. Judicial responses to these efforts are too often framed in a rather simplistic separation of powers argument that sounds to the public suspiciously like "we are above it all; trust us, we will do the right thing." There are better and more articulate responses that can and should be made, but without greater public understanding of the process it is difficult to make them effectively.

Capacity of the Public to Know and Participate

Broad ignorance of the courts does not necessarily indicate a lack of capacity on the part of the public to better understand the American judicial system. There are numerous examples of direct public participation in the operation of the judicial system that suggest that not only does the public have the ability to understand and participate, but that they bring a very special and important perspective to a system that is otherwise operated by insiders. The most obvious example is the jury, even though as mentioned above there are continuing efforts to eliminate the right to a jury trial in highly-complex cases. Yet time and time again in very complicated and controversial cases juries exhibit the capacity to understand and to do justice. Several examples come to mind.

First is the now somewhat infamous Chicago Seven trial that was the federal government's attempt to establish criminal responsibility for the demonstrations and subsequent rioting that occurred surrounding the 1968 Democratic national convention. In that case the defendants, the defense counsel, the prosecutors, and even the judge each made their own individual contributions to generating a circus-like atmosphere that has no place in the courtroom. Despite that atmosphere, extraordinary media coverage, and the simultaneous prosecution of seven quite distinct defendants, the jury of ordinary citizens did a remarkable job fashioning different verdicts for each of the seven defendants. While the judge's contempt rulings were overturned on appeal, all of the jury's verdicts were upheld.

The next example is the well-reported Texaco-Penzoil case. One of the arguments made by Texaco in the trial was that there were industry standards and complex issues that jurors could not understand. But the jury understood rather clearly. Their conclusion was that "a deal is a deal." As intended in our common-law system the jury brought community notions of fairness and justice to bear in their decision making.

A third and final case appropriate to mention in this context is the prosecution of Imelda Marcos. There in the glare of a highly-public prosecution with the investment of enormous amounts of government resources, the jury stood their ground and entered a not guilty verdict.

Other examples of public participation in the judicial process include non-lawyer membership in judicial nominating commissions in merit selection states and in judicial conduct commissions in all 50 states and the District of Columbia. In both of these contexts, non-lawyers bring a very special perspective to selecting and evaluating candidates for judicial office and then determining whether or not judges should be subject to discipline. The experience of the American Judicature Society working with both judicial nominating commissions and judicial conduct commissions suggests that non-lawyers take their roles in those processes extremely seriously. The role of lawyers, and in some case judges, on those bodies is certainly critically important. But non-lawyers

what about a citizen panel to advise those who appt judges - to visit courtrooms + report back — example - re FC judges to mayor ?

often see things quite differently and bring a public perspective that is invaluable. Such public participation may also generate broad support for the institution.

What Can Be Done and Who Is to Do It?

More than a decade ago at the Wingspread Conference a sharp distinction was drawn between "taking the courts' case to the public and recognizing communication as an organic relationship from which courts can learn as well as teach" (Nejelski and Wheeler, 1979:10). There was a call for dialogue between the judiciary and other segments of the society emphasizing that "improved communications is a two-way street: courts must be prepared to listen to 'outsiders' as well as to convey information about themselves" (Mahoney, et al., 1978:91).

A true dialogue requires a degree of mutual respect between participants. Such respect for the public must pervade the system if the courts wish the larger society to believe that they are in the business of providing justice. Despite this, our mechanisms for selecting and evaluating those seeking positions as judges, court managers, or other court personnel give scant attention to these issues.

We neither train nor provide incentives for court personnel to treat the public with respect or to view them as having worthy ideas to improve the administration of justice. It may well be that the courts could learn from private industry how to best serve their customers, to learn what they want and to shape their behavior accordingly. Viewing the public as consumers to be satisfied is not at all natural for institutions that have had a traditional monopoly on services. But as is clear for courts, schools, prisons, and other institutions, competitive alternatives are emerging that are challenging public monopolies. For all of these it is not only a question of losing "customers" but of losing the public support necessary if the courts are to fulfill their role in our system of government.

Much communication with the public necessarily occurs through the media. Here too, the courts are capable of doing much more. While public information officers for court systems may be a good idea, they can play only a small part in the important process of communication. Courts can work with the press and make it easier for them to find answers to their questions. A simple "no comment" is neither required by standards of judicial ethics nor is it very effective. It serves only to enhance public perceptions that this is a system closed to them. Judge Nat Hentel of the Supreme Court of New York, appearing on a panel devoted to "[j]udges, critics and the public interest: balancing competing values," suggested that judges take the responsibility of educating journalists and use them as surrogates to educate the public (*Judicature*, 1989:231). Such efforts, however, cannot be postponed until election time. There must be more general accessibility if genuine communication is to be achieved.

The argument for the courts to increase their interaction with the media is not based solely on the courts' need to be understood. More importantly, the public needs to know what their courts are doing. Ongoing communications also provide opportunities to move from a discussion of an individual case to consideration of the judicial process more generally; it allows an opportunity to clarify the limits that the people, through their legislators, place on judicial decision making. At the appellate level, for example, reporters can be given advance notice of decisions and the date that they will be announced, allowing reporters the opportunity to give more time and thoughtful analysis to the case at hand. Availability to the press and public will of course increase accountability and produce predictable moments of discomfort. Caution is advisable so as to provide appropriate information without violating ethical restraints. But it is unacceptable and dysfunctional for judges to hide behind those restraints and thereby contribute to public misunderstanding of the judicial process.

Many courts are not only aware of a need for increased and better communications with the public, but many have acted upon that belief by developing a variety of creative programs. For example, the Administrative Office of the California Supreme Court has set up public meetings with judges around the state. The meetings last three hours and invite the public to ask general questions about the operation of the courts in that jurisdiction and to get answers directly from their judges. Response has been favorable among the citizens as well as the judges. The State of Colorado has two groups active in giving information about the courts to the public, the Colorado Judicial Planning Council Forum and the Colorado Judicial Institute. The Planning Council Forum, appointed by the Chief Justice, provides a speakers' bureau to citizens' groups. The Judicial Institute provides in-service teacher training, mock trial competition, publications, and public forums for discussion of matters involving the courts. In addition, the Colorado Supreme Court itself holds oral arguments at selected high schools around the state after first supplying teachers with the briefs in the cases to assist them in preparing their students. The State of Nebraska publishes a book for the public on the organizational structure of the Nebraska courts, and in Hawaii there is a simple but effective booklet on the judicial selection method used in that state.

What else can be done? The answer is many things indeed. At a May, 1990 conference on "The Future and the Courts," co-sponsored by the American Judicature Society and the State Justice Institute, participants were required to look into the future and see the justice system as they envisioned it would become. Upon establishing a variety of possible futures, participants were asked to choose their preferred vision and then to develop strategies that would be most likely to achieve it. The range of suggestions reflects a strong preference for judicial proactivity in relationship to the American public.

Suggestions included the following:

- develop a response office to answer questions from the public and interpret the process for them, to refer complainants to appropriate agencies and services, and to develop emergency legal triage;
- create a court ombudsman;
- develop programs to identify the functionally illiterate who could not possibly successfully manage their way through the judicial system as it is currently structured;
- create citizen advisory panels;
- expand court hours to nights and weekends;
- develop courthouses on wheels;
- open court proceedings to real-time media coverage;
- increase use of lay advocates;
- simplify language and procedures; and
- conduct market surveys of the consumers of court services. (1990:17)

While not every suggested strategy constituted efforts to increase the dialogue with the public and/or make the courts more user-friendly, many of those involved in the conference were struck by the consistency of support for more proactive efforts to achieve genuine communication with and provide service for the public at large.

How do we get the public to identify independence and intellectual honesty as virtues to be supported in our judicial system? How do courts get the public support they need if they are to act effectively on behalf of the public? These are difficult questions and we have only scratched the surface of possible answers; but several things are clear. It will take effort and it will take time, and it will take a willingness to accept the criticism and increased demand for accountability that will come with more understanding. Most of all, it will take commitment on the part of those involved in the courts.

Endnote

[1] For a discussion of the emergence of small claims courts see Steele (1981: 293).

References

Adamany, David (1978) *The Implementation of Court Improvement.* Williamsburg, VA: National Center for State Courts.

Birkes, Keith (1990) "Conversation with Kathleen M. Sampson," November.

Brill, Steven (1990) "Watching the Drama of Justice," *The American Lawyer,* July.

Curran, Barbara (1977) *The Legal Needs of the Public.* Chicago: American Bar Foundation.

Dator, James A. and Sharon J. Rodgers (1990) *The Future and the Courts Conference Executive Summary.* Chicago: American Judicature Society.

Easton, David (1975) *The Political System.* Chicago: University of Chicago Press.

Giamatti, A. Bartlett (1983) "The Law and the Public," 38 *The Record of the Association of the Bar of the City of New York* 34.

Goodman, Walter (1990) "TV and the Irresistible Melodrama of America's Legal System of Action," *New York Times,* July 26, B1 and B6.

Judicature (1989) "Judges, Critics and the Public Interest: Balancing Competing Values," 72/4 *Judicature* 226.

Lederer, R. (1987) *Anguished English: An Anthology of Accidental Assaults upon our Language.*

Mahoney, Barry, Austin Sarat and Steven Weller (1978) "Courts and the Public: Some Further Reflections on Data from a National Survey," in *State Courts: A Blueprint for the Future,* T. Fetter (ed.). Williamsburg, VA: National Center for State Courts.

Merry (1990) *Getting Justice and Getting Even, Legal Consciousness Among Working-Class Americans.* Chicago: University of Chicago Press.

Mikva, Abner (1989) "The Verdict on Judge Wapner," *TV Guide,* April 22, 13.

Miner, Roger J. (1989) "Confronting the Communication Crisis in the Legal Profession," 34 *New York Law School Review* 6.

Mnookin, Robert and Lewis Kornhauser (1979) "Bargaining in the Shadow of the Law: The Case of Divorce," 88 *Yale Law Journal* 950.

National Law Journal (1989) "Don't Mess with the Mouse," July 31, 1.

_____ (1990) "How Americans View the High Court," February 26, 1.

Nejelski, Paul and Russell Wheeler (1979) *Conference Report,* Wingspread Conference on Contemporary and Future Issues in the Field of Court Management. Institute for Court Management.

O'Brien, Tim (1990) "The Best Kept Secrets of the Judiciary," 73/6 *Judicature* 341.

Report of the Federal Courts Study Committee (1990).

Report of the Twentieth Century Fund Task Force on Judicial Selection (1989).

Steele, Eric H. (1981) "The Historical Context of Small Claims Courts," *American Bar Foundation Research Journal* 293.

Toward More Active Juries: Taking Notes and Asking Questions (1990) Chicago: American Judicature Society.

Tyler, Tom R. (1990) *Why People Obey the Law.* New Haven, CT: Yale University Press.

Wilde, L. (1987) *The Ultimate Lawyer's Jokebook*.
Yankelovich, Skelly and White (1978) "Highlights of a National Survey of the General Public," *State Courts: A Blueprint for the Future*, T. Fetter (ed.). Williamsburg, VA: National Center for State Courts.

2

On the Myth of Written Constitutions
The Disappearance of Criminal Jury Trial

JOHN H. LANGBEIN

We are accustomed to viewing the Bill of Rights as a success story. With it, the American constitution-makers opened a new epoch in the centuries-old struggle to place effective limits on the abuse of state power. Not all of the Bill of Rights is a success story, however. While we are celebrating the Bill of Rights, we would do well to take note of that chapter of the Bill of Rights that has been a spectacular failure: the Framers' effort to embed jury trial as the exclusive mode of proceeding in cases of serious crime.

I. The Constitutionalization of Jury Trial

The Sixth Amendment says: "In *all* criminal prosecutions, the accused shall enjoy the right to a speedy and public trial, by an impartial jury of the State and district wherein the crime shall have been committed. . . ."[1] "All" is not a word that constitution-makers use lightly. The drafters of the Sixth Amendment used it and meant it. Indeed, the Framers of the Constitution had already used the same word for the same

Reprinted by permission of the *Harvard Journal of Law and Public Policy* from vol. 15, no. 1. (winter, 1992), pp. 119–127.

end when speaking to the same subject two years earlier. Article III of the Constitution insists: "The Trial of *all* Crimes, except in Cases of Impeachment, shall be by Jury. . . ."[2]

Two hundred years later, this Constitution and its Bill of Rights continue to govern our criminal justice system. Indeed, because the Sixth Amendment has been treated as incorporated by the Fourteenth Amendment, the federal jury guarantee now governs not only in the federal courts that the Framers had in mind, but also in the state systems where we process the bulk of our criminal caseloads.[3]

Although the texts mandate jury trial for "all" criminal cases, the reality is far different. In place of "all," a more accurate term to describe the use of jury trial in the discharge of our criminal caseload would be "virtually none." Like those magnificent guarantees of human rights that grace the pretended constitutions of totalitarian states, our guarantee of routine criminal jury trial is a fraud.

This article discusses the astonishing discrepancy between what the constitutional texts promise and what the criminal justice system delivers.

II. Non-Trial Procedure

Why did the Framers call for jury trial in "all" criminal cases? They prescribed "all" because they experienced "all." In the world in which they lived, on both sides of the Atlantic, cases of serious crime systematically went to full jury trial. Jury trial was the routine dispositive proceeding of Eighteenth-Century Anglo-American law. We have historical records from the English sources of a few Eighteenth-Century cases in which some pathetic accused, caught in the act or otherwise sensing the hopelessness of his case, attempted to plead guilty. In these cases, the trial judge resisted accepting the guilty plea. Time and again the judge urged the accused to plead "not guilty" and to take his case to the jury.[4] The great historian of English criminal law, John Beattie of Toronto, has studied this question closely in the surviving Eighteenth-Century records of the county of Surrey, south of London. He reports: "Virtually every prisoner charged with a felony insisted on taking his trial, with the obvious support and encouragement of the court. There was no plea bargaining in felony cases in the eighteenth century."[5]

Return now from the Framers' world of routine jury trial to the practice of our own day. The Constitution has not changed, the Bill of Rights remains in force, and jury trial lives on in the law books as our prototypical mode of discharging cases of serious crime. Furthermore, were you to form your impression of modern American criminal procedure from our popular culture, as nonlawyers and foreigners tend to do, you would scarcely have occasion to notice that anything has changed. Television is busy broadcasting courtroom dramas that culminate in the verdict of a criminal jury trial.

Those who understand our criminal justice system know better. Criminal jury trial has all but disappeared in the United States. Can you find it? Of course, you can find it. You can find it in the show trials of the day, Oliver North, General Noriega, or whatever. But jury trial no longer typifies our system. Can you find a hippopotamus in the Bronx? Yes, there's one in the Bronx Zoo, but it has nothing to do with life in the Bronx. It's a goner. And so, too, stunningly, is criminal jury trial, which has ceased to typify American criminal justice. The criminal justice system now disposes of virtually all cases of serious crime without jury trial, through the plea bargaining system. This non-trial procedure has become the ordinary dispositive procedure of American criminal justice.[6]

The plea bargaining system operates by threat. The authorities who administer our non-jury and non-trial procedure tell the accused in effect: "So you want your constitutional right to jury trial? By all means, be our guest. But beware. If you claim this right and are convicted, we will punish you twice, once for the offense, and once again for having displayed the temerity to exercise your constitutional right to jury trial." Our authorities are, of course, more circumspect in their discourse. They do not need to convey this threat in the bald fashion that I have just expressed it. There is no doubt, however, that plea bargaining works precisely in this way. Whether plea bargaining takes the form of charge bargaining (a lesser offense in exchange for a guilty plea) or sentence bargaining (a reduced sanction in exchange for a guilty plea), the object is to coerce the accused to surrender his right to jury trial by threatening him with a materially greater sanction if he exercises that right.

In observing that the Framers spoke of jury trial in "all" cases of serious crime—that jury trial was their norm—I do not mean to say that they mandated jury trial. Jury trial was indeed waivable. Then as now, the defendant had the option to plead guilty. What he lacked was the inducement. Because prosecutorial authorities were not yet in the business of pressuring people to decline trial, the Framers did not forbid practices that they had no reason to foresee.

III. The Disappearance of Jury Trial

How did criminal jury trial disappear? There is much we do not know, but the historical outline seems tolerably clear.[7] The starting point is to understand that criminal jury trial as the Framers observed it on both sides of the Atlantic in the second half of the Eighteenth Century was a summary proceeding.

The trial that the Framers thought they were constitutionalizing was, by our standards, shockingly brusque and deficient in safeguard. In the Old Bailey in London, the principal court for the trial of serious crime in the Anglo-American world, a dozen or more cases of felony jury trial went forward in a single courtroom in a single day.[8] The procedures were crude. Lawyers were infrequently involved for prosecution or defense.[9] There was almost no law of evidence. The "beyond-reasonable-doubt" standard of proof was neither precisely formulated nor routinely announced.[10] There was no *voir dire* of jurors; challenge rights were virtually never exercised. Jurors sat on many trials during a single session, and many of them were experienced veterans who had sat at previous sessions. They received little judicial guidance and may not have needed much.[11] The accused conducted his own defense, usually without aid of counsel, and without being allowed to testify under oath. There was virtually no appellate review of trials. Indeed, capital convicts were usually executed within days of trial, unless the trial judge took the special step of reprieving the convict in order to allow post-verdict proceedings. Because the system effectively lacked appellate redress, there was no occasion for those features of modern trial practice that are associated with the enterprise of provoking and preserving error for appeal.[12]

We understand that a criminal procedural system so brusque could not have endured. The procedural system that the Framers presupposed when they constitutionalized jury trial was grievously deficient. No one can yearn for the good old days when an Old Bailey judge could try a dozen felons a day. The movement for greater safeguard in criminal procedure that intensified in the later Eighteenth Century and across the Nineteenth and Twentieth Centuries was benign in spirit, and it was in a deep sense inevitable. But there are many ways to increase the level of safeguard and, in the light of hindsight, one can see that the path taken in Anglo-American law was catastrophic. Whereas the Europeans of this period were refining the techniques of an increasingly trustworthy, officialized system of impartial evidence-gathering and prosecuting, the Anglo-American systems turned for safeguard down the path of partisan lawyerization. We came to experience the capture of the criminal trial by lawyers—lawyers for the defense and for the prosecution. The rise of the adversarial system led to the loss of the accused as a testimonial resource, and to the vast elaboration of the law of evidence and of trial procedure that was undertaken in a forlorn effort to regulate adversary combat. Jury trial was redefined as adversary jury trial. The explosive combination of adversary procedure and criminal jury trial produced a system so clumsy, so time-consuming, and so costly that, in the end, Americans found it intolerable to honor the Framers' promise to use jury trial in "all" criminal cases. As a result, the pressure to subvert adversary jury trial has grown ever more intense across the last century.

IV. Evils of Non-Trial Procedure

What is so bad about plea bargaining? A good way to approach that question is to ask why the Framers so valued jury trial. Plea bargaining suppresses both the jury and the trial. There are important virtues to each. The jury disperses power away from the officers of the state. Because the sanctions applied in the criminal justice system are so ominous, the danger of abuse of state power in criminal procedure is serious. Plea bargaining achieves just what the Framers expected the jury to prevent, the aggrandizement of state power. Plea bargaining transfers the power of condemnation to a low-visibility decisionmaker, the prosecutor. Because negotiation replaces trial, plea bargaining substitutes an essentially concealed procedure for the salutary openness of public jury trial. The prosecutor who operates the negotiated plea system exercises awesome powers, powers that were meant to be shared with judges and jurors. As a practical matter, plea bargaining concentrates both the power to adjudicate and the power to sentence in the hands of the prosecutor.

Plea bargaining is also wrong because it is coercive. A legal system that comes to depend upon coercing people to waive their supposed rights is by definition a failed system. The system can no longer function by adhering to its own stated principles. Plea bargaining puts the accused under ferocious pressure to bear false witness against himself.[13] As the disparity grows between the sentence offered for confession and the sentence threatened for conviction upon trial, the inducement to confess becomes ever more intense. I do not think that large numbers of innocent people are confessing themselves guilty to crimes committed by strangers. At the margin, however, such cases do indeed arise.[14]

The want of trial is also costly in another way. There is an important civic interest in having public inquiry and adjudication take place in cases of serious crime—a positive externality, the economists would say. Plea bargaining prevents the citizenry from learning about the circumstances of the crime and punishment. There is, for example, a lingering distaste among substantial sections of the American people about the way that James Earl Ray was sent off to prison in Tennessee. Without trial, we do not feel adequately informed about whether our institutions have responded fully and fairly to events.

In the end, however, the worst aspect of plea bargaining is simply the dishonesty. Charge bargaining has made our criminal statistics into hash. The person who committed murder is pretended to have committed manslaughter; the person whose real crime was child molesting is convicted of loitering around a schoolyard.[15] Not only has this willful mislabelling turned our criminal statistics into a pack of lies, it has also forced us into the widespread practice of preferring arrest records over conviction records for a host of purposes. Continental observers find our reliance upon bare arrest records in matters of sentencing and employment to be incredible.[16] And looming over the whole of the saga of plea bargaining is the lie that has to be lived to escape the Constitution and the Bill of Rights—the lie that persons accused of serious crime really do not want a jury trial.

V. Markets

The Supreme Court's justification for plea bargaining, though wholly unprincipled, possesses the virtue of candor. In *Santobello v. New York*,[17] Chief Justice Burger explained that plea bargaining is to be encouraged because "[i]f every criminal charge were subjected to a full-scale trial, the States and the Federal Government would need to multiply by many times the number of judges and court facilities."[18] Translation: We cannot afford the Constitution and the Bill of Rights. Sheer expediency is rationale enough for disregarding the constitutional texts.

The most prominent academic effort to justify plea bargaining is Frank Easterbrook's chilling paper, "Criminal Procedure as a Market System."[19] Easterbrook correctly observes that the behavior of actors in the plea bargaining system is market-like. Under the constraints of the system, they behave rationally, maximize their utiles, allocate their resources, and so forth.[20] It is indeed quite a glorious Turkish rug market that we have created in lieu of what the Framers designed. Easterbrook's paper assumes away the vital question, which is what purpose the Framers ascribed to jury trial. Did they mean for this entitlement to be sold at the Turkish market with the other rugs? I think not. They had public purposes in mind when envisioning that "all" serious criminal cases would go to jury trial. To say that we have constructed a market in criminal procedural rights is a condemnation, not a justification.

VI. The Fragility of the Written Texts

The disappearance of criminal jury trial offers as telling a lesson as one could wish about the myth of written constitutions. Constitutional texts do not enforce themselves. They require the adherence and support both of the social and political order and of the legal system and legal professionals. Plea bargaining has defeated the Constitution and the Bill of Rights because legal professionals—especially judges, prosecutors, and defense attorneys—have preferred the convenience of doing deals to the rigor of trying cases.

I am left to say that much more attention should be given to how we handle criminal adjudication. I believe that concessionary non-trial procedure is wrong. Condemnation without adjudication, which is effectively what we practice in the plea bargaining system, is wrong. On the other hand, we do not want to recover the procedural world that the Framers envisioned, the world of summary jury trial. Nor can we afford the routine adversary jury trial that is the norm of our formal law.

Events that we cannot foresee but whose happening we can predict with serene certainty will one day force us to rethink our failed system of criminal procedure. We will be driven to re-introduce some component of genuine adjudication into our criminal procedure, perhaps on the platform of the existing Rule 11 hearing that is at present mostly a formalism.[21] When we do, I hope that we might pay attention to the Continental model. More than a century ago, Europeans came to look at Anglo-American criminal justice. They took back with them the notion that lay participation in criminal adjudication is profoundly important, but they also came to the conclusion that systems of mass justice appropriate to urban industrial democracies could not use laypersons in the clumsy, time-consuming, costly fashion of the adversary jury trial. The Europeans devised ways of combining laypersons with professional judges in streamlined procedures that guarantee significant lay participation in every case of serious crime.[22] The result is that they have perpetuated more of our jury tradition than we have. They have a system of routine lay participation in every case of serious crime, whereas we have a system of full-dress adversary jury trial so complex that we must deny it to almost all defendants.

Endnotes

[1] U.S. Const. amend. VI (emphasis added).

[2] Id. art. III, § 2 (emphasis added).

[3] See *Duncan v. Louisiana*, 391 U.S. 145, 149 (1968). State constitutions contain similar guarantees.

[4] See John H. Langbein, "The Criminal Trial before the Lawyers," 45 *U. Chi. L. Rev.* 263, 278–79 (1978) (reporting cases).

[5] John M. Beattie, *Crime and the Courts in England: 1660–1800*, at 336–37 (1986); see id. at 446–47.

6 In the state courts that handle most of the criminal caseload, 95 percent of felony convictions occur without jury trial; 91 percent are plea bargained; 4 percent occur at bench trial. See United States Dep't of Justice, Bureau of Justice Statistics, *Felony Sentences in State Courts: 1988*, at 1 (1990). Bench trial is a latter-day American novelty. See Susan C. Towne, "The Historical Origins of Bench Trial for Serious Crime," 26 *Am. J. Leg. Hist.* 123 (1982).

7 See Albert W. Alschuler, "Plea Bargaining and Its History," 79 *Colum. L. Rev.* 1 (1979); see also Lawrence M. Friedman & Robert V. Percival, *The Roots of Justice: Crime and Punishment in Alameda County, California, 1870-1910* (1981); John H. Langbein, "Understanding the Short History of Plea Bargaining," 13 *Law & Soc'y Rev.* 261 (1979); Mary E. Vogel, "Courts of Trade: Social Conflict and the Emergence of Plea Bargaining in Boston, Massachusetts, 1830-1890" (1988) (unpublished Ph.D dissertation, Harvard University, Univ. Microfilms No. 8901664).

8 See Langbein, supra note 4, at 277.

9 See id. at 282-83.

10 See id. at 284.

11 See id. at 276, 284.

12 See generally Beattie, supra note 5, at 348-50 (describing the "old" form of trial); Langbein, supra, note 4, at 263.

13 See John H. Langbein, "Torture and Plea Bargaining," 46 *U. Chi. L. Rev.* 3 (1978).

14 See Albert W. Alschuler, "The Prosecutor's Role in Plea Bargaining," 36 *U. Chi. L. Rev.* 50, 61 (1968) (discussing an example of coercive plea bargaining).

15 See David Sudnow, "Normal Crimes: Sociological Features of the Penal Code in a Public Defender Office," 12 *Soc. Probs.* 255, 258-59 (1965).

16 See Mirjan Damska, "Evidentiary Barriers to Conviction and Two Models of Criminal Procedure: A Comparative Study," 121 *U. Pa. L. Rev.* 506, 533 (1973).

17 404 U.S. 257 (1971).

18 Id. at 260.

19 12 *J. Legal Stud.* 289 (1983).

20 See id. at 308-09.

21 See *Fed. R. Crim. P.* 11.

22 See John H. Langbein, "Mixed Court and Jury Court: Could the Continental Alternative Fill the American Need?," 1981 *Am. B. Found. Res. J.* 195.

3

Teaching Courts
Some Curriculum and Pedagogy Perspectives

ROBERT H. CHAIRES and *SUSAN A. LENTZ*

The American court system is unique among nations. It is not because it utilizes a hybrid of common law and statute for decision making; many nations do. Neither is it unique because it has a constitutional review power nor because it has hierarchy and operates within a federalistic structure. Again, many nations do. It cannot be said that it is unique because it involves both elected and appointed individuals as legal officials; while uncommon, a few nations do. For every characteristic of the American court system—and there are many more—some nation, somewhere, has had that characteristic in the past, uses it now, or has ultimately rejected it. Within the American system there is only one characteristic that today is legally unique: the civil jury trial, which actually dates back to ancient Athens (Guinther, 1988:2–8).

The true uniqueness of the American court system is its inclusion of so many characteristics, and the great divergence across America in how each aspect is understood and applied. In no other nation on earth do formal judges in an independent court system have such power at so many levels. No other nation relies upon a formal court system to resolve so many disputes, for so many people, on so many issues. Perhaps no other court system engenders so much criticism and critical acclaim at home and worldwide.

Unique—and Complex

The depth and breadth of court integration into American society generates some complex and perplexing issues and problems for teaching about

Written especially for *Courts and Justice*, 2nd ed.

the courts. For example, federalism bred two distinct court systems, but those systems are interlocked in concurrent jurisdiction in many matters, such as civil rights law. At the same time, a legal and political battle over comity, deference to a state court's decisions by the federal courts and other states, has been going on for more than two centuries (Ball, 1987:124–125). Compounding this complexity is the presence of thirteen Federal Circuit Courts of Appeal (two are specialized in subject matter and jurisdiction) that produce often conflicting law in different regions of the United States. Those 13 circuit courts hear appeals from some 800 federal district courts, each encapsulated in the geographic boundaries of a state. Each of those 50 states have their own court systems, which vary even more widely in the law they produce. Added to this are a host of specialized courts at the federal, state and local levels. Administrative law courts, bankruptcy courts, family law courts, juvenile courts, probate courts and tax courts, for example, often operate with substantially different rules of procedure, evidence, burdens of proof and lines of appeal.

Even in the trial courtroom a single judge may be required to wear several different hats. At different times, depending on how a matter is pled, a judge may not only have to shift gears but get into an entirely different vehicle. A federal district court judge, for example, might hear an admiralty case (law of the seas) with its unique rules on one day, the next day conduct a civil trial to a jury, and a week later function as a *de facto* appellate court in a habeas corpus review of a state criminal conviction. At the same time, a state court trial judge in a smaller venue maybe shifting on a daily basis from criminal court judge to civil court judge to juvenile court judge, and more. In some states, they may be asked to reverse their robes and stand not as a court of law but as a court of equity, to use a set of rules dating back to fifteenth-century England's courts of Chancery and Exchequer.

When you multiply all of this by the simple fact that there is political and social context at federal, state, and local levels, square it by wide variances in judicial philosophy and competence, and then introduce "wild card" variables like attorneys and juries, the system may appear not unlike the tangle of a long untamed garden. For the academic studying the courts and the teacher trying to teach about them, this tangle often produces a desire to weed, to straighten, to reduce the seeming disorder.

Contested Ground

Scholarly and practitioner inquiry and comment on the courts necessarily involve specialization. One studies and writes about a particular system of courts such as federal (Ball, 1987), a specific level like appellate (Coffin, 1994), international comparative (Abraham, 1993), or actor-directed as in lawyers (Luban, 1988) and juries (Guinther, 1988). Actors themselves have perspectives on their roles, such as judging (Grodin, 1989) or criminal defense (Kunen, 1983). The inquiry may be law and court specific, as in criminal procedure and the U.S. Supreme Court (Decker, 1992), or subject-group specific, as in race (Wright, 1993). Whether a writing about courts is clearly polemic (Spence, 1989), critical scholarship (Friedman, 1985), or some hybrid intended for general market (O'Brian, 1993) is often in the eyes of the reader.

By the time all this gets distilled down to the usual classroom text, too often the curriculum importance of contextual complexity becomes grayed by focus on process, politics, or neutral descriptiveness. A department in a discipline like political science often resolves context/substance curriculum issues by offering a variety of courts courses at different court-specific levels. For those departments who offer "law" or law-context courses and who also offer, or are considering offering, a dedicated "courts" course, the remedy of multiple courses is not usually present. Most programs can only offer one course. In that course, the uniqueness of the depth and breadth of the American court system should be presented.

One approach to examining the uniqueness and operational complexity of the courts is to consider them "contested ground," a place of ideological conflict. From this perspective, some direction to the task of teaching courts begins to appear. Given that curriculum itself is ideology, pedagogy must transmit that reality. The concept of curriculum being ideological is not new. Apple (1990), for example, holds that curriculum is ideology because it involves choices about what knowledge is important. Apple notes about ideology:

> Interpretations of the scope of ideology vary widely. The phenomena under it can be grouped into at least three categories: (1) quite specific rationalizations or justifications of the activities of particular and identifiable occupational groups (e.g., professional ideologies); (2) broader political programs and social movements; and (3) comprehensive world-views, outlooks, or what Berger and Luckman and others have called symbolic universes (1990:20).

Whether ideology is "false consciousness" or a meaningful system of bringing order to complex social situations, ideology "always deals with legitimation, power conflict, and a special style of argument (rhetoric based on assumptions presented as fact)" (Apple, 1990:20–21). Although Apple writes about educating grades K–12 and educating teachers to blindly accept and teach ideology, his ideas have great relevance to the study and teaching of courts.

Schools, including universities, are contested ground because they are places where conflicts are played out about what knowledge is important, and how it will be taught. The courts are contested ground because they process, create, and legitimate ideological perspectives on: (1) actors and acted upon, i.e., judges, lawyers, criminals, victims, plaintiffs and defendants; (2) institutions and movements (while being an institution and movement themselves); and (3) law, both in the symbolic (what and why) and practical (power) dimensions. Gable and Feinman (1998) give an example of this by invoking an image of the courts as places constrained by ideology and the hegemonic constructs generated by ideology. It is a view of court actors, judges and lawyers, locked into a system they themselves cannot explain except by reference to normative models like politics and power. Arguably, teachers of courts may themselves become locked into normative models and explanations.

Concepts of ideology and contested ground suggest that teaching a critical course on courts involves more than presenting political or policy-oriented perspectives on the courts. Clearly, teaching courts offers some challenging and perplexing problems in curriculum and pedagogy. To address some of these challenges and problems the next sections will: (1) examine the idea of courts as contested ground by looking at the myth and manipulation that generates ideology; (2) put forth that the teaching of courts differs significantly from the teaching of law; and (3) suggest a strategy and set of tactics for "doing courts."

Myth and Manipulation in Courts

While there can be little doubt that the courts are political actors, they are also much more. What that "much more" is, or should be, is the substance of continuing debate, controversy, and accusation. A large part of this debate, controversy, and accusation centers around perspectives on the courts that can be considered mythological in history and application. In this context, myths can be considered as perceptions that drive actions or nonactions. Reich (1987), for example, describes four continuing tales that shape popular thinking and political response in an endless cycle. These four—"rot at the top" (out-of-control big government and big business), "mob at the gates" (foreigners threatening our institutions), "triumphant individual" (entrepreneurs versus drones), and "benevolent community" (fixing the poor)—"have endured throughout American history. But in each era they have been combined and conveyed in slightly different ways" (1987:14). Kappeler, Blumberg and Potter (1996) similarly describe mythologies in criminal justice as unproven or unprovable assumptions and/or negligent, even deliberate, distortions of crime, violence, and safety that tend to polarize and demonize (see also Donzinger, 1996, and in contrast Wilbanks, 1987).

The courts get involved when mythology generates ideology (or perhaps the reverse); the result becomes political agenda, and political agenda becomes law. For example, Reinarman and Duskin (1998) describe the drug war as an ideological construct, and Fisher (1998) describes the perceptions about the reality of crime waves as feeding from ideological roots. While all or many crime waves may just be "myths," they are treated as real. Laws are passed, enforced, litigated. Violators are acquitted or found guilty by plea or trial and then punished. However, things are not quite so simple. Courts are contested ground. Not all follow or believe in a particular myth or ideology. To one person or another (or group), the courts will always be "good" or "bad" depending on how congruent the court's actions are with expectations shaped by ideology. Hence, a mythology about courts develops.

Court Myths

Within the line of thought developed by Kappeler and his colleagues (1996), there are both negative and positive myths (the term "myths and legends of criminal justice" was actually coined by Atkins and Pogrebin, 1978). "Good guy" myths survive, and prosper, in conjunction with "bad guy" myths. While mythology in criminal justice is not simplistic, it is simple in comparison to the mythology of the court system, which has a much broader scope of actors, process and subject. Criminal justice is only one part of the court system. While actors in the criminal justice system may view the courts as part of "their system," even collectively they only deal with a relatively small part of it.

Court myths are no less subject to manipulation than the political myths of Reich (1987) or criminal justice myths. In addition, the courts have a civil dimension that generates its own mythology. Arguably, the "litigation explosion" is another version of Reich's "entrepreneur tale," one in which the drones suck the blood of American corporations by frivolous litigation and plaintiff's lawyers are the civil version of Kappeler et al.'s (1996) "bad guys" (see, for example, Olson, 1991, and in contrast Spence, 1989, both polemics). When ideology drives mythology, facts get lost, manipulated, transformed. As Crossen (1994:19) relates, statistics have become a new battlefield of manipulation, of corrupted information, and "Behind the explosion of corrupted information is, first, money." All this contributes to the courts as contested ground, out of which comes decisions about which myth, which ideology, which set of corrupted information will be legitimized.

Clearly, though, some interests more than others strongly depend on mythology and manipulation. In this vein, an examination of the myths surrounding courts discloses that there are negative and positive myths that have become part of the "court mythology." Each myth will have its promoters, those who consciously or unconsciously support it and/or transmit it. Each myth also will have its manipulators, those who use the myth to obtain an end or effect.

Table 1 Court Myths

POSITIVE MYTHS	Promoters	Manipulators	Effect
David and Goliath— Courts are places where the weak can win over the mighty if their cause is right and just.	"Feel good" movies and novels Optimists K–12 teachers	Plaintiffs' bar	Open courts (see table 2)
Day in Court—Courts are a place where the average person will find wise judges and fair juries who will listen to them.	Individual winners		Open courts
Judges are Wise and Fair—They are special people with vast knowledge and compassion	Court television shows Bench Individual winners	Corporate winners	Decreased incentive for critical examination of judges and system
NEGATIVE MYTHS			
The Hired Gun—There exist attorneys that are so competent that they can win any case no matter what the facts and law are.	Cynical movies and novels News media Individual losers Corporate losers Criminal justice agencies	Defense bar Corporate losers Prosecutors Civil defense bar	Tort reform Criminal procedure reform Restrictions on contingency fees Closing court access Demonizing of criminal defense bar Changes in legal ethics standards
Just Another Bureaucracy—There is nothing special about the courts or judges. What they do could be be done better in other forums.	Social science academics News media Pessimists	Politicians Proponents of ADRs (alternative dispute resolutions) Those who benefit from removing particular subject matter jurisdiction	Emphasis on bureaucratic efficiency Diminishing of co-equal branch of government status Proper law makers are always legislators Changes in legal education
Litigation Explosion— The courts are being overwhelmed by friv- olous lawsuits pushed by greedy plaintiffs' lawyers.	Insurance industry Manufacturers	Insurance industry Manufacturers ADR proponents Defense bar Conservative media	Tort reform Closed courts Increased ADRs
Revolving Door Criminal Courts— Crime waves, weak laws, and liberal judges are making society unsafe.	Law enforcement News media	Politicians Conservative media	Reduction in judicial discretion Sentencing reform Increasing contraction of civil rights Racial disparity

Table 1 is not intended to be exhaustive, nor can it be. However, it does display one of the realities of positive and negative court mythology. Negative mythology generates more controversy and action than positive mythology. In large part, this is the nature of the public beast. Negative mythology is much more newsworthy and manipulable. It is axiomatic that active complainers are more visible and more often heard than those who, if not happy, are at least marginally satisfied. A classic example of this is the American fascination with radio talk shows. Very few, if any, of those shows concentrate on saying how good things are. Even the hallowed halls of academia tend to be dominated by criticism. Few scholars have made reputations by complimenting the status quo or writing about how well something works.

Court mythology persists for many reasons. As table 1 suggests, however, a primary reason is that a particular myth tends to support ideology about the overall role of government. In this vein, a litigation explosion myth can be explained within the ideology that government improves society by helping business interests and that the courts as a branch of government should further that interest, not impede it—in particular, that court resources should be expended on resolving interbusiness litigation, not all those other things. Of course, other interests have different perspectives on what are important or unimportant matters for the courts to handle. Some would close the courts to all but a few things, others would open them to much more.

Opening and Closing the Courts

Black (1976) relates that law increases in quantity as society becomes more stratified, specialized, and organized into separate groups and interests. As the quantity of law increases, it follows that law must intrude into more and more arenas of life. Where the law intrudes, enforcement and the courts follow. Not surprisingly, there are many arenas of life in which some, or many, desire that the law not intrude. Thus, to some, the courts, particularly the United States Supreme Court, should stay out of politics and stick with the law (for example, Bork, 1990). To others, the courts, and most particularly the Supreme Court, are seen as the only practical venue for enforcing and achieving social justice.

To understand this point it may be helpful to view the varying perspectives on the role(s) of the courts as a continuum rather than as an "either/or" division.

As this continuum indicates, subject matter jurisdiction often reflects ideology about the role of courts. For many, the issue of subject matter is a political one; for others it is social and moral. Mensch (1998), in her history of mainstream legal thought, describes the evolution of American law in

---

Continuum of Perspectives on the Courts

| Courts should only ◄─────────────────────► handle contract and criminal matters. Constitution should be narrowly construed. | Courts should be open to all issues and parties. Constitution should be broadly construed. |

---

terms of what is private (outside governmental control) and public (subject to law). For example, for much of American history the family and the workplace were private matters, subjects largely outside legal control. In this sense, the history of American legal evolution has been one of a constant increase in the scope of what is public and hence subject to law.

Individuals and groups vary greatly in their views concerning what government should do, at which level, to whom, and why. Quite simply, courts as contested ground are in the middle of the disputes. In point, some view the courts as generating the disputes by existing as a forum. In this perspective the solution becomes simple: limit the forum. Others see the courts as the only practical place to resolve disputes, particularly among parties with unequal resources, and for those groups who have been traditionally disenfranchised from the political process. The latter perspective operates to expand the forum.

The Quantity of Courts

Ideology by itself, though, is not the only thing driving court expansion and contraction. As more issues become subject to law, the role(s) of the courts expand at a rate even greater than the increase of the law. This occurs for several primary reasons:

- Courts make law in the common law tradition as they resolve claims not covered or controlled by statute (Tarr, 1999:285; Altschuler and Sgroi, 1996:129–159; Abraham, 1993:7–15).

- The American legislative process tends to produce statutes that are subject to various interpretations; legislatures often deliberately offload tough issues onto the courts (Coffin, 1994:309–312).

- Federalism generates ambiguities and conflicts in the law (Coffin, 1994:43–65; O'Brian, 1986:202–271).

- A pluralistic, multi-class society produces "special interest" law that tends to expand the scope of law (Wright, 1993; Friedman, 1985).

- The existence of a civil jury increases the symbolic importance of the courts as a venue (Guinther, 1988; O'Barr and Conley, 1994).

The result of these reasons, and by no means is this list exhaustive, is that increasing quantities of law, for better or worse, increase the need for a court system that can legitimately resolve disputes. The key word is legitimate and a key figure (if not *the* key figure) in legitimacy is the judge.

Judicial Accountability versus Independence

Judicial activism, judges going beyond the law to interpose their own values, is in the eye of the beholder. It is also issue specific. Judges can be activist both by what they do and by what they refuse to do. This single point has generated and sustained the continuing academic debate and political rhetoric about accountability versus independence for judges at all levels. The issue of accountability at a basic level centers on the idea that judges should decide issues in a manner consistent with the popular will of the people. The independence perspective centers around the idea that judges must follow the law even when that decision is unpopular.

The continuing controversy about judicial selection is a classic example of how perceptions of the legitimacy of the courts are heavily tinged with political, moral, and mythological variables. Tarr (1999:61) notes that 29 states use some form (partisan or nonpartisan) of popular election for judges (see also Smith, 1993:100–104). Next in prevalence is some form of merit selection (22 states), and finally appointment by the governor (5 states) and election by legislature (3 states). The number of states exceeds 50 because at different levels of the courts different methods may be used. Arguably, the different methods suggest that there are some common, and conflicting, perspectives as to whom and what judges should be accountable or independent from.

Perhaps ironically, the various methods of judicial selection may make little difference. Slotnick (1995) suggests that for most practical purposes the method of obtaining office makes little difference in judicial decisions. Nationally known plaintiff's trial lawyer Gerry Spence (1989) states essentially the same thing but for different reasons. To him, the law will always serve power and judges will always serve the law. As he states, "Judges administer the laws of both saints and tyrants" (1989:101). Both of their perspectives are consistent with a view that judges respond more to dominant ideology than to political expectation.

In theory, the federal system should be less political. Federal trial and intermediate appellate judges, as well as Supreme Court justices (Article III judges) are nominated by the President and approved by the Senate. Once in office they serve essentially for life. They can only be removed by impeachment of the Senate, which has occurred only a few times in American history. Some argue the federal selection process is, in fact, even more political than that of state systems because of the partisan nature of the appointment and ratification process. This point is problematic. Federal judges at all levels tend to outlast several administrations and changing political currents (see, for example, Ball, 1987). Still, the appointment process is highly political and partisan, as evidenced by the fact that between 5 and 15 percent of the 900 odd federal district court and appellate court seats have been vacant in recent years. As Tarr (1999:73–81) relates, Senators of the party not holding the Presidency tend to create logjams. Their response is, in part at least, a recognition of the great power of the federal bench to shape the law in ideological directions opposed to some interests and favoring others. Arguably, it is a recognition that federal judges do much more than "just law." This last point lends some further dimension to the argument that teaching courts only minimally involves teaching law.

Teaching Law versus Teaching Courts

That courts make and shape law is without doubt. However, the past, present and probable future divisiveness surrounding the role of courts in American society strongly indicates that a meaningful study requires separating the process of courts, and its actors, from a direct study of law. Although on its face this may seem an improbable, even undesirable, task, it is not so.

Law schools, in the other direction, do this quite well. Law schools teach law. They teach substantive and procedural law and generally do not confuse the teaching of law with the social and political context of lawyer advocacy and judicial decisions. In their eyes, to do so would upset the balance of the teaching of law. Imagine, for example, a course in law school in which the law of contracts is taught as an ideological process of determining which economic interests are more important to society (for example, Gable and Feinman, 1998). Contract law is taught as a series of legal doctrines and rules. Without these rules there would be no commonality of theory and practice, of overt legal argumentation and reasoning. Some feminist theorists, however, would contend that this method of teaching law is itself ideological since it is androcentric (for example, Martin and Jurik, 1996).

Many law schools do teach courses in subjects like legal philosophy and legal history. In those courses, budding lawyers might learn about the legal realism school of jurisprudence, which argues that judges are really social engineers who couch their decisions in legal theory (see Fisher, Horwitz and Reed, 1993). In that same course they might learn that others perceive the law, lawyers, and judges to be instruments of oppression, as in Marxist legal theory (Mellossi, 1986), or a hegemonic construct to ensure social and economic replication in an elite, as in critical legal studies (Unger, 1986). They might even read the scholarly works on jurisprudence of some currently sitting federal judicial officials in areas like law and economics (Posner, 1980) or former federal judges like Robert Bork on conservative jurisprudence (1990). (For an overview of legal philosophy see Cotterrell, 1989). However, very few law schools require such courses, and even less require a dedicated course on the courts. After all, law school is filled with courses (civil procedure, criminal procedure) that teach lawyers "process." A teaching of "courts" is considered implicit in law school.

Unfortunately, law students, like students elsewhere, tend to focus on those courses that have to do with graduation, career, and practice. The end effect is that many, if not most, law students who become lawyers have not been exposed to diverse views of courts, society, and law. There is little reason to believe that the few lawyers who become judges (and being a lawyer is not a requirement in some low-level courts) have somehow become "enlightened" about the many dimensions of law and courts. An extension of this point is that many judges may not even know initially about the particular legal subject matter or process of the court to which they are appointed or elected. It is not unusual for a lawyer to become a judge in cases or circumstances in which they have no legal or even intellectual or emotional background. For example, a former prosecutor may become a judge in a domestic relations court, or a corporate attorney who has never actually tried a case may preside in criminal court. In each instance they will bring ideological infrastructure to the contested ground.

The same kinds of issues reverberate throughout the hierarchy of the courts. Appellate judges and justices who may never have tried a case to judge or jury make decisions, often only by simple majority, about what was right or wrong about a trial, about what "is" the law to be followed in the future. Appellate court judges and justices who may never have even practiced law in any form, except for teaching and writing about it, make decisions that affect the life, liberty, and property of people (Coffin, 1994).

While there is specialized education and training for American judges, it is somewhat random. Unlike countries like France, where being a judge is a special area of study and training (Abraham, 1993:255–269), there are only two national centers for training state judges: the National Judicial College at the University of Nevada, Reno (there is a separate College of Juvenile and Family Courts also on campus) and the Center for State Courts in Virginia. Some states offer and require substantial training for judges, others little or none at all. It is not uncommon for judges to pay their own way and use their own vacation time to attend judicial education and training sessions. The federal judicial conference, in contrast, offers a variety of continuing educational and training opportunities.

Teaching Implications

For students, especially undergraduates, issues of legal context like myth and manipulation are much more important than "what the law is." A teacher of a course in courts must assume that students are superimposing ideological assumptions over descriptive statements about the courts. Most particularly, it cannot be assumed by any teacher of courts that students have any common idea about the who, what, and where of the actors: judges, lawyers, and juries. Students may have had law courses before entering a courts course, but the law course(s) may have been taught as if courts processed cases based solely on legal arguments. Where students have had a system overview course, the presentation of the courts may have been even more simplistic. Structural descriptions of the courts system showing hierarchy and appellate routes through the state and federal system are simply inadequate to describe the role of courts in American society. At best such descriptive approaches tend to oversimplify law. At worst they tend to perpetuate the mythology of courts. Smith (1996), for example, argues it would be better to teach criminal justice students a course on courts than a course on criminal procedure without "context" (in critical response, see Zalman, 1996).

Perhaps the most important consideration about differentiating the teaching of law from the teaching of courts is that most students are not going on to graduate or law school. For those programs that are educating and training students for careers and professions that significantly involve applying law to people, more is needed than just "the law." An appreciation of the mythology surrounding courts and court actors serves to demystify law. It helps students understand the law as something over which they have some control. It helps students see law as something they do rather than something that is done to them.

Doing the Law or Being Done To

In many ways the courts are shallow constructs, as is the law. The courts and law are only potentials. No system, no law is self-activating; all work through people. The people who activate the system—plaintiffs, lawyers, and judges—*are* the real system. While the legislative process of making law is fascinating, law is nothing until an attempt at enforcement is made. Statute books are full of laws that cannot be enforced, laws that were just symbolic and were never intended to be enforced, and laws that history and social evolution have passed by. Few states, for example, enforce laws on sodomy. Still, their constitutional right to make and enforce such laws, at least against homosexuals, remains in power. Perhaps the most difficult concept for many to understand is that the law books are full of laws not yet made. Those are the laws that grow out of the interpretation of what already exists.

A *good* courts course educates students in the simple fact that the law is not static. It informs students that the law changes as people change and argue and decide within different contexts. A *great* courts course brings students to realize that they have as much to say about the law as any one else, that they can be doers more than done to. The mythology of the courts may produce conflicting visions, but the courts remain as the only practical venue for testing visions. When the law says many things, the courts are by tradition, and law, the place to find a final word, for a while.

Accessing the courts may be difficult and expensive, but it is less difficult and expensive than the alternatives, such as trying to influence legislation where powerful interests are involved. More importantly, much of what the court does is more specific, more personal, to the parties involved. Indeed, it is in the courts that the major battles of civil rights have been fought and continue to be fought. For example, while many social and historical factors have changed the constitution and statutes regarding race and gender, it took litigation to apply the law to specific people. The process can be expected to continue.

The Color and Gender of Courts

While there has been much written on race and gender in the law, the courts are not of a unified mind as to what it all means, and why (for example, Kennedy, 1997; Wright, 1993). However, in the history of this area, several things are clear:

- *Courts have changed the face of the work force.* The law existed, but it is trial court orders that have brought many employers, public and private, kicking and screaming into the twentieth century. Where will they go in the twenty-first?

- *Courts continue to make policy by what they do and refuse to do.* The final realm of some of America's most important symbolic decisions has always been in the courts, including abortion, crime control, morality, and sexuality. Will a mere change in who is on the court make a real difference in the twentieth century?

- *Courts have changed their public perception in the twentieth century.* Their roles have moved from remote law deciders to agents of change, to unpredictable political actors. While words like conservative and liberal are thrown about, without context such words are meaning-less. Judges change. What will they do in the twenty-first century?

At the cusp of the twenty-first century 1,200,000 people are in prison. Four hundred thousand more are in jails on a daily basis. Millions more bear the stigma of being ex-felons, on probation, or on parole. A simple majority of these are people of color, statistical racial and ethnic minorities. Mauer and Huling (1995) point out that one in three black males between 18 and 28 are in prison, on probation, or on parole. Single mothers with children represent an increasingly large portion of the ultra-poor. In *De-Shaney v. Winnebago County Department of Social Services* (109 S.Ct 998 [1989]), the Supreme Court ruled that the state owed no special duty to pro-tect an abused child, that welfare protection was a gift of state (see Rosen-blatt, 1990). *Proposition 209* in California and a series of cases directed at law schools effectively ended affirmative action in graduate education at public legal institutions. Chaires (1996) addresses some of the bleak future ramifications of the intersections of these trends, and others. He also points out how the courts have played a major role in visiting the sins of the father on the children of the future.

Doing Courts

The pedagogy of teaching courts involves interdependent considerations of description, critical analysis, and philosophic definition. In short, teach-ing courts must necessarily include imposing a multidimensional context on a system that is too often presented and perceived in unidimensional terms. Like other governmental organizations, the courts act and are acted upon. Unlike other government organizations, the courts are multi-tasked and empowered at a level without precedent, barring that of Plato's theo-retical philosopher-kings. Those tasks and that power make the courts evermore contested ground. That this is so places an obligation on teacher and student to continually and critically examine the roles they play in cre-ating or perpetuating the ideology and mythology of that contested ground.

Apple (1990:xvi) states about teaching: "Our task is to teach and to learn; to take our inquiries as seriously as the subject deserves; to take criticism of what we say respectfully and openly; to hunger for it so that we too can be called upon to challenge and reformulate our own commonsense as we ask others. . . ." Apples's call suggests that "doing courts" can never be static, that curriculum and pedagogy must constantly be reevaluated. This in turn would dictate that a major goal of a courts course is demystifying the courts so that critical inquiry can take place in a manner that does not make students unable to "see the forest for the trees."

Perhaps the most valid analogy that can be drawn for the courts is not in the public sector but in the private. The courts can be likened to a huge multinational corporation. The various parts (state and regional circuit courts) often operate with virtual independence because they must exist in the legal, political and cultural confines of the host state or region. Like a multinational corporation, at the very top is a board of directors—the Supreme Court, which sometimes loosely, sometimes closely, supervises and makes policy and enforces the rules. Like a board of directors, which in theory is bound by the limits of the Articles of Incorporation in what they do and how they do it, the Supreme Court is legally bound to follow the Constitution. Like a multinational corporation, which is in theory legally bound to act in the best interests of the stockholders, the courts are, in theory, legally bound to act in the best interests of society. Like a huge multinational corporation, there is seldom consensus as to what the rules are, what the goals are, and how to achieve them. Most of all, like stockholders who only look at their dividend returns, citizens seldom care what the courts do until it personally affects them.

Often, the study of corporations is done by comparing how they are supposed to operate (theory/ideal) with how they really do (practice/reality), and then examining how or why the difference (if any) came about. This methodology can be used as a teaching tool to examine and demystify courts. In teaching courts, simple tools are important. The sheer complexity of the courts can be overwhelming. For this reason, court study can successfully be approached by a series of inquires about what is the theory/ideal and the practice/reality.

Building the Model

What develops out of a multidimensional perspective on the courts is a possible matrix for approaching critical inquiry. If there are issues of myth and manipulation in the courts, then clearly one goal of a courts course is to reconcile what the courts do with what people think the courts do. This can be called a positivistic/organization perspective of courts, the comparison of formal expectations with actual results. If, as suggested, court actors (attorneys, judges, juries) modify the formal law and process in complex ways into informal patterns of law and process consistent with their ideologies, then this personal/ideological dimension should also be subjected to analysis. Finally, if the courts are more than the sum of their parts, if they serve a practical cultural role of being a legitimate place for the resolution of differences and a symbolic role of legitimizing law, then this legitimate/symbolic dimension is also a necessary part of the study of the courts. Each of these dimensions, the positivist/organization, the personal/ideological, and the legitimate/symbolic, can be examined in the context of the differences between theory/ideal and practice/reality.

Placing a few of the current issues of the courts into the matrix generates a table that can be used as a platform from which to approached organized discourse.

Table 2 Teaching Matrix for Courts

	Theory/Ideal	Practice/Reality
Positivist/ Organization	Formal structure Federalism Mixing of common and code law Legal education as training for profession and service	Courts as organizations Courts as subordinate, superior and coordinate political actors Legal and political decision theories Legal education as training for hierarchy
Personal/ Ideological	Lawyers as advocates The bar as a participatory democracy Judges as neutral Judges as wise and learned	Lawyers divided by status and legal subject matter The bar as an instrument of self-interest and restricting competition Judges as politicians in robes Vast variances in skills, knowledge and temperament
Legitimate/ Symbolic	Courts as doing law and justice Juries as important actors Rational legal system Unified legal theory Equal law	Courts as instruments of social control and power Juries' nullification as dangerous to vested interests Juries as mere pawns Law as a hodgepodge of morality, religion, compromise, and greed disguised as rationality Law biased along gender and race lines

Of course what goes into each block of table 2 may, and should, constantly change. Still, however, while each point may not be subjected to inquiry, just cuing the student that a particular point is part of the contested ground of courts may be enough in itself to generate self-inquiry. This is not intended to be *the* way to approach a courts course; it is merely a suggestion of one way to approach some of the major issues that come up in teaching such a course. Hopefully, there will never be one "best way" to teach any course.

In looking at issues in both a descriptive manner and a critical manner, and examining each in the context of myth and manipulation, the study of the courts becomes more dynamic. As curious as it may seem, the study and teaching of courts also becomes easier. Gradually, students begin to understand the ambivalence and contradictions of the court as a natural part of the process. Perhaps, most importantly, students begin to see themselves in their views of the courts. If at the end of any courts course, taught in any manner, students appreciate how different perspectives on opening and closing the court affect the checks and balances of society, and their own roles in imagining or creating those checks and balances, then curriculum and pedagogy has been successful.

Conclusion

The courts are political actors; processors and creators of law; the makers of myth; a series of complex organizations that are in turn part of a greater complex organization; and stages on which many dramas, and occasional comedies, of life and choice are played. The courts are many things to many people. Their roles are so complex that the study of courts should never be dull. Artz (1988) relates that undergraduate legal studies are too important to leave to lawyers, and McCoy (1993) holds that the teaching of courts and law has been marginalized in undergraduate criminal justice programs precisely because lawyers teach the courses. Perhaps there is a message there: the teaching of courts is too important to be taught in a way that does not display the full uniqueness of the American court system.

Bibliography

Abraham, Henry J. (1993). *The Judicial Process*, 6th ed. New York: Oxford University Press.

Altschuler, Bruce E. and Celia A. Sgroi (1996). *Understanding Law in a Changing Society*, 2nd ed. Upper Saddle River: NJ: Prentice Hall.

Apple, Michael W. (1990). *Ideology and Curriculum*, 2nd ed. New York: Routledge.

Artz, Donna E. (1988). "'Too Important To Leave To Lawyers:' Undergraduate Legal Studies and Its Challenge to Professional Legal Education," *Nova Law Review*, Vol. 13:125–163.

Atkins, Burton and Mark Pogrebin, Eds. (1978). *The Invisible Justice System: Discretion and the Law*. Cincinnati: Anderson.

Ball, Howard (1987). *Courts and Politics: The Federal Judicial System*. Englewood Cliffs, NJ: Prentice Hall.

Black, Donald (1976). *The Behavior of Law*. New York: Academic Press.

Bork, Robert (1990). *The Tempting of America*. New York: Simon & Schuster.

Carp, Robert A. and Ronald Stidham (1996). *Judicial Process in America*, 3rd ed.

Washington, DC: CQ Press.

Chaires, Robert (1996). "Visiting the Sins of the Father: The Intersection of Criminal Justice and Social Welfare Policy and Practice in 2006," *Journal of Law and Social Work*, Vol. 6, No. 1:23–32.

Coffin, Frank M. (1994). *On Appeal: Courts, Lawyering, and Judging*. New York: W.W. Norton & Co.

Cotterrell, Roger (1989). *The Politics of Jurisprudence: A Critical Introduction to Legal Philosophy*. Philadelphia: University of Pennsylvania Press.

Crossen, Cynthia (1994). *Tainted Truth: The Manipulation of Fact in America*. New York: Simon and Schuster.

Decker, John F. (1992). *Revolution to the Right: Criminal Procedure Jurisprudence during the Burger-Rehnquist Court Era*. New York: Garland.

Donziger, Steven R. (1996). *The Real War on Crime*. New York: HarperPerennial.

Fisher, William W. III, Morton J. Horwitz and Thomas A. Reed, Eds. (1993). *American Legal Realism*. New York: Oxford University Press.

Fishman, Mark (1998). "Crime Waves as Ideology," in *Constructing Crime: Perspectives on Making News and Social Problems*, W. Potter and V. Kappeler, Eds. Prospect Heights, IL: Waveland Press, pp. 53–73.

Friedman, Lawrence M. (1985). *Total Justice*. Boston: Beacon Press.

Gable, Peter and Jay Feinman (1998). "Contract Law as Ideology," in *The Politics of Law*, 3rd ed. D. Kairys, Ed. New York: Basic.

Grodin, Joseph (1989). *In Pursuit of Justice: Reflections of a State Supreme Court Justice*. Berkeley: University of California Press.

Guinther, John (1988). *The Jury in America*. New York: Facts on File Press (a research project of the Roscoe Pound Foundation).

Holten, N. Gary and Lawson L. Lamar (1991). *The Criminal Courts: Structures, Personnel, and Process*. New York: McGraw-Hill.

Kappeler, Victor E., Mark Blumberg and Gary W. Potter (1996). *The Mythology of Crime and Justice*, 2nd ed. Prospect Heights, IL: Waveland Press.

Kennedy, Randell (1997). *Race, Crime, and the Law*. New York: Random House.

Kunen, James (1983). *"How Can You Defend Those People?"* New York: McGraw-Hill.

Luban, David (1988). *Lawyers and Justice: An Ethical Study*. Princeton, NJ: Princeton University Press.

Martin, Susan Ehrlich and Nancy Jurik (1996). *Doing Justice, Doing Gender: Women in Law and Criminal Justice Occupations*. Thousand Oaks, CA: Sage.

Mauer, Marc and Tracy Huling (1995). "One in Three Young Black Men Ensnared in the Justice System," *Overcrowded Times*, Vol. 6, No. 6:1, 10–12.

McCoy, Candace (1993). "Criminal Courts and Legal Studies: The Marginalized Core," *Journal of Criminal Justice Education*, Vol. 4. No. 2:235–249.

Mellossi, Dario (1986). "Marxist Sociology of Law," *Legal Studies Forum*, Vol. 10, No. 3:341–356.

Mensch, Elizabeth (1998). "The History of Mainstream Legal Thought," in *The Politics of Law*, 3rd ed., D. Kairys, Ed. New York: Basic.

O'Barr, William M. and John M. Conley (1994). "Lay Expectations of the Civil Jury System," in *The Law & Society Reader*, R. Abel, Ed. New York: New York University Press, pp. 382–400.

O'Brian, David M. (1986). *Storm Center: The Supreme Court in American Politics*, 3rd ed. New York: W. W. Norton & Co.

Olson, Walter K. (1991). *The Litigation Explosion: What Happened When America Unleashed the Lawsuit*. New York: Truman Talley.

Posner, Richard A. (1980). "The Ethical and Political Basis of the Efficiency Norm in Common Law Adjudication," *Hofstra Law Review*, Vol. 8, No. 3:487–507.

Reich, Robert B. (1987). *Tales of A New America*. New York: Times Books.

Reinarman, Craig and Ceres Duskin (1998). "Dominant Ideology and Drugs in the Media," in *Constructing Crime*, G. Potter and V. Kappeler, Eds. Prospect Heights, IL: Waveland Press, pp. 317–331.

Rosenblatt, Rand (1990). "Social Duties and the Problem of Rights in the American Welfare State," in *The Politics of Law*, 2nd ed., D. Kairys, Ed. New York: Pantheon, pp. 90–114.

Ryan, John Paul, Ed. (1986). "Proceedings of the ABA National Conference on Law in Undergraduate Liberal Education," *Legal Studies Forum*, Vol. 10:121–130.

Slotnick, Elliot E. (1995). "Review Essay on Judicial Recruitment and Selection," in *Courts and Justice: A Reader*, G. L. Mays and P. R. Gregware, Eds. Prospect Heights, IL: Waveland Press, pp. 200–215.

Smith, Christopher (1993). *Courts, Politics, and the Judicial Process*. Chicago: Nelson-Hall.

Smith, Christopher (1996). "Teaching the Irrelevance of Law on Criminal Procedure," *Journal of Criminal Justice Education*, Vol. 7, No. 1:45–58.

Spence, Gerry (1989). *With Justice For None*. New York: Penguin.

Tarr, G. Allan (1999). *Judicial Process and Judicial Policymaking*, 2nd ed. Belmont, CA: Wadsworth.

Unger, Roberto Mangabeira (1986). *The Critical Legal Studies Movement*. Cambridge: Harvard University Press.

Wilbanks, William (1987). *The Myth of a Racist Criminal Justice System*. Monterey, CA: Brooks/Cole.

Wright, Bruce (1993). *Black Robes, White Justice*. New York: Carol Publishing.

Zalman, Marvin (1996). "Reflections on Christopher Smith's Article 'Teaching the Irrelevance of Law on Criminal Procedure," *Journal of Criminal Justice Education*, Vol. 7, No. 1:59–63.

Questions to Consider

1. The authors describe historical and current conflicts between court officials (judges and lawyers) and ordinary citizens. What conflicts do they cite as examples? Can you think of any current examples in which there are attempts to limit the role of citizens in legal decision making?

2. Some have argued that the demands placed on courts to process cases have led many judges to assume a more "managerial role" in court proceedings. In such a role, judges actively negotiate with the parties about the course and outcome of litigation, seeking to cajole and perhaps pressure the parties to settle or plea bargain before the case goes to a jury trial. As much of this "case management" takes place in judicial chambers, off the record and out of the public eye, there is less and less public contact with judicial process. In addition there are fewer limitations on judicial power, as there is no requirement to provide written and reasoned opinions and no opportunity for appellate review. Are the administrative pressures cited by the authors again causing court personnel to slowly take power away from juries and limit public involvement in, and understanding of, court processes? If so, what might be done to reverse this trend?

3. Myths are assumptions about the nature of reality, and most of us readily recognize such myths. We may choose to believe in some myths and disbelieve others. At this point, using the list of court myths cited by Chaires and Lentz, which myths do you believe to be true and which not? Estimate the strength of each of your beliefs by listing any "facts" you may have to support a particular belief. At this point, what can you say about your list of "facts" in relation to your beliefs?

Section II
Decision Making in the Shadows
Little-Understood Components and Processes in the Criminal Justice System

The three articles in this section highlight aspects of the court system that are seldom talked about, much less widely understood. In addition to providing new images of federal magistrates, Appeals Courts, and de novo trials, each article engages us with questions concerning the conflicting role of the courts in providing justice for those who come before them, while contending with our increasing social demands for efficiency in government operations.

Christopher Smith outlines the benefits of operational flexibility that magistrate judges give to federal courts, but we see a continuation of the problem noticed in the previous section, that of judges "forcing" litigants to forgo a jury trial, thereby obtaining their "consent" to have their issue heard before a magistrate judge. At the same time, such coercive actions remain unreviewable, or even noticed by the public, as such actions are "cloaked in the impenetrable discretionary authority of judges."

Courts depend on our belief in their authority, and Smith's article provides rich insight into the role of, and perceived need for, authority by officials below the rank of full judge. Magistrate judges want lawyers to "jump" when instructed to do so and feel the need to be called by the higher-status term "judge" rather than by the lower-status term "magistrate." Notice also the recent growth in "lesser" judicial actors, such as magistrates and pro se law clerks, who are increasingly being given the ability to judge some aspect of a litigant's case.

Will there always be some conflict in perceived status among judicial actors? Is the responsibility of each case decision getting more and more diffuse as more people have a hand in the decision? Are we creating multiple and inaccessible levels of bureaucracy in the name of efficiency?

53

The empirical caseload analysis of appellate federal courts by Davis and Songer points out how various groups of judges provide different decisional outcomes for the same types of cases. The institutional culture that creates trial courtroom "work groups" also creates different decisional dynamics for each group of judges. Does the law or the politics of each work group determine the outcome of each case?

Numerous public perceptions are also challenged by this article on appellate courts. Predictions in the late 1960s of a mass increase in criminal appeals due to the expansion of a criminal defendant's constitutional rights did not materialize. The assumption, instilled during the 1980s and early 1990s, that the courts were being overwhelmed with criminal appeals simply was not true. In fact, the rate of criminal appeals has expanded less than any other business area of the courts. Similarly, the popular assumption that courts are the appropriate avenue to help the powerless is contradicted by the fact that more powerful government and business institutions win overwhelmingly in the federal appellate courts. Does the law determine the outcome of each case or does the relative power of each party make an impact?

The ongoing conflict between efficiency and justice is again highlighted by David Harris's article on de novo trials. Few are aware that approximately one-half of the states use a system of mandatory judicial, rather than jury, trials to expedite criminal cases. When the justice of this non-jury system was challenged, it was validated by the Supreme Court, which reasoned that no defendant was hurt by this system; if anything, defendants were helped by receiving a second chance at acquittal. Harris now argues in retrospect that these assumptions about harm and justice are incorrect. He finds that the de novo trial structure discourages defendants from requesting new trials, leaves the judging system more open to bias, and shifts power toward the more affluent. Efficiencies may be gained simply because the cases get dismissed due to discouraged witnesses quitting what they see as a long and frustrating process.

4

From U.S. Magistrates to U.S. Magistrate Judges
Developments Affecting the Federal District Courts' Lower Tier of Judicial Officers

CHRISTOPHER E. SMITH

Congress created the office of U.S. magistrate in 1968 to provide additional case-processing resources for the federal district courts. In December 1990, the title for the office was changed to "U.S. magistrate judge" as part of the Judicial Improvements Act.[1] Full-time magistrate judges are appointed by district court judges for renewable eight-year terms and part-timers are appointed for renewable four-year terms.[2] Because they do not possess the attributes of Article III judges (i.e., presidential appointment, senate confirmation, and protected tenure), magistrate judges are considered "adjuncts" of the federal courts who perform tasks delegated by the district judges.

Initially, the magistrates' authority was primarily confined to the limited tasks performed by the old U.S. commissioners, lay judicial officers who handled warrants, arraignments, and petty offenses from 1793 until they were replaced by the newly-created magistrates after 1968.[3] Congress subsequently amended the Magistrates Act in 1976 and 1979 to authorize magistrates to assist district judges with a broad

Reprinted by permission of the American Judicature Society and the author from *Judicature*, vol. 75, no. 4 (Dec./Jan., 1992), pp. 210–215.

spectrum of tasks, including the supervision of complete civil trials with the consent of litigants.[4] After the 1979 Act, magistrates could perform virtually any task undertaken by district judges except for trying and sentencing felony defendants.[5] By June 1990, the 323 full-time magistrates and 153 part-time magistrates were such an integral component of the federal district courts that they were responsible for completing 450,565 tasks, including 4,220 civil and criminal evidentiary hearings, 45,201 civil pretrial conferences, and 1,008 complete civil trials.[6] Article III judges acknowledged that magistrates "contribute significantly to the administration of justice in the United States and are an integral part of the Federal judicial system"[7] by including the magistrates' interests in arguments presented to Congress concerning the need for higher salaries for judicial officers.[8]

Because these subordinate judicial officers were intended to be utilized flexibly according to the needs of each district court, the precise judicial roles performed by magistrate judges vary from district to district. For example, one 1985 study of magistrates' roles found that they could be classified as performing three model roles: "Additional Judge," supervising complete civil cases and otherwise sharing caseload responsibilities with district judges; "Team Player," handling motion hearings, conferences, and other tasks to prepare cases for trial before district judges; and "Specialist," primarily processing Social Security disability appeals and prisoner petitions for the district judges.[9] The specific mix of tasks assigned to magistrate judges within each district depends upon a variety of factors, including district judges' views on magistrate judges' proper judicial role and the nature of the caseload pressures.[10] Because the tasks performed by magistrate judges vary, their roles within each district court are susceptible to change as court reforms, changing caseload compositions, and other factors affect the demands placed upon federal courts and the district courts' case-processing capabilities. This article will discuss how recent developments affecting the federal courts are likely to shape the tasks and roles performed by the district courts' lower tier of judicial officers.

A New Title and Enhanced Status

The magistrate judges' original title, "magistrate," was a source of unhappiness for many of the lower tier judicial officers. District courts throughout the country received authorization to appoint magistrates in the early 1970s. Because neither district judges nor practicing attorneys knew how these new judicial officers, with their vaguely defined authority, ought to be regarded, many judges simply used magistrates as if they were merely permanent law clerks. Practicing attorneys followed suit by failing to treat magistrates with the deference and respect they would normally accord to a recognized judicial officer.[11] As a result, many magistrates believed their effectiveness was hampered because lawyers did not understand that they were indeed authoritative judicial officers. For example, a lawyer interviewed for one study said that "when a [district] judge tells you to do something, you jump. But when a magistrate tells you to do something, well, you do it, but it's not the same."[12]

"Magistrate" is a respected title in the British legal system, but in the United States it is merely a generic term for judicial officer. Because many state court systems employ the title "magistrate" for low-level lay officials, practicing attorneys often confused the authoritative federal judicial officers with the relatively inconsequential lay "justices of the peace" who bear the title "magistrate" in many states. The potential confusion that the title could cause was recognized when the new federal judicial office was created and the Judicial Conference of the United States subsequently discussed the issue in a report to Congress:

> Those who would prefer a change in title state that the term "magistrate" has traditionally referred to a low-level local official who performs a narrow range of functions in criminal cases, i.e., a justice of the peace. They point out that this traditional association of the term is inaccurate when applied to the full-time United States magistrates. They also note that many state magistrates are not well regarded and some have been prosecuted for wrongdoing.[13]

The title "magistrate" contributed to many practical problems when lawyers did not accord the subordinate judicial officers with appropriate deference and respect. If lawyers do not "jump" when instructed to take a specific action by a magistrate, then magistrates must waste time in the aftermath of motion hearings and discovery conferences trying to ensure that attorneys comply with the magistrates' orders. District judges could always force compliance by reiterating the magistrates' orders, but such redundant actions diminish the advantages for saving the judicial system's resources that Congress sought to attain by making magistrates authoritative judicial officers.[14] In addition, because magistrates' authority to preside over civil trials depends upon the consent of litigants,[15] the failure of attorneys to recognize magistrates' status and authority as judicial officers can reduce the likelihood that litigants will consent to magistrates' jurisdiction and thereby hinder the implementation of this mechanism to reduce district judges' civil caseload burdens. The magistrates' title may be an important component of attorneys' willingness to recommend the consent trial option to their clients:

> Some magistrates view the title "judge" not only as an entitlement [for themselves as authoritative federal judicial officers], but as a

functional necessity if they are to perform effectively when presiding over trials. . . . Many litigants may automatically prefer to have their cases heard by someone bearing the title of "judge." As a result, magistrates lose opportunities to gain visibility and build their reputations as judicial officers, and the potential flexibility and judicial economy of the magistrate system are diminished.[16]

In order to combat the confusion over magistrates' title, district judges in some districts addressed the magistrates as "judge" and instructed attorneys to do the same. This action reinforced the magistrates' status as judicial officers within those districts, but it exacerbated morale problems among magistrates in other districts who desired similar recognition but were forbidden by their supervising district judges from using the title "judge."[17]

As a result of the title change contained in the Judicial Improvements Act, the magistrate judges can expect to be more readily addressed as "judge." The new title and form of address will help educate attorneys and litigants about the magistrate judges' status as authoritative judicial officers within the federal courts. This should enhance the magistrate judges' contributions to effective case processing within the district courts by encouraging full cooperation and compliance from attorneys and by increasing the visibility and credibility of the litigants' option to consent to have civil cases tried before magistrate judges.

In 1979, when Congress considered the legislation that authorized magistrates to oversee consent trials, two members of Congress complained that "[f]rom the standpoint of appearance, procedure, and function, an impartial observer will not be able to tell the difference between a magistrate and an Article III judge."[18] In the context in which they raised this concern as part of the debate about the proper authority of non-Article III judicial officers, this was a significant issue to consider. But is this question as compelling today? Now that Congress has explicitly endorsed magistrate judges as "federal judicial officers,"[19] federal appellate court decisions have accepted the constitutionality of magistrates' authority,[20] and magistrates have supervised civil trials for more than a decade, does it matter whether an outside observer, be it a litigant or an attorney, knows the precise difference between a magistrate judge and an Article III district judge?

There may be legitimate, principled reasons to reopen the debate about the appropriate scope of non-Article III judges' authority.[21] However, because legislative and judicial policy makers have endorsed broad authority for magistrate judges, there is strong reason to give magistrate judges the title and status necessary for maximizing their contributions to the work of the district courts. Magistrate judges are different than Article III district judges in regard to their scope of authority and the delegation of tasks.[22] The title change contained in the Judicial

Improvements Act merely indicates that when magistrate judges serve as the presiding judicial officers for matters pending before the district courts, the litigants and attorneys should be made well aware that the magistrate judges are indeed authoritative judicial decision makers who are to be accorded appropriate deference and respect.

Consent Trial Authority

Recent court reform initiatives threatened the magistrates' status and authority within the federal courts. One of the recommendations made in 1989 by the Brookings Institution's task force on civil justice reform[23] was aimed directly at the broad exercise of authority by magistrates: "Procedural Recommendation II: Ensure in each district's plan that magistrates do not perform tasks best performed by the judiciary." The phrase "tasks best performed by the judiciary" seemed to imply that district judges rather than magistrates should preside over civil trials.

The task force report served as the basis for legislative proposals by Senator Joseph Biden, the chairman of the Senate Judiciary Committee. Biden's court reform bill, entitled "The Civil Justice Reform Act," contained, among other things, provisions requiring mandatory discovery-case management conferences and monitoring conferences for complex litigation that would both be "presided over by a judge and not a magistrate."[24] Such mandatory conferences would be designed to force district judges to become involved in case management for each civil case and would consequently reduce the likelihood that entire civil cases would be referred to magistrates by the consent of the litigants. In proposing his court reform legislation, Senator Biden made it quite clear that he did not think that magistrates could manage civil litigation effectively.[25]

Ultimately, Biden's "Civil Justice Reform" bill was scrapped in favor of "The Judicial Improvements Act of 1990," which was developed through negotiations between the Senate Judiciary Committee and the Judicial Conference of the United States.[26] In regard to authority of magistrates,[27] the legislation enacted by Congress followed the recommendation of the Federal Courts Study Committee's 1990 report to encourage more consent trials before magistrates. The Federal Courts Study Committee urged that "Congress . . . allow district judges and magistrates to remind the parties [in civil litigation] of the possibilities of consent to civil trials before magistrates."[28] The statutory change affecting magistrates' consent trial authority suited the interests of both district judges and magistrates by, respectively, maintaining district judges' discretion and autonomy with regard to case management[29] and encouraging the referral of more complete civil trials to the newly retitled magistrate judges.

The Judicial Improvements Act encourages civil consent trials by now permitting district judges and magistrate judges to inform litigants directly about their option of consenting to a trial before a magistrate judge: "[E]ither the district court judge or the magistrate may again advise the parties of the availability of the magistrate, but in so doing, shall also advise the parties that they are free to withhold consent without adverse substantive consequences."[30] The involvement of judicial officers in informing litigants about the consent option represents a significant change from previous statutory language that made clerks of court exclusively responsible for communications about the consent option and precluded any involvement by judges or magistrates.[31] When Congress officially authorized magistrates to preside over complete civil trials with the consent of litigants in 1979,[32] the statute precluded involvement by judicial officers and emphasized the voluntariness of litigants' consent in order to avoid the possibility that judicial officers might pressure litigants to consent."[33]

Magistrate judges in many districts should enjoy increased opportunities to oversee complete civil cases as a result of the statutory change. Some districts had failed to implement regular procedures for educating litigants and their attorneys about the consent option through notices from the clerk of court. Litigants often remained uninformed about their options because the court personnel with whom they came into the most frequent, direct contact through pretrial conferences and hearings, namely the district judges and magistrates, were forbidden from discussing the magistrates' consent authority.[34] Now judicial officers will be able to remind parties about the consent option throughout the stages of civil litigation. Under the previous system, some districts that had routinized the notice process informed litigants about the consent option only at the outset of litigation.[35] If litigants did not understand the scope of magistrates' authority, they would be reluctant to consider immediately consenting to an unfamiliar process under the authority of an unfamiliar judicial officer.[36] Because the parties may not recognize the desirability of consenting to a magistrate judge's jurisdiction for a firm and expedited trial date until after the initiation of discovery and pretrial conferences, the new procedure will provide the opportunity for useful reminders to litigants when judicial officers perceive that such a referral might be beneficial.

Pressure to Consent

Although the new procedure will increase the flexible utilization of magistrate judges and increase their status and authority in some districts, the involvement of judicial officers in informing litigants about the consent option also entails risks. The original statutory provision concerning notice to parties precluded the participation of judicial officers because they might coerce litigants into consenting. Congress was aware of the possibility, for example, that district judges might be "tempted to force disfavored cases into disposition before magistrates by intimations of lengthy delays manufactured in district court if the parties exercise their right to stay in that court.[37] Subsequent research revealed that this was a genuine risk that, in fact, came to fruition in some districts despite the statutory prohibition on communications from judicial officers to litigants concerning consent. A Federal Judicial Center study found that:

> There was a clear consensus among the [California lawyers] interviewed that when a judge raises the question of consent to a magistrate—for whatever reason—lawyers feel that they have little choice but to go along with the suggestion. Attorneys consistently reported feeling some pressure to consent, particularly in a "smaller" case; when interviewees were asked to describe the reasons for consent, the overriding one given was that the judge had suggested it.[38]

Another study found examples of district judges engaging in precisely the behavior that Congress feared, namely pressuring litigants to consent to the referral of disfavored cases to magistrates.[39]

Because the statutory revisions from the Judicial Improvements Act now invite judicial officers to communicate with litigants about the consent option, there are even greater risks that parties will be or will feel pressured to waive their right to have their case heard before an Article III judge. Such actions by judges are not likely to be challenged by attorneys: "Lawyers are not likely to admit publicly that they were weak in the face of improper conduct. They also [may] think twice about directly challenging the ethical conduct of a judge sitting in a court that provides a basis for their legal practice and livelihood."[40] Moreover, even if the issue of coercion is raised, it would be difficult to prove to an appellate court that a district judge had improper motives or undertook improper actions. Judges' coercive actions identified in one study "were essentially immune from external scrutiny because scheduling trial dates and refusing to grant continuances (two of the most frequently-manipulated mechanisms to pressure litigants) are part of a judge's prerogatives. Thus, the coercive actions were cloaked in the impenetrable discretionary authority of judges."[41] Because the new notice provision invites the participation of judicial officers, district judges and magistrate judges must become much more self-conscious about their own motives and the possible coercive consequences of their communications with litigants concerning the consent option.

Task Assignments

Current developments affecting the federal courts are certain to affect magistrate judges' task assignments in various districts, although it is uncertain precisely how those assignments will be affected. Although the changes affecting the subordinate judicial officers' title and consent trial authority should encourage increased references of complete civil cases to the magistrate judges, other factors may impede an increase in trials before magistrate judges.

The Judicial Improvements Act requires each district court to develop and implement a "civil justice expense and delay reduction plan."[42] In the course of examining mechanisms for effective case management and cost-effective discovery, districts may create new procedures that actually limit the exercise of magistrate judges' authority. For example, expense and delay reduction plans may make magistrate judges exclusively responsible for oversight of discovery, pretrial conferences, and other preliminary matters, thus formalizing the subordinate judicial officers' roles as "Trial Preparers" rather than as "Autonomous Judges" presiding over civil consent trials.[43] Because district judges exert significant control over the magistrates' roles through their authority to appoint and reappoint the subordinate judicial officers and through their power over the delegation of tasks,[44] Article III judges will continue to have substantial influence over the definition of magistrate judges' roles within each district court. If the judges within a district believe that magistrate judges should exercise limited authority, the expense and delay reduction plans are likely to reflect that preference.

The precise tasks assigned to magistrate judges within a district depend not only upon the district judges' conceptualizations of the proper role for their judicial subordinates, but also upon the caseload composition within the district.[45] If a magistrate judge works within a district containing large prisons, they may become "Specialists" in prisoner petitions. Similarly, in districts that receive especially large numbers of Social Security disability appeals, the magistrate judges' working lives may be absorbed by the process of reviewing administrative law judges' findings in such cases. Although some districts utilize alternative mechanisms (e.g., staff attorneys, pro se law clerks, district judges' law clerks) for processing prisoner and Social Security cases, these two particular categories of cases have a significant impact upon workloads of magistrate judges in many districts.[46]

How are the federal courts currently being affected by these categories of cases? In regard to Social Security disability appeals, the federal district courts have experienced a steady decline in such cases. Disability cases peaked in 1984 at 24,215[47] in the aftermath of the Reagan administration's attempt to remove summarily 336,000 beneficiaries

In SC, mat cases go to JHO's after all discovery completed

from that Social Security program.[48] By contrast, in 1990 there were only 5,212 of such cases filed in the federal district courts.[49] Thus, unless a magistrate judge serves a district that is especially affected by disability cases, these Social Security cases are becoming less burdensome and therefore are having fewer limiting effects upon magistrate judges' availability for other tasks, such as consent trials.

In regard to prisoners' petitions, the burden upon the federal courts has continued to grow. There were only 29,303 prisoners' petitions filed in the district courts in 1982[50] but that number grew to 42,630 in 1990.[51] After handling only 11,578 prisoner matters in 1980, the magistrate judges' burden peaked at 27,002 in 1987 and then dropped back to a consistent plateau just below 21,000 in 1989 and 1990.[52] Because prisoners' filings in the federal courts have shown steady annual increases throughout the 1980s, the recent reduction in the magistrate judges' burden must indicate district judges are employing alternative mechanisms for processing such cases, such as pro se clerks[53] or their own law clerks. Although the burden upon the magistrate judges generally has, for the moment, stabilized, the tremendous increases in the number of people imprisoned throughout the United States make it likely that the number of prisoners' petitions will increase as well. There were only 329,821 people in prison in 1980, but that number leaped to 771,213 in 1990 as the result of aggressive prosecutions and stiffer sentences for narcotics and other offenses.[54]

Although rising prison populations make it appear likely that magistrate judges will continue to have some portion of their working lives absorbed by prisoners' petitions, other developments may reduce the number of such petitions in the federal courts. The Supreme Court has taken the initiative to create new rules for habeas corpus petitions that have the effect of precluding multiple petitions, enforcing procedural bars, and otherwise limiting prisoners' access to the federal courts.[55] Other potential exclusionary mechanisms have been discussed in justices' opinions[56] and may be on the horizon for implementation in future decisions. In addition, President Bush and Congress are working on legislative proposals that would, if passed, place additional limitations upon prisoners' opportunities to file habeas corpus petitions in the federal courts.[57] Although habeas corpus petitions typically constitute only 25 to 30 percent of the prisoners' petitions filed in federal court, they have constituted 40 percent of the magistrate judges' prisoner tasks in recent years.[58] The current developments aimed at reducing the number of habeas corpus petitions may reduce the magistrate judges' burden or, alternatively, district judges may simply assign their judicial subordinates more prisoner civil rights cases, which typically comprise more than 60 percent of the prisoner filings.[59]

Effect of Felony Prosecutions

Magistrate judges' workload is being affected by the increase in federal felony prosecutions, especially for narcotics offenses. Increases in felony prosecutions tie up the district judges because "speedy trial" requirements make criminal cases move to the head of the docket queue. Because magistrate judges cannot conduct trials and sentence offenders in felony cases, an increase in felony prosecutions should make litigants more inclined to consent to civil trials before magistrate judges as district judges' time becomes increasingly absorbed by felony cases. By consenting to a trial before a magistrate judge, litigants in civil cases can obtain an early and firm trial date. They may also be able to choose which magistrate judge will preside over the trial if the district court's case-processing procedures utilize references to multiple available magistrate judges. Although the increases in felony prosecutions may lead to more civil case responsibilities for magistrate judges, the subordinate judicial officers also have their time absorbed in assisting the felony work of district judges; "Magistrates handled 313 percent more detention hearings in 1990 than in 1985, 111 percent more search warrants, 45 percent more preliminary examinations, 44 percent more arrest warrants, and 38 percent more arraignments."[60]

As with other developments affecting the federal courts, the magistrate judges' task assignments are affected by increases in criminal prosecutions, but it is not clear that such changes will necessarily lead to broader, more flexible utilization of the subordinate judicial officers. For example, although the magistrate judges' responsibilities for preliminary criminal matters increased in conjunction with the increasing criminal caseload in the district courts, the number of civil consent cases for magistrate judges was virtually the same in 1990 as it was in 1986 (4,958 to 4,960).[61] Although the increase in felony cases during the late 1980s did not consistently escalate the number of civil consent cases for magistrate judges, the new statutory notice provisions permitting judicial officers to inform and remind litigants about the consent option may generate such an increase in the future. The number of civil consent trials before magistrate judges is most likely to rise if district judges continue to be preoccupied with felony cases and if those judges evince a concomitant willingness to refer complete civil cases to their judicial subordinates.

Conclusion

Recent and ongoing developments in the federal courts will shape the status, authority, and workload of the U.S. magistrate judges. With their new title and increased opportunities to educate the bar about the breadth of their judicial authority, especially their ability to supervise civil consent trials, magistrate judges are poised to fulfill the potential that their supporters have envisioned for broad, flexible contributions to the case-processing responsibilities within each district court.

Although the subordinate judicial officers received a vote of confidence from Congress in the passage of the supportive Judicial Improvements Act instead of Senator Biden's limiting Civil Justice Reform bill, it remains to be seen whether the magistrate judges will be able to exercise the full range of judicial tasks authorized by statute and desired by many of the incumbent judicial officers themselves.[62] Because the precise tasks assigned to magistrate judges are still significantly influenced by the preferences of the district judges with whom they work and by the nature of their individual districts' caseloads, the recent efforts to enhance magistrate judges' status, authority, and usefulness within the federal courts may, in fact, have little effect upon the subordinate judicial officers' contributions to the court system. The Judicial Improvements Act and the federal courts' continuing docket pressures have set the stage for broader, more innovative use of magistrate judges, but the actual implementation of reforms is dependent on the district judges' willingness to delegate important responsibilities to their judicial subordinates.

Endnotes

[1] References to the lower tier judicial officers concerning their status and authority prior to December 1990 will use the previous title "magistrate" rather than the new title "magistrate judge."

[2] See Smith, "Who Are the U.S. Magistrates?" 71 *Judicature* 143 (1987); Smith, "Merit Selection Committees and the Politics of Appointing United States Magistrates," 12 *Just. Sys. J.* 210 (1987).

[3] See Spaniol, "The Federal Magistrates Act: History and Development," 1974 *Ariz. L. Rev.* 566; Peterson, "The Federal Magistrates Act: A New Dimension in the Implementation of Justice," 56 *Iowa L. Rev.* 62 (1970).

[4] See McCabe, "The Federal Magistrates Act of 1979," 16 *Harv. J. Legis.* 343 (1979).

[5] See, e.g., *Gomez v. United States*, 109 S.Ct. 2237 (1989) (magistrates not authorized to supervise the selection of jurors in felony criminal cases).

[6] Administrative Office of the U.S. Courts, *Annual Report of the Director of The Administrative Office of the U.S. Courts* 25 (1990). Because these figures are drawn from individual magistrate judges' reports concerning their own activities and the categories of activities are not precisely defined (e.g. different activities may be classified as separate "civil pretrial conferences" by different magistrate judges), case processing statistics provide only a rough picture of magistrate judges' responsibilities. Although the statistics from the Administrative Office cannot provide precise information on the magistrate judges' accomplishments, the figures demonstrate substantial contributions to the work of the district courts by the lower tier of judicial officers.

7 Committee on the Judicial Branch of the Judicial Conference of the United States, *Simple Fairness: The Case for Equitable Compensation of the Nation's Judges* 81–82 (1988).

8 See, Smith, "Federal Judicial Salaries: A Critical Appraisal," 62 *Temple L. Rev..* 849 (1989).

9 See Seron, *The Roles of Magistrates: Nine Case Studies* (Washington, D.C.: Federal Judicial Center, 1985); Seron, "Magistrates and the Work of the Federal Courts: A New Division of Labor," 69 *Judicature* 353 (1986).

10 See Smith, *United States Magistrates in the Federal Courts: Subordinate Judges* 115–146 (New York: Praeger, 1990).

11 Smith, "The Development of a Judicial Office: United States Magistrates and the Struggle for Status," 14 *J. Legal Prof.* 175, 184–185 (1989).

12 Smith, supra n. 10, at 135.

13 *The Federal Magistrates System: Report to the Congress by the Judicial Conference of the United States* 62 (1981).

14 Many magistrates can cite examples of incidents in which the judicial officers wasted time reinforcing to attorneys the idea that magistrates are indeed authoritative federal judicial officers: "In some instances, it is very obvious to the magistrate that the attorney regards the magistrate as being of lesser importance. The magistrate may be forced to marshal resources in order to maintain his or her desired judicial role. For example, in a . . . case in which an attorney attempted to go over the magistrate's head to the judge in order to get a conference rescheduled, it was clear that the attorney never would have attempted such a maneuver if the district judge were presiding over the conference. After an attorney approached a judge about rescheduling, there would be nothing that the attorney could do but comply with the judge's orders. [In this] example, the magistrate hurried to contact the judge to ensure that the judge upheld the magistrate's decision. Thus the magistrate, because of the relatively new judicial office and uncertainty about [the] appropriate status and role for the magistrate position, must often actively seek to maintain proper behavior and respect on the part of attorneys." Smith, supra n. 10, at 195.

15 "Upon the consent of the parties, a full-time United States magistrate or a part-time United States magistrate who serves as a full-time judicial officer may conduct any or all proceedings in a jury or nonjury civil matter and order entry of judgment in the case, when specially designated to exercise such jurisdiction by the district court or courts he serves." 28 U.S.C. sec. 636(c)(1).

16 Smith, supra n. 11, at 181–182.

17 Id. at 180–184.

18 H.R. Rep. No. 1364, 95th Cong., 2d Sess. (1978) at 37 (statement of Reps. Drinan and Kindness).

19 The "definition" section of the Judicial Improvements Act clearly endorsed the magistrate judges' status as judicial officers: "As used in this chapter the term 'judicial officer' means a United States district court judge or a *United States magistrate*" (emphasis supplied). 28 U.S.C. sec. 482 (1990).

20 See, e.g., *Pacemaker Diagnostic Clinic of America, Inc. v. Instromedix, Inc.*, 725 F.2d 537 (9th Cir. 1984) (*en banc*), cert. denied, 469 U.S. 824 (1984).

21 See Resnik, "The Mythic Meaning of Article III Courts," 56 *U. Colo. L. Rev.* 581 (1985).

22 For example, district judges control the delegation of tasks to magistrate judges and, unless the parties have consented to a magistrate judge's authority, magistrate judges merely make recommendations to district judges concerning dispositive motions.

23 See Litan, "Speeding Up Civil Justice," 73 *Judiculture* 162 (1989).

24 The relevant provisions proposed: "A requirement that . . . a mandatory discovery-case management conference, presided over by a judge and not a magistrate, be held in all cases within 45 days following the first responsive pleading" (S.2027, 101st

Cong., 2d Sess. sec. 471(b)(3) (1990)); and "[F]or cases assigned to the track designated for complex litigation, calendar a series of monitoring conferences, presided over by judge and not a magistrate, for the purpose of extending stipulations, refining the formulation of issues and focusing and pacing discovery" (Id. at sec. 471(b)(3)(I)).

25 Biden's statement introducing his court reform legislation expressed doubts about the magistrates' effectiveness: "The [pretrial] conference may lose some of its significance in the minds of the attorneys if presided over by a magistrate, since the unfortunate fact is that many attorneys seem to be far more willing to take frivolous positions before a magistrate. . . . [M]agistrates may themselves be more reluctant than judges to frame the contours of litigation, limit discovery, establish a date certain briefing schedule and address the full panoply of discovery case management conference issues." 136 *Cong. Rec.* S414 (daily ed. Jan. 25, 1990) (statement of Sen. Biden).

26 Some aspects of the negotiation process between the judiciary and Congress apparently angered members of the Senate Judiciary Committee: "The [Senate Judiciary] [C]ommittee complied with the request of the Judicial Conference to work with one body [i.e., a four-judge task force appointed by Chief Justice William Rehnquist], only to have the [Judicial] Conference seemingly defer to another body [i.e., the Conference's Committee on Judicial Improvements which rejected the negotiated legislative proposal]—which had no role whatsoever in the discussions and negotiations—at the point of decision. Such actions only serve to undermine the cooperative relationship between Congress and the judicial branch that our citizens rightly expect and deserve." S.416, 101st. Cong., 2d Sess. (1990) at 5.

27 To counteract Senator Biden's perception that magistrates are ineffective because lawyers do not respect their authority, district judges argued that magistrates can be very capable and authoritative, especially in districts in which judges permit them to perform a broad range of tasks: "[Magistrates] have informed me that it is a rare occasion indeed, that any attorney ever takes a frivolous position when appearing before them. If that should occur in some districts, I suspect that it is more of a reflection of how the magistrates are perceived by the Article III judges, and what duties or powers those judges have permitted the magistrates to perform. If that suspicion is true, one way to address the concerns of the [Brookings Institution's] Task Force is to leave the matter of who presides at the conference to the discretion of the district court adopting its plan." Enslen, *Prepared Statement of the Hon. Richard Enslen, U.S. District Court for the Western District of Michigan, presented in Testimony Before the Senate Judiciary Committee During Consideration of S.2027, The Civil Justice Reform Act of 1990* (Mar. 6, 1990) at 45.

28 *Report of the Federal Courts Study Committee* 79 (Apr. 2, 1990).

29 The district judges had argued to Congress that "the proposed diminution of the role of magistrates would hamper the proposed legislation's underlying purpose of improving case-processing efficiency." Robinson, *Prepared Statement of the Hon. Aubrey E. Robinson, Jr., Chief Judge, U.S. District Court of the District of Columbia, Presented in Testimony Before the Senate Judiciary Committee During Consideration of S.2027, The Civil Justice Reform Act of 1990* (Mar. 6, 1990) at 4.

30 28 U.S.C. sec. 636(c)(2) (1991).

31 "[T]he clerk of court shall, at the time the action is filed, notify the parties of their right to consent to the exercise of such jurisdiction. The decision of the parties shall he communicated to the clerk of court. Thereafter, neither the district judge nor the magistrate shall attempt to persuade or induce any party to consent to reference of any civil matter to a magistrate." 28 U.S.C. sec. 626(c)(2) (1982).

32 At least 36 district courts referred civil cases to magistrates for trial before Congress explicitly endorsed this practice with the 1979 Act. H.R. Rep. No. 1364, supra n. 18, at 4.

33 See Smith, "Assessing the Consequences of Judicial Innovation: U.S. Magistrates'

Trials and Related Tribulations,'' 23 *Wake Forest L. Rev.* 455, 474–476 (1988).

[34] See Smith, supra n. 10, at 85–87.

[35] One former magistrate described the old statutory notice provision as ''unworkable on its face'' because the notice was frequently attached to the summons and ''such boilerplate is commonly ignored.'' Sinclair, *Practice Before Federal Magistrates* sec. 2303 (New York: Matthew Bender, 1987).

[36] In the districts in which magistrates were used as ''Additional Judges,'' the practicing bar became familiar with the individual magistrates and knowledgeable about their authority. Thus there was greater willingness to consent. See Seron, *The Roles of Magistrates*, supra n. 9, at 38–39.

[37] H.R. Rep. No. 1364, supra n. 18, at 14.

[38] Seron, *The Roles of Magistrates*, supra n. 9, at 61–62.

[39] Smith, supra n. 10, at 103–104.

[40] Id. at 180.

[41] Id.

[42] 28 U.S.C. sec. 471 (1991).

[43] For a detailed typology of eight possible model roles for magistrates, see Smith, supra n. 10, at 127–132,

[44] Id. at 115–119; see Seron, ''The Professional Project of Parajudges: The Case of the U.S. Magistrates,'' 22 *Law & Soc'y Rev.* 557 (1988).

[45] Smith, supra n. 10, at 140–141.

[46] See Seron, *The Roles of Magistrates*, supra, n. 9, at 83–92.

[47] .Administrative Office of the U.S. Courts, *Annual Report of the Director of the Administrative Office of the U.S. Courts* 180 (1986).

[48] See Mezey, *No Longer Disabled: The Federal Courts and the Politics of Social Security Disability* (New York: Greenwood, 1988).

[49] Administrative Office, supra n. 6, at 138.

[50] Administrative Office, supra n. 47, at 179.

[51] Administrative Office, supra n. 6, at 138.

[52] Id.

[53] See Zeigler & Hermann, ''The Invisible Litigant: An Inside View of Pro Se Actions in the Federal Courts,'' 47 *N.Y.U. L. Rev.* 157 (1972).

[54] Cohen, ''Prisoners in 1990,'' *Bureau of Justice Statistics Bulletin* 1 (May 1991). Increases in prisoner filings are not purely a function of increases in prison populations. See Thomas, Keeler & Harris, ''Issues and Misconceptions in Prisoner Litigation: A Critical View,'' 24 *Criminology* 775 (1986).

[55] See, e.g., *McCleskey v. Zant*, 111 S.Ct. 2841 (1991) (failure to raise claim in initial habeas corpus petition in federal courts barred subsequent petition concerning claim); *Coleman v. Thompson*, 111 S.Ct. 2546 (1991) (procedural default under state court rules barred raising claim in subsequent federal court habeas corpus petition).

[56] In a concurring opinion in *Duckworth v. Eagan*, 109 S.Ct. 2875 (1989), Justice O'Connor argued that the Supreme Court should emulate its decision in *Stone v. Powell*, 428 U.S. 465 (1976), which precludes federal court consideration of habeas corpus ''exclusionary rule'' claims that have been previously raised in state courts, by similarly precluding federal court review of *Miranda* claims.

[57] See Diemer, ''Blood for Blood: Senate Focuses upon Fighting Crime, *Cleveland Plain Dealer*, June 30, 1991, at 15–A.

[58] Administrative Office, supra n. 6, at 25, 140.

[59] Id.

[60] Id. at 24.

[61] Id. at 25.

[62] See Smith, supra n. 10, at 69–75, 182–187.

5

The Changing Role of the United States Courts of Appeals
The Flow of Litigation Revisited

SUE DAVIS and DONALD R. SONGER

Introduction

The United States courts of appeals are approaching their one hundredth birthday.[1] Created to alleviate the workload of the Supreme Court and to increase the power of the federal courts to apply the national law, the intermediate appellate judiciary has become a major political institution that functions not only as a norm enforcer but also as a creator of public policy. Despite their importance, the courts of appeals were the "courts nobody knows"[2] until J. Woodford Howard provided his comprehensive study of three circuits (1981). Howard studied the business and behavior of the second, fifth, and D.C. circuits during the fiscal years 1965–67 in order to describe the functions of the appellate courts in the federal system and their relations with other courts.[3]

Although Howard pointed out changes in the role of the courts of appeal, such as the increase in criminal appeals, he concentrated primarily on describing exactly what the courts were doing in the late 1960s. Other studies have focused more attention on the changes that

Reprinted by permission of the *Justice System Journal* from vol. 13, no. 3 (1988–89), pp. 323–340.

the intermediate appellate courts have undergone over time. For example, Baum, Goldman, and Sarat (1981–82), who analyzed the activity of the second, fifth, and ninth circuits from 1895 through 1975, found that the business of the courts shifted from predominantly private economic disputes to government economic regulation and criminal appeals.

In this article we explore the role of the courts of appeals, paying particular attention to the changes that they have undergone during the last 20 years. We pose the following questions. Has the nature of the business of the courts changed since the 1960s? Have the demands on the intermediate appellate courts increased since that time? Does the diversity in business and behavior that Howard found among circuits currently prevail? And what is the nature of the increasing number of cases that are disposed of without a published opinion? The reader should be aware from the outset that this article is a preliminary report, which outlines a number of important findings, but which does not purport to provide a new theory of the appellate process.

Our study is based upon analysis of data collected by the Administrative Office of the United States Courts for cases decided during fiscal year 1984 as documented by the Federal Judicial Center and made available through the Inter-University Consortium for Political and Social Research. Additionally, we have utilized data collected for the D.C., the fourth, and the eleventh circuits for calendar year 1986.[4]

Our study is grounded on and builds upon Howard's work; consequently, we proceed much as he did in "The Flow of Litigation in Three Courts of Appeals" (1981:ch.2), exploring differences among the circuits and comparing our findings for the 1980s to his.[5] More specifically, we begin by examining the business of the courts of appeals by comparing the sources of the cases, the types of cases, and the parties before the courts in 1984 to those of the earlier time periods in order to suggest ways in which the role of the federal appellate judiciary has changed. In addition to changes in the nature of cases, the volume has also changed—increasing dramatically over time. Thus, we examine the magnitude of the increasing workload. Second, we explore the behavior of the courts of appeals by describing the rates of reversal in different circuits, and for different types of cases, to look further at their role and, particularly, at their relationship to the federal trial courts. We then describe the decisions of the courts of appeals by identifying winners and losers to shed additional light on the role of the courts. Third, we explore the relationship between the courts of appeals and the Supreme Court by describing supervision by the Supreme Court. Finally, moving away from Howard's work, we discuss the importance of unpublished decisions in order to begin to delineate their importance for the future study of the lower federal courts.

The Business of the Courts of Appeals

The role the courts play in the making of public policy is heavily dependent on the nature of their business. The courts of appeals in the nineteenth century with caseloads dominated by tort cases were hardly likely to make policy regarding the constitutional rights of individuals accused of crimes. Conversely, appellate courts that dispose of a large number of criminal appeals inevitably make policy regarding the rights of the accused. Similarly, the source of the courts' business is an important ingredient in their role in public policy. A large proportion of cases from the district courts would indicate that the courts of appeals were correcting errors of the lower courts to ensure the uniform application of the federal law. On the other hand, if the cases coming to the courts of appeals were predominantly appeals from decisions of administrative agencies, it would suggest that the courts were functioning more as overseers of the federal bureaucracy.

Howard found that appeals from the district courts rather than from federal administrative agencies dominated the caseloads. While civil litigation dominated the dockets, criminal appeals rose considerably during the years 1961 through 1979 (1981:26). Moreover, the three circuits differed in the efforts they devoted to criminal cases—the D.C. circuit had the highest percentage of criminal appeals.

Table 1 compares the patterns in the sources of business of the courts of appeals in 1984 to that of 1965–67 in the three circuits that Howard studied. The data for 1984 show that while appeals from the district courts dominated the second and fifth circuits, cases from federal administrative agencies comprised almost half of the cases decided by the D.C. circuit. The proportion of criminal cases also differed in the three circuits. The fact that the rate of criminal appeals to the D.C. circuit decreased from 39 percent to 5.2 percent while remaining about the same for the second and fifth circuit (22.6 percent and 13.7 percent, respectively) is explained by the new policy beginning in 1973 of transferring appeals and petitions for habeas corpus to local courts.[6] Additionally, the proportion of administrative appeals in the D.C. circuit more than doubled from 1967 to 1984.

Table 2 delineates the sources of the cases decided by the courts of appeals for all of the circuits in 1984. Three patterns are noteworthy. First, criminal cases did not become the dominant business of the courts of appeals as the projections during the 1960s suggested. In fact, in nine of the twelve circuits less than 20 percent of the cases were criminal appeals. Moreover, in six of the twelve circuits, criminal cases made up a smaller portion of the business than in any of the three circuits examined by Howard. Second, there was tremendous variation among the circuits. For example, the eleventh circuit led in the percentage of

Table 1.
Nature of Cases* Decided by Three Circuits
FY 1984 v. FY 1965-67**

Circuit	Civil %	Criminal %	Bankruptcy %	Admin. %	Other %	Total N
			1984			
2d	67.8	22.6	2.5	7.1	--	1,749
5th	76.4	13.7	2.1	7.8	--	2,504
D.C.	48.6	5.2	1.5	44.8	--	1,306
			1965-67			
2d	53.9	21.7	6.2	14.4	3.8	1,357
5th	68.4	16.1	3.5	9.7	2.3	2,248
D.C.	39.0	39.0	0.0	16.2	5.7	1,336

*Appeals from U.S. District Courts.
**Source of 1965-67 data: Howard (1981) p. 26, Table 2.1.

Table 2.
Nature of Cases Decided by All Circuits
(FY 1984)

Circuit	Administrative %	Civil U.S. %	Civil Private %	Criminal %	Bankruptcy %	Total N
D.C.	44.8	30.2	18.4	5.2	1.5	1,306
1st	6.4	27.7	44.2	19.8	2.0	763
2d	7.1	18.4	49.4	22.6	2.5	1,749
3d	8.9	17.6	51.6	18.9	3.0	2,027
4th	5.9	20.2	56.2	15.0	2.6	2,010
5th	7.8	12.2	64.2	13.7	2.1	2,504
6th	11.3	20.5	52.4	13.8	1.9	2,021
7th	8.8	20.4	54.0	14.5	2.3	1,941
8th	5.6	21.3	52.5	18.0	2.6	1,364
9th	15.8	20.2	38.9	23.0	2.2	3,195
10th	8.0	24.6	47.7	15.5	4.1	1,409
11th	4.3	15.4	46.1	31.3	2.8	2,540

criminal appeals while the D.C. circuit had a low of 5.2 percent; private civil cases ranged from a low of 18.4 percent in the D.C. circuit to a high of 64.2 percent in the fifth circuit. Finally, it is clear from Table 2 that the D.C. circuit's business is distinguished from that of all the others by its heavy concentration of administrative appeals and low rates of criminal and private civil cases. The shift in the business of the D.C. circuit suggests that the role of that court has changed in a major way. No longer dominated by criminal appeals, the D.C. circuit is now largely occupied by administrative appeals.

Table 3 displays the rate of increase for each of the different types of business during the time periods 1961 through 1979, and 1979 through 1984. Howard found that between 1961 and 1979 criminal appeals increased at a higher rate (507.1 percent) than any of the courts' other business—"criminal justice shifted from a peripheral to a central responsibility of Courts of Appeals in one generation" (1981:27). In sharp contrast, we found that it was not criminal appeals but bankruptcy that increased the most from 1979 to 1984 (299.3 percent); criminal appeals increased the least—only 54.3 percent. The data indicate that, contrary to the dire predictions made in the 1960s (see, for example, Carrington, 1969:547), as well as the folklore of the 1980s, the courts of appeals have not been overwhelmed with criminal appeals. Indeed, the rate of criminal appeals has expanded less than any other business of the intermediate appellate courts.

Who are the parties in the cases decided by the courts of appeals? Identifying parties in litigation before the judiciary is important for several reasons. First, a description of the parties will shed light on the role that various groups and individuals play in bringing issues before the judiciary. Second, identifying parties may suggest that some types

Table 3.
Caseload Increases for All Circuits
1961,* 1979,* 1984

Case Type	1961 N	1979 N	1984 N	1961-79 Increase	1979-84 Increase
Administrative Appeals	457	887	2,454	94.1%	176.7%
Civil, U.S.	621	1,882	4,483	203.1%	138.2%
Civil, Private	1,101	3,650	11,136	231.5%	205.1%
Criminal	448	2,720	4,197	507.1%	54.3%
Bankruptcy	93	140	559	50.5%	299.3%
Total	2,712	9,279	22,829	242.1%	146.0%

* Source: Howard (1981) p. 27, Table 2.2.

of individuals and groups have a better chance of prevailing (see, for example, Galanter, 1974). Moreover, if there are variations among the circuits, interest groups would be encouraged to shop for the most favorable forum. Third, attention to the parties will provide some insight into the dynamics of interest group activity (see, for example, Gates and McIntosh, 1988).

Howard's analysis of the parties for 1965–1967 revealed that the federal government was a litigant in more cases than either state governments or private parties. While Howard did not present the actual breakdown in the role of each class of litigant as either appellant or respondent, he nevertheless concluded that "the federal government, *both as appellant and appellee*, was their primary consumer" (1981:28, emphasis added). In stark contrast, the data presented in Table 4 demonstrate that for 1986 all three levels of government appeared much more frequently as respondents than as appellants.[7] In all three circuits, the majority of appeals were brought by individuals, with the highest rate of 84.8 percent recorded in the fourth circuit. Next in frequency among appellants in all three circuits were private corporations. In none of the circuits were governments at any level a major source of appeals. Even in the D.C. circuit only 5 percent of the appeals were brought by the federal government. Governments, however, frequently appeared as respondents in all three circuits. In the D.C. circuit more than two-thirds of all appeals were against the federal government. In the fourth and eleventh circuits the federal government appeared as respondent less frequently than in the D.C. circuit but still more frequently than either

Table 4.
Parties Before the Three Circuits
(FY 1986)

Circuit	Business	Non-profit	U.S. Govt.	Local Govt.	State Govt.	Individual	Total
	%	%	%	%	%	%	N
			Appellants				
4th	10.0	0.6	2.0	0.5	0.9	84.8	2,032
11th	16.3	0.9	3.4	2.1	1.5	74.0	1,298
D.C.	24.6	11.4	5.2	1.3	2.2	50.4	228
			Respondents				
4th	16.7	1.0	28.3	13.9	29.7	8.8	2,032
11th	22.0	1.4	41.6	7.9	13.6	11.7	1,298
D.C.	17.1	3.1	70.2	0.4	0.4	7.0	228

business or individuals. In addition, in both circuits state and local governments were frequently present as respondents. Thus, while significant differences among the three circuits studied are evident, overall, the business of the courts consists largely of appeals brought by private parties against governments.

When Howard examined the business of the three circuits according to substantive field, he found specialization and regionalization to an extent that suggested to him that "[r]egionalization of appellate structures, for some subjects at least, may well spawn regional socialization and regionalized national law" (1981:33). Analyzing those differences, he divided sixty-two subjects into three categories (1981:Appendix 2). First, he labeled fields as "staple litigation" if they comprised two percent or more of a circuit's caseload. By such a measure, labor relations, taxation, and criminal procedure were "staple litigation" for all three circuits. Second, he designated as "marginal activity" those subjects that were only sparsely litigated in all three circuits: kidnapping appeals, embezzlement, extortion, racketeering, food and drugs, and migratory birds. He designated a third class of litigation as fields of "circuit concentration"—certain fields that were heavily represented in one circuit but not the others. For example, admiralty, civil rights, and social security were prevalent in the fifth circuit but sparse in the D.C. circuit (1981:29–33).

Analyzing the data from 1984, using slightly different categories than Howard's twelve broad issue fields and including all the circuits, we also found variations in the business of the circuits. As Table 5 indicates, certain fields were substantially adjudicated in all circuits (civil rights and prisoner petitions), while other areas were only sparsely dealt with (anti-trust, tax, environment, bankruptcy). Table 5 also shows how the proportion of cases in the issue categories varied among the circuits. In fact, in eight of the eleven substantive issue areas the circuit with the highest percentage of cases had at least twice the proportion of cases observed in the circuit with the lowest percentage of cases. Moreover, while Howard suggested that there were regional differences in the business of the circuits, the variation displayed in Table 5 appears to be completely unrelated to geographical regions. In fact, no systematic pattern is observable: all that is apparent is that the twelve circuits differ widely from each other. For example, for contract cases the geographically distant second and eleventh circuits have the highest rates while the sixth and ninth are the two lowest. In contrast, in the area of torts, the second circuit has the lowest rates while the tenth and fifth circuits have the highest. While the South is often considered the most distinctive region, the patterns of the three southern circuits are not noticeably similar.

Table 5.
Business of the Circuits
(in percent; FY 1984)

Issue	D.C.	1	2	3	4	5	6	7	8	9	10	11
Contrct	6.4	9.2	9.8	8.8	7.1	9.0	6.4	7.5	8.8	6.8	10.9	9.5
Torts/ Prop	16.9	9.7	5.8	9.7	7.0	18.7	8.2	5.8	11.2	8.4	13.8	7.3
Civil Rts	18.4	19.8	10.5	11.3	11.1	14.3	14.5	16.5	16.6	10.1	12.7	11.0
Prsner Petns	8.3	9.3	17.9	18.9	37.0	20.7	23.4	29.4	17.8	10.9	13.7	19.8
Labor	5.3	4.6	3.0	5.3	2.0	2.5	3.9	3.1	3.5	3.8	2.6	2.1
Patent/ Copyrt	.8	1.7	2.6	1.4	.5	1.0	.9	1.1	1.0	1.4	.5	.8
Social Sec	2.1	7.6	5.1	4.6	5.7	2.2	8.6	2.2	4.6	2.6	2.2	4.0
Anti- trust	1.8	1.0	1.2	1.4	.5	1.2	1.0	1.2	1.7	2.1	1.5	.7
Tax	0	.7	1.3	.5	.7	.9	1.5	1.4	2.1	2.3	2.9	1.0
Envir- nmnt	3.1	.4	.2	1.0	.4	.7	.3	.3	.1	.8	.3	.1
Bank- rptcy	0	0	.1	0	0	.1	0	.1	.1	.1	.2	.1
Other	36.9	36.0	42.6	37.0	27.8	28.9	31.1	31.5	32.6	50.8	38.8	43.5
Total (N)	1,306	763	1,749	2,027	2,020	2,504	2,021	1,941	1,364	3,195	1,409	2,540

Workload

Much has been written during the last twenty years about the proliferating caseload of the courts of appeals.[8] Increase in demands on the courts are most often attributed to changes in American society that have resulted in "ligitigiousness,"[9] to developments in the law that have provided more access to the federal trial courts for adjudication of the rights of the accused and for civil rights, or to the "activism" of the Supreme Court. Characterizations of the courts of appeals as overburdened, strained, and at risk of becoming bureaucracies abound and have often been colored by ideological orientations that include preferences for relegating adjudication to the state courts (Powell, 1982; Rehnquist, 1974, 1976). The major significance of empirical analyses of caseloads, therefore, lies in their ability to provide the basis for objective assessments of the demands on the courts of appeals. Although we do not attempt to resolve the debate over whether or not the courts are overburdened, we provide a description of their present workload. We found that the workload has increased rapidly since the 1960s. The number of cases in which judges made a final decision increased by 314 percent among circuits in rates of reversal of decisions by district courts. We also found variation in reversal rates based on the subject matter of the litigation. Likewise, the data for 1984 revealed substantial variations according to subject matter as well as among the different circuits. As Table 6 shows, the high reversal rate of 32.2 percent for Social Security contrasts with the lows of 13.7 percent for patent/copyright and 12.3 percent for the twenty years from 1967 through 1987. Moreover, the number of authorized judgeships increased during that period by only 77 percent, making it clear that the number of cases decided per judge has grown significantly since the late 1960s.[10]

Table 6.
Reversal Rates by Subject Matter
(FY 1984)

Issue	Affirm %	Reverse %	Dismissed %	Total N
Contract and Torts/ Property	56.4	20.6	16.5	4,161
Civil Rights	54.2	18.8	19.8	3,008
Prisoner Petitions	52.0	12.3	32.7	4,467
Labor	52.9	24.9	14.5	763
Patent/ Copyright	56.6	13.7	16.8	256
Social Security	55.3	32.2	10.2	931
Antitrust	44.6	21.8	17.3	294
Tax	53.8	20.4	21.1	299
Environment	48.2	24.1	13.5	141
Other	64.0	15.6	16.1	8,409
Total	57.7	17.5	19.7	22,829

Rates of Reversal

Howard noted that it is useful to describe reversal rates because they reveal "something about the range of appellate oversight, the cohesion within circuits, and the frequency of formal decisional controls, [although] they are crude indicators of judicial functions and relationships with other courts" (1981:41). Howard's analysis revealed a great deal of variation in prisoner petitions. Still, it is important to note that more than two-thirds of the decisions by district courts in every issue category were left undisturbed by the courts of appeals.

Table 7 shows that the rates of reversal varied substantially among the circuits. The rate of reversal in the first circuit, for example, was

Table 7.
Reversal Rates By Circuit

	1984				
Circuit	Affirm %	Reverse %	Mixed %	Dismissed %	Total N
D.C.	33.3	21.4	8.6	36.8	1,306
1st	63.4	22.5	.4	13.6	763
2d	58.0	16.4	5.9	19.7	1,749
3rd	61.9	14.1	1.0	23.0	2,027
4th	65.9	18.7	5.6	9.9	2,010
5th	54.5	20.5	8.1	16.9	2,504
6th	64.5	18.9	4.4	12.2	2,021
7th	58.4	13.6	3.4	24.6	1,941
8th	58.4	14.7	8.3	18.6	1,364
9th	55.7	20.5	4.5	19.2	3,195
10th	47.9	17.7	5.0	29.4	1,409
11th	63.1	12.7	5.4	18.8	2,540
Total	57.7	17.5	5.2	19.7	22,829

	1965-67[*]					
Circuit	Affirm %	Reverse %	Mixed %	Avoid %	Other %	Total N
D.C.	68.9	19.6	2.9	3.6	4.9	1,336
2d	73.6	17.2	5.8	1.7	1.6	1,357
5th	63.9	24.4	6.0	1.5	4.3	2,248

*Source: Howard (1981:Appendix 4)

nearly twice as high as that in the eleventh. Still, those differences did not seem to follow regional lines.

Winners and Losers

In order to learn more about the functions of the intermediate appellate courts we extended our investigation to ask a question that Howard did not: "Who were the winners and losers in the courts of appeals?" While we are aware that the concepts of winning and losing are ambiguous (see Kritzer et al., 1985), we found them to be useful at this stage in our study. For this portion of the analysis we used our data for the fourth, eleventh, and D.C. circuits because the Administrative Office data does not identify winners and losers.

Table 8 presents the results of the analysis of "who wins" considering unpublished as well as published decisions. The United States and state and local governments were winners in a high percentage of cases in all three circuits while individuals won least frequently in all circuits. While there was some variation among the three circuits, the differences among litigant classes was far greater than inter-circuit differences for any given type of litigant. For example, business was most successful and individuals least successful in the fourth circuit, but the difference between the success rate for individuals and that of state governments in the fourth circuit (80.1 percent) was far greater than the range among circuits in the success rates for either individuals (11.4 percent) or business (15.8 percent). It is risky to draw firm conclusions from our cursory examination of winners and losers in the courts of appeals. Still, the data make it possible to hypothesize tentatively that in contrast to the popular view of the courts as an avenue of redress for those who are otherwise powerless, the courts do not frequently disturb the political status quo (governments win most cases), and those with greater resources (for example, business) win more frequently than those who

Table 8.
Winners and Losers in the 4th, 11th, and D.C. Circuits
(Calendar Year 1986—All Decisions)

Party	4th		11th		D.C.	
	% win	N	% win	N	% win	N
Business	61.9	491	51.4	453	46.1	89
Non-profit	50.0	30	69.2	26	36.7	30
U.S. Govt.	85.9	594	83.2	562	81.8	154
State & Local Govt.	93.7	892	71.7	300	55.6	9
Individual	13.6	1,823	25.0	1,050	18.2	121

lack corresponding organizational and financial resources (for example, individuals). Further research is clearly needed to explore such a possibility.

Supreme Court Review

Howard found that in the 1960s the Supreme Court exercised very little direct supervision over the courts of appeals. While 20 percent of circuit decisions were appealed, the Supreme Court heard only 9 percent of those requests for review. Thus, in only 1.9 percent of all appeals court cases was the circuit decision reviewed by the Supreme Court; two-thirds of those were reversed.

An examination of the decisions of the courts of appeals for 1986 suggests that review by the Supreme Court of circuit decisions has now become even less frequent. As Table 9 shows, the rate of appeal by the losing party in the courts of appeals has not changed much over the last twenty years.[11] During these two decades, however, the number of cases heard in the courts of appeals has approximately tripled while the number of decisions reviewed by the Supreme Court has remained relatively stable. As a result, the proportion of circuit decisions reviewed by the Supreme Court has dropped dramatically from the already low rates reported in Howard's earlier study and is now less than 1 percent in each of the three circuits. The figures in Table 9 indicate that the Supreme Court still reverses the decision in nearly two-thirds of the cases it accepts for review, but since so few cases are accepted, the result is that in 99.5 percent of all appeals court cases the circuit decision is left undisturbed by the Supreme Court.

Table 9.
Supreme Court Review of Three Courts of Appeals
(1986)

Circuit	Pblsh'd Circuit Decisions Appealed to Supreme Court		All Circuit Decisions							
			Total	Revw'd* by S Ct		Afrm'd by S Ct		Revrs'd by S Ct		Other**
	%	n	N	%	n	%	n	%	n	%	n
4th	23.1	347	2,032	0.5	11	0.1	3	0.3	7	--	1
11th	21.8	294	1,601	0.4	6	0.1	2	0.2	3	0.1	1
D.C.	16.9	59	228	0.9	2	0.4	1	0.4	1	--	0
Total (3 circuits)	22.0	700	3,861	0.5	19	0.2	6	0.3	11	0.1	2

*Cases accepted for review by Supreme Court
**Cases accepted for review, with Supreme Court decision pending

Howard reported that during the 1960s the nature of the cases reviewed by the Supreme Court was not identical to the type of cases on the appeals courts' agendas. Although the agendas of both of these levels of the judiciary have changed over the past twenty years, we found that they remain quite different from each other. First, there are major differences in the frequency of appeals in different types of cases. Close to one third of the civil rights decisions of the courts of appeals were appealed, but only 3.5 percent of individual benefits cases (for example, social security disability claims) and only 10.5 percent of diversity cases. Second, the Supreme Court was quite selective in the types of cases it chose to review. The Court was almost four times as likely to grant a request for review in a civil rights case as it was in a criminal appeal, and none of the petitions to review an individual benefits or diversity decision were granted. But even in the area with the most frequent review by the Supreme Court (civil rights), fewer than 5 percent of the decisions were reviewed. In most areas, review was much less likely. The low rates of appeal in most areas guarantee that the courts of appeals will have the "final say" in most areas of judicial policy.

In the 1960s, the United States sought review by the Supreme Court in only 10 percent of all of the cases it lost in the courts of appeals. Our data revealed that requests for review by the United States dropped to a rate of 7.4 percent in 1986. Other types of litigants sought review much more frequently when they lost in the courts of appeals (business, 13.3 percent; individuals, 22.8 percent). But while the rates at which they appealed differed, we found that each of these three groups of litigants were nearly equally successful in securing Supreme Court review in those cases in which they requested review (United States, 12.5 percent; business, 12.1 percent; individual, 13.4 percent). Still, because individuals lost most frequently in the courts of appeals (426 losses as opposed to 249 for business and 108 for the United States), and since they had the highest rate of appeal from their losses, it turns out that over half (68.4 percent) of the petitions for review were brought by individuals.

The Importance of Unpublished Decisions

In order to improve their efficiency in the face of growing caseloads the lower courts have begun to dispose of an increasingly large number of cases without a published decision. During the 1960s and 1970s there were several efforts to develop some systematic way to limit the number of published opinions. In 1964 the Judicial Conference of the United States requested that the federal courts limit the number of published opinions by publishing only opinions that have precedential value.[12]

In 1974 and 1975 the Commission on Revision of the Federal Court Appellate System (the Hruska Commission) held hearings to consider many of the questions raised by limiting publication, particularly that of policies regarding citation. In its final report, however, the Commission declined to make a recommendation and passed the questions back to the Judicial Conference. The Judicial Conference issued a statement in 1978 concluding that limited publication had resulted in increased dispositions, but:

> At this time we are unable to say that one opinion publication plan is preferable to another, nor is there a sufficient consensus on either legal or policy matters, to enable us to recommend a model rule. We believe that continued experimentation under a variety of plans is desirable.[13]

The twelve circuits of the courts of appeals have subsequently adopted widely diverging rules and practices regarding publication of decisions. For example, the first and third circuits have a written rule that the court should weigh the precedential value of a disposition before publishing it; the second circuit's rule states that summary orders are not formal opinions and should not be reported; the eleventh circuit adopted a rule according to which only signed opinions are published.[14]

We were not at all surprised to find that the rate of nonpublication has increased tremendously since the 1960s. While Howard found the non-publication rate to be 16.3 percent during the years 1965–1967 (1981:24) we found that 62.8 percent of the cases decided in 1984 were unpublished. Analyzing the differences between circuits, which Howard did not do, we found dramatic variations in the rates of publication by the different circuits as shown in Table 10. Those rates ranged from a high of 66.4 percent by the eighth circuit to a low of 20.8 percent by the third circuit.

We found the reversal rate for unpublished decisions to be 10.2 percent—considerably lower than the 29.7 percent for those that were published. The rate of reversal in unpublished decisions suggests that those cases are not trivial, as has been generally assumed.

We also found significant differences in the tendencies of the courts of appeals to publish opinions in cases raising different types of issues. For example, none of the circuits published opinions in more than a quarter of the prisoner petition cases they decided, while each circuit published more than 80 percent of their environmental decisions. Such findings make clear that if researchers continue to rely solely on published opinions, they will be unable to obtain an accurate picture of the business of the courts of appeals.

Circuits also differ significantly in their propensities to publish certain types of decisions. For example, the D.C. circuit was more than five times

Table 10.
Rates of Publication by Circuit
(FY 1984)

Circuit	Published %	Published n	Unpublished %	Unpublished n	Total N
D.C.	45.8	598	54.2	708	1,306
1st	54.0	412	46.0	351	763
2d	37.6	658	62.4	1,091	1,749
3rd	20.8	422	79.2	1,605	2,027
4th	23.6	475	76.4	1,535	2,010
5th	44.1	1,105	55.9	1,399	2,504
6th	30.4	614	69.6	1,407	2,021
7th	38.6	750	61.4	1,191	1,941
8th	66.4	906	33.6	458	1,364
9th	34.0	1,085	66.0	2,110	3,195
10th	33.9	477	66.1	932	1,409
11th	38.9	987	61.1	1,553	2,540

$X = 1141.03$
$df = 11$
$p < .001$

as likely as the fifth circuit to publish opinions in social security cases but was much less likely to publish patent/copyright decisions. Such variation demonstrates that there are significant differences in practice among the circuits in their operational definitions of the criteria for publication. Our findings strongly suggest that if unpublished decisions are not taken into account, sets of cases across circuits will not be comparable.

Conclusion

Variation among the circuits of the courts of appeals in both their business and behavior dominated our findings. While Howard found variation among three circuits, we found that diversity in all twelve circuits. But contrary to Howard, we did not discern any pattern that would indicate that regional effects are responsible for the variations.

Our analysis of the business of the intermediate appellate judiciary indicated that criminal cases have not overwhelmed the courts, contrary to the predictions of the 1960s. Additionally, in contrast to the 1960s, when governments dominated the dockets both as appellants and respondents, cases brought by private parties against government are more prevalent in the 1980s.

We found that the demands on the courts of appeals have continued to increase into the 1980s and that judicial resources, in the form of authorized judgeships, have not kept pace with the surging caseloads. Also, our findings were consistent with Howard's conclusion that the decisions of the district courts are only rarely disturbed by a court of appeals, which attests to the importance of the federal trial courts and to the limited role of the intermediate appellate courts as supervisors of the district courts. Although variation among circuits was the theme that dominated our study, there was one major exception: the United States was the winner in an overwhelmingly high percentage of cases. Our examination of review of the courts of appeals by the Supreme Court revealed that the latter court supervises the intermediate appellate courts to an even lesser extent than it did during the 1960s. Thus, the importance of the courts of appeals in defining circuit precedent and policy has continued to grow. The Supreme Court appears to prefer to review certain types of cases, but even among the preferred types it disturbs very few decisions of the courts of appeals.

Although one of the purposes of studying the courts at any level is to assess the need for reform, we make no attempt to do so here. Neither do we offer speculations regarding the causes of increasing caseloads. Our goal has been to shed light upon the role of the courts of appeals in the 1980s. How have they performed the function of uniformly applying federal law? We found that Howard's conclusion regarding the intermediate appellate courts remains true after 20 years. The courts of appeals do not comprise an institution for the creation of national policy; rather, they are twelve different courts that are marked by wide diversity in their business and behavior. The patterns of diversity among the circuits in their business, the parties litigating before them, their behavioral tendencies, and their publication practices is one area that has not yet been adequately explored.

Finally, our findings point out that future research must be based on unpublished as well as published decisions. Our analysis raises serious questions about the traditional view that unpublished opinions have little or no precedential value, contribute little to the development of public policy, and do not involve any discretion by federal judges.[15] Indeed, we have demonstrated that the study of unpublished decisions will be essential if we are to achieve a full understanding of the courts of appeals.

Endnotes

[1] The courts of appeals were created by the Circuit Court of Appeals Act of 1891.

[2] Stephen L. Wasby, "Extra Judges in 'The Court Nobody Knows': Some Aspects of

Decision Making in the United States Courts of Appeals," paper presented at the annual meeting of the American Political Science Association, Washington, D.C., 1979, as noted by Howard (1981:xvi).

[3] Additionally, he utilized the reports of the Administrative Office of the United States Courts from fiscal years 1960 to 1979. Howard's data consisted of 4,135 cases published in the Federal Reporter, plus 806 unpublished cases obtained from the Administrative Office of the United States Courts for a total of 4,941 cases. Those cases comprised roughly 40 percent of total decisions made by all circuit courts after hearing or submission on briefs during these years. He chose the years 1965–67 because they represented "the last span of relative stability before an avalanche of appeals descended upon larger circuits, forcing expansion of judicial manpower by one-third after 1978" (1981:xix).

[4] The data include all of the published and unpublished decisions of the fourth, eleventh, and D.C circuits,

[5] "The Flow of Litigation in Three Courts of Appeals" was originally published in 1973 as "Litigation Flow in Three United States Courts of Appeals," 8 *Law and Society Review* 35.

[6] The transfer to District of Columbia courts took place under the Court Reorganization Act.

[7] In multiple party cases only the first listed appellant and respondent were coded.

[8] See, for example, Carrington (1969): "The existing framework is being strained by the rapidly increasing number of appeals in the federal system." See also Powell (1982), Griswold (1983), Posner (1985).

[9] For examinations of the connection between American legal culture and the propensity to use the courts, see, Lieberman (1981), Friedman (1985), Neubauer (1986).

[10] Baum, Goldman, and Sarat also attested to the growth in the demands on the appellate courts through 1975 (1981–2).

[11] It was not possible to determine which unpublished decisions were appealed. Therefore our findings are based on a sample of 700 of the published decisions for 1986. According to custom, if a decision initially designated to be unpublished is accepted for review the Supreme Court, the circuit will publish the decision. Therefore, while the rate of appeal from our sample of unpublished decisions is unknown, the rate of review of such decisions is zero.

[12] Reports of the Proceedings of the Judicial Conference of the United States 11 (1964) as quoted in Stienstra (1985:6).

[13] Opinion Publication Plans in the United States Courts of Appeals: Report of the Subcommittee on Federal Jurisdiction of the Committee on Court Administration of the Judicial Conference of the United States, as quoted in Stienstra (1985:13).

[14] For a summary of the rules, see Stienstra (1985:28–46).

[15] See, for example, Fra (1977); Reynolds and Richman (1978); Shuchman and Gelfand (1980).

References

Baum, Lawrence, Sheldon Goldman and Austin Sarat (1981–82) "The Evolution of Litigation in the Federal Courts of Appeals," 16 *Law and Society Review* 291.

Carrington, Paul D. (1969) "Crowded Dockets and the Courts of Appeals: The Threat to the Function of Review and the National Law," 82 *Harvard Law Review* 542.

Fra, Pamela (1977) "A Snake in the Path of the Law: The Seventh Circuit's Non-Publication Rule," 39 *University of Pittsburgh Law Review* 309.

Friedman, Lawrence M. (1985) *Total Justice.* New York: Russell Sage Foundation.

Galanter, Marc (1974) "Why the 'Haves' Come out Ahead: Speculations on the Limits of Legal Change," 9 *Law and Society Review* 95.

Gates, John B. and Wayne V. McIntosh (1988) "Interest Groups and Litigation: From Advocacy to Symbolism," paper presented at the Annual Meeting of the Law and Society Association, Vail, Colorado.

Griswold, Erwin N. (1983) "Helping the Supreme Court by Reducing the Flow of Cases into the Courts of Appeals," 67 *Judicature* 58.

Howard, J. Woodford, Jr. (1981) *Courts of Appeals in the Federal Judicial System: A Study of the Second, Fifth, and District of Columbia Circuits.* Princeton, NJ: Princeton University Press.

Kritzer, Herbert M., Austin Sarat, David M. Trubek and William L. F. Felstiner (1985) "Winners and Losers in Litigation: Does Anyone Come Out Ahead?" paper presented at the Annual Meeting of the Midwest Political Science Association, Chicago.

Lieberman, Jethro K. (1981) *The Litigious Society.* New York: Basic Books.

Neubauer, David W. (1986) "Review Essay: Are We Approaching Judicial Gridlock?" 11 *The Justice System Journal* 363.

Posner, Richard (1985) *The Federal Courts: Crisis and Reform.* Cambridge, MA: Harvard University Press.

Powell, Lewis F. (1982) "Are the Federal Courts Becoming Bureaucracies?" 68 *American Bar Association Journal* 1370.

Rehnquist, William H. (1976) "The Cult of the Robe," 15 *The Judges Journal* 74.

_____ (1974) "Whither the Courts?" 60 *American Bar Association Journal* 787.

Reynolds, William L. and William M. Richman (1978) "The Non-Precedential Precedent: Limited Publication and No-Citation Rules in the United States Courts of Appeals," 78 *Columbia Law Review* 1167.

Shuchman, Philip and Alan Gelfand (1981) "The Use of Local Rule 21 in the Fifth Circuit: Can Judges Select Cases of 'No Precedential Value'," 29 *Emory Law Journal* 194.

Stienstra, Donna (1985) *Unpublished Dispositions: Problems of Access and Use in the Courts of Appeals.* Washington, DC: Federal Judicial Center.

6

Justice Rationed in the Pursuit of Efficiency
De Novo Trials in the Criminal Courts

DAVID A. HARRIS

For the last three decades, the ever-expanding caseload of the nation's courts has attracted the attention of judges and scholars. All have sought ways—some old, some new—for courts to cope with the growing number of cases. The Supreme Court entered this debate on the criminal side in 1971, by formally sanctioning plea bargaining as an essential and a highly desirable tool for disposing of most criminal cases. Most commentators claimed that plea bargaining was inevitable; it was, and would always remain, the major method for disposing of criminal cases. In the civil arena, numerous efforts have been made in the last ten to fifteen years intended to cut the backlog of civil cases by using alternative dispute resolution and other mechanisms. Proponents of these techniques have hailed them as cost-effective methods of case disposition that benefit litigants at little cost.

During the 1980s, however, scholars challenged these almost universally accepted propositions. Notwithstanding its wide use, they argued, plea bargaining is not a desirable way to dispose of cases. On the contrary, plea bargaining taints the criminal justice process, damages the defendant, and offends the Constitution. Further, plea bargaining is not inevitable; a large court system can exist without reliance on it.

Reprinted with changes by permission of *Connecticut Law Review* and the author from vol. 24, pp. 382–431. Copyright 1992 by the *Connecticut Law Review*.

Opponents of plea bargaining have also recommended the use of procedures from other nations as alternatives. In civil cases, critics have argued that the alternative dispute resolution movement's single-minded striving for case disposition ignores and exacerbates the imbalance of power inherent in much litigation, and thereby disadvantages litigants who are least powerful.

With their emphasis on novel devices, these debates have ignored one traditional vehicle for expediting criminal litigation—the two-tiered de novo trial system. For many years, about half of the states have used this court structure to obtain rapid, efficient disposition of criminal cases. Misdemeanors and less serious felonies make up ninety percent of the nation's criminal caseload. De novo systems handle misdemeanors and less serious felonies; de novo systems therefore affect overall case disposition profoundly.

In de novo court systems, defendants initially are tried in a lower court. These lower courts lack many of the basic protections associated with due process. If the lower court finds a defendant guilty, and the defendant is dissatisfied with the lower court's verdict or sentence, the defendant cannot appeal to a traditional appellate court for review of the trial record. Rather, the dissatisfied defendant may request, and is entitled to receive, a brand new trial—a trial de novo—in the court of general criminal jurisdiction. In the new trial, the full spectrum of constitutional safeguards apply, and all issues—legal and factual—are determined afresh. The Supreme Court says the defendant loses nothing in the de novo process because the second, full-dress trial is available to her simply for the asking; indeed, she gains a second opportunity for an acquittal. For its part, the state gains efficiency, as it realizes savings of time and resources for every case permanently disposed of in the lower court without the full range of costly due process protections.

Closer examination, however, shows that de novo systems do not perform as promised. This article demonstrates that de novo systems do indeed yield efficiency and savings for the state, but for the wrong reason: New trials are *not*, in fact, freely available. On the contrary, the structure of de novo systems discourages defendants from requesting new trials. De novo systems operate invisibly but forcefully to deter the exercise of the express right to a new trial. De novo systems also leave lower court judges free to resolve cases on whatever basis they find desirable—personal proclivities, whim, or gut feeling—with virtually no enforceable requirement that the law govern their decisions. Further, like alternative dispute resolution, de novo systems shift power away from those who are already least advantaged. The fate of these individuals is easily disregarded by advocates of efficiency, who focus exclusively on decreasing the size of the caseload. Moreover, de novo systems handle a large portion of the criminal cases. Consequently, they represent the only contact many people have with the criminal justice system, and perhaps the system's only chance to keep first offenders from becoming repeat and felony offenders. These opportunities are squandered, however, in the pursuit of efficiency. Thus, examination of de novo systems engenders skepticism regarding mechanisms that are claimed to handle cases more efficiently than at present, at no cost to the defendant and with few implications for substantive change.

For these and other reasons, de novo systems should be abolished outright. Abolition, however, is unlikely. The combination of tradition and the siren song of efficiency ensures their survival. Accordingly, the goal of this article is to urge the reform of de novo systems so that they can at least function with the minimal degree of fairness expected from American courts. After Part I describes de novo systems, . . . [Part II] demonstrates the falsity of the premise underlying all three decisions— that a new trial in the court of general jurisdiction is readily available. . . . [Part II] also shows that de novo systems pose other, substantial problems for both the criminal justice system and society in general. . . . [Part III] proposes eight ways to improve these courts.

I. Characteristics of De Novo Court Systems

A. De Novo Appeal

The signal characteristic of de novo courts is the right to request and receive a new trial in the superior court after a verdict of guilty in a lower court. In a typical de novo system, the lower court has jurisdiction over a specified group of offenses. At trial in the lower court, the defendant may plead not guilty and litigate the case, or plead guilty, with or without an agreement with the prosecutor. If the defendant is found guilty, the court sentences the defendant. After sentencing, if the defendant wants a new trial—based on the judge's legal rulings before or during the course of the trial, the severity of the sentence, the mere possibility that the defendant will "do better" in the superior court, or any other reason—the defendant can request and receive a new trial in the superior court. This new trial will take place without reference to the prior trial or its outcome. Traditional review of legal issues by an appellate court is not available.

Twenty-four states utilize de novo systems. At least eight of these twenty-four states have more than one lower court. Five other states have de novo systems that allow new trials only when the lower court does not generate any record of the trial proceedings.

B. Unavailability of Juries

In half of the de novo systems, a judge or some other judicial officer hears the case in the lower court. If the defendant wants a jury trial, she may either make a pretrial request that the lower court transfer the case to the superior court, or have a trial in the lower court and then request a trial in the superior court. Some states allow the defendant to choose either option. Other states require that the defendant go through the lower court proceeding.

In the other states with de novo court systems, the defendant may elect to have a jury in the lower court determine her guilt or innocence. If dissatisfied in any way with the lower court proceeding, the defendant may request and receive a new trial in the superior court.

C. Streamlined Procedures

In approximately one-third of all de novo systems, certain basic procedures are either streamlined or eliminated in the lower court. Those procedures often include discovery rules, procedures requiring written briefing and separate hearings on legal issues, and the availability of bills of particulars. Presumably, the elimination or abbreviation of these procedures make the lower courts more efficient.

D. Judges Without Legal Training

In approximately two-thirds of the de novo court systems, judges need not be members of the bar. While statutes may require these lay judges to attend a basic training course or successfully complete an examination, they will nevertheless preside without the basic legal background required of the least experienced practitioner. Some systems require only a high school diploma for a person to be eligible for the bench. Thus, many lower court judges are marginally qualified to rule on complex legal issues, decide guilt and innocence, and pass sentence.

E. Limited Jurisdiction

All states using de novo systems limit the jurisdiction of their courts. Some limit jurisdiction to less serious felonies, misdemeanors, violations of local ordinances, or some combination of the three. Other de novo systems limit jurisdiction according to the severity of the penalty authorized for an offense. Still others have jurisdictional limitations which combine these and other criteria. Notwithstanding these jurisdictional limitations, courts in many de novo systems still have substantial power over the persons they convict.

F. Suspension or Vacation of Sentence Pending Appeal

In most de novo systems, the sentence of the lower court remains in effect pending a new trial unless the defendant meets bail conditions set by the lower court. In a few de novo systems, a request for a new trial automatically vacates or suspends the sentence imposed by the lower court.

* * *

II. Purposes and Premises Examined

In *Colten*, *Ludwig*, and *North*, the Supreme Court made numerous assumptions about the way de novo systems operate. As the next section of this article demonstrates, these assumptions are questionable. Moreover, other problems inherent in the structure of de novo systems, not hinted at in the Supreme Court's cases, also present major difficulties.

A. How Can De Novo Systems Be Efficient?

The common thread that runs through *Colten*, *Ludwig*, and *North* is that de novo systems efficiently handle criminal cases. For a variety of reasons, however, de novo systems are not structured to be efficient; if they are efficient, it is for exactly the wrong reasons.

1. Two Trials for the Convicted

In the view of the Supreme Court, a defendant loses nothing by proceeding through the lower court before her case comes before a superior court. If conviction and sentence in a lower court dissatisfies the defendant for any reason, she simply requests and receives a new trial. Surely, if the lower court incarcerates her, the request for a new trial will quickly restore the status quo. In other words, defendants have nothing to lose and everything to gain by requesting a new trial. It would seem therefore that all defendants convicted in lower courts except those receiving obviously lenient sentences would request a new trial.

If these assumptions are true, de novo courts actually would be the least efficient of all possible arrangements. The accused usually will request a new trial and receive not only a full-dress trial in a superior court, complete with a jury and the full complement of constitutional rights, but also will receive a bench trial in the lower court, with all the attendant opportunities for discovery and acquittal. Moreover, this double portion of legal nourishment goes only to those already convicted by a lower court. A single trial in a superior court would serve just as well to determine guilt, without the cost of the lower court trial. Thus, the de novo court system is the least efficient rather than the most efficient arrangement: for those most likely to be convicted, the system provides two trials when one would suffice, complete with an additional set of courts and attendant bureaucracy.

2. Appeals Resulting from Severe Sentences

In *Colten*, the Supreme Court stated that sentences in lower courts usually are not severe. The Court, however, offered no support for this proposition. The statutes limiting the jurisdiction of de novo court systems often do so according to the maximum penalties a court may impose. Maryland allows lower court judges to impose penalties up to twenty years of imprisonment. Other states give their lower courts jurisdiction over offenses that carry penalties of up to one year or up to five years. Nothing restrains judges in the lower courts from making full use of this sentencing power. This power also is available to judges in the superior court, of course. In at least one important respect, however, the consequences of severe sentences in the lower court are much different from the consequences of severe sentences in the superior court. If judges in the lower court consistently sentence more severely than judges in the superior court, the logic of *Colten*, *Ludwig*, and *North* dictate that this will result in a flood of requests for new trials in the superior court; defendants will have two trials when one would do. Indeed, if the defendant has little to lose by any request for a new trial, a severe sentence—especially one considered severe not just in and of itself, but in relation to what one would expect from a superior court— would prompt a request for a new trial almost automatically. Lower court judges need not concern themselves with the systemic effects of their sentencing practices, however, because nothing obligates lower court judges to mete out sentences similar to those used by superior court judges in similar cases. Thus, if a defendant finds the trial and verdict otherwise unobjectionable, the severity of the sentence alone may cause a request for a new trial. From the point of view of a defendant who receives a harsh sentence, there is little risk in a new trial because the sentence already is severe.

3. Process Prolonged and Witnesses Discouraged

De novo systems also create inefficiencies that, in at least one respect, pose a direct threat to the prosecution's case. When a defendant goes through both the lower and superior courts, the number of times that the principals in the case—the defendant, the police and the civilian witnesses—must appear may double. While a case in the lower court theoretically could be resolved in a single court appearance, necessitating only one appearance by witnesses, this probably is not the norm. At least two or three trial dates in each lower court case is not out of the ordinary; for each one, witnesses would need to be summoned. If the defendant requests a new trial in the superior court, the whole process would start over, necessitating a new round of appearances. As this process grinds on, one or more of the state's witnesses could lose interest or become frustrated with the case and not come to court, especially in a case that may not seem that important from the start. The defendant may count on this phenomenon; witness attrition may be the goal of the defense in requesting continuances or a new trial. In fact, the new trial may be nothing more than the invocation of a whole new set of continuances and delays. Adding another layer to the process simply multiplies the chances that the defendant may be able to "wear out" the opposition. The opportunity for a new trial thus provides a direct incentive for the defendant to protract the proceedings, making them as costly and as slow as possible. Indeed, the only possible respect in which this war of attrition may be efficient is that many cases that the prosecution could otherwise bring to a successful conclusion may die prematurely instead.

4. Costs of Lower Courts and Lower Court Trials

The efficiency arguments assume that it is faster and less expensive to handle cases in lower courts than in superior courts. If misdemeanors and less serious felonies are resolved without a jury and other trappings of due process, the criminal justice system saves the costs of, and time necessary for, these "luxuries." Given that these cases make up about ninety percent of all criminal cases, the argument goes, these savings add up.

This argument, however, ignores the costs involved in allowing a second trial. To the extent that defendants avail themselves of the opportunity for a second trial, the costs of these superior court proceedings must be part of the calculus. If defendants request a second trial not to actually receive a second trial but simply to gain tactical advantage through delay, this too represents a cost that the efficiency arguments must include. To the extent that the defendant is incarcerated either before her lower court or her superior court trial, the efficiency equation must also include the costs of this confinement, along with concomitant loss of job opportunities and productivity.

5. How Is Efficiency Maintained?

The discussion so far exposes several flaws in the argument that de novo systems dispose of their cases more efficiently than do single level courts. Yet states retain de novo systems, evidently finding them efficient enough that abolishing them seems unattractive. If requests for new trials make de novo systems inefficient, and de novo systems are already performing efficiently, defendants must be failing to request new trials. Given the Supreme Court's assumptions that new trials would be relatively easy for defendants to obtain and not costly, what dissuades a defendant convicted in the lower court from rejecting the "offer of settlement" made by the lower court? The answer must be that defendants are not as free to request new trials as the Supreme Court claims. In fact, defendants are discouraged from exercising their right to a new trial. Justice Stevens neatly captured this point in his dissent in *Ludwig*, when he discussed the requirement that the defendant had to endure the lower court proceeding before he could obtain a full-dress trial in front of a jury:

> A defendant who can afford the financial and psychological burden of one trial may not be able to withstand the strain of a second. Thus, as a practical matter, a finding of guilt in the first-tier proceeding will actually end some cases. . . . [W]hy does [Massachusetts] insist on the *requirement* that the defendant must submit to the first trial? Only, I suggest, because it believes the number of jury trials that would be avoided by the required practice exceeds the number that would take place in an optional system. In short, *the very purpose of the requirement is to discourage jury trials by placing a burden on the exercise of the constitutional right.*

As the next section of this article will show, requiring that defendants go through a lower court before they can get to a superior court is only one of many ways that de novo systems discourage requests for new trials in the superior court.

B. Discouraging Requests for New Trials: Direct Process Barriers

Defendants who wish to receive a new trial in the superior court after a trial in the lower court face numerous obstacles. The Court acknowledged and minimized some of them; others went unrecognized. These obstacles take the form of direct process barriers that are part of, or generated by, the dual-level de novo system itself.

1. Monetary and Nonmonetary Costs

Costs that discourage new trials come in both monetary and nonmonetary forms. For defendants who are not indigent, retaining counsel will carry a definite, dollars-and-cents price tag. While some defendants may find the cost of counsel for one trial manageable, the cost for a second appearance may be prohibitive. Similarly, most de novo court systems require a defendant appealing for a new trial to pay a fee. If the defendant is indigent, she may ask that the court waive the fee. A waiver, however, does little for a person who, while impoverished, does not meet the applicable criteria for indigence. Further, courts might also pass on to the defendant the cost of summoning defense witnesses to trial. Because the Constitution explicitly protects the right to compulsory process, an indigent defendant should be able to attain a waiver of this cost. "Court costs" represent another toll imposed on those who wish a second trial. Add to this the costs of any out of the ordinary expenses, such as retaining an expert for two trials instead of one, and it becomes clear that the defendant must run a financial obstacle course to obtain a second trial.

Nonmonetary costs also discourage defendants from taking appeals. These costs reach indigent as well as nonindigent defendants. For example, inasmuch as a request for a new trial in a de novo system starts the cycle of appearances, motions, and trial dates again, defendants face a new series of dates upon which they must choose to go to court rather than to engage in some other activity. For many defendants, the other activity will be employment. To the extent that defendants charged with misdemeanors as a group have limited discretion to take days off, this can become costly not only in terms of lost wages but also in terms of lost employment. A second trial may also entail further meetings and preparation with counsel, especially if the second trial will be before a jury, or will require separate hearings preceding the second trial on matters such as motions to suppress and dismiss.

Another type of nonmonetary cost comes in the form of atrophy or damage to the defendant's case. In the same way that de novo systems may cause prosecution witnesses to lose interest, defense witnesses may also disengage. Like the defendant, defense witnesses may have only limited flexibility in employment schedules. Subpoenae notwithstanding, witnesses also have much less at stake in the outcome of a trial than the accused. As a consequence, defense witnesses may fail to attend a second trial. Witnesses and evidence will also become harder to locate and gather the more time passes. Having testified once in a trial in the lower court, defense witnesses will be vulnerable to impeachment in a second trial in a superior court. Both witness discouragement and impeachment may cause the defendant to feel additional pressure either not to pursue a second trial, or to plead guilty in the superior court. All of these costs deter the assertion of the right to a new trial in the superior court.

2. Psychological Burdens

Having to proceed through the lower court before gaining access to a superior court represents a significant psychological burden. Unresolved charges carry a stigma, regardless of the court in which the charges are to be tried. Because the Supreme Court recommends that the defendant admit guilt in the lower court in order to avoid the expense of two trials, the defendant must also live with a lower court conviction until the superior court trial. Moreover, obligating the defendant to defend herself in a de novo court system increases the amount of time it takes for the defendant to obtain a full-dress trial by jury.

3. The Risk of a Greater Sentence

Whenever a defendant requests a new trial, she runs the risk that she will receive a more severe sentence at the hands of the superior court than she did in the lower court. If anything is a direct deterrent to exercise of the right to a new trial, it is this risk. Nevertheless, the Supreme Court stated in *Colten* that the possibility that the superior court might impose a greater sentence than the lower court did not violate the Constitution because the higher sentence would not result from vindictiveness. Few would disagree, however, that the risk exists and may actually deter; the gamble the defendant must take is intuitively obvious. Further, some have advanced strong arguments that the threat of a harsher sentence would indeed rise to the level of a constitutional violation. While scholars debate these constitutional arguments, a lay person—a person incarcerated after one trial who successfully petitioned for another—puts the point more forcefully:

> I know it is usuelly [sic] the courts prosedure [sic] to give a larger sentence when a new trile [sic] is granted. I guess this is to discourage petitioners. Your Honor, I don't want a new trile [sic] I am afraid of more time. . . . Your Honor, I know you have tried to help me and God knows I apreceate [sic] this but please sir don't let the state re-try me if there is any way you can prevent it.

4. Incarceration Pending New Trial

In any criminal trial system, a court may incarcerate defendants pending trial by setting bail conditions defendants cannot meet. Defendants in de novo systems face this prospect not once, but twice. The mere filing of a request for a new trial is insufficient to vacate or suspend the lower court verdict and sentence in most courts. This incarceration is ironic in light of the Supreme Court's characterization of the lower court verdict as an offer the defendant may freely accept or reject. Defendants who are too poor to meet even minimal bail conditions prior to trial are likely to remain incarcerated until the resolution of the case, or until a bail reduction, in the superior court. The amount of bail may have less to do with the likelihood that the defendant will appear for trial than with a preset "schedule" of bail amounts based solely on the offense charged.

Incarceration between a lower court verdict and trial in the superior court has profound implications. First, defendants serve more time in jail prior to a superior court trial than as a result of any superior court sentence. Second, a positive correlation exists between commitment to incarceration before trial and findings of guilt after trial, between commitment to incarceration before trial and the likelihood of a jail sentence, and between being Caucasian and receiving a bond that does not require the deposit of money with the court. Thus, persons incarcerated pending a new trial in superior court are more likely to remain there after trial, and non-whites are at higher risk for this treatment. It would be surprising indeed to find defendants eager to appeal under these circumstances.

5. *Failure to Inform Defendant Adequately of Rights*

In all de novo systems, defendants have an unconditional right to a new trial in the superior court. This right supposedly saves de novo court systems from constitutional infirmity. Ability to exercise this right presupposes knowledge of the right's existence and of the method of its exercise. Courts are duty bound to inform defendants of these critical facts; indeed, the Supreme Court explicitly assumed that lower court judges inform defendants that they have the right to a new trial in a superior court.

Unfortunately, courts do not always inform defendants of their constitutional rights. In fact, the available evidence suggests that defendants usually do not receive full and effective advice of rights in misdemeanor courts. Courts treat the obligation to inform defendants of their rights as a mere clerical function they must perform repeatedly, if they perform it at all. Many courts advise defendants of their constitutional rights in large groups, or even address advice of rights to the courtroom as a whole. That this phenomenon has persisted over a long period of time, surviving even the requirement that most misdemeanor defendants receive appointed counsel, is disheartening. More importantly, these practices weaken the argument that the availability of a new trial in the superior court serves as an adequate constitutional savior for de novo systems. Mileski sums up the likely effects of these practices well:

> If a defendant happens to be talking to his neighbor, if he is for some other reason inattentive, or if he arrives in court later than the scheduled ten o'clock, he is not formally informed of his rights unless the judge later informs him in a face-to-face encounter, as he sometimes does. Inattention or tardiness, then, may carry with it whatever are the consequences of ignorance of constitutional rights. Moreover, there is the matter of the defendant's inability to comprehend various rights—something that is inaccessible to an observer. The degree of comprehension may vary according to the form of apprising.

Thus, failure to inform defendants properly—or at all—of their rights effectively hides the right to a new trial from the defendant's view.

C. Collateral Costs and Lack of Benefit to Defendant

In *Colten*, *Ludwig*, and *North*, the Supreme Court concluded that the efficiencies that de novo systems provide to the states come at little or no cost to defendants. The Court even assumed that defendants in de novo systems have opportunities to improve their cases that defendants whose cases begin in superior courts do not. In reaching these conclusions, however, the Court ignored a host of realities that defendants face. These realities render absurd the idea that defendants suffer no hardship by virtue of the workings of de novo systems. The previous section of this article highlighted problems that are generated by, and take place in, the adjudicative process in the lower court itself. The following section focuses on hardships that are generated by the adjudicative process in the lower court but which find expression elsewhere. This latter group of problems will therefore be referred to as collateral costs.

1. Revocation of Probation

Courts often make use of probation as a form of punishment and supervision in lieu of incarceration. Probation usually takes the form of an agreement: the court refrains from executing all or part of a sentence if the defendant agrees to abide by rules for probation. These obligations, which could include reporting to a probation officer, maintaining steady employment and a place of residence, and participating in special programs, always include the obligation to obey all federal, state, and local laws. If a defendant in a new case in a lower court is already on probation in a previous case, a conviction in the new case violates the terms of the probation in the previous case. This violation of probation occurs unless, under state law, a request for a new trial in the superior court vacates the lower court conviction. State law, however, usually does not vacate the prior conviction. This poses potentially devastating problems for the defendant. Because the new lower court conviction violates the terms of the probation imposed upon the defendant in the earlier case, the judge assigned to the earlier case is free to revoke the probation immediately and impose any suspended sentence. Thus, even if the defendant has a right to a new trial in the superior court, the new lower court conviction may force her to await the superior court trial in jail. This belies the Supreme Court's benign characterization of lower court verdicts.

2. Sentencing Problems in Pending Cases

Defendants often encounter more than one set of criminal charges at one time. If one set of charges results in a conviction in the lower court, and if this conviction stands pending a new trial in a superior court, this conviction carries consequences into other cases. For example, a number of states and the federal government use sentencing guidelines that typically give courts a range within which to sentence a defendant, based on facts about both the offense and the defendant. Among the most important facts about the defendant these guidelines consider is the defendant's record of prior convictions. If a lower court conviction stands pending a new trial in a superior court, guidelines applied to the defendant in another case might not distinguish this conviction from others, regardless of the fact that the superior court trial could arrive at a different outcome. Even without guidelines, sentencing judges might well count lower court convictions from cases in which a new trial in superior court is pending against the defendant's record until the final resolution of any new trial in the superior court.

3. Damage to Reputation

A lower court conviction that stands pending a new trial in the superior court may also damage the reputation of the person convicted. The conviction is a clear, dry fact that few people have trouble understanding; the fact that there will be a new trial, with every issue open to redetermination is complex enough that few people will take the time and effort to understand. Therefore, unless the appeal to the superior court automatically vacates the lower court conviction, the damage to reputation may remain. The final resolution of the case in the superior court comes too long afterward to make a difference.

4. Deportation

Under the laws governing immigration, a noncitizen convicted of a crime may be deported in a variety of circumstances. This power is not confined to large-scale or felony crimes. The government may deport persons convicted of misdemeanor-type offenses. Lower court convictions for any of these crimes serve as bases for deportation, regardless of the possibility or likelihood of exoneration in a new trial in the superior court. Indeed, the government might deport a noncitizen on these grounds even before the opportunity arrives for the superior court trial.

5. Loss of Licenses

Another category of hardships the Supreme Court ignored is the loss of licenses. For example, states have made the loss of driver's license a statutorily required result of convictions for driving under the influence of alcohol and other misdemeanors. Given that many people cannot work without transportation to and from their jobs, a lower court conviction that results in a suspension of a driver's license before the opportunity for a new trial in a superior court damages the defendant's ability to earn a living.

Newer statutes have a more direct impact on employment. These statutes can result in the revocation of state licenses necessary to engage in a variety of occupations and trades upon convictions for misdemeanors such as the possession of controlled substances. Unlike the revocation of a driver's license, these statutes may not just make it more difficult to work; depending on the defendant's occupation, they may make employment impossible.

6. Negative Impact on Defendant's Superior Court Trial

A lower court trial can have a negative impact on the superior court trial. Witnesses become discouraged and unavailable through simple disinterest, and loss of income due to lost work. Witnesses also become vulnerable to impeachment with prior testimony. The lower court trial will likely polarize and harden witnesses' positions, and gives the state a chance to polish its case, curing defects that arose in the lower court. The state's witnesses may even become more prosecution oriented.

The greatest negative impact, however, may involve an even larger, overarching issue: the shadow that the lower court trial casts upon the presumption of innocence. No one questions the central place of this presumption to due process of law. Even so, convictions from lower courts burden the all-important presumption of innocence during any trial in the superior court. For example, potential jurors, especially in a small-town setting, will likely know that the defendant appears in superior court because she failed to win an acquittal in the lower court. Certainly, the judge in the superior court trial knows this even if the jurors do not. This knowledge may infiltrate the proceedings—through the judge's rulings, attitude, or even through the judge's direct statements to the jury.

7. Loss of Job

The two-stage de novo system presents numerous difficulties for the employed defendant. Some of these were discussed earlier—for example, a doubling of the number of court appearances if the defendant wishes to have a trial in the superior court, the lack of transportation due to the revocation of a driver's license, and incarceration pending a new trial. The lower court need not incarcerate the defendant, however, to cause problems with employment prior to a new trial in a superior court.

Sentences that include reporting to a probation officer or attendance at special programs restrict freedom, albeit in a less direct way than incarceration. Being under the continuing control of the criminal justice system can cause defendants to miss work, to be unable to work necessary overtime, and to fail to perform other tasks for the employer. At best, these may make the defendant a less valued employee; at worst, the defendant may lose a job.

8. Lack of Benefits to Defendants

Beyond the collateral costs to the defendant that de novo systems carry, another assumption of the Supreme Court should be questioned. If, as the Court claims, defendants receive unique opportunities in de novo systems to improve their cases, collateral costs should be viewed less harshly. At least, an intelligent assessment of collateral costs would require that they be balanced against these benefits. According to the Court, these benefits are the potential for discovery of the state's evidence during the lower court trial, and the fact that the de novo court system provides two opportunities for acquittal. Careful thought, however, reveals little in the way of any real benefits to balance against collateral costs.

Use of the lower court trial for discovery presupposes the presence of an attorney. This type of discovery requires more than simply listening to the state's evidence. The right questions must be asked in the right form. Questions unartfully phrased might, at best, elicit answers indicating the general direction of the state's case, but have little value in establishing the specifics of the evidence through the possibility of later impeachment of witnesses. Having an attorney to conduct discovery during the lower court trial requires that the defendant invest resources, in the form of money to employ private counsel or time to meet with counsel (whether privately paid or court appointed). This drains resources available for the trial in superior court.

Further, many de novo systems do not generate any record of their proceedings. To the extent that the defendant seeks a general idea of the direction of the state's case and its evidence, she may find the lower court trial of some value. Without a record, however, even if the defendant has an attorney who knows how to ask the right questions in the right manner, there is little hope of holding the state's witnesses to their lower court testimony during the superior court trial through impeachment. Apart from the issue of impeachment, nothing requires that the prosecution use the same witnesses, evidence, or theory in the superior court that it used in the lower court. While an entirely new direction in the superior court might be uncommon, a second trial affords the state the opportunity to gather evidence and witnesses not available for the first trial, to prepare for defense motions, arguments and general strategy, and to repair any holes in its case illuminated by the defense in the lower court.

Moreover, one cannot assume, as the Supreme Court does, that the defendant will receive these benefits without having to expose her own case. In order to take advantage of the opportunity to use the lower court trial for discovery, the defense must at least cross-examine; standing silent will yield little not disclosed by the charging papers. For the court to allow the questioning, the questions must be relevant. Thus, even without offering defense evidence, the defendant may expose strategy or weaknesses in her case.

D. Judicial Accountability

The de novo feature of the courts studied in this article has an important corollary: the actions of lower court judges seldom receive any scrutiny or review from higher courts. As de novo systems are structured, traditional review of lower court actions by appellate courts simply has no place. In the event of an erroneous legal decision or interpretation, the defendant has the same remedy that she may use in the event of a determination of the facts she finds unfavorable: a new trial in the superior court. This runs contrary to traditional, well-established conceptions of appellate review. In the most basic sense, the de novo feature means that these courts never receive guidance concerning the decisions and interpretations of the law that they render on a daily basis. Cases never return to these judges after review by a higher court and there are no opinions assessing the lower court judge's actions. In sum, lower court judges have no ongoing accountability for their decisions. This means that several important functions of traditional appellate review go unserved in de novo court systems.

1. Correction of Mistakes in Individual Cases

In traditional types of appellate review, the appellate court reviews the record of the trial court for errors by the trial judge. If the appellate court finds reversible error, and even when it does not, the trial judge receives guidance, usually in the form of a written opinion. The opinion tells the trial judge how she erred and how to correct the mistake—for example, hold a new trial or grant a particular kind of hearing. Appellate review may also inform the trial court that it acted correctly, indicating that a similar response to similar situations will be acceptable in the future. Thus, a traditional appeal not only corrects mistakes in individual cases, it also allows the monitoring of the general practices of the trial court by reviewing a particular case. By acting in this fashion, the appellate court insures that all individuals before the trial court receive fair treatment.

2. Systemic Correction: "Quality Control"

The review of trial court actions by appellate courts also serves to guide trial courts other than the one in which the particular case under review occurred. Written opinions by appellate courts allow all courts to take advantage of the experience of the trial court in question and learn from its successes and failures. The process educates both the particular trial judge and all other participants in the system—judges, prosecutors, defense attorneys, and other court personnel—concerning the correct interpretation of rules, statutes, and precedent. The possibility of appellate review, therefore, tends to control judicial misconduct in all reviewable cases, not just those particular cases that reach appellate courts. Thus, the criminal process is "guided, in large part, from the top down. Traditional appellate review of trial court actions in criminal cases form the ultimate guarantee of fairness of the process; review on appeal explained in written opinions is the "quality control mechanism" for the system as a whole.

3. Uniformity

Traditional appellate review also serves the function of assuring uniform interpretation and application of the law throughout judicial institutions. Uniformity was a chief preoccupation of American courts in the eighteenth and nineteenth centuries. Throughout the history of the American judicial system, some form of review of trial court decisions, including those of early petty offense courts, has always been available to ensure that the law was applied evenly. Lack of uniformity creates disparities between courts, placing a premium on local knowledge rather than general principles, and disadvantages outsiders to any community. Thus, the law becomes more a matter of experience than general rules by which persons may measure and formulate conduct. Further, the lack of appellate review manifests itself by destroying any incentive to develop a system of uniform court rules. Without any recorded set of collective experiences, such as appellate court opinions reviewing the actions of trial judges, a rule maker will find little experiential grist for the mill and little reason to think any particular rule necessary. All of this tends to tolerate and promote sloppy, nonstandard procedures.

4. Lower Court Judges Need not Follow the Law

Without the possibility of review by an appellate court, the actions of lower court judges need have nothing to do with the law. In fact, lower court judges' actions may be based on the judges' own proclivities rather than on the law. Judges who are not reviewed may make decisions based on a personal world view, gut feeling of rough justice, local knowledge, or personal feelings about discipline and punishment, rather than on general legal principles. The law, with its logical application of technical rules, need be paid little heed, because no one will scrutinize the actions of lower court judges to see how they meet legal standards. This ultimately leaves the lower court judge's power unchecked, an especially worrisome result in a system in which many judges need not have legal training.

Unchecked judicial power undermines the legitimacy of these courts in the eyes of those who move through them. Courts derive their authority to decide disputes—be they disputes between individuals in civil cases or between the state and individuals in criminal cases—from the law itself. The law empowers courts to decide cases according to general principles and rules. If judges in de novo systems do not operate and decide cases according to law, the legitimacy and authority of courts as institutions and of government in general is undermined. Review of trial court decisions by appellate courts comprises one of the chief devices for ensuring that trial courts follow the law and are not governed by personal whim or caprice. Lack of appellate review unshackles the judge to roam the decisional landscape at will, with little regard for criteria and conclusions the law deems proper.

5. Discipline Provided by the Jury

Juries impose discipline on a judge. The presence of the jury obligates the judge to follow the law more closely than she might otherwise. The judge must handle the jury carefully, scrupulously assuring that the jury is correctly selected, that the lawyers respect the jury and its functions vis-a-vis the evidence during the trial, and that the jury is instructed correctly. Without traditional appellate review, none of the necessary scrutiny of the judge's handling of the jury function can take place. The presence of a jury also causes the judge to invest the process with more attention to the law and a greater degree of overall seriousness and dignity. Juries are also more likely to acquit than judges presiding alone; this shows the judge a conception of reasonable doubt different from her own, and breeds necessary judicial skepticism of the government and its actors. At the very least, use of juries puts citizens in courtrooms who are not part of the usual courtroom working group of judge, prosecutor, defense attorney, and staff. The mere presence of outsiders, especially as decisionmakers, causes the judge to modify behaviors and methods of proceeding inappropriate for public observation. The Supreme Court has acknowledged this tendency as part of the function of the jury: The jury guards against government oppression, in the form of "the corrupt or overzealous prosecutor and against the compliant, biased, or eccentric judge."

6. The Only Accountability: Court Administrative Systems

To the extent that any accountability exists for judges in de novo systems, it takes the form of regulations for court administration. These regulations, often implemented by chief judges, clerks of the court, professional court administrators, or other members of the court bureaucracy, emphasize the orderly, rapid disposition of cases and the efficient functioning of the bureaucracy above all else. Each of the states with a de novo system has a web of statutes, regulations, and administrative personnel to move cases through the criminal justice system as quickly and inexpensively as possible.

When combined with the lack of any accountability for legal decisions through traditional appellate processes, these administrative imperatives move judges away from the time- and resource-consuming requirements of due process of law toward the goal of efficiently clearing the docket, regardless of the effect on defendants. When all that matters to the "superiors" of a lower court judge are caseload disposition figures, what happens in any one case becomes largely irrelevant. No higher authority scrutinizes the judge's actions in any one case. Considerations such as fairness and the accuracy of determinations of guilt recede; interest in the caseload and its effects on the rest of the system becomes paramount.

E. Courts as Teachers

Courts, especially criminal courts, do more than simply adjudicate disputes. They also educate the members of the public that pass through them about the real meaning of concepts central to our society—the rule of law, fairness, the importance of the individual, the needs of society, and the proper accommodation of each of these to the other. The structure of de novo court systems undermines the ability of the lower courts to play this role.

Despite the fact that serious crimes more often capture public attention, courts that handle less serious cases, such as the lower courts in de novo systems, remain vitally important. To the extent that most citizens have just a few contacts in their lifetimes with the judicial system, such contacts are likely to be with the lower courts. Therefore, these courts are largely responsible for forming citizens' impressions of the judiciary. The experiences citizens have in these courts will either build or undermine confidence in and respect for law. Lower courts also represent one of the few points at which the judicial system might intervene before young offenders become repeat offenders.

The nature of proceedings in misdemeanor courts is well documented. Suffice it to say that lower courts' lack of respect for individuals and lack of awareness of the critical effects their actions can have on an individual's life are well known. The implications of these attitudes and the practices they foster loom large when combined with the lack of accountability of lower court judges, the lack of requirements of legal training for these judges, and other features of the lower courts in de novo systems. For all those that pass through the lower courts, whether as a complainant, witness, defendant in a traffic case, or defendant in a criminal case, the treatment they receive and the practices they observe hold a lesson. Lower courts may teach that the judge, not the law, is what matters, that there is little thought given to individuals in the lower courts, and that not even the appearance of justice is important. Courts may also teach that the law is a set of abiding principles worth respecting, a source of moral authority deserving of deference, and that due process is not just a burden but a "valuable privilege worth claiming." Lessons of the former nature seem likely to engender disrespect for the law, to alienate people and to influence "the quality and extent of order found in society." Only one point is certain: Citizens will learn whatever lessons the lower courts teach them.

III. Recommendations

Thus far, this article has described the characteristics of lower courts and demonstrated that the Supreme Court's analysis in *Colten*, *Ludwig*, and *North* is unsatisfactory. For a variety of reasons, de novo systems are not structured to produce efficiency; they invite waste, encourage duplicative actions by defendants, and require a redundant court bureaucracy. States retain de novo court systems, however, because by discouraging requests for new trials de novo systems dispose of criminal cases more quickly and less expensively than a system consisting only of superior courts. Lower courts also impose many costs on defendants, and the benefits the Court says defendants receive in the lower courts are illusory.

Viewed as a whole, the situation tempts the reformer to decry de novo systems as structurally defective and inherently unjust, and to call for their outright abolition. Certainly, abolishing de novo court systems could help to ensure that all defendants receive the consideration and fair treatment due process dictates, regardless of the court in which they are tried.

Yet the weight of tradition is considerable; outright abolition of de novo systems is unlikely. In lieu of abolition, this section of this article contains recommendations. They are aimed at enabling de novo systems to continue to benefit states by handling the large number of less serious criminal cases more rapidly and efficiently than a single, unified court system could, while providing some assurance that those whose cases move through the lower courts receive their due.

A. New Trial Request as Stay of Conviction and Consequences

A request for a new trial in the superior court should operate to stay or vacate any lower court conviction and its consequences. Statutes should make this process automatic upon the request for a new trial. Several state systems already operate this way. This would give the Supreme Court's characterization of the verdict of lower courts as "an offer in settlement" some substance. Currently, defendants convicted in the lower courts in most states must bear their convictions, and the consequences of these convictions, unless and until the superior court acts to the contrary. Some states allow a stay of incarceration upon the posting of a bond with the court. Because most bonds contain some financial condition, the availability of a stay only with the posting of a bond assures that only those without money are incarcerated pending appeal; those with money go free. If we intend that the defendant be free to accept or reject the lower court verdict or sentence, an automatic stay ensures real choice and equal treatment.

If a stay of lower court conviction and its consequences is not made automatic, legislatures should trim the power of lower courts to incarcerate defendants prior to trial in superior courts. Given the positive correlation between incarceration prior to trial, the probability of both being found guilty and further incarceration, and given the fact that a white person has a better chance of staying free pending trial than does a black person, courts should hesitate to use incarceration prior to trial in any case. A court should be especially cautious in choosing to incarcerate a defendant if the defendant has an unfettered right to a new trial, as in de novo systems. Unfortunately, courts in de novo systems lack any such caution. For example, in Feeley's study, ten percent of those arrested were detained until disposition, twice as many as were incarcerated after disposition. As Feeley notes, this pretrial incarceration may exact a penalty heavy enough by itself that many defendants prefer to opt out of the system through an early guilty plea. At the very least, therefore, when defendants seek release pending a new trial in the superior court, there should be a rebuttable presumption that no conditions of release more severe than those set prior to the lower court trial should be set after the lower court trial in the absence of evidence that those conditions will not secure the defendant's appearance at the new trial. The lower court conviction alone should not be sufficient to rebut this presumption.

B. Optional Traditional Appellate Review

Instead of a new trial, de novo systems should allow the defendant to opt for a traditional appeal, in which a higher court reviews the record for erroneous legal decisions by the trial court. Currently, one jurisdiction makes this option available. Making a stay of conviction and any adverse consequences automatic will encourage defendants to take this route. The option of filing a traditional appeal would put lower court trial judges on notice that appellate courts will be looking over their shoulders, and will therefore encourage judges to improve the caliber of lower court proceedings above their normally abysmal state. To the extent that the appellate process teaches judges the law, the entire criminal justice system will benefit. Mistakes in individual cases can be corrected, and the law will be more uniformly applied.

C. A Record for All Lower Court Proceedings

The option of traditional appellate review requires that lower courts generate a record. This record might take forms other than traditional stenographic recordings, such as audio or video tape. A lower court record allows the use of lower court testimony in the superior court for purposes of impeachment and discovery. These records lend themselves to the documenting of abusive practices in the lower courts, whether by individual judges or by the lower court system in general. Records could also be important tools in any effort to see that defendants are properly advised of their rights and the possibility and consequences of waivers of those rights.

D. Full Legal Education for All Judges

The irony in *North v. Russell* cannot have gone unnoticed by the members of the Supreme Court. In the very case in which the Court found the use of lay judges in de novo and other criminal court systems constitutionally defensible, a lower court lay judge sentenced to jail a defendant who was not, in fact, legally eligible to be incarcerated. One could hardly imagine a more serious type of mistake than jailing a person who should remain free. While a judge with a full legal education could make the same mistake, this seems less likely. Beyond mistakes, lack of legal training influences the way a judge views the proceedings and parties before the court. Lack of legal training causes decisions to be based on judges' personal proclivities instead of law and principle, and shifts the balance in favor of the government.

E. Limit the Authority of Lower Courts to Impose Penalties

The Supreme Court's opinions repeatedly refer to the limited powers of lower courts, especially the limited powers of these courts to incarcerate defendants. Unfortunately, this is not the case. Many states give these courts a wide range of sentences to impose, including lengthy incarceration. In courts in which the power of the judge is unchecked by judicial review, and in which the only remedy for a mistake or an injustice—a new trial—is actively discouraged, and where the judge may not have legal training, such broad power is indefensible. Even sentences of thirty days' incarceration could cause damage to careers and lives. The power of lower courts to impose sentences should be limited so that they can do only small amounts of damage.

F. Individualized Advice of Rights

States should address the failure to advise defendants of their rights to a new trial, and to other rights as well, by requiring that lower court judges advise defendants individually. The court should also supply defendants with a written version of the court's advice, a copy of which the defendant could initial to indicate that she had received the information. While this would not make absolutely certain that all who heard or saw their rights explained actually understood them, such a procedure could provide some assurance that defendants leave court knowing they had a right to a new trial, and with some understanding of the basic mechanics of the process.

G. Sentencing Guidelines

A number of states and the federal government use sentencing guidelines in their criminal justice systems. While the particular purposes of these systems vary, all utilize the same basic mechanism: use of a formula to calculate "scores" for the defendant, the offense, and other relevant factors, all of which are combined on a numerical matrix to calculate a particular range of punishment that the court may impose. Under some guidelines, the range of punishment binds the court; the court may depart from the prescribed range only under extraordinary circumstances or not at all. Under other systems, the guidelines are advisory, requiring only that the reason for the departure appear on the record.

States with de novo systems should require lower court judges to follow binding sentencing guidelines that would prohibit lower court judges from exceeding the punishment that the defendant would receive in the same case in superior court. This would address the problem of superior court trials that are generated by the disparity between the more severe sentences of lower court judges and the less severe sentences of superior court judges. By keeping lower court sentences in line with superior court sentences, sentencing guidelines remove a major incentive for new superior court proceedings in cases in which the defendant is not dissatisfied with either the trial process or the court's finding of guilt. Guidelines would also promote institutional uniformity; persons charged with the same crime in the same jurisdiction could expect the same outcome, regardless of the fact that the cases come before different courts. Use of such guidelines would also forestall the use of adaptive strategies by superior court judges to discourage new trials, such as presumptively concluding that the sentence of the lower court is appropriate in every appealed case. Though the guidelines should be binding, they need not be inflexible. The circumstances under which departure from the guidelines is allowed should be carefully specified; in the event of a departure, the lower court should be required to write an opinion demonstrating that the departure from the sentencing ranges met the specified criteria. This opinion should be made subject to traditional appellate review by a higher court. The point is that guidelines help prevent unnecessary appeals from overwhelming the superior court and turning efficiency into a cruel joke.

H. Optional Use of Juries

Use of juries in lower courts tempers the vast power of the judge in these courts, if for no other reason than that it is the jury that ultimately decides the case. Using juries in these courts also obligates judges to exercise more self-discipline and care in following procedures and applying the law. If juries are available in lower courts in the first instance, defendants need not bear the costs of a lower court trial before having a jury trial in the superior court.

I. Opting Out of the Lower Court

States should allow defendants to choose to avoid the lower court and proceed to superior court without the necessity of a lower court trial or guilty plea by making a simple request for a superior court trial. Like the use of juries in the lower court, this allows the defendant to obtain the advantages she perceives as important to her case, including the presence of a jury, the use of superior court procedures, or a legally trained judge, without the costs associated with a first trial. Some states already allow the defendant this choice. To ensure that this procedure is not abused, defendants should be required to make this request within a sufficient number of days before trial to allow sufficient notification of witnesses and court personnel. If the defendant violates this requirement and makes the request for a superior court trial on the day of his lower court trial, the request would be honored immediately— that is, the case would be put before a jury on the day of the request, eliminating the use of requests for superior court trials as de facto continuances.

J. Availability of Full Discovery

Few commodities are as important to the making of an intelligent decision as complete and accurate information. The need for complete information is particularly strong in the criminal justice system because a journey through the system is replete with serious implications. More complete and accurate information will lead all actors in the process, including defense counsel and defendants, to make better decisions, whether these decisions concern trial strategy, the wisdom of accepting an offer to plead guilty, the length of a sentence, or even the guilt or innocence of the defendant. Better decisions mean fewer requests for superior court trials because fewer defendants will be dissatisfied. Further, with more information, decisions of lower courts will resemble the decisions of superior courts more closely, making a gamble on an improved decision in the superior court less likely to pay off.

V. Conclusion

This article has examined a set of courts that are both vitally important and largely invisible. Lower courts in de novo systems hear misdemeanor and less serious felony cases in criminal courts in approximately half the states. Given the proportion of all criminal cases these courts handle, the significance of these courts looms large. Because they receive virtually no oversight in the form of traditional appellate review, and because they serve generally poor and noninfluential constituencies, lower courts attract little attention. Careful scrutiny shows that, notwithstanding the speculation of the Supreme Court, de novo systems do not benefit defendants. On the contrary, de novo systems increase the pressure on defendants to resolve cases as quickly as possible by making the exercise of constitutional rights, such as the right to trial by jury, more costly than in single-level systems that operate without the trial de novo feature. The availability of a new trial, which supposedly saves de novo systems from numerous constitutional maladies, is worse than an empty promise; it actually causes the defendant further damage. As with alternative dispute resolution, however, the goal of de novo court systems is efficiency and conservation of resources in the disposition of cases. Other concerns are secondary.

Thus, de novo systems teach us to proceed with caution when asked to embrace new, more efficient methods of case disposition that supposedly benefit all concerned.

Perhaps the best course is the elimination of de novo systems and the processing of all cases through single level systems, regardless of the seriousness of the offense. Given the historic resistance to such proposals, the changes proposed here may serve as a useful middle ground. If our lower court systems cannot be uprooted, perhaps they can be reconstructed to work better and to preserve some of their advantages. At least these proposals might make for better decisions by the lower courts and for better trials for defendants in them; perhaps they will also help teach citizens who have contact with lower courts the lessons about our government that we would all prefer.

Questions to Consider

1. Researchers have provided evidence that judges prefer to handle civil cases rather than criminal cases (most federal judges having come from corporate/business law backgrounds), but under federal law judges must try criminal cases themselves and can not shunt them to less judicial officers. Note that as felony caseloads have increased, there has not been an accompanying increase in civil magistrate trials. Rather, magistrates have seen a dramatic increase in activity related to criminal trials, even though they may not be the ultimate trial judges. Are federal judges avoiding work on criminal trials? Why would they do this? Why would there be a rule that only a full federal judge be able to try a felony case? Is it appropriate for multiple "judges" to handle different segments of each criminal proceeding? Should judges be told what cases they can try, or should the decision be left to each judge?

2. As electronic datebases expand, the public has more and more access to the published opinions of courts. Yet Davis and Songer cite the fact that approximately 63 percent of federal appellate court case decisions are never published. How is the public's right to know being affected by this lack of publication?

3. The number of cases decided per judge has grown significantly since the 1960s. Given the growth in the number of judicial assistants, is it clear that the actual workload of each judge has grown significantly? Why might judges ask for more resources?

4. Justice Stevens asserts that efficiencies are potentially gained in de novo trials only because this system discourages people from exercising their right to a jury trial. Do you agree or disagree? Why? How does the de novo trial system provide further evidence for those who assert that our jury trial rights are being continually eroded?

5. Malcolm Feeley has argued that putting someone through the criminal justice adjudication process often becomes the actual punishment, regardless of whether the person is innocent or guilty. How might the

de novo trial process in this country support or detract from his assertion?

6. How does the de novo trial system allow the guilty to "play the system"? How might one argue that it allows the innocent to "get played" as well?

7. Citizens most often come in contact with lower-level courts such as de novo trial courts. What impact would the "rough justice" of these courts have on citizens' perceptions about the quality of justice being provided? What might be the long-term consequences for our society?

Section III
Limiting or Trusting Juries?

The preceding sections have raised the issue of public involvement in legal decision making, and with this issue come many questions. Who has ultimate ownership of our nation's courts? Are the courts the exclusive domain of lawyers and judges, upon whom the public must rely to obtain needed services? What problems arise if we leave our court system to the total control of lawyers and judges? Does the public in effect subsidize the business of lawyers by paying the institutional overhead of courts? To what extent do citizens have a say in how their justice system operates?

One central method of public involvement in our system of justice is the jury. Up to twelve people, selected from a larger group of community members, observe the trial process and make decisions about the many disputes generated by our society. There is probably not a more democratic institution in our society than the jury—citizens making day-to-day decisions about their community. For many years after this country was formed, it was understood that juries had more power than judges or lawyers. Their group decisions were seen as the best method of ensuring that justice was applied in individual cases. To do this, the jury was given the power to decide issues of fact, and the jury had the power and responsibility of making sure that the law provided for justice in the case before them. Slowly judges took away the jury's power to decide issues of law as well as some issues of fact. Given this historical pattern of decreasing jury power, one must ask just how healthy our democratic institution of the jury is and what challenges it faces.

The articles in the following section seek to provide some insight into these basic questions. Most of the historical and scientific evidence presented seems to indicate that the power and responsibility of juries has been, and is still, steadily eroding. In each article, we examine the current limits on jury decision making and the problems these limits create in achieving the goal of justice.

The first three articles highlight several limits which have been placed on jury decision making, raising the question of who ultimately controls court process. Steele and Thornberg focus on juror confusion caused by judicial instructions given in complex legal language and the reasons why judges fail to correct this confusion. This failure is particularly problematic because studies show that juries who receive plain English instructions are more likely to reach reliable verdicts. The authors argue that judges continue to use the legalese that causes juror confusion because legal instructions are designed to appease appellate court judges rather than to enhance jury comprehension.

Saul Kassin next uses mock jury studies to argue that many lawyer trial tactics, which continue to be allowed by judges, unfairly affect the jury. These unfair tactics are allowed due to our deference to the adversary method, a deference based on the assumption that the truth will emerge if opposing lawyers each are given maximum freedom to promote their clients' self-interest. We might ask whether we promote falsity in the name of truth by allowing lawyers to manipulate the justice process.

James Levine highlights the problem of jury sequestration, a paternalistic approach toward jurors in which, in an attempt to insulate jurors from non-courtroom influences, they are kept together as a group and forbidden to have significant contact with anyone but each other. Analyzing the jury decision-making process he concludes that on balance, sequestration seems to undermine the pursuit of justice. Given the perpetuation of this practice, one might ask whether justice is the ultimate goal in setting rules for court process or whether court professionals maintain an unstated goal of jury control as the operative management guideline.

Hartmus and Levine then address the theme of a judge's ability to control the jury's exposure to evidence by exploring the possibility of video-taped trial transcripts for juror deliberations. Instead of refusing to let juries take notes during trials or making them rely on a written record, they suggest that the quality of juror decision making would be substantially improved by giving jurors access to all relevant information that occurred during the trial. In a class, should we make students take exams based on their recollection of the lectures and a single reading of the text, or should we allow students to revisit the material? How much more important are the decisions of jurors? How do we enhance the ability of jurors to make the right decision? And again, do we trust jurors enough to give them what they need to make good decisions, or do we continue to rely on judicial discretion to maintain controls?

Finally, in Scheflin and Van Dyke's article on jury nullification, we explore the range of appropriate jury power. Over the last two hundred years, American judges have taken from the jury the ability to determine law. Is this simply an appropriate deference to judicial expertise, or can juries best "complete" or "perfect" the law given their joint perceptions of community justice? The stakes over who controls the court system are high and the conflict between court professionals and juries is escalating. In 1998, the U.S. Court of Appeals for the 2nd Circuit ruled that judges could dismiss jurors who refuse to follow the law as defined by the judge. Similarly, in 1997, Colorado prosecutors obtained an obstruction-of-justice conviction against a juror who failed to reveal before trial that she had concerns with the underlying law in question.

This controversy reflects a much larger conflict over the goals of our society: Are we to promote the rule of law, which is theoretically applied equally to everyone, by deferring to judicial expertise, or do we promote fairness and democracy by allowing a group of community citizens to decide by consensus what is just in each unique situation that is brought before them? The authors use empirical studies to argue that informing juries that they have the power to do justice seems to lead juries, in fact, to do just that.

7

Jury Instructions
A Persistent Failure to Communicate

WALTER W. STEELE, JR. and
ELIZABETH G. THORNBURG

Jury instructions play an essential role in the American judicial system, bridging the gap between the law, the evidence as presented in court, and the jury. Because jury instructions do play such a central role in any trial, one would expect jury instructions to be carefully drafted to maximize juror comprehension, but they are not. Research shows that most jurors do not understand their instructions,[1] and that the level of juror comprehension of instructions would improve dramatically if the instructions were rewritten with the jury in mind.

This article documents the existence of juror confusion and identifies the forces that lead to the continued use of incomprehensible instructions. It then suggests specific changes in the law and efforts that the organized bar and judiciary must make in order for understandable instructions to become the norm rather than the exception.

Documented Jury Confusion

Case Law

It is difficult to discover the extent to which jurors comprehend court instructions, because rules of evidence and procedure usually protect

Reprinted by permission of the American Judicature Society and the author from *Judicature*, vol. 74, no. 5 (Feb./March, 1991), pp. 249–254.

the mental processes of jurors from inquiry.[2] There are two lines of cases, however, that document jury misunderstanding: cases in which juries send judges notes during deliberations,[3] and cases from states that allow testimony about conversations among jurors during deliberations.[4] Both demonstrate the existence of juror confusion, and both demonstrate the courts' reluctance to correct the confusion.

The problems of confusion and judicial nonintervention are present in *Whited v. Powell*,[5] a Texas supreme court case. In *Whited*, a juror misunderstood the court's charge and misstated the law to another juror, who then changed his vote based on the misstatement. The supreme court characterized this as "express misconstruction of the court's charge," but refused to order a new trial.[6] The court noted that "it would be most unrealistic to expect that all members of the jury as ordinary laymen would thoroughly understand every portion of a complicated charge . . . Most of our jury verdicts would be of little value" if the misunderstanding of one or more jurors were grounds for new trial.[7] *Whited* is just one of many cases that demonstrate the judiciary's reluctance to require that instructions be comprehensible.[8] Apparently, the inclination of most courts is to let sleeping dogs lie rather than to undertake a campaign to improve the comprehensibility of jury instructions.[9]

Social Science Research

Social scientists have also proved that juries misunderstand instructions: there is an empirically demonstrable gap between what judges instruct and what juries understand.[10] Their studies reveal that a large percent of jurors fail to understand their instructions.[11] In fact, some studies showed that jurors who receive typical pattern instructions do not comprehend the issues better than jurors who receive *no instructions at all*.[12]

Fortunately, the social science studies also provide the basis for hope. Jurors who receive instructions rewritten into plain English are significantly more likely to reach a reliable verdict.[13] More important, researchers have identified the linguistic features of jury instructions that cause comprehension problems in jury instructions.[14] For example, constructions such as nominalizations,[15] phrases beginning with "as to," misplaced phrases, multiple negatives, and passive verbs confuse jurors; instructions rewritten to eliminate these constructions are significantly better understood.[16] In addition, instructions which are poorly organized or which use unnecessarily difficult vocabulary tend to confuse jurors. Using this information, lawyers and judges willing to make the effort can write comprehensible jury instructions, and appellate courts can test those instructions on appeal.[17]

Empirical Research

We decided to test some pattern jury instructions to see if jurors understood them. The subjects for our test were people called to jury service in Dallas County, Texas, who had not yet served on a jury. We selected five Texas pattern jury instructions for testing: (1) proximate cause; (2) new and independent cause; (3) negligence; (4) presumption of innocence; and (5) accomplice testimony.[18] These instructions present an even mix of short and long sentences, simple and difficult vocabulary, and straightforward and convoluted syntax.

We suspected that the instructions would confuse jurors for a number of reasons. Some of the pattern instructions were poorly organized; all of the instructions used difficult vocabulary; and some instructions were hard to understand due to their length. We rewrote the instructions, trying to eliminate these problems without changing the meaning of the instructions (see pages 116–118).

The next step was to test whether the rewritten instructions were more comprehensible than the pattern instructions. To do this we created four audio tapes. Each tape contained a recording of a ''judge'' reading each of the five instructions, some in pattern form and some in rewritten form. We then played one of the tapes for each juror. After each instruction, we stopped the tape and asked the juror to paraphrase the instruction.[19] Each juror heard and paraphrased all five instructions on the tape. We then analyzed the jurors' responses to see whether the jurors correctly paraphrased each legally significant element of the instructions:[20]

Results

The results of the experiment confirmed what other researchers had found: jurors' comprehension of the pattern instructions was low, and jurors understood the rewritten instructions better than the pattern instructions (see table 1).[21] For example, the jurors correctly paraphrased only 5.83 percent of the pattern instruction on ''new and independent cause,'' but correctly paraphrased 29.67 percent of the rewritten instruction. Similarly, the jurors correctly paraphrased 19.49 percent of the pattern instruction on ''negligence,'' but correctly paraphrased 35.28 percent of the rewritten instruction.[22]

The subjects' improved comprehension was dramatic. The overall gain in juror comprehension was 408 percent for the ''new and independent cause'' instruction, 112 percent for the ''accomplice testimony'' instruction, 81 percent for the ''negligence'' instruction, 60 percent for the ''proximate cause'' instruction, and 34 percent for the ''presumption of innocence'' instruction.

Table 1 Paraphrases of five pattern/rewritten instructions

	Percent legally incorrect	Percent of no paraphrase	Percent legally correct
New & independent cause			
pattern	1.67	92.50	5.83
rewritten	1.00	69.33	29.67
Accomplice testimony			
pattern	0.44	90.26	9.30
rewritten	1.07	79.17	19.76
Negligence			
pattern	1.54	78.97	19.49
rewritten	0.00	64.72	35.28
Proximate cause			
pattern	0.91	84.55	14.55
rewritten	0.77	75.90	23.33
Presumption of innocence			
pattern	3.86	78.77	17.37
rewritten	0.61	76.06	23.33

The percentage figures represent the percentage out of the total variables for each instruction. For example, if an instruction had ten variables (ten legally significant elements), and two of the ten were correctly paraphrased, the percentages would be 0% legally incorrect, 80% no paraphrase, and 20% legally correct. The results for multiple jurors were cumulated to get the results set out in the table. Note that the most frequent response by far was "no paraphrase." In other words, for the most part the jurors failed to comprehend large portions of the instruction, and thus were unable to paraphrase it.

Our experiment indicates that the jurors who participated failed to comprehend large portions of the instructions. This result should be of deep concern to both lawyers and judges, because jurors who do not understand their instructions may not render the verdict they intend or the verdict that they would render if they understood their instructions.[23]

This concern should be translated into action. We did successfully rewrite the instructions, and neither of us has any advanced training in English composition. We want practicing lawyers and judges to view our experiment as realistic and as a task within their reach. Jurors do not adequately understand instructions as currently drafted, but can understand significantly more when instructions are rewritten for clarity.

Can the System Change?

Although the research makes a convincing case for change to plain English in our jury instructions, overwhelming forces supporting the status quo may present an insurmountable obstacle. A number of factors make it difficult to bring about meaningful change in the way jury instructions are drafted. One set of factors arises from lawyer attitudes. Some lawyers and judges resist change, believing erroneously that jurors understand their instructions. Other lawyers believe that the confusion benefits their clients and, therefore, support the status quo rather than exert efforts to achieve greater clarity. Some lawyers and trial court judges are willing to change, but are afraid to do so because of the risk that the clearer instructions will be reversed by appellate courts because they are not the "pattern" instructions.

Lawyers and judges who do not resist change are still faced with some difficulties in rewriting jury instructions. Some are inherent in the nature of the law and cannot be eliminated. One inherent difficulty in writing jury instructions stems from the complexity of the law itself. Complicated concepts are more difficult to express clearly than simple ones. It is difficult to explain in a paragraph concepts that first-year law students spend months learning. Difficult, however, does not mean impossible.

The complexity of the law, and the difficulty of rewriting it, often stems from the subtleties of meaning acquired by legal terms of art and other legal language. This subtlety of meaning, however, "attaches as a function of usage, and not because of any inherent property of the word itself."[24] As lawyers speaking to each other use certain words, their knowledge of the underlying case law communicates something more to them than a simple dictionary definition of the word would show. This kind of extra communication, however, is restricted to members of the profession who understand the usage behind the word. It does not extend to lay people on juries. An explanation that would communicate a term of art to a jury with all its professional resonances, then, might need to be extremely long.[25]

A related roadblock to simplicity is the law's occasional vagueness. Some legal concepts are inherently general: "reasonable person"; "reasonable doubt"; "preponderance of the evidence"; "unconscionable." To redefine such concepts so that they can be standardized or quantified could have two unfortunate results. First, it might make the cost of litigation prohibitive by requiring quantifiable proof.[26] Second, greater specificity might rob the law of its flexibility and its ability to reflect community standards. Because of these problems, we do not propose a redefinition of such concepts to achieve greater clarity.

Other factors preventing change arise from the law surrounding instructions. Some of the rules of procedure governing the submission

Pattern and Rewritten Instructions

Pattern Charge

Proximate cause means that cause which, in a natural and continuous sequence, produces an event, and without which cause such event would not have occured; and in order to be a proximate cause, the act complained of must be such that a person using ordinary care would have foreseen that the event, or some similar event, might reasonably result therefrom. There may be more than one proximate cause of an event.

New and independent cause means the act of a separate and independent agency, not reasonably foreseeable, which destroys the causal connection, if any, between the act inquired about and the occurrence in question, and thereby becomes the immediate cause of the occurrence.

Negligence means failure to use ordinary care; that is to say, failure to do that which a person of ordinary prudence would have done under the same or similar circumstances, or doing that which a person of ordinary prudence would not have done under the same or similar circumstances.

Presumption of innocence All persons are presumed to be innocent and no person may be convicted of an offense unless each element of the offense is proved

Rewritten

An event often has many causes. In order to be a "proximate cause," three things must be true. First, the cause naturally and continuously led to the event. Second, the event would not have happened without the proximate cause. Third, a person using ordinary care would have foreseen that the proximate cause might reasonably lead to the event or to some similar event. There may be more than one proximate cause of an event.

Sometimes when a natural chain of events is set in motion, that chain is broken by a "new and independent cause." The law defines "new and independent cause" in its own particular way. To be a "new and independent cause" the cause must be all of the following:

First: The cause must, indeed, break a chain of events already set in motion so that it becomes the immediate cause of what happens.

Second: The cause must come from a source that is separate and independent from the defendant.

Third: The cause must be one that the defendant could not have foreseen using ordinary care.

A person can become negligent in two ways. The first way a person becomes negligent is by doing something that a person of ordinary care would not have done in the same situation or in a similar situation. The second way a person becomes negligent is by failing to do something that a person of ordinary care would have done in the same situation or in a similar situation.

My job as judge is to tell you about the laws that apply to this case. As jurors, you have two jobs.

First: In reaching your verdict you must

Pattern Charge

beyond a reasonable doubt. The fact that the defendant has been arrested, confined or indicted for, or otherwise charged with, the offense gives rise to no inference of guilt at his trial. In case you have a reasonable doubt as to defendant's guilt after considering all of the evidence before you, and these instructions, you will acquit him. You are the exclusive judges of the facts proved, and of the credibility of the witnesses and the weight to be given their testimony, but the law you shall receive in these written instructions, and you must be governed thereby.

Accomplice testimony An accomplice, as the term is here used, means anyone connected with the crime charges, as a party thereto and includes all persons who are connected with the crime, as such parties, by unlawful act or omission on their part transpiring either before or during the time of the commission of the offense. A person is criminally responsible as a party to an offense if the offense is committed by his own conduct, by the conduct of another for which he is criminally responsible, or by both. Mere presence alone, however, will not constitute one a party to an offense.

A person is criminally responsible for an

Rewritten

follow the laws that I am explaining to you; and

Second: You must decide what the facts are in this case. In other words, you must decide what happened.

To decide what the facts are you will have to decide how much of each witness's testimony you believe, and how much weight to give what is believed.

Our law states that anyone charged with a crime is presumed to be innocent unless the prosecution proves each part of the crime beyond a reasonable doubt. In deciding whether the prosecution has proved each part of the crime beyond a reasonable doubt, you must think about all of my instructions and about all of the evidence before you. After you have done this, if you have a reasonable doubt about the existence of any part of the crime you must find the defendant not guilty.

As part of the normal legal process, the defendant has been arrested, jailed, and charged, but these facts do not suggest that the defendant may be guilty, and you must not consider these facts as any evidence of the defendant's guilt.

This instruction is in two parts. First, I am going to tell you about the kind of witness known as an accomplice. The second part of the instruction will tell you when you can consider testimony from an accomplice.

To be an accomplice, a person must intend to help with the crime, and with that intention, a person must engage in one or more of the following activities by act or by omission either before or during the commission of the offense:

1. Solicit another person to commit the crime;
2. Encourage another person to commit the crime;

Pattern Charge

offense committed by the conduct of another if, acting with the intent to promote or asssist the commission of the offense, he solicits, encourages, directs, or aids or attempts to aid the other person to commit the offense. The term "conduct of another" means any act or omission and its accompanying mental state. A conviction cannot be had upon the testimony of an accomplice unless the jury first believes that the accomplice's evidence is true and that it shows that the defendant is guilty of the offense charged against him, and then you cannot convict the defendant upon said testimony unless the accomplice's testimony is corroborated by other evidence tending to connect the defendant with the offense charged, and the corroboration is not sufficient if it merely shows the commission of the offense, but it must tend to connect the defendant with its commission.

Rewritten

3. Direct another person to commit the crime;
4. Help another person to commit the crime; or
5. Try to help another person to commit the crime.

Merely being at the scene of a crime does not make a person an accomplice.

Now, when can you use testimony from an accomplice? You cannot use the testimony of an accomplice to convict the defendant unless:

First, you believe that the accomplice's testimony is true.

Second, you believe that the evidence from the accomplice shows that the defendant is guilty of the crime charged in this case.

Third, there is some evidence *other than* the evidence from the accomplice which tends to connect *the defendant* with the commission of the crime. It is not enough that this other evidence shows that the crime was committed by *someone*. It must tend to show that the defendant committed the crime.

Without all three things you must totally ignore the evidence from an accomplice.

---

of jury instructions hinder efforts at rewriting. Two notable examples are the rules prohibiting the judge from commenting on the evidence and the rules prohibiting the judge from informing the jury of the effect of its answers. Common law traditionally allowed the judge to aid the jury in comprehension of the instructions.[27] Unfortunately, this common law tradition has been abandoned in most states, although it still thrives in the federal system.[28] Pervasive as these rules may be, they make the instructions extremely awkward and difficult for the jurors to comprehend.

Another point of resistance arises because the drafting of jury instructions often gets a low priority in trial preparation. Because of time and financial constraints, many trial lawyers delay writing the instructions until the trial has started, anticipating that the case may settle on the courthouse steps or a plea bargain may be reached as the jury is impaneled. The inevitable result is a confused set of hastily prepared instructions.[29]

Finally, change is difficult because the instructions are proposed and drafted in a process driven by the adversary system. Each lawyer is primarily concerned with presenting instructions that benefit his or her client and is only secondarily concerned with improving the legal system as a whole by drafting clear instructions. Also, the ultimate decision on the form of instruction is made by the trial judge. Unfortunately, judges are the ones with the least to gain by using comprehensible but unorthodox instructions. Lawyers, at least, may be interested in rewriting instructions if they preceive that clarity benefits their clients. Trial court judges, however, lack that motivation and instead risk reversal by deviating by one word from the pattern instruction or the language of appellate opinions. The adversary system, then, tends to discourage lawyers from writing the clearest possible instructions and puts the ultimate control in the hands of the party with the least incentive to change.

Forces for Change

In order for the legal system to produce comprehensible instructions, three changes must occur. First, the law must be changed to create incentives for lawyers and judges to worry as much about comprehensibility as they do about technical correctness. Appellate courts could adopt a standard of clarity, judging the instructions by standards which have been developed by linguistic researchers in this field.[30] Second, changes must be made in the law governing the submission of jury instructions to eliminate requirements that hinder comprehension. Judges should be permitted to comment on the evidence and to inform the jury of the effect of their answers. Third, the movement to draft clear jury instructions must be taken out of the realm of the adversary system.

How would the process of change work, given adequate motivation? The models are found in the experience of the bench and bar in formulating codes of procedure and codes of evidence. Although the process is painful and costly, the American bench and bar have managed to come together in compromise to improve codes of trial procedure and codes of evidence. When these efforts are undertaken on a high plane, with a recognition of the need for improvement, and with a selfless willingness to make uncomfortable changes in the interest of justice, they have worked.

In fact, committees of lawyers and judges have created pattern jury instructions in a number of jurisdictions. Unfortunately, these commit- tees have rarely managed to draft pattern instructions that are comprehensible to jurors. Because pattern instructions are drafted by committees of judges, lawyers, and law professors, concerns about legal accuracy and comparative advantage tend to outweigh concerns about clarity. Indeed, most of the social science research that has proved instructions to be unintelligible, including the research reported in this article, has been done using pattern instructions.

Two relatively minor changes in the techniques of the committees drafting pattern instructions would go a long way towards solving the problem. First, the emphasis of the lawyers and judges charged with the responsibility of drafting pattern jury instructions must change from one of stating the law in every minute detail to one of clearly stating the law so that jurors can understand it.[31] Second, the membership of such drafting committees must include lay persons. Lawyers and judges must realize that the education and experience that produce good lawyers and judges do not necessarily produce good writers of conventional prose. Further, the socialization of lawyers into legal discourse prevents them from "hearing" the instruction as jurors would. It may take a person without legal training to anticipate certain comprehension problems. Better yet, the proposed instructions could be empirically tested for juror comprehension, with problem areas rewritten and eliminated.[32] Such an effort could be undertaken by the courts or bar association of any state.[33]

The problem is clear: juror comprehension of instructions is pitifully low. Likewise, the general scheme of solutions is evident. Unfortunately, prospects for actual change appear dim. Real change would require all parties involved—trial and appellate courts, state bar committees, and the trial bar—to rise above their narrowly perceived self-interest and act instead in the interests of the judicial system as a whole.

Endnotes

[1] Lawyers and judges have suspected for some time that many jurors do not understand their instructions. See e.g. Cook, "Instructionese: Legalistic Lingo of Contrived Confusion," 7 *J. Mo. B.* 113 (1951); Head, "Confessions of a Juror," 44 F.R.D. 330 (1967); Hoffman & Brodley, "Jurors on Trial," 17 *Mo. L. Rev.* 235 (1952); Hunter, "Law in the Jury Room," 2 *Ohio St. L. J.* 1 (1935); Winslow, "The Instruction Ritual," 13 *Hastings L. J.* 456 (1962).

[2] See e.g., Fed R. Evid. 606(b), Tex. R. Evid. 606(b); Pope, "The Mental Operations of Jurors," 40 *Tex. L. Rev.* 849, 851–52 (1962).

[3] Meyer & Rosenberg, "Questions Juries Ask: Untapped Springs of Insight," 55 *Judicature* 105, 106 (1971).

[4] See, for example, the Texas cases *Compton v. Henrie*, 364 S.W.2d 179 (Tex. 1963) (one juror's repeated incorrect statement regarding "preponderance of the evidence"), and *Whited v. Powell*, 155 Tex. 210, 285 S.W.2d 364 (1956).

5 155 Tex. 210, 285 S.W.2d 364 (1956).

6 Id. at 215, 285 S.W.2d at 367.

7 Id. at 216, 285 S.W.2d at 368.

8 Case law shows that juries are often confused about instructions regarding: (1) the measure of damages [*Hoffman v. Deck Masters, Inc.*, 662 S.W.2d 438 (Tex. App. 1983) (jury miscalculation of damages due to misunderstanding of instructions would not justify retrial)]; (2) causation and the apportionment of negligence [*Kindle v. Armstrong Packing Co.* 103 S.W.2d 471, 473 (Tex Civ. App. 1937) (jury thought proximate cause meant whole cause; not ground for new trial)]; and (3) definitions of words such as "actual notice" [*Coakley v. Crow*, 457 S.W.2d 431, 435 (Tex. Civ. App. 1970), cert. denied, 402 U.S. 90 (1971))], "undue influence" [*Stephens County Museum, Inc. v. Swenson*, 517 S.W.2d 257, 259–60 (Tex. 1974)], "pledge" [*Martin v. U.S. Trust Co.*, 690 S.W.2d 300, 309 (Tex. App. 1985)], and "consent" [*Cortez v. Medical Protective Co.*, 560 S.W.2d 132, 135 (Tex. Civ. App. 1977)]. Such mmistaken notions lead to mistaken verdicts, yet courts refuse to grant new trials.

9 "Any attempt to rewrite the current approved jury instructions raises the fear that differences in interpretation will come to the surface and create disruption, while if you leave it in legalese everyone can nod and smile and believe whatever they want." Mathewson, "Verbatim," 15 *Student Lawyer* 6 (1986).

10 See e.g., Hastie, Penrod & Pennington, *Inside the Jury* (Cambridge: Harvard University Press, 1983); Charrow & Charrow, "Making Legal Language Understandable: A Psycholinguistic Study of Jury Instructions," 79 *Colum. L. Rev.* 601; Strawn & Buchanan, "Jury Confusion: A Threat to Justice," 59 *Judicature* 478 (1976); Strawn, Buchanan, Pryor & Taylor, "Reaching a Verdict, Step by Step," 60 *Judicature* 383 (1977); Elwork, Sales & Alfini, "Judicial Decision: In Ignorance of the Law or in Light of It?", 1 *Law & Hum. Behav.* 163, 173 (1970); Severance, Greene & Loftus, "Toward Criminal Jury Instructions that Jurors Can Understand," 75 *J. Crim. L. & Criminology* 198 (1984).

The American Bar Association has recently sponsored a study of jury comprehension in complex cases. The ABA researchers videotaped shadow juries composed of alternate jurors who had seen the same evidence and heard the same instructions as the actual juries hearing real cases in federal court. They found that jury instructions written in legalese were confusing and unclear. For example, the jurors in a criminal case were unable to define "beyond a reasonable doubt" despite an instruction on the burden of proof. 6 *BNA Civil Trial Manual* 116 (April 4, 1990).

11 For example, in one test jurors received detailed background information regarding a case, read a set of instructions, and took multiple choice retention and comprehension tests. The results showed that 86 percent of the criminal juries were unable to answer accurately questions concerning proof of guilt, and less than half of the civil juries were able to answer a question about proximate cause. Forston, supra n. 10, at 615.

12 Elwork, Sales & Alfini, *Making Jury Instructions Understandable* (Charlottesville, VA: Michie, 1982); Elwork, Sales & Alfini, "Judicial Decisions," supra n. 10, at 173. After seeing a personal injury trial on video tape, jurors were given either no instructions, pattern instructions, or rewritten instructions. Id.

13 Strawn, Buchanan, Pryor & Taylor, supra n. 10, at 387–88; Elwork, Alfini & Sales, "Toward Understandable Jury Instructions," 65 *Judicature* 432, 434–35 (1982).

14 Charrow, supra n. 10, at 1307–08.

15 A nominalization is a verb turned into a noun. Nominalizations are grammatical, but are difficult to understand because they do not communicate a scene that the juror can picture. For example: NOMINALIZATION: *Recovery* by Mr. Smith is predicated upon *circumvention* of the adultery statute. VERB: Mr. Smith can *recover* if he *circumvents* the adultery statute.

¹⁶ Charrow, supra n. 10, at 1335–58. In the Charrows' experiment, for example, comprehension of instructions regarding agency increased 93 percent, comprehension of instructions about assumption of the risk increased 78 percent, and comprehension of an instruction about the use of evidence increased 52 percent, Id. at 1370 (Table 14).

¹⁷ We suggest, for example, that any lawyer trying to write clear instructions should consult Elwork, Sales & Alfini, *Making Jury Instructions Understandable*, supra n. 12, at ch. 7. This book provides empirically supported, easy to follow advice for improving jury instructions.

¹⁸ The civil instructions are from State Bar of Texas, 1 Texas Pattern Jury Charges (Supp. 1986). The criminal instructions are from McClung, *Jury Charges for Texas Criminal Procedure* (1987).

¹⁹ This method of research is known as paraphrase testing. In a paraphrase task, the subject either listens to or reads some material and is then asked to explain it in his or her own words. The validity of paraphrase testing is supported by extensive psychological literature, and is based on the notion that a test subject will discuss (i.e. paraphrase) that which is understood and fail to discuss that which is not understood or is ignored. For a thorough discussion of paraphrase testing, see Charrow, supra n. 10, at 1309–11.

²⁰ For a full text of the pattern and rewritten instructions, the score sheets, and the statistical results, see Steele & Thornburg, "Jury Instructions: A Persistent Failure to Communicate," 67 *N.C.L. Rev.* 77, 88–94 and 110–119 (1988).

²¹ An average of all five of the pattern instructions revealed that only 12.85 percent of the paraphrases were correct, as compared to 23.59 percent correct paraphrases from rewritten instructions, an impressive 91 percent gain in understanding.

²² The comprehension figures, even for the rewritten instructions, are still quite low. Note, however, that these figures represent comprehension of instructions given in isolation. The subjects did not hear voir dire, opening statements, evidence, or closing arguments. It is likely that these parts of a trial also serve to increase their understanding of the instructions. Our purpose, however, was to test juror comprehension of instructions in and of themselves, so we did not provide them with these external clues to meaning.

²³ Social science researchers, for example, showed identical videotaped trials to juries, half using pattern instructions and half using rewritten instructions. They found a statistically significant difference in the verdicts reached by the two groups. See Elwork, Sales & Alfini, *Making Jury Instructions Understandable*, supra n. 12, at 174–76.

²⁴ Perlman, "Pattern Jury Instructions: The Application of Social Science Research," 65 *Neb. L. Rev.* 520, 536 n. 65 (1986).

²⁵ Id.

²⁶ Perlman notes, for example, that to change "substantial likelihood of confusion among consumers" to a quantified standard such as confusion of 65 percent of prospective customers would greatly increase the cost of trademark litigation. Id. at 538.

²⁷ See e.g., Walker, "Judicial Comment on the Evidence in Jury Trials," 15 *A.B.A.J.* 647 (1929).

²⁸ See *United States v. Block*, 755 F.2d 770, 775 (11th Cir. 1985).

²⁹ Farrell, "Communication in the Jury Room: Jury Instructions," 85 *W. Va. L. Rev.* 5, 21 (1982).

³⁰ Charrow, supra n. 10, at 1359–60.

³¹ Pattern instructions have, in the past, tended to take their language from appellate opinions. But appellate opinions, while acceptable as intraprofessional communications, are not written for the purpose of explaining the law to lay persons. There are separate linguistic universes here: one for members of the bar, and one for the lay persons who serve on juries. When language written for one audience is directed instead to another, the resulting confusion should not be surprising.

[32] These suggestions are so minor that one wonders why they have not already been adopted. Some have. In Pennsylvania, a subcommittee headed by two psycholinguists tested proposed pattern instructions for clarity. Nieland, *Pattern Jury Instructions: A Critical Look at a Modern Movement to Improve the Jury System* 25 (Chicago: American Judicature Society, 1979). Two law professors have written an exemplary set of instructions for the Alaska court system. Perlman & Saltzburg. *Alaska Pattern Civil Jury Instructions* (1981).

[33] Other practices unrelated to the way in which instructions are written can affect the jury's ability to understand its job and follow the instructions. For example, studies have demonstrated that jurors who receive written copies of their instructions pay more attention to the instructions and reach more accurate results, yet only 16 jurisdictions currently allow the jury to take copies of the instructions into the jury room. Foston, supra n. 10, at 619. Also, some studies have indicated that jurors who are instructed in certain aspects of the law at the beginning as well as at the end of the trial are better able to evaluate evidence and understand their instructions. See e.g., Prettman, "Jury Instructions—First or Last," 46 *A.B.A.J. 1066 (1960).*

8

The American Jury
Handicapped in the Pursuit of Justice

SAUL M. KASSIN

Whether it is true or not, the story is a favorite among students of trial advocacy: Clarence Darrow, smoking a cigar during the presentation of his opponent's case, stole the jury's attention by inserting a thin wire into the cigar and producing an ash that grew like magic with every puff.[1] In a more recent case involving personal injury in which the plaintiff had lost a leg, Melvin Belli carried into court a large L-shaped package wrapped in yellow butcher paper and tied with a white string, and placed it on counsel's table as a visible reminder. Then during his closing argument, Belli unwrapped the package, only to reveal a prosthesis.[2] These courtroom pranks as well as other, more common trial practices, are clever, entertaining, and perhaps even effective. But at what cost to the jury's pursuit of justice?

This article examines nonevidentiary social influences on the jury, influences that emanate from various trial practices and threaten to compromise a litigant's right to a fair trial. Broadly defined, there are two phases in the jury's decision-making task that are at risk. The first is the factfinding competence of *individual jurors*—that is, their ability to make accurate judgments of the evidence (e.g., by distinguishing among witnesses of varying credibility), and disregard information that is not in evidence (e.g., material received from the news media, voir

Reprinted by permission of the *Ohio State Law Journal* and the author from vol. 51 (1990), pp. 687–711.

dire questions, opening statements, closing arguments, and inadmissible testimony). The second phase of a jury's task is the deliberation of the *jury as a group*—that is, the process by which individual members contribute independently and equally to a joint outcome, exerting influence over each other through information and rational argument rather than heavy-handed social pressure.[3]

The following evaluation of juries is based on the results of controlled behavioral research, not on abstract legal theory, isolated case studies, or trial anecdotes. The reader should thus be mindful of both the strengths and weaknesses inherent in this approach. The most appropriate way to obtain a full and rich understanding of how juries function is to observe the decision-making process in action. Juries, however, deliberate in complete privacy, behind closed doors. Unable to observe or record actual jury deliberations, researchers have had to develop alternative, less direct strategies (e.g., analysis of court records in search of statistical relationships between various trial factors and jury verdicts; post-trial interviews with jurors, alternates, and other trial participants; jury simulation experiments). Most of the research reported in this paper was conducted within a mock jury paradigm.[4]

I. Factfinding Competence of Individual Jurors

As individual factfinders, jurors must competently process all evidence and instructions, disregard information that is not in evidence, and reconstruct disputed events by distinguishing among witnesses of varying credibility. We will see that the task is difficult, and that it is complicated even further by various questionable practices.

A. Jurors as Arbiters of Truth and Deception

Confronted with opposing sides and inevitably conflicting testimony, jurors must accept the testimony of some witnesses, and reject others. Toward this end, the courts instruct jurors to pay close attention not only to the content of the witness's testimony but to his or her demeanor while testifying. Indeed, many judges prohibit jurors from taking notes for fear that they will overlook informative nonverbal cues.[5]

Unfortunately, psychological research suggests that people perform at only slightly better than chance levels in evaluating truth and deception. Even individuals who make these judgments for a living (e.g., customs inspectors, law enforcement officers) are prone to error.[6] Based on a review of over thirty studies, Miron Zuckerman and others conclude that there is a mismatch between the nonverbal behaviors actually associated with deception and those cues used by perceivers.[7] People tend to focus on a speaker's face, for example, even though facial expressions are under conscious deceptive control.[8] At the same time, there is a tendency to overlook kinesic and paralinguistic cues, even though they are more revealing.[9] In short, there is reason to believe that jurors tune into the wrong channels of communication. Seduced by the silver tongue and the smiling face, they may fail to notice the restless body and the quivering voice.[10]

Human imperfections aside, the rules of evidence and trial procedure that guide the questioning of witnesses are intended to facilitate the jury's quest for the truth.[11] In theory, direct and cross examination should thus enhance the credibility of witnesses who are accurate and honest, while diminishing the credibility of those who are inaccurate or dishonest—in other words, it should heighten the jury's factfinding competence. There is no way to know how frequently the law's objectives are actually achieved. While much is written about effective questioning techniques, surprisingly little research has examined their prevalence or their impact on the jury.[12] One problem, however, seems evident. Even though trial attorneys are expected to adhere to rules of evidence and keep their trial strategies within the boundaries of ethical conduct,[13] they often bend the rules and stretch the boundaries.[14] Thus we ask, to what extent can the examination of witnesses be used to subvert a jury's quest for the truth?

There are several ethically questionable trial practices, or "dirty tricks," that could make it difficult for jurors to make sound credibility judgments. Coaching witnesses, leading their testimony in court, distracting the jury at critical moments in an opponent's case, making frivolous objections, and asking questions that invite the leakage of inadmissible evidence, are among the possibilities.[15] In this section, two such practices are evaluated: the presentation of deposition testimony, and the use of presumptuous cross-examination questions.

B. Deposition Testimony and the Surrogate Witness

As difficult as it is to evaluate witnesses by their demeanor, the task is needlessly complicated when jurors must make judgments of credibility without ever seeing the actual witness. Often, people who are scheduled to testify are not available to appear in court.[16] In order to secure the substance of what these prospective witnesses have to say, counsel may take a deposition and enter that deposition into the trial record.

The use of deposition testimony in lieu of the live witness raises an interesting procedural question: How is such testimony entered into the trial record? How is the information presented, and what effect does it have on the jury's ability to evaluate the witness? In most courts, depositions are transcribed and then read aloud from the witness stand by a clerk or by an individual appointed by the witness's attorney. Usually, the clerk reads the answers, while the attorney reads the questions; sometimes, the attorney reads the entire script.

As one might expect, the practice of using what I call "surrogate witnesses" in an adversarial context paves the way for abuse. In one case, for example, I observed pretrial auditions of more than thirty professional actors and actresses who were called to play the roles of various absent witnesses who had been deposed. The actors all read the transcripts flawlessly. What distinguished those who were hired from those who were not was their ability to project through subtle nonverbal behaviors—crossing legs, rolling eyes, smiling, or sighing at a critical moment—specific impressions of the witnesses they were supposed to represent.[17]

It should not be permissible to use surrogates in this manner. Indeed, deposition readers should not unduly emphasize any words or engage in suggestive conduct. Nevertheless, many litigators appreciate the potential for gain in this procedure. For example, one trial advocate advises that "whoever is playing the part of the witness on the stand will, most assuredly, be identified with that witness. True, he is nothing more than an actor, but human beings tend to associate a voice with a person; so be certain that the 'actor' projects a favourable image."[18] It is even suggested that when faced with a witness with undesirable characteristics, the "imaginative" lawyer should consider taking a deposition and then replacing that witness with an attractive surrogate.[19] Research on the social psychology of persuasion offers little guidance. It is clear that audiences are influenced by the *source* of a communication,[20] but do characteristics of the *messenger* have the same effect? Is it truly possible to alter the impact of a deposition and mislead the jury by manipulating the surrogate's demeanor?

To test this hypothesis, I conducted the following mock jury experiment.[21] Eighty-eight subjects read a summary of a case in which the plaintiff sought damages from a security company because he had been harassed and then shot by one of its guards. The defense claimed the plaintiff was drunk and had inadvertently shot himself in a scuffle with their guard. There were no eyewitnesses to the shooting, and the physical evidence was ambiguous. For all practical purposes, a jury's verdict would thus hinge on the relative credibility of opposing witnesses, the plaintiff and the guard. After reading a summary of the case, subjects watched a carefully staged videotape of the plaintiff's testimony. An actor was hired to play this critical witness in two contrasting roles. In one tape, he was attentive, polite, cooperative, and unhesitating in his response to questions; in the other, he read the same testimony, but was impolite, often annoyed, cautious and fumbling in his style. The actor read exactly the same transcript in both conditions, varying only his tone of voice, facial expressions, and body language.

Since a witness's demeanor is considered relevant, one would expect that even though subjects heard the same testimony read by the same actor, those who viewed the positive-demeanor witness would prove more favorable to the plaintiff than those who viewed the negative-demeanor witness. This expectation was confirmed. Subjects rated the positive witness as more likeable, sincere, and trustworthy, and his testimony as more believable, accurate, and persuasive. Seventy-two percent of those in the positive-demeanor group voted for the plaintiff, compared to only twenty-two percent in the negative-demeanor group. But what if subjects were told—both before and after watching the tape—that they were not seeing the actual witness, but an individual assigned to read the witness's deposition? Since the demeanor of a surrogate is not relevant to judging the credibility of a witness, and since the two tapes were identical in verbal content, jurors should not be affected by what they saw. But they were. Even though subjects were aware that they were merely watching a clerk reading from a transcript, those who watched the positive- rather than negative-demeanor tape rated the witness and the testimony itself as more credible, and were more likely to return a verdict for the plaintiff—sixty-one percent to thirty-three percent.

As noted earlier, deposition readers are not supposed to embellish their performances. But can judges necessarily detect the subtle nuances and manipulations of a professional actor? People are often not conscious of the nonverbal cues that guide their impressions. Moreover, what about *nonbehavioral* sources of bias such as the deposition reader's physical appearance? Persuasion researchers have found that communicators who are attractive elicit a greater change in attitudes and behavior than those who are not.[22] To examine whether jurors are likewise influenced by the physical appearance of a surrogate, I conducted an experiment similar to the one just described.[23] Mock jurors read about a criminal conspiracy case, and then listened to an audiotape of the testimony of a female witness accompanied by a series of slides taken in a courtroom. All subjects heard the same tape, but viewed slides of either an attractive or unattractive woman who was believed to be either the witness or a deposition reader.[24] Paralleling the results of the first study, perceptions of the witness's credibility were affected not only by the physical attractiveness of the witness, but by the surrogate's appearance as well.

Taken together, these studies suggest that jurors may be unable to separate a witness and his or her testimony from the messenger who delivers it. Thus, it seems that jurors—despite their best efforts to make sound credibility judgments—may be seriously misled by the behavior and appearance of those who read depositions. The solution to this problem is clear, and easily implemented: videotaped depositions. Since the opportunity for mischief is inherent in the mere substitution of one individual for another, videotape should be used to preserve the witness's demeanor for the record without introducing additional extraneous information. Jurors would then watch these tapes on a monitor stationed in the courtroom.[25]

C. Presumptuous Cross-Examination Questions and the Power of Conjecture

The opportunity to confront opposing witnesses through cross-examination is an essential device for safeguarding the accuracy and completeness of testimonial evidence. What impact does cross-examination have on the jury's ability to reconstruct the truth about an event? What are the dangers? Ideally, cross-examination should enhance a jury's factfinding competence by increasing the credibility of witnesses who are accurate and honest relative to those who are not. To be sure, cross-examination is an indispensable device. Many a mistaken and deceptive witness has no doubt fallen from the stand, exposed, scarred, and discredited from the battle of cross-examination. But cross-examination can also be used to exert an influence over the jury in a way that subverts its quest for truth.

Asking questions provides more than simply a mechanism for eliciting answers. Leading questions in particular may impart information to a listener through imagery, implication, and conjecture.[26] Carefully chosen words can obscure and even alter people's impressions, as when tax increases are called "revenue enhancements," and the strategic defense initiative is referred to as "star wars." Consider the following exchange between an attorney and the defendant in an illegal abortion case:

> Q: You didn't tell us, Doctor, whether you determined that the *baby* was alive or dead, did you Doctor?
>
> A: The *fetus* had no signs of life.[27]

In this example, the witness resisted the lawyer's imagery. Often, however, answers can be shaped by how a question is worded. In a classic experiment on eyewitness testimony, for example, Elizabeth Loftus and John Palmer had subjects watch films of an automobile collision. Those who were subsequently asked, "About how fast were the cars going when they *smashed* into each other?" estimated an average speed of forty-one miles per hour; those who were asked "About how fast were the cars going when they *hit* each other?" estimated an average of only thirty-four mph.[28] In fact, the wording of this critical question had a lasting effect on subjects' memories of the event. When asked one week later whether they could recall broken glass at the scene of the accident (there was none), only fourteen percent of those previously asked the hit question said they did, compared to thirty-two percent of those who had been asked the smash question. Once the seed of misinformation was planted, it took on a life of its own.

Even when a question does not mislead its respondent, it may still mislead the jury. When a question implies something that is never explicitly stated, for example, the listener may confuse what is said with what is only implied. Cognitive studies of pragmatic implications reveal that such confusion is common. In one study, mock jurors listened to an excerpt of testimony and indicated whether certain statements were true or false. After hearing the statement, "I ran up to the burglar alarm," for example, most subjects recalled that the witness had said, "I *rang* the burglar alarm." Apparently, people process information between the lines and assume they heard what was only implied.[29]

Due to the nearly unrestricted use of leading questions, cross-examination provides additional opportunity to influence jurors through questions that are designed to impart misleading information to the jury. In *Trial Ethics*, Underwood and Fortune note that "one of the most common abuses of cross-examination takes the form of a question implying a serious charge against the witness, for which counsel has little or no proof. All too often, trial attorneys ask such questions for the sole purpose of wafting unwarranted innuendo into the jury box."[30] When lawyers ask questions that suggest their own answers, are jurors influenced by the information implied by those questions? Is cross-examination by innuendo an effective device?

Research in non-legal settings tentatively suggests an affirmative answer. For example, William Swann and his colleagues examined the effects of hearing an interview in which the questioner implies that the respondent has certain personal characteristics.[31] They had subjects listen to question-and-answer sessions in which the interviewer probed for evidence of either extroverted behavior (e.g., "What do you do when you want to liven things up at a party?") or introverted behavior (e.g., "Have you ever felt left out of some social group?"). One-third of the subjects heard only the questions, one-third heard only the answers, and one-third heard both sides of the interview. When subjects heard only the questions, they inferred that the respondent had the traits sought by the interviewer (i.e., they assumed that the interviewer knew enough to ask extroverts about parties and introverts about difficult social situations). Suggestive questions thus serve as proof by conjecture.

In the context of a trial, of course, jurors hear not only the questions asked but the answers they elicit. It stands to reason that under the circumstances, conjectural evidence may be buried under the weight of the witness's testimony. Yet those subjects in the Swann study who—

like jurors—heard both sides of the interview, were also misled. Consider the implications. The respondents in these experimental interviews did not actually possess the implied traits, so it seems odd that their answers did not override the effects of the interviewers' questions. In fact, however, the result makes sense. Limited to answering specific questions, respondents provided evidence to confirm the interviewers' conjecture. Subjects who heard the full interview were thus left with false impressions shaped by the questions. As Swann and his colleagues put it, "once respondents' answers 'let the cat out of the bag,' observers saw no reason to concern themselves with how the bag was opened."[32]

In light of these provocative findings, it is important to examine the effects of presumptuous cross-examination questions in legal proceedings in which jurors have the benefit of knowing the context of the questions (e.g., the adversarial relationship between the cross-examiner and witness) and hearing the responses they evoke (e.g., the witness's admission or vehement denial of the implication, or an objection from the witness's attorney).

In a recent study, 105 mock jurors were randomly assigned to one of seven groups.[33] All subjects read a transcript of a rape trial in which the defense argued that the victim was mistaken in her identification. Some subjects read a version of the case in which the cross-examiner asked a presumptuous derogatory question of the victim (i.e., "Isn't it true that you have accused men of rape before?" followed by "Isn't it true that, four years ago, you called the police claiming that you had been raped?"); others read a version in which such questions were asked of an expert for the defense (i.e., "Isn't it true that your work is poorly regarded by your colleagues?" followed by "Hasn't your work been sharply criticized in the past?"). Within each version, the cross-examiner's questions were met with one of three reactions: an admission ("yes," "yes it is [has]"), a flat denial ("no," "no it isn't [hasn't]"), or an objection by the witness's attorney, after which the question was withdrawn before the witness had a chance to respond. An additional group of subjects read a transcript that did not contain any presumptuous questions.

Our results provided strong but qualified support for the hypothesis that negative presumptuous questions would diminish a witness's credibility. When the recipient of the question was the victim, the question did not significantly diminish her credibility. In fact, except when the question elicited an admission, female subjects—who are generally less sympathetic to the defense in this case than males— disparaged the defense lawyer who conducted the cross-examination. When the recipient of the presumptuous question was an expert, however, the technique of cross-examination by innuendo proved highly effective. When the expert's professional reputation was called into question—even though the charge was not corroborated by other evidence—subjects lowered their ratings of his credibility as a witness (i.e., he was perceived as less competent, believable, and persuasive). Indeed, among female subjects, subjective estimates of guilt were elevated in all the innuendo groups, a result that reflects the diminished impact of the defense expert. These effects were obtained regardless of whether the presumptuous question had elicited a denial, an objection, or an admission. It is particularly interesting that this effect was obtained even though many of our subjects reported that they did not actually *believe* the derogatory implications concerning the expert. In short, even when the expert denied the charge, even when his attorney objected to the question, and even though many subjects in both situations did not accept as true the cross-examiner's presumption, the witness became "damaged goods" as soon as the reputation question was raised.

Why were our mock jurors so influenced by uncorroborated presumptions? There are at least two possible explanations. First, research in communication suggests that when people hear a speaker offer a premise in conversation, they naturally assume that he or she has an evidentiary basis for that premise.[34] Within the context of a trial, it is conceivable that jurors—naive about the dirty tricks of cross-examination—adhere to a similar implicit rule. In other words, jurors may assume that a lawyer who implies something about an expert's reputation must have information to support that premise, and treat it though it were a foregone conclusion. A second possible reason for the impact of presumptuous questions is that after all the evidence in a case has been presented, jurors may be unable to separate in memory the information communicated within the questions from those contained within the answers. Studies indicate that people often remember the contents of a message but forget the source,[35] and that people often cannot discriminate among the possible sources of their current knowledge.[36] This kind of confusion is particularly likely to occur when the different sources of information are distant in time and equally plausible—as when jurors must recall after days, weeks, or months of testimony, whether a particular belief was derived from a lawyer's questions or a witness's answers.

From a practical standpoint, this study suggests that the use of presumptuous questions is a dirty trick that can be used to distort juror evaluations of witness credibility. As cross-examiners regularly employ such tactics, judges should be aware of the dangers and make a serious effort to control them. According to Rule 3.4(e) of the American Bar Association 1981 Rules of Professional Conduct, counsel "shall not allude to any matter that the lawyer does not reasonably believe is relevant or that will not be supported by admissible evidence." In practice, however, many judges demand only a "good faith belief" in the truthfulness of the assertions contained in cross-examination questions.[37]

Two approaches can be taken to the problem. Since witnesses have an opportunity to deny false assertions, and since lawyers have an opportunity to object or "set the record straight" on redirect examination, one approach is to allow cross-examiners a good deal of latitude, and trust the self-corrective mechanisms already in place. Our study suggests, however, that both a witness's denials and an attorney's objections may fall on deaf ears. In the case of our expert, subjects lowered their ratings of his credibility even when he flatly denied the charge and even when his attorney won a favorable ruling on an objection. In fact, these strategies may well backfire. People are suspicious of others who are forced to proclaim their innocence too vociferously.[38] Likewise, research indicates instructions to disregard objectionable material are often ineffective, perhaps even counterproductive.[39]

Rather than taking a hands-off policy, our results lead me to believe that judges should intervene to control presumptuous leading questions. As a matter of judicial discretion in trial management, judges may admonish counsel who insert false premises into their questions.[40] Perhaps cautionary instructions to the jury would prove effective. If jurors are moved by conjecture because they follow the implicit rule of conversational logic that speakers have an evidentiary basis for their premises, then perhaps jurors should be forewarned about the use of dirty tricks. Recall that Swann's experiment had subjects listen to an interviewer ask questions that presumed the respondent to be introverted or extraverted. Hearing the questions, subjects inferred that the interviewee possessed the implied traits. When they were told, however, that the interviewer's questions were chosen at random (i.e., without a reason), subjects did not make the inference. Thus, it may be similarly effective to caution jurors that the premises contained within questions are not evidence, and alert them to possible abuses.

To summarize, psychological research indicates that suggestive examination questions can mislead a jury in two ways. First, the questions themselves can misinform others through the power of conjecture. Second, suggestive questions can actually produce support for that conjecture by shaping the witness's testimony. If counsel wants to portray a witness as greedy, lazy, neurotic, introverted, or extraverted, he or she can do so by asking a series of biasing questions. Since a witness can tell a story only in response to specific inquiries, it is not impossible to get that witness to provide the necessary evidence. Redirect examination offers a possible safety valve, and to some extent its rehabilitative potential is self-evident. It is important to note, however, that first impressions often resist change despite subsequent contradictory information,[41] and that neither denial nor judicial admonishment is likely to have fully curative effects.

D. Nonevidentiary Temptations

As part of their factfinding role, jurors are instructed to recognize and disregard nonevidentiary sources of information—much of which is revealed within the courtroom (e.g., voir dire questions, inadmissible testimony, opening statements, closing arguments). Can human decisionmakers maintain separate files in memory for evidence and nonevidence? And can they delete the latter from awareness upon instruction to do so?

In a series of experiments on "reality monitoring," Marcia Johnson and her colleagues have found that people are often unable to recall the sources of their knowledge.[42] Under certain circumstances people remember the *content* of a message, while forgetting the *source*. People are especially vulnerable to confusion when the possible sources of information are equally plausible—as when jurors must recall after a trial presentation whether their beliefs are based on what was said by the lawyers or witnesses, or whether they are the product of their own self-generated inferences. In the end, it means that jurors may erroneously attribute their own versions of reality, or counsel's version, to reality itself.

Research on the effects of opening statements illustrates the possible consequences of source confusion in the courtroom. In a series of mock jury experiments, Lawrence Wrightsman and others consistently found that strong opening statements are persuasive—even when they are not subsequently borne out by the evidence.[43] In one study, for example, subjects read one of three versions of an auto theft trial. In one version, defense counsel promised in his opening statement that he would provide evidence of an alibi, evidence that was never forthcoming. In contrast to subjects to whom the claim was never made, those who received the empty promise were more likely to vote for the defendant's acquittal. The strategy failed only in the third version of the trial, where the prosecutor reminded the jury in his closing argument of the discrepancy between what was promised and what was proved.[44] Absent reminder, jurors may simply lack the necessary awareness of the sources of their trial beliefs.

Additional problems arise when jurors are exposed to inadmissible testimony, prompted by an attorney's question and subsequently stricken from the record. It should come as no surprise that jurors are often influenced by this leakage of nonevidentiary information. In one study, for example, mock jurors read a transcript of an armed robbery and murder trial. When the only available evidence was weak and circumstantial, not a single juror voted guilty. In a second version of the case that also contained a recording of a suspicious telephone conversation between the defendant and a bookmaker, and in which the judge ruled the tape admissible, the conviction rate increased to twenty-six percent. In a third version of the case in which the judge ruled the wiretapped conversation inadmissible and admonished to disregard the tape, the conviction rate increased even further, to thirty-five percent.[45] Additional research has shown that when the judge embellishes his or her ruling by admonishing jurors at length, they become even more likely to use the forbidden information.[46]

Judicial admonishment may well backfire for a variety of reasons. First, it draws an unusual amount of attention to the information in controversy, increasing its salience relative to the evidence. Indeed, the psychology of instructions-to-disregard parallels recent studies on the paradoxical effects of thought suppression. For example, Daniel Wegner and his colleagues found that when people were told to actively suppress thoughts of a white bear, that novel image intruded upon consciousness with remarkable frequency.[47] A second problem is that instructions to disregard are a form of censorship, a restriction on the juror's decisionmaking freedom. Again, research in other contexts indicates consistently that people react against prohibitions of this sort in order to assert their right to consider all possible information.[48] A third reason why instructions-to-disregard may be counterproductive is that jurors do not share the law's "due process" model of what constitutes a fair trial, the assumption that a verdict is just if procedural fairness is achieved. Ask jurors what they seek, and most will cite outcome accuracy as the main objective (i.e., "to make the *right* decision"). Thus, it is notable that jurors seem most likely to succumb to the temptation to use inadmissible evidence when that evidence exonerates the criminal defendant.[49]

Sometimes inadmissible evidence is properly introduced via the "limited admissibility rule" which permits the presentation of evidence for one purpose, but not another.[50] In such cases, the judge admits the evidence, restricts its proper scope, and instructs the jury accordingly (e.g.. when a defendant's criminal record is admitted for its bearing on the issue of credibility, not guilt). Can jurors compartmentalize evidence in this manner, using it to draw one inference, but not another? This rule is one of the paradoxes of evidence law, and is viewed by many as a lesson in futility. One survey revealed that ninety-eight percent of the lawyers and forty-three percent of the judges questioned believed jurors could not comply with this instruction.[51] They are probably right. Mock jurors who learn that a defendant has a criminal record and are limited in their use of that evidence are more likely to vote for conviction even though their judgments of the defendant's credibility are unaffected by that information.[52] Likewise, mock juries spend a good deal of time discussing a defendant's record—not for what it implies about credibility, but for what it suggests about criminal predispositions.[53]

E. Voices from an Empty Chair

In one trial, a defendant accused of armed robbery claims he was drinking in a bar at the time, but does not bring in alibi witnesses who were supposed to have been with him. In another trial, a party involved in a traffic accident fails to call to the witness stand a friend or relative who was a passenger during the collision. Cases such as these pose a dilemma: When a prospective favorable witness does not take the stand, should opposing counsel be permitted in closing argument to cite that witness's absence as proof of his or her adverse testimony? Should the judge invite jurors to draw negative inferences from that missing witness?

The courts are divided on how they manage this situation. Nearly a century ago, in *Graves v. United States*, the United States Supreme Court introduced what has come to be known as the missing witness rule, or empty chair doctrine. The rule states that "if a party has it peculiarly within his power to produce witnesses whose testimony would elucidate the transaction, the fact that he does not do it creates the presumption that the testimony, if produced, would be unfavorable."[54] In operational terms, this rule enables lawyers to comment on a witness's absence in closing arguments and judges to suggest possible adverse inferences to the jury. The reasons for this doctrine are straightforward.[55] The courts assume that litigants who fail to call knowledgeable witnesses are concealing evidence and should be pressured to come forward with that evidence. In addition, it is argued that jurors on their own will draw adverse inferences from the absence of an expected witness. Stephen Saltzburg, for example, suggested that once jurors are presented with a theory about a case, they naturally come to expect certain kinds of supporting proof and are likely to make adverse inferences about any party that fails to satisfy these expectations. Carrying this analysis one step further, Saltzburg argued that judges should take juror expectations and inferences into account before ruling to exclude evidence considered relevant but prejudicial.[56]

The empty chair doctrine has been criticized on at least three grounds. First, it is said to be unfair to draw adverse inferences from missing evidence because there are many other possible reasons for a witness's failure to appear in court.[57] Second, constitutional issues arise in cases where an expected witness does not testify on behalf of a criminal defendant, whose own silence is protected by the fifth amendment.[58]

A third criticism of the empty chair rule is that it sends a confusing mixed signal to jurors about their role as factfinders. Although jurors are admonished time and again to base their judgments only on evidence produced in court, the missing witness instruction may encourage them to speculate on other matters not in evidence.[59]

On their own, do jurors make adverse inferences concerning absent witnesses? What are the effects of empty chair comments? Indirectly, psychological research suggests an "it depends" answer to these empirical questions. When a prospective witness is central to a case and, hence, conspicuously absent, juries are likely to speculate, even without prompting. This suggestion is based on studies indicating that people are biased against criminal defendants who remain silent, even when they are specifically admonished not to draw negative inferences.[60] In contrast, when a witness is not clearly essential to a case, juries are not likely to be influenced by his or her absence. This suggestion is based on studies on the "feature-positive effect," the finding that humans are relatively insensitive to events that do *not* occur.[61]

To examine more directly the effects of missing witnesses on legal decision-making, my students and I conducted the following mock jury study.[62] Upon arrival in a mock courtroom, fifty subjects—participating in small groups—read one of four versions of an insanity murder trial in which either a central witness (the defendant's close friend) or a peripheral witness (a co-worker of the defendant) was absent,[63] and in which the judge and opposing counsel either did or did not suggest an adverse inference.[64] Opinions of the case were assessed both before and after subjects deliberated.

The results of this experiment were generally consistent with the predictions derived from other research. Three findings in particular are noteworthy. First, all subjects were aware of the witness's absence, but when asked if they needed additional information, far more subjects in the comment than no-comment condition expressed a need for testimony from that witness. Second, there was an effect on case-related opinions: among subjects who read the missing-central transcript, empty chair comments increased the likelihood of conviction and enhanced their evaluations of the prosecuting attorney. In the missing-peripheral condition, however, the same empty chair comments decreased the likelihood of conviction and diminished subjects' evaluations of the prosecuting attorney. Third, subjects in the comment condition, after deliberating, were somewhat more likely than those in the no-comment condition to express a desire for testimony from the defendant (who did not testify). This latter result suggests the possibility that jurors who read the empty chair comments had discussed the defendant's failure to testify during their deliberations.

Is the missing witness inference "natural," an argument made by proponents of the empty chair doctrine? No, the inference is not as natural as it may seem. Subjects in the no-comment group knew that the prospective central or peripheral witness had not testified, but they did not hold the defendant responsible unless prompted to do so by the judge and opposing counsel. To be sure, all subjects recognized that the missing witness was absent, but only those in the comment condition were moved by his absence. Should empty chair comments, then, be permitted? Our study does not provide a clear answer to this second question. For trial attorneys, there are potential costs and benefits associated with empty chair comments, depending on the status of the witness in question. Lawyers who comment on a missing-central witness may draw the jury's attention to a gap in the opponent's case, reap the benefits of the inferences likely to be drawn, and elicit the perception that they themselves are competent. On the other hand, attorneys who drag a missing-peripheral witness into evidence risk alienating the jury by making what appears to be an implausible argument, and eliciting the perception that they themselves are desperate, if not incompetent. Our results thus support the conclusion that the empty chair doctrine cannot easily be used for unfair strategic purposes, without regard for the extent to which the jury already expects testimony from that witness.

II. The Jury Deliberation Process

It is often said that the distinctive power of the jury is that it functions as a group. Indeed, although the jury meets in complete privacy, the courts have articulated a clear vision of how juries should deliberate to a verdict. Basically, there are three components to this ideal.

The first component is one of independence and equality. No juror's vote counts for more than any other juror's vote. A twelve-person jury should thus consist of twelve independent and equal individuals, each contributing his or her own personal opinion to the final outcome. Unlike other task-oriented groups, the jury's role is ideally structured to promote equal participation. The cardinal rule of jury decisionmaking is that verdicts be based only on the evidence introduced in open court. By limiting the task as such, jurors are discouraged from basing their arguments on private or outside sources of knowledge. The courts try to foster this ideal in a number of ways. For example, jurors are told to refrain from discussing the trial until they deliberate, thus ensuring that each juror develops his or her own unique perspective on the case, uncontaminated by others' views. In addition, the courts often exclude from service people who are expected to exert a disproportionate amount of influence over other jurors (such as lawyers or others who have expertise in trial-relevant matters).

The second component of an ideal deliberation is an openness to informational influence. Inside the jury room, members have a duty to share information, exchange points of view, and debate the evidence. This deliberation requirement means that jurors should maintain an open mind and withhold their judgment until "an impartial consideration of the evidence with his fellow jurors."[65] It also means that consensus should be achieved through rational, persuasive argument. As the Supreme Court put it almost a century ago, "[t]he very object of the jury system is to secure unanimity by a comparison of views, and by arguments among the jurors themselves. . . . It cannot be that each juror should go to the jury-room with a blind determination that the verdict shall represent his opinion of the case at that moment; or, that he should close his ears to the arguments of men who are equally honest and intelligent as himself."[66]

The third ideal of deliberation follows from the second. Although juries should strive for a consensus of opinion, that goal should not be achieved through heavy-handed social pressure. Obviously, those who dissent from the majority should not be beaten, bullied, or harangued into surrendering their convictions for the purpose of returning a verdict. The reason is simple: if jurors comply with the majority to avoid rejection or terminate an unpleasant experience, then their final vote might not reflect their true beliefs. In the Supreme Court's words, "the verdict must be the verdict of each individual juror, and not a mere acquiescence in the conclusion of his fellows. . . ."[67]

As in other decisionmaking groups, juries reach a verdict through two processes—informational and normative.[68] Through informational social influence, individuals conform because they are genuinely persuaded by majority opinion; through normative influence, individuals comply in order to avoid the unpleasant consequences of social pressure. Indeed, groups often reject, ridicule, and punish individuals who frustrate a common goal by taking a deviant position.[69] The importance of both processes has been well documented in recent conformity research,[70] and in jury research as well.[71] As Kalven and Zeisel noted in *The American Jury*, the deliberation process "is an interesting combination of rational persuasion, sheer social pressure, and the psychological mechanism by which individual perceptions undergo change when exposed to group discussion."[72]

Although jury verdicts should follow a vigorous exchange of information and a minimum of normative pressure, the delicate balance between these competing forces can be altered by various aspects of a jury's task.[73] For example, normative influences are heightened in groups that decide on questions of values rather than facts,[74] and in groups that take frequent public ballots.[75] In addition, recent research implicates two procedural factors that may compromise the integrity of jury deliberations: (1) the dynamite charge, and (2) the acceptance of nonunanimous verdicts.

A. The Dynamite Charge

Recently, I received a phone call from a criminal lawyer whose client had been convicted on six counts of tax fraud. After two days of testimony, arguments, and instructions, the twelve-person jury spent three days deliberating. On the second day of deliberation, the jury informed the judge that it was at an impasse on some counts. The jurors were reconvened, but then on the third day said they were hopelessly deadlocked on all counts, with no verdict in sight. At that point, the judge issued a special instruction, one that is designed to prod hung juries toward a verdict. Twenty minutes later, as if a spell had been cast, the jury reached unanimous guilty verdicts on all counts.

The instruction that preceded the jury's decision was modeled after the *Allen* charge, first used in Massachusetts,[76] and approved by the United States Supreme Court in *Allen v. United States*.[77] Used to blast deadlocked juries into a verdict, this supplemental instruction is believed to be so effective that it is commonly known as the "dynamite charge."[78] For judges confronted with the prospect of a hung jury, this instruction can be used to avert a mistrial by imploring jurors to reexamine their own views and to seriously consider each other's arguments with a disposition to be convinced. In addition, it may state that "if much the larger number were for conviction, a dissenting juror should consider whether his doubt was a reasonable one which made no impression on the minds of so many men, equally honest, equally intelligent with himself."[79]

Trial anecdotes suggest that the dynamite charge is effective. Those who believe the effect is desirable argue that it encourages all jurors to reevaluate their positions and that, after all, those who are in the voting minority are typically obstinate holdouts who should "properly be warned against stubbornness and self-assertion."[80] Opponents, however, fear that legitimate dissenters, "struggling to maintain their position in a protracted debate in the jury room, are led into the courtroom and, before their peers, specifically requested by the judge to reconsider their position.[81] The charge places the sanction of the court behind the views of the majority, whatever they may be. . . ."[82]

The dynamite charge has its share of proponents and critics. In 1968, the American Bar Association opposed this instruction on the grounds that it coerces the deadlocked jury into reaching a verdict and places inordinate amounts of pressure on those in the minority.[83] The dynamite charge has been prohibited or restricted in certain state and federal courts.[84] In 1988, however, the United States Supreme Court ruled that the dynamite charge is not necessarily coercive, and reaffirmed its use on a routine basis.[85]

Although the dynamite charge has stirred controversy for many years, and although the Supreme Court has now upheld its use, until recently no empirical studies had examined its impact on the jury's deliberation process. Thus, my colleagues and I sought to test the hypothesis that the dynamite charge upsets the delicate balance of social influence forces, causing those in the majority to exert increasing amounts of normative rather than informational pressure, and causing those in the minority to change their votes.[86]

In order to test this hypothesis in a controlled setting, we contrived an artificial experimental situation in which lone subjects "deliberated" by voting and passing notes. Overall, seventy-two individual subjects read about a criminal tax case, thinking they would participate on a mock jury. In fact, subjects were taken to a cubicle and told they would communicate with three others in different rooms by passing notes. These so-called deliberations were structured by discrete rounds. After reading the case summary, subjects wrote down a verdict and a brief explanation. They signaled the experimenter over an intercom. The experimenter collected the subject's note, supposedly collected other subject's notes, photocopied them, and distributed the copies to each subject. After reading the other notes, subjects began a second round of deliberation voting, writing an explanation, signaling the experimenter and receiving written feedback from three fictitious peers. Subjects were instructed that this procedure would be reiterated until the group reached unanimity. In fact, unless subjects changed their votes, the session was terminated after seven rounds. At that point, a questionnaire was administered and subjects were debriefed.

Six sets of notes—three guilty, three not guilty—were written and photocopied.[87] All subjects received three notes at a time. Those assigned to the majority received two randomly selected sets of notes that agreed with their guilty or not guilty verdicts, and one set that did not. In contrast, subjects assigned to the minority received three randomly selected sets of notes that all disagreed with their verdicts. By the end of the first round, subjects thus found themselves in either the majority or minority faction of a three-to-one split. Unless subjects changed their vote, these divisions persisted.[88] After the third round, half the subjects were reminded that since verdicts had to be unanimous, they would continue to "deliberate."[89] For the other half, the experimenter—acting as judge—delivered an instruction patterned after the *Allen* charge.

Three results were consistent with the hypothesis that the dynamite charge is effective because of normative pressure on those in the voting minority. First, among subjects caught in a deadlocked jury (i.e., who remained committed to their initial votes after the third round), those in the minority changed their verdicts more often than those in the majority after receiving the dynamite charge, but not in the no-instruction control group. Second, minority subjects who heard the dynamite charge reported feeling heightened pressure from the judge—more than in the majority and minority-no-instruction groups.[90] Third, compared to all other subjects, those in the majority who received the dynamite charge exhibited in their notes diminishing amounts of informational influence strategies (e.g., citing facts or laws relevant to the case), coupled with a significant increase in normative social pressure (e.g., derogating those who disagreed, refusing to yield) immediately following the judge's instruction. Clearly, the dynamite charge tipped in an undesirable direction the balance of forces operating on our subjects, subjectively empowering the voting majority relative to the minority.

Taken as a whole, our results call into question the use of the dynamite charge as a means of eliciting verdicts from deadlocked juries. This study should be considered tentative, however, with regard to its generalizability to real trials. To systematically test the impact of the dynamite charge on the votes, perceptions, and behaviors of individual jurors, we contrived an artificial situation in which lone subjects "deliberated" by passing notes.[91] It remains to be seen whether the same results would emerge within live, interacting groups of jurors. It also remains to be seen whether alternative forms of instruction yield better results (i.e., verdicts from deadlocked juries through informational rather than normative influence).[92]

B. Less-Than-Unanimous Verdicts

The problem with the dynamite charge is that it may produce verdicts in which the jury's unanimity is more apparent than real. However, even the appearance of unanimity is often not necessary. In a pair of 1972 decisions, the United States Supreme Court ruled that states may allow juries to return verdicts without having to secure agreement from all members.[93] Finding neither a legal nor historical basis for the unanimity tradition, the Court concluded that, as a practical matter, juries function similarly under unanimous and nonunanimous decision rules. Writing for the *Johnson* majority, Justice White argued that majority jurors would maintain an open mind and continue to deliberate in good faith even after the requisite majority is reached.[94] In dissent, Justice Douglas argued that once a requisite majority is reached, majority jurors will become closed-minded, and vigorous debate would give way to "polite and academic conversation."[95]

Are unanimous and nonunanimous juries equivalent in the extent to which they achieve the ideals of deliberation? Several studies have addressed the question, and the results converge on the same answer: the differences are substantial. In one study, Charlan Nemeth had several hundred students at the University of Virginia read about a murder trial and indicate whether they believed the defendant to be guilty or not guilty.[96] Three weeks later, these students participated in six-person mock juries constructed to split four to two in their initial vote, favoring either conviction or acquittal. The groups were given two hours to reach a decision. Half were instructed to return a unanimous verdict, the other half needed only a two-thirds majority. Compared to those driven toward unanimity, majority-rule juries took less time to settle on a decision (many of these groups, in fact, concluded their deliberations without a single change in vote). When subjects were given an opportunity to evaluate the quality of their deliberations, those who had participated in majority juries were less satisfied, less certain of their verdicts, and less influenced by others' arguments.

In a more extensive study, Reid Hastie and his colleagues recruited over 800 people from jury pools in Massachusetts.[97] After a brief voir dire, these subjects were randomly assigned to participate in sixty-nine twelve-person mock juries, all of whom watched a videotape of a reenacted murder trial. An approximately equal number of juries were instructed to reach a verdict by either a twelve to zero, a ten to two, or an eight to four margin. Based on objective analyses of the deliberations as well as jurors' own subjective reports, the results were striking. Compared to unanimous juries, those that deliberated under a more relaxed rule spent less time discussing the case and more time voting. After reaching their required quorum, these groups usually rejected the hold-outs, terminated discussion, and returned a verdict within just a few minutes. Needless to say, those who participated in majority juries viewed their peers as relatively closed-minded, felt less informed about the case and less confident about the final verdict. Hastie and his colleagues also observed that many of the majority jurors were quite combative during their deliberations, as "larger factions in majority rule juries adopt a more forceful, bullying, persuasive style because their members realize that it is not necessary to respond to all opposition arguments when their goal is to achieve a faction size of only eight or ten members."[98]

C. Summary Policies that Compromise the Deliberation Process

In nineteenth century England, juries that were unable to achieve unanimity "were locked up in a cart, without meat, drink, fire, or candle, and followed the judge from town to town. Only their verdict could secure their release."[99] American juries were similarly subverted. Judges used to urge deadlocked juries to resolve their disagreements through such coercive measures as the denial of food and drink, excessive deliberation hours, and the threat of confinement. Today, the strategies may differ, but the objective is the same. The dynamite charge and the relaxation of a unanimous verdict requirement are driven by a contempt for the hung jury and the costs incurred by a mistrial. Proponents of these policies seem to base their opinions on the assumption that a jury becomes deadlocked because of one obstinate holdout, the chronic anti-conformist. Opponents, on the other hand, base their views on the belief that juries are hung as a genuine response to close, difficult cases in which the evidence allows for well-reasoned disagreement and does not compel a particular verdict. To be sure, not all deadlocked juries are created equal, and anecdotes can be found to support either position. Kalven and Zeisel's research, however, suggests that hung juries occur in only about five percent of all criminal jury trials, and do so especially in close cases in which the minority consists of a group rather than one member—a finding that lends support to the latter, more rational image.[100]

Neither the dynamite charge nor suspension of the unanimity requirement have desirable effects on the quality of the jury's decisionmaking apparatus. Used to implore the deadlocked jury to return a verdict, the dynamite charge may well encourage members of the voting majority to exert increasing amounts of normative pressure without added informational influence, thus intimidating members of a voting minority into compliance. The net result, of course, is an illusion of unanimity. Even worse is the outright acceptance of nonunanimous verdicts. This policy weakens and inhibits dissenting jurors, breeds closed-mindedness, impairs the quality of discussion, and leaves many jurors unsatisfied with the final verdict. And yet, without a potent and vocal dissent based on legitimate differences of opinion, the jury is reduced to a mere collection of individuals, losing its strength as a vital decisionmaking group.

III. Conclusions

The American trial jury is a truly unique institution. In the words of Kalven and Zeisel, "[i]t recruits a group of twelve laymen, chosen at random from the widest population; it convenes them for the purpose of the particular trial; it entrusts them with great official powers of decision; it permits them to carry on deliberations in secret and to report their final judgment without giving reasons for it; and, after their momentary service to the state has been completed, it orders them to disband and return to private life."[101]

This article rests on a conviction that juries should not be evaluated by case studies, autobiographical accounts, and news stories, but by hard empirical research designed to answer concrete, behavioral questions. With that objective in mind, trial practices that influence the decisionmaking process were examined for their effects on both individual jurors and the jury as a group.

Jurors are expected to base their opinions on an accurate appraisal of evidence to the exclusion of nonevidentiary sources of information. Thus, trials are structured by an elaborate network of rules to focus jurors on the evidence, to facilitate their search for the truth, and to insulate them from various social influences. Research on how jurors assess the credibility of witnesses, and their ability or willingness to resist the lure of certain kinds of extraneous information, gives rise to the conclusion that there is much room for improvement. To begin with, jurors are supposed to distinguish among witnesses of varying credibility, an often difficult task. Yet that task is more complicated than is necessary. To be sure, the occasional intrusion into the trial record of inadmissible testimony and objectionable arguments is an inevitable fact of life in an adversarial system. But too often, American courts compound the problem by permitting counsel to (1) use surrogates to present deposition testimony for absentee witnesses, leaving the jury to disentangle the appearance and demeanor of the messenger from the message and its original source; (2) impart information through conjecture and innuendo, leaving jurors to assume the truth of uncorroborated matters and confuse in memory the sources of their knowledge; and (3) invite jurors to draw adverse inferences from missing witnesses, leading them to create evidence from the absence of evidence, and sending a confusing mixed signal concerning speculation and the boundaries of their fact-finding role.

Turning to the jury as a group, it is perhaps the greatest asset of the jury that a group of independent citizens, strangers to one another, are placed behind closed doors and directed to reach a common decision. Bringing a diversity of perspectives to bear on the task, these jurors share information, clash in their values and argue over competing interpretations. Remarkably, out of this conflict, ninety-five percent of all juries succeed in returning a verdict. Intolerant of lengthy deliberations and the five percent of juries that declare themselves hung, however, the courts have sanctioned procedures and structural changes in the jury that widen the gap between the ideals and realities of deliberation. One example is the *Allen* instruction, otherwise known as the dynamite charge. Used to implore the deadlocked jury to return a verdict, research suggests it may tip in an undesirable direction the balance of informational and normative forces operating within the jury, further empowering the voting majority relative to the minority, and intimidating the latter into compliance. A second example is provided by the United States Supreme Court's decisions to uphold the right of states to relax the jury's unanimity requirement. Indeed, research clearly indicates that a less-than-unanimous decision rule weakens dissent, breeds closed-mindedness, impairs the quality of discussion, and leaves many jurors unsatisfied with the final verdict.

In light of recent research on human decisionmaking and behavior, consciousness should be raised in American courtrooms about common trial practices and procedures that lead individual jurors and the groups to which they belong to exhibit less-than-ideal performance. Prescriptions for how juries should function are clear. In reality, however, the American jury is too often handicapped in the pursuit of justice.

Endnotes

[1] McElhaney, "Dealing with Dirty Tricks," 7 *Litigation* 45, 46 (1981).

[2] M. Belli, *Melvin Belli: My Life on Trial* 107–9 (1976).

[3] *Allen v. United States*, 164 U.S. 492, 501 (1986).

[4] The mock jury paradigm involves simulating trials in the form of transcripts, audiotapes, or videotapes, and recruiting subjects to act as jurors. This method has two advantages. First, it enables researchers to secure control over events that take place in the "courtroom" and design controlled experiments that can establish causal relationships between specific trial characteristics and jury verdicts. Second, it offers a good deal of flexibility, enabling researchers to manipulate variables that cannot be touched in real cases (e.g., evidence, arguments, trial procedures, judge's instructions, the composition of the jury) and obtain measures of behavior that are otherwise too intrusive (e.g., mid-trial opinions, attention, comprehension, and recall; physiological arousal; videotaped deliberations). In short, trial simulations enable us to observe not only the outcome but the process of jury decisionmaking. A more extensive discussion of this technique appears in Bray & Kerr, "Methodological Considerations in the Study of the Psychology of the Courtroom," *The Psychology of the Courtroom* 287, 296–98 (1982). For a description of practical applications, see Kassin, "Mock Jury Trials," 7 *Trial Dipl. J.* 26 (1984).

As with other indirect methods of inquiry, the mock jury paradigm is not without its shortcomings. In exchange for a highly controlled environment, the approach suffers from the problem of external validity (i.e. generalizability to real trials). As a general rule, generalizability is enhanced by research conditions that approximate the real event. Still, legitimate empirical questions can be raised. For more detailed critiques, see Dillehay & Neitzel, "Constructing a Science of Jury Behavior," *Review of Personality and Social Psychology* 246 (1980); Ebbesen & Konecni, "On the External Validity of Decision-Making Research: What do we Know about Decisions in the Real World?" *Cognitive Processes in Choice and Decision Behavior* (1980).

[5] For a review of arguments against notetaking, see S. Kassin & L. Wrightsman, *The American Jury on Trial: Psychological Perspectives* 128 (1988).

[6] DePaulo & Pfeifer, "On-the-Job Experience and Skill at Detecting Deception," 16 *J. Applied Soc. Psychology* 249, 261–62 (1986); Kraut & Poe, "Behavioral Roots of Person

Perception: The Deception Judgments of Customs Inspectors and Laymen," 39 *J. Personality & Soc. Psychology* 784, 788 (1980).

[7] Zuckerman, DePaulo & Rosenthal, "Verbal and Nonverbal Communication of Deception," 14 *Advances in Experimental Soc. Psychology* 1, 38–40 (1981).

[8] Deceivers often wear false smiles to mask their real feelings; see Ekman, Friesen & O'Sullivan, "Smiles When Lying," 54 *J. Personality & Soc. Psychology* 414, 415 (1988).

[9] Deception is often accompanied by fidgety movements of the hands and feet, and restless shifts in posture. When people lie, especially when they are highly motivated to do so, there is also a rise in their voice pitch and an increased number of speech hesitations. See DePaulo, Lanier & Davis, "Detecting the Deceit of the Motivated Liar," 45 *J. Personality & Soc. Psychology* 1096 (1983); see also, Streeter, Krauss, Geller, Olson & Apple, "Pitch Changes During Attempted Deception," 35 *J. Personality & Soc. Psychology* 345, 348–49 (1977).

[10] People sometimes become more accurate in their judgments of truth and deception when they are too busy to attend closely to what a speaker says. See Gilbert & Krull, "Seeing Less and Knowing More: The Benefits of Perceptual Ignorance," 54 *J. Personality & Soc. Psychology* 193, 201 (1988). Although distracting jurors from the content of a witness's testimony is a ludicrous idea, it is possible that credibility judgments would be improved by a more specific demeanor instruction, one that redirects attention toward cues that are more diagnostic than facial expressions. Research suggests, for example, that when people are encouraged to pay more attention to the voice than to the face, they make more accurate judgments of truth and deception. See DePaulo, Lassiter & Stone, "Attentional Determinants of Success at Detecting Deception and Truth," 8 *Personality & Soc. Psychology Bull.* 273, 277 (1982). Liars are also betrayed by movements of the lower body, so jurors could be instructed to consider these cues as well. Ironically, however, the witness's body is often hidden from view—by the witness stand.

[11] E. Cleary, *McCormick on Evidence* § 5 (2d ed. 1972).

[12] For a review of this literature, see Loftus & Goodman, "Questioning Witnesses," *The Psychology of Evidence and Trial Proc.* 253 (1985).

[13] *Model Rules of Professional Conduct* Rule 3.4 (1983).

[14] See generally R. Underwood & W. Fortune, *Trial Ethics* (1988); Underwood, "Adversary Ethics: More Dirty Tricks," 6 *Am. J. Trial Advoc.* 265 (1982).

[15] McElhaney, supra note 1, at 45–48; Underwood, supra note 14, at 269–89.

[16] The death of a prospective witness is an obvious problem. Those who live beyond a certain distance from the courthouse, or who are sick, handicapped, out of the country, or in prison, may also be excused. See *Fed. R. Civ. P.* 32(a)(3).

[17] See generally, Kassin, supra note 4, at 27.

[18] A. Morrill, *Trial Diplomacy* 52 (1972). Conversely, it is advisable to present the testimony of witnesses who are "singularly impressive" live rather than via deposition. See R. Keeton, *Trial Tactics and Methods* 18 (1973).

[19] A. Morrill, supra note 18, at 52.

[20] For a recent review of this literature see R. Petty & J. Cacioppo, *Communication and Persuasion* 204–9 (1986).

[21] Kassin, "Deposition Testimony and the Surrogate Witness: Evidences for a 'Messenger Effect' in Persuasion," 9 *Personality & Soc. Psychology Bull.* 281, 283–84 (1983).

[22] E.g., Chaiken, "Communicator Physical Attractiveness and Persuasion," 37 *J. Personality & Soc. Psychology* 1387, 1395 (1979); see also Pallak, "Salience of a Communicator's Physical Attractiveness and Persuasion: A Heuristic versus Systematic Processing Interpretation," 2 *Soc. Cognition* 158, 168 (1983).

[23] Kassin, "Deposition Testimony and the Surrogate Witness: Further Evidence for a 'Messenger Effect' in Persuasion," Unpublished data (1990).

[24] Attractiveness was determined through pretesting.

[25] See, e.g., McCrystal, "Videotape Trials: Relief for Our Congested Courts," 49 *Den. U.L. Rev.* 463, 465-66 (1973); see also Kornblum, "Videotape in Civil Cases," 24 *Hastings L.J.* 9, 23-26 (1972).

[26] See Conley, O'Barr & Lind, "The Power of Language: Presentational Style in the Courtroom," 6 *Duke L.J.* 1375, 1386-89 (1978).

[27] Danet, "'Baby' or 'Fetus'?: Language and the Construction of Reality in a Manslaughter Trial," 32 *Semiotica* 187, 206 (1980).

[28] When other verbs were substituted for these, estimates varied considerably, e.g., "collided" yielded 39 mph; "contacted" yielded 32 mph. See Loftus & Palmer, "Reconstruction of Automobile Destruction: An Example of the Interaction Between Language and Memory," 13 *J. Verbal Learning & Verbal Behav.* 585, 586 (1974).

[29] See Harris & Monaco, "Psychology of Pragmatic Implication: Information Processing Between the Lines," 107 *J. Experimental Psychology: General* 1, 6-9 (1978); see also Johnson, Bransford, & Solomon, "Memory for Tacit Implications of Sentences," 98 *J. Experimental Psychology* 203 (1973).

[30] R. Underwood & W. Fortune, supra note 14, at 346.

[31] Swann, Giuliano & Wegner, "Where Leading Questions Can Lead: The Power of Conjecture in Social Interaction," 42 *J. Personality & Soc. Psychology* 1025, 1034 (1982); see also Wegner, Wenclaff, Kerker & Beattie, "Incrimination Through Innuendo: Can Media Questions Become Public Answers?," 40 *J. Personality & Soc. Psychology* 822, 830-32 (1981).

[32] Swann, Giuliano & Wegner, supra note 31, at 1033. This effect is so powerful that it even influences the self-perceptions of the respondents themselves. After being interviewed, they took personality tests in which they were asked to describe themselves on various dimensions. Those who had answered questions about introverted or extroverted behaviors later rated themselves as such on the questionnaires.

[33] Kassin, Williams & Saunders, "Dirty Tricks of Cross Examination: The Influence of Conjectural Evidence on the Jury," 14 *Law and Human Behavior* 373 (1990).

[34] Grice, "Logic in Conversation," 3 *Syntax and Semantics* 41, 44 (1975); Hopper, "The Taken-For-Granted," 7 *Human Communication Research* 195, 198 (1981).

[35] Kelman & Hovland, "'Reinstatement' of the Communicator in Delayed Measurement of Opinion Change," 48 *J. Abnormal & Soc. Psychology* 327, 332-35 (1953); Pratkanis, Greenwald, Leippe & Baumgardner, "In Search of Reliable Persuasion Effects: III. The Sleeper Effect is Dead. Long Live the Sleeper Effect," 54 *J. Personality & Soc. Psychology* 203, 205 (1988).

[36] Johnson, "Discrimination the Origin of Information," *Delusional Beliefs: Interdisciplinary Perspectives* (Otmanns & Maher eds. 1987); Johnson & Raye, "Reality Monitoring," 88 *Psychological Rev.* 67, 82 (1981).

[37] *U.S. v. Brown*, 519 F.2d 1368 (6th Cir. 1975).

[38] Shaffer, "The Defendant's Testimony," *The Psychology of Evidence and Trial Procedure* (Kassin & Wrightsman eds. 1985); Yandell, "Those Who Protest Too Much are Seen as Guilty," 5 *Personality & Soc. Psychology Bull.* 44, 47 (1979).

[39] Carretta & Moreland, "The Direct and Indirect Effects of Inadmissible Evidence," 13 *J. Applied Soc. Psychology* 291, 291-93 (1983); Sue, Smith & Caldwell, "Effects of Inadmissible Evidence on the Decisions of Simulated Jurors: A Moral Dilemma," 3 *J. Applied Soc. Psychology* 345, 351-53 (1973); Wolf & Montgomery, "Effects of Inadmissible Evidence and level of Judicial Admonishment to Disregard on the Judgments of Mock Jurors," 7 *J. Applied Soc. Psychology* 205, 216-18 (1977).

[40] In some cases, the courts have even sustained the right of an opposing party to call a cross-examiner to the witness stand to inquire into the "good faith basis" for a specific

line of questions. See *United States v. Cardarella*, 570 F.2d 264, 268 (8th Cir. 1978); *United States v. Pugliese*, 153 F.2d 497,498-99 (2d Cir. 1945).

[41] See, e.g., Asch, "Forming Impressions of Personality," 41 *J. Abnormal & Soc. Psychology* 258, 288-90 (1946); Darley & Gross, "A Hypothesis-Confirming Bias in Labeling Effects," 44 *J. Personality & Soc. Psychology* 20, 21-22 (1983); Greenwald, Pratkanis, Leippe & Baumgardner, "Under What Conditions Does Theory Obstruct Research Progress?", 93 *Psychological Rev.* 216, 227 (1986); Hamilton & Zanna, "Context Effects in Impression Formation: Changes in Connotative Meaning," 29 *J. Personality & Soc. Psychology* 649, 652-54 (1974); Hayden & Mischel, "Maintaining Trait Consistency in the Resolution of Behavioral Inconsistency. The Wolf in Sheep's Clothing?" 44 *J. Personality* 109, 129-31 (1976); E. Jones & G. Goethals, *Order Effects in Impression Formation: Attribution Context and the Nature of the Entity*, 42-43 (1971); Kruglanski & Freund, "The Freezing and Unfreezing of Lay Inferences: Effects on Impressional Primacy, Ethnic Stereotyping, and Numerical Anchoring," 19 *J. Experimental Soc. Psychology* 448, 461-65 (1983); Lord, Ross & Lepper, "Biased Assimilation and Attitude Polarization: The Effects of Prior Theories on Subsequently Considered Evidence," 37 *J. Personality & Soc. Psychology* 2098, 2108 (1979).

[42] See, e.g., Johnson, Bransford & Solomon, "Memory for Tacit Implications of Sentences," 98 *J. Experimental Psychology* 203, 204 (1973); Johnson & Raye, supra note 36, at 81-82.

[43] Pyszczynski & Wrightsman, "The Effects of Opening Statements on Mock Jurors' Verdicts in a Simulated Criminal Trial," 11 *J. Applied Soc. Psychology* 301, 309-10 (1981); Wells, Wrightsman & Meine, "The Timing of the Defense Opening Statement: Don't Wait Until the Evidence Is In," 15 *J. Applied Soc. Psychology* 758, 769 (1985).

[44] Pyszczynski, Greenberg, Mack & Wrightsman, "Opening Statements in a Jury Trial: The Effect of Promising More Than the Evidence Can Show," 11 *J. Applied Soc. Psychology* 434, 442 (1981).

[45] Sue, Smith & Caldwell, supra note 39, at 350-51; see also Caretta & Moreland, supra note 39, at 305-6.

[46] Wolf & Montgomery, supra note 39, at 216.

[47] Wegner, Schneider, Carter & White, "Paradoxical Effects of Thought Suppression," 53 *J. Personality & Soc. Psychology* 5, 8-9 (1987).

[48] This explanation is based on Brehm's 1966 theory of psychological reactance. See S. Brehm & J. Brehm, *Psychological Reactance: A Theory of Freedom and Control* 3-7 (1981); see also Worchel, Arnold & Baker, "The Effect of Censorship on Attitude Change; The Influence of Censor and Communicator Characteristics," 5 *J. Applied Soc. Psychology* 227, 237 (1975) (for relevant empirical support).

[49] Thompson, Fong & Rosenhan, "Inadmissible Evidence and Juror Verdicts," 40 *J. Personality & Soc. Psychology* 453, 460 (1981).

[50] *Fed. R. Evid.* 404(a)(3).

[51] Note, "To take the Stand or Not to Take the Stand: The Dilemma of the Defendant with a Criminal Record," 4 *Colum. J. L. & Soc. Probs.* 215, 218 (1968).

[52] Wissler & Saks, "On the Inefficacy of Limiting Instructions: When Jurors Use Prior Conviction Evidence to Decide on Guilt," 9 *L. & Hum. Behav.* 37, 47 (1985).

[53] See Shaffer, supra note 38, at 145. The inherent prejudice of this rule is indicated by the finding that mock jurors told of a defendant's criminal record view the remaining evidence as more damaging than those who are uninformed. See Hans & Doob, "Section 12 of the Canada Evidence Act and the Deliberations of Simulated Juries," 18 *Crim. L.Q.* 235, 244-46 (1975).

[54] *Graves v. United States*, 150 U.S. 118, 121 (1893).

[55] E. Cleary, *McCormick on Evidence* § 272 (3d ed. 1984); J. Chadbourn, *Wigmore's Evidence*, § 286 (3d ed. 1970).

[56] Saltzburg, "A Special Aspect of Relevance: Countering Negative Inferences Associated with the Absence of Evidence," 66 *Calif. L. Rev.* 1011, 1012 (1978).

[57] For example, a litigant may choose to protect family members and friends from the stress of cross-examination, or may fear that a witness will lack credibility. See Stier, "Revisiting the Missing Witness Inference: Quieting the Loud Voice from the Empty Chair," 44 *Md. L. Rev.* 137, 144–45 (1985).

[58] In *Griffin v. California*, the United States Supreme Court ruled that neither judges nor prosecuting attorneys may comment on a defendant's failure to take the witness stand. 380 U.S. 609, 615 (1965). Indeed, judges may instruct jurors *not* to draw adverse inferences from a defendant's silence. *Lakeside v. Oregon*, 435 U.S. 333, 340–41 (1978). Questions are thus raised about whether the fifth amendment is compromised by comments concerning absent witnesses other than the defendant. See McDonald, "Drawing an Inference from the Failure to Produce a Knowledgeable Witness: Evidentiary and Constitutional Consideration," 61 *Calif. L. Rev.* 1422, 1423–26 (1973); see also Tanford, "An Introduction to Trial Law," 51 *Mo. L. Rev.* 623, 680–81 (1986).

[59] S. Kassin & L. Wrightsman, supra note 5, at 113.

[60] Shaffer & Case, "On the Decision Not to Testify in One's Own Behalf: Effects of Withheld Evidence, Defendant's Sexual Preferences, and Juror Dogmatism on Juridic Decisions," 42 *J. Personality & Soc. Psychology* 335, 344 (1982).

[61] Fazio, Sherman & Herr, "The Feature-Positive Effect in the Self-Perception Process: Does Not Doing Matter as Much as Doing?," 42 *J. Personality & Soc. Psychology* 404, 409–10 (1982); Newman, Wolff & Hearst, "The Feature-Positive Effect in Adult Human Subjects," 6 *J. Experimental Psychology: Hum. Learning & Memory* 630, 647–48 (1980).

[62] Webster, King & Kassin, "Voices from an Empty Chair: The Missing Witness Inference and the Jury," *Law and Human Behavior* (in press).

[63] Id. To establish juror expectations for a missing witness, defense counsel's opening statement included mention of the fact that the defendant had talked about his emotional difficulties to a close friend and to a co-worker. In the missing-central version of the case, the close friend did not testify. In the missing-peripheral version, the co-worker did not testify. All versions of the transcript thus contained the same information, varying only in the present and absent sources of that information.

[64] In the *no-comment* condition, neither the prosecutor nor the judge made reference to the missing witness. In the *comment* condition, the prosecutor argued in closing, "I put it to you, ladies and gentlemen—where is Mr. Steven Marshall (John Mills)? Is it possible that Mr. Marshall (Mills) would not have corroborated the misinformed opinion of the psychiatrists? I think it is. Members of the jury, if your best friend (co-worker) were in this kind of trouble, wouldn't *you* want to be here to help him? I think, in weighing the evidence, you will come to the conclusion that I have." Id.

Also in the comment condition, the judge's charge to the jury included the following instruction, approved for use in federal courts: "If, according to appropriate procedures, the court is shown that a witness is available to one of the parties alone, and the anticipated testimony of the witness would elucidate some material issue, and the party who fails to produce the witness offers no explanation, then the factfinder may be permitted, but is not required, to infer that the testimony would have been unfavorable to the party who failed to call the witness." See I. Devitt & C. Blackmar, *Fed. Jury Prac. and Instructions*, § 17.19 (3d ed. 1977); see also Fed. Judicial Ctr. Comm. to Study Crim. Jury Instructions, *Pattern Crim. Jury Instructions* 49 (1982) (for alternative language).

[65] American Bar Association Project on Minimum Standards for Criminal Justice (1968), Standards Relating to Trial by Jury, Section 5.4. Open-mindedness is such an important aspect of deliberation that if a juror dies before a verdict is announced, the jury cannot

return a verdict even if all the remaining jurors swear that the deceased had agreed with their decision. The reasoning behind this rule is that "[t]he jurors individually and collectively have the right to change their minds prior to the reception of the verdict. . . ." E. DeVitt & C. Blackmar, *Fed. Jury Pract. and Instructions*, § 5.23 (3d ed. 1977).

66 *Allen v. United States*, 164 U.S. 492, 501–2 (1896).

67 Id. at 501.

68 Asch, "Studies of Independence and Conformity: A Minority of One Against a Unanimous Majority," 70 *Psychological Monographs*, Whole No. 416 (1956); Deutsch & Gerard, "A Study of Normative and Informational Social Influence Upon Individual Judgment," 51 *J. Abnormal & Soc. Psychology* 629 (1955).

69 See, eg., Schacter, "Deviation, Rejection, and Communication," 46 *J. Abnormal & Soc. Psychology* 190 (1951); for a review see Levine, "Reaction to Opinion Deviance in Small Groups," *Psychology of Group Influence* (P. Paulus ed. 1980).

70 See, e.g., Campbell & Fairey, "Informational and Normative Routes to Conformity: The Effect of Faction Size as a Function of Norm Extremity and Attention to the Stimulus," 57 *J. Personality & Soc. Psychology* 457, 458 (1989).

71 See, e.g., Kaplan & Miller, "Group Discussion and Judgment," *Basic Group Processes* 65 (P. Paulus ed. 1983); Kaplan & Miller, "Group Decision-Making and Normative Versus Information Influence: Effects of Type of Issue and Assigned Decision Rule," 53 *J. Personality & Soc. Psychology* 306 (1987); Stasser, Kerr & Bray, "The Social Psychology of Jury Deliberations," *Psychology of the Courtroom* 221 (Kerr & Bray eds. 1982).

72 H. Kalven & H. Zeisel, *The American Jury* 489 (1966).

73 There are important reasons to protect individual jurors from normative influences that elicit mere public compliance. First, justice is undermined when a jury renders a verdict not supported even by its membership (e.g., criminal defendants should not be convicted by juries internally plagued by a reasonable doubt). Second, unanimous votes produced by normative influences may undermine perceptions of justice among those who serve on juries.

74 Kaplan & Miller, supra note 71, at 311.

75 Hawkins, "Interaction Rates of Jurors Aligned in Factions," 27 *Am. Soc. Rev.* 689 (1962) (public vote in jury deliberation).

76 *Commonwealth v. Tuey*, 62 Mass. 1 (1851).

77 164 U.S. 492 (1896).

78 It has also been called the "shotgun" instruction, the "third degree" instruction, the "nitroglycerin" charge, the "hammer" instruction, and the "hanging" instruction. See Marcus, "The *Allen* Instruction in Criminal Cases: Is the Dynamite Charge About to be Permanently Defused?" 43 *Mo. L. Rev.* 613, 615 (1978).

79 *Allen*, 164 U.S. at 501. The full text of the charge reads as follows:

That in a large proportion of cases absolute certainty could not be expected; that although the verdict must be the verdict of each individual juror, and not a mere acquiescence in the conclusion of his fellows, yet they should examine the question submitted with candor and with a proper regard and deference to the opinions of each other; that it was their duty to decide the case if they could conscientiously do so; that they should listen, with a disposition to be convinced, to each other's arguments; that, if much the larger number were for conviction, a dissenting juror should consider whether his doubt was a reasonable one which made no impression upon the minds of so many men, equally honest, equally intelligent with himself. If, upon the other hand, the majority was for acquittal, the minority ought to ask themselves whether they might not reasonably doubt the correctness of a judgment which was not concurred in by the majority.

Id.

[80] *People v. Randall,* 9 N.Y.2d. 413, 214 N.Y.S.2d 417, 174 N.E.2d 507 (1961) (quoting *People v. Faber,* 199 N.Y. 256, 260–61.

[81] Id. at 850, 139 Cal. Rptr. at 869, 566 P.2d at 1005 (quoting *United States v. Bailey,* 468 F.2d 652, 662 (5th Cir. 1972)).

[82] *People v. Gainer,* 19 Cal.3d 835, 850, 139 Cal. Rptr. 861, 869, 566 P.2d 997, 1005 (1977).

[83] American Bar Association Project on Minimum Standards for Criminal Justice, Standards Relating to Trial by Jury, Standards 5.4 (1968).

[84] See Jensen, "After *Lowenfield:* The *Allen* Charge in the Ninth Circuit," 19 *Golden Gate U.L. Rev.* 75, 85 (1989); Marcus, supra note 78, at 617; Notes and Comments, "On Instructing Deadlocked Juries," 78 *Yale L.J.* 100, 103–6 (1968).

[85] *Lowenfield v. Phelps,* 484 U.S. 231 (1988).

[86] Kassin, Smith & Tulloch, "The Dynamite Charge: Effects on the Perceptions and Deliberation Behavior of Mock Jurors," 14 *Law and Human Behavior* 537 (1990).

[87] Each set consisted of six notes written in the same handwriting.

[88] As one might expect, several members of the minority capitulated; in these instances, the session was terminated and questionnaires administered.

[89] This no-instruction control procedure was designed to resemble what often happens when jurors are deadlocked and the judge directs them to return for further discussion.

[90] It is interesting that even though all subjects received the same deliberation notes, those in the minority-dynamite group imagined they were under greater pressure from the other jurors.

[91] Further research is clearly needed. One approach would be to conduct field experiments on real cases in which deadlocked juries are randomly assigned to receive either the *Allen* charge or a control instruction. Because random assignment of real juries is not feasible, however, a more realistic approach is to conduct a large-scale laboratory study involving interacting mock jurors.

[92] The American Bar Association, for example, offered an alternative charge, one which emphasizes jurors' duty to consult with one another without singling out those in the minority. The instruction reads:

> It is your duty, as jurors, to consult with one another and to deliberate with a view to reaching an agreement, if you can do so without violence to individual judgment. Each of you must decide the case for yourself, but do so only after an impartial consideration of the evidence with your fellow jurors. In the course of your deliberations, do not hesitate to reexamine your views and change your opinion if convinced it is erroneous. But do not surrender your honest conviction as to the weight or effect of evidence solely because of the opinion of your fellow jurors, or for the mere purpose of returning a verdict.

See American Bar Association Project on Minimum Standards for Criminal Justice, Standards Relating to Trial by Jury, Standard 5.4 (1968).

[93] *Apodaca v. Oregon,* 406 U.S. 404 (1972) (the Court upheld convictions by votes of 11 to 1 and 10 to 2); *Johnson v. Louisiana,* 406 U.S 356 (1972). Current practices are varied. The federal courts still require unanimous verdicts, but a handful of states permit non-unanimous verdicts in criminal trials, and over 30 states allow these verdicts in civil actions.

[94] We have no grounds for believing that majority jurors, aware of their responsibility and power over the liberty of the defendant, would simply refuse to listen to arguments presented to them in favor of acquittal, terminate discussion, and render a verdict. On the contrary it is far more likely that a juror presenting reasoned argument in favor of acquittal would either have his arguments answered or would carry enough other jurors with him to prevent conviction.

Johnson, 406 U.S. at 361.

95   [N]onunanimous juries need not debate and deliberate as fully as must unanimous juries. As soon as the requisite majority is attained, further consideration is not required either by Oregon or by Louisiana even though the dissident jurors, might, if given the chance, be able to convince the majority. . . . It is said that there is no evidence that majority jurors will refuse to listen to dissenters whose votes are unneeded for conviction. Yet human experience teaches that polite and academic conversation is no substitute for the earnest and robust argument necessary to reach unanimity.

Id. at 388–89.

96   Nemeth, ''Interactions Between Jurors as a Function of Majority vs. Unanimity Decision Rules,'' 7 *J. Applied Soc. Psychology* 38, 42–43 (1977).

97   R. Hastie, S. Penrod & N. Pennington, *Inside the Jury* 45 (1983).

98   Id. at 112.

99   *Walker v. United States,* 342 F.2d 22, 28 (5th Cir. 1965).

100   H. Kalven & H. Zeisel, supra note 72, at 453.

101   H. Kalven & He. Zeisel, supra note 72, at 3.

9

The Impact of
Sequestration on Juries

JAMES P. LEVINE

Wander into the Holiday Inn on New York City's Staten Island most any evening and you will encounter a rather puzzling sight. At either end of one or more corridors armed law enforcement officials will be on guard, poised to jump into action should one of the doors on the floor open. The visitor observing this scene might well proceed with trepidation, imagining that the room of a criminal suspect or fugitive is under surveillance. In fact, what is taking place is the routine monitoring of a sequestered jury.

Jury sequestration refers to the physical isolation of the jury from the rest of society. It is the opposite of what is technically called "separation of the jury," the condition that exists when jurors are permitted to go their separate ways when court is not in session. Sequestration can take place at two points in the judicial process, during the trial itself (a rare phenomenon) or during deliberations. Its primary purpose is to shield jurors from biasing outside influences that might vitiate the integrity of the trial and deprive defendants of their right to verdicts based on law and evidence. It is thus seen as an instrument to further due process of law.

When sequestration is ordered, jurors are kept together as a group and forbidden to have significant contact with anyone but each other. Access to the media is denied or strictly limited: exposure to trial coverage is prevented; newspapers are banned or censored; television viewing is off limits or highly restricted. Jurors are cut off from family, friends, and

Reprinted with permission from *Judicature*, Vol. 79, No. 5, March–April 1996, pp. 266–272.

neighbors; they become a world unto themselves. They are confined to the courtroom or the juryroom during working hours, and they are required to eat and sleep in special quarters. Court officers keep track of their every activity, sometimes even following them into bathrooms. Sex is normally off-limits, physical activity is severely constrained, and solitude is all but impossible.

Jurors can be held in contempt of court and are subject to fines and imprisonment if they depart from court-imposed restrictions. Says University of Texas law school professor Michael Tigar, an opponent of sequestration: "There are prison systems that provide more privileges than some sequestered jurors receive."[1] It is no exaggeration to call sequestered juries prisoners of the court.

Much attention has recently been focused on sequestrations during the trial itself. There have been celebrated cases featuring long periods of isolation, such as the eight-and-one-half month Charles Manson case in the 1970s, the second Rodney King case, which lasted 57 days, and the O.J. Simpson case, which went on for 266 days—setting the record for sequestration. While such lengthy confinements are rare, it is more common for juries to be sequestered for several nights during deliberations. Until New York State changed its law in June 1995, *all* criminal juries in that state had to be sequestered while they were deliberating and even now sequestration is mandatory in cases of serious felonies. In other cases New York now follows the more flexible policy of the federal court system and the other 49 states where judges have the discretion to keep the jury apart from the community during the entire trial or during deliberations.

This article assesses some of the impacts of sequestration on jury decision making, a topic that has received little scholarly analysis. This may to some extent be due to the infrequency of sequestration outside New York, but it also reflects the paucity of solid information about how sequestration works in practice. Mock jury research, which has been so helpful in learning about a wide range of influences on jurors, has not been used, in part because of the impracticality of isolating and confining subjects as part of an experiment.

In assessing sequestration we are by default forced to rely on theoretical speculation about human behavior, a smattering of tangentially related empirical data, and insights garnered from reportage. Because this is no substitute for systematic evaluation done in a methodologically rigorous fashion, the following analysis suffers from over-reliance on anecdotes and an insufficient grounding in rigorous studies. It is in truth a collection of hypotheses and a consideration of their plausibility rather than a definitive demonstration of how sequestration works in practice. But it does subject a controversial judicial practice to the spotlight of systematic analysis and raises issues that have received insufficient scrutiny: Does sequestration make jury decision makers fairer and more rational, or does it put undue pressures on jurors that undermine their capacity for objectivity? Does it prompt the jury to concentrate on the evidence by fending off improper external influences, or does it trigger counterproductive psychological and social dynamics that debase the decision-making process? Is it a protection for defendants, as originally anticipated, or does it ironically function to promote convictions? Are the benefits worth the costs? Does sequestration further the ideals of justice?

Shielding the Jury

The historic rationale for sequestering juries was to insulate them from the insidious invasions of the press and the pressures of the community. Preventing communications from sources other than fellow jurors was supposed to focus attention on the evidence introduced at the trial and the instructions of judges, the only material that was to be the basis of verdicts.

The media in particular are thought to be a contaminating source of prejudice. News coverage is ubiquitous and even an innocuous radio program of music and weather can burst forth with commentary about a trial in progress. Newspaper headlines dramatize the latest information or rumors about cases, and the most obedient jurors trying to follow judges' orders that they not follow the case might lay their eyes on such potentially biasing words in print.

There is much controversy about the effectiveness of sequestering juries in warding off publicity. In certain notorious cases the press is saturated with prejudicial pre-trial commentary, in which case sequestration during either the trial or deliberations may be too late to do any good. Any number of mock jury experiments have shown that pre-trial publicity increases convictions, the judges' admonitions to disregard such publicity notwithstanding.[2] A thorough review of this research prompted jury expert Norbert Kerr to conclude that "intense pretrial publicity can adversely affect . . . jury verdicts" and to doubt the effectiveness of common remedies.[3]

Another intrusion from which jurors are spared by sequestration is community opinion. Frightful cases entailing violence often create public fervor for convictions that can result in a rush to judgement. Where the defendant is the subject of public scorn there can be pressures to convict. Less frequently, those on trial who engender sympathy can receive public support.

Since jurors' identities are part of the public record except in the rare instances when anonymous juries are used, any number of individuals who happen to cross paths with jurors are in a position to offer their views and influence the verdict. Going home when court is out of session can entail encounters with merchants, neighbors, family, and other acquaintances who may be all too eager to volunteer opinions.

When jurors are permitted to commingle with the community, judges warn them to avoid any exposure to discussion of the trial. But such instructions may well fall on deaf ears, as jurors thirst to find out more about the case than they heard in court. The most conscientious of jurors may inadvertently find themselves at the center of discussions about the case, whether at the local bar or in the family living room. Telling jurors to shut themselves off to normal communications and to tune out all trial-related discourse may well be in vain.

Even in the absence of propaganda or pressure, sequestration may shield jurors from distractions that interfere with their concentration on the case. Being limited to dreary hotel rooms and meaningless banter during group meals may sharpen their wits when it comes to jury room exchanges. While going home provides all kinds of creature comforts and may be an outlet for relieving pent-up stress, it can also confront jurors with the woes and worries that beset everyone—overdue bills, leaking roofs, truant children, marital problems, and the like. Carrying these problems back to the court may well subject jurors to fits of daydreaming and self-absorption when they are supposed to be attending to discussions about the case.

Some trial procedures intended to protect defendants' rights are difficult to carry out in practice, such as the rule of *Batson v. Kentucky* prohibiting the use of peremptory challenges to exclude people from juries because of their race.[4] But it is a relatively straightforward task to quarantine jurors physically. While stories are told of jurors smuggling newspapers, unblocking their telephones,[5] watching banned television programs,[6] and sneaking out of their hotel rooms,[7] such breaches of sequestration are hopefully uncommon. Sequestration thus seems quite effective in screening out potentially biasing publicity, and it may at times contribute to more objective fact-finding.

Fostering Juror Intimacy

Being thrown together in close quarters engenders closer relations among jurors. While even non-sequestered juries often develop close attachments as a result of socializing with one another for days on end, the cutting off of contact from the outside world occasioned by sequestration can intensify the bonding process. Jurors have referred to themselves as having become a family, warmly recounting after trials are over how close they had become even in the face of acute differences of opinion about the evidence.[8]

How might such camaraderie impact deliberations? First, becoming emotionally connected with each other might well incline jurors to listen to competing arguments. Communications tend to be more positive when one has a personal relationship with someone else than when people confront one another as anonymous functionaries. Relatively few juries are unanimous at the outset of deliberations;[9] some degree of persuasion is normally necessary to achieve the unanimity that most jurisdictions still require. Positive personal feelings may well be one ingredient impelling jurors to open themselves up to other perspectives.

A second consequence of juror bonding may be to enable people to overcome barriers to communication based on differences in background. Juryroom tensions based on race, ethnicity, or class that may accentuate prejudicial responses to defendants or victims may be defused when jurors get to know each other. Social psychology evidence demonstrates that gaining information about specific individuals who are part of a stereotyped group diminishes reliance on stereotypes.[10] Moreover, personal contact with members of a disliked group produces positive attitudes toward such individuals if not to the entire group.[11]

By its very nature sequestration generates potentially beneficial contact among people who have little in common and who might share mutual disdain for one another. Jurors cloistered together tend to talk to each other about the petty details and diversions of life. They also wind up commiserating with each other about the travails of their jury experience, lamenting everything from lawyer monotones to hard juror chairs to inadequate ventilation. What they find is greater rapport than they might have expected. Jurors from different worlds who by force of their sequestered circumstance wind up spending hours idly talking with one another may well hear each other more when the focus turns to the case at hand.

There can, of course, be a deleterious consequence of being brought together in close quarters against one's will. Cliques can emerge, sometimes based on background factors such as race or ethnicity, which can reduce inter-group contact; there are reports that the O. J. Simpson jury was so plagued.[12] Even in the absence of such clustering, one can develop animosities toward co-jurors that obstruct effective deliberations. Thus, one of the jurors in the Joel Steinberg murder case dealing with the death from child abuse of his six-year-old illegally adopted girl later chastised some of his co-jurors in no uncertain terms: "Hate is too strong a word, but I have no desire to run into them again."[13]

The intimacy foisted onto jurors by sequestration can thus be a two-edged sword, a means of bringing juries together as a concerted decision-making team or a source of aggravation that serves to promote greater discord. Social psychological theories are of limited use in determining which way the sword most commonly strikes, as an aid or a hindrance to rational deliberation.

Compounding Stress

Jury experience is inherently trying. Not only do jurors have their personal lives disrupted, but they are often required to deal with gruesome factual details, emotionally charged testimony, incomprehensible legal jargon, unpleasant disagreements with co-jurors, and agonizing decisions. Considerable research has now demonstrated the ubiquity of juror stress.[14]

The length and complexity of modern trials can take its toll. The aggravation they experience, normally held within, surfaced during a libel case in White Plains, New York, which had run four months and showed no signs of reaching a conclusion. A contingent of the despairing jury demanded a meeting with the judge where they exploded in anger. So distraught were the jurors that the judge declared a mistrial and dismissed the jury.[15]

Cases entailing violence are especially distressing for the jury. Jurors hearing the case of serial sex killer Jeffrey Dahmer, after listening to weeks of very graphic descriptions of dismemberment, mutilation, and sex with corpses, later revealed the toll the trial had taken on them. Said one juror: "I think that there are fourteen other victims in this case and that is the fourteen jurors. They have been through some traumatic times . . . I am beginning to think there is no such thing as normal after this."[16] While the Dahmer case was horrifying in the extreme, even less upsetting cases can afflict the psyches of jurors.

Sequestration surely compounds this stress. Not a single former juror who contacted New York State's Jury Project created in 1993 by Chief Judge Judith Kaye had good things to say about it.[17]

Studies have shown that persons forced to co-exist with strangers in conditions of isolation against their will sometimes become frustrated, angry, and aggressive.[18] What is true of those like disaster victims confined to close quarters with people they do not know is surely true of some sequestered jurors: they can become disoriented and distressed. Thus, one juror sequestered during the Reginald Denny beating case emerging from the Los Angeles riots that took place after the Rodney King verdict was reported to have suffered a breakdown. He was kept on the jury despite having been witnessed running up and down the corridor of the hotel where the jurors were staying, shouting: "I can't take it any more."[19]

Juror Retaliation

Jurors who resent the experience of sequestration and are disturbed by it may vent their wrath on one of the trial adversaries. The physical and psychological discomfort of having one's life disrupted may be attributed to the accused, who is blamed for having caused the entire unpleasant situation. To avenge the ordeal of sequestration, the juror comes down hard on the persons thought to have been responsible for triggering it—even if the defendants are in fact innocent. One study comparing sequestered and unsequestered New York juries showed that the former produced 16 percent more convictions than the latter, although there were insufficient controls for case differences in the research to provide confidence in the findings.[20] Jurors may also take out their anger on the prosecution. Since it is the state that initiates the entire trial process, it is the state who deserves to be punished.

Juror Capitulation

Jurors can cope with stress in another way that is adverse to the ideal of justice. Those unduly upset by their ordeal may capitulate to the will of the majority in hopes of speeding up a verdict. In the classic movie *Twelve Angry Men*, one of the jurors switches his vote from guilty to not guilty to hasten a verdict, because he did not want to waste the tickets he had to a night baseball game. While such flippancy is probably rare, any number of real jurors have confessed how desperately they wanted to get out.

The tension of juryroom conflict can itself erode a juror's fortitude. Many a juror has spoken of the anguish they experienced simply by being part of a minority holding out against dominant sentiment. A juror who believed John Hinckley guilty of attempting to murder President Ronald Reagan but who eventually submitted to fellow jurors who thought him not guilty by reason of insanity minced no words: "I changed because of the pressure. I had the shakes all day. I had to get out of there."[21]

Feelings of intimidation experienced by dissidents on the jury may well be intensified by the pangs of sequestration. It is bad enough to be isolated in a minority position within the jury; it is worse to have no escape. As another member of the Steinberg jury put it: "Until you've been sequestered, you can't imagine how horrible it is. It makes you feel powerless and helpless."[22]

The irritation if not downright hostility of those in the majority against dissenters can become a nagging undercurrent during the hours spent away from the jury room. Even idle chitchat and exchange of pleasantries can become unnerving when the atmosphere is fraught with tension. The agony of being "odd person out," the stubborn one or two or three jurors holding up a verdict, may be heightened by the omnipresence of one's adversaries. When your antagonists are constantly "in your face," it may be hard for beleaguered jurors to resist the temptation to yield to their point of view. We know from previous field and experimental research that majorities within juries tend to prevail,[23] and sequestration may reinforce such majoritarian pressure. Thus, one reason why two jurors who initially voted to convict O.J. Simpson reversed themselves after less than four hours of discussion might have been the desire to end their "captivity" and resume their normal lives. Unanimous verdicts so achieved, rather than representing the triumph of the majority's persuasiveness, may be the flawed results of a terribly stressful decision-making context.

Short of making complete about faces, jurors who are fed up may agree to compromise verdicts.[24] Jury deliberations in the "Chicago Seven" cases arising out of the clash between antiwar protesters and police during the 1968 Democratic National Convention ended in just such fashion. After five days of anguish, the sequestered jury acquitted all of the defendants of conspiracy; they convicted five of inciting a riot; and they absolved two completely. The juror who engineered the deal later said that the negotiated verdict was reached "although a majority of jurors felt all the defendants guilty on both counts—and three jurors felt all of them were innocent."[25] This groping for middle ground has also been observed in mock jury research.[26]

Juror Obstinacy

An opposite effect of experiencing the isolation of sequestration, equally pernicious, is juror stubbornness. The constant presence of one's adversaries may be perceived by some jurors as a challenge to their willpower, and holding out becomes an act of face-saving defiance as much as an assertion of confidence in one's point of view. The intimidating effects of sequestration can thus engender closed-mindedness, creating a siege mentality that stymies productive deliberations.

On the other hand, judges tell of unsequestered juries who quickly resolve their apparent deadlocks after getting "a good night's sleep."[27] The support system provided by those at home can provide an outlet for stress and a reinforcement of ego that permits jurors to open their minds to the arguments of peers. Replacing intensely charged juror interactions with intervals of normal routines and relationships can take the edge off of the taxing psychodynamics of the jury room. Avoiding sequestration can thus prevent needlessly hung juries.

Influence of Court Officers

It has been suggested that sequestration can improperly favor the prosecution due to the continuous interaction between jurors and court officers, who are generally perceived to be affiliated with the law enforcement system. Bailiffs, marshals, court-employed bus drivers and the like are sometimes the sequestered jurors' sole contact with the outside world. Those guarding the jurors are often sworn peace officers who carry guns, hardly to be distinguished from police. The association that develops between such personnel and the jury can foster a connection that compromises the neutrality of the jurors.

This can happen in two ways. First, court personnel may pass along their own predispositions, which are more likely than not oriented toward conviction. It was in recognition of this biasing effect that the Supreme Court of Nebraska overturned a murder conviction rendered by sequestered jurors who had played black jack with the local sheriff who dropped in on them in the course of supervising the sequestration.[28]

A second even more subtle biasing impact can paradoxically occur when court officers are acting most professionally. The American Bar Association's Committee on Jury Standards stipulates that procedures should be put into place so that "the inconvenience and discomfort of the sequestered jurors is minimized."[29] Jurors who are treated well in furtherance of this policy may develop a certain fondness towards their keepers—a peculiar manifestation of the "Stockholm syndrome," the surprising tendency of some kidnapping victims to become attached to their abductors. Jurors who feel positive toward court officers may generalize such good will to other law enforcement officials.

Dissuading Service

Fear of sequestration is one reason some people try to avoid jury service. Worries about being pent up with strangers in an unfamiliar environment for an unspecified period of time may be one factor accounting for the fact that only about two out of every five people called for jury service actually come to court.[30] Those receiving notices in the mail often simply disregard them, knowing full well that there will probably be no follow-up and certainly no drastic consequences.

Those who do show up will commonly allege all kinds of problems that would ensue from being sequestered to justify getting excused—medical conditions, young children in need of supervision, elderly parents in need of assistance, and the like. For example, 95 percent of the pool of 4,482 people contacted as possible jurors in the second trial of the police officers who beat Rodney King said sequestration would create prohibitive hardships.[31]

Among those precluded from serving by the risk of sequestration are the physically disabled who require special assistance and members of religious groups whose beliefs would be compromised if they could not go home on weekends. Court personnel have reported that many women have asked to be excused from serving on juries due to nighttime child care duties.[32] This obstacle to jury service may actually put the practice of sequestration in legal jeopardy in that the right of women to fair representation on juries is now constitutionally protected.[33]

What part sequestration plays in decisions to avoid jury duty is anyone's guess. It may well be a minor element, but to the extent that people are creatures of routine, the threat of abrupt and unpredictable changes in one's daily regimen posed by sequestration may be decisive. It is one thing to come to court every day, engaging in what may actually be a welcome diversion from the tedium of work or school or retired life; it is another thing to put oneself at the mercy of the court after hours.

Sequestration, then, can have pernicious impacts *prior to* its imposition. Court administrators, in attempts to make jury duty less onerous, have been coming up with various strategies to encourage more cooperativeness from citizens—from one day/one trial to cleaner bathrooms in the courthouse. But perhaps one of the least palatable aspects of jury service is being removed from one's home and family as a ward of the court. This facet of jury service, while a relatively rare occurrence, may well be scary enough to deter some from serving at all and an impediment to attempts to further democratize the jury system.

Costs of Sequestration

Sequestration is expensive. New York's former policy of requiring it in all criminal cases cost about $4 million annually. Each of the 1,400 juries sequestered in the year ending April 30, 1994 cost the state an average of $2,816 per night: $709 for lodging; $208 for meals; and $1,899 for court officers' overtime.[34] Sequestering the O.J. Simpson jury cost about $1 million.

Although these expenditures are a tiny fraction of the total criminal justice budget, opportunity costs are at stake: the money could be spent otherwise. Thus, abolishing mandatory sequestration in New York freed up funds which will help defray the cost of recent legislation raising jurors' compensation from the paltry $15 a day paid through the end of 1996 to $27.50 in 1997 and $40 in 1998. Since low juror pay is a significant deterrent to jury service, such re-allocation broadens the pool of jurors and presumably creates more representative panels.

Learning More

Jury research is now a veritable cottage industry. Social scientists study the effects of virtually every imaginable factor on juries: race, gender, and class of defendants; social demography of the jurors themselves; type of crime; different kinds of evidence and testimony; public attitudes toward crime and criminals; size of jury; unanimous versus non-unanimous decision rules; and so forth.[35] Practitioners serving as consultants have used a potpourri of investigative methods to study jury selection and claim to know a great deal about the relationships between jurors' backgrounds and their decision-making proclivities.[36] Yet an issue of considerable moment for both the integrity of the judicial process and the welfare of jurors has escaped systematic scrutiny; we remain relatively uninformed about the effects of sequestration.

State legislatures have over the years grappled with the issue of sequestration as they fashion and refashion their rules of criminal procedure. Trial judges must determine which cases warrant the drastic step of sequestration, and appellate courts often have to decide whether verdicts rendered in the absence of sequestration violated constitutional rights.[37] Yet these policy makers and legal authorities must act in an empirical vacuum, resting decisions on vague cogitations about the impact of trial publicity and the nature of the deliberative process. This situation needs correcting: we need to learn more about how the jury actually functions when it is quarantined from the community.

A number of research strategies could prove fruitful. It might be possible to sequester mock juries experimentally if subjects were permitted to terminate their participation on demand. A more feasible approach would be to interview ex-jurors about their experiences under sequestration, just as the Capital Jury Project has quite poignantly captured the sentiments of former jurors in capital cases who were eager to talk about the life-or-death decisions they made.[38]

In the aftermath of New York's abolition of mandatory sequestration in many cases, there is a golden opportunity to do a "before-and-after" study: the viewpoints and the verdicts of jurors sequestered before the law took effect can be compared with the behavior of subsequent juries allowed to go home during deliberations. A number of useful questions could be posed and answered: Do conviction rates go up? Are there more hung juries? Do juries reach verdicts more quickly? Do more prospective jurors show up in court? Are jurors more satisfied with their experiences?

The Pursuit of Justice

The negative impacts of sequestration normally appear to outweigh its virtues. Its potential for unnerving and even infuriating jurors is apparent, offsetting whatever advantages it may have in shielding jurors from prejudicial publicity and the distractions of personal life. Its effect on the quality of deliberations is also problematic: while it may bond some juries it may fracture others. It may foster a too-cozy relationship between jurors and court officers; and it is surely a deterrent to jury service.

On balance, sequestration seems to undermine the pursuit of justice. Both the personal well-being of jurors and the public interest in quality decision making seem best served by keeping the jury free unless there is substantial reason to do otherwise. Sequestration should be used quite selectively, reserved for cases that promise to receive frenzied, inescapable media saturation.

This condemnation of sequestration is expressed with some uneasiness. Cost-benefit analysis is always a problematic and subjective endeavor, belying precision. Assessing whether sequestration comes at too high a price in both money and human costs involves the making of personal value judgments. Is sequestration worth it if it spares a single innocent defendant from a wrongful verdict? Would curtailing press coverage as the British do be a less harmful means of providing a fair trial? How much stress and strain on jurors is *too* much stress and strain? Social science cannot answer these questions, but it can provide better measurement of the costs and benefits of sequestration.

Endnotes

[1] Quoted in Hansen, Sequestration Little Used, Little Liked, 81 *ABA* J. 16, 17 (October 1995).

[2] Kramer, Kerr, and Carroll, Pretrial Publicity, Judicial Remedies, and Jury Bias, 14 *Law and Hum. Behav.* 409 (1990); Otto, Penrod, and Dexter, The Biasing Impact of Pretrial Publicity on Juror Judgments, 18 *Law and Hum. Behav.* 453 (1994).

[3] Kerr, The Effect of Pretrial Publicity on Jurors, 78 *Judicature* 120 (1994).

[4] 476 U.S. 79 (1986).

[5] A sequestered New York juror deciding the case of a teen-ager on trial for the murder of his parents made an illicit phone call during which he was told about a news conference held by detectives who said that even the defendant's sister thought him guilty—information that was conveyed to other jurors. Glaberson, Compulsory Jury Seclusion: New York Benefit or Waste? *N.Y. Times,* July 5, 1991, at A1.

[6] A case has been reported of a jury that rigged a coat hanger into a television antenna to watch forbidden programs. Letter from G. Thomas Munsterman of the National Center for State Courts (Arlington, Virginia), March 14, 1995.

[7] In one New York case, court officers captured a juror who was observed at night using bed sheets to escape from his second story hotel window. *People v. Conyers*, 189 A.D. 2d. 607 (1993).

[8] Yarrow, Jury Renders Mixed Verdict in Attica Case, *N.Y. Times*, February 5, 1992 at B4.

[9] Kalven and Zeisel, *The American Jury* 488 (1966).

[10] Locksley, Hepburn, and Ortiz, Social Stereotypes and Judgments of Individuals: An Instance of the Base-Rate Fallacy, 18 *J. Res. and Dev. in Educ.* 23 (1982).

[11] Cook, Interpersonal and Attitudinal Outcomes in Cooperating Interracial Groups, 12 *J. Res. and Dev. in Educ.* 97 (1978).

[12] Margolick, Excused Juror Tells Judge That Racial Hatred Permeates and Divides Simpson Panel, *N.Y. Times*, April 14, 1995, at A13.

[13] Polsky, Trials and Tribulations, *N.Y. Newsday*, February 1, 1995, at B4.

[14] Hafemeister and Ventis, Juror Stress: What Burden Have We Placed on Our Juries? 1992 *St. Ct. J.* 35 (1992); Hafemeister, Legal Report: Juror Stress, 8 *Violence and Victims* 177 (1993); Hafemeister and Ventis, Juror Stress: Sources and Implications, 1994 *Trial* 68 (1994).

[15] Hernandez, Westchester Trial Illustrates the Burdens of Jury Services, *N.Y. Times*, December 19, 1994, at A1.

[16] Quoted in Hafemeister and Ventis, Juror Stress: What Burden . . ., supra n. 14, at 35, 37–38.

[17] New York State Office of Court Administration, *The Jury Project: Report to the Chief Judge of the State of New York* 114 (1994).

[18] Schulman and Winick. Some Aspects of Sequestration in Jury Trials: Does It Aid the Defense or the Prosecution? 18 *IJA Rep.* 1 (1985).

[19] Hamilton, Denny Beating Trial Judge Releases Juror Transcripts: Record Reveals Behavior before Removing 2, Retaining 1, *Washington Post*, October 15, 1993, at A2.

[20] Winick and Smith, Past-Trial Sequestered Juries Tilt Toward Guilty Verdicts, *N.Y. Law Journal*, December 12, 1986, at 1.

[21] Jurors Assert That Pressure Forced Them to Alter Votes, *N.Y. Times*, June 23, 1982, at B6.

[22] Polsky, supra n. 13, at B5.

[23] Kalven and Zeisel, supra n. 9, at 488; Stasser, Opinion Change During Group Discussion, 3 *Personalty and Soc. Psychology Bull.* 252 (1977); Tanford and Penrod, Jury Deliberations: Discussion Content and Influence Processes in Jury Decision Making, 16 *Applied Soc. Psychology* 16 (1986).

[24] Levine, Jury Room Politics, 16 *Trial L. Q.* 21 (1984).

[25] Richards, Juror for Chicago 7 Convinced Panel Reached Proper Verdict, *The Oregonian*, March 1, 1970, at 1.

[26] Hastie, Penrod, and Pennington, *Inside the Jury* 60 (1992): Greene, On Juries and Damage Awards: The Process of Decisionmaking, 52 *Law and Contemp. Prob.* 241 (1989).

[27] Letter from G. Thomas Munsterman, March 14, 1995.

[28] *Simants v. State*, 202 Neb. 828, 277 N.W. 2d. 217 (1979).

[29] American Bar Association. Judicial Administration Division, Committee on Jury Standards, *Standards Relating to Juror Use and Management* 173 (1993).

[30] Levine, *Juries and Politics* 44 (1992).

[31] Jury Pool Small for Beating Trial, *N.Y. Times*, January 5, 1993, at A8.

[32] New York State Office of Court Administration, supra n. 17, at 115.

[33] *J.E.B. v. Alabama* ex rel. T.B., 114 S.Ct. 1419 (1994).

[34] New York State Office of Court Administration, supra n. 17, at 133.

[35] For a compilation of much of this research, see Kassin and Wrightsman, *The American Jury on Trial: Psychological Perspectives* (1988) and Frederick, *The Psychology of the American Jury* (1987).

36 Fukurai, Butler, and Booth, *Race and the Jury: Racial Disenfranchisement and the Search for Justice* (1993); Abramson, *We, the Jury: the Jury System and the Ideal of Democracy* 143–176 (1994).

37 *United States v. Carter*, 602 F.2d 799 (1979); *West Virginia v. Young*, 173 W. Va. 1, 311 S.E.2d 118 (1983); *Livingston v. Florida*, 438 So. 2d 235 (1984); *Minnesota v. Sanders* 376 N.W.2d 196 (1985).

38 Bowers and Vandiver, *The Capital Jury Project* (1991).

10

Videotaped Trial Transcripts for Juror Deliberations

DIANE M. HARTMUS and JAMES P. LEVINE

In the aftermath of a string of controversial verdicts, criticism of juries abounds. Not the least of the charges is that jurors simply cannot remember, decipher, and integrate the evidence; they get the facts all wrong. The fate and even the lives of countless defendants are said to hinge on a decision-making process mired in confusion.

Perhaps the problem lies not with the aptitudes of jurors but with the inadequacies of the trial process, which deprives jurors of resources that would enhance their capability to reach correct verdicts. Many jurisdictions refuse to let jurors take notes during trials, consigning them to the role of passive observers who must rely on memory alone during the deliberation stage when they must sort out the testimony they have heard. Many judges are opposed to permitting jurors to ask or submit questions to witnesses, thus depriving the jury of answers to critical questions that the lawyers may not have asked. Jurors are ordered not to discuss evidence until the end of the trial, even though it might make more sense to let them confer intermittently during the trial when testimony is fresh in their minds. The jury's opportunity to act rationally is constrained by an overreliance on traditional practices.

Any number of innovations in trial practices might well enhance the quality of jury decision making, including the use of technological

Reprinted with permission from *Judicature*, Vol. 82, No. 2, September–October 1998, pp. 84–96.

advances in the communications field. In particular, this article explores the idea that trials ought to be videotaped routinely and that the resulting video transcripts ought to be made available to juries during the course of their deliberation. Videocassette recorders have wended their way into virtually every aspect of modern life. They should be made a standard piece of equipment in the jury room, a means of ready access to testimony that helps jurors discover the truth and do a better job of rendering justice.

In the early 1980s Kentucky became the first state to use videotape to record the official trial record. Courts in other states have since followed the example, implementing videotape on a permanent or trial basis as the method of taking the record. Many courts favor the reliability and cost effectiveness of video.

Modern technology has provided video equipment that is inconspicuous and does not interfere with courtroom proceedings. One New Jersey court described its set-up as follows: "There are a number of cameras mounted on the walls, with microphones on each counsel table, one on the witness box and one on the bench. The cameras in the courtroom are voice activated. Anyone who speaks in the courtroom is not only sound recorded but videotaped as well." Furthermore, the court noted that at the end of court each day, each party in the proceedings may buy a videotape of the day's proceedings for $10.

As early as 1981, the United States Supreme Court noted that the cumbersome electronics previously required for camera coverage ". . . are less substantial factors today. . . ." (*Chandler v. Florida*) Today, it is possible to videotape court proceedings using one small, noiseless stationary camera located inconspicuously in the courtroom. No specialized lighting is necessary and existing microphone systems can usually be utilized. Modern electronic equipment is inexpensive and efficient, readily at hand to improve jurors' fact finding without any deleterious side effects.

Advantages

There may be much to be gained from using video transcripts. First, it is commonly thought that visual portrayals of events have a bigger cognitive impact than verbal renditions alone. A court reporter's reading back of portions of a trial transcript can have a numbing effect on juries, especially if a lengthy bit of testimony is involved. Rereading testimony, particularly large amounts, is largely ineffective and can be confusing. Allowing jurors to peruse and study the entire transcript might remedy this inadequacy, but in general jurors are not provided with a copy of the trial transcript. Transcripts that have been properly admitted into evidence, such as that of a deposition, or the transcript of a tape recorded conversation, may be allowed to accompany a jury into the deliberation room, but this is at the discretion of the judge. Jurors are thus often left to rely on their own recollections of the testimony, an inherently unreliable process.

On the other hand, watching witnesses spontaneously respond to lawyers' questions can be quite riveting; the human presence captured by the video draws the jurors' attention. This squares with common experience: almost all of us can recall times when our attention gravitated to a television set and distracted us from other activities. Televised presentations of testimony are simply more engrossing than second-hand oral regurgitations, no matter how accurate the latter may be. It is the promise of gaining and keeping the concentration of jurors that makes the video transcript so appealing.

Another advantage of the video transcript is that it enables the deliberating juror to be more proactive in figuring out the facts and applying the law. With proper cataloging of tapes, jurors have the ability to switch quickly to different parts of the trial to compare and contrast testimony. It is generally thought that jurors are in search of the "story" of events that is most credible, but the standard presentation of witnesses entailing cross-examination, redirect, and recross does anything but present facts in a logical, sequential order. The opportunity to move back and forth on a videotape can put jurors in control, permitting them to reconstruct the trial in a meaningful way that answers the legal questions put before them. Jurors can thus become purposive investigators of facts rather than somewhat helpless recipients of disordered information.

Video transcripts of the trial can enhance the forensic skills of jurors in yet another way. One of the most difficult judgments to be made by the jury is to figure out who is lying and who is telling the truth. Verdicts often hinge on choosing from among witnesses who contradict one another, but resolving "he said, she said" conflicts is no mean feat. The chance to view and re-view the testimony afforded by video transcripts enables jurors to rely on body language and voice inflections as they seek to distinguish truth-tellers from liars. Whereas the court reporter's affectless recitation of witnesses' words eliminates the revealing physical side to testimony, the videotape captures revealing bodily reactions and vocal intonations, which can provide clues about veracity. Seeing whether people sweat, fidget, wave their hands, tap their feet, or avoid their questioners' eyes, and hearing whether their voices are halting or forceful, provides a source of data that has a bearing on determining truthfulness. Guilty defendants may concoct excellent alibis, but how they relate their tale in open court can impeach their credibility. While such kinesics can themselves be misleading and should not be relied on exclusively, they are relevant information neatly captured by videotapes. As a supplement to logical consistency and external corroboration of testimony, they can help jurors figure out whether someone is telling the truth.

Potential Problems

There are problematic aspects to using videotranscripts. One concern is the handling of sidebar conferences. Obviously, the jury is not to be exposed to what is said at a sidebar, yet a record must be maintained of these conferences for purposes of appeal. Thus, it will be necessary to either use a different method of recording these conferences, perhaps a second camera, or the jury must be given an edited copy of the videotranscript, with all sidebar conferences edited out.

Likewise, "struck" testimony not to be heard by jurors will have to be expurgated. This is not a complex process, as modern video equipment allows for quick editing and accurate locating of previously recorded material. Indeed, it is probably less time-consuming than deleting from old-fashioned stenographer machines.

Beyond the logistical issues, there will be those who claim that replacing transcripts with videotapes and allowing juries the freedom to replay any portion of the trial is antithetical to sound judicial process. As noted, video transcripts will allow jurors to switch quickly between parts of the trial; this may give rise to images of a juror repeatedly playing the testimony of one particular witness over and over, or jumping from witness to witness, in a manner reminiscent of "channel-surfing." At worst, the videotranscript could be used as a source of entertainment, with jurors replaying their favorite "episodes" and thereby needlessly lengthening time spent in the jury room. However, studies of the deliberation process have shown that jurors take their mission very seriously and stick to the business at hand. It is unlikely that they would engage in such frivolity.

The use of technology always raises concerns, particularly among individuals who are not familiar with its use. Equipment failure is frequently cited, but mechanical fallibility is probably no greater than the chance of human errors that occur in trials. A videorecorder may break down, just as stenographers get sick or have trouble with their machines. Courts have always had to work around such happenings, and will continue to do so even with the increased use of technology. Backup copies of tapes will be necessary, in case of accidental erasure or other misfortune, but duplicating tapes is an inexpensive and easy process.

The presence of a camera in a courtroom, even if it is not for use by television, always raises questions about its possible adverse effects on witnesses and others involved in a trial. Fears arise that a camera will be distracting to witnesses, or will increase nervousness, or entice some to "play" to the camera. However, numerous studies have found that the impact of electronic coverage of courtroom proceedings is "virtually nil." California conducted a study on the effect of electronic coverage of court proceedings and found that there "was virtually no impact upon jurors, witnesses, judges, counsel or courtroom decorum when cameras were present during judicial proceedings. . . ."

Legality

Whether or not a jury can have portions of a trial transcript read to it during its deliberations is a decision left to the discretion of the judge. A number of United States courts of appeals have stated that such a decision will be reviewed only to assure there was no abuse of discretion. Judges must weigh the benefits of allowing the jury to rehear evidence with the risk of slowing down the trial and of selectively emphasizing particular evidence by allowing the jury to hear it more than once. The risk can be tempered by reminding the jury to consider the evidence as a whole. Courts have applied the same standards to the replaying of audio-taped testimony.

When the testimony the jury wishes to rehear is on videotape the standard is not so clear. The U.S. Court of Appeal for the Ninth Circuit has specifically addressed the issue of allowing a jury to replay videotaped testimony. In *U.S. v. Binder* (1985), the defendant appealed a conviction for child molestation. The children had been permitted to testify on video, on the agreement of the parties, to relieve their apprehensiveness about appearing in court. During deliberations, the jury requested the court to replay, in the jury room, the videotaped testimony of the children. Following argument in chambers, the court granted the jury's request. The defendant was not present during the proceedings in chambers or the playing of the tape in the jury room. During the replay of the tape, the jury asked to skip preliminary sections of the tape, and to selectively replay the tape. The court granted the first request and denied the second. Both these communications between the judge and jury occurred without consulting counsel or the defendant.

Noting that "the rereading of a witness' testimony is disfavored when it unduly emphasizes that testimony" the court of appeals held that "[a]llowing the jury to see and hear the children's videotaped testimony a second time in the jury room during deliberations unduly emphasized their testimony." Interestingly, the court noted that the experience of viewing videotaped testimony ". . . serves as the functional equivalent of [viewing] a live witness." Because of this, the court reasoned that such exposure would unduly emphasize the children's testimony over other evidence in the case.

In a later case, *U.S. v. Sacco* (1989), the ninth circuit clarified its views, noting that *Binder* did not establish a per se rule against replaying video-taped testimony, but that "[t]he decision to replay testimony is within the broad discretion of the trial judge to be exercised on a case-by-case basis." In *Sacco*, the ninth circuit held that the court had not erred in permitting the jury to replay the videotaped deposition of a prosecution witness after deliberation had begun.

It distinguished *Binder* in several ways, noting that there was ample physical evidence aside from the tape of the defendant's conduct, the credibility of the defendant was not at stake, and the videotaped testimony did not directly conflict with that of other defense witnesses. The court also noted that the tape was played in its entirety, in open court, with the defendant and his attorneys present. Thus, while federal law is inconclusive, there does seem to be an openness to allowing selective use of videotapes in the jury room.

State courts faced with the question of whether to allow a videotape to be given to a jury during deliberations have generally made a distinction between videotapes that are testimonial in nature, such as depositions or confessions, and those that are nontestimonial. Some states allow video-tapes that have been properly introduced into evidence and are determined to be nontestimonial to accompany the jury into the deliberation room at the judge's discretion. Other states allow nontestimonial video-tapes to be replayed at a jury's request, under controlled conditions in open court.

Some states will not allow videotapes that are determined to be testimonial to accompany a jury into the deliberation room, but may allow those tapes to be replayed in open court under controlled conditions, in response to a jury's request. First, however, the court must consider the exact nature of the jury's difficulty, if the testimony that will solve the jury's question can be isolated, and whether the probative value of the testimony outweighs the danger of undue emphasis. Other states do not allow testimonial videotapes to be reviewed by a jury under any conditions.

The courts are thus just beginning to grapple with the use of video-taped testimony by juries. At this time, in most jurisdictions, it is a decision left to the discretion of the judge, bound by the dictate that, presumably since the jury does not have exposure to all the testimony, the judge must guard against undue emphasis of particular testimony. With the inevitable increase of the use of videotape, courts are undoubtedly going to be forced to confront this issue again.

Resistance to Change

Videotaping a trial and providing the videotape to the jury for use during deliberations is a significant change in trial procedures. Certainly there will be resistance. Most notably, court reporters will fear the erosion of their profession. This is an understandable concern that encompasses matters far beyond the videotaping of trials. The pressures facing the court reporting profession are extreme, and videotaping trials is merely one of many technologies that threaten to make their profession obsolete. But saving jobs should not be the primary concern driving judicial policy making.

Perhaps the strongest resistance will come from judges themselves. Providing a jury with a videotape of the trial for unfettered use significantly diminishes the ability of the judge to control the jury's exposure to evidence. No longer will the judge be called upon to balance the benefits of allowing the jury to rehear evidence with the risk of selectively emphasizing particular evidence by allowing the jury to hear it more than once. The judge's opinion of what is important enough for the jury to hear again will be replaced by the jury's sentiments of what it needs to hear again in order to reach a sound verdict. Judicial discretion will be replaced by jurors' needs. Certainly this is a big change in the role of a judge. Some will be bitterly opposed to such a change, just as some resisted the imposition of sentencing guidelines. In either case, judges' self-interest in maintaining control should not be permitted to block seemingly useful reform.

Future Research

Neither the merits nor the pitfalls of videotaping have been tested empirically. Research would provide a sounder basis for assessment than the above speculations. Mock juries looking at videotapes of a simulated trial while deliberating can be compared with mock juries deprived of tapes but dealing with the identical simulated case to see which does a better job of getting the facts right. In addition, ex-jurors can be asked their opinion about whether videotapes would have been helpful and whether they felt handicapped in being unable to revisit the live testimony, and the opinions of practitioners, such as lawyers, judges, and court officers can be obtained. Finally, field experiments could be undertaken in which cases in a given jurisdiction are randomly assigned to a "tapes-permitted" and "tapes-prohibited" condition; both the verdicts and jurors' post-trial reactions could be compared.

Technological breakthroughs are revolutionizing American criminal justice. Police cars on patrol in many cities have computer links to the National Crime Information Center in Washington, enabling them to immediately determine if suspects have criminal records. Prosecutors have sophisticated management information systems allowing them to track cases through complex court systems; fingerprint identification is done electronically. DNA analysis is routinely done in crime labs to solve sex crimes. Prisons use sophisticated video surveillance to maintain order.

At the adjudication stage, many jurisdictions are now using teleconferencing to conduct arraignments in jail cells, which not only eliminates the cost of transporting prisoners to the courthouse but also helps protect their right to a prompt judicial hearing. A more ambitious endeavor is a "high tech" trial court in Manhattan that, among other things, allows jurors to view physical evidence closely through the use of special video-imaging tools and flat-screen monitors set up in the jury box.

Videotaped trial transcripts is a simpler idea, using now commonplace technology to make jury decision making more enlightened. Unlike many criminal justice reforms that seem to pit conflicting values like crime control and due process against each other, the use of video transcripts in the jury room involves no such agonizing choices, although there will be some technical and procedural difficulties to be overcome. By giving juries a better chance to get the facts right, more guilty people who would otherwise have been wrongfully acquitted will be convicted and more truly innocent people who would have been convicted will be exonerated. Videotaped trial transcripts may thus be a modest means of helping the much-maligned American jury and a powerful instrument in the pursuit of justice.

11

Merciful Juries
The Resilience of Jury Nullification

ALAN W. SCHEFLIN and JON M. VAN DYKE

The power of a jury to soften the harsh commands of the law and return a verdict that corresponds to the community's sense of moral justice has long been recognized.[1] Widely disputed, however, is whether jurors should be told they have this authority. Proponents have seen a right to a jury nullification instruction as an inalienable part of the heritage of democracy,[2] whereas opponents have argued that it is tantamount to anarchy.[3] Although in the past judges did instruct jurors about their role,[4] and judges in Maryland and Indiana still do,[5] most courts now refuse to explain honestly to jurors that they have the ultimate power to decide whether it is appropriate to apply the law to the facts presented to them.[6]

This judicial lack of candor has been periodically challenged; during the past few years a persistent grass roots movement has developed to promote the notion that our juries should be fully informed of their powers. Information about jury nullification has been spreading to an increasingly larger group of citizens and potential jurors. This movement serves to illustrate the resilience of the "jury nullification" concept and its link to fundamental notions of democracy.

This article discusses this new populist movement, analyzes some recent court decisions, reports some of the significant developments related to jury nullification during the past decade, and concludes that

Reprinted by permission of the *Washington and Lee Law Review* and the authors from vol. 48, no. 1 (winter, 1991), pp. 165–183.

our judicial system would be better served if judges instructed jurors of their true powers.[7]

What's in a Name?

Persuaders have long been aware of the significance of what something is called. For example, when President Ronald Reagan wanted financial and other support for the "Contras" who were fighting the Sandanista government in Nicaragua, he found it advisable to rename them "freedom fighters," which had a patriotic and positive tone, rather than "Contras," a term with negative connotations. Similarly, people who believe abortion is immoral have stopped calling themselves "anti-abortionists," opting instead for the more positive "pro-lifers."

Jury nullification debate similarly has been hampered by semantics. The term "jury nullification" is widely used by commentators and will also be used here by the authors, but it is not a term that accurately describes what is being advocated. The jury power at issue here is not a power to "nullify" statutes or precedents in order to create or substitute a new version of the law.[8] Instead, it is a power to "complete" or "perfect" the law by permitting the jury to exercise that one last touch of mercy where it may not be appropriate and just to apply the literal law to the actual facts.

According to Professor George Fletcher, the term "jury nullification"

> is unfortunate and misleading, because it suggests that when the jury votes its conscience, it is always engaged in an act of disrespect toward the law. The acquittal, supposedly, nullifies the law. In place of the law, it is said, the jury interposes its own moral judgment or political preferences.[9]

Fletcher rejects the view that jury nullification is an affront to the rule of law, and he provides a healthier and more accurate image:

> [T]he function of the jury as the ultimate authority on the law [is] not to "nullify" the instructions of the judge, but to complete the law, when necessary, by recognizing principles of justification that go beyond the written law. It would be better if we abandoned the phrase "jury nullification" and spoke instead of the jury's function in these cases of completing and perfecting the positive law recognized by the courts and the legislature.[10]

If "jury nullification" originally had been call "jury mercy," some of the emotional opposition might not have developed. Fletcher is correct to observe that this opposition has been based on a sense that when juries "nullify" they are acting *extra*-legally, outside the bounds of law. Under this view, the act of "nullification" appears to stand in opposition to the law.

Fletcher's perspective is more cordial. Jury nullification is not *extra-legal*; quite the opposite. Nullification is an integral part of the law itself, serving the unique and vital function of smoothing the friction between law and justice, and between the people and their laws. Nullification then becomes a tolerable, and occasionally beneficial, side-effect of the power to return general verdicts of acquittal not subject to judicial review. Take, for illustrative purposes, the case of Leroy Reed.

"Inside the Jury Room": *Wisconsin v. Leroy Reed* [11]

Leroy Reed, a sincere but dull-witted convict on parole, was arrested by his parole officer for illegal possession of a weapon. Reed enjoyed the television detective program "The Equalizer" and thought he might like to become a private investigator himself. Off went letters to mail-order detective companies for brochures, books, and courses. Some of the information he received stated he would need a gun. Reed obediently bought one, not fully realizing that he was violating a condition of his parole. No one in the courtroom doubted that Reed was only vaguely aware of what was going on and that he had not caused harm, was not likely to cause harm, and certainly did not have any intent to cause harm or violate rules. Punishing him would be like rebuking a five-year-old for not knowing algebra. Under the technical wording of the law, however, Reed was guilty. His defense lawyer pleaded for a jury nullification instruction, but the trial judge called it "an invitation to anarchy."

Once in the jury room, it was clear that the jurors were unanimous about two things: that Reed was guilty under the law, but morally was innocent. The just thing to do would be to acquit him. But the jurors had been told they had to follow the letter of the law. What should they do? During the spirited two-hour debate, some jurors argued that their oath required them to convict even though it meant doing an injustice. Others argued that they must follow what their consciences told them was the right thing to do in this case.

Both sides, however, seemed upset that the law had left them in this predicament. In the end, the conscience arguments converted the last remaining holdout. When he reluctantly retreated from his belief that the jury had no moral leeway, a verdict was reached.

Leroy Reed was acquitted. Some jurors went home having less respect for the legal system than when they had first reported for jury duty. Imagine how much worse they would have felt upon learning that an honest jury nullification instruction could have solved their dilemma and made them proud and respectful of the legal process. Other jurors, however, when finally told about jury nullification, did not condemn the failure to receive the instruction.[12]

The doctrine of jury nullification strikes a resonant chord in the community. Professors Hans and Vidmar report on the results of a 1979 Canadian survey "where people were asked whether jurors should be instructed that they are entitled to follow their own conscience instead of strictly applying the law if it will produce a just result."[13] The survey showed that

> over three-quarters of the respondents said yes. Furthermore, people who had actually served on a jury were even more supportive; 93% of them endorsed the idea of giving these instructions. (On the other hand, Canadian judges were overwhelmingly opposed: Fewer than five percent agreed that jurors should receive such instructions.)[14]

Despite its popular appeal, judges in the United States, like their Canadian counterparts, are not kind to arguments for nullification.

Judicial Decisions

The decisions concerning jury nullification during the past decade have been relatively predictable, with most courts acting defensively and negatively when litigants have requested a jury nullification instruction.[15] The nullification doctrine is raised by defendants with some regularity in cases of tax protests,[16] abortion protests,[17] antinuclear protests,[18] and euthanasia,[19] but it usually meets an icy judicial reception.

One particularly illuminating example is *State v. Ragland*,[20] decided by the New Jersey Supreme Court in 1986. The defendant, a prior convicted felon, was charged with four separate crimes all stemming from the same incident—(1) conspiracy to commit armed robbery, (2) unlawful possession of a weapon, (3) unlawful possession of a weapon without a permit, and (4) possession of a weapon by a convicted felon. The trial court severed the last charge "to avoid the inevitable prejudice in the trial of the other charges that would be caused by introducing defendant's prior felony conviction, an essential element in the severed charge."[21]

After the jurors found the defendant guilty of the first three charges, the trial judge gave the jury the following instruction and asked them to give their verdict on the fourth charge:

> If you find that the defendant, Gregory Ragland, was previously convicted for the crime of robbery and that he was in possession of a sawed-off shotgun, *as you have indicated* . . . then you *must* find him guilty as charged by this Court.[22]

The defendant appealed on the ground that this instruction took from the jurors their right to reach an independent verdict and, indeed, constituted a ''directed verdict'' from the judge.

All seven justices on the New Jersey court agreed that the above instruction was improper because the instruction included the ''as you have indicated'' phrase. The court reasoned that the use of this phrase denied the jury the power to evaluate the evidence anew to determine whether the prosecutor had proved beyond a reasonable doubt that the defendant had violated the fourth charge.

The justices divided sharply, however, on whether the use of the word ''must'' in this charge was proper, with four concluding that it was and three arguing that it was not. The three judges in the minority argued that the use of language such as ''must'' should be discontinued ''because of its potential to be interpreted in a manner that compromises jury independence and blurs the accepted dichotomy between judge and jury.''[23]

The majority opinion of Chief Justice Wilentz acknowledged that precedents are divided on this issue,[24] but argued in strongly emotional language that ''must'' is an appropriate word to use because New Jersey juries do not have a '''right' to announce a verdict of acquittal despite its determination of guilt.''[25] Chief Justice Wilentz argued that no evidence exists that jury nullification serves society well,[26] that an instruction to jurors about their power ''would confuse any conscientious citizen''[27] and produce ''total arbitrariness''[28] and ''cynicism,''[29] and that a system that included a jury nullification instruction would be ''almost ludicrous.''[30]

Although *Ragland* remains the judicial norm, a decision that strikes a dramatically different tone is *Stevenson v. State*,[31] in which the Maryland Court of Appeals reaffirmed the constitutionality of Article 23 of the Maryland Declaration of Rights, which states that:

> In the trial of all criminal cases, the Jury shall be the Judges of Law, as well as of fact, except that the Court may pass upon the sufficiency of the evidence to sustain a conviction.[32]

The majority's decision in this case also helps explain how this provision is to be interpreted and applied.

Dorothy Lou Stevenson was convicted by a jury of murdering her husband by pouring gasoline on him while he slept and then igniting the gas with a match. At the beginning of the trial, the trial judge explained to the jurors the unique constitutional role that juries play in Maryland and, pursuant to Article 23, informed them that:

> Under the Constitution of Maryland, [you are] the judge of the law as well as of the facts. Therefore, anything which I may say about

> the law, including any instructions which I may give you, is merely
> advisory and you are not in any way bound by it.[33]

After the evidence was presented, the judge did not again make such a statement, but instead gave instructions on the issues of law and "couched all of his remarks in mandatory language."[34] Mrs. Stevenson argued that the preliminary instruction violated her right to due process under the Fourteenth Amendment of the United States Constitution and specifically infringed upon her privilege against self-incrimination, the presumption of innocence, and the requirement of proof beyond a reasonable doubt.[35]

The majority opinion rejected these arguments and reaffirmed the propriety of issuing the preliminary instruction under Article 23. It also clarified exactly what the jury's power includes and thus responds to the fears expressed by Chief Justice Wilentz in New Jersey. The Maryland jury's role under Article 23 "is confined 'to *resolv[ing] conflicting inter-pretations of the law [of the crime]* and to decid[ing] whether th[at] law should be applied in dubious factual situations,' *and nothing more.*"[36]

The Maryland jury's responsibility thus is to determine whether it is equitable and just to apply the law defining a crime to the facts presented to it. The jury has no role in determining whether evidence should be admitted, whether witnesses are competent to testify, whether the court has jurisdiction, or whether the statutes are constitutional.[37] In summary, the Maryland Court of Appeals stated:

> Implicit in the decisions of this Court limiting the jury's judicial role to the "law of the crime" is a recognition that all other legal issues are for the judge alone to decide.
>
> Because of this division of the law-judging function between judge and jury, it is incumbent upon a trial judge to carefully delineate for the jury the following dichotomy: (i) that the jury, under Article 23, is the final arbiter of disputes as to the substantive "law of the crime," as well as the "legal effect of the evidence," and that any comments by the judge concerning these matters are advisory only; and (ii) that, by virtue of this same constitutional provision, all other aspects of law (e.g., the burden of proof, the requirement of unanimity, the validity of a statute) are beyond the jury's pale, and that the judge's comments on these matters are binding upon that body. In other words, the jury should not be informed that all of the court's instructions are merely advisory; rather only that portion of the charge addressed to the former areas of "law" may be regarded as nonbinding by it, and it is only these aspects of the "law" which counsel may dispute in their respective arguments to the jury. On the other hand, the jury should be informed that the judge's charge with regard to any other legal matter is binding and may not be disregarded by it.[38]

In 1981, the Maryland Court of Appeals addressed this matter once again and said that the jury's role in evaluating the law of the crime was limited to those instances where the law is unclear or in dispute: "[I]n those circumstances where there is no dispute nor a sound basis for a dispute as to the law of the crime, the court's instructions are binding on the jury and counsel as well."[39]

A subsequent case that illustrates the leeway still given to a jury in Maryland is *Mack v. State.*[40] The defendant in *Mack* was charged with assault and battery and use of a handgun in the commission of a crime of violence. The trial court instructed the jurors that they had to find the defendant guilty of a crime of violence (assault and battery) in order to find him guilty of the second crime, which required a violent crime as a prerequisite. The trial judge also informed the jury that this instruction was binding.[41] Nonetheless, the jury found the defendant not guilty on the first charge and guilty on the second. When the defendant challenged this decision as inconsistent with the "binding" instructions, the trial judge ruled "that the jury's verdict was 'in all probability, a compromise verdict' that could stand."[42] The Court of Appeals accepted this illogical result as within the jury's power and affirmed the verdict.

An Empirical Study

The general judicial hostility to nullification ignores the popular sentiment for the doctrine and does not seem to be influenced by the data suggesting that a nullification instruction would not spawn "runaway" juries.

It is extremely difficult to develop definitive studies that illustrate how a jury nullification instruction affects a jury's deliberation, but Professor Irwin A. Horowitz of the University of Toledo Department of Psychology attempted such a study recently.[43] Professor Horowitz sought to study "whether the jury functioned differently if it was given nullification instructions; whether the impact of such instructions depended on the precise form in which they were given; and whether their impact also depended on the type of case in which they were given."[44]

Horowitz assembled forty-five six-person juries, drawing names from the official jury pool used in Toledo, Ohio.[45] He then chose three different factual situations and asked fifteen of the juries to evaluate each of three situations presented with professionally-acted audio tapes and slides. The cases involved (1) the murder of a grocer during a robbery attempt, (2) the killing of a pedestrian by a drunk college student driving in a foggy night, and (3) the "mercy" killing of a terminally ill and suffering cancer patient by a sympathetic nurse who had the consent of the patient and her family.

The fifteen juries were in turn broken into groups of five and each group was given one of three jury instructions: (a) a standard instruction taken from the Ohio Pattern Juror Instructions, which does not make any reference to nullification; (b) the Maryland Instruction, which contains nullification language;[46] and (c) what Professor Horowitz characterizes as a "radical" nullification instruction, taken from one of the present authors' earlier articles.[47] The result was that all fifteen of the juries convicted the alleged murderer of the grocer despite the three different instructions they received, but variations occurred in their evaluations of the other two fact situations. Two of the five juries that received the "standard" and "Maryland" instructions acquitted the drunk college student but *none* of those receiving the "radical" instruction reached a verdict of acquittal. And in the "mercy" killing case, one of the five "standard" juries acquitted the nurse, two of the "Maryland" juries acquitted, and *four* of the "radical" juries acquitted.[48]

Although the sample Horowitz used is small and more work clearly is required, this study does show that juries told that they have power are more likely to exercise it and to reach results that—at least in these cases—appear to be more just and equitable.[49]

From the Judicial to the Political Arena

The controversy over the propriety of a jury nullification instruction lay dormant for most of this century until resurrected in the 1960s as part of the defense strategy in anti-Vietnam War demonstration trials.[50] As mentioned above, it did not meet with a warm judicial reception, and most judges still refuse to instruct juries honestly about their nullification power. Such refusal in the 1960s did not significantly undermine the legitimacy of the judiciary because few people knew about nullification. This is no longer true in the 1990s. The jury nullification movement is more active now than at any previous period. Journalists have noted that juries have appeared to invoke their nullification power in many prominent recent cases.[51] More significantly, frustration with the judicial system, and in particular the perception that judges are dishonest with juries, has caused proponents of jury nullification to seek satisfaction from two more hospitable forums—voters and legislators.

Voters and Legislators

Debate about jury nullification raises fundamental, and unanswered, questions about sovereignty in a constitutional democracy. It was therefore natural that nullification proponents would seek out the two major forums for lawmaking, the popular vote and legislation.

In the summer of 1989, Larry Dodge, a Montana businessman, joined with his friend Don Doig to found the Fully Informed Jury Association (FIJA). This "national nonprofit nonpartisan group [is] dedicated to jurors being fully informed of their rights."[52] Within eighteen months, the organization had jury rights lobbyists in thirty-five states.[53]

FIJA sponsored the first Bill of Jury Rights Conference in November 1990. The purpose of the gathering was to plan strategy to lobby legislators to enact "fully informed jury" statutes, and to urge voters to pass initiatives, referenda, or constitutional amendments to protect the heritage of the jury's right of nullification.[54] The Conference concluded with a ceremony at the federal courthouse to kickoff a national Jury Rights Campaign.

Because public sentiment supports jury nullification,[55] FIJA's appeal spans the political and social spectrum:

> Conservatives and constitutionalists, liberals and progressives, libertarians, populists, greens, gun owners, peace groups, taxpayer rights groups, home schoolers, alternative medicine practitioners, drug decriminalization groups, criminal trial lawyers, seat belt and helmet law activists, environmentalists, women's groups, anti-nuclear groups, ethnic minorities, . . . and judges (yes, some judges are sympathetic).[56]

As of January 1991, FIJA had successfully persuaded legislators to introduce bills in the state legislatures of Alaska, Arizona, Georgia, Louisiana, Massachusetts, New York, Oklahoma, Tennessee, and Wyoming.[57]

These bills differ widely in language. One of the more interesting options is the Massachusetts bill, introduced by Senator Robert L. Hedlund,[58] which seeks to soften the confrontation between the legislature and the judiciary. Senator Hedlund has strong feelings about its importance: "I see this bill as supporting one of the two pillars of freedom—the right to a fully informed jury. The other pillar is the right to vote."[59] If passed, the bill will amend the handbook all potential trial jurors receive and would add a new segment to the video presentation they watch. Senator Hedlund's bill states:

> In informing the jurors of the nature and extent of their duties and responsibilities . . . the handbook shall inform the jurors that in all cases they have the historical, constitutional, and natural right to judge not only the liability, guilt, or innocence of the defendant(s) under the law as charged, but to exercise their conscience in doing so and that, if they determine according to their conscience that the law as charged by the judge is unjust or wrongly applied to the defendant(s), it is their obligation, right, and duty to judge according to their conscience.

By its wording, the bill would apply both to civil and criminal jury trials. Application of jury nullification in civil cases is less pressing an issue because the judge always maintains the authority to alter or reject the verdict. Thus, a jury that votes its conscience can be judicially reversed. Discussions of jury nullification in the context of civil cases thus tend to be rare.[60]

Senator Hedlund's bill contains one great virtue and one great vice. Its virtue is that it attempts to avoid a direct confrontation with judges and therefore does not order them to instruct juries about their nullification power. The jurors will receive accurate information from their handbook, and judges will not be compelled to give it to them.[61]

The one great vice in the bill is that it makes a statement of jury power that is far too broad. Under its terms, for example, a jury could *convict* on the basis of conscience if the jurors feel the law is too soft or lenient. The bill needs to be amended to remove that impression. Language must be added to convey to the jury that it may exercise its conscience or "mercy" power only for leniency. No defendant may be judged by a standard harsher than the law on the books. *Ex post facto* convictions are unacceptable.

Another illustration of the breadth of the bill's language is to be found in the sentence that permits jurors to exercise conscience if the law as charged by the judge "is unjust or wrongly applied" to the defendant(s). It would be better to say that jurors, in the exercise of their consciences, "may acquit the defendant if the application of the law, as given by the judge, would result in an unjust conviction."

Having jurors speculate on the "justness" of a law is to distract them from their central task of applying the facts to the law in that particular case. If a law is unjust, its application in any case is unjust, and voters, legislators, or judges should remove it from the books. Juries do not have this power. Their power is limited to refusing to apply the law in the single case presented to them, and then only when following the technical mandate of the law would offend the community's sense of justice.

Senator Hedlund's bill undoubtedly will undergo language changes as it moves through the legislative process. In rewritten form, it may serve as a model for laws that truly make our nation a "government of the people, by the people and for the people."[62]

Legislation has not been the only path to jury nullification law reform. FIJA has been busy circulating petitions for ballot initiatives in many states, including Arkansas, California, Colorado, Florida, Idaho, Montana, Utah, and Washington. In some of these states, amendments to the state constitutions are sought. By the end of 1991, FIJA hopes to have electoral campaigns in all fifty states.

One of the most elaborate jury nullification provisions appeared as an initiative to amend the Oregon Constitution:[63]

> It is the natural right of every citizen of the state of Oregon, when serving on a criminal-trial jury, to judge both the law and the facts pertaining to the case before the jury, in order to determine whether justice will be served by applying the law to the defendant. It is mandatory that all jurors be informed of this right. Before the jury hears a case, and again before jury deliberation begins, the court shall inform the jurors of their rights in these words: "As jurors, your first responsibility is to decide whether the prosecution has proven beyond reasonable doubt every element of the criminal charge. If you decide that the prosecution has proven beyond reasonable doubt every element of the criminal charge but that you cannot in good conscience support a guilty verdict, you are not required to do so. To reach a verdict which you believe is just, each of you has the right to consider to what extent the defendant's actions have actually caused harm or otherwise violated your sense of right and wrong. If you believe justice requires it, you may also judge both the merits of the law under which the defendant has been charged and the wisdom of applying that law to the defendant. Accordingly, for each charge against the defendant, even if review of the evidence strictly in terms of the law would indicate a guilty verdict, you have the right to find the defendant not guilty. The court cautions that with the exercise of this right comes the full moral responsibility for the verdict you bring in." As part of their oath, the jurors shall affirm that they understand the information concerning their rights which this section requires the court to give them, and that no party to the trial may be prevented from encouraging jurors to exercise this right. For the jurors to be so informed is declared to be part of the defendant's fundamental right to trial by jury, and failure to conduct any criminal trial in accordance with this section shall not constitute harmless error, and shall be grounds for a mistrial. No potential juror may be disqualified from serving on a jury because he or she expresses willingness to judge the law or its application, or to vote according to his or her conscience.

As the Oregon Supreme Court succinctly stated, this initiative, if adopted, "would enshrine in the Oregon Constitution the concept of 'jury nullification.'"[64] The Court expressed hostility toward the initiative,[65] but did not strike it down.

Juridical Dishonesty

Essential to the success of the grass roots jury nullification movement is publicity. People need to be informed about the right to fully informed juries. Jury nullification makes news in most major criminal trials where a clash of values attracts public attention. Articles about jury nullification now appear in newspapers and magazines with great frequency. When the Public Broadcast System (PBS) aired "Inside the Jury Room," an estimated twenty-five million viewers saw the program.[66] Jury nullification is getting more press coverage than ever before. Millions of people are learning what the judges refuse to tell them.

Contacting Potential Jurors

Press coverage has the advantage of reaching many people, but it does so at a time in their lives when the jury nullification issue is not very pressing. For potential jurors, however, information about jury nullification may have a more direct impact on the juror's deliberations.

On January 25, 1990, the *San Diego Reader* published a three-quarter page advertisement[67] with the following headline:

ATTENTION JURORS & FUTURE JURORS
You Can Legally Acquit Anti-Abortion
"Trespassers" Even If They're "Guilty"

The advertisement began by saying "[s]uppose you're on the jury in the trial of pro-life 'rescuers' who blocked the entrances to an abortion facility. The judge will probably tell you it makes no difference whether you agree with their actions. . . . He's Not Telling the Truth." The text went on to praise a Philadelphia jury that had used its "common-law right to 'nullify'" a trespass law.

The timing of the appearance of the advertisement was well planned. Trials were beginning for Operation Rescue defendants accused of trespass and other offenses at the site of a medical clinic. That the advertisement was designed to influence jury verdicts cannot be in doubt. Indeed, the publisher of *The Reader* was one of the defendants and his lawyer told the press that he was aware the advertisement would be run.[68]

Three weeks before the San Diego advertisement appeared, leaflets were distributed outside the courthouse in El Cajon, California. The demonstrators stopped when warned by the marshal that they could be arrested for felony jury-tampering. To combat the information being handed out, judges gave jurors special instructions to disregard the leaflets.

California was not the first location where such leaflets appeared. Operation Rescue adherents in Jackson, Mississippi, distributed leaflets urging jurors to "nullify every rule or 'law' that is not in accordance with the principles of Natural, God-given, Common, or Constitutional Law."[69]

Many of these leaflets present a distorted and incorrect discussion of nullification. Potential jurors who read them may taint the deliberations of actual juries with misinformation. Only an accurate jury nullification instruction from the judge can eliminate this problem.

In fact, many of the pamphlets and leaflets go further than presenting misinformation. They suggest or hint that potential jurors should deceive judges.

Should Jurors Be Honest with Judges?

Sir Walter Scott wrote the much quoted phrase, "Oh! what a tangled web we weave [w]hen first we practise to deceive!"[70] Proponents of jury nullification have written about the lack of candor involved when the judge fails to tell the jury about nullification. This dishonesty now has spawned a more virulent deception in the reverse direction: jurors lying to judges.

In 1988, the authors received a four-page pamphlet entitled "The Informed Juror." Written by Paul deParrie and sponsored by an Oregon group called Advocates for Life, the pamphlet gives a very brief description of nullification before calling on conservatives, "especially Christians," to refrain from showing during voir dire that they have strong feelings about abortion. The pamphlet's author advises:

> During jury selection it may be wise to refrain from elaborating on answers to questions asked by attorneys. Any appearance of being educated, involved or opinionated may be sufficient cause to be rejected, thus being removed from the opportunity to be a watchman for abuses by the executive and judicial departments of government. This does not mean that you would be untruthful in answering questions. Simply keep your answers brief if you would like to improve your chances of serving on a jury.

Not all anti-abortion activists have been content with silence or brevity. For some, outright deception appears justified. One such illustration surfaced in San Diego where a published advertisement stopped just short of advocating lying.[71] Noting that "before you even get on the jury, they may ask you whether you know about your right to 'nullify,'" the advertisement then offered a suggested response:

> *Don't believe a word they say. . . .*
> *Here's How to Do It*
> It's easy. The most important rule is, *don't let the judge and prosecutor know that you know about this right.*
> It is unjust and illegal for them to deny you this right. So, if you have to, it's perfectly all right for you to make a "mental reservation."

> Give them the same answer you would have given if you were
> hiding fugitive slaves in 1850 and the 'slave catchers' asked if you
> had runaways in your attic. Or if you were hiding Jews from the Nazis
> in Germany.

This recommendation for "pious dishonesty" was then followed by
two other suggestions:

> The second rule is, *educate the other jurors* about jury nullification
> and, if possible, persuade them to vote "not guilty."
> The third rule is *stick to your guns.* Don't let other jurors make
> you change your position.

Millions of potential jurors may be exposed to similar advertisements,
leaflets, or pamphlets. That means that countless juries may contain
members who have concealed their awareness of nullification, who hold
seriously incorrect views about it, and who intend to "educate" the other
jurors to rebuff laws they do not like.

When jury nullification was a judicial secret, it was easier to refuse
to give jury nullification instructions.[72] Such refusal today, however,
may seriously compromise the justice of our jury verdicts.

Should Judges Be Honest with Jurors?

What should the judge do about the fact that jurors may know something
about nullification, accurate or not? Suppose, for example, we have a
panel of potential jurors in a criminal case that has attracted media
attention. Some of these jurors have seen literature about a right to nullify
laws. What they read contained many errors. The defense lawyer or
prosecutor may request to ask questions about nullification on voir dire.
Should the lawyers be allowed to voir dire about nullification? If not,
these jurors will contaminate the jury deliberations. If so, information
about nullification will be made public. The judge may decide to give
an antinullification instruction, but this, of course, will reinforce what
the literature said would happen and would not correct any errors about
the doctrine.

Judicial failure to give honest and correct instructions on nullification
may thus directly contribute to contamination of jury deliberations. It
is a sad irony that while judges continue to refuse to give accurate jury
nullification instructions, they in fact are creating the anarchy they seek
to avoid.

Conclusion

The renewed grass roots interest in a "fully informed jury" reinforces
our earlier views that judges should give jurors an accurate and honest

instruction about the jury's role and power. The instruction should state that the judge must properly make rulings on procedural matters and will be guiding the trial so that all constitutional protections are provided to the litigants. The instruction should also say that the jury does not have the power to create new statutes or evaluate the constitutionality of the statutes before them. The jury should be encouraged to pay respectful attention to the acts of the legislature which, after all, reflect the democratic wishes of the community's majority. But the jurors should also be told that their function is to represent the community in this trial and that their ultimate responsibility is to determine the facts that occurred and to evaluate whether applying the law to these facts will produce, in the eyes of the community, a just and equitable verdict.

This type of honest instruction would reinforce our nation's commitment to a government where the people are sovereign, and it would serve to bring the people and their laws together in closer harmony.

Endnotes

[1] See, e.g., *Lessard v. State*, 719 P.2d 227, 231 (Wyo. 1986) (citing numerous other cases).

The topic of "jury nullification" has been discussed in detail by the authors in their previous writings: J. Van Dyke, *Jury Selection Procedures: Our Uncertain Commitment to Representative Panels* 225-51 (1977); Scheflin & Van Dyke, "Jury Nullification: The Contours of a Controversy," 43:4 *Law & Contemp. Prob.* 51 (1980); Scheflin, "Jury Nullification: The Right to Say No," 45 *So. Cal. L. Rev.* 168 (1972); Van Dyke, "The Jury as a Political Institution," 16 *Cath. Law.* 224 (1970); Van Dyke, 3 *The Center Mag.* 17 (No. 2, March-April 1970).

[2] Among those advocating giving jurors an honest instruction about their powers, in addition to the authors in the articles cited supra in note 1 are: Timko, "Jury Nullification Thru the Initiative Process," in *Jury Nullification* Vol. 1 (1987); Becker, "Jury Nullification: Can A Jury Be Trusted?," 16 *Trial* 41 (Oct. 1980); Freeman, "Why Not A Jury Nullification Statute Here Too?," 131 *New L.J.* 304 (March 19, 1981); Kaufman, "The Right of Self Representation and the Power of Jury Nullification," 28 *Case W. Res. L. Rev.* 269 (1978); Kunstler, "Jury Nullification in Conscience Cases," 10 *Va. J. Int'l L.* 71 (1969); McCall, "Sentencing By Death Qualified Juries and the Right to Jury Nullification," 22 *Harv. J. on Legis.* 289 (1985); Osterman, "Should Jurors Be Told They Can Refuse To Enforce The Law?: Law Must Respect Consciences," 72 *A.B.A.J.* 36 (March 1986); Sax, "Conscience and Anarchy: The Prosecution of War Resisters," 57 *Yale Rev.* 481 (1968); Schultz, "Will 'Jury Nullification' Save Ollie North?," 11 *Legal Times* 18 (March 6, 1989); Note, "Jury Nullification and Jury-Control Procedures," 65 *N.Y.U.L. Rev.* 825 (1990); Note, "Laws That Are Made to Be Broken: Adjusting for Anticipated Noncompliance," 75 *Mich. L. Rev.* 687 (1977); Note, "The Jury's Role Under the Indiana Constitution," 52 *Indiana L.J.* 793 (1977); Note, "Toward Principles of Jury Equity," 83 *Yale L.J.* 1023 (1974); Note, "Jury Nullification: The Forgotten Right," 7 *New Eng. L. Rev.* 105 (1971).

Articles discussing jury nullification or the "dispensing power" of juries which provide support for nullification but do not reach an explicit conclusion on whether an instruction should be given include: Barkan, "Jury Nullification in Political Trials," 31 *Soc. Prob.* 28 (Oct. 1983); Howe, "Juries As Judges of Criminal Law," 52 *Harv. L. Rev.* 582 (1939); Jacobsohn, "A Right to Disagree: Judge, Juries, and the Administration of Criminal Justice in Maryland," 1976 *Wash. U. L. Q.* 571; Kamins, "Jury Nullification—A Rarity in Criminal-Law Practice," 194 *N.Y.L.J.* 1 (Aug. 20, 1985); Levine, "The Legislative Role of Juries," 1984 *A.B.F. Res. J.* 605; Myers, "Rule Departures and Making Law: Juries and Their Verdicts," 13 *Law & Soc. Rev.* 781 (1979); Pacelle, "Sanctuary Jurors' Dilemma: Law or Justice?," 8 *Am. Law.* 95 (Sept. 1986).

3 Recent works arguing that such an instruction should not be given to the jurors include: M. Kadish & S. Kadish, *Discretion to Disobey: A Study of Lawful Departures from Legal Rules* (1973); Allen, "Editorial: Nihilism at Santa Barbara," 57 *A.B.A.J.* 999 (Oct. 1971); Christie, "Lawful Departures from Legal Rules: 'Jury Nullification' and Legitimated Disobedience," 62 *Cal. L. Rev.* 1289 (1974); Goldsmith, "Jury Nullification and the Rule of Law," 17 *The Colo. Law.* 2151 (1988); Kadish & Kadish, "On Justified Rule Departures by Officials," 59 *Cal. L. Rev.* 905 (1971); Marshall, "Should Jurors Be Told They Can Refuse To Enforce The Law?: Jurors Must Respect The Law," 72 *A.B.A.J.* 36 (March 1986); McBride, "The Jury is Not a Political Institution," 11 *Judge's J.* 37 (April 1972); Scott, "Jury Nullification: An Historical Perspective on a Modern Debate," 91 *W. Va. L. Rev.* 389 (1989); Simson, "Jury Nullification in the American System: A Skeptical View," 54 *Tex. L. Rev.* 488 (1976); Tavris, "The Law of An Unwritten Law: A Common Sense View of Jury Nullification," 11 *West St. L. Rev.* 97 (Fall 1983); Note, "Jury Nullification in Historical Perspective: Massachusetts as a Case Study," 12 *Suffolk U.L. Rev.* 968 (1978); Comment, "Jury Nullification and the Pro Se Defense: The Impact of *Dougherty v. United States*," 21 *U. Kan. L. Rev.* 47 (1972).

4 See Scheflin & Van Dyke, supra note 1, at 56–63.

5 Id. at 79–85.

6 Id. at 59–68.

7 We will not revisit the major arguments rejecting or supporting nullification. These may be found in our prior work, see supra note 1, and in the work of others, see supra notes 2 and 3. Nor will we discuss two evolving questions: the application of jury nullification in civil trials, and the expansion of jury powers to influence the admission of evidence. Our focus in this article is on the emerging politics of the nullification debate as it shifts from the courthouse to the statehouse and ballot box.

8 Some opponents of jury nullification have argued that juries will have the power to "ignore" or "disregard the law," or to return a verdict that may "fly in the face of both the evidence and the law." Indeed, the more radical proponents like jury nullification for just this reason. But this rhetoric does nullification a disservice. Lawless "Rambo" juries have no place in the legal system; the supremacy of the rule of law is essential in a constitutional democracy. Juries should not act as quasilegislators deciding which laws to eliminate or revise.

9 G. Fletcher, *A Crime of Self-Defense: Bernhard Goetz and the Law on Trial* 155 (1988). The quote continues: "There are some who defend this residual power in juries as the highest expression of democracy and community control over the machinery of the state, and others who decry the same power as an invitation to anarchy." Id.

10 Id.

11 The story of Leroy Reed is told in a remarkable television documentary where, for the first time, television cameras were allowed to film an actual jury deliberating to verdict. "Inside the Jury Room" (1986) was a segment of the PBS show "Frontline." The film was written and produced by Alan M. Levin and Stephen J. Herzberg.

12 Law Professor Stephen J. Herzberg, co-producer of "Inside The Jury Room," met with the jurors immediately after the trial. He explained jury nullification to them and said

that they did have the right to return an acquittal. It was a highly emotional session. Many of the jurors were crying. Herzberg, "Inside the Jury Room," presented at the Bill of Jury Rights Conference, St. Louis, Missouri (No. 10, 1990). The authors wish to thank Franklin M. Nugent for an audiotape of Professor Herzberg's talk. The authors also wish to thank Professor Herzberg for supplying us with additional information about the case and with a videotape of his postverdict discussions with the jurors and the judge.

A case in which the failure to give a nullification instruction may have produced a conviction is reported in Pacelle, supra note 2, at 95. According to Pacelle, many of the jurors are still suffering from their experience.

[13] V. Hans & N. Vidmar, *Judging the Jury* 158 (1986), (citing Doob, "Public's View of Criminal Jury Trial," and Doob, "Canadian Trial Judges' View of the Criminal Jury Trial," in *Law Reform Commission of Canada Studies on the Jury* (1979)).

[14] V. Hans & N. Vidmar, supra note 13, at 158.

[15] See, e.g., *Medley v. Commonwealth*, 704 S.W.2d 190 (Ky. 1985); *People v. St. Cyr*, 341 N.W.2d 533 (Mich. App. 1983); *State v. Perkins*, 353 N.W.2d 557 (Minn. 1984); *State v. Maloney*, 490 A.2d 772 (N.H. 1985); *State v. Champa*, 494 A.2d 102 (R.I. 1985).

[16] See generally *United States v. Krzyske*, 836 F.2d 1013 (6th Cir. 1988); *United States v. Wiley*, 503 F.2d 106 (8th Cir. 1974).

In *United States v. Ogle*, 613 F.2d 233, 236 (10th Cir. 1980), Ogle, a tax protester, was convicted of trying to influence potential jurors by supplying them with a "Handbook for Jurors." The Handbook contained an inaccurate description of jury nullification ("it is unnecessary for jurors to follow the law of the land where they conceive of the law being contrary to their concepts of morals").

[17] See, e.g., *United States v. Anderson*, 716 F.2d 446 (7th Cir. 1983).

[18] See, e.g., *State v. Champa*, 494 A.2d 102 (R.I. 1985).

[19] See S. Kassin & L. Wrightsman, *The American Jury On Trial: Psychological Perspectives* 157–58 (1988). Kassin and Wrightsman describe two euthanasia cases. In the first, the jury acquitted. In the second, the jury convicted because, as one juror explained, "We had no choice. The law does not allow for sympathy." Id. at 158.

In their book *Judging the Jury*, supra note 13, professors Hans and Vidmar observe that euthanasia cases demonstrate the unique value served by jury nullification. In these cases, "the legal authorities feel compelled to bring charges, but they rely on the jury's sense of fairness to acquit the defendant." Id. at 158.

[20] 105 N.J. 189, 519 A.2d 1361 (1986).

[21] *State v. Ragland*, 105 N.J. 189, 192, 519 A.2d 1361, 1362 (1986).

[22] Id. (emphasis added).

[23] Id. at 220, 519 A.2d at 1377 (Handler, J., concurring in part and dissenting in part). The dissenting judges did not, however, advocate giving a jury nullification instruction. Id. at 221, 519 A.2d at 1378.

[24] Id. at 198–99, 519 A.2d at 1365–66. One decision subsequent to *Ragland* that strikes a very different tone and criticizes a trial judge for confining a jury too narrowly is *Cheek v. United States*, 59 U.S.L.W. 4049 (1991). The jury indicated that it felt constrained by "the narrow and hard expression" of the law as given by the judge, id. at 4051 n.6, and the United States Supreme Court agreed that the instruction was too strict, reversing and remanding for a new trial.

[25] Id. at 204, 519 A.2d at 1369.

[26] Id. at 206, 519 A.2d at 1370.

[27] Id. at 208, 519 A.2d at 1371.

[28] Id. at 210, 519 A.2d at 1372.

[29] Id. at 209, 519 A.2d at 1371.

[30] Id. at 210, 519 A.2d at 1372.

[31] 289 Md. 167, 423 A.2d 558 (1980). The majority opinion was written by Judge Digges for himself and three other judges. Judges Eldridge and Davidson dissented, arguing that Article 23 of the Maryland Declaration of Rights violates the 14th Amendment of the United States Constitution. Id. at 194, 423 A.2d at 572. Judge Cole also dissented with regard to the specific manner in which the instructions were given in this case, reserving the question of the status of Article 23 under the United States Constitution. Id. at 204, 423 A.2d at 577.

[32] *Md. Const. Declaration of Rights* art. 23.

[33] *Stevenson v. State*, 289 Md. 167, 171, 423 A.2d 558, 560 (1980).

[34] Id. at 171, 423 A.2d at 561.

[35] Id. at 188, 423 A.2d at 569.

[36] Id. at 179, 423 A.2d at 564 (emphasis in original) (quoting from *Dillon v. State*, 277 Md. 571, 581, 357 A.2d 360, 367 (1976) (emphasis in original)).

[37] Id. at 178, 423 A.2d at 564.

[38] Id. at 179–80, 423 A.2d at 565.

[39] *Montgomery v. State*, 292 Md. 84, 89, 437 A.2d 654, 657 (1981). In *Allnutt v. State*, the Maryland Court of Special Appeals noted that:

> Instances of dispute of the law of the crime are an endangered species rapidly approaching extinction. Once an appellate court has ruled on the "law of the crime," the matter then becomes settled law, and thereafter the jury is no longer the judge of the law with respect to that particular matter. Consequently, disputes of the law of the crime will decrease in number with each successive appellate ruling.

59 Md. App. 694, 703, 478 A.2d 321, 325 (1984).

[40] 300 Md. 583, 479 A.2d 1344 (1984).

[41] *Mack v. State*, 300 Md. 583, 600, 479 A.2d 1344, 1352 (1984).

[42] Id.

[43] See Horowitz, "The Effect of Jury Nullification Instruction on Verdicts & Jury Functioning in Criminal Trials," 9 *Law & Hum. Behav.* 25 (1985); Horowitz, "Jury Nullification: The Impact of Judicial Instructions, Arguments, and Challenges on Jury Decision Making," 12 *Law & Hum. Behav.* 439 (1988).

[44] V. Hans & N. Vidmar, supra note 13, at 159 (describing studies of Professor Irvin Horowitz). The quote ends "The answer he got was yes to all three questions." Id.

[45] All 170 participants had previously served as jurors in Ohio courts. Horowitz (1985), supra note 43, at 30.

[46] The instruction used by Professor Horowitz was as follows:

> Members of the Jury, this is a criminal case and under the Constitution and laws of the State of Maryland in a criminal case the jury are the judges of law as well as the facts in the case. So that whatever I tell you about the law while it is intended to be helpful to you in reaching a just and proper verdict in the case, it is not binding upon you as members of the jury and you may accept or reject it. And you may apply the law as you apprehend it to be in the case.

Horowitz (1985), supra note 43, at 29 (quoting Scheflin & Van Dyke, supra note 1, at 83, quoting *Wyley v. Warden*, 372 F.2d 742, 743 n.1 (4th Cir. 1967)).

[47] The instruction is taken from Van Dyke (1970), supra note 1. Jurors were told the following:

> 1. "Although they are a public body bound to give respectful attention to the laws, they have the final authority to decide whether or not to apply a given law to the acts of the defendant on trial before them";
> 2. That "they represent (the community) and that it is appropriate to bring into their deliberations the feelings of the community and their own feelings based on conscience";

    3. And, jurors were told that despite their respect for the law, "nothing would bar them from acquitting the defendant if they feel that the law, as applied to the fact situation before them, would produce an inequitable or unjust result." Horowitz (1985), supra note 43, at 30–31.

[48] Horowitz, supra note 43, at 32.

[49] Kassin & Wrightsman identify two potential problems arising from the Horowitz study. First, "jury nullification is like a door that can swing both ways. Just as it can license jurors to acquit the guilty, it is argued, it can enable them to convict those who are innocent." S. Kassin & L. Wrightsman, supra note 19, at 161. Carefully worded jury instructions should all but eliminate this possibility. Even if such a conviction occurred, it could be reversed. Jury convictions, unlike jury acquittals, are not final.

    The second concern is that when the jury nullification instruction is made explicit, jurors will become "diverted from the external to the internal, from the evidence onto their sentiments." Id. at 161. It seems more likely to us that jurors will deal more openly and honestly with their sentiments, but would not be "diverted" from their initial task of finding the true facts.

[50] Credit goes to Professor Sax for rekindling the flame of jury nullification. See Sax, supra note 2.

[51] Among the recent highly publicized trials where jury nullification appears to have played a role are those of Mayor Marion Barry of Washington, D.C., for drug use, Oliver L. North for his role in the Iran-Contra Affair, and Bernhard Goetz for his assault in a New York City subway.

    After Mayor Barry's jury returned a conviction for a relatively minor charge and acquittals on the other counts, the trial judge Thomas Penfield Jackson spoke at Harvard Law School and expressed his dismay that the jurors had failed to return more convictions even though the evidence was "overwhelming" on at least a dozen counts. Bruce Fein then wrote a column chastising Judge Jackson for his "acid carping at jurors for nullifying the law." Fein, "Judge, Jury . . . and the Sixth," *Wash. Times*, Nov. 8, 1990, at G3. Judge Jackson had said:

> The jury is not a minidemocracy or a minilegislature. They are not to go back and do right as they see fit. That's anarchy. They are supposed to follow the law.

Commentator Fein responded by saying:

> Jury nullification in a particular case is no more a legislative repeal of a criminal law, or anarchy, than are the commonplace decisions of prosecutors to resist prosecutions where the crime is deemed inconsequential or mitigated by special circumstances.

Id.; see also Thompson, "Sifting the Pool; Juror Questionnaires Explore Drug Addiction, Prejudice," *Wash. Post*, June 5, 1990, at A1.

    The jury in Oliver North's trial similarly returned a verdict that indicated sympathy with the accused, convicting him on only three of the twelve charges against him. Georgetown University Law Professor Paul F. Rothstein analyzed the trial by saying: "It's jury nullification. . . . The instructions on aiding and abetting left [the jurors] little choice, but I think they sort of vaguely felt in their minds that his superiors ordered it and he was in a bind. . . ." Strasser, "Jury in North's Trial Settled on the Concrete; Abstractions Rejected," *Nat'l L.J.*, May 15, 1989, at 9; see also Schultz, supra note 2.

    Regarding the Goetz case and jury nullification, see G. Fletcher, supra note 9; Pinsley, "Goetz Appeal Explores Jury Nullification Issue," *Manhattan Lawyer*, Nov. 1, 1988, at 11; April 5, 1987, sec. 4, at 6, col. 1.

[52] *Fully Informed Jury Association, Media Handout* 2 (Oct. 30, 1990).

[53] Adler, "Courtroom Putsch?," *Wall St. J.*, Jan. 4, 1991, at A1, col. 1.

[54] FIJA has many other jury reform proposals besides the nullification issue. Discussion of them is beyond the scope of this article.

⁵⁵ See sources cited supra note 13.

⁵⁶ *The FIJActivist* 1 (Special Outreach Issue, 1990).

⁵⁷ Some of these bills, such as the ones in Arizona and Wyoming, have been defeated. Others remain to be debated.

⁵⁸ The authors would like to thank David J. Shagoury, aide to Senator Hedlund, for helpful discussions about jury nullification.

⁵⁹ Telephone interview with Massachusetts Senator Robert L. Hedlund (January 28, 1991). The authors would like to thank Senator Hedlund for providing us with additional information about his bill.

⁶⁰ See *Zenith Radio Corp. v. Matsushita Electric Indus. Co., Ltd.*, 478 F. Supp. 889 (E.D. Pa. 1979); V. Hans & N. Vidmar, supra note 13, at 160–63; Scheflin & Van Dyke, supra note 1, at 69–71.

⁶¹ With this silver lining, however, comes a dark cloud. If judges do not give nullification instructions, or, worse yet, give a strong statement that jurors must follow the judge's instructions, jurors may rightly become confused about their role. Some judicial cooperation inevitably will be necessary.

⁶² A. Lincoln, Address at Gettysburg (Nov. 19, 1863).

⁶³ Oregon's Constitution presently recognizes a right of jury power. Article I section 16 provides "In all criminal cases whatever, the jury shall have the right to determine the law, and the facts under the direction of the court as to the law, and the right of new trial, as in civil cases." *Ore. Const.* art. I, § 16.

⁶⁴ *Fauvre v. Roberts*, 309 Ore. 691, 694, 791 P.2d 128, 130 (1990).

⁶⁵ The Court ruled against proponents of the initiative who were challenging the wording of the description of the provision in the Attorney General's certification of the ballot title. Id. at 696, 791 P.2d at 132.

⁶⁶ Herzberg, supra note 12.

⁶⁷ At the bottom right of the advertisement there is a small box, labelled "ATTENTION LAWYERS," which contains a reference to our article in 43:4 *Law & Contemp. Prob.* 52 (1980). Neither of us was contacted before this reference was used. Statements in the advertisement are in direct contradiction to our position. We categorically and emphatically do not endorse jurors lying to judges nor do we endorse telling jurors to disbelieve everything they hear from judges.

⁶⁸ See Jackson, "DA's Office Decries 'Jury Nullification' Ad," *San Diego Union*, Jan. 26, 1990, at B1.

⁶⁹ The authors thank Jerry Mitchell, reporter for the Jackson, Mississippi *Clarion-Ledger*, for sending us the leaflet. This particular leaflet was sponsored by the Christian Action Group of Jackson, Mississippi.

⁷⁰ Sir Walter Scott, "Marmion," Canto VI, Stanza 17, in *Complete Poetical Works* 145 (1900).

⁷¹ See supra text at note 65.

⁷² Larry Dodge has reported a case from New York in which one of the jurors began to explain jury nullification to the others, but they sent a note to the judge about him. The judge permitted him to continue to deliberate after telling him to "keep his politics out of the case and apply the law as given." The juror agreed, went back to the deliberations, and hung the jury. He was later threatened with perjury and contempt charges, but they were never brought. Dodge, "A Complete History of the Power Rights and Duties of the Jury System," a talk delivered at the State of the Nation Conference, sponsored by the Texas Liberty Association (July 7, 1990).

Questions to Consider

1. In the Steele and Thornberg article about confusing jury instructions, what institutional interests prevent change? Some argue that trial court judges are merely following legal rules, but who makes these rules?

2. The issue of lawyers trying to manipulate the jury often becomes a matter of public discussion when celebrity criminal trials, such as the Rodney King and O.J. Simpson trials, are broadcast by the media. There are usually two poles of argument. Some argue that we must let lawyers do what they will: "If they were your lawyers, wouldn't you want them to have the freedom to help you?" Others argue that the judge must prevent lawyers from using misleading tactics because jurors, throughout the whole process of the trial, may not be able to distinguish between misleading tactics and facts. Kassin points out that our current system of giving lawyers the ability to confuse while encouraging jury ignorance creates problems. Consider a third option: Give the jury as much information as possible and trust in the joint common sense of twelve people. This option would include giving juries information on the potentially manipulative language of lawyers. What do you think would be the merits or demerits of such a system? Why haven't judges or lawyers accepted this third option? What, if any, shift in courtroom power would occur if this were put into effect?

3. If you were required to take a group test in your class based on the lectures up to a certain point, do you believe your decision would be better if you had access to tapes of the prior lectures? How is this situation similar to or different from that of a jury?

4. Suppose your class had to obtain unanimous agreement about the answers to the test questions but had as much time to answer as you

wished. Do you believe you would arrive at a better decision if you were allowed to go home and later come back to class or if you were kept together until you made the decision? How is this situation the same as or different from a jury situation?

5. Our society has created many institutional systems in an attempt to meet our community needs, but invariably people try to play that system to their own personal advantage. For example, Scheflin and Van Dyke point out how some groups in society have tried to play the jury system by getting jurors with pre-determined conclusions on specific cases. Does "playing the system," whether the system is a tax system, a welfare system, or a justice system, create pressures to destroy that system even though it attempts to provide some level of justice for all? How do we retain a relatively good system in the face of such abuse?

6. Scheflin and Van Dyke argue that judicial failure to inform jurors that they have the power to nullify a law only makes things worse. Do you agree or disagree? Why?

Section IV
Problems for the Judiciary

Courts, like all public institutions, face ongoing administrative problems. This section explores one of the most compelling and complex questions confronting court operation: who ultimately makes the decisions? To understand why this question is so complex, one must understand that courts are inherently political institutions, with judges and other members of the legal profession trying to maintain their independence from outside control.

David Orrick first looks at the growing societal trend to professionalize the administration of public institutions. The need for efficiency and competence, given limited resources, puts pressure on professional groups, such as doctors with hospitals and lawyers with courts, to yield some of their traditional power to others specifically trained to manage these complex institutions. While there is a valid need for professional independence, professional competence does not necessarily translate into administrative competence. The lack of competence leaves ordinary people to cope with disorganized and ineffective courts. The problem of improving disorganized courts is inhibited not only by the desire of judges to retain the reins of power but also by the political nature of courts. For example, Orrick points out that political patronage rather than competence is often the basis for appointing court administrators and that local authorities continue to battle with state authorities over control of court processes.

Elliot Slotnick continues the discussion of judicial independence by looking at how we choose our judges. If we want our judges to be less political, we need to give them some measure of independence, yet in a democratic society we need to make our officials accountable. The tension between these needs is reflected in the various ways judges are chosen and retained. Slotnick points out that the balance is currently skewed, for the concept of democratic accountability is unfortunately more a potentiality than a reality.

The two final articles in Section IV continue the theme of politics and power by addressing the pressing societal issues of race and gender. Courts are part of our social fabric, and they do not escape from the problems faced by other institutions. Barbara Graham begins by looking at the racial composition of judges in this country. At issue is the question of diversity: should our judges, to whom we give power over crucial issues in our lives, reflect who we are as a society? How good is that reflection, and how might we make the image more clear? Graham explains some of the structural problems inhibiting diversity in our judiciary, such as the fact that the pool of lawyers from which judges are chosen contains relatively few minorities. Interestingly, while politics may keep some minorities from being elected, the political perspective of state governors makes a major difference in whether minorities get appointed to the bench. Once minorities have their foot in the door, they, as other such appointees, are almost universally retained by the electorate.

Just as a variety of viewpoints is important in obtaining fair jury decisions, a variety of viewpoints is also important in achieving better overall justice from judicial decisions. Men and women often have different perspectives, such that judicial diversity arguably should include not only racial and ethnic but also gender representation. Early studies indicate that including women's perspectives may not greatly change the outcome pattern of current court decisions; rather, their new and varied participatory styles may change the way courts conduct everyday business.

Such new styles in conducting the everyday business of courts becomes important especially when considering gender bias in such business, as reviewed by Hemmens and his colleagues. Studies in more than thirty states make it clear that gender bias is quite prevalent, an unsurprising result as court personnel share the prevailing attitudes of the larger society. This raises the question of what being a professional within the court system really means. If such professionals are to be given power and discretion, what obligations do they have toward those whom they serve, and to what extent can we expect more of them than simply reflecting prevailing social biases? In addition, we are faced with the broader question of how we protect ourselves from abuses of power while giving judges the power and independence to do justice.

12

Court Administration in the United States
The On-Going Problems

DAVID ORRICK

In any review of the system by which justice is delivered in the United States, the concept of "court administration" now plays an important role, particularly since the publication of the presidential Commission Report in 1967.[1] In that extraordinary document, specific reference was made to the need for improved administration in the courts, pursuant to the theme of the whole report:

> States should provide for clear administrative responsibility within courts and should ensure that professional court administrators are available to assist the Judges in their management functions.[2]

The report went on immediately to provide a useful working definition of the contribution a court administrator can make to the efficient operations of the courts:

> (administrative officers can) aid the judiciary by collecting judicial statistics, managing fiscal affairs, supervising court personnel and performing duties in connection with the assignment of Judges and scheduling of cases.[3]

The passage of more than 20 years since that statement provides that civilized distance in time to review the extent to which this recommendation has been followed, and to offer some explanation for the failure,

Reprinted by permission of the author from the *Anglo-American Law Review*, vol. 19 (Jan./March, 1990), pp. 36–54.

if any, to have reached that goal. It is, unfortunately, the premise of this paper that those goals have not been met, and that under the current and foreseeable circumstances, the problems in reaching them will be neither easily nor quickly solved.

For the courts' colleagues in the criminal justice system, the police and correctional agencies, the significance in this Presidential report lies in its terrible stimuli, the specific trauma of the assassination of President Kennedy, and the general, miserable deterioration in human relations experienced in American cities during the 1960s, reflected in both the type and amount of crime, drug abuse and riots which were taking place. These problems for those other parts of the criminal justice system, developing at the same time as an unprecedented expansion in criminal defendants' rights and the rights of access to the courts by poor people, have led to unprecedented stress on all components of the justice system, including the courts. Until the 1960s, America's courts may have been able to stumble along in an inefficient, poorly administered way. Since the 1960s, the need for well-administered courts, to handle an ever-increasing workload of more difficult cases, has been obvious to all.

It would be improper to begin by suggesting that the United States' concerns for court administration only began in the 1967 report. The recommendations for improved court administration provided they should more properly be considered as part of what is at least the second, perhaps even the third generation of high visibility efforts at such improvements. It is generally accepted that the original stimulus to recognize the need for efficient administrative practices in the courts came as far back as 1906, with Roscoe Pound's speech to the American Bar Association (the ABA).[4] It was not until the mid 1930s, however, that the ABA really made any major efforts to come up with recommendations for improvement in this area. After this original sloth, the ABA must be given much credit, to this day, for its on-going contributions, as most recently reflected in its Model State Judicial Article,[5] and comprehensive *Standards*.[6]

In the actual terms of concerns for administration being translated into positions with administrative duties, it is generally acknowledged[7] that the states of Ohio (1923) California (1926) and North Dakota (1927) were the first to do something. North Dakota's place in this early group is particularly interesting: even now, it is still one of the United States' most sparsely settled units, with the very generous ratio of one trial judge for every 3,430 population. It would not be the first American state court system one would think of in considering the possibilities of the usual administrative stress on the courts caused by high population numbers and the general problems government faces in America's heavily metropolitan states. North Dakota's numbers, for example, compare with the ratio in California, whose coastal area most certainly is heavily metropolitan, of one judge for every 17,634.[8]

More recently, New Jersey, under the leadership of the legendary Chief Justice Vanderbilt, is usually acknowledged as producing the first state-wide administrative office in 1948. At the local level, the first trial court administrative office was established in the Los Angeles Superior Court—that forum of Sergeant Joe Friday and *Dragnet* fame—in 1957.[9]

Even prior to the production of the 1967 President's Commission report, 25 of the states had established state-wide court administrative offices.[10] In the 20 years since, all the rest of the states have established some sort of state-wide function to deal with these administrative concerns, with jurisdiction-wide offices in the District of Columbia, Guam and Puerto Rico as well. The incumbents of these offices together form the Conference of Court Administrators, (COSCA) which began life in the mid-1950s as the National Conference of Court Administrative Officers (NCCAO).

National organizations for trial court administrators have existed for some time: the original National Association for Court Administration, (NACA) merged with the National Association of Trial Court Administrators, (NATCA) to become the National Association of Court Managers (NACM) in the early 1980s. These organizations are able to interact nicely with groups such as the Conference of Chief Justices (CCJ) and the various groups representing the interests of the states' trial Judges. The very existence of these groups is a positive sign.

Yet in some states there is still sufficient wariness about the credibility and authority of an administrator *per se* in the court system that the incumbent holds a judge's title and rank, perhaps on the feeling that one judge will only listen to another judge, whatever the topic. New York calls its equivalent to other states' State Court Administrator "Chief Administrative Judge." In New York's neighbouring state, Connecticut, another of the United States' oldest and most established state court systems, the State Court Administrator also holds judicial rank.

Because of details like this, there is still much substance to the general feeling in the 1967 Presidential Report's observation:

> In many . . . states (having such an office) the functions of this office
> are limited, and its potential has not yet been realized.[11]

This observation could even be shared with those offices which have been created since 1967. In Vermont, for example, the State Court Administrator's office, created in 1968, has had to contend all along in its trial court of general jurisdiction with lay Judges, whose position there seems sacrosanct. The anachronistic assignment system for the lawyer Judges on that court dates back to the circuit riding days of Chief Justice John Marshall: it seems equally sacrosanct. This is a specific example;

in the remainder of this paper we suggest some general reasons why that potential has not been realized.

The Court Administrator and the Judicial Role

To the extent to which the professional literature is a barometer of the concerns in the (academic) field, the need for court administrators has long been part of the conventional wisdom. One searches in vain for monographs with titles which suggest otherwise. Yet it is possible that a properly conducted research exercise might raise the possibility that there is still some doubt among the Judges as to this need. It is the basic justification for the court administrator's position that he can relieve the Judge of many of the routine tasks which go along with the management of any agency, inside or outside the justice system.

Ideally, this frees up the Judge to concentrate on providing justice in the individual case, resolving the specific dispute between the litigants or determining the guilt or innocence of the defendant to the criminal charge—the "micro" sense of justice, to steal the shorthand of Malthus' dismal science—while allowing the administrator to provide justice in the broader, "macro" sense, by keeping that court running at its most efficient, on an overall, day-by-day basis.

When the Judge and administrator can work together in close harmony, the Judge's adjudicative skills, ultimately what he is being paid uniquely to provide, can be exercised to the fullest in a *sequence* of individual cases.

Reality suggests otherwise. In many of the American states, the judge continues to be an elective official, at both the trial and appellate levels. This can even include the Chief Justice himself of the Supreme Court, or its terminological equivalent (is it reflective of the problems courts face that there is not even agreement among the states on the title of that court of last resort?). It has been one of the provocative, but time-honoured traditions of the American governmental process that "to the winner go the spoils."[12] In many elective positions in America, the successful candidate, whether or not in the judiciary, has several positions which are his to fill under the general power of patronage.[13] The newly elected Judge can "bring on his own team," to include such close assistants as private secretaries, law clerks, court officers, etc.

It does not necessarily follow that these team members are in any way qualified to hold the positions to which they are appointed. In the usual way of things, they are people who have been (financial) supporters or campaign workers for the Judge during his election campaign, people to whom the Judge is returning a favour. It does follow that such a court system is subject to interruption in the experience level of people holding important, if sometimes low visibility jobs. A Judge's private secretary, who organizes his calendar, and his law clerk, who does his legal research, can have a lot to do with the pace with which he delivers his findings of fact, for example.

In some instances, this susceptibility to change may affect the Chief Court Administrator for the state himself, a very high visibility position. In the controversial and hard-fought election for Chief Justice in Ohio in November 1986, the incumbent was defeated for re-election. That defeat also led to a change in State Court Administrators, to nobody's surprise, since the incumbent Administrator was correctly perceived to be very personally associated with the defeated Chief Justice.

The spoils system is totally contrary to the English tradition of governmental support jobs—the Civil Service, in the crudest embrace of that term—being protected from such change. It is not the purpose here to discuss the advantages and disadvantages of the spoils system. Rather, we emphasize the effect it can have on the experience level of those involved in administrative matters in the court. Decisions from the bench get made in the individual case, regardless of who the decision-maker is and the turnover in Judges. But great value is lost to the on-going process of administration when the incumbent administrator's position is tied too strongly to that of the Judge, so that if the Judge goes, the administrator, and all the *in loco* experience he has gained, goes too. As long as judicial positions continue to be elective, and the feeling persists that patronage is still an appropriate part of the judicial scenario, there is no easy end in sight to this problem.

Job Qualifications and Experience

There are not likely to be many formal job qualifications in situations where the administrator position is a patronage appointment for the Judge. The person who took over the State Court Administrator's position in Ohio in November 1986, though legally trained, had no prior experience as a court administrator at any level.

But even in states with appointive Judges, and the possibly stronger sense of continuity in administrative matters that this may allow, the issue of the experience and the qualifications the court administrator brings to his job is still an open book. An assertive judiciary could go a long way to curing this by imposing its own standards. But it would be hard for the Judges to impose strict criteria on formal educational and experience attainments. In many of the individual United States, the Judges themselves have no formal job credentials other than having been admitted to the state bar for a period of time. Their own context is no guide for them, nor can they look to outside bodies such as universities for assistance in establishing job credentials for their administrators. The fault here lies in the nation's educational system, and the lack of university level programmes training people to be court administrators.

In large part because of the stimuli provided by the 1967 Presidential Commission, the number of degree programmes in "criminal justice", so-called—approximately the same area of study that Europe knows as "criminology"—has exploded since 1967. They now number well over 600. Inside that number, there may be no more than 10 to 15 programmes emphasizing court administration matters through major programmes or actual degrees.[14] Compared to the almost limitless opportunities he would have to pursue a career in police or correctional administration, where a programme is available in each of the 50 states, with most states having such a programme in one of the state-funded colleges or universities, the would-be court administrator has few choices. In a land 3,000 miles from coast to coast, he may have to go a long way from home to pursue the court choice. Attending a programme in some state other than his own ensures much larger tuition and travel costs. This possibility of great expense may well mean that some capable would-be court administrators have not been able to read for a degree for financial reasons. This is another problem with no easy end in sight.

The explanations for this lack of programmes quickly become circular. The earliest consequence of the presentation of the 1967 Report was legislation, the Omnibus Crime Control and Safe Streets Act of 1968.[15] Among other things, this statute led to financial assistance being given to universities in developing criminal justice programmes: perhaps at least as importantly, financial assistance was also offered to students pursuing careers in criminal justice, who wanted to take university-level courses, and/or read for a degree in that field.

One of the most provocative statements in the whole 1967 Report opened the Courts Chapter:

> the criminal court is the central, crucial institution in the criminal justice system . . .[16]

but it did not lead, via the 1968 Safe Streets Act, to the development of a lot of degree courses or programmes emphasizing court administration. This paper is not the appropriate forum to grumble too long about those missed opportunities. What can and must be done is to emphasize the impact of this lack of an educational infra-structure on the position of court administrators in the United States.

As a direct result of this lack of educational underpinning to the field of court administration, there is no generally accepted *academic*, i.e., university degree based, credential for entry to field position in court administration, in the same way, for example, that the Master's degree in Social Work (MSW) has been accepted for so long as the Probation Officer's union card. There is now some healthy challenge to the MSW from the development of those Master's level programmes in Criminal Justice. That competition has been healthy, even to the point that it may have produced an embarras de riches. It has certainly helped to lead to a re-examination of the direction for Probation, with a heightened awareness of its place as a sanction.[17] Court administration has no such luxury available to it.

The closest the nation has to an accrediting body for court administrators is the Institute for Court Management (ICM), now an arm of the National Center for State Courts (the National Center). The Institute offers a variety of courses, unquestionably of great relevance for the court administrator-to-be, which can eventually lead to the credential of "Fellow."

In something of a Catch 22 situation, these courses are usually aimed at people already in administrative positions: in something approaching academic incest, it has been traditional in recent years for incumbent senior members of the National Center's own staff to become ICM fellows. Moreover, ICM is not a degree granting institution, and is unlikely ever to become so, unless it can be formally associated with an accredited university. It would for that reason not attract someone interested in receiving a "relevant" college degree to use in his career.

It would be wrong, even by implication, to lay blame for the lack of development of courses and degree programmes in court administration at the feet of those energetic souls who developed the field of criminal justice as a whole into the thriving component of academe that it represents today. The lack of courses and programmes in court administration is simply a mysterious absence in face of the important contribution that the field of public administration as a whole has made to American academe. Courses in public administration are a vital part of the skeleta of degree programmes in Politics, (sometimes called Political Science or Government in American university nomenclature).

It cannot be easily explained why courses in court administration did not develop as a natural part of courses on public administration and other parts of Politics curricula, when courses in Constitutional Law, the Supreme Court and Judicial Theory are time-honoured areas of study. There did not need to be those terrible stimuli provided by the social upheaval of the 1960s, which led to programmes in criminal justice being developed, for programmes in court administration to have developed at universities.

Over the years, the best 'court-watchers' in academe, able to explain appellate court voting patterns at the drop of a note-pad—these days, the personal computer—have been the researchers in Politics faculties.[18] This contact refutes the argument that is occasionally made, suggesting that courses in court administration have not developed because non-legally trained scholars are intimidated by the court environment. It makes the failure of academe to be more interested in matters of court administration all the more of a mystery, again with no obvious resolution in sight.

Management Skills

As a direct result of the general lack of qualifications for the court administrator positions, it is not surprising to find that the most sophisticated management techniques, whether or not dependent on the use of the most up-to-date technology, are not being used in America's courts. It is not to criticize the incumbent court administrator to note this, when the explanation is probably that most of these incumbents have never received any formal management training. In far too many of America's courts, even highly cost-effective personal computers are still not being used for much of the humdrum repetitive accounting and word processing work the courts must perform. One would not, could not expect to see them in operation if the administrator himself is unaware of their capabilities. The lack of up-to-date equipment in a court may be more apparent to the casual visitor than the lack of up-to-date management techniques, but both absences reduce the highest efficiency of the courts.

At its worst, this lack of use of top management skills can cost the government, and vicariously, the individual tax-payer, large sums of money. One of the characteristics about courts which is so easily overlooked is their responsibility as money handlers. Without any of the hoopla attached to a bank, an extraordinary amount of money is taken in by the average court in America on a routine, continuing daily basis.

The combination of court filing fees, court costs and fines is in addition to the comparatively staggering amount of money which the court now handles in its more recently developed role as broker in enforcing child support payment against the obligated parent, which itself adds up to millions of dollars. In many instances, because of a lack of sophisticated money-management skills in the court administrator's office, this money, which could have been placed in (short-term) interest-bearing accounts from which the government would profit, sits around idly in a current account. These are the harsh consequences of the lack of skills. It may be hard to measure the impact of unskilled administrators not being able to produce maximum efficiency from their judicial and non-judicial staff. A lack of dollars is very easily measured.

Upsetting the Apple Cart

Reference has been made above to the influence of the President's Commission, via its own literature, and more importantly, the legislation it spawned, on the administration of justice. Notwithstanding its view of the centrality of the criminal court to the criminal justice process, the basic theme of the Commission's legacy has been crime control. In that respect, the title of the enabling act speaks volumes in its reference to "safe streets."

One of the immediate results of that Safe Streets Act was the creation of a federal funding agency, the Law Enforcement Assistance Agency, (LEAA) which served for many years as a conduit for federal funds to the states' criminal justice systems. That this money was necessarily provided via the conduit of an executive branch agency was an on-going source of irritation to the courts, in a problem distinctive, if not unique to the United States, with their dedication to maintaining the separation of (governmental) powers.

The reality of the delivery of LEAA funds was that the courts perceived themselves as having to deal with executive agencies, invariably attached to the governor's office in the individual states, to receive these moneys, in competition with other executive agencies, the police and corrections. In comparative terms, the courts did not receive as much from the LEAA coffers as seemed appropriate to their role as one-third of the criminal justice system, in the crude breakdown of "Police, Courts and Corrections." And even inside that breakdown, much of the money technically identified for the courts' use was spent on prosecutorial and other matters:

> expenditures for "purely courts" . . . include(d) "alternatives to institutionalization," "community-based detention," "pretrial detention," "investigating units," "youth services," "probation programs," and other non-court functions.[19]

Even though it was "raided" by these other recipients, the pot of money received by the courts in absolute terms from the federal government through LEAA was quite substantial. During the existence of LEAA, approximately $256 million from LEAA discretionary funds, and approximately $344 million from LEAA formula funds (the former block grants) were allocated for state court improvements.[20] But still, by comparison with what the other components received, it did not seem like much. For the courts, this was the worst of both worlds: comparatively an inadequate amount of money, provided through an awkward funding mechanism.

The courts' interaction with LEAA through the state's funding agencies was at best an unhappy marriage. This is not to imply that an infusion of money is a complete solution to the courts' administrative problems and planning capabilities. Rather, we suggest that many energetic people in the state court systems were needlessly distracted by the mechanisms by which the money was provided, and spent more of that energy on changing those mechanisms than in improving the courts.

These plaints were heard. By the mid-1970s, the Crime Control Act of 1976 led to the creation of separate state judicial planning committees. The Conference of Chief Justices created a Task Force on a State Court Improvement Act in 1978, largely because those planning concepts introduced in the 1976 legislation had not seemed to work. That action led, in 1984, to the creation of the State Justice Institute (SJI) as a direct mechanism to fund state courts with federal money. The Act specifies that the recipients, either by grant or contract, of the Institute's funds would be:

> "state and local courts and their agencies" and "national non-profit organizations controlled by, operating in conjunction with, and serving the judicial branches of state governments."[21]

With the establishment of the State Justice Institute, the gauntlet has been thrown squarely at the courts' feet, to make those improvements in court administration, unencumbered by influence from the other branches of governments as to the use of that money.

Jurisdictional Variety

In documenting the history of the creation of court administrative offices earlier, proper distinction was made between the establishment of the first state-wide office and the first local office. As local courts expand in size, it is most appropriate to have local administrative offices established. The sheer size of many of the American states makes it hard for a central office in the state capital effectively to administer the local courts spread round the jurisdiction. It makes great good sense if the state-wide office can thus have the link of the local administrative office, when it is the same state-wide law which is being processed through all the different locations.

Yet, in a matter not unrelated to the on-going influence of an elective judiciary, the problem exists of the local court administrator serving two masters—his local (chief) trial Judge, and the state court administrator in the state capital. With this influence of local tradition, it is not hard to see why there are some states, such as Illinois—where the local influence is still so strong that even justices of the State Supreme Court are elected on a regional basis—in which the influence of the state-wide administrator is by no means as great as it could be. This is that unreached potential to which the President's Commission referred. The disturbing point is that the potential will remain as unattainable for the foreseeable future.

Funding Source Variety

One of the key explanations for the ongoing local influence on the courts, even in face of a long-established state-wide administrative office, is the influence of the funding source, a dependency which can range from paper clips to new buildings. The majority of courts in the United States continue to be funded locally, typically at the county level. This invariably means that administrative improvements which the state-wide administrator and his local trial court colleague want to make have to be funded locally. Both may want computers to be installed to assist in coordinating court statistics across the state, and for the myriad repetitive tasks for which the machines are pre-eminently suited. But without their ability to sell the idea to the local legislators, the idea will go a-wasting. Again, the role of the local Judge cannot be ignored. In an elective situation, he may not want to alienate the local political power base to which he undoubtedly owes much assistance in his own election by looking greedy, by making his own court too "fancy". He may well have run an election campaign based on frugal efficiency in the court system, totally in conflict with the legitimate needs of both the local and state-wide court administrators.

Adequacy of Physical Plant

The role of bricks and mortar in the orderly administration of justice cannot be downplayed. The great majority of America's courthouses were built in the 19th century. They are a wonderful living monument to the architectural and popular attitudes toward government of that century:

> A committee from Pike County, Illinois visited the court house at Clinton, Missouri [and] reported to its own constituents that ". . . after you have gone through [it] leaves you feeling you are sorry you entered . . . It gives you a mean opinion of the people of the County." There was widespread sentiment, then, that the beauty sometimes and the size often of the local dispensary of justice was in fact a mirror of the aspirations and character of the county which it served.[22]

They are proof of the preparedness of the tax-payers to invest hard-earned dollars in visual proof of the role of the court in society. The typical American county courthouse dominates the older part of the county seat's skyline in much the same way as the church or cathedral influences the landscape of English municipal life. This is proper in a society which does not espouse an established religion, where the courthouse plays much the same role as the church in England. It is the courthouse to which one goes in the United States to look for birth records at the local level: it was at the Appomattox courthouse that the Civil War surrender took place.

Unfortunately, these courthouses must now be damned with much faint praise. Although many of them are architectural masterpieces, they are by and large unsuited to the way in which justice is "dispensed" in the 1990s. These are courthouses where the courtroom dominates the building, and where there are proportionately few support offices: in the 1890s, there was little need for them. The typical mid-nineteenth century courthouse in America was an extravagant building. In many instances, the courthouse at the time of its construction was the most expensive government building in the county. Unfortunately, this extravagance often took the form of sheer size and splendour, and not in office space which may have been excessive at the time of construction, but into which the court could have moved as its needs changed.

The roll of time has made many of America's courthouses into architectural white elephants. Because of the methods of construction, often they cannot easily be adapted to suit the modern needs of multiple support offices, with separate needs. On top of this, there is the unrelentless increase in the number of records to be stored. Needs may change, but records just continue to build up. In fact, as many American historians have discovered, the county courthouse in America is a veritable goldmine of information. When it is the instinct, if not the very definition of the law to preserve, the not infrequent problem one sees in the American courthouse is of an information repository bursting at the seams. It should not be the court administrator's job at the local or even the state level, to be an archivist. All too often, he has to be.

In short, many of America's courthouses need to be rebuilt, or extensively renovated. The latter option is not always available to the court's leadership because of the construction of the building. So, even in that situation where the court administrator has been able to persuade the county commissioners to provide him with the computer support, for example, that he so badly needs to keep up with all those records he keeps accumulating, he may then turn round and find he is in a building totally unsuited both electrically[23] and environmentally to the sensitive requirements of high technology. The temperature and humidity levels which must be contended with during the summer in many of the American states are beastly. The observation that court folks in the late 1800s, in the days before central air-conditioning, were wise enough not to hold court in high summer is no solution to those who must sweat through the year-round exercise represented by modern court processing demands.

What is equally clear is that the court administrator who would strive for a new courthouse, in order to take fullest advantage of modern management skills and technology does not have the support for government expenditure which the court system enjoyed in the late 1800s. The fiscal reality of the early 1990s is one of taxpayer revolts, tax caps, limitations on government spending in the states, etc. Nor is this to suggest that the typical modern court administrator is as concerned with the grandeur of the building as court-related people seemed to be in the later 1800s. Even the hard-nosed attitude of producing a functional building will be hard to translate into bricks and mortar, when government expenditures are proportionately so limited. It would also be difficult to sell the county electorate and legislature on the need for some characterless modern "office building" to replace that magnificent structure on the corner of America's equivalent of High Street and Church Street.

The Rays of Hope

The above cannot be pictured as too happy an image of the constraints on effective court administration in the United States: more than once, pessimism has been expressed in this paper over the likelihood of the problem-causing conditions being changed. In some instances, the problems are not even distinctively American in nature. Courts all over the western world are faced by such problems as increasing caseloads and a build-up of records. But by injecting some optimism into the view of the future, certain developments and characteristics of the court administration scene should be listed as possible aids in alleviating the problems.

The Role of Organizations

Roscoe Pound's rallying cry was delivered at the annual meeting of the American Bar Association (the ABA). We repeat here the compliment, that after its sloth in not reacting to Pound's goads earlier, the ABA has consistently been at the forefront in recommending improvements in court administration, and, for that matter, in the whole of the criminal justice system. The maturation of the professional organizations representing the interests of both state-wide and local court administrators has helped those involved in the field to have a better sense of their own identity, a crucial detail in the absence of official credentialing bodies and some other sense of fraternity. COSCA now has routine and useful dialogues with CCJ, itself no less valuable as a linking device for the Chief Justices in the individual states, and is able to speak on behalf of the state courts with a national voice. The two organizations are even smart enough to hold their annual meetings back to back, to enhance the fluidity of that dialogue.

LEAA and Its Progeny

For all the controversy which has been attached to LEAA and the comparative amount of help which it gave to the courts, that help was substantial in absolute terms. Whatever the "procedural" problems, LEAA was the direct or indirect stimulus for many major developments in the courts. It must be hoped that the State Justice Institute, designed as the "courts-only" federal support agency, will be able to make progress from that original awkward stimulus through delivery mechanisms the courts find more acceptable.

Publications

In addition to the *Standards* published by the ABA, another important reference document was produced with LEAA support—the findings of the National Advisory Commission on Criminal Justice Standards and Goals.[24] These national standards provide a useful comparison with, and, in most instances, a supporting view for the ABA's proposals. Although the number of texts and ordinary reference material—such stuff as the routine products of university-based textbook writers—for court administration is minuscule in comparison to the amount of such material available for the other components of the criminal justice system, some important work has been done. One example is the Gallases' text, *Managing the Courts*,[25] which has been argued as providing the first comprehensive definition of court administration.[26] There are also now referred journals, such as the *Justice System Journal*, beginning in 1975, published by the ICM., and the *Judge's Journal*, from the ABA, both emphasizing matters concerning the courts. These are more recent publications coming along to help out *Judicature*, for so long the only worker in the vineyard. All these are in addition to the coverage routinely given to court-related matters in the main *ABA Journal*.

Major Independent Meetings

In recent years, important publicity has been given to the problems of court administration through several meetings held in their own right, and not just as part of annual meetings of such organizations as the American Society of Criminology and the American Society of Public Administration. These include the aptly titled reprise of the title of Pound's speech, "The National Conference on the Causes of Popular Dissatisfaction with the Administration of Justice," (affectionately known as the "Pound Conference"). This was held in 1976, and spawned local versions in many of the individual states in that same year. There have also been the First (1971) and Second (1978) National Conferences on the Judiciary, the latter of which (both were held in Williamsburg, Virginia) also served as the opening ceremony of the headquarters of the newly-moved National Center for State Courts. Later, in 1988, the National Center was itself to host the most important conference held to date on the issue of technology in the courts.[27]

Independent Technological Developments

Notwithstanding the possibly disparaging comments made above about the level of managerial skills displayed by the largely untrained court administrators, there have been independent technological developments, as discussed so fully at the Denver conference, which are almost allowing court administrators to succeed despite their own limitations in their workplace. It is as if those three legs of the tripod— Word Processing,[28] the Data Base, and Spreadsheets[29]—on which the enormous success of the Personal Computer (the PC) has been built, were specially designed for the courts. This is immediately useful assistance available to even the smallest courts.

So, at that local level, advances in technology may already be allowing the court administrator to ignore somewhat the problem issue of a building ill-suited to some technological upgrades. Ironically, in the smaller courts, some of those problems identified with the first computer revolution, that generated by affordable main-frames, have never been faced, as those courts move straight into the second revolution in computers, the rise of the (networked) PC's and desk-top publishing, developments of great value to courts. PC's are less much demanding of controlled humidity environments than main-frame computers, supported by "dumb" terminals.

Similar advances have been made in video technology, with systems now available for the video recording of depositions, and for the taping of the courtroom activity to serve as the *verbatim* transcript of proceedings. This is one of the requirements for the efficient implementation of the appellants' procedural rights in America's reviewing courts to which English appellate courts are not (yet?) subject. When video transcripts are by their nature available immediately, they can reduce to nothing the court administrator's concerns about getting the ordinary written transcript converted from the court stenographer's unique code into ordinary written form with that promptness demanded by the appellate process in the United States.

The Role of Key Individuals

For years in England, the small field of those interested in the delivery of (criminal) justice teaching and research was another tripod, or perhaps, troika—Max Grunhut, Herman Mannheim, and (now Sir) Leon Radzinowicz, with no hierarchy in that order other than the alphabet! In many respects, court administration now is where criminal justice administration was in general in those 1950s and 1960s, as to the influence of a comparative handful of key figures. In an unusual family heritage, Geoff Gallas is carrying on the concerns of his parents, displayed in their seminal *Managing the Courts*,[30] through his doctoral research, ongoing authorship of scholarly monographs, and his position as Director of Research at the National Center for State Courts. Ernest Friesen, co-author with the elder Gallases of *Managing the Courts*, served as the original Director of the Institute for Court Management (ICM). Now a Law School Dean, he continues to be among the most productive authors and speakers on court management issues.

Edward McConnell, President of the National Center for State Courts, came to that position after 20 years' service as the State Court Administrator for New Jersey, beginning with the challenging early years of that office in 1953, when it was serving as the research laboratory for all the wonderful ideas of Chief Justice Vanderbilt, one of the true pioneers in court administration among the ranks of the Judges. One of the key points in the intellectual and moral leadership of court administration concerns in the United States will come with the imminent retirement of Mr. McConnell, whose grasp of the National Center's helm has been synchronous with that body's national reputation on court matters. With respect to those who are already aligning themselves as announced and unannounced candidates to replace him, none of them can bring to the position the eminence in the field that McConnell has developed. Court watchers in America may find out just how much the field in general, and the National Center for State Courts in particular, owes to McConnell.

In a rather delightful irony, one of the great forces since 1969 in pushing the concerns of the state courts—Chief Justice Vanderbilt's trenches, where the common man's law suits and criminal troubles are dealt with, as opposed to those matters of national concern and high finance which concern America's federal courts—has been the recently retired Chief Justice of the United States, Warren Burger, *ex officio* the top federal judicial officer in the country. Now properly honoured as the Honorary Chairman of the National Center for State Courts, Burger successfully invested a lot of his enormous political capital in getting the National Center successfully resettled to its headquarters in Williamsburg.

The National Center's headquarters are unquestionably the most anachronistically modern architecture in that restored colonial town, less than 200 miles from, and hence so much closer and more visible to those in the nation's seat of power in Washington, D.C., than it had been when it was based in Denver. Without sounding too cynical, it is reasonable to assume that those involved with the Law School at the College of William and Mary, one of America's oldest and most prestigious colleges, were quite happy to be landlords to, (they own that modern anachronism!) and associated with a rather new organization when it was so vigorously supported by the nation's Chief Justice. Burger was almost alone in seeing the need for a support agency for the states' courts, to offer a similar assistance to them as could be provided to the Federal Courts by the Administrative Office of the U.S. Courts, established back in 1939,[31] and its "daughter," the Federal Judicial Center.

In comparison to England, where the voluntary movement of Judges off the bench to other careers is frowned upon, as if the resignation is the violation of a lifetime non-revocable trust, such voluntary movement is a common occurrence in the United States. At times, the move is to another area of public service related to the law. It was U.S. Senator Heflin, erstwhile Chief Justice of Alabama, who was the main sponsor of the Bill which became the State Justice Institute Act. Similarly, one of the most productive authors on court matters is Professor Leflar, who had once served as Associate Justice of the Arkansas Supreme Court. There have also been many lively septuagenarians, such as ex-Chief Justice Trainor of California, forced by mandatory retirement ages in the individual states, who have been able to continue to pass on their intellectual energy to young law students at law schools not bound by such mandates. Unfortunately, America's court administrators do not come from its law schools. Still, it is good to know that at least some of its future lawyers are being sensitized to the administrative difficulties faced by the courts.

That key individuals can have such an impact is a reflection of the small size of the field of court administration. As valuable as the contribution of the people mentioned above and the others of whom space precludes a mention here has been, it must be tempered by the bitter-sweet observation that the field of those interested in court administration matters is small—too small, particularly in the academic community.

Unlike the ordinary tradition, where the ideas of the great scholars at the universities can be handed down via their students, the absence of a sufficient number of major academic institutional bases for the field of court administration means that the ideas and spirit of the pioneers will not be as easily handed down to the next generation, when those pioneers are working in the courts.

In a different scenario, McConnell would be just about to step down from his Chair at the College of William and Mary. His disciple, both in New Jersey and at the National Center for State Courts, Sam Conti, would be Professor of Court Administration at the University of Illinois (one of America's many superb state-funded universities with no degree in Court Administration), instead of being the State Court Administrator in that state, a role where his extraordinary instructional skills can hardly be used.

The National Center for State Courts and Other Organizations

Reference has been made above on several occasions to the National Center for State Courts, which now includes the Institute for Court Management. In many respects, particularly in the absence of a decent scholarly base, the single most optimistic contribution to addressing ongoing concerns in court administration in the individual states is the ongoing vigour of the National Center.

Established in 1971, with some financial support from that LEAA with which the courts had such difficulty working, and as a direct result of the First National Conference on the Judiciary in 1971, the National Center was originally based in Denver, along with the Institute for Court Management, (ICM) which had been founded in the previous year. ICM, still based in Denver, has since merged with the National Center, and is essentially its educational and training arm. The articles of incorporation explain the National Center's perception of its own role:

> to conduct research projects on courts and court-related topics in order to identify needs and provide both short and long-term solutions to state court problems;
>
> to conduct education and training programs, seminars and conferences;
>
> to serve as a technical assistance resource for the transfer and adaptation of improvement in court standards, operations, management and technology; and
>
> to serve as a clearinghouse through which members of the courts community and others interested in courts can exchange information and encourage improvement in court administration, practices and procedures.[32]

The range of services offered by the National Center has grown perhaps even further than its founders envisaged. The National Center fills a special role as the Secretariat for many of the court-related organizations in the country, assisting in the production of their documents and the provision of services to their constituents and members. Many reports are completed each year. Their titles attest to the concerns expressed by the courts—inasmuch as the great majority of their reports are written in direct response to a request by the host court—and to the National Center's consistency. Its best work rivals in quality any work that a university-based research team could produce, but it is an oasis in the desert.

The National Center was a vigorous user of LEAA funds during their availability. Now, after the creation of the State Justice Institute, (SJI) it has already become a major recipient of funds from that agency. The funding base of the National Center is the combination of SJI and other federal money, with charges (the equivalent of a membership fee), assessed against the states on a population *per capita* basis. This is together with the funds provided in the contracts entered into between the National Center and the states on the individual projects, and the receipt of generous contributions from dedicated people in the legal and lay communities committed to supporting the National Center.

Now the most visible organization assisting the state courts in their administrative and management concerns, the National Center can probably attribute its ongoing success to its continuing ability to meet the goals stated in its articles of incorporation. The wording of the legislation creating the State Justice Institute suggests that the National Center's role as that most visible agency assisting the state courts will gain an added security in the years to come, through the funding it will receive from that source.

However, the impression should not be gained that the Center is the only agency assisting the state courts in their administrative concerns. The American Judicature Society, (AJS) founded in 1913, with a structure that incorporates representatives from each of the states regardless of size, in much the same way as the U.S. Senate, continues to assist the courts, but seems to have taken something of a back seat since the development of the National Center. Like ICM's *Justice System Journal*, AJS's eponymous *Judicature* journal serves as a valuable provider of written material related to the courts.

Other groups which have provided valuable assistance on court related matters over the years include the American Academy of Judicial Education, the National Association of State Judicial Educators and the National Judicial College. For a long time, the Institute for Judicial Administration, at New York University, was the only university-based research organization interested in court matters.

Finally, in a development illustrative of the "American way," for-profit organizations such as the Rand Corporation are showing more and more interest in the courts, providing healthy competition for the National Center for State Courts, the American Judicature Society and the other non-profit groups, in those many situations where a court wanting to have work done for it must submit its request for assistance to competitive bid for the resulting contract.

Conclusion

Although the problems faced by the courts in America's states are large, not easily solved, and in some instances (e.g. the variety of funding sources and jurisdictions) uniquely American, the dedication of those working in courts, and the support the courts can theoretically receive, gives some confidence that the courts will be able to continue to address and master the most serious of these problems as they arise.

Endnotes

[1] President's Commission on Law Enforcement and Administration of Justice, *The Challenge of Crime in a Free Society* (hereafter, *The 1967 Presidential Commission Report*), Washington, D.C.: U.S. Government Printing Office, 1967, p. 156.

[2] Id at p. 156.

[3] Ibid.

[4] "The Causes of Popular Dissatisfaction with the Administration of Justice," as originally reprinted in 20 *J. Am. Jud. Soc'y*, 178 (1937). Like Gilbert and Sullivan librettos, its title and content have proven to be disturbingly timeless.

[5] This was incorporated into the President's Commission Task Report, *The Courts*, at pp. 92–95.

[6] Including *Standards Relating to Court Organization* (1974); *Standards Relating to Trial Courts*, (1976) *Standards Relating to Appellate Courts*, (1976) all published in Chicago.

[7] See e.g. Ernest C. Friesen, Jr., Gallas, Edward C. and Gallas, Nesta M., *Managing the Courts*, Indianapolis, IN: Bobbs Merrill, 1971 at pp. 16–17.

[8] Adapted from Appendix E and Figure J in State Court Caseload Statistics: *Annual Report, 1984*, Williamsburg, VA: National Center for State Courts.

[9] Friesen et al., op cit. supra at pp. 239–270.

[10] U.S. Bureau of Justice, Bureau of Justice Statistics, *State Court Organization*, 1980.

[11] *1967 Report* at p. 156.

[12] See generally Raymond J. Wolfinger, "Why Political Machines Have Not Withered Away and Other Revisionist Thoughts," *Journal of Politics*, 34 (May 1972), 265–398.

[13] It is estimated, for example, that the elective District Attorney in Cook County, Illinois, which includes Chicago, and which is the United States' largest single court jurisdiction, has nearly 400 such patronage positions at his disposal.

[14] Charles P. Nemeth, *Directory of Criminal Justice Education*, Cincinnati: Anderson Publishing Co., 1986.

[15] 42 U.S.C. Sec. 3701 (Pub. L. 90–351).

16 *1967 Report* at p. 125.

17 Harry E. Allen and Clifford E. Simonsen, *An Introduction to Corrections*, New York: Macmillan, 5th edition, 1989, at p. 718.

18 Scholars such as Glendon Schubert and Sheldon Goldman, for example, have based excellent careers on their analyses for judicial behaviour.

19 See Twentieth Century Fund Task Force on the Law Enforcement Assistance Administration, *Law Enforcement: The Federal Role*. New York: McGraw Hill, 1976, at p. 108.

20 U.S. Senate Committee on the Judiciary, *Senate Report No. 98–480*. U.S. Code Congressional and Administrative News, 5728, 5738 (1984).

21 42 U.S.C. Sec. 10705(b)(1)(A) & (B).

22 Paul Reardon, "The Origins and Impact of the County Court System," in Richard Pare (ed.), *Courthouse*, New York: Horizon Press, 1978 at p. 27. This is an excellent illustrated appraisal of America's courthouses from an architectural standpoint, producing a document which has justly received high praise in the photographic press.

23 It is not at all hard, for example, to find a county courthouse whose electrical service capacity is less than the typical American single family house of today.

24 *Courts* volume. Washington, D.C.: U.S. Government Printing Office, 1973.

25 op.cit. supra at endnote 7.

26 James Maddex, "Major Developments in Court Administration since 1967," paper delivered at the 1986 annual meeting of the Academy of Criminal Justice Sciences, Orlando, Florida, March 1986, at p. 10. This is one of several instances where we share Maddex' somewhat optimistic view of the courts' future.

27 National Conference on Court Technology, April 24–27, 1988, Denver, Colorado.

28 See the favourable review of the "WordPerfect" word-processing software in Donna Baron, "Verdict on WordPerfect," *American Bar Association Journal*, vol. 73, May 1987 at pp. 106–107. That this article, with its need for legally oriented footnotes was itself composed with that same software, by the author, the world's most incompetent typist, may be an independent confirmation of the value of this kind of help.

29 See e.g. David P. Anderson, "Spreadsheet Software: Making the Microcomputer Work for the Court Administrator," *Justice System Journal*, vol. 10, #2 (1985).

30 Op. cit. supra at endnote 7.

31 42 U.S.C. Sec. 3701 et seq. If there has been little emphasis on the concerns of administration of justice in America's *federal* courts in this paper, it is largely because of the general observation that in comparative terms, the same enormity of problems simply do not exist in the nation's federal courts.

32 Reprinted in the National Center for State Courts, *1983 Annual Report*. Williamsburg, VA: N.C.S.C., 1983, at p. 7.

13

Review Essay on Judicial Recruitment and Selection

ELLIOT E. SLOTNICK

Introduction

Research in the area of the recruitment and selection of judges for state and federal tribunals has historically occupied a home near the center of the concerns of judicial politics scholars, legal practitioners, and nonprofessional analysts and observers of American judicial systems. As noted by Dubois, "It is fairly certain that no single subject has consumed as many pages in law reviews and law-related publications over the past 50 years as the subject of judicial selection" (1986a:31). (For a representative annotated bibliography see Chinn and Berlsson [1980].) Underlying this concern is the premise stated by Peltason (1955:29) that "the decision as to who will make the decisions affects what decisions will be made." The scene in which discussion unfolds is set by the premise that courts occupy a unique position in the American political system for, while "ours is a government of laws and not men," the judiciary, nevertheless (and, perhaps, ironically) clearly plays a major policymaking role. A great deal has been written about judicial recruitment and selection, but it has been argued that much allegedly social scientific scholarship has been of a rather polemical nature, with authors joining a debate aimed at deciding which method

Reprinted by permission of the *Justice System Journal* from vol. 13, no. 1 (1988), pp. 109–124.

of judicial selection is "best" and most suited to bringing about an often inadequately articulated, but clearly preferred result. The focal point for such writing is often the balance that a particular selection mechanism strikes between the values of accountability of American judges, arguably maximized in electorally-based selection systems, and judicial independence and expertise, arguably best served by appointive selection systems (see Dubois, 1986a).

Skeptical analysts have, however, questioned the relevance of research seeking the answer to the largely normative question of which judicial selection system is "best," and have asked whether examination of judicial selection is an important enterprise at all—raising the possibility "that selection procedures are formalities with little impact on types of judges selected or upon the quality of judicial decision . . ." (Flango and Ducat, 1979:25). Happily, the eclectic research conducted during the past several years on judicial recruitment amply demonstrates the value of this area of inquiry.

Researchers continue to address the question of the "best" selection method, yet they often state their motivating assumptions, goals, and axes-to-grind at the outset, and examine fundamental issues empirically. In addition, research on judicial recruitment mechanisms is pursued for reasons other than the supposition that alternative systems produce judges with particular characteristics who, as judges, will favor certain decisional outcomes. Even if scholars were convinced that different decisional propensities did not flow from alternative selection procedures, judicial selection processes would constitute an important research focus. Critical issues of democratic theory, including questions · relating to what political forces exercise control over recruitment processes and could structure their rewards, would remain. To the extent that the concepts of representation, access, and participation remain important constructs in democratic theory, and to the degree that elite recruitment, campaigns and elections, executive/legislative relationships, etc. remain concerns of broad interest to students of politics, studying judicial treatment and selection remains of compelling importance.

In this article I shall attempt to review the contributions to our knowledge about judicial recruitment and selection at the state level with primary focus on research published since 1983. Unprecedented attention has been focused on all facets of judicial recruitment in recent years for several complementary reasons. At the federal level, Presidents Carter and Reagan enjoyed unique opportunities to remake the lower federal bench by filling large numbers of newly created judgeships. Increased attention has been placed on recruitment to the U.S. Supreme Court, reflecting the resignations of Chief Justice Burger and Justice Powell, the promotion of William Rehnquist, the appointment of

Antonin Scalia, and the nominations Robert Bork, Douglas Ginsburg, and Anthony Kennedy.

Attention to state judicial recruitment has been less subject to the ebbs and flows associated with such contextual events, largely because the coexistence of disparate state procedures has always invited comparative empirical research, and because the state judicial recruitment arena has always been a hotbed of reform-oriented writing and activity. Inasmuch as changes in state selection procedures could be accomplished through processes less demanding than altering the federal constitution, increased attention has been focused on those mechanisms. Increasingly, interests seeking to utilize courts to pursue their policy goals have found state tribunals a congenial route to policy success, thus helping to politicize state selection processes and make them more competitive.

State Judicial Selection Research

The staple of state judicial selection research has been judicial elections, perhaps best represented by the broad based writing of Dubois, whose pathbreaking analysis (1980) address citizens' levels of electoral interest, knowledge, participation, and the determinants of voting choice. The study also focused on the extent of electoral competition, the implications of incumbency, and the role of interests such as bar associations. The research shed light on numerous issues about which little systematic was known and, understandably, helped to generate a great deal of research that refined and extended our understanding.

Hall (1984) provided a temporal expansion of our scholarly gaze with an historical analysis of the relationship of judicial elections to the value of democratic accountability in four states (California, Ohio, Tennessee, and Texas). Hall's analysis initially demonstrated that between 1846 and 1912 every new state entering the union adopted partisan elections as mechanisms for reinforcing judicial professionalism and accountability. As governmental bureaucracies expanded, desires for legal professionalism no longer seemed best served by the simple following of the democratic will. Indeed, judicial accountability became intimately linked with professionalism, and subsequent reform of selection procedures gravitated first towards nonpartisan balloting and, ultimately, merit selection procedures.

By examining turnout rates and roll-off figures (turnout for a judicial election compared to turnout for the major statewide partisan office) for judicial elections in his four-state sample between 1850 and 1920, Hall was able to assess comparatively the implications of such devices as the Australian ballot, nonpartisan elections, and separation of judicial from other elections. Hall's analysis also supplied historical context for the advantages of judicial incumbency, while demonstrating that there are explicable reasons when incumbency fails, such as a judge's failure to stay within "prevailing majoritarian norms on major public issues" (1984:363), a finding that rings true when applied to contemporary judicial electoral settings.

Despite incumbents' occasional losses, Hall concluded, "Democratic accountability was usually a potential rather than a real threat" (1984:368) in the four states studied. Existing accountability tended to be party oriented, and only under highly controversial circumstances did it extend to curbing judges as individuals. Moreover, democratic accountability declined as the mode of judicial selection moved further from direct partisan election, creating a scenario where "judicial elections became the tail on the electoral kite . . . and the public lost its best means of regulating judicial policy making" (1984:369).

Hall, of necessity, relied heavily on aggregate electoral data supplemented by documentation of contextual political concerns. Aggregate voting data remains the central focus for most studies of contemporary judicial elections (see Atkins et al., 1984; Baum, 1983; Dubois, 1984; Scheb, 1983), but analysts have also relied on sample survey techniques to produce greater understanding of individual voting decisions in the judicial electorate (see, e.g., Griffin and Koran, 1983; Lovrich and Sheldon, 1983 and 1985; Sheldon and Lovrich, 1983). Unfortunately, the substantial costs of such analyses have tended to limit their scope and breadth.

Dubois' effort (1984) to examine voting cues in 123 contested nonpartisan primary and subsequent runoff elections for California's major trial courts between 1976 and 1980 utilized more sophisticated analytic techniques than did previous research. Employing a multivariate model that included numerous potential voting cues such as incumbency, occupational ballot labels, ethnicity of a candidate's surname, campaign spending levels, and newspaper and bar association endorsements, Dubois had much success in post-dicting election results.

Dubois' research confirmed the importance of voting cues in nonpartisan elections where shorthand guides may be critical for voters acting with limited information. More broadly, it indicated a gradual rise in judicial electoral competition, slight chinks in the armor of judicial incumbency, and a shift in the nature of judicial campaigning which, tied to a rapid rise in election costs, has helped create greater public clamor for judicial accountability. Such trends collectively attest to the increased visibility of, and public interest in, judicial elections, while also raising questions and concerns for future research. How do judicial elections compare to other low visibility electoral contests, and how does incumbency fare as compared to alternative electoral arenas? If incumbency is no longer as potent as it used to be, why is this so?

What will the rise in electoral competition auger for the nature of judicial campaigns, their cost, and their ability to attract candidates?

Dubois' findings also clearly differentiated between primary and runoff elections and between those in small counties and those in metropolitan areas. Incumbency, one of the most powerful factors in primary elections, appeared to be a hindrance in runoff campaigns, while several factors seemingly unimportant in primaries, such as higher campaign spending, information in voter pamphlets, and/or candidacy endorsements, were far better predictors of runoff election results. Ballot cues were dominant in explaining Los Angeles County results, but were insignificant for understanding results in small and medium-sized counties, while in small counties the impact of campaign spending was clearly greater than in Los Angeles. These findings attest to the complexity of judicial elections and the necessity of narrowly focused research which attempts to understand the diversity of such elections.

Such efforts isolating critical variables in narrow research settings are well represented by the recent work of Baum (1983), Atkins et al. (1984), and Scheb (1983). Baum's research provided an in-depth examination of the electoral fate of incumbents—previously elected judges seeking re-election—and appointed judges seeking election on one set of lower courts in Ohio from 1962 through 1980, with attention to the size and urbanism of judicial constituencies and the implications for voting outcomes of partisan balance and electoral tides. Baum's findings confirmed, for the most part, past research and conventional wisdom. A scant 8 percent of primary or general election campaigns by incumbents resulted in defeat, and only 13 percent of new judges were recruited through the competitive electoral route. Rather, paths to judicial office followed gubernatorial appointment or election to open seats. Baum's findings clearly have implications for the debate over the form that judicial elections should take, for although "Common Pleas elections are more dangerous for incumbents than are retention elections under merit selection systems, . . . the similarities are more striking than the differences" (1983:429). The "competitiveness" of contested elections may, in fact, closely resemble noncontested retention ballots. In full agreement with Dubois, Baum cautions against drawing too many conclusions from limited research contexts. Underlining the differences between Common Pleas and Supreme Court elections in Ohio, Baum asserts, for example, that "a particular system may vary in its working not only among states but within them—between higher and lower courts, between urban and rural counties. . . . The certainty of many commentators' conclusions about judicial election seems unjustified in light of the uncertainties that remain" (1983:430).

In light of these uncertainties, focused analyses which isolate interesting electoral variables are clearly warranted. In an important addition to the literature offering counterpoint to most studies which suggest that judicial elections do not provide voters with salient cues that generate electoral interest and participation, Atkins, DeZee, and Eckert (1984) focused on the significance of racial cues in 1976 Florida Supreme Court races, only one of which contained a black candidate. Race made a clear difference in a landmark election in which the first black statewide candidate was successful in a southern state since Reconstruction: in predominantly black precincts, there were higher voter participation rates and support levels for the black candidate than were evidenced for the victorious candidates in the other Supreme Court races decided in the same election. More broadly, the study demonstrated that elections historically of low salience can, under important contextual circumstances, generate increased voter mobilization. The low saliency of judicial elections appears to be tied only partially to the invisibility of the office and/or its perceived unimportance. Analysts must make a more concerted effort to isolate additional factors which render such elections more salient affairs.

In a related study illuminating another facet of judicial elections, Griffin and Koran (1983) examined retention election processes. Their analysis of two Wyoming Supreme Court retention elections was based on a survey of respondents' voting behavior, levels of information, and specific reasons for voting decisions, and thus was subject to the generic problems of perceptual recall associated with this mode of analysis. There was great symmetry in respondents' answers across the two elections, clearly suggesting that voters were not differentiating between their two retention ballots. One of the interesting findings was that low levels of information were related to nonvoting or failure to recall one's vote, yet among those voting, some information increased one's propensity to vote ''yes'' on retention while a great deal of information was related to a greater likelihood of voting ''no.'' This finding is somewhat analogous to that from earlier studies of public opinion about the U.S. Supreme Court (e.g., Kessel, 1966)—that to know the court was not, necessarily, to love it, with the most critical evaluations coming from among the most knowledgeable.

The larger picture that emerges from the Griffin and Koran study is that retention elections are prototypical landslides attributable to a lack of information, particularly unfavorable information, which would induce a voter to defeat an incumbent with a ''no'' vote. Because negative voting was not anti-institutional in character, but associated with unfavorable information about the judge, the authors view the retention election process as one fostering only limited accountability: judges may be held accountable if questionable behavior becomes public, yet their retention is assured in the absence of such negative information.

The broadest-based study of retention elections was recently published by Hall and Aspin (1987). Eschewing the strategy of examining a single retention election or retention elections in a single state, Hall and Aspin empirically examined all such elections in each of 10 states between 1964 and 1984. The analysis provides historical context and examines the most frequent criticisms of retention elections, including the charges that they insulate judges from popular control, create life-tenured judges, lack voting cues, are issueless, and are met by low voter turnout.

Hall and Aspin found a mean affirmative vote of 77.2 percent in retention elections and an affirmative vote below 60 percent less than 3 percent of the time. Only 22 retention elections (1.2%) resulted in defeat, with 10 such occurrences in Illinois. In 9 of these 10 instances the incumbent received more than 50 percent, but less than the 60 percent affirmative vote uniquely required under Illinois law. The average rolloff rate across all retention elections was a robust 36.2 percent. The analysis confirmed that voters did not differentiate significantly among judges, while also noting that the rare defeat of a judge did not tend to affect the affirmative votes for other candidates appearing on the same retention ballot. Defeats did not follow gradual erosion of support for a judge, but occurred instead somewhat precipitously often in one's first retention bid. While the mean affirmative vote has appeared to decline over time, the authors positively link retention voting to temporal patterns of public trust in government.

Mention should also be made of research examining efforts by the organized bar to assess candidacies in retention elections. Griffin and Murdock (1985) utilized data from the 1978, 1980, and 1982 Wyoming State Bar Judicial Polls to determine how attorneys' perceptions of personal and judicial attributes related to whether a judge's retention was favored. Interestingly, the factors correlating most highly in linking attorneys' evaluations with their retention recommendations were attributes over which the judges did have some control, including their fairmindedness and deliberateness in reaching decisions, their openmindedness and impartiality, and their courteousness towards litigants, witnesses, and lawyers. In a related, methodologically-oriented study concerned with the potential problem of bias in judicial evaluation surveys, Koebel (1983) concluded that when carefully designed and administered, no systematic biases necessarily existed in bar evaluation polls. The impact of such polls, however, may be another matter, as revealed by Scheb's assessment (1983) of the 1978, 1980, and 1982 Florida Advisory Preference Polls on appellate judges, where none of 54 incumbents were denied retention. The aggregate correlation found between bar poll results and voter support was negligible, leading to the conclusion that idiosyncratic factors such as ballot design and voter ignorance of retention election procedures were more helpful for understanding retention majorities than the bar's advisory input.

Focus on individual electoral behavior in the context of contested primary and general judicial elections emerges as the major concern of Sheldon and Lovrich whose studies (Lovrich and Sheldon, 1983, 1985; Sheldon and Lovrich, 1983) examined, albeit somewhat differently, registered voters' responses to surveys regarding elections in Oregon and Washington. They explored voter knowledge and voting behavior while also addressing the complex question of how different recruitment systems influenced electoral behavior and voter attitudes towards the tenuous balance between accountability and independence that lies at the heart of popular concern with judicial elections.

While not necessarily so characterized in that light by the authors, the picture they draw of the judicial electorate's lack of knowledge is not a very encouraging one, with only a slight majority able to identify more correct than incorrect candidate names from a proffered list (Sheldon and Lovrich, 1983). Over two-thirds of the voters admitted to being unable to name both candidates in a contested race (Lovrich and Sheldon, 1985), over one-third admitted to having no information at all about the judicial election, and a plurality of voters claimed some, but not enough information. It is striking that nearly half of those claiming to have no information actually voted and that fewer than one in five actual voters felt that they had enough information on which to base their vote (Sheldon and Lovrich, 1983). As one might expect, participation increased among those who perceived themselves as more knowledgeable, and voters across all knowledge levels supported nonpartisan judicial elections. Apparently such an electoral process, unencumbered by partisan mediation, was perceived by the voters as assuring the most direct judicial accountability.

The most interesting facet of the Lovrich and Sheldon studies is their exploration of public attitudes on the appropriate balance between judgeship accountability, and judicial independence. The most highly informed voters (based on candidate knowledge) were the least favorably disposed towards the most widely held model of accountability whereby judges are expected to act as "delegates" and strictly follow the public will. Rather, these relatively informed voters favored a more equal balance between independence and accountability and, indeed, they were the least critical of the "trustee" model of adjudication, whereby judges act most independently on behalf of the public and not simply through their mandate. Those with lower levels of knowledge were most favorably disposed to a view of elections as "sanctions," whereby judges acting independent on the electorate's desires could be removed. Based on their data the authors concluded that successful efforts to educate the public would have beneficial consequences by producing public support of a significant degree of judicial independence, a goal they clearly favor (Lovrich and Sheldon, 1983:250).

These preferences were also supported by Lovrich and Sheldon's analysis of the relationship between the "articulation" of an electoral system—that is, the number of actors involved in the initiation, screening, and affirmation of candidates—and the voters' preferred model of judicial elections. Highly articulated electoral settings coincided with greater electoral participation, varied information sources, and a greater likelihood of informed voting. Voters in such settings adopted "a position most in line with a balance between democratic accountability and judicial independence." They resembled "a responsible electorate which comes to the polls relatively well informed to cast ballots, and reflect an appreciation of the special character of judicial elections" (Lovrich and Sheldon, 1985:290–291).

Throughout their research Sheldon and Lovrich cast their findings in a reform mold, asserting that nonpartisan elections can aid in maintaining an appropriate balance between judicial accountability and judicial independence as long as voters are knowledgeable. The onus for ensuring such a system is seen to lie with candidates and legal professionals who have inadequately met their responsibility to supply the information to the electorate that the authors claim they want (Sheldon and Lovrich, 1983:245). Such research has taken important first steps in going beyond simple analysis of voting results to a richer examination of the perceptions of the judicial electorate. The work is clearly suggestive of important questions at the nexus of the judicial process and democratic theory. How can candidates effectively establish name recognition and offer useful and more information to the electorate in a manner consistent with the unique constraints of judicial elections? How does the problem of the "ignorant" judicial voter compare with other electoral settings? How could policymakers frame electoral settings so as to minimize the possibility that the "unknowledgeable" will decide electoral outcomes? Would such engineering be justified? Similarly, how could policymakers ensure a highly articulated selection system? Most broadly, the research resuscitates the timeless normative questions of what role should courts play in a democratic polity and, further, what role could or should judges play in fostering that role.

Sheldon and Lovrich are, perhaps, too optimistic about the level of accountability implicit in contemporary judicial elections given the thrust of their data. Interestingly, Dubois is even more sanguine and argues that such elections should be assessed by "their ability to allow voters to control the general direction and broad boundaries of public policy. . ." (1986a:41–42), not voters' specific knowledge of candidates and their issue stances. Further, Dubois argues, there are inherent tradeoffs and, at times, mutually inconsistent objectives and goals in alternative selection mechanisms which analysts must deal with more realistically and with greater sophistication.

Another facet of the judicial electoral process to which attention has been turned is campaign financing (Dubois, 1986b; Dubois, 1986c; Nicholson and Weiss, 1986). Dubois' broad-scaled analysis of judicial campaign spending examines the generic questions of the overall costs of such campaigns and the difficulties such costs can create for candidates. Useful comparisons are drawn between the costs of judicial campaigns and the contesting of other low visibility elections. Dubois examined over 400 candidates competing in 153 contested nonpartisan primary and runoff elections for seats on the major California trial court between 1976 and 1982. Given the dearth of research in this area, Dubois' limited objectives of describing overall spending levels and identifying "factors that drive those costs upward and . . . affect candidates' attitudes and expectations" about how much money they will need are understandable and warranted (1986c:267). Dubois showed that significant increases in the absolute cost of judicial elections occurred between 1976 and 1978, but electoral costs remained relatively constant since 1976 in real dollar terms and have actually gone down when one controls for inflation. Campaign spending does not increase proportionately with constituency size suggesting, perhaps, that activists' fundraising efforts in such elections cannot keep pace with the growth of a mass electorate. "Open" races lacking incumbents—with a greater amount of competition—cost more than races contested by incumbents. Average spending by candidates, however, is approximately 25 percent higher in races with incumbents, predominantly because of the incumbent candidates' spending.

In a conclusion which runs somewhat counter to emerging conventional wisdom, Dubois asserts that, viewed from the systemic level, "judicial election costs are neither extraordinarily high nor caught in an inexorable upward spiral" (1986c:281). Indeed, the amount of money spent appears to be so minimal as to raise serious questions about the relative ability of judicial candidates to "compete" in the electoral marketplace with higher spending candidates seeking more visible offices. Thus, Dubois questions "whether a sufficient amount of money is being spent on judicial elections to help voters make intelligent choices among competing candidates" (1986c:283). However, despite the relatively small amounts of money involved, judicial candidates operate under numerous constraints which can make even the minimal expenditures at stake seem quite formidable to the individual contestant, with the constraints perhaps such "as to limit judicial candidacies only to the wealthy" (1986c:283).

Researching contributions rather than expenditures, Dubois examined the conflict of interests that might arise when candidates rely on contributors, particularly lawyers, for their solvency (1986b). Viewing 1980 elections, Dubois challenged, in part, emerging conventional wisdoms about judicial campaign financing. The data revealed that lawyers, although the largest source of funds, contributed under 40 percent of the total and made relatively small contributions. The vast amount of borrowed money for these campaigns was derived from candidates and/or their families. Dubois concluded that "the contributor base for judicial elections is actually quite varied, with well more than half of all the dollars contributed in larger amounts originating with groups and individuals who are outside the legal community" (1986b:12). While the dominance of personal financing may dispel allegations of undue influence by contributors on judges, concerns about access to judicial office on an equitable basis are clearly exacerbated. Indeed, in research on funding of election to Cook County Circuit Courts in 1984 which produced similar results, Nicholson and Weiss (1986) are clearly unhappy about the implications of their findings. They note that heavy reliance on personal funding disadvantages potential candidates of modest means, while the stockpiling of large sums of money by the financially strongest candidates can add an aura of impropriety to the electoral setting. They conclude, "The problems inherent in the funding of judicial elections may be one more reason for seriously considering . . . alternative selection methods" (Nicholson and Weiss, 1986:25).

The studies of judicial campaign finance raise numerous questions including that of the object of campaign expenditures. Do candidates attempt to develop judicial campaign issues or, alternatively, are they simply seeking name recognition? What kinds of issues are pressed? How do expenditures in such campaigns compare with those in other low-cost elections and how might this relate to the unique constraints of judicial campaign competition? What do judicial campaign contributors want for their participation? Are they more altruistic than donors in other electoral settings? How does the pattern of personal versus third party financing compare to other electoral settings? Most broadly, do the concerns about the representativeness of an elective judiciary, the role of incumbency and money in competition, and the sources of campaign funding suggest that the option of public financing needs to be considered in an electoral arena rarely suggested as fertile ground for that reform movement?

While much analysis has focused on judicial electoral processes, there has been little examination of alternative methods of state judicial selection, particularly gubernatorial appointment. Such appointment processes are often analogous to federal judicial recruitment and researchers can adopt approaches resembling work on federal judicial selection as exemplified by Dubois' "State Trial Court Appointments: Does the Governor Make A Difference?" (1985). The analysis examined 658 appointments by three governors between 1959 and 1977 to

California's major trial court. In addition to providing a comparison of the appointee's demographic, educational, career, and political characteristics, sitting judges were surveyed about the processes through which they were appointed.

The data clearly revealed that different gubernatorial administrations open up distinct paths to the bench, like Slotnick's finding (1984a) that different paths to federal judgeships characterize appointees in a single administration on racial and gender lines. Partisan political activity was one factor distinguishing the three governors' selection processes, which led to distinct ideological results as well. While Governor Reagan's Judicial Selection Advisory Boards appeared to remove the governor somewhat from the selection process, partisan ideology remained facilitated through prior staff screening. Appointees' perceptions also varied across administrations, with Reagan's most likely to view support by the bar and business leaders as critical, while Governor "Pat" Brown's designates felt that support of local political leaders and personal friendship with the governor was a key to their success (Dubois, 1985:23–24).

Although Dubois demonstrated politicization of gubernatorial appointment processes across administrations, it is noteworthy that "characteristics related to professional preparation and experience did not vary much by governor" (Dubois, 1985:28). Indeed, as research on the federal level has suggested (see Slotnick, 1983b), "quality" of the judicial branch in an absolute sense may not be affected by alternative selection processes as much as such processes help to determine whose definitions of judicial merit will prevail. Thus, white males appointed by President Carter to the federal bench had higher incomes, were older, enjoyed more years at bar, were admitted to practice before higher level tribunals, were more likely to be private practitioners in traditional legal practices, and were more likely to receive higher ABA ratings than their "nontraditional" (female and/or nonwhite) counterparts (Slotnick, 1984b). The paths to federal judgeships for nontraditional appointees were more likely to emerge from the academy (for women) or from other judgeships (for nonwhites) than for white males. Most importantly, Slotnick's analysis suggested that, "while differences abounded among the candidates . . . , they did not . . . underline the inherent superiority of . . . the white male nominees." Rather, differences between the career paths of white male and nontraditional appointees reflected "the different socio, economic, and political roles played in the aggregate by the groups to which nontraditional candidates belong . . . and the opportunities available to members of these groups" (1984b:388).

Much comparative research across presidential administrations (Goldman, 1965, 1972, 1981, 1985, 1987; Fowler, 1983, 1984) offers further testimony to the relationship between the values of the appointing authority and the characteristics of an administration's nominees. Thus, Fowler argued that President Carter's "merit" appointment process was a mechanism for broadening participation and accomplishing affirmative action, while the centralized Reagan approach best furthered his ideological goals (1983). Indeed, formal judicial selection mechanisms may not be central to understanding the outcomes of appointment processes. Such formal processes may be highly visible "and an easy target for the reformer's criticisms," yet they may also serve as smoke-screens "tending to obscure from the analyst's view the most important concerns for understanding recruitment outcomes" (Slotnick, 1984a:237–238). The lessons learned from research at the federal level were reflected in Dubois' findings and his conclusion in California that "the two parties draw their support from different social classes and have distinct commitments to particular ethnic and sexual groups," which is "reflected in the different demographic mix of judges appointed under each governor" (1985:28). These case studies, as well as work on the federal level, demonstrate the need for systematic analyses of executive management style, party organization, and other variables which might affect recruitment outcomes.

Concluding Thoughts

An examination of judicial selection literature published during the past several years reveals that this is an area in which a great deal of wide-ranging scholarly activity is taking place at both the federal and state judiciary levels. Clearly, from the perspective of the academic social sciences, while many research approaches and diverse methodologies have been utilized by analysts to examine judicial recruitment concerns, this is not an area where great theoretical advances of broad interest and applicability are likely to be made. Studies have tended to take place in limited research contexts where analysts have viewed the trees but not the forest. Research approaches have often been idiosyncratic and many case studies have been accompanied with little synthesis and integration of knowledge. In part, this may reflect a healthy situation in which judicial selection research and commentary is undertaken from many quarters, and "any discussion of the subject must include diverse viewpoints and recognize the potential contributions to be found in the alternative perspectives brought . . . by practicing attorneys, judges, academic researchers, public office holders, journalists, and members of the public" (Dubois, 1986a:31). Scholars are raising numerous interesting and important questions about the processes which exist for the recruitment of judges, and they are receiving answers which have greatly expanded our substantive understanding of judicial selection while also providing the grist for the mill of future research.

Often, the findings of the studies discussed throughout this essay have had significant policy implications for actors participating in judicial selection processes in some capacity. Thus, for example, studies of judicial elections have made it clear that the dearth of information about candidates and races is a major roadblock to such elections playing their intended role in a democratic polity. We have also learned that institutional arrangements may affect voter turnout more than information and knowledge. Clearly, the research in this area is suggestive of directions that reforms of judicial campaigns can take as well as of strategic alterations that might be made by judgeship candidates contesting those elections. At the federal level, analysts have underscored the complexity of judicial selection behavior, while documenting that reforms in processes, per se, may not be directly translatable into alternations in judicial behavior. At bottom, our discussion has also demonstrated that there are numerous questions which have not been addressed or about which much remains unsaid.

Little research has attempted to bridge the gap between state and federal selection arenas. Thus, for example, while research has documented systemic differences among federal judges at different levels of the bench (Slotnick, 1983a), it might be instructive to compare and contrast judges across state and federal benches. Such a linkage could lead to a broadened assessment and understanding of the strengths, weaknesses, capabilities, and unique roles of judiciaries operative at diverse governmental levels. More broadly, analysts of judicial recruitment have failed to incorporate their research with studies of elite recruitment in other political contexts. This is particularly telling with regard to understanding the emergence of individuals from underrepresented groups, particularly minorities and women, to governmental positions.

In addition, it should be stressed that studies of judicial selection have implications which go well beyond the primary concern of who gets chosen to fill judgeship vacancies. Rather, research in this area has clear implications for a broader understanding of elite recruitment, elections and voting behavior, political participation, political campaigns, executive-legislative relations and, ultimately, questions about the very nature of representative democracy and the requirements of democratic theory.

Fortuitous circumstances such as the large numbers of vacant judgeships at the federal level and contested judgeships in the state judiciaries have surely given an impetus and momentum to research in this area. The breadth and scope of the studies discussed throughout this essay clearly suggest that the area will continue to be a productive and provocative one for research scholars in the years ahead.

References

Atkins, Burton, Mathew DeZee, and William Eckert (1984) "State Supreme Court Elections: The Significance of Racial Cues," 12 *American Politics Quarterly* 211.

Baum, Lawrence (1983) "The Electoral Fate of Incumbent Judges in the Ohio Court of Common Pleas," 66 *Judicature* 420.

Chinn, Nancy and Larry Berkson (1980) *Literature on Judicial Selection*. Chicago: American Judicature Society.

DuBois, Philip (1980) *From Ballot to Bench: Judicial Elections and the Quest for Accountability*. Austin: University of Texas Press.

_____ (1984) "Voting Cues in Nonpartisan Trial Court Elections: A Multivariate Assessment," 18 *Law & Society Review* 395.

_____ (1985) "State Trial Court Appointments: Does the Governor Make a Difference?" 69 *Judicature* 20.

_____ (1986a) "Accountability, Independence, and the Selection of State Judges: The Role of Popular Judicial Elections," 40 *Southwestern Law Journal* 31.

_____ (1986b) "Financing Trial Court Elections: Who Contributes to California Judicial Campaigns?" 70 *Judicature* 8.

_____ (1986c) "Penny For Your Thoughts? Campaign Spending in California Trial Court Elections, 1976–1982," 38 *Western Political Quarterly* 265.

Flango, Victor and Craig Ducat (1979) "What Difference Does Method of Judicial Selection Make?" 5 *The Justice System Journal* 25.

Fowler, W. Gary (1983) "A Comparison of Initial Recommendation Procedures: Judicial Selection Under Reagan and Carter," 1 *Yale Law and Policy Review* 299.

_____ (1984) "Judicial Selection Under Reagan and Carter: A Comparison of Their Initial Recommendation Procedures," 67 *Judicature* 265.

Goldman, Sheldon (1965) "Characteristics of Eisenhower and Kennedy Appointees to the Lower Federal Courts," 18 *Western Political Quarterly* 755.

_____ (1972) "Johnson and Nixon Appointees to the Federal Lower Courts," 34 *Journal of Politics* 934.

_____ (1981) "Carter's Judicial Appointments: A Lasting Legacy," 64 *Judicature* 344.

_____ (1985) "Reorganizing the Judiciary: The First Term Appointments," 68 *Judicature* 313.

_____ (1987) "Reagan's Second Term Judicial Appointments: The Battle at Midway," 70 *Judicature* 324.

Griffin, Kenyon and Michael Horan (1983) "Patterns of Voting Behavior in Judicial Retention Elections for Supreme Court Justices in Wyoming," 67 *Judicature* 68.

Griffin, Kenyon and Margaret Maier Murdock (1985) "Practicing Attorneys and Judicial Retention Decisions: Judging the Judges in Wyoming," 69 *Judicature* 37.

Hall, Kermit (1984) "Progressive Reform and the Decline of Democratic Accountabilty: The Popular Election of State Supreme Court Judges, 1850–1920," 2 *American Bar Foundation Research Journal* 345.

Hall, William and Larry Aspin (1987) "What Twenty Years of Judicial Retention Elections Have Told Us," 70 *Judicature* 340.

Kessel, John (1966) "Public Perceptions of the Supreme Court," 10 *Midwest Journal of Political Science* 167.

Koebel, C. Theodore (1983) "The Problem of Bias in Judicial Evaluation Surveys," 67 *Judicature* 224.

Lovrich, Nicholas, Jr. and Charles Sheldon (1983) "Voters in Contested, Non-Partisan Judicial Elections: A Responsible Electorate or a Problematic Public," 36 *Western Political Quarterly* 241.

_____ (1985) "Assessing Judicial Elections: Effects upon the Electorate of High and Low Articulation Systems," 38 *Western Political Quarterly* 276.

Nicholson, Marlene and Bradley Weiss (1986) "Funding Judicial Campaigns in the Circuit Court of Cook County," 70, *Judicature* 17.

Peltason, Jack (1955) *Federal Courts in the Political Process*. New York: Random House.

Scheb, John II (1983) "Is Anyone Listening? Assessing Bar Influence in Merit Retention Elections in Florida," 67 *Judicature* 112.

Sheldon, Charles and Nicholas Lovrich, Jr. (1983) "Knowledge and Judicial Voting: The Oregon and Washington Experience," 67 *Judicature* 234.

Slotnick, Elliot (1983a) "Federal Trial and Appellate Judges: How Do They Differ?" 36 *Western Political Quarterly* 570.

_____ (1983b) "Lowering the Bench or Raising It Higher?: Affirmative Action and Judicial Selection During the Carter Administration," 1 *Yale Law and Policy Review* 270.

_____ (1984a) "Judicial Selection Systems and Nomination Outcomes: Does the Process Make a Difference?" 12 *American Politics Quarterly* 225.

_____ (1984b) "The Paths to the Federal Bench: Gender, Race, and Judicial Recruitment Variation," 67 *Judicature* 370.

14

Judicial Recruitment and Racial Diversity on State Courts
An Overview

BARBARA LUCK GRAHAM

The informal and formal processes of determining who becomes a judge evoke intense interest and debate among various groups that seek to influence the nature, character and policy outcomes of our nation's courts. Political parties, bar associations, political elites, and interest groups (business, union, environmental, or civil rights organizations, etc.) struggle to participate and influence the processes of judicial recruitment and selection at the national and state level with the desired goal of shaping judicial policy outcomes favorable to their interests. The political struggle over judicial recruitment and selection also raises the issue of diversity on the bench whereby members of racial and ethnic minority groups and women seek representatives of their groups to serve on courts in order to insure that they have a voice in judicial decision-making. Viewed in this context, judicial recruitment is an important area of study because it speaks to the broader theoretical issue of minority group elite recruitment and representation in the judicial arena.

The issue of racial diversity on courts is one that has been given uneven scholarly attention in the literature on judicial recruitment.[1] On one hand, considerable attention has been paid to minority group representation at the federal court level. For example, conventional wisdom

Reprinted by permission of the American Judicature Society and the author from *Judicature*, vol. 74, no. 1 (June/July 1990), pp. 28–34.

now posits that representational criteria such as race, gender, and religious factors figure prominently for nomination to the U.S. Supreme Court and the lower federal courts.[2] To be sure, the determination of how much weight will be attached to representational factors varies among presidents and is usually dependent upon partisan and ideological considerations. Yet the literature seems to suggest that there is an expectation that diversity on the federal bench will continue to be an issue as long as the federal courts are accorded special status in our dual legal system.

Only recently, however, has similar attention been given to minority judicial recruitment at the state level. Recognizing the importance of state courts in the administration of justice and that most minority citizens are likely to come into contact with state, not federal courts, minority groups are now focusing on the extent to which state judicial systems provide opportunities to serve on the bench. Minority group efforts to penetrate access to the state bench become more problematic when we consider the existence of 50 state court systems accompanied with varied formal and informal judicial recruitment and selection processes to fill vacant seats on these courts. Whether states become and remain committed to a diverse bench will be a major challenge for minority groups and women in the 1990s.

An examination of the literature on judicial recruitment and black representation on the state bench reveals that additional research is necessary to address the important questions raised in this area. This study seeks to fill a major gap in the literature in its examination of minority judicial recruitment at the state level. The purpose of this article is to examine characteristics of judicial recruitment as it pertains to racial diversity on the state bench. It focuses on four major areas of concern. First, data are examined which explore the extent to which blacks are represented on state courts at all levels of the judicial hierarchy. Next, it looks at the structural and contextual explanations of black underrepresentation on state courts. Third, it examines two remedies for correcting the problem of black underrepresentation on the state bench. Finally, it considers the consequences and implications of the lack of racial diversity on the state bench for the administration of justice.

The research population under investigation is the universe of black judges presiding over state courts of general and limited jurisdiction in the United States. The data source for identifying black judges comes from a list of black judges in the United States compiled by the Joint Center for Political Studies (JCPS) and the Judicial Council of the National Bar Association.[3] This roster includes names, addresses and indication of the court presided over by the judge as of July 1986. Attempts were made to verify the existence of the judges on the specified courts and to determine how they initially obtained their seats for the highest general jurisdiction and special jurisdiction courts (civil or criminal) in the states. These data collection efforts involved gathering information from state court clerks and administrators,[4] court biographical directories,[5] state reporters and state official manuals. As a result, this study analyzes data on 714 state court judges covering 41 states for 1986.

Several major developments compel a reexamination of how characteristics of judicial recruitment affect racial diversity on the state bench. Greater attention to the policymaking activities of state courts raises the issue of whether women and minorities will have the opportunity to influence outcomes at all levels of the state judiciary. This development comes at a time when the U.S. Supreme Court and the lower federal judiciary are becoming increasingly conservative on issues of civil liberties and civil rights. The importance of this research is also underscored in light of several states' reexamination of their methods of selecting state judges. A contemporary assessment of black representation on state courts is expected to reveal additional insights into the problem of minority judicial recruitment at the state level.

Are Blacks Underrepresented?

The few empirical studies that analyze black judicial recruitment largely draw upon a data base in the early 1970s; a period in which there were extremely small numbers of black judges on state courts.[6] In 1972, Cook noted that one of the major research problems that occurs in an examination of black representation in the judiciary was identifying and locating black judges on state courts.[7] In order to assess the factors that affect black judicial recruitment, it is first necessary to offer a recent profile of black representation on state courts. In this section, two major issues are addressed. First, data are presented which show the nationwide distribution of black judges on state courts by level of court. In analyzing these data, I attempt to address the substantive question of whether blacks are actually underrepresented on state courts.

The JCPS publication identified 714 black judges presiding over state courts of general and limited jurisdiction and included a listing of quasi-judicial officials as of July 1986.[8] These data were coded and classified according to the distribution of black judges on the state bench by level of court and are presented in table 1. The number of seats on states' major appellate and trial courts are also included. As of 1986, we find that 41 states had black representation on their major and minor courts. Specifically, the data in table 1 reveal that nine states; Alaska, Hawaii, Maine, Montana, New Hampshire, North Dakota, South Dakota, Vermont and Wyoming, lacked black representation on their state courts. One might argue that opportunities for recruitment would be increased or limited depending on the size of the black population in the state. If the percentage of the black voting age population in the state is used as a measure of black population size,[9] we find that among the nine states listed above, seven had a black voting age population of less than one-half of 1 percent. Contrastingly, Idaho and Utah, states with less than one-half of 1 percent black voting age population, had black representation on their state courts.

Table 1   Distribution of black judges on state bench by level of court, 1986

State	State supreme court	Intermediate appellate court	General trial court	Total major courts	Limited juris. courts	Total all
Alabama	1 (9)	— (8)	4 (124)	5	14	19
Arizona	— (5)	— (18)	1 (101)	1	1	2
Arkansas	— (7)	— (6)	— (62)	0	2	2
California	1 (7)	4 (77)	29 (724)	34	54	88
Colorado	— (7)	— (10)	3 (107)	3	2	5
Connecticut	— (7)	— (9)	7 (139)	7	—	7
Delaware	— (5)	*	1 (13)	1	4	5
Florida	1 (7)	1 (46)	7 (362)	9	7	16
Georgia	— (7)	1 (9)	4 (131)	5	15	20
Idaho	— (5)	— (3)	1 (33)	1	—	1
Illinois	— (7)	3 (34)	42 (780)	45	—	45
Indiana	— (5)	— (12)	2 (206)	2	3	5
Iowa	— (9)	— (6)	1 (153)	1	—	1
Kansas	— (7)	1 (10)	2 (215)	3	—	3
Kentucky	— (7)	— (14)	2 (91)	2	—	2
Louisiana	— (7)	1 (48)	5 (192)	6	27	33
Maryland	1 (7)	1 (13)	11 (109)	13	10	23
Massachusetts	— (7)	1 (10)	4 (61)	5	12	17
Michigan	1 (7)	2 (18)	22 (196)	25	44	69
Minnesota	— (7)	— (12)	4 (224)	4	—	4
Mississippi	1 (9)	*	1 (79)	2	31	33
Missouri	— (7)	1 (32)	6 (303)	7	4	11
Nebraska	— (7)	*	— (48)	0	1	1
Nevada	— (5)	*	2 (35)	2	—	2
New Jersey	— (7)	1 (28)	11 (321)	12	21	33
New Mexico	— (5)	— (7)	— (59)	0	1	1
New York	1 (7)	3 (47)	24 (484)	28	35	63
North Carolina	1 (7)	2 (12)	1 (72)	4	14	18
Ohio	— (7)	2 (53)	6 (330)	8	19	27
Oklahoma	— (12)**	— (12)	1 (143)	1	2	3
Oregon	— (7)	— (10)	1 (85)	1	1	2
Pennsylvania	1 (7)	1 (24)	24 (330)	26	10	36
Rhode Island	— (5)	*	— (19)	0	1	1
South Carolina	1 (5)	1 (6)	1 (31)	3	51	54
Tennessee	— (5)	— (21)	8 (125)	8	3	11
Texas	— (18)**	1 (80)	6 (374)	7	27	34
Utah	— (5)	— (7)	— (29)	0	1	1
Virginia	1 (7)	1 (10)	2 (122)	4	2	6
Washington	— (9)	— (16)	3 (133)	3	1	4
West Virginia	— (5)	*	2 (60)	2	1	3
Wisconsin	— (7)	— (13)	3 (197)	3	—	3
Total	11 (289)	28 (741)	254 (7402)	293 (8432)	421	714

( ) Number of seats on state courts. *See* Council of State Governments. *The Book of the States, 1988-89 Edition.* (Lexington. KY) 157-160 for a complete description of how these figures were derived.
— No black judges on court.
* Court does not exist in state.
** Includes state supreme court and court of criminal appeals seats.

Table 1 also demonstrates that 41 percent (N = 293) of the black judges identified by the JCPS roster were classified as general jurisdiction judges and 59 percent (N = 421) were either limited jurisdiction judges or quasi-judicial officials. This finding indicates that black judges are more likely to be found on limited jurisdiction courts such as municipal courts, small claims courts, family courts or justice of the peace courts. It is likely that limited jurisdiction courts serve as important access routes for black judgeships in the state judiciary and subsequently advancing through judicial hierarchy.[10] An examination of biographical data on black judges serving on general jurisdiction courts indicates that many of them served on limited jurisdiction courts prior to their 1986 positions.

The fact that most black judges in the state judiciary are located on limited jurisdiction courts also suggests that they currently have limited opportunities to participate in judicial policymaking at the trial and appellate levels. The data presented in table 1 show that 87 percent (N = 254) of the black judges preside over trial courts of general jurisdiction and 13 percent (N = 39) preside over intermediate appellate courts and state supreme courts. General jurisdiction courts address a wide range of issues on matters such as criminal offenses, personal injury actions, divorce cases and the overall important policymaking function of allocating resources (in terms of gains and losses) that affect millions of individuals. Moreover, issues of discrimination in a variety of contexts are frequently before state courts; thus minority judges may be able to bring additional sensitivity and insight in dealing with these issues. Without greater numbers of black judges at the major trial and appellate levels, one can argue that the black community is deprived of the minority perspective on legal matter's and the development of the law at the state level.

The judicial recruitment literature also indicates the importance of region as a contextual factor in contributing to our understanding of the distribution of judicial selection systems throughout the country. An overview of the distribution of the five major selection systems indicates the nonrandom tendency of states to choose one selection system over another. For example, we find that elective systems (partisan and nonpartisan) dominate among southern states, merit systems are most often found in the midwest and western regions, and gubernatorial appointment systems are primarily found in the northeast. A breakdown of table 1 by region indicates that the north central states have the highest number of general jurisdiction black judges (N = 88), followed by the northeast (N = 70), south (N = 56) and the west (N = 40).[11] These findings are somewhat striking given that 15 states make up the south as defined in this study and that the south has the highest black voting age population and the highest percentage of black elected officials compared to other regions of the country. This finding illustrates a wide disparity in regional distributions of general jurisdiction black judges. In contrast, the south leads the other regions for limited jurisdiction judges (N = 210), followed by the northeast (N = 79), north central (N = 71) and the west (N = 61). Region, then, is a useful contextual variable when examining recruitment patterns of blacks to the state bench.

Have black attorneys made progress in obtaining seats on state courts? The American Judicature Society reported in 1973 that slightly more than 1 percent of judges on the state bench were black.[12] The trends presented in table 2 indicate that progress has been made for obtaining general jurisdiction seats over time. What is significant about the figures presented in table 2 is that a large percentage of black judges (46 percent) for which data were available obtained their seats since 1980. If this trend continues, one can speculate that black attorneys will continue to make progress in obtaining seats on the state bench in the 1990s.

Table 2 Year general jurisdiction judges initially obtained seats*

Year	N	%
1957-1969	14	6%
1970-1974	40	17%
1975-1979	72	31%
1980-1986	109	46%
Total	235	100%

*The year the judge initially reached the bench could not be determined for 58 judges.

Against this background, are blacks underrepresented in the state judiciary? Of course, representation can be defined in several ways such as symbolic, substantive, and proportional.[13] Symbolic representation is exemplified by the presence of judges by identifiable members of their race or gender. Smith and Crockett have shown how black judges provide symbolic pride, inspiration and serve as a symbol of law and justice for members of their group.[14] Once on the bench, it is argued that black judges provide substantive representation by deciding cases in a manner which reduces the vestiges of racism in the legal system.[15] Empirical studies have shown that once on the bench, black judicial decisionmaking increases equality of treatment among defendants.[16]

The most prevalent definition of representation found in the judicial recruitment literature is proportional representation; that is, the proportion of black judges should reflect the same proportion of blacks in the general population. Indeed, if this definition is used, unquestionably blacks are underrepresented on the state bench. Yet, using proportional representation as the yardstick is problematic since for a large majority of seats on state courts, only licensed attorneys are eligible to serve as judges. From another perspective then, an argument can be raised that the black attorney population is the most relevant population to measure against the proportion of black judges on the state bench.

Recent figures indicate that black judges make up approximately 3.8 percent of all the full- and part-time seats on the state bench.[17] Similarly, black attorneys constitute approximately 3 percent of the legal profession. Tentatively, one could conclude from these figures that black judges are not underrepresented on the state bench since the proportion of judges on the state bench are roughly equal to the number of attorneys. On the other hand, we should consider the point that black attorneys are grossly underrepresented in the legal profession; figures indicate that there are about 25,000 black attorneys out of a total pool of 750,000.[18] From this perspective, using the proportion of black attorneys as the population to measure against is misleading for it does not take into account the small pool of available black attorneys to serve on the bench. In the following section, I will consider the utility of this contextual factor in explaining black representation on the state bench.

Explaining a Homogeneous Bench

What explains black underrepresentation on the state bench? The judicial recruitment and selection literature advances two dominant approaches in accounting for the lack of racial diversity on the state bench: structural and contextual explanations. The theoretical underpinnings of the empirical research that highlights structural characteristics of judicial recruitment and selection are generally linked to elite recruitment in other political contexts. This view suggests that structural and systemic forces in the political environment affect the extent to which underrepresented groups gain access to positions at all levels of government. For example, the political participation literature has demonstrated that barriers to voting (e.g., vote dilution techniques and registration requirements) have enhanced black nonvoting and engenders the inability of black citizens to choose representatives of their choice. Drawing on this literature, studies have sought to determine whether judicial selection mechanisms are central to our understanding of recruitment outcomes for minority groups.

Contextual explanations have also emerged in explaining the paucity of black judges on the state bench. This approach suggests that other factors besides judicial selection affect the extent to which blacks will be represented on the state bench. The contextual variable that has received the most attention in the literature is the availability of black attorneys to serve on the state bench. The expectation is that the lack of black attorneys correlates with the lack of black judges on the bench. State statutory qualifications are likely to affect the size of the pool of available attorneys from which judges are selected. The primary ones include age, residency requirements, and legal qualifications such as being a member of the state bar or having practiced law for a certain period of time. These requirements[19] vary among the states, but because of the lack of nationwide data on black attorneys by state, it is difficult to assess the impact of these qualifications or the extent to which they affect the numbers of black attorneys to serve on the state bench.

Three early studies offer some insights on the effects of judicial selection and black representation on the state bench. Cook found that in southern courts, electoral systems did not produce black judges on major courts but a large majority of blacks served on rural courts of limited jurisdiction where in many instances a law degree was not a necessary qualification.[20] Her examination of black representation on northern courts revealed that nonpartisan elections were more favorable in enhancing black representation on state courts, partisan elections were least favorable and that gubernatorial appointment tended to produce idiosyncratic results. In her study, Cook also demonstrated that the very low percentage of black lawyers correlated with the lack of black judges on both northern and southern courts, but this variable did not account entirely for the small number of black judges.

Smith examined black judicial attitudes toward recruitment and selection based on an early 1970s survey of 185 state and federal judges.[21] His study indicated that while 55 percent of the judgeships were listed as elective, 77 percent of the black jurists surveyed were appointed to the bench. His analysis also demonstrated that judicial elections tended to be less influential in the recruitment of black judges. Black voters, according to Smith, were less influential in getting blacks to judicial office than professional standing, political party and friendship.

A 1973 American Judicature Society study revealed that black judges constituted approximately 1.3 percent of the judiciary.[22] Despite the argument that black attorneys stand a better chance of acquiring judgeships through the elective rather than the appointive process, the study showed that most black jurists surveyed attained their positions through some form of appointment. The study found that the prime reason for the small proportion of black judges was the small number of black lawyers available to serve on the bench.

Recent attempts to address the question of whether different methods of judicial selection result in different degrees of access to the bench depending on such factors as gender and race include a 1985 study published by the Fund for Modern Courts.[23] In a nationwide survey, the study demonstrated that the success of women and minorities in achieving judicial office depends on methods of selection—that a higher percentage of women and minorities attained more judicial positions through appointment than an elective process.

When statistical controls were employed, Dubois found only minor differences between elective and appointive systems for female and nonwhite judges recruited to sit on the California trial court bench.[24] He attributed this finding to the underrepresentation of women and nonwhites in the legal profession. Utilizing the Fund for Modern Courts data, Alozie directly addressed the question of whether methods of formal judicial selection account for the differential distribution of black judges on state judiciaries.[25] He found that the percentage of black lawyers in the state was the most significant factor in explaining the degree of variation of black judges in the state, not formal methods of judicial selection.

In another study, Graham addressed the question of whether formal and informal methods of judicial selection predict the likelihood of a black or white attorney serving as a trial judge.[26] In an examination of individual level data collected on 3,823 black and white trial court judges in 36 states, Graham found that formal structures made little difference in black representation because black judges who were formally elected were actually appointed to the bench. Moreover, the study showed that informal methods to the bench, that is, actual routes, were significant. Specifically, gubernatorial appointment and legislative appointment systems seemed to increase black representation on the state trial bench. Overall, the study provided support for the contention that structural arrangements of state judicial selection are significant in accounting for black underrepresentation on the state bench.

A closer examination of these competing approaches in explaining black underrepresentation on the state might reveal that scholars have viewed the trees but not the forest in addressing this problem. The research that suggests that blacks will increase their judgeships by increasing the proportion of black lawyers does not adequately consider the extent to which structural forces in the political and legal environments not only affect the proportion of black judges, but also the availability of black attorneys. Walton's observation is noteworthy here, for he argues that "by barring blacks from the voting booths, the bar rosters and associations, law schools, and full participation in the political arena, states have determined to a great extent the parameters of the black judiciary."[27] Focusing on contextual factors alone does little to expand our substantive understanding of how state judicial recruitment affects outcomes for minority participants. What this literature does reveal is that we are only beginning to make advances in our understanding of the impact of structural characteristics of judicial recruitment for minority representation on state courts.

Patterns of Accession

For descriptive purposes, the data presented in table 1 were reexamined within the context of how black judges reach the state bench by the states' formal designation and by actual routes. The judicial selection literature identifies five major formal routes to the state bench: gubernatorial appointment, Missouri Plan, legislative appointment, partisan election and nonpartisan election. As Berkson pointed out, almost no two states are alike in the methods used to select their judges and few states employ the same method for choosing judges at all levels of the state judiciary.[28] Table 3 presents the patterns of accession to the state bench by formal and actual routes for the general jurisdiction judges.

Table 3   How black judges reach the bench: formal and actual routes, 1986

Selection system	Formal route[1]	%	Actual route	%
Gubernatorial appointment	18	6.1	18	6.2
Missouri Plan	39	13.3	36[2]	12.4
Legislative appointment	14	4.8	12[3]	4.1
Partisan election	106	36.2	50	17.2
Nonpartisan election	97	33.1	24	8.2
Circuit court appointment	19	6.5	19	6.5
Supreme court appointment	—	—	14	4.8
Vacancy	—	—	113	38.8
Court reorganization/consolidation	—	—	5	1.7
Total	293	100.0	291[4]	99.9

— not applicable
1. In some states, different formal selection systems may be used for trial and appellate courts. The figures for the formal designation category were derived by first calculating the total for trial and appellate courts separately and then collapsing both totals into one category. The coding for the formal routes is: appellate courts 1×gubernatorial appointment (CA); 2×Missouri Plan (FL, KS, MD, MA, MO, NY); 3×legislative appointment (SC, VA); 4×partisan election (AL, IL, MS, NC, PA, TX) and 5×nonpartisan election (GA, LA, MI, OH); trial courts 1×gubernatorial appointment (NJ, NC [special judges of superior courts in NC are appointed by governor]); 2×Missouri Plan (AZ, CO, DE, IA, MD, MA, MO, IN); 3×legislative appointment (CT, SC, VA); 4×partisan election (AL, IL, IN, KS, MS, NY, PA, TN, TX, WV); 5×nonpartisan election (CA, FL, GA, ID, KY, LA, MI, MN, NV, OH, OK, OR, WA, WI) and 6×circuit court appointment (IL-associate circuit court judges).
2. Excludes 3 judges who initially reached the bench through court reorganization.
3. Excludes 2 gubernatorial appointments in filling vacancies in Virginia and South Carolina.
4. The author was unable to identify how 1 Ohio judge and 1 Louisiana judge reached the bench.

An examination of the formal route category shows that most black general jurisdiction judges preside over courts in states which formally use partisan and nonpartisan elections.[29] This was not an unexpected finding since 25 of the 36 states with black representation on their major courts formally use elective systems for all or some of their judgeships. When the actual routes to the major state court bench were determined, the figures presented in table 3 indicate the prevalence of interim appointments in formal selection systems, primarily partisan and non-partisan systems. With the exception of Illinois and Louisiana, all states with elective systems examined in this study permit the governor to fill vacancies occurring between elections. Most of the black judges in elective systems initially obtained their seats by gubernatorial appointment. Moreover, vacancy appointments were more common in non-partisan systems than partisan systems. These findings are compatible with prior research which indicates that in elective systems, a considerable proportion of judges initially reach the bench by executive appointment.[30]

The data presented in table 3 are significant in that they demonstrate the importance of the politics of the appointing governor in determining the extent to which minorities will occupy seats on our nation's state courts, despite the formal method used to select judges. Glick observed that "governors usually pick individuals who have been involved in state politics and whose past activity either has been of personal benefit, or has benefited a political party or political allies."[31] He also acknowledged that governors make symbolic appointments to these positions in their attempt to satisfy several constituencies. This analysis suggests that greater attention to the appointment politics of governors might reveal important insights for understanding minority recruitment outcomes.

Remedies

What can be done to remedy the problem of the lack of racial diversity on the state bench? The two remedies discussed here seek to address the broad problem of a racially homogeneous state bench. The first remedy involves the development of affirmative action policies to overcome past inequities in judicial recruitment and selection. Such efforts could be successfully implemented among appointive systems of judicial selection, including the filling of vacancies in elective systems. Since representational criteria are generally among the host of other factors in determining recruitment outcomes, affirmative action goals are clearly consistent with attracting legally qualified minority candidates to the state bench. President Carter's innovations on the federal level in the creation of merit panels among the states serves as a model.[32] Carter's appointments of minorities and women to the federal bench during his single term in office was a dramatic departure from the appointment practices of previous presidential administrations.[33] In addition, various groups (civil rights organizations, women's groups, bar associations) will have to play a greater role in state judicial recruitment and selection in order to realize the goals of a diverse state bench.

Elective systems have structural components not found in appointive systems that are likely to affect the chances of minorities in obtaining seats on the state bench in greater numbers. Several states use at-large or multi-member boundaries as the geographic basis for electing judges.[34] Lawsuits have been filed by minorities challenging the use of at-large and multimember districts in state judicial elections because they have not been successful at the polls.[35] Lower federal court decisions have responded to black voters' claims by expanding the concept of minority vote dilution to judicial elections.[36] The Fifth and Sixth Circuit Courts of Appeals have subsequently applied Sections 2 and 5 of the Voting Rights Act of 1965 as amended to judicial elections.[37] In response to these decisions, several jurisdictions must redraw their judicial districts in order to insure that black voters will have the opportunity to elect judicial candidates of their choice. The immediate effect of these decisions will be felt in the south where much of the litigation originated. Consequently, judicial redistricting is expected to be successful in bringing minorities to the bench in those areas where there [is] a heavy concentration of minorities.[38]

Conclusion

The purpose of this article was to present an overview of the characteristics of judicial recruitment and selection as they contribute to our understanding of black representation on the state bench. Viewed in this context, this research has important implications about the ongoing debate with respect to who gets chosen to fill judgeships on the state bench. This study revealed that although black attorneys have made significant gains on the state bench since the 1970s, black underrepresentation still remains a problem. An examination of the literature that attempted to explain the problem demonstrates the need for systematic analyses of structural variables which might affect minority recruitment outcomes. It was also suggested that the application of affirmative action criteria and judicial redistricting were expected to enhance minority representation at the state level. This article has clear implications about the direction future research should take in addressing the problem of a racially homogeneous state bench. Slotnick has argued that analyses of judicial recruitment have failed to take into account studies of elite recruitment in other political contexts.[39] Since this research suggests that minority representation is as important in the state judiciary as it is in other branches of government, perhaps future research should consider the extent to which institutional arrangements, political participation and elite behavior reveal insights about judicial recruitment and selection.

Endnotes

[1] For an overview and annotated bibliography of this extensive literature, see Chinn and Berkson, *Literature on Judicial Selection* (Chicago: American Judicature Society, 1980); Slotnick, "Review Essay on Judicial Recruitment and Selection," 13 *Just. Sys. J.* 109 (1988).

2 See, for example, Abraham, *The Judicial Process* (New York: Oxford University Press, 5th ed., 1986).

3 See Joint Center for Political Studies, *Black Judges in the United States* (Washington, D.C.: 1986).

4 The author would like to thank the state court clerks and administrators for their assistance in the collection of the data.

5 Two directories are: *The American Bench: Judges of the Nation* (Sacramento: Reginald Bishop Foster & Associates, Inc., 3rd ed., 1985/86); *California Courts and Judges* (San Francisco Law Book Service Co., 4th ed., 1985).

6 See Cook, "Black Representation in the Third Branch," 1 *Black L. J.* 260 (1972); Smith, *Race Versus Robe* (Port Washington, NY: Associated Faculty Press, 1983); American Judicature Society, "The Black Judge in America: A Statistical Profile," 57 *Judicature* 18 (1973). But see Alozie, "Black Representation on State Judiciaries," 69 *Soc. Sci. Q.* 979 (1988).

7 Cook, supra n. 6 at 261.

8 "Quasi-judicial officials are defined as officers required to investigate facts, hold hearings, and recommend official actions on the basis of those facts." See Joint Center for Political Studies, supra n. 3 at 11.

9 See Joint Center for Political Studies, "Black Elected Officials: A National Roster" (Washington, D.C., 16th ed., 1987).

10 See Smith, supra n. 6; Ryan et al., *American Trial Judges: Their Work Styles and Performance* (New York: Free Press, 1980).

11 The geographic divisions used in this study are compatible with those found in JCPS, *Black Elected Officials*, supra n. 9. They are south = MD, WV, VA, KY, NC, SC, TN, GA, MS, AL, FL, TX, LA, OK, AK, DE; northeast = PA, NJ, NY, CT, MA, RI; north central = OH, IL, IN, WI, MO, MI, MN, IA, KS; WEST = CA, OR, WA, ID, AZ, CO, NM, UT, NV.

12 American Judicature Society, supra n. 6, at 18.

13 See Pitkin, ed., *Representation* (New York: Atherton Press, 1969).

14 Smith, supra n. 6; Crockett, "Judicial Selection and the Black Experience," 58 *Judicature* 438 (1971).

15 See Crockett, "Racism in the Courts," 20 *J. of Pub. L.* 685 (1970).

16 See, for example, Welch, Combs and Gruhl, "Do Black Judges Make a Difference?", 32 *Am. J. of Pol. Sci.* 126 (1988).

17 Fund for Modern Courts, *The Success of Women and Minorities in Achieving Judicial Office: The Selection Process* 13 (New York: 1985).

18 These figures were supplied by the National Bar Association, Washington, D.C., January 22, 1990.

19 See National Center for State Courts, *State Court Organization*, 1987 (Williamsburg, VA: 1988) for a listing of state trial and appellate court qualifications to serve on the bench.

20 Cook, supra n. 6.

21 Smith, supra n. 6.

22 American Judicature Society, supra n. 6.

23 Fund for Modern Courts, supra n. 17.

24 Dubois, "The Influence of Selection System on the Characteristics of a Trial Court Bench: The Case of California," 8 *Just. Sys. J.* 59 (1983).

25 Alozie, supra n. 6.

26 Graham, "Do Judicial Selection Systems Matter? A Study of Black Representation on State Courts," forthcoming. *Am. Pol. Q.* (1990).

27 Walton, *Invisible Politics* 224 (Albany: SUNY Press, 1985).

28 Berkson, "Judicial Selection in the United States: A Special Report," 64 *Judicature* 179 (1980).

29 Data were not collected on the limited jurisdiction judges in this study because of the difficulty in obtaining biographical data for these judges and the fact that judicial selection mechanisms vary considerably among these judgeships and they frequently do not conform to the five major methods of judicial selection discussed in this article. See Berkson, supra n. 28.

30 See Herndon, "Appointment as a Means of Initial Accession to Elective State Courts of Last Resort," 38 *N. Dak. L. Rev.* 60 (1962); Atkins and Glick, "Formal Judicial Recruitment and State Supreme Court Decisions," 2 *Am. Pol. Q.* 427 (1974); Dubois, *From Ballot to Bench* (Houston: University of Texas Press, 1980).

31 Glick, *Courts, Politics, and Justice* 89 (New York: McGraw-Hill, 2nd ed., 1988).

32 See, for example Goldman, "Should There Be Affirmative Action for the Judiciary?," 62 *Judicature* 488 (1979); Slotnick, "The U.S. Circuit Judge Nominating Commission," 1 *L. & Policy Q.* 465 (1979); Slotnick, "Federal Appellate Judge Selection During the Carter Administration: Recruitment Changes and Unanswered Questions," 6 *Just. Sys. J.* 283 (1981).

33 See Goldman, "Reagan's Judicial Legacy: Completing the Puzzle and Summing Up," 72 *Judicature* 318 (1989) for a comparative analysis.

34 See National Center for State Courts, supra n. 19.

35 See American Judicature Society, "The Voting Rights Act and Judicial Elections: An Update on Current Litigation," 73 *Judicature* 74 (1989).

36 See Davidson, ed., *Minority Vote Dilution* (Washington, D.C.: Howard University Press, 1984) for a discussion of this concept. See also *Voter Information Project, Inc. v. City of Baton Rouge*, 612 F.2d 208 (5th Cir. 1980).

37 See *Haith v. Martin*, 618 F.Supp. 410 (E.D.N.C. 1985) aff'd 477 U.S. 901(1986); *Mallory v. Eyrich*, 839 F.2d 275 (6th Cir. 1988); *Chisom v. Edwards* 839 F.2d 1056 (5th Cir. 1988), cert. denied, *Roemer v. Chisom* 109 S.Ct. 390 (1988).

38 For example, the first election after judicial redistricting in Mississippi produced two black winners in contested judicial elections—the first in the history of Mississippi elections. See Canerdy, "Black Candidates Appear to Do Poorly in Judicial Races," *The Clarion-Ledger*, June 21, 1989, at 1, col. 1. See also McDuff, "The Voting Rights Act and Judicial Elections Litigation: The Plaintiffs' Perspective," 73 *Judicature* 82 (1989).

39 Slotnick, supra n. 1.

15

Gender Bias in the Courts
A Review of the Literature

CRAIG HEMMENS, KRISTIN STROM, and ELICIA SCHLEGEL

In theory, all persons involved in court proceedings are supposed to be treated equitably. A number of states have conducted studies which indicate that in actuality men and women receive differential treatment in court. As is the case in many aspects of American society, women are most often victims of gender bias (Schafran 1990b; Washington 1989). Female litigants face an uphill battle in pursuing their cases in both civil and criminal courts. Gender bias can take several forms. Gender discrimination often affects domestic violence, divorce, and sexual assault cases. Gender bias can also affect everyday courtroom interactions and operations. Gender bias is harder to detect than in the past because it is more subtle, but it continues to exist (Belknap 1996; Moyer 1992).

In the 1980s, a program called the National Judicial Education to Promote Equality for Women and Men in the Courts (NJEP) was formed by the National Organization for Women Legal Defense and Education Fund, which then invited the National Association of Women Judges to become a cosponsor of the program (Wikler 1980; Schafran 1990a). The NJEP promoted the creation of task forces to study gender bias in the courts. By 1989 thirty states had established gender bias task forces (Schafran 1990a). State task forces were established by state bar association or state court administrative offices and funded largely through donations and research grants (Roberts and Knoebel 1989). In 1989 the National Conference on Gender

Reprinted with permission from *Sociological Imagination*, 35(1): 22–42 (1998).

Bias in the Courts was held in Virginia, and the results of the nine completed bias task force reports were made available for national dissemination. The majority of task force reports discovered gender bias in virtually every stage of the justice system (Schafran 1990b).

This article presents a comprehensive review of the state gender bias studies. While at least thirty states have conducted gender bias research, to date there has been no effort made to examine these studies in toto. Consequently these studies have been examined in isolation, without any effort to explore commonalties among the various states. This article attempts to fill this gap in the literature.

Defining Gender Bias

Before determining the impact of gender bias on the courts, the term "gender bias" must first be defined. There are many different definitions of gender bias, but all share common traits. Gender bias is "actions or attitudes that negatively impact an individual or group primarily because of gender" (Washington 1989:3). Gender bias occurs when decisions are made or actions taken based on stereotypes about men and women (Hawaii 1989). The Utah task force (1990) noted that stereotypes affect society's attitudes about the value of men's and women's work. Gender bias can also involve insensitivity towards certain aspects of men's and women's lives that are genuinely different and may require the inclusion of gender as a factor in decision making (Wisconsin 1991).

Bias can additionally be "intentional and reflect ill will" (California 1996:27). Intentional bias, according to the California report, is the easiest to understand but also the least likely to occur. Biased treatment can further be defined as differential treatment of the sexes in situations where gender should not be considered (Colorado 1990). Gender bias is often based on "misconceptions about the economic and social realities of women's and men's lives manifested in judicial decision and court interaction" (Texas 1994:13). One report defined gender bias as conduct which reflects attitudes and behavior based on stereotypical beliefs about the sexes' "true natures" and "proper roles" rather than independent evaluation of each individual's abilities, life experiences, and aspirations (Louisiana 1992:40).

Surprisingly, several of the state task force studies of gender bias do not explain what the term "gender bias" means. Failure to operationalize the term makes it difficult to determine what is meant by "gender bias."

Bias in Domestic Violence Cases

The state task force studies found that one of the areas in criminal justice where gender bias is most common is domestic violence cases. All of the state task force reports found that women are victims of domestic violence far more often than men. Ninety-eight percent of domestic violence victims are women (Nebraska 1994). Nationwide, 28% of female homicide victims are killed by former husbands or boyfriends, whereas only 5% of male homicide victims are killed by former wives or girlfriends (Wisconsin 1991). Domestic violence is the number one cause of physical injury to women in the United States (Utah 1990).

Gender biased treatment is often based on stereotypes about how domestic violence cases should be handled. Courtroom actors often believe that domestic violence is a private, family matter and should not be dealt with by the courts (Washington 1989). Domestic violence situations are often minimized relative to comparable incidents involving strangers (Utah 1990). In Massachusetts, juries expect more physical injuries to domestic violence victims than to victims of other violent crimes (Massachusetts 1989). In Maryland, 51% of the male attorneys and 68% of the female attorneys believed that judges sometimes failed to view domestic violence as a crime (Maryland 1989). The misconceptions that victims of domestic violence provoke the offender, or that the victim must like it or they would leave, are also a problem (Washington 1989). A state trial court judge commented, "I have difficulty finding where this defendant's [the husband] done anything wrong, other than slapping her [his wife]. Maybe that was justified" (Utah 1990:44). The Massachusetts study revealed that some victims report improper or irrelevant questions during court proceedings. Over three-fourths of the responding attorneys said judges sometimes allow questions as to what the victim did to provoke the battering. Comments made by judges included, "Why don't you get a divorce?" and "Why are you bothering the court with this problem?" (Massachusetts 1989:90).

Bias Towards Victims of Domestic Violence

Female victims of domestic violence encounter many problems when they enter the court system because of biased opinions about domestic violence. The California (1996) task force found that 53% of the male court personnel surveyed "agreed" or "strongly agreed" that declarations of abuse are often exaggerated. Only 26% of the female court personnel surveyed felt this was the case. Additionally, 40% of the men felt that domestic violence cases should be diverted or that counseling should be used rather than criminal prosecution, compared to only 21% of the women surveyed (California 1996).

Iowa's (1993) study found that 45% of the females were only "somewhat confident" or "not that confident" that they would be treated fairly by the court system if they were victims of domestic violence. Their fears appear justified by the Washington (1989) study, which found that 57% of the respondents believe that while police "rarely" or "never" handle domestic violence cases informally, and the perpetrator is usually arrested or cited, prosecutors "rarely" or "sometimes" prosecute domestic violence cases vigorously. Even when the offender is arrested it is unlikely he will spend any time in prison (Illinois 1990). In most cases, the guilty party is merely required to attend counseling sessions (Illinois 1990).

Prosecution When Victim Withdraws Complaint

Further problems in the prosecution of domestic violence cases are created when a victim withdraws her complaint. The Wisconsin (1991) task force found that when victims recant, 32% of the cases are dismissed, 39% of the cases are prosecuted, and 29% are diverted. Victim cooperation is viewed as essential to the prosecution, which often makes the victim responsible for the survival of the case (Minnesota 1989). Holding victims responsible, even indirectly, for the prosecution of a domestic violence case is completely contrary to the principles of the criminal justice system, according to the Minnesota (1989) task force.

Protection Orders

Female victims of domestic violence also have problems obtaining protection orders. The Nevada task force (1988) found that 43% of the attorneys and judges believed that seriously endangered victims of domestic violence are not always granted protection orders. In many cases women are given no assistance in filing protection orders and court personnel may even discourage women from obtaining protection orders (Nebraska 1994). The New Mexico task force (1990) found that 44% of the attorneys surveyed believe court personnel do not provide adequate assistance to women who attempt to get protection orders. This finding is significant because nearly a third of the service providers in the Washington (1989) survey said that victims "usually" or "frequently" had problems completing the paperwork required to obtain a protection order. The Michigan task force (1989) found that there may be a long delay between the granting of a protection order and the protection order becoming effective. The Missouri task force (1993) reported that many times a petitioner attends protection order proceedings underrepresented. Of the judges surveyed, almost half said a petitioner was seldom, if ever, represented by counsel when seeking a protection order (Missouri 1993). This lack of representation may affect the chances of success for female litigants.

Enforcement of Protection Orders

Even when a victim of domestic violence can obtain a protection order, there is no guarantee it will be enforced. According to the Washington (1989) study, 45% of the respondents "usually" or "frequently" violate the "no contact" provisions of protection orders. In the Nebraska (1994) study, only 47% of the attorneys questioned said that misdemeanor violators of protection orders were sentenced to jail. Texas (1994) attorneys said that sanctions, including civil commitments, are only "rarely" or "sometimes" used when protection orders are violated. Maryland (1989) found victims of domestic violence had difficulty receiving protection during divorce proceedings. Although violence often escalates after a victim attempts to leave the batterer, 4 of 10 judges responded that protection order petitions are sometimes or always rejected when other domestic relations cases are pending (Maryland 1989).

Another problem is the inadequate enforcement of protection orders. Police fail to arrest, district attorneys fail to prosecute, and judges fail to adequately punish men who commit crimes against their spouses or violate court orders (Louisiana 1992). In Missouri, 65% of the female attorneys and 64% of the male attorneys believe judges are reluctant to use criminal sanctions in domestic violence cases. In one example, a judge fined a woman $500 and sentenced her to two years probation for shoplifting cigarettes and in the next case only fined a husband $35 for breaking his wife's nose by kicking her in the face (Missouri 1993). This implied to many attorneys that domestic violence cases are not accorded high priority in Missouri courtrooms.

Mutual Protection Orders

Mutual orders for protection imply that both parties are abusive, even when there is no proof of wrongdoing by the petitioner (Michigan 1989). Granting mutual orders for protection can also create problems because police often arrest both parties when called to enforce the protection orders even when only one of them is abusive (Minnesota 1989). The issuing of mutual protection orders also encourages the idea that victims are responsible for their abuse. Granting mutual protection orders proves to women that the court is not serious about holding the abuser accountable for his behavior (Minnesota 1989). Victims of domestic violence who have not committed acts of violence are embarrassed and confused by mutual protection orders (California 1996).

A further problem with the issuance of protection orders is that the majority of judges grant mutual protection orders, even when only one party petitioned for the order (Nebraska 1994). The Texas (1994) task force found comparable results. Approximately 80% of the lawyers surveyed said that mutual protection orders were issued even when only one party had presented evidence of abuse. The Missouri task force (1993) reported that 64% of the female attorneys and 48% of the male attorneys agreed that the issuance of mutual protection orders without evidence of joint fault was at least sometimes the practice in Missouri courts.

Bias in Sexual Assault Cases

Another area in which women experience bias is sexual assault. Much like domestic violence, there are many misconceptions about sexual assault. A study of 1,500 Rhode Island junior high school students found some surprising results about their understanding of sexual assault. The students were asked when a man was justified in having sexual intercourse with a woman who did not consent. Fifty-seven percent of the boys and 39% of the girls said the act was justified if the woman allowed the man to touch her above the waist. Sixty-five percent of the boys and 47% of the girls said that rape was acceptable if the two had a long-term dating relationship. Finally, 24% of the boys and 16% of the girls said the act was reasonable if the man had spent a lot of money on the date (Rhode Island 1987). Although these opinions do not necessarily reflect the attitudes of criminal justice professionals, they do indicate that, among certain segments of the public at least, there is a lack of sensitivity to gender equality issues.

Bias Against Victims of Sexual Assault

Stereotypes about females being responsible for their victimization permeate the criminal justice system, reflecting larger societal perceptions (Belknap 1996). Attitudes of criminal justice personnel often affect whether or not a victim reports sexual assault. As a result of biased attitudes, women seldom report sexual assault (Washington 1989). The misconception that sexual assaults are crimes of passion, not violence, often leads to bias against sexual assault victims (Michigan 1989). As one judge remarked: "Rape is simply a case of poor salesmanship" (Minnesota 1989:894). The New Mexico (1990) task force survey found that 30% of the males and 50% of the females believe that judges sometimes believe that women invited sexual assault by their appearance or behavior.

The main reasons why women do not report sexual assault, according to the Texas (1994) task force report, are fear that the police either will not believe the victim or will blame the victim for the assault. Victims of sexual assault often are not considered believable by criminal justice workers. Half of the female attorneys surveyed in Texas reported that police officers "sometimes" or "frequently" accord less credibility to victims of sexual assault than to victims of other types of assaults (Texas 1994). Forty percent of the female lawyers felt that judges and prosecutors also believe that sexual assault victims are less credible (Texas 1994). Police may feel that they are doing other criminal justice agencies a favor by making judgments about a victim's credibility (Utah 1990).

The Massachusetts task force (1989) also reported bias against sexual assault victims by court employees and courtroom actors. Of the responding district attorneys and public defenders, 47% believe that juries accord less credibility to sexual assault victims than victims of other felonies. Sixty-four percent of these attorneys agreed that juries are less likely to convict if the defendant does not have any physical injuries (Massachusetts 1989). Almost three-fourths of the attorneys and 63% of the judges surveyed in one state agreed that gender stereotypes are commonly used to discredit victims of sexual assault cases (Vermont 1991).

Connecticut (1991) reported that 26% of the responding judges believed that a woman's character and past sexual behavior were relevant to the sexual assault charges to determine the seriousness of the charges. Thirteen percent of the judges believe that provocative dress or the actions of the victim could have provoked the attack (Connecticut 1991). The Washington (1989) task force found that 24% of the judges surveyed believe that victim attire or behavior "sometimes" or "frequently" precipitates sexual attacks. This finding is rather ironic, because rape by definition is forced or coerced sexual intercourse (Klotter 1994).

Prior Relationship with the Perpetrator

The predominant cultural stereotype of "real rape" remains the violent stranger hidden in the shadows (Minnesota 1989). However, one-third of all reported rapes do not fit this stereotype (New Mexico 1990). Sexual assaults are most often committed by family members, friends, coworkers, employers, neighbors, or other acquaintances (Minnesota 1989). These "acquaintance" rapes are often considered less serious than "real" rapes by the criminal justice system. In the Washington (1989) survey, 68% of the attorneys indicated that they believe judges give shorter sentences in acquaintance rape cases. The Nebraska task force (1994) had similar findings. Eighty-three percent of the attorneys surveyed said that "date rape" defendants receive lighter sentences than "stranger rape" defendants. Sixty-six percent of the female attorneys and 40% of the male attorneys surveyed in Colorado (1990) felt that judges inappropriately reduce charges in acquaintance rape cases on some occasions. Seventy-two percent of the attorneys questioned in the Utah (1990) survey said that conviction is "always" or "often" less likely when the victim knew the defendant. Attorneys in the Texas (1994) survey felt that in sexual assault cases involving acquaintances, the offenders receive more lenient sentences than when the victim and assailant were strangers.

The Nebraska task force (1994) found that 85% of the female attorneys believe bail is set lower in cases where the parties know one another. Police are also more likely to take sexual assaults seriously when they are committed by a stranger (Texas 1994). Attitudes regarding the victim's relationship to the offender are significant because 80% of sexual assaults are perpetrated by someone known to the victim (Nebraska 1994).

Ninety percent of the judges surveyed in Missouri (1993) believe juries are less likely to convict in a sexual assault case in which the victim has been sexually active. Eighty-one percent of the judges, 87% of the female attorneys, and 85% of the male attorneys believe that acquaintance rape offenders receive shorter sentences than offenders who had no prior relationship with the victim (Missouri 1993). Similarly, in the state of Vermont (1991), 78% of the attorneys and 47% of the judges believe shorter sentences are given to offenders who had a prior relationship with the victim.

Treatment of a Victim Who Reports a Rape

If a woman decides to report her rape she may face the possibility of being re-victimized by the courts. In the Texas (1994) survey, 37% of the male judges, compared to only 8% of the female judges, agreed that the victim's sexual history is relevant to the issue of her consent. A woman who does not conform to society's expectation that she be chaste and virginal must have been asking to be raped (Michigan 1989). Ninety-two percent of the female attorneys and 76% of the male attorneys in the Nebraska (1994) survey believe that defense attorneys use stereotypes such as "women say no when they mean yes" to discredit victims.

In Nebraska (1994), 62% of the attorneys and 60% of the judges responded that during trial "date rape" victims are questioned beyond what is necessary to present a consent defense. Minnesota (1989) found that 75% of the attorneys surveyed felt defense attorneys "always," "often," or "sometimes" used stereotypes to discount sexual assault victims. The attorney may badger or harass the victim witness (Michigan 1989). When asked how often judges intervene when there is improper questioning about the victim's sexual history, 33% of the attorneys surveyed in Colorado (1990) felt that judges "never" or "almost never" intervene.

Bias in Divorce Cases

Divorce cases are, for obvious reasons, an area in which the possibility of gender bias looms large. There are several issues which arise, including alimony, division of property, child support, and child custody. All state task force reports are unanimous in their findings that women suffer from gender bias in all areas of divorce cases. Several studies also found that men suffer from gender bias in regard to child custody issues.

Alimony Awards

A major issue in divorce cases is whether to grant alimony. Popular belief about divorce is that men are generally the most affected economically. Many divorced men claim that their ex-spouse received the majority of their personal belongings and was awarded a substantial amount of alimony (New York 1986). Research shows that this perception is false. The Georgia (1992) study concluded that it is women who experience a dramatic decrease in their standard of living following a divorce. This is especially true when the woman is a homemaker and has put aside further education and training for marriage. When the marriage ends in divorce, the woman is forced to enter a work force where her earning capacity is extremely low (New York 1986). The Nebraska (1994) survey found that 55% of the attorneys believed that judges are more likely to sacrifice the current lifestyle of the wife when determining the amount of maintenance awards. The Florida (1990) survey found that men were routinely awarded over half of the marital assets, even when women were awarded custody.

The failure of the courts to provide adequate support has resulted in significant economic variation between former husbands and wives which greatly disadvantages women (Iowa 1993). The average awards issued to women in one state are completely insufficient and provide a standard of living close to the poverty line (California 1996). In another state, fathers experienced a 73% *increase* in their standard of living after a divorce, while the wives who retained custody of the children experienced a 32% *decrease* in theirs (Utah 1990).

Part of the problem is due to the fact that judges do not have a realistic understanding of the future earnings of a homemaker who has not worked outside of the home for a significant amount of time (Nebraska 1994). Another reason for this problem is the lack of enforcement of alimony awards may result in a long-term reduction in a woman's standard of living (New Mexico 1990). The Missouri task force (1993) also found that maintenance or alimony is detrimental to custodial women. Their research found that women with children following a divorce are the fastest growing poverty group. The percentage of children in poverty almost doubles from

19% to 36% after their family splits up. Other research found indicated that judges often decide the amount of alimony based on the amount the ex-husband could afford without altering his standard of living.

In Maryland (1989) 30% of the judges, 20% of the male attorneys and 44% of the female attorneys responded that upholding the husband's current lifestyle is often or always a deciding factor when deciding the amount of alimony awarded. Half of the female attorneys and 20% of the male attorneys in another state believe judges seldom or never have a realistic understanding of the likely future earnings of a longtime homemaker (Missouri 1993). Without a realistic understanding of a woman's earning capacity, a judge is unable to grant an appropriate alimony settlement. The District of Columbia (1992) report found that 35% of the attorneys believe judges rarely or never grant sufficient alimony awards.

Division of Marital Property

The division of marital property is an area where most would believe women generally benefit. Such is not the case, however. A majority of the attorneys surveyed in Nebraska (1994) felt that judges believe husbands are entitled to a greater share of the marital property when the wife's primary contribution has been that of a homemaker. This finding reflects the notion that "whoever earns it, owns it" and neglects the contribution female homemakers provide (Nebraska 1994). In New Mexico (1990) 63% of survey respondents felt the division of property generally results in a long-term reduction in the standard of living for women but not for men. Forty percent of the female attorneys in Hawaii believe women are at a disadvantage in division of property, as compared with only 23% of the male attorneys (Hawaii 1989). Property division and alimony are often treated as a package, which also creates problems for women (Colorado 1990).

Child Support Awards

Women also face problems with child support awards. While 90% of children in divorced families reside with their mother (Kentucky 1992), only 45% of the lawyers surveyed in Washington (1989) believe that child support awards realistically reflect the cost of raising children. The Nebraska (1994) study found that 37% of the attorneys felt that judges' awards for child support "rarely" or "never" reflect the costs of actual child rearing.

Judges also have a tendency to follow child support guidelines that do not adequately reflect the needs of children (Minnesota 1989). Judges rarely give mothers more money than the guidelines recommend. If the judge deviates from the guidelines at all, it is usually to grant less child support than is suggested (Minnesota 1989). This practice is problematic because child support guidelines were designed to be the floor for determining support levels, not the ceiling (Minnesota 1989). Following child support guidelines "often" or "always" leads to a reduced standard of living for women and children after a divorce, according to 49% of respondents in the New Mexico (1990) survey.

Enforcement of Child Support

Even when suitable child support is awarded, it may not be enforced by the courts. In 1990, the Census Bureau reported only 44% of children nationally receive the court-ordered child support payments (Vermont 1991). Failure to pay child support is one of the most blatant violations of court orders (California 1996). In Minnesota (1989) child support agencies said they collect on their cases about 40% of the time. In Nebraska (1994) only 15% of the child support payments due were collected. Many fathers do not pay child support because they receive no punishment from the court system. The Washington (1989) task force found that half of the lawyers surveyed said judges "never" use jail as a sentence for failure to pay child support. However, 81% of attorneys in the Nebraska (1994) survey said that judges are willing to use the court's contempt powers to enforce child support. The majority of attorneys (73%) also believe judges are willing to jail non-payers of child support, which indicates that some states are willing to use sanctions to enforce child support awards (Nebraska 1994). Although 51% of the judges in Maryland reported entering earnings withholdings orders on delinquent child support payments, 62% of the female attorneys and 56% of the male attorneys regarded this statement as rarely or never true (Maryland 1989).

Massachusetts has used wage assignments to enforce support payments since 1986. Wage assignment involves deducting the child support payment directly from the non-custodial parent's paycheck (Massachusetts 1989). This procedure was later adopted as a model for national legislation. Several other states argued that in theory this is an effective measure, but too many judges fail to use it. Attorneys reported to the Kentucky task force (1992) that some judges do not use wage assignments because they fear doing so will jeopardize a man's job or embarrass him in front of his coworkers.

Child Support as a Bargaining Chip

An additional problem with child support is that it is often used as a bargaining chip in custody hearings. "Many fathers threaten a custody battle (even though they do not want custody) to browbeat their wives on economic issues—i.e., accept low support or I'll go after custody. Unhappily, it works. Women feel so powerless and frightened, they will allow their ex-husbands to reduce them and their children to poverty, just to preserve custody of their children" (Utah 1990:25). Sixty-one percent of the lawyers and 71% of the judges in the Washington (1989) survey believe that women "occasionally" or "usually" accept lower child support.

Bias Against Courtroom Actors

Female court employees and lawyers also suffer from gender bias, often at the hands of other courtroom actors. The Nevada task force summarizes the existence of gender bias in the courts very well: " . . . from time to time male judges, lawyers, and other participants in the legal system have conducted themselves in a manner that is offensive and intolerable to women participants in the legal system" (Nevada 1988:67). Seventy-four percent of the lawyers and 54% of the judges surveyed in Washington believe that gender bias is present in the courts (Washington 1989). Between 20% and 40% of respondents perceived bias in some form in Hawaii's legal system (Hawaii 1989). The perception of the existence of bias is clearly related to gender, however. Forty-four percent of the female lawyers as compared to only 11% of the male attorneys surveyed in Texas believe that bias is widespread (Texas 1994). The Colorado task force (1990) found similar results. Four of ten of the female attorneys compared to just 6% of the male attorneys felt that bias was widespread. The Nebraska task force (1994) found that 48% of the male attorneys surveyed believe bias was nonexistent in the courts, while only 3% of the female attorneys felt this was the case. Clearly, males and females in the courts have different opinions about the existence of bias in the courts.

Bias Against Female Attorneys

Females working in the courts perceive much more gender bias than male actors do (Colorado 1990). Bias was most often reported by female attorneys (Nebraska 1994). Eighty-two percent of the female attorneys in Texas reported that they experienced biased behavior from opposing counsel, and 64% experienced bias from male judges (Texas 1994). Rhode Island (1987) identified male attorneys as being responsible for the majority of discrimination against women in the courtroom. Male attorneys were identified as being responsible 45% of the time, while judges were identified 31% of the time. In the Missouri task force survey (1993), 42% of the female attorneys admitted hearing demeaning remarks about women by judges, either in the courtroom or in chambers (1993). Female attorneys in New Jersey reported similar experiences. Seventy-six percent of the female attorneys reported being treated disadvantageously by judges because of their gender. Eighty-six percent of the female attorneys and 49% of the male attorneys reported incidents of discriminatory treatment of female attorneys by their fellow male attorneys in the courtroom (New Jersey 1984).

Maryland (1989) surveyed attorneys on the different types of gender bias behavior they had observed. Fifty-seven percent of the female attorneys reported judges giving less credibility to the statements of female attorneys than statements of male attorneys. Fifty-six percent of the female attorneys, compared to 20% of the male attorneys, were repeatedly asked by judges if they are attorneys. Fifty-four percent of the female attorneys have experienced comments about their personal appearance. In one case, a female attorney was assigned to an adoption case. When she entered the courtroom the judge looked at her and said: "They don't make the stork like they used to!" (Maryland 1989).

Not only are male attorneys not exposed to the types of gender bias that female attorneys report, they are often not even aware that it exists (Ninth Circuit 1993). As noted above, male lawyers consistently report fewer observations of gender bias than female lawyers (Kansas 1992). A comment from one male attorney is instructive: "This sounds to me like someone fishing for problems that don't exist. In eleven years, I have never seen a judge treat a woman with less respect than a man" (Utah 1990:94).

The most common form of gender bias mentioned was the practice of judges and attorneys addressing female attorneys in a demeaning manner (Kansas 1992). Many females reported that judges would refer to them by their first name during court procedures while addressing male attorneys by their formal names. Many female attorneys reported being addressed by familiar terms such as "sweetie," "little lady lawyer," "pretty eyes," and "dear" (Michigan 1989:927). Female attorneys in Missouri reported being addressed by judges in familiar terms twice as often as male attorneys (Missouri 1993). Fifty percent of the female attorneys in Nebraska said they were addressed in familiar terms by attorneys (Nebraska 1994). The New Mexico task force (1990) found that 48% of the female attorneys said that counsel sometimes addressed females in an inappropriate manner while only 12% of the male attorneys said this sometimes happened.

Another common form of gender bias suffered by female attorneys is sexist remarks or jokes (New Hampshire 1988). When asked if inappropriate jokes about their sex had been made in their presence, 21% of the female attorneys in the Iowa survey reported that it had occurred on many occasions, while only 1% of the male attorneys said it occurred frequently (Iowa 1993). Half of the female lawyers surveyed in California said that they had heard jokes or remarks demeaning to women from fellow attorneys. In addition, 45% of the females indicated that they had heard judges make such comments at least occasionally (California 1996).

Females are also often asked whether or not they are attorneys while men are not questioned (Nebraska 1994). Seventy percent of the female attorneys responding to the Minnesota (1989) survey said they were sometimes asked if they are attorneys. "When I accompany a senior partner to court, I am often asked if I am his daughter (by attorneys, judges), I am not assumed to be a competent associate attorney working on a case." (Utah 1990:97). Female attorneys may also endure comments about their personal appearance (Washington 1989). Just over half of the female attorneys in the Nebraska survey responded that comments had been made about their personal appearance by other attorneys. Further, female attorneys may experience bias if they attempt to act aggressively (Nebraska 1994). "I have found that if I don't immediately agree to something the other side wants, they consider me a 'bitch' and difficult to work with. . . . If a man says no to a demand, he is being an aggressive litigator" (Nebraska 1994:9).

Gender bias also often affects the hiring and promotion of female attorneys (Kansas 1992). Thirty-five percent of the females surveyed in New Mexico felt that women have trouble being hired, while only 10% of the male respondents felt that females have trouble getting hired (New Mexico 1990). California (1996) found that 62% of the female attorneys believed they had less chance for advancement than men and 96% of the females said they had more trouble balancing work and family than male attorneys. Over half the women surveyed by the Ninth Circuit Court task force believe that promotion is tilted in men's favor (Ninth Circuit 1993). The types of law female attorneys practice may reflect bias as well. Judges may believe that capital cases or major drug cases are too difficult for female attorneys. Unfortunately, because women are rarely involved in major cases, it is difficult for them to establish a reputation as being a good criminal attorney (Michigan 1989).

Female attorneys are also paid less than male lawyers for the same work. "It is my perception that the partners believe that women will work at least as hard as men and will accept lower salaries" (Ninth Circuit 1993:38). The New Mexico task force (1990) found that the average mean income of male lawyers was always higher than that of female attorneys in similar types of practices. After twenty years in practice male lawyers can expect to earn, on average, $92,000 while female attorneys make approximately $66,100 a year (New Mexico 1990). Female lawyers, on average, earn $100 less per case than male attorneys (Michigan 1989).

Bias Against Female Judges

Female attorneys are not the only actors in the court system that experience bias. Many female judges also report encountering gender bias. Several judges in the Minnesota survey reported being addressed in familiar terms and even referred to by their first names by court personnel, bailiffs, and janitors (Minnesota 1989). Half of the female judges responding to the Colorado (1990) survey said that they were sometimes treated with less respect by counsel. Additionally, 35% of the female judges surveyed in Colorado said they were treated with less respect than their male counterparts (Colorado 1990). "Difficult white male judges are referred to as 'irascible' while female judges are characterized as 'bitches'" (Michigan 1989:87).

The most common gender bias perceived by female judges was the hiring practices and placement of female judges (New Hampshire 1988). Women are greatly underrepresented on the bench. The Minnesota task force (1989) found that women made up only 10% of the state's judiciary. In Louisiana (1992), the task force found that of 525 judicial appointments made in three years, women received only 15% of the available appointments. In Vermont, in 1991, only 5 out of the 33 appointed judges were women. In Missouri, 75% of the male attorneys and judges, and 96% of the female attorneys felt that gender was a significant factor in judicial nominations. Eighty-four percent of the female attorneys and 36% of the male attorneys believe that a court will not nominate another female or minority member if one has already been selected.

Female judicial applicants are sometimes asked inappropriate questions by male judicial commission members (Vermont 1991). The female applicants may be asked who will care for their children if they are appointed or how they would handle their job if they had children (Nebraska 1994). Twelve percent of the female attorneys responding to the Iowa survey indicated they had been asked during interviews for judgeships if they intended to have children, while none of the male attorneys said they had been asked that question (Iowa 1993).

Do Judges Intervene to Stop Biased Behavior?

Because gender bias is present in the courts it is important to know how often judges intervene to stop the behavior. Judges have a great deal of influence on the conduct of courtroom actors. Judges who intervene when bias occurs have a lasting impression and may encourage others to follow suit (Michigan 1989). Unfortunately, 81% of the females and 62% of the males surveyed in Texas said that male judges "rarely" or "never" intervene when court personnel make comments demeaning to women (Texas 1994).

Only 9% of the female attorneys in the New Mexico survey said judges intervene to correct biased conduct. The majority of attorneys (both male and female) surveyed by the Colorado task force (1990) felt that judges "rarely" or "never" intercede when biased behavior takes place. However, the majority of judges felt they "always" or "almost always" reprimand counsel or court personnel for behaving in a manner demeaning to women (Colorado 1990). A survey in New Jersey (1984) found that only 18% of the female attorneys and 7% of the male attorneys have seen judges intervene to correct discriminatory behavior. According to the Vermont task force (1991), 70% of the female attorneys surveyed reported that judges rarely, if ever, intervene in the demeaning or differential treatment of women.

The Effect of Gender Bias on Case Outcome

When judges do not attempt to stop bias in the courtroom the case may be affected by it. Twenty-five percent of the females and 8% of the males responding to the New Mexico survey felt that gender bias does affect the outcome of the case (New Mexico 1990). Fifty-nine percent of the female attorneys and 30% of the male attorneys surveyed in Texas believe that the gender of the attorney affects case outcome (Texas 1994). Over one-third of the female attorneys responding to the Colorado survey believe that male judges assign more weight to arguments made by male attorneys (Colorado 1990).

Bias Against Men

Bias against men does exist in the courts. However, the extent to which men experience biased behavior is not clear. Two areas in which there is evidence that men routinely suffer from gender bias are child custody cases and criminal sentencing (Daly 1987; Price & Sokoloff 1995).

Child Custody

The area in which men most often experience gender bias is child custody. A father who wants to pursue custody faces stereotypes about who should raise children. The Georgia (1991) task force collected research on gender bias in child custody hearings. The data indicated that, in most cases, mothers are given the sole custody of their children after a divorce. In the majority of cases women receive sole (61%) or joint (27%) custody of their children, while fathers receive sole custody only 13% of the time according to the Washington (1989) survey. The Nebraska (1994) task force found that half of the attorneys surveyed felt judges assume that children belong with their mothers. In Iowa's survey an even greater percentage (72%) of attorneys said judges presume mothers should receive custody (Iowa 1993). A judge in a custody dispute was quoted as saying, "I don't buy that the father is better for a 22-month old girl than the mother. And I can't swallow it. I'm going to vomit on it. I can't handle it" (Michigan 1989:62). Less than one-fourth of the attorneys in the Texas (1994) survey believe judges give serious consideration to fathers who seek custody. Thirty percent of the attorneys in Nebraska (1994) said they discourage fathers from seeking custody because they believe judges will not give the father's petition fair consideration.

The Georgia (1991) study found several biased attitudes which influence a judge's custody decision. These include the belief that a father is not as good a parent as the mother, and the belief that children need to be with their mothers. Missouri (1993) found that 86% of the female and 94% of the male attorneys felt that judges indicated, by action or statement, that young children should be with the mother. The Maryland task force (1989) reported similar assumptions in 49% of judges, 79% of female attorneys, and 95% of male attorneys.

Sentencing

Another area in which bias against men is perceived to exist is criminal sentencing (Curran 1983; Daly 1987). Jail sentences are imposed less often on women, and when women are sent to jail they serve less time than men (Minnesota 1989). However, women are usually convicted of property crimes, which are considered less serious than crimes against persons under sentencing guidelines (Minnesota 1989). Approximately 103,000 men and 7,000 women were convicted of violent felonies in 1986 (Wisconsin 1991). The smaller number of women in prison is explained by the distribution of offenses (Minnesota 1989). Defendants with similar criminal histories, charged with similar crimes, receive like sentences, regardless of gender (New Mexico 1990).

Although many of the studies found women's and men's sentences to be comparable, the perception exists that women receive lighter sentences. Sixty-three percent of the judges questioned in the Texas (1994) survey believe men are "frequently" treated more harshly by the criminal justice system than women. Forty-two percent of the attorneys in the Texas (1994) survey believe women receive lighter sentences than men convicted of similar crimes. The largest area of biased sentencing appears to be probation (New Mexico 1990). Seventy-nine percent of respondents in the New Mexico (1990) survey believe women are more likely to receive probation than men. Judges in the Washington (1989) study said they do consider gender related issues in sentencing. For example, judges are reluctant to sentence women with small children to prison (Washington 1989).

Conclusion

Clearly women experience gender bias in the courts of this country. While a review of the state task force reports makes the extent and prevalence of the problem clear, the solution is not so obvious to determine or easy to achieve. A major problem in dealing with gender bias is that it is not a practice created by the court system. Rather, it is a reflection of prevailing attitudes in society. The implication of gender bias is that women are still not being viewed as equal to their male counterparts. Although current laws and affirmative action plans have furthered women's equality, they cannot by themselves change the attitudes of individuals. It is the individual attitudes that require change if gender bias is to be eradicated.

One of the most important recommendations for change mentioned by all the studies is education. It is extremely important that courtroom actors develop a better understanding of how gender bias affects the justice system. Another recommendation was extending greater sensitivity to victims of sexual assault and domestic violence. These two crimes are particularly degrading to victims and must be handled with a great deal of compassion. Additionally, judges must develop a better understanding of economic issues facing women after a divorce.

The task force reports on gender bias provide strong evidence that gender bias exists in all aspects of the court system, and in virtually all courts. The reports also indicate that there is a wide variation in the perception of the existence of bias, depending on the gender of the observer. Females perceive much more bias than do males. While it is possible that this is due to females being overly sensitive to the issue, the evidence suggests it is the males who misperceive the situation. Remedying gender bias requires convincing those most often guilty of it that they are acting in a biased fashion. If this can be accomplished, a major step will have been taken.

Task Force Reports

California. 1990. *Achieving Equal Justice for Women and Men in the Courts: The Draft Report of the Judicial Advisory Committee on Gender Bias in the Courts.*

Colorado. 1990. *Colorado Supreme Court Task Force on Women in the Courts, Gender and Justice in the Colorado Courts.*

Connecticut. 1991. *Gender, Justice and the Courts: Report of the Connecticut Task Force.*

District of Columbia. 1992. *District of Columbia Courts Final Report on Racial and Ethnic Bias and Task Force on Gender Bias in the Courts.*

Florida. 1990. *Report of the Florida Supreme Court Gender Bias Study Commission.*

Georgia. 1991. *Gender and Justice in the Court: A Report to the Supreme Court of Georgia by the Commission on Gender Bias in the Justice System.*

Hawaii. 1989. *Achieving Gender Fairness: Designing A Plan to Address Gender Bias in Hawaii's Legal System.*

Illinois. 1990. *The 1990 Report of the Illinois Task Force on Gender Bias in the Courts.*

Iowa. 1993. *Final Report of the Equality in the Courts Task Force.*

Kansas. 1992. *Report of the Kansas Bar Association Task Force on the Status of Women in the Profession.*

Kentucky. 1992. *Kentucky Taskforce on Gender Fairness in the Courts: Equal Justice for Women and Men.*

Louisiana. 1992. *Louisiana Task Force on Women in the Courts: Final Report.*

Maryland. 1989. *Report of the Special Joint Committee on Gender Bias in the Courts.*

Massachusetts. 1989. *Gender Bias Study of the Court System in Massachusetts.*

Michigan. 1989. *Final Report of the Michigan Supreme Court Task Force on Gender Issues in the Courts.*

Minnesota. 1989. *Minnesota Supreme Court Task Force for Gender Fairness in the Courts.*

Missouri. 1993. *Report of the Missouri Task Force on Gender and Justice.*

Nebraska. 1994. *Nebraska Supreme Court Task Force on Gender Fairness in the Courts, Final Report.*

Nevada. 1988. *Justice for Women: First Report of the Nevada Supreme Court Task Force on Gender Bias in the Courts.*

New Hampshire. 1988. *Report of the New Hampshire Bar Association Task Force on Women in the Bar.*

New Jersey. 1986. *Second Report of the New Jersey Supreme Court Task Force on Women in the Courts.*

New Mexico. 1990. *Final Report of the New Mexico State Bar Task Force on Women and the Legal Profession.*

New York. 1986. *Report of the New York Task Force on Women in the Courts.*

Ninth Circuit. 1993. *The Effects of Gender in the Federal Courts: The Final Report of the Ninth Circuit Gender Bias Task Force.*

Rhode Island. 1987. *The Final Report of the Rhode Island Committee on Women in the Courts: A Report on Gender Bias.*

Texas. 1994. *The Gender Bias Task Force of Texas Final Report.*

Utah. 1990. *Utah Task Force on Gender and Justice: Report to the Utah Judicial Council.*

Vermont. 1990. *Gender and Justice: Report of the Vermont Task Force on Gender Bias in the Legal System.*

Washington. 1989. *Washington State Task Force on Gender and Justice in the Courts.*

Wisconsin. 1991. *Wisconsin Equal Justice Task Force Final Report.*

References

Belknap, J. 1996. *The Invisible Woman: Gender, Crime, and Justice.* Cincinnati: Wadsworth.

Curran, D. 1983. "Judicial Discretion and Defendant's Sex." *Criminology* 21:4158.

Daly, K. 1987. "Discrimination in the Criminal Courts: Family Gender, and the Problem of Equal Treatment." *Social Forces* 66:152–175.

Klotter, J. 1994. *Criminal Law.* Cincinnati: Anderson.

Moyer, I. L. 1992. *The Changing Roles of Women in the Criminal Justice System: Offenders, Victims, and Professionals.* Prospect Heights, IL: Waveland Press.

Price, B. R., and N. S. Sokoloff. 1995. *The Criminal Justice System and Women: Offenders, Victims, and Workers.* New York: McGraw-Hill.

Roberts, A. and W. Knoebel 1989. "National Conference on Gender Bias in the Courts." *State Court Journal* 13:12–21.

Schafran, L. H. 1990a. "Overwhelming Evidence: Reports on Gender Bias in the Courts." *Trial* 26:28–35.

Schafran, L H. 1990b. "Gender and Justice: Florida and the Nation." *Florida Law Review* 42:181–207.

Wikler, N. J. 1980. "On the Judicial Agenda for the 80s: Equal Treatment for Men and Women in the Courts." *Judicature* 64:202–209.

Questions to Consider

1. Have you ever considered the career option of being a court administrator? What challenges must one confront in order to become such a professional? What do you think are some of the major issues a court administrator must deal with in his or her job?

2. Slotnick recounts studies that show that the more citizens know about courts, the more likely they are to be critical of them. How might court officials benefit by keeping their activities low profile? As you learn more about courts, how do you feel about courts?

3. Other studies indicate that increasing a person's knowledge about the social role of courts leads to higher support for judicial independence. If court officials really seek to address their problems and publicize these efforts, how might they gain more power and prestige in the long term?

4. How would you go about choosing judges for your community? How would you insure that they are "just" judges?

5. How would having a representative level of minority and women judges affect the decisions made in our court system? Is it important to look at the collective as well as individual decisions of such judges? If our courts reflect who we are, how does our society benefit?

6. If you were in a courtroom and witnessed obvious gender or racial bias against another by a court professional, how would you feel? Would you feel differently if the person being discriminated against was you? Given the level of bias evidenced by the readings, how do you think this affects people's perceptions of the courts?

7. Should we hold court professionals, who are given power over others, to a higher standard regarding racial and gender discrimination than we use with each other? What kind of accountability system should we have to enforce the standard you selected? Does it exist?

Section V
Politics in the
Decision-Making Process

It has often been claimed that law is politics. In the context of courts, this would mean that decisions made by our court systems are made politically. For our purposes, we will define decisions made politically as decisions that are substantially influenced by factors outside of the immediate facts in controversy. Thus, political legal decisions would be those influenced by negative factors such as racial bias or by positive factors such as understanding cultural differences. The results of such politically influenced decisions, therefore, may be less just or more just than if one strictly followed a legal rule.

Some legalists argue that legal decisions are not political because legal decision makers are simply following the law. Whether the actors are judges, prosecutors, defense lawyers, or juries, the following articles point to numerous political components in their decision making. These six articles argue that this nonpolitical perspective is a naive picture of the legal process. Whether the actors are judges, prosecutors, defense lawyers, juries, or even those who choose judges under a "merit" system, the articles point to numerous political components in their decision making.

An even more important lesson from these articles is that all decision makers have perspectives that they bring to new issues. This "outside" perspective can bring wisdom as well as prejudice. The challenge for our criminal justice system is to devise methods to harness this wisdom while limiting the prejudice.

In the first article, Bennett Gershman explains why prosecutors act unfairly and why the justice system fails to stop such unfair practices. He argues that prosecutors often act unfairly because such tactics "work"; they know that juries often act politically by considering information (even illegal and prejudicial statements) that has been presented by prosecutors. Little is done to correct this situation because the governing rules, such as the harmless error doctrine, are very vague and subjective. Such vagueness allows judicial values to become more prominent, leading to inconsistent decisions. Further, even if prosecutors are found to have acted unfairly, there are few if any sanctions. Once again we see the need to confront the dilemma of power; how do we give needed discretionary independence to court officials yet effectively control abuses of that power?

The articles by Rodney Uphoff and Alissa Worden reflect similar problems with defense attorneys. Uphoff updates a classic 1967 study by Abraham Blumberg, who argued that defense attorneys were coopted by the legal system to serve its organizational ends. Uphoff finds more variety in defense functions but still uncovers multiple ways in which outside forces, such as economic realities, court procedures, and methods of delivering legal services, affect the decisions defense attorneys make in representing their clients.

Alissa Worden compares defense attorney delivery systems in her focus on the growing method of private contracting. While this system seems like it would be more efficient, she points to the many pitfalls, such as price fixing and monopoly practices, which debilitate logical and efficient decision making.

Mary Dodge and John Harris, along with Martha Minow, explore alternatives to the traditional belief that we must eliminate all politics from our legal system. Dodge and Harris used the "three strikes" laws in California to show that while most judges do not allow jurors to be told that defendants face mandatory severe sanctions for minor felony charges, jurors still act politically by often refusing to convict when three-strike punishment for relatively minor offenses is a possibility. They argue instead that not trusting juries engenders this kind of haphazard response, and that we need to give jurors all the facts as well as some voice in sentencing. A Decision Quest/*National Law Journal* poll in October 1998 found that three out of four Americans eligible to serve on a jury say they would act on their own beliefs of right and wrong regardless of legal instructions from a judge. Clearly juries are as potentially political as judges and prosecutors, and efforts at control are really battles over levels of control and dominance. Also in question is our underlying trust in democracy and in ourselves.

Martha Minow expands the perspective that our legal system is inherently political, arguing that we have the seeds of a solution in our current legal system. She states that fairness means one must include notions of both representation and neutrality. We want our legal decision makers to be political by bringing in outside experiences sufficient to make a just decision, yet not to be biased by their experiences. She argues that the best way to ensure an accommodation between representation and neutrality is to use collaborative decision making, a system we now have with the institution of the jury.

16

Why Prosecutors Misbehave

BENNETT L. GERSHMAN

The duties of the prosecuting attorney were well-stated in the classic opinion of Justice Sutherland fifty years ago.[1] The interest of the prosecutor, he wrote, "is not that he is in a peculiar and very definite sense the servant of the law, the twofold aim of which is that guilt shall not escape or innocence suffer. He may prosecute with earnestness and vigor—indeed, he should do so. But, while he may strike hard blows, he is not at liberty to strike foul ones."[2]

Despite this admonition, prosecutors continue to strike "foul blows," perpetuating a disease which began long before Justice Sutherland's oft-quoted opinion. Indeed, instances of prosecutorial misconduct were reported at least as far back as 1897[3] and as recently as the latest volume of the *Supreme Court Reporter*.[4] The span between these cases is replete with innumerable instances of improper conduct of the prosecutor, much of which defies belief.

One of the leading examples of outrageous conduct by a prosecutor is *Miller v. Pate*,[5] where the prosecutor concealed from the jury in a murder case the fact that a pair of undershorts with red stains on it, a crucial piece of evidence, were stained not by blood, but by paint. Equally startling is *United States v. Perry*,[6] where the prosecutor, in his summation, commented on the fact that the "defendants and their counsel are completely unable to explain away their guilt."[7] Similarly,

[in] *Dubose v. State*,[8] the prosecutor argued to the jury: "Now, not one sentence, not one scintilla of evidence, not one word in any way did this defendant or these attorneys challenge the credibility of the complaining witness."[9] At a time when it should be clear that constitutional and ethical standards prevent prosecutors from behaving this way,[10] we ought to question why prosecutors so frequently engage in such conduct.

Much of the above misconduct occurs in a courtroom. The terms "courtroom" or "forensic misconduct" have never been precisely defined. One commentator describes courtroom misconduct as those "types of misconduct which involve efforts to influence the jury through various sorts of inadmissible evidence."[11] Another commentator suggests that forensic misconduct "may be generally defined as any activity by the prosecutor which tends to divert the jury from making its determination of guilt or innocence by weighing the legally admitted evidence in the manner prescribed by law."[12] For purposes of this analysis, the latter definition applies, as it encompasses a broader array of behavior which can be classed as misconduct. As will be seen, prosecutorial misconduct can occur even without the use of inadmissible evidence.

This article will address two aspects of the problem of courtroom misconduct. First, it will discuss why prosecutors engage in courtroom misconduct, and then why our present system offers little incentive to a prosecutor to change his behavior.

Why Misconduct Occurs?

Intuition tells us that the reason so much courtroom misconduct by the prosecutor[13] occurs is quite simple: it works. From my experience as a prosecutor for ten years, I would hypothesize that most prosecutors deny that misconduct is helpful in winning a case. Indeed, there is a strong philosophical argument that prosecutorial misconduct corrupts the judicial system, thereby robbing it of its legitimacy. In this regard, one would probably be hard pressed to find a prosecutor who would even mention that he would consider the thought of some form of misconduct.

Nonetheless, all of this talk is merely academic, because as we know, if only from the thousands of cases in the reports, courtroom misconduct does occur. If the prosecutor did not believe it would be effective to stretch his argument to the ethical limit, and then risk going beyond that ethical limit, he would not take the risk.

Intuition aside, however, several studies have shown the importance of oral advocacy in the courtroom, as well as the effect produced by such conduct. For example, the student of trial advocacy often is told of the importance of the opening statement. Prosecutors would undoubtedly agree that the opening statement is indeed crucial. In a University of Kansas study,[14] the importance of the opening statement was confirmed. From this study, the authors concluded that, in the course of any given trial,[15] the jurors were affected most by the first strong presentation which they saw. This finding leads to the conclusion that if a prosecutor were to present a particularly strong opening argument, the jury would favor the prosecution throughout the trial. Alternatively, if the prosecutor were to provide a weak opening statement, followed by a strong opening statement by the defense, then, according to the authors, the jury would favor the defense during the trial. It thus becomes evident that the prosecutor will be best served by making the strongest opening argument possible, thereby assisting the jury in gaining a better insight into what they are about to hear and see. The opportunity for the prosecutor to influence the jury at this point in the trial is considerable, and virtually all prosecutors would probably attempt to use this opportunity to their advantage, even if the circumstances do not call for lengthy or dramatic opening remarks[16]

An additional aspect of the prosecutor's power over the jury is suggested in a University of North Carolina study.[17] This study found that the more arguments counsel raises with respect to the different substantive arguments offered, the more the jury will believe in that party's case. Moreover, this study found that there is not necessarily a correlation between the amount of objective information in the communication and the persuasiveness of the presentation.

For the trial attorney, then, this study clearly points to the advantage of raising as many issues as possible at trial. For the prosecutor, the two studies taken together would dictate an "action packed" opening statement, containing as many arguments that can be mustered, even those which might be irrelevant or unnecessary to convince the jury of the defendant's guilt. The second study would also dictate the same strategy for the closing argument. Consequently, a prosecutor who, through use of these techniques, attempts to assure that the jury knows his case may, despite violating ethical standards to seek justice,[18] be "rewarded" with a guilty verdict. Thus, one begins to perceive the incentive that leads the prosecutor to misbehave in the courtroom.[19]

Similar incentives can be seen with respect to the complex problem of controlling evidence to which the jury may have access. It is common knowledge that, in the course of any trial, statements frequently are made by the attorneys or witnesses, despite the fact that these statements may not be admissible as evidence. Following such a statement, the trial judge may, at the request of opposing counsel, instruct the jury to disregard what they have heard. Most trial lawyers, if they are candid, will agree that it is virtually impossible for jurors realistically to disregard these inadmissible statements. Studies here again demonstrate that our intuition is correct, and that this evidence often is considered by jurors in reaching a verdict.

For example, an interesting study conducted at the University of Washington[20] tested the effects of inadmissible evidence on the decisions of jurors. The authors of the test designed a variety of scenarios whereby some jurors heard about an incriminating piece of evidence while other jurors did not. The study found that the effect of the inadmissible evidence was directly correlated to the strength of the prosecutor's case. The authors of the study reported that when the prosecutor presented a weak case, the inadmissible evidence did, in fact, prejudice the jurors. Furthermore, the judge's admonition to the jurors to disregard certain evidence did not have the same effect as when the evidence had not been mentioned at all. It had a prejudicial impact anyway.

However, the study also indicated that when there was a strong prosecution case, the inadmissible evidence had little, if any, effect.[21] Nonetheless, the most significant conclusion from the study is that inadmissible evidence had its most prejudicial impact when there was little other evidence on which the jury could base a decision. In this situation, "the controversial evidence becomes quite salient in the jurors' minds."[22]

Finally, with respect to inadmissible evidence and stricken testimony, even if one were to reject all of the studies discussed, it is still clear that although "stricken testimony may tend to be rejected in open discussion, it does have an impact, perhaps even an unconscious one, on the individual juror's judgment."[23] As with previously discussed points, this factor—the unconscious effect of stricken testimony or evidence—will generally not be lost on the prosecutor who is in tune with the psychology of the jury.

The applicability of these studies to this analysis, then, is quite clear. Faced with a difficult case in which there may be a problem of proof, a prosecutor might be tempted to sway the jury by adverting to a matter which might be highly prejudicial. In this connection, another study[24] has suggested that the jury will more likely consider inadmissible evidence that favors the defendant rather than inadmissible evidence that favors conviction.[25]

Despite this factor of "defense favoritism," it is again evident that a prosecutor may find it rewarding to misconduct himself in the courtroom. Of course, a prosecutor who adopts the unethical norm and improperly allows jurors to hear inadmissible proof runs the risk of jeopardizing any resulting conviction. In a situation where the prosecutor feels there is a weak case, however, a subsequent reversal is not a particularly effective sanction when a conviction might have been diffi-cult to achieve in the first place. Consequently, an unethical courtroom "trick" can be a very attractive idea to the prosecutor who feels he must win.[26] Additionally, there is always the possibility of another conviction even after an appellate reversal. Indeed, while a large number of cases are dismissed following remand by an appellate court, nearly one half of reversals still result in some type of conviction.[27] Therefore, a prosecutor can still succeed in obtaining a conviction even after his misconduct led to a reversal.

An additional problem in the area of prosecutor-jury interaction is the prosecutor's prestige; since the prosecutor represents the "government," jurors are more likely to believe him.[28] Put simply, prosecutors "are the good guys of the legal system,"[29] and because they have such glamour, they often may be tempted to use this advantage in an unethical manner. This presents a problem for the prosecutor in that the "average citizen may often forgive, yea urge prosecutors on in ethical indiscretions, for the end, convictions of criminals certainly justifies in the public eye any means necessary."[30] Consequently, unless the prosecutor is a person of high integrity and is able to uphold the highest moral standards, the problem of courtroom misconduct will inevitably be tolerated by the public.

Moreover, when considering the problems facing the prosecutor, one also must consider the tremendous stress under which the prosecutor labors on a daily basis. Besides the stressful conditions faced by the ordinary courtroom litigator,[31] prosecuting attorneys, particularly those in large metropolitan areas, are faced with huge and very demanding case loads. As a result of case volume and time demands, prosecutors may not be able to take advantage of opportunities to relax and recover from the constant onslaught their emotions face every day in the courtroom.[32]

Under these highly stressful conditions, it is understandable that a prosecutor occasionally may find it difficult to face these everyday pressures and to resist temptations to behave unethically. It is not unreasonable to suggest that the conditions under which the prosecutor works can have a profound effect on his attempt to maintain high moral and ethical standards. Having established this hypothesis, one can see yet another reason why courtroom misconduct may occur.

Why Misconduct Continues?

Having demonstrated that courtroom misconduct may, in many instances, be highly effective, the question arises as to why such practices continue in our judicial system. A number of reasons may account for this phenomenon. Perhaps the most significant reason for the continued presence of prosecutorial misconduct is the harmless error doctrine.

Under this doctrine, an appellate court can affirm a conviction despite the presence of serious misconduct during the trial. As Justice Traynor once stated, the "practical objective of tests of harmless error is to conserve judicial resources by enabling appellate courts to cleanse the judicial process of prejudicial error without becoming mired in harmless error."[33]

Although the definition advanced by Justice Traynor portrays the harmless error doctrine as having a most desirable consequence, this desirability is undermined when the prosecutor is able to misconduct himself without fear of sanction. Additionally, since every case is different, what constitutes harmless error in one case may be reversible error in another. Consequently, harmless error determinations do not offer any significant precedents by which prosecutors can judge the status of their behavior.

By way of illustration, consider two cases in which the prosecutor implicitly told the jury of his personal belief in the defendant's guilt. In one case, the prosecutor stated, "I have never tried a case where the evidence was so clear and convincing."[34] In the other case, the prosecutor told the jury that he did not try cases unless he was sure of them.[35] In the first case the conviction was affirmed, while in the second case the conviction was reversed. Interestingly, the court in the first case affirmed the conviction despite its belief that the "prosecutor's remarks were totally out of order."[36] Accordingly, despite making comments which were "totally out of order," the prosecutor did not suffer any penalty.

Contrasting these two cases presents clear evidence of what is perhaps the worst derivative effect of the harmless error rule. The problem is that the stronger the prosecutor's case, the more misconduct he can commit without being reversed. Indeed, in the *Shields* case, the court stated that "the guilt of the defendant was clearly established not only beyond a reasonable doubt, but well beyond any conceivable doubt."[37] For purposes of our analysis, it is clear that by deciding as they do, courts often provide little discouragement to a prosecutor who believes, and rightly so, that he does not have to be as careful about his conduct when he has a strong case. The relation of this factor to the amount of courtroom misconduct cannot be ignored.

Neither can one ignore the essential absurdity of a harmless error determination. In order to apply the harmless error rule, appellate judges attempt to evaluate how various evidentiary items or instances of prosecutorial misconduct may have affected the jury's verdict. Although it may be relatively simple in some cases to determine whether improper conduct during a trial was harmless, there are many instances when such an analysis cannot properly be made, but nevertheless is made. For example, consider the situation when an appellate court is divided on whether or not a given error was harmless. In *United States v. Antonelli Fireworks Co.*,[38] two judges (including Judge Learned Hand) believed that the prosecutor's error was harmless. Yet, Judge Frank, the third judge sitting in the case, completely disagreed, writing a scathing dissent nearly three times the length of the majority opinion. One wonders how harmless error can be fairly applied when there is such a significant difference of opinion among highly respected members of a court as to the extent of harmfulness of trial errors. Perhaps even more interesting is the Supreme Court's reversal of the Court of Appeals for the Second Circuit's unanimous finding of harmless error in *United States v. Berger*.[39] As noted, *Berger* now represents the classic statement of the scope of the prosecutor's duties. Yet, in his majority opinion for the Second Circuit, Judge Learned Hand found the prosecutor's misconduct harmless.

The implications of these contradictory decisions are significant, for they demonstrate the utter failure of appellate courts to provide incentives for the prosecutor to control his behavior. If misconduct can be excused even when reasonable judges differ as to the extent of harm caused by such misbehavior, then very little guidance is given to a prosecutor to assist him in determining the propriety of his actions. Clearly, without such guidance, the potential for misconduct significantly increases.

The *Shields* case presents yet another factor which suggests why the prosecutor has only a limited incentive to avoid misconduct. In *Shields*, the court refused to review certain "potentially inflammatory statements" made by the prosecutor because of the failure of the defense to object.[40] Although this approach has not been uniformly applied by all courts, the implications of this technique to reject a defendant's claim are considerable. Most important, it encourages prosecutors to make remarks that they know are objectionable in the hope that defense counsel will not object. This situation recalls the previous discussion which dealt with the effect of inadmissible evidence on jurors. Defense counsel here is in a difficult predicament. If he does not object, he ordinarily waives any appealable issue in the event of conviction. If he does object, he highlights to the jury the fact that the prosecutor has just done something which, some jurors may feel, is so damaging to the defendant that the defense does not want it brought out.

The dilemma of the defense attorney in this situation is confirmed by a Duke University study.[41] In that study, jurors learned of various pieces of evidence which were ruled inadmissible. The study found that when the judge admonished the jury to disregard the evidence, the bias created by that evidence was not significantly reduced.[42] Consequently, when a prejudicial remark is made by the prosecutor, defense counsel must act carefully to avoid damaging his client's case. In short, the prosecutor has yet another weapon, in this instance an arguably unfair aspect of the appellate process, which requires preservation of an appealable issue.[43]

A final point when analyzing why prosecutorial misconduct persists is the unavailability or inadequacy of penalties visited upon the prosecutor personally in the event of misconduct. Punishment in our legal system comes in varying degrees. An appellate court can punish a prosecutor by simply cautioning him not to act in the same manner again, reversing his case, or, in some cases, identifying by name the prosecutor who misconducted himself.[44] Even these punishments, however, may not be sufficient to dissuade prosecutors from acting improperly. One noteworthy case[45] describes a prosecutor who appeared before the appellate court on a misconduct issue for the third time, each instance in a different case.

Perhaps the ultimate reason for the ineffectiveness of the judicial system in curbing prosecutorial misconduct is that prosecutors are not personally liable for their misconduct. In *Imbler v. Pachtman*,[46] the Supreme Court held that "in initiating a prosecution and in presenting the state's case, the prosecutor is immune from a civil suit for damages under Section 1983."[47] Furthermore, prosecutors have absolute, rather than a more limited, qualified, immunity. Thus, during the course of a trial, the prosecutor is absolutely shielded from any civil liability which might arise due to his misconduct, even if that misconduct was performed with malice.

There is clearly a need for some level of immunity to be accorded all government officials. Without such immunity much of what is normally done by officials in authority might not be performed out of fear that their practices are later deemed harmful or improper. Granting prosecutors a certain level of immunity is reasonable. Allowing prosecutors to be completely shielded from civil liability in the event of misconduct, however, provides no deterrent to courtroom misconduct.

Conclusion

This analysis was undertaken to determine why the issue of misconduct seems so prevalent in the criminal trial. For the prosecutor, the temptation to cross over the allowable ethical limit must often be irresistible because of the distinct advantages that such misconduct creates in assisting the prosecutor to win his case by effectively influencing the jury. Most prosecutors must inevitably be subject to this temptation. It takes a constant effort on the part of every prosecutor to maintain the high moral standards which are necessary to avoid such temptations.

Despite the frequent occurrences of courtroom misconduct, appellate courts have not provided significant incentives, to the prosecutor to avoid misconduct. It is not until the courts decide to take a stricter, more consistent approach to this problem, that inroads will be made in the effort to end it. One solution might be to impose civil liability on the prosecutor who misconducts himself with malice. Although this will not solve the problem, it might be a step in the right direction.

Endnotes

1 *Berger v. United States*, 295 U.S. 78 (1935)

2 Id. at 88.

3 See *Dunlop v. United States*, 165 U.S. 486 (1897) where the prosecutor in an obscenity case, argued to the jury, "I do not believe that there are twelve men that could be gathered by the venire of this court . . . , except where they were bought and perjured in advance, whose verdict I would not be willing to take. . . ." Id. at 498. Following this remark, defense council objected and the court held that statement to be improper.

4 See *Caldwell v. Mississippi*, 105 S. Ct. 2633 (1985) (improper argument to capital sentencing jury); *United States v. Young*, 105 S. Ct. 1038 (1985) (improper argument but not plain error).

5 386 U.S. 1 (1967). In this case, the Supreme Court overturned the defendant's conviction after the Court of Appeals for the Seventh Circuit had upheld it. The Court noted that the prosecutor "deliberately misrepresented the truth," and that such behavior would not be tolerated under the Fourteenth Amendment. Id. at 67.

6 643 F.2d 38 (2d Cir. 1981).

7 Id. at 51.

8 531 S.W.2d 330 (Texas 1975).

9 Id. at 331. The court noted that the argument was clearly a comment on the failure of the defendant to testify at trial.

10 See *Griffin v. California*, 380 U.S. 609 (1965), where the Supreme Court applied the Fifth Amendment to the states under the Fourteenth Amendment.

11 Alschuler, "Courtroom Misconduct by Prosecutors and Trial Judges," 50 *Tex. L. Rev.* 627, 633 (1972).

12 Note, "The Nature and Function of Forensic Misconduct in the Prosecution of a Criminal Case," 54 *Col. L. Rev.* 946, 949 (1954).

13 Of course, there is also a significant amount of defense misconduct which takes place. In this respect, for an interesting article which takes a different approach than this article, see Kamm, "The Case for the Prosecutor," 13 *U. Tol. L. Rev.* 331 (1982), where the author notes that "courts carefully nurture the defendant's rights while cavalierly ignoring the rights of the people."

14 Pyszczynski, "The Effects of Opening Statement on Mock Jurors' Verdicts in a Simulated Criminal Trial," 11 *J. Applied Soc. Psychology* 301 (1981).

15 All of the cited studies include within the report a caveat about the value of the study when applied to a "real world" case. Nonetheless, they are still worthwhile for the purpose of this analysis.

16 In some jurisdictions, attorneys may often use the voir dire to accomplish the goal of early influence of the jury.

17 Calder, "The Relation of Cognitive and Memorial Processes to Persuasion in a Simulated Jury Trial," 4 *J. Applied Soc. Psychology* 62 (1974).

¹⁸ See *Model Code of Professional Responsibility* EC 7-13 (1980) ("The duty of the prosecutor is to seek justice.").

¹⁹ Of course, this may apply to other attorneys as well.

²⁰ Sue, "The Effects of Inadmissible Evidence on the Decisions of Simulated Jurors—A Moral Dilemma," 3 *J. Applied Soc. Psychology* 345 (1973).

²¹ Perhaps lending validity to application of the harmless error doctrine, which will be discussed later in this article.

²² Sue, note 20 supra, at 351.

²³ Hastie, *Inside the Jury* 232 (1983).

²⁴ Thompson, "Inadmissible Evidence and Juror Verdicts," 40 *J. Personality & Soc. Psychology* 453 (1981).

²⁵ The author did note that the defendant in the test case was very sympathetic and that the results may have been different with a less sympathetic defendant.

²⁶ Of course, this begs the question: "Is there a prosecutor who would take a case to trial and then feel that he didn't have to win?" It is hoped that, in such a situation, trial would never be an option. Rather, one would hope for an early dismissal of the charges.

²⁷ Roper, "Does Procedural Due Process Make a Difference?" 65 *Judicature* 136 (1981). This article suggests that the rate of nearly 50 percent of acquittals following reversal is proof that due process is a viable means for legitimatizing the judiciary. While this is true, the fact remains that there is still a 50 percent conviction rate after reversal, thereby giving many prosecutors a second chance to convict after their original misconduct.

²⁸ See *People v. McCoy*, 220 N.W.2d 456 (Mich. 1974), where the prosecutor, in attempting to bolster his case, told the jury that "the Detroit Police Department, the detectives in the Homicide Bureau, these detectives you see in court today, and myself from the prosecutor's office, we don't bring cases unless we're sure, unless we're positive." Id. at 460.

²⁹ Emmons, "Morality and Ethics—A Prosecutor's View," *Advanced Criminal Trial Tactics* 393-407 (P.L.I. 1977).

³⁰ Id.

³¹ For an interesting article on the topic, see Zimmerman, "Stress and the Trial Lawyer," 9 *Litigation* 4, 37-42 (1983).

³² For example, the Zimmerman article suggests time off from work and "celebration" with family and friends in order to effectively induce relaxation.

³³ R. Traynor, *The Riddle of Harmless Error* 81 (1970).

³⁴ *People v. Shields*, 58 A.D.2d 94, 96 (N.Y.), aff'd, 46 N.Y.2d 764 (1977).

³⁵ *People v. McCoy*, 220 N.W.2d 456 (Mich. 1974).

³⁶ *Shields*, 58 A.D.2d at 97.

³⁷ Id. at 99.

³⁸ 155 F.2d 631 (2d Cir. 1946).

³⁹ 73 F.2d 278 (1934), rev'd, 295 U.S. 78 (1935).

⁴⁰ *Shields*, 58 A.D.2d at 97.

⁴¹ Wolf, "Effects of Inadmissible Evidence and Level of Judicial Admonishment to Disregard on the Judgments of Mock Jurors," 7 *J. Applied Soc. Psychology* 205 (1977).

⁴² Additionally of note is the fact that if the judge rules the evidence and did not admonish the jury, then the biasing effect of the evidence was eliminated. The authors of the study concluded that by being told not to consider certain evidence, the jurors felt a loss of freedom and that in order to retain their freedom, they considered it anyway. The psychological term for this effect is called reactance.

[43] Of course, this does not mean that appeals should always be allowed, even in the absence of an appealable issue. Rather, one should confine the availability of these appeals to the narrow circumstances discussed.

[44] See *United v. Burse*, 531 F.2d 1151 (2d Cir. 1976), where the Court named the prosecutor in the body of its opinion.

[45] *United States v. Drummond*, 481 F.2d 62 (2d Cir. 1973).

[46] 424 U.S. 409 (1976).

[47] Id. at 431. 42 U.S.C. § 1983 authorizes civil actions against state officials who violate civil rights "under color of state law."

17

The Criminal Defense Lawyer
Zealous Advocate, Double Agent, or Beleaguered Dealer?

RODNEY J. UPHOFF

In theory, the criminal defense lawyer is called to be a zealous advocate vigorously representing those persons accused by the state of violating the law.[1] As the champion of the accused, the criminal defense lawyer plays an essential role in the adversary system by challenging the prosecutions' efforts to secure a conviction.[2] Defense counsel's responsibility is to probe and test the state's evidence to ensure that the accused is convicted only if the prosecution can muster sufficient evidence to prove the defendant's guilt beyond a reasonable doubt.[3] Moreover, it is counsel's duty to defend the accused zealously, even if counsel knows the defendant is guilty.[4]

In principle, therefore, a criminal defense lawyer, through counsel's legitimate efforts, may actually frustrate the search for the truth. Indeed, defense counsel may be ethically required to do so.[5] Defense counsel's zealous representation of a client is not, of course, without bounds. As an officer of the court, a defense lawyer's advocacy is constrained by various ethical rules.[6] Nevertheless, although disagreement exists as to how far a criminal defense lawyer may go on behalf of a client in certain

Reprinted by permission of West Group from the *Criminal Law Bulletin*, Vol. 28, No. 5 (Sept./Oct. 1992), pp. 419–456. Copyright © 1992 by West Group, 610 Opperman Drive, St. Paul, MN 55164. All rights reserved.

tough ethical situations,[7] there is little question that defense counsel is required to be an able, devoted defender standing with the accused in an adversarial struggle with the state.[8]

However, is defense counsel, in practice, really a zealous advocate striving to provide a vigorous defense to the accused? Or is defense counsel too often a "double agent" merely seeking to persuade the client to accept a plea bargain, which is designed primarily to redound to the benefit of the lawyer and the criminal justice system?[9] Is there, in fact, a significant gap between the theoretical role of defense counsel and the actual practices of most criminal defense lawyers? To answer these questions, the first section of this article explores the observations made by Abraham Blumberg in 1967 that led him to conclude that defense lawyers were co-opted by the criminal justice system to serve organizational ends rather than their clients' interests.[10] The second section examines the behavior of defense lawyers in three counties to ascertain whether Blumberg's portrayal of defense counsel as double agent indeed is accurate. After discussing a number of important systemic variables that adversely affect the behavior and zeal of criminal defense lawyers, the second section concludes that "beleaguered dealer" more aptly describes the role of defense counsel in these counties. Finally, the third section considers the extent to which strengthening the system for the delivery of indigent defense services will enhance zealous advocacy and improve the quality of representation provided to most criminal defendants.

Defense Lawyer as "Double Agent"

In his oft-cited article "The Practice of Law as Confidence Game: Organization Co-optation of a Profession," Abraham Blumberg turned his attention to the question of whether the traditional legal conception of the role of a criminal defense lawyer actually squared with social reality.[11] Blumberg correctly noted that the traditional view was based on the notion of a criminal case as an adversary, combative proceeding in which defense counsel zealously defended the accused. In fact, Blumberg stated, few cases actually are decided by trial.[12] Rather, the vast majority of cases are resolved by the plea-bargaining process, a process dictated by the organizational structure of criminal courts.[13] This court organization has its own set of goals and discipline, which in turn impose certain demands and conditions of practice on the actors in the system, including defense counsel.[14] As a result of organizational pressure, defense lawyers abandon their ethical commitment to their clients and instead "help the accused redefine his situation and restructure his perceptions concomitant with a plea of guilty."[15]

According to Blumberg, the formal and informal relations of all of the various actors in the criminal justice system were more important than the needs of any client.[16] Hence, in order to ensure continued positive relations and to cope with an intolerably large number of cases, these actors were bound together in "an organized system of complicity."[17] Blumberg described a variety of different systemic practices and institutional evasions that serve to pressure the accused to plead guilty while permitting the system to maintain an outward commitment to due process.[18] Defense lawyers were key players in the successful operation of the system. Owing their primary allegiance to the system, defense lawyers, whether public defenders or retained counsel, were concerned largely with strategies designed to manipulate clients into pleading guilty.[19]

Blumberg focused much of his attention on the efforts of criminal defense lawyers to "con" their clients.[20] To pull off this con, the criminal defense lawyer had to collect a fee, convince the client to accept a guilty plea, and still terminate the litigation as quickly as possible." Counsel was a double agent because she pretended to help the client when, in fact, her main objective was to limit the scope and duration of the client's case, not to do battle.[22] Thus, defense counsel utilized her unique role in the organization to persuade or cajole the client to accept a result—a plea bargain—that served the interests of the organization and the lawyer above those of the client.[23]

But do Blumberg's damning observations about criminal defense lawyers really reflect the reality of the contemporary criminal justice system? To address this question, this article examines the practices of criminal defense lawyers in three counties: Milwaukee County, Wis., Dane County, Wis., and Cleveland County, Okla.[24] There is no methodological significance to the selection of these three counties. They were selected simply because the author has been a participant observer in each.[25] As with Blumberg's article, no empirical data supports the author's observations about the behavior of criminal defense lawyers in these counties. Nonetheless, the picture of the criminal defense bar portrayed in this article is quite similar to that painted by others looking at defense lawyers in other criminal justice systems.[26]

Defense Lawyer as Beleaguered Dealer: Observations of Lawyers at Work

Blumberg presented a very cynical, negative picture of criminal defense lawyers and of their relationships with their clients. With broad strokes, Blumberg painted the portrait of the criminal defense lawyer as a manipulative con artist who succumbs to the pressures of making a living in a closed community by "duping" clients to enter pleas that benefit the system more than the clients.[27] Although it is true, as it was in 1967, when Blumberg's article appeared, that the vast majority of clients in Milwaukee, Dane, and Cleveland Counties plead guilty instead of going to trial.[28] Nevertheless, it does not follow that the large number of guilty pleas is simply the product of defense lawyer double-dealing. Rather, numerous factors, including some of the systemic pressures described by Blumberg, affect a defendant's plea decision and the behavior of a criminal defense lawyer. Indeed, the varied conduct of defense lawyers in these three counties confirms that Blumberg's premise that court organization dictates defense counsel's role, that of double agent, is suspect.

Admittedly, many of Blumberg's observations about certain systemic pressures and practices accurately reflect similar aspects of the criminal justice systems in Milwaukee, Dane, and Cleveland Counties. In all three counties, private defense lawyers almost always want their fees in advance and routinely look to the client's family and friends to contribute to the client's defense.[29] Certainly, there are lawyers in each county who prey on the ignorance or anxieties of their clients and their clients' families to increase their fees and to enhance the collection of those fees.[30] At times, court personnel, prosecutors, or judges will aid defense counsel's efforts to collect a fee, and this assistance may subsequently be used to pressure defense counsel.[31] And there are lawyers who manipulate their clients by lying to them about the complexity of the case, the working of the system, or the dangers of going to trial in order to maximize the lawyer's financial return on a particular case.[32] There are, therefore, lawyers in each county who fit Blumberg's double agent profile.

Simply to characterize all criminal defense lawyers as double agents, however, grossly distorts the overall picture of the criminal defense bar in these counties. Not all defense lawyers "ultimately are concerned with strategies which tend to lead to a plea."[33] Nor is it true that "it is the rational, impersonal elements involving economics of time, labor, expense and a superior commitment of the defense counsel to these rationalistic values of maximum production of court organization that prevail, in his relationship with a client."[34] If Blumberg's image of defense counsel is entirely accurate, what explains those cases that do go to trial: stubborn clients, bad salesmanship by the lawyers, ideological zealots, or desire to deflect "outside" scrutiny?[35] Blumberg's analysis offers no explanation.

Unquestionably, however, each county has a number of criminal defense lawyers, especially public defenders in Dane and Milwaukee Counties, who are committed professionally and ideologically to obtaining the best possible results for their clients.[36] Although heavy case loads affect the ability of public defenders—and, in some instances, their willingness and enthusiasm—to go to trial, most public defenders in Milwaukee and Dane Counties bargain as aggressively as possible on behalf of their clients. These public defenders, in turn, usually advise their clients of the available, albeit often quite limited, options, in an honest, unbiased manner.

Moreover, in each county there are private lawyers specializing in criminal cases who can and will aggressively defend those clients with the economic resources to pay for a zealous defense. Instead of seeking to limit the litigation, some lawyers file numerous motions in an effort to wear down the prosecution and achieve a favorable outcome for their clients.[37] Finally, there are lawyers in each county who have zealously defended their clients at great personal sacrifice. Dedication, commitment to principle, and personal values, not financial gain, drive some criminal defense lawyers.[38]

Blumberg posited that criminal defense lawyers function as double agents because conning the client into a quick plea ensured that a case would be profitable and enabled counsel to serve the ends of a complicitous, closed system.[39] Yet, if court structure and organization dictate defense counsel's role, why is it that not all defense lawyers in Milwaukee, Dane, and Cleveland Counties behave alike? Why do only some criminal defense lawyers in these counties succumb to personal or systemic pressure and function as double agents while others do not? Why is it that some defense lawyers in these counties conduct vigorous defenses and others put up only a staged or token resistance?

There is no single explanation for why criminal defense lawyers play their role so differently. Nor is there a simple answer as to why some public defenders and private lawyers operate some of the time as double agents.[40] A public defender may be lazy, inexperienced, incompetent, overwhelmed, burned out, focused on a particularly difficult and time-consuming case, subject to personal problems, or distracted by a combination of such factors.[41] Private lawyers must not only cope with these factors but also try to earn a living. Only infrequently does a criminal defense lawyer command a fee commensurate with the time it takes to investigate and defend a criminal case fully and competently. Simply put, most people accused of a crime cannot afford to pay for effective assistance of counsel.[42] Most low-income defendants who do not qualify for public defenders in Wisconsin or for court-appointed counsel in Cleveland County cannot obtain adequate legal representation.[43] It is these defendants in all three counties who face the real prospect of being represented by double agents. Although, at times, a defendant will be advised by defense counsel that the meager retainer paid will only cover a negotiated plea, too often the accused neither understands nor ever learns of the real limits of counsel's representation. Unhappily, it may not be until the client insists on a trial that the defense lawyer's limited zeal becomes obvious.[44]

Often, however, it is not defense counsel's lack of zeal but the defendant's lack of money that dictates counsel's actions. Often a defendant who wishes to hire a lawyer can only raise a minimal retainer. Once retained, the lawyer may prod and push the prosecutor for a dismissal or a favorable plea bargain, but if the prosecutor refuses, the client is often left with an unhappy choice: Accept the negotiated deal or go to trial. Even if the lawyer wants to fight the charge and is willing to go to trial for an additional $1,500, the client rarely chooses to do so. The economic realities of the system, not counsel's lack of zeal, frequently pressure the defendant to accept a plea.[45]

In Milwaukee, Dane, and Cleveland Counties, there also are some defense lawyers who are afraid of trying cases, view trials personally as losing ventures, or do not want to alienate a judge or prosecutor by refusing a settlement. These lawyers are not really responding to economic forces or case load pressure but to personal needs or psychological limitations that interfere with their ability to perform in accordance with their professional responsibilities.[46] For many defense lawyers, however, the spirit is willing, but the resources are lacking.

What is clear, then, is that most criminal defense lawyers in Milwaukee, Dane, and Cleveland Counties cannot be characterized simply as double agents. Systemic pressures and organizational obligations certainly influence but do not dictate the behavior of the criminal defense lawyer. As with many of his observations, Blumberg's generalizations about defense lawyers as double agents simply sweep too broadly.[47]

Are most defense lawyers, then, zealous advocates? If so, why is it that the vast majority of cases end in guilty pleas?[48] Blumberg's focus on the role played by defense lawyers in producing guilty pleas underplays the fact that a defendant's decision to plead guilty is shaped by a variety of individual factors and systemic features.[49] For many defendants, the plea decision has little to do with the zeal or even the availability of defense counsel. Rather, a significant number of defendants simply want to plead guilty. Some defendants plead guilty because they really are willing to accept responsibility for their actions. Others want to end the matter quickly and see a guilty plea as the fastest way out of a bothersome predicament. Still other defendants engage in their own simple cost-benefit analysis and conclude that fighting the charge is not worth the time, money, or risk.[50] For some defendants, then, the decision to plead guilty does not depend on the availability or actions of defense counsel.

Nonetheless, for other defendants, various systemic factors, including the availability, cost, and quality of counsel, profoundly influence the plea-bargaining process and, ultimately, the plea decision.[51] A comparison of the features and the culture of the criminal justice system in Milwaukee, Dane, and Cleveland Counties reveals many striking similarities in the plea-bargaining process. However, that comparison also reveals significant differences in the delivery of indigent defense services, local bail practices, and the workings of the local prosecutor's office. These systemic variations not only have an impact on the plea-bargaining process in each county, but also affect the general zeal of the local defense bar.

The most significant systemic feature distinguishing Cleveland County from the two Wisconsin counties is the absence of a public-defender system in Cleveland County. Rather, Cleveland County uses an assigned-counsel system to provide representation to indigent defendants.[52] An indigent defendant in Cleveland County obtains representation, therefore, only if the court chooses to appoint counsel. Only those defendants able to retain counsel are represented at their initial appearance. Defendants unable to make bail generally must wait at least three weeks before the court will act on their application for court-appointed counsel.[53] Those defendants who bail out or have a bond posted for them are presumed to be able to afford counsel.[54] Hence, no lawyer is appointed until the defendant appears before the court and demonstrates an inability to hire counsel. Even then, the defendant is generally denied appointed counsel, told to make additional efforts to secure retained counsel, and threatened with bail revocation if counsel is not obtained. Defendants have had their bail revoked and been forced to return to jail in order to secure appointed counsel.

Felony defendants who remain in jail for at least three weeks are usually deemed indigent, and counsel is appointed. Appointments are made by the local judges from a list of all of the lawyers in the county who practice criminal law.[55] Appointed lawyers in Cleveland County are not paid on an hourly basis. Rather, defense lawyers are paid at a fixed rate of $250 for a misdemeanor case and $500 for a felony.[56] Except in a capital case, therefore, a lawyer will not be compensated more than $500 regardless of the amount of time devoted to a case. Any appointed lawyer wishing an investigator or expert assistance must apply to the judge. Judicial approval of such litigation expenses, however, is very rare.[57]

Milwaukee and Dane Counties have local public-defender offices that are part of a statewide program.[58] Public-defender staff attorneys are state employees with salaries and benefits comparable to those provided to the lawyers in the Wisconsin Attorney General's Office.[59] These staff lawyers answer to the lawyer who directs their office, not to the local judges. Moreover, indigency determinations are made not by the judges but by the local public defender's office. Hence, any person charged with a crime will obtain representation as long as that person meets the eligibility standards set by statute.[60] The public defender's office then assigns the indigent defendant a staff attorney or a private lawyer from a list maintained by the local office. Some clients secure representation even prior to charges being issued.[61]

Although public defenders represent the majority of indigent defendants in Milwaukee and Dane Counties, private lawyers in each county defend roughly 25 percent of the clients served by the public-defender program.[62] Private lawyers presently are paid $45 per hour for in-court time and $35 per hour for out-of-court work with no specified limit on the number of hours to be spent on a case.[63] The bills generated by private lawyers handling assigned cases are paid by the public-defender program. In addition, private lawyers can also obtain funds for investigative and expert services from the local office.[64] Finally, the Milwaukee and Dane County offices have their own investigative staff, some access to social workers, and the ability to fund expert services. Even though the Wisconsin public-defender program definitely needs increased funding, the funding problem is not at the same crisis level experienced by Cleveland County and numerous other jurisdictions.[65]

Many indigent defendants in Milwaukee and Dane Counties are in custody at the time of their initial appearance, but, unlike in Cleveland County, defendants usually are represented by counsel at that court appearance. Not only does defense counsel's early intervention allow him to argue about bail but it enhances counsel's ability to mount an effective defense. Finally, in stark contrast with the judicial reluctance to appoint assigned counsel in Cleveland County, judges in Milwaukee and Dane Counties actively encourage defendants to seek legal assistance from the public defender's office. As a result, many more defendants come to court with a lawyer in these Wisconsin counties than in Cleveland County. Thus, the system's structure for delivering indigent defense services encourages representation in Milwaukee and Dane Counties while discouraging it in Cleveland County. Unrepresented defendants in Cleveland County have little ability to do more than just accept whatever plea bargain is offered to them.[66] Easy access to free defense services or the imposition of barriers to obtaining such representation substantially affects the plea-bargaining process and the actors involved in that process.

A second significant systemic difference between Cleveland County and the two Wisconsin counties is Cleveland County's more limited use of personal recognizance bonds and its heavy reliance on bail bondsmen. When a person is arrested, that person's family and friends generally make every effort to post bail. Unable to raise sufficient funds on their own, many people in Cleveland County turn to a bail bondsman to obtain the needed bond. Money paid to a bail bondsman, however, is no longer available to secure counsel, pay fines, or satisfy court costs. For many defendants and their families, the lack of additional funds compels them either to forgo defense counsel or hire counsel at a bargain price. Unfortunately, it is defense counsel retained for an inadequate fee who is least likely to act as a zealous advocate and most likely to function as a double agent.[67]

In addition, those defendants who do not secure a bond prior to their initial court appearance rarely are represented at that initial appearance. Without counsel to make a bail argument on their behalf, fewer defendants in Cleveland County are released on their own recognizance than in Milwaukee or Dane County. Continued incarceration increases the pressure on defendants to use a bail bondsman or plead guilty to obtain their release. In Cleveland County, defendants unable to make bail at times are provided counsel solely to facilitate the entry of a guilty plea. At other times, defendants will languish in jail for periods well beyond the normal sentence meted out for a particular charge simply because counsel is never appointed and the matter is not brought to the attention of the judge or prosecutor. When the case finally surfaces, the defendant is allowed to plead guilty for time served.[68]

Although, infrequently, a defendant unable to post low bail in Milwaukee or Dane County will be held for an inordinate length before the case is located and resolved, the system generally operates to avoid such cases. Indeed, the Wisconsin bail provisions specifically "are designed to see that a maximum number of persons are released prior to trial with a minimum of financial burden upon them."[69] A sizable number of persons arrested for a misdemeanor are given a citation and released.[70] If the person is detained and the accused's family or friends cannot post the necessary cash bail, the defendant will remain incarcerated until the initial court appearance. Fortunately, most defendants have an initial court appearance within twenty-four hours of their arrest. Moreover, most defendants in Milwaukee and Dane Counties are represented at the initial appearance, usually by a public defender. Counsel's bail arguments regularly lead either to a recognizance bond or a reduction in the amount of bail.[71]

Some defendants in Milwaukee and Dane Counties fail to make bail and are subject, therefore, to some of the same pressure experienced by detainees in Cleveland County. Nevertheless, these defendants at least have had a lawyer assigned to them who now is working on their behalf. For the unrepresented defendant in Cleveland County, the pressure is much greater.[72]

Finally, for those defendants in Milwaukee or Dane Counties who do post cash bail, that money will be returned to the person posting it unless the defendant fails to appear for a court appearance. Sometimes a defendant can retain counsel by offering the lawyer a lien on this bail money. Often the bail money can be used to pay a fine, restitution, or court costs. In short, a comparison of Milwaukee, Dane, and Cleveland Counties demonstrates that the bail practices in a given community have a considerable impact on the plea decisions of many defendants in that community.[73]

The operation of the district attorney's office in Milwaukee, Dane, and Cleveland Counties represents the third significant systemic feature affecting defendants' plea decisions and the behavior of criminal defense lawyers in these three counties. There are many similarities in the attitude of the staff and in the workings of the three offices,[74] but there also are some significant differences. With over ninety attorneys, the size of the Milwaukee office allows for more specialization and more overall expertise. Nevertheless, the volume of cases handled by the system and each prosecutor, the number of courts, and the greater time it takes for cases to work through the system increase the opportunity for defense counsel in Milwaukee to "shop" for a better plea bargain, to leverage defense strengths to the defendant's advantage, and to resist prosecutorial pressure to "play ball."

In contrast to Milwaukee's large staff, Dane County has twenty-six prosecutors and Cleveland County nine. Operating in smaller, more closed courthouse communities than in Milwaukee County, the prosecutors in Dane and Cleveland Counties tend to be more cohesive and communicative about defense lawyers and their practices. Because they know most defense lawyers very well, Dane and Cleveland County prosecutors have an edge over their Milwaukee counterparts.

Although news travels faster in the courthouse communities of Dane and Cleveland Counties, the systemic pace is slower than in Milwaukee County. Thus, prosecutors in Dane and Cleveland Counties seemingly have more time to spend on minor charges and are less willing either to divert cases from the system or dismiss them once they are filed.[75] This reluctance to divert or dismiss charges in part reflects the fact that Dane and Cleveland Counties rely on a deputy district attorney to issue virtually all charges.[76] Accordingly, once charges have been issued, most assistant district attorneys are very hesitant to dismiss a case. This is so even though the initial charging decision rested primarily on the deputy's review of police reports with little opportunity to evaluate the strengths or weaknesses of the case or the existence of any mitigating factors. This is particularly so in Cleveland County because the office relies on law student interns to handle almost the entire misdemeanor case load.[77] The interns' limited discretion makes it difficult to negotiate the dismissal of any issued charge or to secure a significant reduction in the standard offer for a particular offense.

In Milwaukee County, however, charges generally are issued following a charging conference in which one of the prosecutors on duty that week meets with the complainant, police officers, witnesses, and, at times, the defendant and defense counsel, before deciding what, if any, charges to file.[78] Although the charging system used in Milwaukee County involves an enormous front-loading of prosecutorial resources, the system produces better-informed and more accurate charging decisions. This charging process also eliminates many weak or unsubstantiated cases that otherwise would clog the system.

There are several lessons to be learned in studying the systems in Milwaukee, Dane, and Cleveland Counties. First, variations in significant systemic features influence the behavior of a system's defense lawyers. In Cleveland County, for example, the system for appointing counsel works to discourage defendants from actually obtaining counsel. Defendants are pressured to waive their rights and plead guilty without the assistance of counsel. In other cases, the delay in appointing a lawyer or the system's bail practices pressure the defendant simply to "get it over with." Once a lawyer finally is appointed, the client may instruct the attorney simply to obtain the best plea bargain possible.[79] The defense lawyer may be very willing to challenge the state's case and even argue with the defendant about the shortsightedness of a guilty plea.[80] Nonetheless, if the client persists in wanting a plea bargain, defense counsel may be left simply securing the best deal possible, even though counsel believes a conviction is unjust and a guilty verdict unlikely.

Second, a criminal justice system driven by plea bargaining exerts substantial pressure on a criminal defendant not to go to trial. Defendants face considerable moral, psychological, physical,[81] and economic pressure to plead guilty. Many defendants confess and few suppression motions are granted, so that most defendants battle tough odds should they choose to go to trial. Even if the evidence is less than overwhelming, a defendant may be reluctant to risk trial because of numerous prior convictions, the fear of judicial retaliation for going to trial, or the amount of pretrial incarceration to be endured before a trial will occur. Above all, the prosecutor usually has a wide range of bargaining threats— charging additional offenses, adding sentence enhancers, and including a charge with a mandatory minimum sentence, to name a few—that also deter defendants from turning down proposed deals.[82]

Although most defendants want to plea bargain, they often are not satisfied with the deals they receive. Yet, few defendants actually want to go to trial. For criminal defense lawyers, then, much of their time is spent negotiating a deal against an adversary who generally can dictate the terms. Under such circumstances, defense counsel is not a double agent but a beleaguered dealer negotiating from a position of weakness. It is not defense counsel's profit motive but the structure of the system that primarily influences the decision of many defendants to accept a plea bargain.

Third, because so many defendants are unable to afford counsel, the local structure for delivering indigent defense services largely determines the overall quality of representation provided to criminal defendants in a particular community. Thus, the existence of a reasonably well-funded public-defender program in Milwaukee and Dane Counties explains in large part why more defendants in these counties receive competent, zealous representation than in Cleveland County. As full-time criminal practitioners, the Wisconsin public defenders are better trained and have more resources than the appointed lawyers in Cleveland County. It is not surprising, then, that these public defenders generally pursue more aggressive defense tactics.[83] Moreover, by filing motions, taking cases to trial, and disseminating information to private lawyers who do not specialize in criminal law, the public defenders encourage and educate other defense lawyers to be more zealous. In addition, retained counsel in these two counties tend to be more aggressive, knowing that they will not be singled out by the prosecutor's office and retaliated against for taking cases to trial. Finally, not only do appointed lawyers in Wisconsin have access to experts and investigative assistance but they also receive adequate compensation without imposed limits. Private lawyers appointed to represent indigent defendants in Wisconsin, therefore, are provided with a financial incentive to prepare adequately and to take cases to trial.[84]

On the other hand, the appointed-counsel system in Cleveland County, based on a fixed flat-compensation scheme, serves to encourage the very behavior by defense counsel condemned by Blumberg.[85] A defense lawyer earns a modest or, at times, even a decent fee if the client enters a quick plea. There is, however, an economic disincentive to investigate, to research, or, above all, to take a case to trial. A lawyer who chooses to spend time, energy, and money in the defense of a case does so at his own expense. In Cleveland County, as in other jurisdictions around the country, not enough lawyers are willing to make that personal sacrifice.[86] Defense counsel may not be a con but feels pressure to strike a deal. Frequently, appointed counsel enters the negotiation process without much leverage. In fact, the prosecutors in Cleveland County know full well the economic realities confronting appointed counsel.

Nonetheless, it is not just profit motive or financial pressure that causes some criminal defense lawyers to be less than zealous. Heavy case loads create time pressure and stress that can overwhelm even the best-intentioned, most competent defense lawyer.[87] Certainly there are some public defenders in Milwaukee and Dane Counties who respond to case load pressures by cajoling, threatening, or manipulating their clients into pleading guilty.[88] Like private lawyers who accept an insufficient retainer and then force a plea bargain on an unwitting client, some public defenders will oversell the advantages of a plea bargain, conduct an inadequate investigation, or fail to prepare properly for trial, thereby coercing guilty pleas from reluctant defendants.

Most public defenders in Milwaukee and Dane Counties, however, do not respond to heavy case loads by operating as double agents. Rather, they attempt to cope with their heavy case loads by allocating their time and limited investigative resources in the best possible way.[89] Consequently, some cases are not adequately researched or investigated. Some defendants, therefore, receive better representation at the expense of others. Moreover, overworked public defenders have less time to spend with their clients and this hampers their ability to develop trusting, meaningful attorney-client relationships.[90] Absent a good attorney-client relationship, the defendant is even more susceptible to buckle under the pressure to plead guilty.

Despite serious time pressure and heavy case loads, the public defenders in Milwaukee and Dane Counties, for the most part, bargain effectively for many of their clients. They know the system well and thus are able to evaluate the worth of a proposed plea bargain and the merits of taking a case to trial.[91] In addition, faced with their own case load pressures and the knowledge that these public defenders generally have the capacity and willingness to fight if an acceptable deal is not struck, the prosecutors in these counties have some incentive to bargain reasonably. Unlike appointed counsel in Cleveland County, defenders of the indigent in Wisconsin, albeit beleaguered, pose a credible threat.

But as their resources become increasingly strained, overburdened public defenders in Milwaukee and Dane Counties are more vulnerable to prosecutorial pressure and less able to use tactics, such as filing a well-briefed motion, that apply pressure on the prosecutor.[92] In short, the final lesson to be learned from examining these three counties is that even the lawyers in a well-structured indigent defense system will find it difficult to act aggressively without adequate time and resources. Large case loads exert added pressure on public defenders to obtain acceptable plea bargains for most of their clients. There is that subtle but constant pressure when negotiating numerous cases not to push a prosecutor too hard in one case so that counsel will obtain favorable consideration in other cases.[93] And there is real pressure to avoid antagonizing prosecutors because of the tremendous discretion they have to reward or punish defendants in the plea bargain process. Faced with these pressures, the overworked public defender may produce the same results as the underpaid private lawyer: ''plea bargains too easily accepted by one-shot clients on the advice of lawyers trying, either out of self-interest or for the good of their clients as a class, to maintain good personal relations with the judges and prosecutors with whom they must regularly work."[84]

Defense Lawyer as Effective Advocate: Structuring the System to Enhance Zeal

Criminal defense lawyers in Milwaukee and Dane Counties appear to defend their clients more zealously and effectively than lawyers in Cleveland County primarily because of the superior resources allotted to the representation of indigent defendants in Wisconsin. Simply put, zealousness comes with a price tag. Until society is prepared to increase the resources allocated to the defense of persons accused of crimes, few defendants will receive effective zealous assistance of counsel.

Because most criminal defendants are indigent, improving the delivery of indigent defense services in a local system constitutes the best means of enhancing the overall quality of representation in that system. Moreover, improving the indigent defense system in a community heightens the zeal and effectiveness of the private defense bar. This improvement, however, cannot be attained simply by sleight of hand or minor structural tinkering. In most jurisdictions, substantial resources are needed to correct serious shortcomings in the delivery of indigent defense services.[95] In light of the keen competition for dollars in austere state budgets and the incessant clamor for a war on crime, the prospects for major funding increases for defense services are dim. And yet, increased funding is imperative if the crisis in the delivery of indigent defense services occurring in many counties across the United States is to be adequately addressed.[96]

Assuming, therefore, that some additional funds are made available for indigent defense services, how must the system be structured for delivering those services to ensure that more defendants are provided a zealous defense? Again, there is no simple answer. It is clear, however, that if the system truly is to enhance zeal and effective advocacy, it must lessen defense counsel's vulnerability to the pressures inherent in the plea-bargain-driven criminal justice system.[97]

An adequately funded, independent, "mixed" statewide program of salaried public defenders and assigned private counsel represents the indigent defense system least susceptible to these insidious pressures.[98] First, a mixed system is desirable because it blends experienced, well-trained criminal law specialists together with private lawyers who may bring fresh, creative approaches to systemic problems as a result of their civil experience. In addition, a strong assigned-counsel component of the program ensures that the local defense bar will continue to play an active role in criminal defense litigation. If the private bar lacks an investment in the indigent defense program, the organized bar may not rally enthusiastically behind the program. Without the vigorous support of the bar, the public-defender program will have difficulty garnering legislative votes for needed funding.[99] Finally, the continued involvement of private lawyers in the criminal justice system lessens the institutionalization of criminal defense work with its concomitant dangers.[100]

Next, this mixed public-defender program must be structured to insulate defense counsel from direct economic pressure. Counsel should not have to curry favor with the judiciary to be appointed to cases or face economic retaliation for not settling or defending a case as a judge sees fit. The program must control the hiring and firing of its staff lawyers as well as the selection of appointed counsel. Neither the judiciary nor any local government entity should control the salaries or compensation paid to indigent defenders.[101] Economic control includes the real threat of interference with counsel's representation.[102] Defense counsel's independence must be respected and encouraged.

So, also, assigned counsel must be adequately compensated. Flat, fixed fees, especially with low maximum limits, discourage lawyers from being effective advocates. Instead, lawyers are rewarded for resolving cases as quickly as possible without an adequate inquiry into the merits of the case. Any contract or assigned-counsel system relying on a fixed-fee method of compensation builds into the system an economic disincentive to take cases to trial.[103] This does not mean that many cases should or would be tried even under this proposed public-defender system. Indeed, the systemic pressures that already coerce many defendants into pleading guilty will continue to force most defendants to accept plea bargains. But the indigent defense system should not add to that pressure. Rather, the system must be structured to facilitate access to counsel. As in the Wisconsin public-defender system, defendants must get representation early with as few procedural hurdles as possible.[104]

Early representation is meaningless, however, unless defense counsel has ready access to the resources needed to mount a vigorous defense. Adequate support staff and investigative resources are crucial if effective representation is to be provided.[105] Care must be taken to ensure that assigned counsel as well as staff lawyers have sufficient access to investigators and expert services. Moreover, adequate training must be provided for public-defender staff lawyers, and low-cost continuing education programs must be developed for assigned counsel.[106] A lawyer cannot practice criminal law competently without keeping current on changes in substantive law and criminal procedure.[107]

In addition, this public-defender system must provide reasonable salaries with manageable case loads. Excessive case loads create undue pressure to settle, not to try jury trials. The public defender's compensation package must be designed to reward effective, aggressive lawyering, not to encourage the mere processing of a set number of cases. Adequate performance measures together with merit raise incentives[108] improve the likelihood that public defenders will act zealously.[109]

A statewide public-defender program must secure adequate funding if it is to provide competent defense services. Given the budget pressures confronting virtually every state legislature, however, even an adequately funded program will still face tough choices on allocating funds.[110] The history of the Wisconsin public-defender program since 1977 suggests that it is extremely difficult to balance reasonably high salaries, excellent benefits, good working conditions, and strong support and litigation services with reasonable case loads.[111] In striking an appropriate balance, program administrators must bear in mind that together with the lawyer actually handling a case, they are responsible for the quality of representation ultimately provided.[112] Administrators and legislators also must remember that requiring public defenders to handle too many cases invariably results in deficient representation.

The top priority for a public-defender program, therefore, must be to keep case loads at a level that allows staff attorneys to perform in accordance with the standards of a competent criminal defense lawyer.[113] This means, in part, developing a mechanism to divert cases to assigned counsel when case loads get too heavy. In addition, this means giving public defenders sufficient time to interview their clients, to investigate, to research, and to prepare adequately for negotiations, trials, and sentencings.[114]

There is no cost-free method for generating more time. Faced with the challenge of keeping case loads light while providing quality representation to an increasing number of clients, the program may have to use a salary structure that is unlikely to produce career public defenders. Thus, it may be necessary to keep salaries fairly low and hire more new law school graduates, thereby creating more positions but with fewer cases per attorney. Staff lawyers would earn less money but have improved working conditions, less stress, and more job satisfaction.[115] Any loss of expertise due to increased lawyer turnover would arguably be offset by the increased zeal of the larger staff and the greater use of senior staff lawyers as supervisors.[116]

Moreover, some additional time may be created by providing staff lawyers with better litigation support. It may be desirable to spend more money on investigators or paralegals, who could assume many of the tasks that are often inefficiently handled by lawyers. Finally, difficult and complex cases often strain the resources of a small public-defender office. One advantage of a statewide program would be the central administration's ability to shift resources or use special units to defend selected cases efficiently and effectively.[117]

Yet, even though improving the indigent defense system in a community would affect the quality of representation afforded many defendants, a significant number of low-income defendants would remain largely unaffected. The working poor, many making only minimum wage, do not qualify under existing indigency standards for an indigent defender.[118] Unable to afford to hire a zealous advocate, the low-income defendant is forced to take whatever bargain the prosecutor proffers.

The prospects for improving the representation of these defendants are particularly bleak. It may be that a percentage of low-income defendants could qualify as partially indigent and, therefore, for a small retainer, receive the same representation provided to other defendants by the public-defender program.[119] Expanding the number of indigent clients served by the program, however, increases case load pressure and decreases the time available to provide zealous representation to others in the program. In light of the substantial financial needs already facing most jurisdictions, expansion of the program to cover more low-income people is highly unlikely.[120]

There are limits, then, to the extent to which dramatic change can occur in the criminal justice system. Undoubtedly, improving indigent services will lead to greater zeal and more effective lawyering. And yet, even though the overall zeal of the defense bar may increase, the nature of the plea-bargaining process and the system itself substantially limit a dramatic difference in the role of the criminal defense lawyer. That is because in most cases, the defendant, the case itself and the system substantially limit the options available to the defendant and to counsel.

Given the pressure that the prosecutor and the system bring to bear on criminal defendants, even zealous defense lawyers generally will be beleaguered dealers. If negotiations fail, however, the zealous advocate must have the will and ability to fight on behalf of a client. Unless we give defense lawyers the necessary resources and incentives to challenge the state, our adversary system indeed will drift further toward the co-optative system Blumberg described.

Endnotes

[1] "The basic duty defense counsel owes to the administration of justice and as an officer of the court is to serve as the accused's counselor and advocate with courage and devotion, and to render effective, quality representation." ABA, *Standards for Criminal Justice* Standard 4-1.2(b) (3d ed. 1991). The ethics codes enshrine the principle of zealous partisanship. See, e.g., *Model Code of Professional Responsibility* DR 7-101, EC 7-1, EC 7-4, EC 7-19 (1981); *Model Rules of Professional Conduct* Preamble (1983). As Charles Wolfram observes, "[T]he American lawyer's professional model is that of zeal: a lawyer is expected to devote energy, intelligence, skill and personal

commitment to the single goal of furthering the clients' interests as those are ultimately defined by the client." C. Wolfram, *Modern Legal Ethics* 585 (1986). Moreover, numerous cases trumpet the lawyer's obligation to be a vigorous defender. See, e.g., *Von Moltke v. Gillies*, 332 U.S. 708, 725–726 (1948) (the right to counsel demands undivided allegiance and service devoted solely to the interests of the client).

2 As Justice Powell has noted:

> In our system a defense lawyer characteristically opposes the designated representative of the State. The system assumes that adversarial testimony will ultimately advance the public interest in truth and fairness. But it posits that a defense lawyer best serves the public not by acting on behalf of the State or in concert with it but rather by advancing "the undivided interests of his client."

Polk County v. Dodson, 454 U.S. 312, 318–319 (1981). For an excellent summary of the basic principles of the U.S. adversary system of criminal justice, see W. LaFave & J. Israel, *Criminal Procedure* 24–32 (1985).

3 Justice White eloquently summarized the role of the criminal defense lawyer:

> But defense counsel has no comparable obligation to ascertain or present the truth. Our system assigns him a different mission . . . . Defense counsel need present nothing, even if he knows what the truth is. He need not furnish any witnesses to the police, or reveal any confidences of his client, or furnish any other information to help the prosecution's case. If he can confuse a witness, even a truthful one, or make him appear at a disadvantage, unsure or indecisive, that will be his normal course. Our interest in not convicting the innocent permits counsel to put the State to its proof, to put the State's case in the worst possible light, regardless of what he thinks or knows to be the truth. Undoubtedly there are some limits which defense counsel must observe, but more often than not, defense counsel will cross-examine a prosecution witness, and impeach him if he can, even if he thinks the witness is telling the truth, just as he will attempt to destroy a witness who he thinks is lying. In this respect, as part of our modified adversary system and as part of the duty imposed on the most honorable defense counsel, we countenance or require conduct which in many instances has little, if any, relation to the search for truth.

United States v. Wade, 388 U.S. 218, 256–258 (1967) (White, J., dissenting in part and concurring in part).

4 Id. See also C. Wolfram, note 1 supra, at 586–587.

5 "The procedural and legal system are supposedly designed to produce results based on just laws fairly applied on the basis of accurate facts; but a lawyer's objective within that system is to achieve a result favorable to the lawyer's client, possibly despite justice, the law, and the facts." C. Wolfram, note 1 supra, at 585. Because defense counsel must be a zealous partisan, counsel's efforts may well interfere with the search for the truth. M. Freedman, *Understanding Lawyers' Ethics* 161–171 (1990); A. Amsterdam, *Trial Manual for the Defense of Criminal Cases* 2–327 (1984); C. Wolfram, note 1 supra, at 588–589, 641, 650–651. Even commentators critical of the legal profession's commitment to the principles of partisanship and nonaccountability generally recognize that the criminal defense lawyer must pursue the defendant's interests even at the expense of an accurate outcome. D. Luban, *Lawyers and Justice: An Ethical Study* 58–63 (1988).

6 As Chief Justice Burger noted in *Nix v. Whiteside*, 475 U.S. 157 (1986), the lawyer's "overarching duty" to advocate and advance the client's interests is limited by the lawyer's "equally solemn" responsibilities and duties as an officer of the court. Id. at 166–168. In certain situations, ethical provisions require defense counsel to take action or to disclose information adverse to the interests of the client. See J. Burkoff, *Criminal Defense Ethics* ch. 6 (1986). Nonetheless, there is considerable disagreement regarding the extent to which defense counsel's advocacy must be tempered by his

duties as an officer of the court. Compare Chief Justice Burger's view in *Nix v. Whiteside*, supra, at 157, 168 (emphasizing defense counsel's role as an officer of the court) with that of Justice Brennan in *Jones v. Barnes*, 463 U.S. 745, 761–762 (1983) (Brennan, J., dissenting) (stressing that counsel must function as an advocate as opposed to a friend of the court). See also Justice White in *United States v. Wade*, note 3 supra, at 218, 257–258 (White, J., dissenting in part and concurring in part) (defense lawyer's mission is not to ascertain or present the truth); Justice Black in *Von Moltke v. Gillies*, note 1 supra, at 708, 725–726 (right to counsel demands undivided allegiance and service devoted solely to the interests of the client); Justice Powell in *Polk County v. Dodson*, note 2 supra, at 312, 318 (defense counsel best serves the public by advancing the individual interests of the accused); Commission on Professional Responsibility of Roscoe Pound-Am Trial Lawyers Found., *The American Lawyer's Code of Conduct* preamble (1982) ("It is clear that the lawyer for a private party is and should be an officer of the court only in the sense of serving a court as a zealous, partisan advocate of one side of the case before it, and in the sense of having been licensed by a court to play that very role.").

⁷ Even after *Nix v. Whiteside*, note 6 supra, at 157, for example, there is a continuing controversy as to how the criminal defense lawyer should respond when counsel knows or suspects that the client is going to testify falsely. Lefstein, "Client Perjury in Criminal Cases: Still in Search of an Answer," 1 *Geo. J. Legal Ethics* 521 (1988). For a discussion of various resolutions to the perjury issue, see M. Freedman, note 5 supra, at 109–141.

⁸ As Justice Powell observed:

> [T]he duty of the lawyer, subject to his role as an "officer of the court," is to further the interests of his clients by all lawful means, even when these interests are in conflict with the interests of the United States or of a State. But his representation involves no conflict of interest in the invidious sense. Rather, it casts the lawyer in his honored and traditional role as an authorized but independent agent acting to vindicate the legal rights of a client, whoever it may be.

In re Griffiths, 413 U.S. 717, 724 n.14 (1973).

To vindicate the rights of an accused, a lawyer must be an effective as well as loyal advocate. *Polk County v. Dodson*, note 2 supra, at 312, 322. At a minimum, therefore, a criminal defendant is guaranteed the right to "reasonably effective assistance of counsel." *Strickland v. Washington*, 466 U.S. 668, 687 (1984). The line between ineffective and adequate assistance of counsel is difficult to draw. See Mounts, "The Right to Counsel and the Indigent Defense System." 14 *N.Y.U. Rev. L. & Soc. Change* 221–241 (1986). Yet, unquestionably, defense counsel ethically bound to provide competent, timely, and informed representation. See *Model Rules of Professional Conduct* Rule 1.1, 1.3, 1.4 and commentary (1983) *Model Code of Professional Responsibility* DR 6-101, DR 7-101 (1981); ABA, note 1 supra, Standard 4-1.3.

⁹ See Blumberg, "The Practice of Law as Confidence Game: Organizational Co-optation of a Profession," 1 *Law & Soc'y Rev.* 15, 28–31 (1967) (describing criminal defense lawyers as double agents because they serve organizational ends while appearing to help their clients).

¹⁰ Id. at 15–39. See also M. Heumann, *Plea Bargaining* 80 (1978) (concluding that defense lawyers ultimately succumb to the culture of the court system, a culture that rewards cooperation and sanctions a formal adversarial approach).

¹¹ Blumberg, note 9 supra, at 18. Blumberg's work continues to be cited regularly. See, e.g., D. Luban, note 5 supra, at 60–61; Schneyer, "Sympathy for the Hired Gun," 41 *J. L. Educ.* 11, 23–24 (1991).

¹² Blumberg indicated that usually over 90 percent of criminal convictions followed a negotiated guilty plea. Blumberg, note 9 supra, at 18.

¹³ Intolerably large case loads must be disposed of by a court system lacking sufficient resources. As a result, "the principals, lawyer and assistant district attorney, rely upon one another's cooperation for their continued professional existence, and so the bargaining between them tends usually to be 'reasonable' rather than fierce." Id. at 22–23.

¹⁴ Id. at 19.

¹⁵ Id. at 20.

¹⁶ Blumberg reasoned:

Accused persons come and go in the court system schema, but the structure and its occupational incumbents remain to carry on their respective career, occupational and organizational enterprises. The individual stridencies, tensions, and conflicts a given accused person's case may present to all the participants are overcome because the formal and informal relations of all the groups in the court setting require it. The probability of continued future relations and interaction must be preserved at all cost.

Id.

¹⁷ Id. at 22.

¹⁸ Id. at 22–23.

¹⁹ Id. at 23. See also Sudnow, "Normal Crimes: Sociological Features of the Penal Code in the Public Defender's Office," 12 *Soc. Probs.* 255–277 (1965) (public defenders are mere functionaries primarily concerned with quickly disposing of cases).

²⁰ Blumberg detailed at length the nature of this "confidence game," in which the criminal defense lawyer manipulated the client into accepting a guilty plea that the client was "conned" into believing was the desirable fruit of counsel's vigorous efforts on the client's behalf. Blumberg, note 9 supra, at 24–31.

²¹ Id. at 27.

²² Id. at 28–29.

²³ Blumberg expressed this conclusion in the following language:

[T]he lawyer's role as agent-mediator may be seen, as unique in that he is in effect a double agent. Although, as "officer of the court" he mediates between the court organization and the defendant, his roles with respect to each are rent by conflicts of interest. Too often these must be resolved in favor of the organization which provides him with the means for his professional existence. Consequently, in order to reduce the strains and conflicts imposed in what is ultimately an over-demanding role obligation for him, the lawyer engages in the lawyer-client "confidence game" so as to structure more favorably an otherwise onerous role system.

Id. at 38.

²⁴ Milwaukee County is a large urban county of 959,275 people, most of whom live in the city of Milwaukee. Dane County's population of 367,085 is concentrated in Madison, the capital of Wisconsin. Like Dane, Cleveland County is a moderate-size county of 174,253 people. Norman, the home of the University of Oklahoma, is the largest city in Cleveland County.

²⁵ The author practiced law in Milwaukee from 1978 to 1984 as a public defender and in a private firm from 1988 to 1990. He directed a clinical program at the University of Wisconsin in Dane County from 1984 to 1988. The students in this program defended indigent clients charged with misdemeanor offenses. Since joining the faculty at the University of Oklahoma College of Law in 1990, he has supervised law students handling criminal cases in the Cleveland County courts. His comments, therefore, are based on his own observations as a participant in each system as well as discussions with and observations of third-year law students working in these three systems. He also interviewed criminal defense lawyers, prosecutors, and judges in each county.

Similarly, Blumberg's article was "based upon observations made by the writer

during many years of legal practice in the criminal courts of a large metropolitan area."
Blumberg, note 9 supra, at 18.

26 See, e.g., L. McIntyre, *The Public Defender* (1987); J. Casper, *Criminal Courts: The Defendant's Perspective* (1978); Coyle, Strasser & Lovelle, "Fatal Defense," *Natl L.J.* June 11, 1990, at 30; Alschuler, "The Defense Attorney's Role in Plea Bargaining," 84 *Yale L.J.* 1179 (1975); Skolnick, "Social Control in the Adversary System," 11 *J. Conflict Resolution* 52 (1967); R. Herman, E. Single & I. Boston, *Counsel for the Poor* (1977); Arthur Young & Co., *Seattle-King County Public Defender Association Evaluation Project: Final Report* (1975).

Moreover, many of the author's observations about the representation provided by assistant public defenders in Milwaukee and Dane Counties mirror those of the Spangenberg Group, a nationally recognized consulting firm offering technical assistance and research concerning indigent defense systems. See Spangenberg Group, *Caseload/Workload Study for the State Public Defender of Wisconsin, Final Report* (1990).

27 Blumberg, note 9 supra, at 18–38.

28 It is difficult to obtain exact figures on the percentage of cases actually tried in each jurisdiction. In Cleveland County, 38 cases were tried in 1989 and 29 in 1990. In comparison, 5,724 criminal cases were disposed of by guilty pleas in Cleveland County in 1989 and 5,029 in 1990. In Dane County, 165 cases were decided by trial in 1989 and 141 in 1990. This compares with 5,095 cases disposed of by guilty pleas in Dane County in 1989 and 6,184 in 1990. The Director of State Courts Office for Wisconsin does not maintain statistics on the manner in which cases were disposed of in Milwaukee County. The statistics maintained by the Milwaukee County Clerk of Courts Office reflect that in 1989 there were 428 criminal jury trials out of 14,756 cases that either were pleaded out or dismissed. In 1990, there were 461 criminal jury trials held in Milwaukee County while 16,029 cases were pleaded out or dismissed.

29 These observations are borne out not only by the author's experiences and conversations with defense lawyers but also by clients unable to raise sufficient funds to retain or keep private counsel, who subsequently looked to the public-defender office or the author's clinical program for assistance.

30 For a similar observation, see Alschuler, note 26 supra, at 1190–1194.

31 Id. at 1195. See also M. Mayer, *The Lawyers* 161–162 (1967) (reporting that the courts commonly grant postponements to private lawyers to aid them in collecting fees). Judicial willingness to tolerate numerous continuances is not surprising given the willingness of many of these lawyers to contribute to judicial reelection campaigns.

32 Unfortunately, it is not only defense lawyers who sometimes lie to their clients. Others have observed that both civil and criminal lawyers lie to their clients for reasons of self-interest. See Lerman, "Lying to Clients," 138 *U. Pa. L. Rev.* 659 (1990); Hellman, "The Effects of Law Office Work on the Formation of Law Students' Professional Values: Observation, Explanation, Optimization," 4 *Geo. J. Legal Ethics* 537 (1991); Alschuler, note 26 supra, at 1194–1198.

33 Blumberg, note 9 supra, at 23.

34 Id.

35 According to Blumberg, the criminal justice system shrouds itself in secrecy to avoid close scrutiny, which would reveal the complicitous nature of the system. Id. at 22. See also A. Dershowitz, *The Best Defense* (1982).

36 In their study of the Wisconsin public-defender program, the Spangenberg Group was particularly impressed with the quality and dedication of the public defenders in the Milwaukee office. See Spangenberg Group, note 26 supra, at 39. For a similar positive reaction to the lawyers in the Cook County public defender office, see McIntyre, note 26 supra, at 172–173.

37 Good criminal defense lawyers frequently use an aggressive motion practice to further their clients' interests. *The Champion*, a monthly magazine put out by the National Association of Criminal Defense Lawyers, regularly contains articles urging defense lawyers to file a variety of different motions. See, e.g., Hingson, "State Constitutions and the Criminal Defense Lawyer: A Necessary Virtue," 14 *The Champion* 6 (Dec. 1990); Preiser & Swisher, "Aggressive Defense of White Collar Clients," 15 *The Champion* 6 (June 1991).

38 Not all lawyers are willing to make a financial sacrifice like that of Connecticut lawyer Chester Fairlie, who ruined his private practice and exhausted his own savings by spending over 650 hours to defend an accused murderer. See ABA & National Legal Aid & Defender Ass'n, *Gideon Undone: The Crisis in Indigent Defense Funding* 11, 14–15 (1982).

Nonetheless, there are numerous examples in all three counties of lawyers who have unselfishly made personal and financial sacrifices on behalf of their clients. See also Spangenberg, "Why We Are Not Defending the Poor Properly," 1 *Crim. Just.* 48 (1986) (noting that despite many problems, many public defenders and private lawyers were dedicated to providing quality representation to indigent defendants).

39 Blumberg, note 9 supra, at 28.

40 Indeed, as Ted Schneyer suggests, there are many forces and pressures at work that discourage zealousness and tempt the criminal defense lawyer to be an indifferent advocate. Schneyer, note 11 supra, at 23–24. See also Alschuler, note 26 supra, at 1180 (nature of plea-bargaining system necessarily tempts lawyers to make decisions not really in their clients' interest).

41 A number of commentators complain that public defenders provide perfunctory representation. See, e.g., Sudnow, note 19 supra. Many have linked the public defender's cooperative approach to defending their clients to the defender's deferential attitude toward the judiciary. See M. Levin, *Urban Politics and the Criminal Court* (1977); Dimock, "The Public Defender: A Step Towards a Police State," 42 *A.B.A.J.* 219–221 (1965); C. Silverman, *Criminal Violence, Criminal Justice* (1978); G. Robin, *Introduction to the Criminal Justice System* (1984). More commonly, inadequate representation by public defenders has been traced to excessive case loads and underfunded programs. See, e.g., Klein, "The Emperor Gideon Has No Clothes: The Empty Promise of the Constitutional Right to Effective Assistance of Counsel," 13 *Hastings Const. L.Q.* 625, 661–662 (1986). Other commentators as well as numerous empirical studies suggest, however, that defendants represented by public defenders fare no worse than those represented by retained private counsel. See, e.g., J. Casper, note 26 supra; Herman, Single & Boston, note 26 supra; L. McIntyre, note 26 supra. Nonetheless, these commentators report that public-defender clients often mistrust their lawyers and believe they receive inadequate representation. See also note 90 infra and accompanying text.

42 As overhead costs and inflation drive legal costs up, few defendants are able to raise sufficient money to pay a significant retainer. Even fewer are able to afford the cost of the investigator or expert needed to mount an effective defense.

43 The problem is particularly acute in Cleveland County because the judges apply such a low indigency standard that few defendants qualify for court-appointed counsel. See notes 52–57, 60 infra and accompanying text.

44 On numerous occasions, defendants would come to the Milwaukee public-defender office seeking assistance after their lawyer successfully withdrew from a case. The lawyer would have claimed irreconcilable differences as the basis for the motion to withdraw. In reality, however, it was the defendant's insistence on a trial and counsel's unwillingness to go to trial for the meager retainer the defendant could scrape up that prompted the motion to withdraw.

⁴⁵ Alschuler, note 26 supra, at 1203.

⁴⁶ Trial work is often incredibly stressful. Stress, fear, and personal convenience shape the behavior of some lawyers and influence the recommendations made to their clients. See L. McIntyre, note 26 supra, at 150–151. Moreover, given the uncertainty of predicting trials, the cautious nature of most lawyers, and the fear of a severe sentence after a guilty verdict, even well-intentioned lawyers may present clients with their options in a manner that influences them to plead guilty rather than go to trial. See Alschuler, note 26 supra, at 1205–1206.

⁴⁷ For a similar conclusion based on her study of the Cook County public defender, see L. McIntyre, note 26 supra, at 47–48.

⁴⁸ Although statistics vary from jurisdiction to jurisdiction, most studies indicate that over 90 percent of the convictions in the state courts are the result of guilty pleas. See Bureau of Justice Statistics, U.S. Dep't of Justice, *Bulletin: Felony Sentences in the State Courts, 1988*, at 6 (1990). Undoubtedly, the percentage of misdemeanor cases disposed of by a guilty plea is even higher. See Smith, "Forgotten in the Courts," 2 *Crim. Just.* 14, 17 (1987). In Milwaukee County, for example, out of 38,202 misdemeanor cases disposed of during 1986, there were only 114 trials. See G. Barczak, *Milwaukee County Circuit Court Annual Report* (1986).

⁴⁹ To Alschuler, the whole plea-bargaining system is structured to coerce guilty pleas and thereby to deprive defendants of their right to trial. See Alschuler, note 26 supra, at 1199–1206, 1306–1314.

⁵⁰ The author shares Malcolm Feeley's observation that most defendants are concerned primarily with resolving their cases quickly with a minimal expenditure of time and money. See generally M. Feeley, *The Process Is the Punishment: Handling Cases in a Lower Criminal Court* (1979). Indeed, one of the most common observations of the clinical students both at the University of Wisconsin and the Oklahoma College of Law is that so many defendants are uninterested in their own cases. Often, the students were frustrated by clients' indifference and decision to just get the matter over with despite the weakness of the state's case.

⁵¹ Numerous variables affect the working of a criminal justice system. The local crime rate, funding for the different systemic actors, effectiveness of the local police, arrest policies, economic health of the local community, and availability of social services and treatment programs are among the many factors contributing to the number of cases in the system and the manner in which these cases will be handled. Also, events and decisions at the state and national level influence the local system. For example, statewide prison overcrowding and parole release policies may influence local plea-bargaining practices and sentencing decisions. Or federal funding for the war on drugs may mean an additional position in the district attorney's office, allowing for more aggressive prosecution of defendants charged with drug offenses.

⁵² There are four primary systems for the delivery of defense services to indigent defendants:

1. A public-defender program, in which full-time or part-time salaried staff attorneys handle cases as part of a public or private nonprofit agency;

2. An assigned-counsel system, in which the court appoints a private attorney from a list of available attorneys to handle a particular case;

3. A contract system, in which an individual attorney, a group of attorneys, or a bar association agrees to provide defense services for a fixed amount; and

4. A mixed system, in which both salaried and public defenders and assigned counsel represent a significant number of indigent defendants.

See N. Lefstein, *Criminal Defense Services for the Poor* 7–8 (1982); Bureau of Justice Statistics, U.S. Dep't of Justice, *Special Report, Criminal Defense Systems—A National Survey* 3 (1984).

As of 1988, sixty-eight of Oklahoma's seventy-seven counties used the assigned counsel method. Oklahoma's two largest counties had public defender agencies, and seven counties used a contract system. See Spangenberg Group, *Oklahoma Indigent Defense Systems Study Final Report* 9–10 (1988).

[53] Prior to July 1991, however, defendants who appeared at their initial arraignment without counsel were to be informed of their right to counsel and assigned a lawyer if they were financially unable to employ counsel. Okla. Stat. tit. 22, § 464 (Supp. 1985).

[54] This practice is inconsistent with *McGraw v. State*, 476 P.2d 370 (Okla. Crim. App. 1970), in which the court held that the fact that defendant was free on bond did not preclude a finding that he lacked the financial ability to retain counsel. As the court noted, "[I]t is understandable that an accused with limited resources might use them to pay for a bond to secure his freedom rather than paying a lawyer's fee." Id. at 373. It appears that the problem of denying counsel to persons who make bail may be widespread in Oklahoma. See Spangenberg Group, note 52 supra, at 50–51. It also is not uncommon for judges around the country to view the defendant's ability to post bond as a significant factor in determining indigency. See National Legal Aid & Defender Ass'n, *The Other Face of Justice: A Report of the National Defender Survey* 60–61 (1973). According to Alschuler, Texas trial judges apply the same "unfair and unrealistic" test: Anyone who can make bond is not indigent. See Alschuler, note 26 supra, at 1257 no. 214. But see ABA, note 1 supra, Standard 5-6.1 ("counsel should not be denied because of a person's ability to pay part of the cost of representation, because friends or relatives have resources to retain counsel, or because bond has been or can be posted.").

[55] The judges insist that any lawyer with any criminal experience who practiced in Cleveland County take several criminal appointments each year. Given the minimal compensation available for handling these cases, many lawyers consider these cases a financial burden. The burden becomes very onerous in serious felony or capital cases. See *State v. Lynch*, 796 P.2d 1150 (Okla. 1990) (holding that Oklahoma's statutory scheme for compensating lawyers appointed to represent indigent defendants provides an unreasonable, arbitrary rate of compensation).

[56] Prior to July 1, 1991, the maximum fees by statute that an appointed Oklahoma lawyer could receive were as follows: Title 22, Section 1271 of the Oklahoma Statutes provided that compensation should be "reasonable and just" but should not exceed $500 per case, regardless of the severity of the charges; Title 22, Section 464 of the Oklahoma Statutes provided that fees for services rendered until the defendant is discharged or bound over after a preliminary hearing were not to exceed $100; Title 22, Section 701.4 of the Oklahoma Statutes provided for "reasonable and just" compensation in capital cases with a maximum of $200 for services prior to a preliminary hearing, $500 for the preliminary hearing, and $2,500 for services from the time a defendant is bound over through final disposition in trial court.

For administrative ease, Cleveland County judges for years have simply awarded lawyers the set amount of $250 for a misdemeanor and $500 for a felony, regardless of the actual time spent. The judges assume that most lawyers in most cases put in a sufficient number of hours of work that it is unlikely that any lawyer will reap a significant financial windfall from handling these cases. The judges recognize, however, that in some cases, especially ones that go to trial, lawyers are grossly undercompensated.

In *State v. Lynch*, note 55 supra, at 1164, the Oklahoma Supreme Court recognized the inadequacies of Oklahoma's statutory scheme and set up guidelines for compensating appointed counsel based on the hourly rate of prosecutors and the public defenders in Oklahoma's two largest counties. It held off implementing these guidelines in noncapital cases until August 24, 1992 to give the legislature an opportunity to address the problem.

In response to *Lynch*, the Oklahoma legislature passed the Indigent Defense Act, Okla. Stat. tit. 22, § 1355 (Supp. 1990). Pursuant to this statute, each judicial district is to develop its own system for delivering indigent defense services. This legislation is still being implemented, and its effects on Cleveland County have yet to be felt.

[57] Throughout Oklahoma, courts seldom approve requests for investigators, forensic testing, or experts. See Spangenberg Group, note 52 supra, at 46–48. Lack of access to investigative assistance or expert services is a common weakness of many indigent defense systems, especially assigned counsel or contract systems. See Mounts & Wilson, "Systems for Providing Indigent Defense: An Introduction," 14 *N.Y.U. Rev. L. & Soc. Change* 193, 199 n.33 (1986); Coyle, Strasser & Lavelle, note 26 supra, at 30; Smith, note 48 supra, at 17.

[58] In 1977, the Wisconsin legislature created the Office of the State Public Defender, an independent agency under the direction of the Public Defender Board. Wis. Stat. § 15.78 (1989). The governor, with the advice and consent of the Senate, appoints the nine members of the board, who, in turn, select the state public defender. The state public defender supervises the operation of the program, which is divided into two divisions: appellate and trial. As of September 1990, there were 258 staff attorneys located in 37 offices throughout Wisconsin and approximately 1,400 private lawyers certified to accept appointment cases. See Office of the State Pub. Defender, 1989–91 *Biennial Report* (1991). The Milwaukee trial office had 46 staff lawyers compared with 18 in the Dane County office.

[59] In most jurisdictions, salaries of public defenders lag behind those of their prosecutorial counterparts. In Wisconsin, however, public defenders as state employees generally earned more during the past decade than most assistant district attorneys with comparable experience. This lack of salary parity led the Wisconsin District Attorneys Association to push for legislation that created state funding for the operation of all local district attorney offices and made assistant district attorneys state rather than county employees. See Wis. Stat. Ann. § 978.001–978.14 (West 1991).

[60] Wis. Stat. § 977.07(2) (1989) provides:

If the person's assets, less reasonable and necessary living expenses, are not sufficient to cover the anticipated cost of effective representation when the length and complexity of the anticipated proceedings are taken fully into account, the person shall be determined to be indigent in full or in part. The determination of the ability of the person to contribute to the cost of legal services shall be based upon specific written standards relating to income, assets and the anticipated cost of representation.

The specific written standards are set forth by administrative rule. See Wis. Admin. Code § S.P.D. 3.01 (1990).

In Cleveland County, on the other hand, judges determine the defendant's right to appointed counsel based on their subjective assessment of the defendant's indigency. The judges use the pauper's affidavit set forth in Okla. Ct. Crim. App. R. 1.14 to obtain information, but no guidelines exist as to how that information is to be analyzed. Accordingly, there is considerable variance in indigency determinations. This problem is not unique to Cleveland County. See Spangenberg Group, note 52 supra, at 49–51. For an extended discussion of the need to develop specific eligibility criteria that compares liquid assets with the anticipated cost of counsel, including litigation expenses, and the merits of removing the eligibility determination from judicial control, see National Study Comm'n on Defense Servs. *Guidelines for Legal Defense Systems in the United States* 72–96 (1976).

[61] Section 969.06 of the Wisconsin Statutes, read in conjunction with Section 977.05(b) of the Wisconsin Statutes, provides for representation of an indigent "as soon as

practicable after a person has been detained or arrested." In practice, however, the public defender's office represents eligible persons seeking assistance even before any arrest or detention. For a discussion of the importance of early representation, see ABA, note 1 supra, Standard 5-5.1 and commentary (2d ed. 1980); National Study Comm'n on Defense Servs., note 60 supra, at 48–71.

[62] In his last report to Governor Thompson and the Wisconsin legislature, State Public Defender Nicholas Chiarkas noted that the public-defender trial staff was now handling 62.3 percent of all indigent cases statewide, with the remainder handled by assigned private lawyers. See Office of State Pub. Defender, note 58 supra, at 5–6. Since 1977, staff lawyers in the Milwaukee and Dane County offices generally have defended about 75 percent of the program's clients in each county.

[63] As of December 1, 1992, the rate will be $50 per hour for in-court work and $40 for other work. Id. at 15.

[64] Private lawyers must seek prior approval from the local public-defender office before hiring an expert or investigator. See Wis. Admin. Code § S.P.D. 2.12 (1990).

[65] For a discussion of the Wisconsin funding needs, see Spangenberg Group, note 26 supra, at 28–49. Clearly, there are other jurisdictions, including Cleveland County, where the funding shortfalls are much worse. See, e.g., Coyle, Strasser & Lavelle, note 26 supra, at 30–44; Special Comm. on Criminal Justice in Free Soc'y, Criminal Justice Section, Criminal Justice in Crisis (1988). For a discussion of the serious funding crisis in Oklahoma, see Spangenberg Group, note 52 supra, at 30–46.

As Spangenberg noted in the fall of 1989, "[T]he problem has grown substantially worse for most indigent defense systems since 1986. With a few exceptions, indigent defense delivery in the country once again has reached a crisis stage." Spangenberg, "We Are Still Not Defending the Poor Properly," 4 Crim. Just. 11 (1989). Norman Lefstein detailed the extent of the national crisis in his study done at the behest of The American Bar Association. See N. Lefstein, note 52 supra. For other accounts of the continuing crisis in the delivery of indigent defense services in this country, see Spangenberg, note 38 supra, at 13–15, 48; Murphy, "Indigent Defense and the U.S. War on Drugs," 6 Crim. Just. 14, 14–20 (1991); Monahan, "Who Is Trying to Kill the Sixth Amendment," 6 Crim. Just. 24, 24–28, 51–52 (1991).

[66] Some unrepresented defendants do obtain better plea bargains by negotiating their own deals. Like Alschuler, this author has observed some sympathetic prosecutors make offers to unrepresented defendants that went well below the norm given the person's record and the charge. See Alschuler, note 26 supra, at 1274–1278. If the unrepresented defendant wants to contest the charge or the prosecutor's initial offer is harsh, however, the defendant has little leverage or ability to obtain the desired result.

[67] Many commentators have decried the inadequate representation provided by poorly paid courthouse "regulars" or "pleaders," who turn over cases as quickly as possible to maximize their profits. See, e. g., Bazelon, "The Defective Assistance of Counsel," 42 U. Cin. L. Rev. 1, 8–11 (1973); Alschuler, note 26 supra, at 1182–1186.

[68] After the arraignment, the next court appearance in Cleveland County is referred to as the call docket. At the call docket, each defendant must announce whether he wants a jury trial, court trial, or date to plead guilty. Call dockets are held roughly six weeks apart. At the call docket on November 19, 1991, it was "discovered" that seven misdemeanor defendants had each been incarcerated for almost six weeks because of their inability to post minimal bond. Each was charged with public intoxication in violation of Title 37, Section 8 of the Oklahoma Statutes (1990), which carries a maximum jail sentence of thirty days. The usual disposition for this offense is a small fine, some community service, or a weekend in jail. Upon learning that these defendants were still incarcerated—the jail was checked when the defendants did not appear in

person at the call docket—the cases were set for disposition. Each defendant pleaded guilty for time served.

    This problem is, of course, not unique to Cleveland County. For a brief look at the problems with "forgotten" detainees in the Baltimore city jail, see Presser, "Lost and Found," *A.B.A.J.*, Nov. 1991, at 42.

[69] Wis. Stat. Ann. § 969.03 comment L. 1969, ch. 225 (West 1985). Sections 969.02 and 969.03 of the Wisconsin Statutes spell out the procedures for releasing persons charged with misdemeanors and felonies. Although surety bonds by individuals or corporate sureties are still permitted, such bonds are rarely used.

[70] See Wis. Stat. § 968.085 (1989).

[71] Moreover, in Milwaukee County there is a nonprofit social service agency, the Wisconsin Correctional Service, which runs various programs for the Milwaukee court system. These programs further facilitate the pretrial release of a number of defendants, especially those with drug, alcohol, or mental health problems, who would otherwise remain incarcerated. Success on a release program enhances a defendant's chance to obtain a favorable outcome. Dane County has some similar programs, but they are not as structured or as extensive as those of Milwaukee County. Cleveland County does not have any agency involved in a pretrial release program.

[72] The pressure on indigent defendants is compounded by the policy of the Cleveland County sheriff not to permit pretrial detainees any visitors except for a lawyer for their first seven days in jail.

[73] For an article making the same point based on a study of the pretrial detention practices in Houston, Texas, see Wheeler & Wheeler, "Reflections on Legal Representation of the Economically Disadvantaged: Beyond Assembly Line Justice," 26 *Crime & Delinq.* 319 (1982). See also H. Zeisel, *The Limits of Law Enforcement* 47–49 (1982) (discussing the inequities of a bail system that exerts undue pressure on incarcerated defendants to plead guilty).

[74] None of the offices adheres to a policy of no plea bargaining. Presumably, a major policy decision such as this would have a substantial impact on the behavior of defendants and their lawyers. See Spangenberg, note 65 supra, at 12 (policies of limited or no plea bargaining have great impact on indigent defense resources).

[75] Although assistant district attorneys in all three counties complained of heavy case loads and serious time pressures, the prosecutors in Milwaukee County seemingly labored under heavier work loads. As a result, the Milwaukee prosecutors were more responsive when defense counsel demonstrated the weakness of the state's case. Prosecutors in both Dane and Cleveland Counties routinely filed and then more aggressively pursued cases that either would not have been issued or would have been quickly dismissed in Milwaukee County.

[76] Dane County has two deputy district attorneys, while Cleveland County has one. In both counties, the district attorney is also involved in charging decisions in certain cases. Additionally, in Cleveland County, all drug charges are filed by one assistant district attorney and all child molestation cases by another. Occasionally, the deputy district attorney will speak to the complainant, other witnesses, the arresting officers, or the suspect in making a charging decision. Charges usually are issued, however, based on a review of the police reports and the suspect's criminal record.

[77] The law student interns are authorized to practice pursuant to Okla. Sup. Ct. R. 2. Although the intern program is designed to give the students "real-world" experience under the supervision of an experienced lawyer, the students are all supervised by one prosecutor who rarely appears with them in court. The interns generally seek advice from their supervisor, however, before reducing or dismissing a charge.

[78] This charging conference procedure is used in all felony and serious misdemeanor

cases. All other misdemeanor charges are filed based on the prosecutor's review of police reports and rap sheets.

[79] Generally, a lawyer should not even begin plea negotiations without the consent of the client. See ABA, note 1 supra, Standard 4-6.1(b) (2d ed. 1980). In the latest edition of *Standards for Criminal Justice*, Standard 4-6.1(b) has been modified by the deletion of the phrase "although ordinarily the client's consent to engage in such discussions should be obtained in advance." Because the commentary to this standard has yet to be published, the rationale for this change is unclear. Nevertheless, because a lawyer may find it necessary to discuss information revealed by the client while plea bargaining, counsel generally should secure the client's permission before negotiating with the prosecutor. Compare *Model Code of Professional Responsibility* DR 4-101(B), DR 4-101(C) (1981) with *Model Rules of Professional Conduct* Rule 1.6(1983).

[80] Because the defendant ultimately controls the decision whether to plead guilty or to go to trial, defense counsel should present the available options as clearly and as objectively as possible. See *Jones v. Barnes*, note 6 supra, at 745, 751; *Model Rules of Professional Conduct* Rule 1.2 (1983); ABA, note 1 supra, Standard 5.2(a). Even when the defendant is anxious just to plead guilty to get the matter over with, counsel must ensure that the defendant is cognizant of the consequences of a guilty plea. This is particularly so when representing young defendants, who often do not recognize the potential impact of a criminal conviction on their employment opportunities, eligibility for military service, or insurance rates. Like Feeley, this author has frequently seen public defenders or clinical law students attempt to dissuade defendants who are anxious to get their cases over quickly from pleading guilty. See M. Feeley, note 50 supra, at 222. See also ABA, note 1 supra, Standard 4-4.1 (defense counsel's duty to investigate exists regardless of defendant's admission of guilt or stated desire to plead guilty).

[81] Unquestionably, the deplorable conditions in many county jails, including the real risk of physical harm to pretrial detainees, spur some defendants to plead guilty. For a brief look at some of the hardships endured by pretrial detainees, see *Wallace v. Kern* 371 F. Supp. 1384 (E.D.N.Y. 1974), rev'd., 499 F.2d 1345 (2d Cir. 1974).

[82] There is little question to anyone familiar with the criminal justice system that the prosecutor wields extraordinary power, and has enormous discretion. See ABA, note 1 supra, Standard 3-1.1, at 3–7 (2d ed. 1979). For a summary of the scope of the prosecutor's discretion, see W. LaFave & J. Israel, note 2 supra, at 559–594. Moreover, the "give and take" of plea bargaining gives the prosecutor considerable leverage to coerce a guilty plea. See *Bordenkircher v. Hayes*, 434 U.S. 357 (1978) (not improper for prosecutor to carry out threat to prosecute defendant as a habitual offender because of defendant's unwillingness to plead to underlying felony).

[83] Not all public defenders have a reputation for providing aggressive, zealous representation. See Klein, note 41 supra, at 657–663. For a thorough and damning account of the abysmal quality of representation provided to indigents in New York by both assigned counsel and the Legal Aid Society, see McConville & Mirsky, "Criminal Defense of the Poor in New York City," 15 *Rev. of L. & Soc. Change* 581 (1986–1987). See also Sudnow, note 19 supra. Most of the criticism leveled against public defenders, however, springs from underfunded, overloaded programs that provide substandard representation. Adequately funded programs tend to get high marks for the quality of representation delivered to the program's clients. See, e.g., U.S. Dep't of Justice, *An Exemplary Project: The D.C. Public Defender Service* (1975); Arthur Young & Co., note 26 supra.

[84] Arguably, reasonable rates paid by the Wisconsin public-defender program provide a financial incentive for lawyers to spend unnecessary time defending a case, turn down reasonable plea offers, or go to trial on hopeless cases. Admittedly, some lawyers

may overwork a case. While at the Milwaukee public-defender office, the author reviewed a private lawyer's voucher that included twenty-five hours for time spent calling every Brown in the Milwaukee phone book trying unsuccessfully to make initial contact with his newly assigned client. The public-defender program would selectively cut bills such as the one submitted in Brown's case. Although this power is used sparingly, it does discourage abuse. See Wis. Stat. § 977.08(4) (1989) (Public Defender Board reviews decisions of the state public defender regarding payment of private lawyer vouchers). Finally, the client makes the ultimate decision on pleading guilty or going to trial. The client's reluctance to go to trial, fear of an increased sentence, and interest in a quick resolution generally will override the desire of an overzealous assigned lawyer looking to make some extra money by "milking" an appointed case.

[85] See *State v. McKenny*, 582 P.2d 573, 577 (Wash. 1978) (compensation scheme unrelated to work actually performed creates "an economic disincentive against satisfactory representation"); ABA, note 1 supra, Standard 5-2.4, at 5–33 (2d. ed. 1979) (flat payment rates should be discouraged because the inevitable result is lawyers doing only what is minimally necessary to qualify for flat payment). For a chilling study of the inadequate representation provided to many capital defendants in several Southern states using an assigned-counsel method, see Coyle et al., note 26 supra, at 30–44. A number of courts have struck down statutory schemes for compensating assigned counsel with low maximum awards on the ground that as administered, such systems unfairly and arbitrarily compelled some lawyers to shoulder a heavy financial burden that properly should be borne by the state. See, e.g., *State v. Lynch*, note 55 supra, at 1150; *State v. Smith*, 242 Kan. 336, 747 P.2d 816 (1987).

Nevertheless, it is evident that in many jurisdictions, the compensation provided to appointed lawyers in an assigned-counsel system still is woefully inadequate. Unfortunately, too often these assigned lawyers also provide woeful representation. See N. Lefstein, note 52 supra at 17–24; McConville & Mirsky, note 83 supra at 899–901: Smith, note 48 supra, at 17; Herman, Single & Boston, note 26 supra, at 161.

[86] See Mounts & Wilson, note 57 supra, at 194; N. Lefstein, note 52 supra, at 19–20. For personal accounts of private lawyers laboring under financial pressure to induce clients to plead guilty and not go to trial, see ABA & National Legal Aid & Defender Ass'n, note 38 supra, at 10–11, 14–15. As Dean Paul Carrington observed, "while there will be admirable exceptions of lawyers laboring to do what few will ever know or care about, a system that desires zealous advocacy on the whole will have to reward it." Carrington, "The Right to Zealous Counsel," 1979 *Duke L.J.* 1291, 1294. See also Spangenberg Group, note 52 supra, at 37–46 (commending Oklahoma lawyers for continuing to take indigent appointments despite inadequate compensation but noting that experienced lawyers increasingly were opting out of such appointments).

[87] "No attorney, no matter how skilled, trained, and committed, can provide competent representation under working conditions which do not allow such skill, training, and commitment to be practiced." Mounts, note 8 supra, at 221. See also ABA, note 1 supra, Standard 5-4.3, at 5–48 (2d ed. 1979); ABA & National Legal Aid & Defender Ass'n, note 38 supra, at 5.

[88] For a summary of the adverse effects of an excessive case load on a public defender's ability to prepare, investigate, research, and consult with clients, see Klein, note 41 supra, at 662–675.

[89] In his recent report, Spangenberg praised the Wisconsin public defenders for their dedication and quality. Yet, he concluded that an increasing number of the public defenders' clients were suffering because the lawyers were laboring under the strain of an excessive case load and work load. See Spangenberg Group, note 26 supra, at 32–49.

[90] See Mounts, "Public Defender Programs, Professional Responsibility and Competent

Representation,'' 1982 *Wis. L. Rev.* 473, 486. As many commentators have noted, defendants often mistrust their lawyer, especially when counsel is appointed, not retained. See *Jones v. Barnes*, note 6 supra, at 745, 761 (Brennan, J., dissenting); Herman, Single & Boston, note 26 supra, at 153. For a detailed count of the reasons clients mistrust their lawyers, especially public defenders, See J. Casper, note 26 supra; L. McIntyre, note 26 supra, at 62–73.

[91] Like any experienced criminal practitioner, most public defenders can assess realistically the value of a proffered plea bargain because they know the prosecutor's standard offers and the judge's sentencing proclivities. See Alschuler, note 26 supra, 1229–1230.

[92] See Spangenberg Group, note 26 supra, at 34.

[93] ''Defense counsel should not seek concessions favorable to one client by any agreement which is detrimental to the legitimate interests of a client in another case.'' ABA, note 1 supra, Standard 4-6.2(d). Although public defenders probably do not often explicitly ''trade off'' one client to secure a favorable deal for another, the give-and-take process involved in bargaining numerous cases with a handful of prosecutors invariably works to the advantage of some clients and the disadvantage of others. For a brief look at this troublesome and, perhaps, unresolvable problem, see Alschuler, note 26 supra, at 1210–1224.

[94] Schneyer, note 11 supra, at 24 (emphasis in the original). See also Alschuler, note 26 supra, at 1254–1255; Klein, note 41 supra, at 669–673.

[95] See note 65 supra.

[96] As Mounts and Wilson point out, there are many political factors contributing to this serious underfunding of defense services. Mounts & Wilson, note 57 supra, at 200–201. Because increased spending for defense services is so politically unpopular, the litigation model may well be one of the most effective means of securing additional funding. See Wilson, ''Litigative Approaches to Enforcing the Right to Effective Assistance of Counsel in Criminal Cases,'' 14 *N.Y.U. Rev. L. & Soc. Change* 203 (1986). In Oklahoma, for example, it was not until the Supreme Court of Oklahoma forced the legislature's hand by adopting its own statewide compensation scheme for court-appointed counsel in *State v. Lynch*, note 55 supra, at 1150, that the Oklahoma legislature finally passed a measure creating the Indigent Defense Act. See note 56 supra.

[97] Alschuler argues that the intolerable nature of the plea-bargaining system is such that all defense lawyers are ''subject to bureaucratic pressures and conflicts of interest'' that can only be avoided by ''restructur[ing] our criminal justice system to eliminate the overwhelming importance of the defendant's choice of plea.'' Alschuler, note 26 supra, at 1313. He calls, therefore, for the abolition of the plea-bargaining system and sufficient resources to pay for the added costs of more trials. Id. at 1180, 1314.

While the author of this article concurs with many of Alschuler's observations, especially his descriptions of the destructive impact of plea bargaining on the attorney-client relationship, the author does not agree that the abolition of plea-bargaining is either feasible or desirable. Given the existing crisis in the criminal justice system at all levels, with only a small percentage of cases going to trial, the resources needed to adequately fund this restructured system would be staggering. Moreover, the working poor and many middle-class defendants would be unable to afford aggressive advocacy under this restructured system. In a system devoid of plea-bargaining, these defendants may face far harsher dispositions. It is more desirable, therefore, to expand and adequately fund defense services and, thus, permit defense lawyers to function as effective adversaries of the state. See also Mounts, note 90 supra, at 488 (suggesting that budgetary problems are the primary stumbling block to a public defender's ability to provide quality representation).

⁹⁸ In a mixed system, both staff public defenders and assigned private lawyers represent a "substantial number" of indigent clients. N. Lefstein, note 52 supra. at 8. For an excellent summary of the advantages of a mixed system, see ABA, note 1 supra, Standard 5-1.2 and commentary (2d. ed. 1979). See also National Study Comm'n on Defense Servs. note 60 supra, at 124-136 (recommending mixed defender and assigned-counsel system, with each handling a substantial share of cases) 144-180 (recommending a state defender office to organize, coordinate, and monitor the delivery of defense services throughout each state).

⁹⁹ See Spangenberg, note 38 supra, at 15; National Study Comm'n on Defense Servs., note 60 supra, at 134-135. In Wisconsin, the support of the state bar has been instrumental in enabling the Wisconsin public-defender program to avert financial crisis. See Gimbel, "The Public Defenders' Changing Image," *Wis. B. Bull.*, Sept. 1985, at 9, 10.

¹⁰⁰ Echoing earlier observations by Alschuler, Spangenberg noted that a substantial diminution of the role of the private bar in the criminal system raised the specter of a system dominated by institutional lawyers too comfortable and too cooperative to protect their clients' rights. See Spangenberg, note 38 supra, at 14-15; Alschuler, note 26 supra, at 1210-1222. For an extended look at the dangers of an institutional defender program primarily committed to the cost-efficient processing of defendants, see McConville & Mirsky, note 83 supra, at 582-695.

¹⁰¹ The ethics codes clearly require a defense lawyer to exercise independent judgment on behalf of a client without allowing an employer or administrator to direct or regulate counsel's advocacy. See *Model Code of Professional Responsibility* DR 5-107(B) (1981); *Model Rules of Professional Conduct* Rule 5.4(c) (1983). See also *Polk County v. Dodson*, note 2 supra, at 312, 321-322 (concluding that the state must respect the professional independence of the individual public defender, who, in turn, must make case decisions free from administrative control). There is little question that assistant public defenders and appointed counsel are unlikely to feel free to engage in legitimate but judicially unpopular defense tactics if they are economically dependent on the judiciary. See National Study Comm'n on Defense Servs., note 60 supra, at 218-221; ABA, note 1 supra, Standards 5-1.3, 5-3.1 and commentary (2d. ed. 1979).

Similarly, a county's interest in obtaining defense services at the lowest possible cost cannot be permitted to compromise defense counsel's independence and the quality of representation provided by counsel. See *State v. Smith*, 140 Ariz. 355, 681 P.2d 1374 (1984).

¹⁰² To guarantee the professional independence of the defender program, most commentators urge the creation of a board that sets general policies for the operation of the program but is removed from the day-to-day operation of the program and precluded from interfering in any cases. See ABA, note 1 supra, Standards 5-1.3, 5-1.6, 5-2.4; National Study Comm'n on Defense Servs., note 60 supra, at 224-231.

¹⁰³ "Since a primary objective of the payment system should be to encourage vigorous defense representation, flat payment rates should be discouraged. The inevitable effect of such rates is to discourage lawyers from doing more than what is minimally necessary to qualify for the flat payment." ABA, note 1 supra, Standard 5-2.4, at 5-33 (2d. ed 1979). See also notes 85-86 supra and accompanying text. For an unduly optimistic view of the contract system, see Spears, "Contract Counsel: Different Way to Defend the Poor," 6 *Crim. Just.* 24-31 (1991) (arguing that quality criteria in the initial bidding process, prior approval by the funding agency of any change in the lawyers in the contracting firm, and a noncause termination clause in the contract ensures quality representation by the contracting firm). Most commentators, however, believe that the contract system provides an economic incentive to turn over cases quickly without regard for quality representation. See, e.g., National Study Comm'n on Defense Servs.,

note 60 supra, at 169–170: Wilson, *Contract Bid Programs: A Threat to Quality Indigent Defense Services* (Mar. 1982,) (unpublished report for National Legal Aid and Defender Association). See also *State v. Smith*, note 101 supra (finding that contract system in Mohave County based on flat payment for one-fourth of county's total case load militated against inadequate representation by overburdened defense counsel).

[104] See notes 61–66 supra and accompanying text.

[105] As a national study has concluded:

> Quality representation is not only related to the compensation of counsel. It also depends upon the availability of supporting services and facilities as these are not only vital to the presentation of the defense's case, they are often required to disprove the prosecution's case. Since the state already has the police to conduct investigations and supply expert testimony, assigned counsel would be forced to operate under a distinct disadvantage without the availability of necessary supporting services and facilities. This is an inequity which no system of justice should tolerate.

National Study Comm'n on Defense Servs., note 60 supra, at 272. See also ABA, note 1 supra, Standard 5-1.4.

Although it is evident that defense counsel can seldom function effectively without adequate support, it is abundantly clear that support services are virtually nonexistent or badly underfunded in most jurisdictions. See N. Lefstein, note 52 supra, app. at F-1–F-68. Even though the Wisconsin public-defender program is better funded than most, it is seriously deficient in investigative and support services. See Spangenberg Group, note 26 supra, at 33, 43–44.

[106] See ABA, note 1 supra, Standard 5-1.5.

[107] "The practice of criminal law has become highly specialized in recent years, and only lawyers experienced in trial practice, with an interest in and knowledge of criminal law and procedure, can properly be expected to serve as assigned counsel." ABA, note 1 supra, Standard 5-2.2, at 5–27 (2d ed. 1979). Many courts and commentators have noted the increased complexity of handling a criminal case. See, e.g., *State v. Smith*, note 85 supra, N. Lefstein, note 52 supra, at 18; National Study Comm'n on Defense Servs., note 60 supra, at 433–439.

[108] My experience as the chief staff attorney of the Milwaukee office confirms that to encourage zeal and productivity, merit raises are essential. See also Carrington, note 86 supra, at 1305–1307 (arguing for bonus system for staff attorneys to inspire zeal together with the right to fire one's appointed lawyer); National Study Comm'n on Defense Servs., note 60 supra, at 454–458.

[109] Developing adequate performance measures poses a serious problem for any public defender administrator or board. There are national case load standards, but they are only a crude starting point for assessing the adequacy of a staff lawyer's performance. Local case load standards must be tailored to reflect local variations such as the prosecutor's charging system, local plea-bargaining practices, and court congestion. For a detailed look at one approach to developing case load standards weighted to reflect various local factors, see Spangenberg Group, note 26 supra, at 16–93.

Setting reasonable case load standards, however, only solves part of the problem. A public defender may meet case load requirements and handle a prescribed number of cases but provide poor representation. An effort must be made to ensure that aggressive, competent lawyering is rewarded and that quality representation is not sacrificed at the altar of case load statistics. Supervision and evaluation by experienced senior lawyers constitutes the best mechanism for ensuring quality representation. See National Study Comm'n on Defense Servs., note 60 supra, at 440–441.

[110] Given the demonstrated inability of local government to fund indigent defense services adequately, the author assumes that this proposed program is state funded and administered as an independent state agency. For the advantages of this approach,

see National Study Comm'n on Defense Servs., note 60 supra, at 242–258.

[111] See Spangenberg Group, note 26 supra, at 1–15. For additional background on the often heated political battles over the budget for the Wisconsin public defender program, see Phelps, "Dust Settles After Legislative Battle," *Wis. B. Bull.*, Sept. 1985, at 20–23; Phelps, "Mounting Stress on Wisconsin's Justice System," *Wis. B. Bull.*, Mar. 1987, at 32.

[112] Program administrators who are lawyers are bound to ensure that the lawyers in their program are not violating the rules of professional conduct. *Model Rules of Professional Conduct* Rule 5.1 (1983). If the supervising lawyers know that their lawyers are handling so many cases that they are neglecting the rights of their clients, these supervisors as well as the staff lawyers are in violation of their ethical responsibilities. For a further discussion of the ethical problems confronting supervisors and staff lawyers grappling with excessive case loads, see Klein, "Legal Malpractice, Professional Discipline, and Representation of the Indigent," 61 *Temp. L.Q.* 1171 (1988); Mounts, note 90 supra, at 473.

[113] See note 109 supra.

[114] Public defenders also must recognize the importance of spending more time talking with their clients about their cases and then devote the necessary time. See, e.g., Wilkerson, "Public Defenders as Their Clients See Them," 1 *Am. J. Crim. L.* 141, 142 (1972) (most widely shared grievance among public-defender clients is lack of contact with or visits from their lawyer). Absent increased and improved communications, public defenders will not be able to overcome the mistrust most clients feel toward their assigned lawyers. See, e.g., J. Casper, note 26 supra. at 36 (lack of time spent with clients is a significant factor contributing to the poor image of public defenders).

[115] Keeping salaries low is not a desirable solution. but it is preferable to making do with inadequate support services or excessive case loads, both of which compromise the quality of defense services. The issue in part turns on whether good lawyers could still be attracted to and retained by the program if salaries were not comparable to those in the prosecutor's office as recommended by the National Study Commission. See National Study Comm'n on Defense Servs., note 60 supra, at 278–284. Given the poor job market, the increased number of clinical students anxious to get into defender programs, and the attractiveness of a public-defender job for lawyers looking for litigation experience, attracting good candidates is unlikely to be a problem. A loan forgiveness program for students going to a public defender's office or doing other public service work would encourage even more quality graduates to apply for public-defender positions.

Although it is possible that a lower salary structure will lead to increased turnover, the job market and enhanced job satisfaction may counter that trend. Moreover, it is clear that many lawyers do public-defender work for reasons other than money. See L. McIntyre, note 26 supra, at 80–84, 89. Finally, it is not clear that higher turnover and loss of experience necessarily results in lower-quality representation. That depends on the extent of the turnover, the quality of the training programs, and the zeal and quality of the new recruits.

[116] For a discussion of the importance of monitoring training and supervision, see National Study Comm'n on Defense Servs., note 60 supra, at 434–447.

[117] Not only does a statewide program best serve the goal of quality representation, it "offers the most efficient and flexible means of allocating available resources." National Study Comm'n on Defense Servs., note 60 supra, at 175.

[118] Even using the Wisconsin indigency test, which is more generous than the standardless determinations made in Cleveland County and many other jurisdictions, see note 59 supra, many people on small fixed incomes do not qualify for public-defender

representation. Realistically, however, a person receiving a monthly Social Security benefit cannot hire counsel. Unfortunately, public-defender administrators facing case load increases on top of existing crushing case loads are not inclined to argue for a loosening of indigency standards. In fact, the Wisconsin public-defender office continues to use outdated figures as to the anticipated cost of retaining counsel by applying their indigency test to hold dawn their case load. See Wis. Admin. Code § S.P.D. 3.02(1). See also *State v. Dean*, 163 Wis. 2d 503, 471 N.W.2d 310 (Wis. Ct. App. 1991) (Wis. Admin. Code § S.P.D. 3.02 use $300 for cost of hiring lawyer in criminal traffic case when evidence suggests real cost is $500 to $1,000). The use of outdated figures works to deny counsel to low-income persons who really cannot afford representation. As a result, some low-income defendants are challenging the public defender's denial of counsel. In *State v. Dean*, the Wisconsin Court of Appeals held that the trial court should have exercised its inherent power to appoint counsel despite the indigency determination of the public defender. Most needy defendants, however, do not challenge the public defender's denial of counsel but simply go without counsel.

[119] Such an approach was recommended by the National Study Commission in its 1976 report on defense services. See National Study Comm'n on Defense Servs., note 60 supra, at 104–122.

[120] Indeed, it already appears that overtaxed indigent defense systems are being asked to handle more indigent cases each year, thus exacerbating existing case load problems. See Spangenberg Group, note 26 supra, at 4. Budgetary pressures are likely to produce a tightening of indigency standards rather than an expansion of coverage to include the working poor. In fact, the drive toward a tightening of eligibility requirements is already under way in many states. See Spangenberg. note 38 supra, at 48. The problem, of course, is that people squeezed out of the indigent defense system usually are left with two bad alternatives: pro se representation or hiring a cheap lawyer.

Some public-defender programs have urged decriminalization as a means to retard case load growth and the spiraling costs both of the public-defender program and the criminal justice system as a whole. See Phelps, "Mounting Stress on Wisconsin's Justice System," *Wis. B. Bull.*, Mar. 1987, at 33–34. As Nicholas Chiarkas noted in his agency's annual report, the public defender's office achieved several major goals with the enactment of the latest Wisconsin biennial budget: Various misdemeanor offenses were decriminalized and the line between misdemeanor and felony property offenses was raised from $500 to $1,000. See Office of State Pub. Defender, note 58 supra, at 7, 9. While these legislative changes are desirable from the standpoint of many defendants, the result will be the greater use of civil forfeiture actions where no right to counsel exists.

18

Privatizing Due Process
Issues in the Comparison of Assigned Counsel, Public Defender, and Contracted Indigent Defense Systems

ALISSA POLLITZ WORDEN

Since 1963, when the U.S. Supreme Court declared that indigent defendants are entitled to counsel in felony prosecutions, the task of providing representation for the poor has taken on increasing significance and complexity. In recognizing the "widespread belief that lawyers in criminal courts are necessities, not luxuries," (*Gideon v. Wainwright*, 372 U.S. 335, 1963), the Court acknowledged the transformation of criminal courts from the relatively simple tribunals of the nineteenth century into today's complicated procedural mazes of strategy and negotiation. More importantly, rejecting the convenient but improbable assumption that as officers of the court in an adversarial system prosecutors and judges adequately protect defendants' interests, the Court attempted to correct the imbalance of power between prosecutors and the accused by ensuring that all defendants be afforded the opportunity for expert advocacy.

This guarantee has been the subject of controversy, however, as the Court has expanded the right to counsel to cover many misdemeanor and some juvenile proceedings, increasing the burden on state and local governments to supply representation to the poor. This responsibility

Reprinted by permission of the *Justice System Journal* from vol. 14, no. 3 and vol. 15, no. 1 (1991), pp. 390–418.

cost taxpayers almost one billion dollars in 1986 (Criminal Defense for the Poor, 1988)—a burden that is highest in communities with greatest need and fewest resources, those with high crime rates and large poverty populations. Careful implementation of the Court's policy, therefore, is important for practical and fiscal reasons. But designing and operating effective programs for providing representation is important from a due process perspective as well. Justice in an adversarial system depends in large measure on the balance of skill and experience between opposing counsel; and court-appointed counsel is the rule rather than the exception in most felony proceedings.[1] The quality of representation afforded indigents, therefore, not only affects defendants' experiences in the criminal justice system, but also cumulatively determines the character of justice itself.

However, although there has been much debate over the best way to provide counsel for the poor, evaluation studies have been inconclusive and sometimes unsystematic. In particular, there have been few studies of contracting with private attorneys for indigent defense, an increasingly popular alternative to assigned counsel and public defender programs. This article attempts to offer a more stable foundation for empirical research by drawing upon theories of privatization to provide a framework for analyzing the potential comparative benefits and drawbacks of contracting.

A second and related purpose of this article is to explore conceptual and methodological issues associated with evaluative research on indigent defense and to derive recommendations for future research from these explorations.[2] Evaluation studies comparing publicly paid counsel with privately retained attorneys have found little evidence that the quality of representation differs significantly across program types. However, these studies seldom examine more than two or three courts and hence are of limited generalizability (particularly insofar as they do not permit comparison of features within program types) and very few studies include contract systems. Furthermore, there is little agreement on how to best measure program effectiveness and efficiency. The steady increase in contracting prompts a reconsideration of ways of evaluating programs offering counsel for the poor.

The Right to Counsel and the Contracting Innovation

Although the right to counsel for indigents was not constitutionally guaranteed in state felony courts until 1963, in some jurisdictions a tradition of representation for the poor had already existed for decades. The two dominant forms of providing counsel from these traditions developed (McConville and Mirsky, 1989; McIntyre, 1987).[3] The most common means of providing representation for the poor is the assigned counsel system, used in 52 percent of all counties. Assigned counsel systems distribute the burden of indigent representation among members of the private bar through case-by-case assignment by judges or magistrates. For decades this service was formally or informally provided *pro bono* in many jurisdictions, but today virtually all assigned counsel jurisdictions reimburse attorneys for indigent representation with either state or county funds. The public defender system, which had its origins in rapidly growing urban areas at the turn of the century, is now in use in 37 percent of all counties, including many of the most heavily populated urban areas (Criminal Defense for the Poor, 1988). Public defender systems are comprised of centrally staffed and administered offices, whose salaried attorneys represent all or most defendants deemed indigent.

Recently a small but growing number of jurisdictions began to contract with private practitioners or firms to provide this service. The administration of contract systems varies considerably, but in its simplest and perhaps most common form, contracting involves bidding by private attorneys and law firms for representation of all criminal defendants found indigent during the term of the contract, in return for a fixed payment. The use of contracting for indigent defense, as for other state and local services, has grown considerably over the past decade, and there is reason to believe it will become a more rather than less popular option for implementing the Supreme Court's mandate.[4]

While the best means of providing counsel for the poor has been a matter of debate within the bar and among academics for many years, contracting has become the object of political and professional controversy. The American Bar Association and the National Legal Aid and Defender Association have both debated the merits of this increasingly popular alternative to traditional programs (Lefstein, 1982; Moran, 1982), and several national studies of indigent defense have recently been completed (Criminal Defense for the Poor, 1988; Spangenberg et al., 1986a; Spangenberg et al., 1986b). Concerns about the quality and accountability of contract programs have been added to a longstanding agenda of issues including the competing merits of state and county administration and funding, the relative effectiveness of public defender and assigned counsel programs, and the feasibility of continued local bar involvement in criminal defense during an era of increasing professional specialization. The growing popularity of contracting as an alternative to traditional programs has rekindled professional and academic interest in understanding and evaluating alternative means of representing the poor.

The Premises of Privatization

The concept of privatization encompasses a variety of arrangements by which government responsibility for a function is shifted in whole or in part to the private sector. In the United States, privatization typically involves a change in the production rather than in the provision of a service or product: while government continues to *provide* a service or product by arranging for its production—by ensuring that specified members of society in fact receive the service or product—responsibility for *production* is turned over to the private sector (Kolderie, 1986; Morgan and England, 1988)[5] The most common form of privatization in this country is contracting, whereby government retains responsibility for defining the service to be offered and the population to be served, as well as for selecting producers of that service, and arranges through written contract with private individuals or firms for the actual production of the service.

Privatization in general, and contracting in particular, have become increasingly popular means of performing public functions at the state and local level in the wake of diminishing federal support for subnational government, increasing agitation for taxpayer relief, and a consequent drive to cut unnecessary programs and reduce the costs of mandated functions (Donahue, 1989; Poole and Fixler, 1987).[6] In some cases privatization has been adopted as a corrective to perceived public management problems. In corrections, for example, privatization has been endorsed as a solution to a host of administrative problems, including overcrowding, failure of rehabilitation programs, and the rising costs of liability for inmate and employee safety (Robbins, 1986). Moreover, privatization, especially contracting, is seen as a means of imposing some predictability and stability on program costs, an especially important concern in local governments that are unprepared to absorb unexpected budget overruns (Houlden and Balkin, 1985b). More generally, the use of private entrepreneurs has been seen as a promising alternative to the pathologies of bureaucracies—organizational and procedural rigidity, excessive regulation, self-protective civil service systems, and the absence of internal and external incentives to operate innovatively and efficiently (Savas, 1987).

Proponents argue that contracting produces three important and related improvements in service production.[7] First, contracted service production is thought to be more efficient than public production because competition for contracts motivates all would-be producers to bid at a price that represents minimum production costs and profit; in contrast, public agencies have few incentives to conserve resources. Second, privatization is thought to induce more flexibility in production compared with rule-bound public agencies, contractors are better situated to take advantage of economies of scale and production innovations, staying competitive by simultaneously improving service quality and minimizing costs. Third, under some conditions private producers are exempt from regulations that govern public agencies, and therefore may expeditiously secure resources and bypass costly reporting and accounting procedures (Salamon, 1989).

Of course, since the assigned counsel and public defender alternatives do not neatly correspond to classic bureaucratic organization, the virtues of flexibility, minimal regulation, and efficiency may not exclusively characterize contractual service provision of indigent defense. Assigned counsel systems are typically quite decentralized, and may be flexible, innovative, and efficient.[8] Public defender offices more closely approximate bureaucracies in that they are vulnerable to rigidity and routinization (Sudnow, 1965). However, public defender offices differ from classic bureaucracies insofar as they are only loosely hierarchical and are staffed by attorneys who, unlike many other public servants, are socialized to see themselves as autonomous professionals. Furthermore, despite negative images and reports of client distrust (e.g., Casper, 1972), some public defender offices are characterized by strong advocacy cultures (McIntyre, 1987; Bohne, 1978; Eisenstein and Jacob, 1977: Ch. 6).

The extent to which improvements over traditional public service provision are actually realized in the privatization of any particular function is a matter for empirical analysis, not mere speculation, and many agree that there has been far too little empirical research supporting these claims. Even the most committed advocates of privatization concede that it is not an appropriate alternative to public production for all services (Savas, 1987), although there exists some disagreement about the conditions that favor privatization. Chamberlin and Jackson suggest that privatization is appropriate

> . . . when purchases are frequent, information is abundant, the costs of a bad decision are small, externalities are minimal, and competition is the norm. . . . At the other extreme . . . where externalities and collective interests abound, natural monopolies are dominant, distributional goals are important, or debate and experience will alter preferences, then governmental determinations of service levels and public provision should continue. (1987: 604)

In other words, when there exists (1) ongoing competition among producers, (2) the opportunity for informed and repeated choices among producers, and (3) consensus on the specific characteristics and benefits of the service, contracting is an acceptable and often desirable substitute for public production. To what extent do these conditions hold for the market of indigent defense services?[9]

Characteristics of the Market: Competition

The bars of many jurisdictions include enough attorneys to generate competition for indigent defense contracts, but in some small communities there may be only a few attorneys specializing in criminal defense, and of these only a handful willing to combine their civil practices with a substantial number of criminal cases. Because criminal law is not a lucrative subspecialty and defense work is more psychologically and emotionally taxing than many other fields, meaningful competition for indigent defense contracts may exist only in jurisdictions whose bars are sufficiently diverse and specialized to generate competition among general practitioners and criminal defense specialists (see Meeker et al., 1989). Paradoxically, contracting appears to be most appealing in jurisdictions with few lawyers willing or able to handle poverty cases and too few cases to justify a public defender office. Not surprisingly, contracting has been adopted most widely in western states with small and scattered populations (Criminal Defense for the Poor, 1988), perhaps in part because the political culture of western states is more receptive to entrusting public functions to the private market (Donahue, 1989; Poole and Fixler, 1987).

Characteristics of Selection Process

The appropriateness of the contract alternative for indigent defense also hinges on characteristics of the producer selection process: specifically, the degree of rationality with which a choice can be made and, if the selecting agent is not also the consumer or beneficiary of the product, the closeness of communication between decision makers and actual consumers regarding product quality. Of course, the ideal conditions for rational selection involve full information about the likely quality and costs of services offered by each bidder; consequently, in the absence of reliable predictions about quality, the process of decision making is presumably improved by the opportunity to review (or repeat) the decision process frequently.[10]

The policy environment for indigent defense departs from these conditions in several ways, largely because attorney performance is difficult to evaluate and because there is little communication between implementors and consumers regarding service quality. In the first place, except at the point of contract renewal, policy implementors (typically county commissioners and judges) can make only prospective judgments about the quality of bidders' work. While the quality of an attorney's performance in private practice can be evaluated indirectly and informally by reputation and observation, these evaluations are usually based on work performed by the attorney under a set of economic incentives quite different from those prevailing under a contract arrangement.[11]

Even if implementors were capable of overseeing and evaluating contract attorneys, they would find little consensus among professionals regarding the differences between exemplary, acceptable, and marginally adequate representation. While in some policy areas the work of would-be contractors can be readily evaluated by informed experts following established professional standards (the work of civil engineers, for example), even the Supreme Court agrees that evaluating the quality of counsel is difficult, and it has generally avoided the issue in claims of defective assistance of counsel (see *United States vs. Cronic*, 104 Supreme Court 2039 (1984) and *Strickland vs. Washington*, 104 Supreme Court 2052 (1984)). Moreover, implementors' ideas about desirable characteristics may conflict. Contracts for indigent defense are made by elected commissioners, often with the advice of local trial judges and sometimes even prosecutors. Commissioners may be primarily concerned with minimizing expenditures, judges may prefer attorneys who will heed the court's crowded calendars, and prosecutors may lobby for contractors with whom they can build comfortable working relationships. Moreover, the constituents represented by these actors, although probably generally indifferent or ignorant, may agree that they do not want to pay for zealous defense of accused criminals.

Those for whom the quality of counsel is most important, of course, have no voice in the selection process. While in some policy areas beneficiaries of contracted services are able to express their satisfaction or dismay with services, such as garbage collection or the provision of school lunches, the consumers of indigent defense have little voice in selecting or assessing the representation they receive in criminal court. Policy officials' fiscal concerns are effectively balanced by consumer reactions when consumers are also taxpayers and voters; a county commission that tries to save money by contracting with inexperienced or incompetent garbage collectors, for example, will soon learn of its mistake. But implementors feel little political pressure to award bids for representing accused criminals to the attorney or firm offering the highest quality service at a reasonable price, and accused criminals, especially poor ones, do not constitute an important segment of most office-holders' constituencies.[12]

Finally, while frequent evaluation and review of contractors' performance may be desirable in theory, one of the often cited drawbacks of contracting is that it introduces the possibility of service interruption and discontinuity as contracts are renegotiated or awarded to new producers (Morgan and England, 1988). From the point of view of funding authorities, contracts for indigent defense can be made no more frequently than once a year; indeed, given the backlogs in many criminal courts and the complex and prolonged nature of criminal defense work, there are sound ethical and professional reasons for preferring multi-year contracts to single-year agreements. However, long-term agreements may compromise the efficiency and cost effectiveness of contracting by reducing lawyers' incentives to process cases quickly.

Characteristics of the Product: The Defense Attorney's Role

Contracting may be desirable when there is little ambiguity about the nature of the service to be contracted, but professionals do not always concur on the proper role of the criminal defense attorney. Some see the defense lawyer as little more than a check against prosecutorial exploitation in the plea bargaining process (see McConville and Mirsky, 1989);[13] others point out that defense counsel's failure to assume more vigorous roles is a flaw in what should be a more adversarial system (Alschuler, 1975). At a minimum, defense lawyers are professionally obligated to safeguard basic due process rights; therefore, counsel may be expected to not only render advice but also consider all reasonable legal defenses for their clients.

Others argue further that lawyers defending the poor should not only effectively represent individual clients, but should also pursue thorough litigation policy reforms that would benefit the poor as a class, sometimes noting that other public officials in the courts, including prosecutors and attorneys general, are expected to initiate or pursue policy change through litigation (Carlin et al., 1966; Sykes, 1969; Bohne, 1978).[14] Some advocate the establishment of public defender offices for this purpose, reasoning that an institutionalized "repeat player" free of competing obligations is better able to protect the specific and general interests of indigents accused of crime (see Houlden and Balkin, 1985b; National Advisory Commission on Criminal Justice Standards and Goals, 1973). Clearly these alternative roles demand different amounts of time, skill, effort, and perhaps idealism in the provision of legal representation. Therefore, evaluating the quality, or effectiveness, of contract programs is complicated by the lack of agreement on exactly what kinds of services participating lawyers should provide.

Contracting may be less than ideal for functions that incorporate social objectives other than specific products or services, since such objectives (which may have few vocal constituents) may be sacrificed to visible and politically popular goals such as minimizing public expenditures (Chamberlin and Jackson, 1987). Morgan and England point out that the cost savings that may be possible through contracting must be balanced against other, less tangible values: "Efficiency remains a laudable goal,

but not to the exclusion of other equally fundamental principles—
constitutional protections, equity, citizenship, and community"
(1988:986). Some argue that contracting of functions such as corrections
represents a threat to civil rights because unlike government agents,
contractors performing government functions are not clearly bound to
constitutional restrictions on state actions toward individuals (Sullivan,
1987). Of course, because canons of ethics guide the actions of attorneys
regardless of the financial terms of their relationship, there is no *prima
facie* reason to presume that contract systems for indigent defense are
any more or less protective of constitutional rights than any other
arrangement, including representation of fee-paying clients.[15] Moreover,
contracting, in theory at least, should present no threat to the equity
of program administration provided that clear definitions of eligibility
are established and overseen by government.

A more subtle trade off is suggested by what Morgan and England call
the "second face" of privatization: the diminished conception of
community responsibility for public functions that accompanies
delegation of public functions to private organizations (1988). While
Morgan and England focus on supplementing more than on substituting
public producers with private ones (as exemplified in the trend toward
employment of private security companies to accomplish ends that are
in fact the formal responsibility of public law enforcement), their general
argument regarding the value of maintaining some functions as public
or collective responsibilities may apply to indigent defense. The relevant
public, in this case, is the bar rather than the general citizenry. Contract
systems relieve private attorneys of what would otherwise be their
periodic ethical obligation to represent the poor. As a profession, the
bar seeks responsibility for its own regulation and quality control; but
the concentration of indigent defense work in the offices of only one
or a handful of attorneys reduces the bar's involvement in, and hence
commitment to, monitoring this work. That this concern is real rather
than merely rhetorical is evidenced by the task forces and commissions
created at national and state levels to study the contracting option and
to develop guidelines and regulations governing its use.[16]

In sum, the premises of privatization are not altogether consistent with
the function of criminal representation of the poor, although it must be
remembered that some of the potential problems with contracting might
be identified just as readily with assigned counsel or public defender
programs. The following section addresses some of the specific pitfalls
of privatization as they apply to indigent defense contracts, with a view
toward developing a research agenda that would not only examine the
claims of contracting advocates, but would also specify the conditions
under which contracting is most compatible with the needs of the poor
and the ethics of the legal profession. In particular, the following section

discusses, first, the need to carefully evaluate claims that contracting is inherently more efficient than other forms of service production, and second, the difficulties of maintaining the accountability of contract attorneys.

The Promises and Pitfalls of Privatization

The Efficiency Assumption. There have been few studies that model the decision to privatize at the local level, but those that exist unsurprisingly reveal that policy makers are most likely to privatize under conditions of fiscal strain (see Ferris, 1987; Worden and Worden, 1989).[17] This suggests that privatization may result from public officials' concern with program efficiency (Morgan and England, 1988; Dunleavy, 1986; Wilson, 1988). Contracting potentially offers a superior means of reducing and capping the costs of indigent defense. The costs of traditional assigned counsel systems can be only imperfectly predicted, since caseloads fluctuate, lawyers vary in the time they are willing to spend on indigent defendants, and in small jurisdictions one or two major felony cases can dramatically increase annual program costs. Public defender systems operate like any other government agency: they typically submit budget requests for annual allocations based on estimates of their workload over the upcoming year. However, because contract systems often provide for lump sum payments in return for representation of all or a specified proportion of indigent defendants, in theory they permit officials to precisely predict program costs even without knowing what the year's caseload will bring.

But there is reason to question whether contracting lives up to its promise of efficiency. The efficiency of contracting may be compromised by price-fixing and collusion among apparent competitors, as well as by the inadvertent creation of private monopolies as losing bidders drift out of the market of potential suppliers leaving providers dependent upon the original contractor (Morgan and England, 1988; McEntee, 1985; Kolderie, 1986). There is little danger of this occurring when the market of suppliers includes a large number of approximately equivalent bidders who will continue to conduct private business if they fail to receive government contracts. When the government is the major or sole purchaser of the service in question, however, the successful bidder may have little or no competition when the contract comes up for renewal.

In some jurisdictions these problematic conditions may obtain for criminal defense work. In most courts at least half, and sometimes virtually all, felony defendants are found eligible for court-appointed counsel.[18] As more lawyers choose to specialize rather than maintain general practices, fewer attorneys will be interested in (or capable of) sustaining criminal practices to serve the small number of non-indigent criminal defendants who seek counsel. Informal agreements among bidders is also more likely when few wish to compete for the contract; and just as fees for privately retained counsel are established by local norms, expectations about the going rate for advising the indigent may be established over several bidding cycles. Therefore, although competitive bidding may in fact reduce service production costs, the conditions that permit competition do not exist (or cannot be sustained) in all jurisdictions.

Discerning whether or not contracting represents an *improvement* in program efficiency is also complicated by the difficulty of accurately estimating comparability and program costs. Across jurisdictions or within jurisdictions where only a portion of indigent defense work is contracted, the comparability between cases represented by the contractor and cases represented by assigned counsel or public defenders must be assessed, lest the work for which costs are compared in fact represent systematically different degrees of difficulty or seriousness.[19] Moreover, reported expenditures for different program types may underestimate the true costs of functions turned over to the private sector (Kolderie, 1986; McEntee, 1985). The costs of administrative oversight, record-keeping, client screening, and program monitoring are seldom included in estimates of assigned counsel or contract program costs because in many jurisdictions these functions are performed by regular court staff or are not performed at all (Houlden and Balkin, 1985b), although they are included in the program budgets of public defender programs.

Maintaining Accountability and Program Monitoring

Contracting also raises potential problems of accountability (Moe, 1987). As James Gentry points out,

> A particular sort of market failure occurs when the purchaser of a good is unable to observe its consumption. In such a case, the purchaser cannot accurately gauge the quantity and quality of the good delivered. The supplier may therefore provide to the consumer less than was purchased and retain the residual without fearing sanctions from the unwitting buyer. (1986:356)

In the case of indigent defense, consumption of the good delivered is not only difficult to observe—it is largely concealed by the lawyer-client privilege. Moreover, the lines of accountability between policy implementors and service producers is quite attenuated. After all, county (and state) officials are the involuntary implementors of an indigent defense policy promulgated by the Supreme Court, and as such their motivation to ensure effective implementation of indigent defense may be shaped by concerns other than a commitment to the policy itself (Johnson and Canon, 1984).

As is the case with many policies designed to benefit the poor, few community leaders advocate greater expenditures for better representation of indigent criminal defendants. Indeed, one might reasonably hypothesize that even those community organizations that monitor the effectiveness and equity of programs designed to benefit the poor invest few resources in lobbying for better provision of legal assistance to accused criminals. Therefore, efficiency (defined as minimum cost per case) may be pursued at the expense of quality or comprehensiveness of service.

The problem of maintaining accountability (ensuring the delivery of an acceptable level of service) is further complicated by the difficulty of monitoring attorney performance. The danger in contracting indigent defense, of course, is that having secured the contract, attorneys may invest minimal effort in indigent clients in order to maximize time invested in fee-paying clients. A possible solution to this problem is careful structuring of provider incentives in the contract-writing stage (Sullivan, 1987; Donahue, 1989). Separate budget lines could be established for attorney fees and associated investigative expenses, to encourage more assiduous investment in pretrial preparation. Attorneys could be required to demonstrate a commitment to (and experience in) criminal defense work prior to seeking the contract, and secondary defense systems could be established to accommodate cases with multiple defendants. Maximum caseloads could be established to allow bidders to more accurately estimate their expected costs. Agreements could be struck only with attorneys who establish non-profit organizations. However, many and probably most contracts for indigent defense contain no such provisions. Contracts typically do not reimburse attorneys in proportion to their actual investment in cases, but instead specify a lump sum for a certain number of cases, a term during which the attorney is responsible for all defendants found indigent, or a fixed amount per case.

Of course, carefully structured contracts may raise the costs of representation above that generated by a simple lump-sum low-bid process, and they potentially pose some of the same difficulties generated by assigned counsel systems (for instance, caps on caseloads require counties to provide for the possibility that these caps will be exceeded, and that additional resources will be needed to accommodate the overflow). However, these conditions do permit an indirect form of accountability, by structuring the bidding decisions of participating attorneys and, further, by minimizing the disincentives to provide careful and effective representation.

Toward a Systematic Evaluation of Alternatives

Despite its significance for defendants and for the bar (or perhaps because of it) debate over alternative means of representing the poor has sometimes been shaped by ideology and self interest. Advocates of privatization as well as policy implementors often merely assume the relative efficiency of contracting, questioning neither the actual prospects for cost savings nor the fate of equally important goals, such as program effectiveness and equity, under a contract arrangement. On the other hand, members of the bar may view contracting, as they have sometimes viewed public defenders, as a threat to private practice, particularly in urban areas where some attorneys build substantial practices on court assignments (McConville and Mirsky, 1989; Blumberg, 1967).

While indigent defense is not a policy problem for which contracting is indisputably a superior alternative, that is not to say that a carefully structured contract program would not provide equal or better representation (at reasonable cost) in many communities now served by other program forms. There is, at any rate, little doubt that a growing number of jurisdictions will experiment with this alternative, rendering further research on the actual operation of these programs imperative. Despite the large number of studies conducted over the past three decades, we still cannot conclude with certainty that either the public defender or the assigned counsel programs are superior; so few studies have examined contract programs that their claimed benefits and drawbacks must be considered speculative rather than known. The final section of this article considers some of the conceptual and methodological issues confronting researchers working in this area and offers some specific suggestions for future analyses.

Measurement Issues: Efficiency, Effectiveness, and Equity

Some of the issues associated with measuring program efficiency or cost effectiveness have already been discussed. For example, researchers should be careful to include all relevant costs for any program, and should ensure that programs under comparison are in fact responsible for similar types of work. Moreover, because efficiency is typically measured as cost per case (e.g., Grier, 1971; Spangenberg, 1986b), care should be taken to ensure that the number of cases processed accurately reflects the number of defendants eligible for representation in each jurisdiction studied. Anecdotal evidence suggests that eligibility for free counsel is sometimes determined by the amount of money left in program budgets rather than by actual need for the service; while on the other hand, assigned counsel programs that appear extremely efficient may in fact be programs that exhaust their budgets before the end of the fiscal year and rely thereafter on the *pro bono* representation of private counsel.

Extant studies illustrate the importance of careful attention to differences within as well as across program types. Public defender programs appear to be less expensive per case than assigned counsel systems (Grier, 1971; Cohen et al., 1983; Singer and Lynch, 1983). While some of the few studies that compare contract with assigned counsel or public defender programs find no differences in costs per case (Worden and Worden, 1989; Lefstein, 1982), other studies have found that the efficiency of contract systems depends on program characteristics. Houlden and Balkin found, for example, that contract attorneys operated more efficiently than did assigned counsel on a per-case basis, but that was because the former spend much less time with indigent clients. The two programs' costs per attorney hour were almost identical (1985b). (Of course, an alternative conception of efficiency could explain this finding: perhaps contract attorneys' expertise and experience in criminal law, and their familiarity with other criminal court actors, permits them to handle cases more expeditiously than assigned counsel, who may seldom practice criminal law outside of court appointments.) A study of programs operating in Michigan counties found that while overall contract programs' costs per case were little different from those of other program types, whether or not contracts were competitively bid made a very important difference in costs. Competitively bid contracts were much less expensive and non-bid programs much more expensive than either assigned counsel or public defender programs (Worden, 1990).

Evaluating program effectiveness or quality has proven even more problematic than assessing program costs. Evaluation requires not only the establishment of a baseline for comparison but also determination of appropriate measures of attorney performance. The comparative studies of indigent defense programs that have appeared in academic journals over the past twenty years represent a range of judgments about the proper baseline for evaluation of program quality. Many studies draw direct comparisons between attorneys handling indigent cases (whether as private counsel assigned by the court, or as public defenders) and privately retained counsel (e.g., Gitelman, 1971; Stover and Eckart, 1975; Wheeler and Wheeler, 1980), while others simply compare alternative means of representing indigents (e.g., Clarke and Kurtz, 1983; Grier, 1971; Benjamin and Pedeleski, 1969). Still others, perhaps by virtue of access to more diverse jurisdictions, attempt comparisons of more than one indigent defense program with privately retained counsel (Flemming, 1986; Houlden and Balkin, 1985a; 1985b; Hermann, et al., 1977; Levine, 1975; Casper 1972; Taylor et al., 1972). While some suggest that it is not altogether reasonable to compare indigent defense programs with the representation provided by the private bar (Houlden and Balkin, 1985b), in fact most such comparisons reveal only slight differences in performance measures. As a baseline for evaluation, the performance of privately retained attorneys may provide an ethically sound starting point; after all, it is difficult to make a normative or ethical argument that accepts or condones representation of a significantly different caliber for fee-paying and indigent defendants. So perhaps research should be directed toward discerning the nature and extent of differences between the representation provided to the poor and that provided to fee-paying clients.

An alternative, of course, is to formulate standards independent of empirically established reference points. Cavender, for example, focused his comparison of private attorneys and public defenders on the American Bar Association's standards regarding effective representation at sentencing (1987). These standards state specific responsibilities for defense attorneys, including the explanation of sentencing alternatives, discussion of rehabilitative sentencing, and review of pre-sentence investigations and recommendations (American Bar Association, 1971). As guidelines for effective representation are further developed at both the national and state levels (and particularly as guidelines for contract systems are articulated), these standards might be used as practical operationalizations of effective counsel.

Regardless of the nature of their comparisons, most researchers have focused on one or more of three overlapping conceptualizations of effectiveness of counsel: process measures, outcome measures, or attorney-client relationship measures. Process measures assess the number of formal opportunities taken by an attorney to defend his or her client's case, as well as the investment of effort made in developing the case. They include, for example, the frequency of appearances, number of motions filed, and number of days taken to dispose of cases (Luskin and Luskin, 1987; Flemming, 1986; Houlden and Balkin, 1985a; 1985b), as well as the time spent on investigation and research (Lefstein, 1982; Levine, 1975). In the few studies that have employed these measures only small differences have emerged among program and attorney types, (Luskin and Luskin, 1987; Houlden and Balkin, 1985a; 1985b; Levine, 1975), although there is suggestive evidence that contract attorneys invest less effort in formal pre-trial proceedings (Flemming, 1986) and in investigation (Lefstein, 1982).

These measures must be used with caution. While some are no doubt valid indicators of effective representation (e.g., effort invested in investigation and research) others may not be. For example, despite constitutional guarantees of speedy trial, lengthy delays between arrest and final disposition may be in a defendant's best interests if such delays in fact represent strategic efforts to weaken a prosecutor's case;[20] while in some courts, under some circumstances, insisting on preliminary hearings may be a misguided violation of local norms.

Outcome measures assess performance in terms of dispositions and sentences, and include mode of disposition (guilty plea or trial), frequency of dismissals, and frequency of acquittals, as well as measures of sentence severity. While some early studies found that attorney type was related to differences in dispositions and sentences (Benjamin and Pedeleski, 1969; Summer, 1969; Gitelman, 1981; Cohen et al., 1983), most studies that control for defendant and case characteristics have uncovered few differences between privately retained attorneys and public defenders (Sterling, 1983; Nardulli, 1986; Stover and Eckart, 1975; Wheeler and Wheeler, 1980; Flemming, 1986; Taylor, et al., 1972). Some studies suggest, however, that public defenders secure more dismissals than assigned counsel, but that their clients suffer more severe sentences (Clarke and Kurtz, 1983; Cohen et al., 1983). There are too few studies of contract systems to permit generalization about their relative effectiveness (see Houlden and Balkin, 1985b).[21]

Dispositional characteristics appeal to researchers because they are readily available in public records. However, some of these variables, such as acquittal rate, vary little across jurisdictions. Furthermore, outcomes reflect numerous contextual influences which must be controlled to isolate the effects, if any, of type of counsel. For example, variation in guilty plea rates across clients in different programs may tell us more about prosecutors' policies than about defense lawyers' skills (Flemming, 1990). Sentence severity may reflect attorney effectiveness only under some conditions where, for example, sentence negotiation is not constrained by sentencing guidelines or probation officers' recommendations. Thus these measures should be employed with caution and only in studies of sufficient scope to ensure that contextual variables are controlled.

More generally, these measures tend to presume that the quality of counsel rests largely in the ability to get clients off—through acquittal or lenient sentencing—but a broader view of advocacy embraces activities designed to preserve or establish a place for clients in their communities. Additional potentially useful measures would include the frequency with which attorneys secure constructive and rehabilitative outcomes such as diversion and first offender treatment, or, in less serious cases, the frequency with which attorneys propose restitution as a means of restoring defendant-victim relationships.

Attorney-client relationship variables include some of the measures used by Cavender (1987), such as attorneys' explanation of sentencing alternatives and time spent with clients (Levine, 1975; Stover and Eckart, 1975), as well as client perceptions of attorney competence (Casper, 1972; Hermann et al., 1977). Although they have been few in number, studies of defendant attitudes suggest that clients of publicly paid attorneys, particularly of public defenders, are less trustful, cooperative, and deferential than are clients of privately retained lawyers (Casper, 1972; Hermann et al., 1977; and see Flemming, 1986; but see also Atkins and Boyle, 1976). Given that indigent defendants are of course represented by publicly rather than privately *paid* counsel, the important research and policy questions are first, whether or not this distrust compromises effective representation, and second, whether some indigent defense programs engender better client-attorney relationships than others. For example, Casper's finding that indigent defendants were less trusting of public defenders than of counsel employed in a private non-profit (albeit publicly funded) office suggests that the more attenuated the apparent relationship between court authorities and counsel, the more confidence clients feel in their lawyers' independence (19____). If this observation is generalizable, with all other things being equal, contract programs may engender more satisfied clients than traditional public defender offices.

Future research should be directed toward two goals in developing measures of effectiveness of counsel. First, research should explore the relationships among the measures already in use in order to determine whether there exist patterns or clusters of behaviors that define the boundaries between effective and ineffective counsel. Extant studies typically compare alternative program types across several of the variables mentioned above, but fail to examine the possibility that correlations among these measures might permit the building of scales and indices that constitute more sensitive gauges of effectiveness.[22]

Second, for the purpose of comparing program types (and in particular, for the purpose of comparing variations on the contract system), institutional or programmatic characteristics should be employed as indirect indicators of effectiveness. Some such characteristics are informal; for example, it has long been conventional wisdom that some of the strengths of public defender programs are the informal socialization and training that new attorneys receive in such offices, and the pooled experience and resources that can be brought to each new case (McIntyre, 1987; Hermann et al., 1975). Institutional subcultures of this sort may develop in contracting attorneys' offices as well (see Eisenstein et al., 1987). On the other hand, much has been written about the institutional defects of centralized programs that process defendants in an assembly-line fashion (Gilboy and Schmidt, 1979; Gilboy, 1981), and the dangers of organizational cooptation by powerful judges and prosecutors (Sudnow, 1965; but see Battle, 1973). Other indicators of institutional effectiveness are formal and may even appear in contracts themselves. For example, contracts (as well as assigned counsel and public defender systems) that set aside part of program budgets for investigatory expenses, training, or secondary systems (to handle conflict cases or overloads) increase incentives to conduct thorough defenses, but programs lacking such features create incentives to provide minimal defense. Examination of these institutional characteristics might better illuminate dimensions of effectiveness that are overlooked in individual level studies of attorney performance.

These issues speak indirectly to a final normative concern, program equity. Indigent defense programs are equitable to the extent that they offer services of similar quality to defendants who are similarly situated financially. Very little research has been conducted on variation in eligibility guidelines across jurisdictions (for one example, see Spangenberg et al., 1986b). Some of this work relies on statutory definitions that may have little operational meaning. Research is needed on formal and informal means of determining eligibility, and on their comparability across jurisdictions within states. Furthermore, equitable programs must provide representation of equivalent quality to co-defendants, an increasingly common problem as narcotics offenses assume a larger share of the criminal justice system's caseload. Viewed from another angle, indigent defense systems are equitable to the extent that they provide approximately equal compensation to attorneys charged with representing the poor. Because representing the poor is an ethical obligation that often takes time away from attorneys' private practices, fairness requires that this burden be distributed evenly among members of the legal profession.

Research Design Issues

Studies of indigent defense systems have been handicapped by a variety of data collection and methodological problems that may account in part for the difficulty of drawing conclusions from these studies. The problem of comparability across jurisdictions, especially when those jurisdictions are in different states, plagues all criminal court research. Indigent defense programs that are not state organized and administered may be organized by county or circuit, or may include multiple circuits, and counties may opt to use different program forms for misdemeanor and felony courts.

Moreover, information about locally administered indigent defense programs is seldom available in central locations such as state archives or even state bar associations. The result of this fragmentation of information is that multi-jurisdictional studies—studies that permit not only comparison of two or three programs, but also the rigorous testing of hypotheses about the consequences of variation in program form— are very difficult to execute in many states. Case study comparisons have generated interesting and important hypotheses about how (and to some extent, why) programs differ, but more extensive studies are needed to test these predictions. In particular, studies that examine differences between types of contracts, different ways of organizing public defender offices, and varying degrees of centralization in assigned counsel systems may tell us a great deal about the best ways to design these programs (e.g., Houlden and Balkin, 1985b).

Furthermore, as previously noted many studies, even those that rely upon coded data from case records, fail to control for important defendant and case attributes, despite evidence from many courts that factors such as bail status, offense seriousness, and prior record—factors that may be correlated with defendants' socioeconomic status—are strong predictors of outcomes (Spohn et al., 1981). Failure to control for these factors may produce a distorted picture of the differences between various indigent defense programs and privately retained counsel.

Finally, studies that have commendably sought to assess variation in soft but significant measures of effectiveness such as attorney-client relationships have relied more heavily on the attorney than on the client (e.g., Levine, 1975; Cavender, 1987), while some studies of client evaluations suffer from sample selection bias, insofar as only convicted defendants are interviewed (e.g., Atkins and Boyle, 1976). Defendants' reports may prove more reliable indicators or actual practices than formal rules or even attorneys' recollections, so future research should not only incorporate measures of defendant perceptions when possible, but should also seek validation of attorneys' self-reports by eliciting evaluations of specific instances of performance from their colleagues, from prosecutors, and from the bench.

Conclusions

This article begins and ends with the modest objective of stimulating reconsideration of the ways in which we evaluate indigent defense in trial courts. As contracting becomes an increasingly common but controversial means of representing the poor accused of crimes, a systematic consideration of the premises and problems of contracting, as well as a thoughtful reconsideration of traditional assigned counsel and public defender systems, is in order. One might reasonably conclude from this discussion that no system is inherently preferable to all others, but rather, that some program features may be desirable accompaniments to one or more program types. Moreover, it is sensible to assume that some means of providing representation are better suited for some types of jurisdictions than for others; for example, a full-time public defender office is ill-suited for a sparsely populated and isolated rural county, while assigned counsel systems may be an inadequate option in communities with few criminal defense practitioners.

One need not conclude, as some have, that contracting is an inherently flawed means of ensuring that the poor are represented in criminal court; indeed, under some conditions contracting may produce higher quality representation than do other systems. However, policy makers' interest in the contracting alternative is motivated by efficiency concerns rather than by the professional standards of bench and bar, and contracting tends to shift responsibility and accountability for effective indigent representation away from the legal profession into the hands of a few private practitioners. The chief danger in the move toward contracting, then, is that efficiency considerations will assume overriding importance in the eyes of elected officials who must design and fund local indigent defense programs and that consequently effectiveness and equity will be sacrificed. The traditional refuge of defendants deprived of adequate counsel is the appellate process, and some state courts have expressed willingness to scrutinize the operations and incentives inherent in simple contract systems (e.g., *Smith v. State of Arizona*, 140 Arizona 355, 1984). But the appellate process should serve only as an occasional check on the errors of policy makers, not as an intrusive corrective. Policy implementors and the legal profession, as well as indigent defendants, are best served by careful consideration of the potential and limitations of alternative means of representation, and by choices based on judgment balanced by efficiency and due process values.

Endnotes

[1] Estimates of felony indigency rates vary considerably, from a low of about 48 percent (Spangenberg et al., 1986) and rising rapidly (Criminal Defense for the Poor, 1988) to 60 percent (Moran, 1982; Gilboy, 1981), to 90 percent in some Michigan counties (Worden, 1990).

[2] The focus of this article is on programs that are primarily county-administered and county-funded; a host of other issues attend programs that are centrally administered and funded, although many of the issues raised in this article are germane to arguments for and against centralization of program administration.

[3] Although the U.S. Supreme Court has stated unambiguously that states must provide counsel to indigents accused of crimes (*Gideon v. Wainwright*, 372 U.S. 335; *Argersinger v. Hamlin*, 407 U.S. 25, 1972), the Court has not specified how such services are to be provided, nor what constitutes indigency for purposes of receiving free counsel; consequently, states have devised various systems and rules for organizing and funding indigent defense programs. In most states indigent defense at the trial

court level is statutorily delegated to county governments. In 33 states indigent defense services are organized wholly or partly at the county or judicial circuit level, and in 24 states funding for indigent defense programs is derived completely or primarily from county rather than state budgets (Criminal Defense for the Poor, 1988).

⁴ In 1982 fewer than 7 percent of all counties had contract programs; by 1986 over 11 percent did (Criminal Defense for the Poor, 1988). It is important to note that jurisdictions employing public defenders are disproportionately urban, and hence a majority of indigent criminal defendants in the U.S. are in fact represented by public defenders rather than assigned counsel or contract attorneys.

⁵ The distinction between provision and production has been a source of confusion among critics and advocates of privatization. Kolderie distinguishes between these two functions: a service is "publicly or socially provided (a) where the decision whether to have it (and the decisions about who shall have it and how much of it) is a political decision, (b) when government arranges for the recipients not to have to pay directly for the service themselves, and (c) when the government selects the producer that will service them" (1986:286). Although referring to legal representation as something produced by attorneys is an awkward twist on conventional usage of the term, for the sake of consistency with the privatization literature this distinction will be adopted here.

⁶ The shift toward privatization may have also been accelerated by the increasing reliance at the city and county level on professional managers, whose training and orientation sensitize them to efficiency issues, and who may also be more up-to-date on innovative ways of providing services than local elected officials (Morgan, 1979).

⁷ Some advocates of privatization also argue that privatizing is good for its own sake: these ideological arguments are premised on the notion that less government is better. Often, however, these arguments are applicable to a more complete form of privatization than contracting, viz., to turning over to the private sector both decisions about provision AND production of the service (see Savas, 1987); indeed, outside the United States privatization usually refers to public divestiture of functions that in this country have always been private, such as health care. Because indigent defense is a constitutionally mandated service, this perspective is not relevant to this discussion.

⁸ In a sense, of course, the assigned counsel systems operating in most counties represent an extremely decentralized form of privatization. However, assigned counsel systems are seldom formally limited to a specified subset of the bar (although informally they sometimes are), and an attorney's commitment to representing indigents in criminal matters is ethically and historically grounded more in professional obligations than in financial or business exchanges between the court and members of the bar (McIntyre, 1987). Public defender systems, at least as they operate in most counties, represent pure public production of indigent representation. Only contract systems represent privatization in the conventional sense.

⁹ The following section sets aside, for the moment, the question of whether contracting is better or worse than existing alternatives, evaluating it from the theoretical perspective on optimal and inappropriate conditions for contracting. Subsequent sections consider the ways in which contracting might or might not be superior to assigned counsel and public defender systems, and suggest ways of evaluating the quality of these alternatives.

¹⁰ An alternative to contracting that gives service production consumers more responsibility for producer selection is the voucher system. Voucher systems depend for their success on the ability of consumers or beneficiaries to make informed and thoughtful choices among producers; she who chooses the producer (usually from among a group of pre-approved individuals or firms) will also directly enjoy or suffer the consequences of her decision, and she is therefore motivated to make the best and

perhaps the most economical selection. Consumer choices about some products, such as food, are made frequently, and from among producers whose relative attractions can be readily assessed; for such products or services some form of privatization (such as food stamps) is quite appropriate (Savas, 1987). However, although voucher systems have been suggested for use in indigent criminal defense (Casper, 1972), and have been used to a limited extent by the Legal Services Corporation for the representation of poor people in civil cases, the assumption of informed consumer choice may not hold for legal representation as well as it does for some other services and products (Meeker et al., 1989).

[11] The most common fee arrangement among attorneys is an hourly charge, secured by a retainer. Contract systems typically do not reimburse attorneys in proportion to their actual investment in cases, but instead pay a lump sum for a specified number of cases, or a specified term during which the attorney is responsible for all defendants found indigent, or a fixed amount per case (Spangenberg et al., 1986; Worden, 1990). Clearly the economic incentives produced by these arrangements differ from those characterizing conventional fee agreements.

[12] This phenomenon was documented in a study of Kalamazoo, Michigan's experiences with contract attorneys; the original attorney group was found to be too enthusiastic in defense of the poor, and failed to cooperate to a satisfactory degree with judges and prosecutors. The contract was subsequently awarded to a more amenable group of lawyers at the urging of the local bench (Eisenstein et al., 1987: Chapter 6).

[13] This viewpoint was recently expressed by the director of California's public defender office, who in rejecting the role of a strong due process advocate characterized his office as the loyal opposition (Panel Urges Abolition, 1988).

[14] The argument that poverty lawyers should handle not only routine litigation but impact litigation as well was an important justification for the founding of the predecessor to the Legal Services Corporation during the Johnson administration. The fate of the Corporation over the past ten years illustrates the controversial nature of such reform-oriented programs.

[15] Indeed, there is some reason to suspect that attorneys in private practice, be they assigned counsel or on retainer, are more protective of their clients' interests at the expense of victims than are public defenders, who may identify more strongly with the court (see Ford and Regoli, 1990).

[16] Concern about the importance of the private bar's role in indigent defense at the local level was expressed even prior to *Gideon*; almost thirty years ago an article in the *Stanford Law Review* recommended that local bars play an active role in providing lists of qualified attorneys, supervising their performance, monitoring the funding process to ensure adequate allocations, establishing referral services for the marginally indigent, and providing training and resources to young lawyers interested in taking appointments ("Representation of Indigents in California," 1961; see also Grier, 1971). An active role was also endorsed by the National Advisory Commission on Criminal Justice Standards and Goals (1973). More recently McConville and Mirskey documented the New York City bar's efforts to improve the quality of appointed representation in response to claims of inadequate counsel (1989); Gilboy illustrates the political conflict that may emerge when local bars attempt to actively participate in the appointment process in the face of judges' preferences for particular lawyers (1981). It is also true, of course, that bar association activity sometimes reflects professional self-interest and a desire to monopolize and manage the availability of legal services, and to restrict the legal activities of groups that do not share lawyers' interests (see Kessler, 1986).

[17] While in some cases political resistance to privatization may affect this choice (in the form of public employee union objections; see Ferris, 1987), indigent defense is of

little interest to constituent groups. One might expect to find, however, that the bar takes an interest in the choice to switch from an assigned counsel to a contract system (Worden and Worden, 1989).

[18] It is important to note in this connection that appointment rates may be only weakly correlated with actual indigency rates, since judges and administrators employ widely differing standards of indigency (Lefstein, 1982).

[19] Casper, for example, attributed defendants' preferences for a non-profit legal aid agency over public defenders to a distrust of the latter; but the lighter caseloads of the former might partially account for the better relationships they developed with defendants (1972; see also Levine, 1975; Meeker et al., 1989).

[20] However, for a privately retained attorney delay may be an attempt to ensure that fees are paid before the case is resolved and the client disappears or is incarcerated (Blumberg, 1967). Furthermore, lengthy disposition time may be more or less valuable to a defendant depending on pretrial detention status. A defendant free on bond can maintain social, family, and perhaps work commitments and thus endure fewer hardships as a result of delayed disposition. However, recent research finds little difference in case processing times for publicly paid and privately retained attorneys (Luskin and Luskin, 1987; Flemming et al., 1987); and another study concluded that local legal cultures is the most important determinant of case processing time (Church, 1978). Given the significance of bail status as a predictor of case outcome (Spohn, et al., 1981), a more important measure of effective representation might be attorneys' success in obtaining reasonable bail. An additional important (but often overlooked) procedural factor, one that varies considerably across systems, is the amount of time elapsed between arrest and attorney appointment; defendants deprived of an advocate for several days after arrest may feel overwhelmed by the authority of law enforcement officers and prosecutors.

[21] Further evidence that lawyers make little difference in sentencing is found in sentencing studies that control for attorney type (Talarico, 1979; Uhlman and Walker, 1979; Willison, 1984; but see Spohn et al., 1981).

[22] For example, Casper examined the relationship between defendants' assessments of the fairness of their treatment and dispositional characteristics; and there exists an intriguing body of theoretical research on the dimensions of perceived fairness in court proceedings which could be fruitfully applied to policy problems. (See Casper, 1978; Thibaut and Walker, 1975; Tyler, 1984; Tyler, 1987; Casper et al., 1988; and especially Landis and Goodstein, 1987.)

References

Alschuler, Albert W. (1975) "The Defense Attorney's Role in Plea Bargaining," *Yale Law Journal* 1179.

American Bar Association Project on Standards for Criminal Justice (1971) *Standards Relating to the Prosecuting Function and the Defense Function.* New York: American Bar Association.

Atkins, Burton and E. Boyle (1976) "Prisoner Satisfaction with Defense Counsel," 12 *Criminal Law Bulletin* 427.

Battle, Jackson L. (1973) "Comparison of Public Defenders' and Private Attorneys' Relationships with the Prosecution in the City of Denver," 50 *Denver Law Journal* 101.

Benjamin, Roger W. and Theodore B. Pedeleski (1969) "The Minnesota Public Defender System and the Criminal Law Process," 4 *Law and Society Review* 279.

Blumberg, Abraham (1967) "The Practice of Law as a Confidence Game: Organizational Cooptation of a Profession," 1 *Law and Society Review* 15.

Bohne, Brenda Hart (1978) "The Public Defender as Policy Maker," 62 *Judicature* 176.

Carlin, Jerome E., Jan Howard and Sheldon L. Messenger (1966) "Civil Justice and the Poor: Issues for Sociological Research," 1 *Law and Society Review* 9.

Casper, Jonathan D. (1972) *American Criminal Justice; The Defendant's Perspective.* Englewood Cliffs, NJ: Prentice-Hall.

_____ (1978) "Having Their Day in Court: Defendant Evaluations of the Fairness of Their Treatment," 12 *Law and Society Review* 237.

Casper, Jonathan D., Tom R. Tyler, and Bonnie Fisher (1988) "Procedural Justice in Felony Cases," 22 *Law and Society Review* 483.

Cavender, Gray, Barbara Cable Nienstedt, and Ronald S. Everett (1987) "Effectiveness of Counsel: An Empirical Analysis," 10 *Journal of Crime and Justice* 195.

Chamberlin, John R. and John E. Jackson (1987) "Privatization as Institutional Choice," 6 *Journal of Policy Analysis and Management* 586.

Church, Thomas W., Jr. (1978) *Justice Delayed: The Pace of Litigation in Urban Trial Courts.* Williamsburg, VA: National Center for State Courts.

Clarke, Stevens and G. Kurtz (1983) "The Importance of Interim Decision to Felony Trial Court Dispositions," 74 *Journal of Criminal Law and Criminology* 476.

Cohen, Larry J., Patricia P. Semple, and Robert E. Crew, Jr. (1983) "Assigned Counsel versus the Public Defender: A Comparison of Relative Benefits," in William F. McDonald, editor, *The Defense Counsel.* Beverly Hills: Sage.

Criminal Defense for the Poor 1986 (1988) Washington, DC: Department of Justice, Bureau of Justice Statistics.

Donahue, John D. (1989) *The Privatization Decision.* New York: Basic Books.

Dunleavy, Patrick (1986) "Explaining the Privatization Boom: Public Choice versus Radical Approaches," 64 *Public Administration Review* 13.

Eisenstein, James, Roy B. Flemming, and Peter F. Nardulli (1987) *The Contours of Justice.* Boston: Little-Brown.

Eisenstein, James and Herbert Jacob (1977) *Felony Justice,* Boston: Little-Brown.

Ferris, James M. (1987) "The Decision to Contract Out: An Empirical Analysis," 22 *Urban Affairs Quarterly* 289.

Flemming, Roy B. (1986) "Client Games: Defense Attorney Perspectives on Their Relations with Criminal Clients," 1986 *American Bar Foundation Research Journal* 253.

_____. (1990) "The Political Styles and Organizational Strategies of American Prosecutors: Examples from Nine Courthouse Communities," 12 *Law and Policy* 25.

Flemming, Roy B., Peter Nardulli, and James Eisenstein (1987) "The Timing of Justice in Felony Trial Courts," 9 *Law and Policy* 179.

Ford, David A. and Mary Jean Regoli (1990) "The Effectiveness and Impacts of Defense Counsel in Cases of Wife Battery." Paper presented at the Law and Society Association annual meeting, Berkeley.

Gentry, James Theodore (1986) "The Panopticon Revisited: The Problem of Monitoring Private Prisons," 96 *Yale Law Journal* 353.

Gilboy, Janet (1981) "The Social Organization of Legal Services to Indigent Defendants," 1981 *American Bar Foundation Research Journal* 1023.

Gilboy, Janet A. and John R. Schmidt (1979) "Replacing Lawyers: A Case Study of the Sequential Representation of Criminal Defendants," 70 *Journal of Criminal Law and Criminology* 1.

Gitelman, Morton (1971) "The Relative Importance of Appointed and Retained Counsel in Arkansas Felony Cases—An Empirical Study," 24 *Arkansas Law Review* 442.

Grier, Richard (1971) "Analysis and Comparison of Assigned Counsel and Public Defender Systems," 49 *North Carolina Law Review* 705.

Hermann, Robert, Eric Single, and John Boston (1977) *Counsel for the Poor: Criminal Defense in Urban America* Lexington, MA: Lexington.

Houlden, Pauline and Steven Balkin (1985a) "Costs and Quality of Indigent Defense: Ad Hoc vs. Coordinated Assignment of the Private Bar Within a Mixed System," 10 *Justice System Journal* 159.

—————— (1985b) "Quality and Cost Comparisons of Private Bar Indigent Defense Systems: Contract vs. Ordered Assigned Counsel," 76 *Journal of Criminal Law and Criminology* 176.

Johnson, Charles A. and Bradley C. Canon (1984) *Judicial Policies: Implementation and Impact.* Washington: CQ Press.

Kessler, Mark (1986) "The Politics of Legal Representation: The Influence of Local Politics on the Behavior of Poverty Lawyers," 8 *Law and Policy* 149.

Kolderie, Ted (1986) "The Two Different Concepts of Privatization," 46 *Public Administration Review* 285.

Landis, Jean M. and Lynne Goodstein (1987) "When Is Justice Fair? An Integrated Approach to the Outcome Versus Procedure Debate," 1986 *American Bar Foundation Research Journal* 675.

Lefstein, Norman (1982) *Criminal Defense Services for the Poor.* Chicago: American Bar Association Standing Committee on Legal Aid and Indigent Defense.

Levine, James P. (1975) "The Impact of 'Gideon': The Performance of Public and Private Criminal Defense Lawyers," 8 *Polity* 215.

Luskin, Mary Lee and Robert C. Luskin (1987) "Case Processing Times in Three Courts," 9 *Law and Policy* 207.

McConville, Michael and Chester A. Mirsky (1989) *Criminal Defense of the Poor in New York City.* New York: Center for Research in Crime and Justice, New York University School of Law.

McEntee, Gerald W. (1985) "City Services: Can Free Enterprise Outperform the Public Sector?" 55 *Business and Society Review* 43.

McIntyre, Lisa J. (1987) *The Public Defender: The Practice of Law in the Shadows of Repute.* Chicago: University of Chicago Press.

Meeker, James W., John Dombrink and Beth Quinn (1989) "Competitive Bidding of Legal Services for the Poor: An Analysis of the Scientific Evidence," paper presented at the 1989 meeting of the Law and Society Association, Madison.

Moe, Ronald C. (1987) "Exploring the Limits of Privatization," 47 *Public Administration Review* 453.

Moran, Thomas, ed. (1982) *Gideon Undone: Crisis in Indigent Defense Funding*. Chicago: American Bar Association and the National Legal Aid and Defender Association.

Morgan, David R. (1979) *Managing Urban America*. North Scituate, MA: Duxbury.

Morgan, David R. and Robert E. England (1988) "The Two Faces of Privatization," 48 *Public Administration Review* 979.

Nardulli, Peter F. (1986) "'Insider Justice': Defense Attorneys and the Handling of Felony Cases," 77 *Journal of Criminal Law and Criminology* 379.

National Advisory Commission on Criminal Justice Standards and Goals (1973) *The Courts*. Washington: U.S. Government Printing Office.

"Panel Urges Abolition of California Defender's Office" (1988) 19 *Criminal Justice Newsletter* 5.

Poole, Robert W. Jr. and Philip E. Fixler, Jr. (1987) "Privatization of Public-Sector Services in Practice: Experience and Potential," 6 *Journal of Policy Analysis and Management*.

"Representation of Indigents in California—A Field Study of the Public Defender and Assigned Counsel Systems" (1961) 13 *Stanford Law Review* 522.

Robbins, Ira P. (1986) "Privatization of Corrections: Defining the Issues," 69 *Judicature* 324.

Salamon, Lester M. et al. (1989) *Privatization: The Challenge to Public Management*. Washington: National Academy of Public Administration.

Savas, E. S. (1987) *Privatization: The Key to Better Government*. Chatham: Chatham House.

Singer, Shelvin and Elizabeth Lynch (1983) "Indigent Defense Systems: Characteristics and Costs," in William F. McDonald, editor, *The Defense Counsel*. Beverly Hills: Sage.

Spangenberg, Robert L., Beverly Lee, Michael Battaglia, Patricia Smith, and A. David Davis (1986a) *National Criminal Defense Systems Study*. Washington: U.S. Department of Justice.

Spangenberg, Robert L., Richard L. Wilson, Patricia A. Smith, and Beverly N. W. Lee (1986b) *Containing the Costs of Indigent Defense Programs: Eligibility Screening and Cost Recovery Procedures*. Washington: U.S. Department of Justice.

Spohn, Cassia, John Gruhl, and Susan Welch (1981–82) "The Effect of Race on Sentencing: A Reexamination of an Unsettled Question," 16 *Law and Society Review* 71.

Sterling, Joyce (1983) "Retained Counsel Versus the Public Defender: The Impact of Type of Counsel on Charge Bargaining," in William F. McDonald, editor. *The Defense Counsel*. Beverly Hills: Sage.

Stover, Robert V. and Dennis R. Eckart (1975) "A Systematic Comparison of Public Defenders and Private Attorneys," 3 *American Journal of Criminal Law* 265.

Sudnow, David (1965) "Normal Crimes: Sociological Features of the Penal Code in a Public Defender Office," 12 *Social Problems* 255.

Sullivan, Harold J. (1987) "Privatization of Public Services: A Growing Threat to Constitutional Rights," 47 *Public Administration Review* 461.

Summer, Marvin R. (1969) "Defending the Poor: The Assigned Counsel System in Milwaukee County," 1969 *Wisconsin Law Review* 525.

Sykes, Gresham M. (1969) "Legal Needs of the Poor in the City of Denver," 4 *Law and Society Review* 255.

Talarico, Suzette M. (1979) "Judicial Decisions and Sanction Patterns in Criminal Justice," 70 *Journal of Criminal Law and Criminology* 117.

Taylor, Jean C., Thomas P. Stanley, Barbara J. DeFlorio and Lynne N. Seekamp (1972) "An Analysis of Defense Counsel in the Processing of Felony Defendants in San Diego, California," 49 *Denver Law Journal* 233.

Thibaut, John and Laurens Walker (1975) *Procedural Justice: A Psychological Analysis.* Hillside, NJ: Lawrence Earlbaum.

Tyler, Tom R. (1984) "The Role of Perceived Injustice in Defendants' Evaluations of Their Courtroom Experience," 18 *Law and Society Review* 51.

_____ (1987) "Conditions Leading to Value-Expression Effects in Judgements of Procedural Justice: A Test of Four Models," 52 *Journal of Personality and Social Psychology* 333.

Uhlman, Thomas and Darlene Walker (1979) "A Plea Is No Bargain: The Impact of Case Disposition on Sentencing," 60 *Social Science Quarterly* 218.

Wheeler, Gerald R. and Carol L. Wheeler (1980) "Reflections on Legal Representation of the Economically Disadvantaged: Beyond Assembly Line Justice," 26 *Crime and Delinquency* 319.

Willison, David (1984) "The Effects of Counsel on the Severity of Criminal Sentences," 9 *Justice System Journal* 87.

Wilson, L. A., II (1988) "Rescuing Politics from the Economists: Privatizing the Public Sector," in Richard C. Hula, editor, *Market-Based Public Policy.* New York: St. Martin's Press.

Worden, Alissa Pollitz (1990) "Counsel for the Poor: An Evaluation of Contracting for Indigent Defense," paper presented at the annual meeting of the Law and Society Association, Berkeley.

Worden, Alissa Pollitz and Robert E. Worden (1989) "Local Politics and the Provision of Indigent Defense Counsel," 11 *Law and Policy* 401.

19

Calling a Strike a Ball
Jury Nullification and "Three Strikes" Cases

MARY DODGE and JOHN C. HARRIS

The 1994 California "Three Strikes and You're Out" ballot initiative received overwhelming public endorsement. The hue and cry over clogged courtrooms and overloaded corrections facilities hardly squelched the fervor for harsher punishment. Few people, however, predicted the discrepancies between public opinion and jurors' reactions to sentences imposed on defendants who committed what appear to be minor crimes and who now face 25 years to life in prison. Increasing juror dissatisfaction, hung juries, and nullification cases suggest that the controversy over the three-strikes policy extends beyond the predicted impact, as jurors have balked at the severe consequences for some defendants.

California's three-strikes law, unlike those of other states, provides that a defendant with a history of "serious" or "violent" conviction is subject to the law's sentencing provisions regardless of the nature of the current felony. It includes a second-strike provision specifying that a person convicted of any felony with one prior conviction of a serious or violent offense is subject to twice the term of punishment that would otherwise apply. The most draconian provisions, however, are reserved for convicted felons with two "strike priors" who can receive three times the punishment that would otherwise apply or 25 years to life in prison,

Written especially for *Courts and Justice*, 2nd ed.

whichever is greater (CA Penal Code §667; §1170.12; §1192.7(c); §667.5(c)). While judges have the authority to dismiss prior allegations (*People v. Romero*, 1996), that authority does not appear to be used frequently (Legislative Analyst's Office, 1997).

The controversy over jury verdicts and sentencing developed as a seemingly large number of offenders were incarcerated for nonviolent crimes. Shichor and Sechrest (1996) note that 70 percent of all defendants charged as second- and third-strikers are currently facing nonserious, nonviolent criminal charges. According to the Legislative Analyst's Office (1997), less than one-fourth of second-strikers were sentenced to prison for a violent or serious offense; the most common second-strike offenses are possession of a controlled substance, petty theft with a prior theft, and second-degree burglary. Slightly less than half of third-strikers were admitted to prison for nonserious, nonviolent offenses. The most common third-strike offenses are robbery and first-degree burglary, followed by possession of a controlled substance, second-degree burglary, and possession of a weapon.

Public opinion may favor harsh punishment, but individual jurors are questioning the applicability of the three-strikes law to certain offenders. Researchers have found that global public response to crime policy differs significantly from specific situational attitudes; punitive global attitudes are diminished under specific situations (Applegate et al., 1996). The research also showed that respondents favored a discretionary application of three-strikes laws when an offender committed a nonviolent crime or posed little physical threat to society. These findings are similar to investigations of mandatory sentencing that suggest that community standards tend to be less punitive than existing law and that the public views long-term incarceration as an inadequate solution to crime (Blumstein & Cohen, 1980; Miller, Rossi & Simpson, 1991; Samuel & Moulds, 1986).

The legitimacy of the three-strikes law and appropriateness of punishment have been questioned in cases involving nonviolent and seemingly nonserious offenses. The California law has been subjected to harsh criticism. Some of these criticisms have come from unexpected sources. A deputy district attorney, for example, stated: "The nonviolent felony provision—it offends the common citizen's sense of justice—'steal a piece of pizza . . . life term'" (Personal Interview). Some third-strike cases have involved relatively minor offenses, including petty theft with a prior and drug possession. For example:

A man was charged with stealing $5.00 worth of meat.

A homeless man, whose only possession was a bicycle, was charged with stealing a $2.00 bicycle lock.

A severely retarded 34-year-old woman, who was homeless and living in a park, was charged with possession of a $5.00 rock of cocaine.

A man who allegedly bought a crushed macadamia nut from the police was charged with attempting to possess drugs.

In other cases, defendants with a history of more serious priors were convicted and sentenced under three strikes for minor current charges:

A man was convicted of stealing a carton of cigarettes from Target. His priors, 15 years earlier, included burglary and assault.

A woman whose priors included robbery, burglary, and prostitution was convicted for taking a $5.00 cut in a cocaine deal.

A man was convicted for receiving stolen property—a 1985 Cadillac. His priors included burglary and drug possession and a robbery that involved a pack of cigarettes taken from another inmate.

Some jurors have expressed regret over their vote for conviction or have requested leniency for the defendant after discovering the severity of the penalty. A juror who voted to convict a three-strikes defendant of petty theft told the defense attorney: "I'd be glad to talk to the judge and ask for a lighter sentence" (Krikorian et al., 1996). After the panel realized the possible punishment for the burglary conviction, two jurors filed declarations with the court. One juror stated in court documents: "This is stupid, I don't think this benefits anyone. Personally, I don't think the three strikes should apply to nonviolent crimes" (Lynch & Cekola, 1995). In the case of a woman convicted of buying $5.00 worth of cocaine, a juror who wished that he had held out for a mistrial expressed his chagrin after he discovered the verdict would send a chronic drug user to prison for life:

I felt deceived by the court. They should have let us know this was a three-strikes case. I'm a firm believer in "don't do the crime if you can't do the time," but this was just ridiculous. (Lynch & Cekola, 1995)

In one dramatic courtroom scene Henry Jackson Jr., who had four previous felony convictions, was found guilty of possession of rock cocaine. After the verdict was announced, Jackson shouted, "I want you all to know you put me away for 25 years" (Sherwood, 1995). The jurors were polled after the outburst and a mistrial was declared after two refused to affirm their previous decision to convict. In San Francisco, a jury refused to continue deliberations when they learned the defendant would be sentenced under the three-strikes law (Cox, 1996).

Juror Ben Sherwood (1995) described his experience in a three-strikes case that resulted in a hung jury. The charges involved two men who were accused of selling 5.3 grams of marijuana to an undercover cop. According to Sherwood:

> The judge instructed us neither to pity the defendants nor to consider their possible punishment. In our first straw poll, nine jurors voted to convict. Three "not guilties" were worried about the dire consequences the defendants faced.

In Silicon Valley, Joe Louis Lugo, who had confessed to possessing a small amount of crack cocaine, was acquitted because the jury disagreed with the three-strikes law. According to Public Defender Edward Nino, "compassion overcame punitive sanctions." He stated:

> All of the jurors could not—or had a real difficult problem with the fact that . . . a conviction in this particular case would send this man away for the rest of his life. This is an example of jury nullification, because the evidence was extremely strong (Gonzales, 1995).

A jury's right to nullify is firmly entrenched in common law and viewed by many as a legitimate part of the legal process (Reed, 1996). Jurors nullify the law when they acquit defendants despite sufficient evidence to convict. Gormlie (1996) notes that nullification has experienced a revival in the 1990s because of the media attention given to high-profile cases. Proponents of nullification argue that the purpose is to promote justice by informing jurors that they have the power to act mercifully if applying the law to the defendant's act would lead to an unjust result (Dorfman & Iijima, 1995).

The controversy often focuses on whether or not jurors should receive nullification instructions. Brody (1995) believes that jurors should be informed of the right to return a verdict of not guilty, despite evidence of guilt. The reluctance of trial courts, with the exception of Georgia, Indiana, and Maryland, to formally implement instructions has promoted grassroots movements to apprize jurors of the available options. The Fully Informed Jury Association, a national, nonprofit organization, promotes nullification through newsletters, a website, and handbills. Prosecutors and judges, however, have pursued charges of contempt, obstruction, or tampering against distributors of nullification propaganda (King, 1998). Some courts have dismissed or replaced jurors who advocate nullification. The Second Circuit Court of Appeals ruled that judges have the duty to dismiss jurors who intend to nullify (*United States v. Thomas*, 1977).

The majority of courts agree that mandatory sentencing laws are insufficient justification for instructions on nullification. In 1996, Dennis Baca filed an appeal after he was found guilty of two counts of petty theft with a prior and sentenced under the three-strikes law. The appellant argued that he "had an absolute right to have the jury made aware of the harsh sentence which the court would be required to impose if he were convicted, and to have the jury acquit him if they felt that the sentence was too harsh, regardless of the strength of the evidence of his guilt" (*People v. Baca*, 1996). The California Court of Appeal rejected Baca's claim that he was entitled to have the jury instructed on the doctrine of nullification. The court, although it acknowledged a jury's right to nullify, rejected suggestions that the "jury be informed of that power, much less invited to use it."

Judges in California have expressed concern over possible nullification in three-strikes cases. One judge commented:

> Generally speaking: Petty theft or minor personal possession of drugs should NOT result in 25 to life in prison. Jurors on these kinds of cases are becoming concerned and reluctant to convict even when guilt is certain (Personal Interview).

Jury speculation over punishment has resulted in problematic outcomes in other cases, as well. San Francisco Superior Court Judge Lucy Kelly McCabe noted:

> We have had two cases in our system already where the jury thought it was a third strike, although it wasn't, and they hung, because people are unwilling, faced face-to-face with the defendant, to give somebody life for a bad check (Alegria, 1994).

Judges rarely allow lawyers to mention possible sentencing, and standard jury instructions prohibit jurors from considering punishment. The majority of courts agree that information about punishment is the exclusive domain of the judiciary. Requests by defendants to inform juries of the sentencing consequences of a guilty verdict have been routinely denied and deemed as "inappropriate and distracting" (*United States v. Patrick*, 1974). Courts have consistently refused to grant requests that would allow the jury to consider punishment (King, 1998).

> A Kentucky court rejected the defendant's claim that he should have been able to tell the jurors that, while convicting on the principle offense, they could refuse to find persistent felony offender status in order to avoid triggering a mandatory sentence enhancement if they concluded that the sentence enhancement was too severe (*Medley v. Commonwealth*, 1985).

> The Sixth Circuit court upheld a district court's refusal to allow defense to inform the jury of the sentence if the defendant is found guilty, and of nullification power (*United States v. Calhoun*, 1995).

> The First Circuit court rejected efforts by the defense attorney to inform the jury of the severity of the punishment as an indirect attempt to provoke jury nullification (*United States v. Manning*, 1996).

In California, trial judges' responses to issues surrounding juries and three-strike have varied widely. One judge, for example, declared a mistrial after discovering mid-trial that four jurors disagreed with the three-strikes law (*Jones v. Hennessey*, 1995). A few California judges, however, now allow lawyers to question potential jurors about their views of three-strikes during voir dire. One deputy district attorney suggested that full information for jurors may not be a bad thing. She spoke to jurors after a three-strikes conviction and was told that the jurors had considered that fact but had " . . . convicted anyway, we knew the judge could sentence the defendant to less than life under the *Romero* decision" (Personal Interview).

Nonetheless, the great majority of judges and prosecutors attempt to keep the fact that the defendant faces severe punishment from the jury.

Defense lawyers are discovering that the introduction of prior record evidence, contrary to past research, may work in favor of their client. A California district attorney stated:

> The defense now tries to communicate to the jury that their client has suffered prior nonviolent felony convictions, hoping that the disproportionate punishment of a life term will create renegade jurors who refuse to convict (Personal Interview).

Baseball analogies are frequently included in opening and closing statements. A defense attorney may simply state, "Let's play ball" or "We're on third base." Lawyers are using arguments that tell the jury to disobey the law. A lawyer who has promoted nullification in several cases says that sophisticated arguments offer jurors a "hook." This tactic gives juries an option and "lets them off the hook for disobeying the judge's instructions" (Personal Interview). Judges have responded by threatening severe sanctions if the defense attorney informs the jury of the defendant's strike status. One judge stated: "I make no bones about it. I let them know they'll (defenders) go to jail if they mention the three-strikes law" (Personal Interview). Nonetheless, baseball analogies abound in strike cases.

Researchers, however, have consistently found that under a variety of circumstances the introduction of prior record information results in increased conviction rates by mock jurors (Borgida & Park, 1988; Doob & Kirshenbaum, 1972; Greene & Dodge, 1995; Hans & Doob, 1976; Wissler & Saks, 1985). Horowitz (1985; 1988) notes that nullification arguments by defense lawyers promote the consideration of social norms in the decision-making process. Mock jurors, for example, were more lenient in euthanasia and possession cases. Mandatory sentencing has increased defense lawyers' arguments that the imbalance between crime and punishment should lead to an acquittal (Gormlie, 1996; Morvillo, 1994).

In rare instances, judges have allowed defense attorneys to disclose a client's criminal record. Attorney Michael J. Cassidy disclosed a client's prior record at trial. Jurors, though troubled by the conviction, felt obligated to obey the judge's instruction to follow the law. Cassidy commented on the case:

> I tried to impress upon the jury that the people who voted for three strikes thought it was only for people who committed violent crime, and I tried to tell them this particular case didn't fit the bill of goods that they were sold. It didn't work. (Lynch & Cekola, 1995)

Defense lawyers are also choosing to forego bifurcation in hopes that by introducing prior convictions during the guilt phase jurors will consider punishment in deliberations and be less likely to convict. This tactic, however, is not always successful. Courts may order bifurcation over the objection of defense counsel in strike cases, when the prosecutor requests it to prevent the specter of jury nullification (*People v. Cline*, 1998). In *Cline*, the court of appeal commented: "Here, the court noted that it had presided over two trials in which the jury apparently had refused to follow the law and had found the defendants not guilty of offenses falling under the three-strikes law."

Prosecutors are opposed to attempts to introduce three-strikes information at trial. Several attorneys believe that the possibility of nullification is greater if the jury discovers the nature of the case before the verdict and starts guessing about a defendant's priors. A prosecutor expressed concern at "jurors being allowed to hear [and therefore consider] the penalty or punishment in a particular case" (Personal Interview). A number of California deputy district attorneys expressed similar sentiments: "Jurors become reluctant to convict or find priors to be true if they learn it is a three-strikes case." Another claimed, "In terms of jury nullification the worst thing that happened to prosecutors was the third strike" (Personal Interview). This is also true in jurisdictions where jurors, particularly African-American jurors, are perceived to be sympathetic to defendants. One deputy district attorney said a problem with the three-strikes law was "racial nullification by black jurors of black defendants regardless of race of victims."

The draconian punishments imposed for relatively minor current offenses under California's three-strikes law have made jury nullification a central concern of the state's trial courts. The common wisdom is that jurors will balk at severe punishments for minor offenses. Jury expert James P. Levine (1997) notes:

> So, whereas mock jurors agree with current policies which penalize recidivists more stringently than first-time offenders and even accept in principle the idea of life imprisonment for habitual offenders which has been approved by the Supreme Court, they resist imposition of draconian punishments when the repeat offenses are relatively trivial; in their minds, "enough is enough."

Despite the relatively few reported cases of acquittal, the possibility of nullification or hung juries is a concern of prosecutors and judges and an area of continuing interest for defense counsel. This has, undoubtedly, led to prosecutors dismissing prior allegations in some cases, though others resist this response. As one prosecutor proudly recollected, "Our jurors will follow the law. One jury came back and convicted—they had tears in their eyes, but they convicted" (Personal Interview). Nonetheless, the potential for nullification is a common subject of comment and concern.

Despite the concern of the courts and arguments of legal scholars, there is as yet little systematic research concerning nullification in three-strikes cases. Judicial and advocate approaches to the issue remain *ad hoc* and without firm social science support or analysis.

The exact number of three-strikes nullification cases is unknown. Incidents of nullification may begin to diminish as a result of the *Romero* decision. Although it appears to have had little impact so far (Legislative Analyst's Office, 1997), the decision may reduce the number of two- and three-strikes cases (Clark, Austin, & Henry, 1997). If the possibility of judicial discretion becomes widely known, it may influence jurors and lead to conviction even when they have concern over application of the law.

Our current research efforts include the identification and analysis of cases that have resulted in hung juries and known nullification. A juror questionnaire has been designed to assess whether juror knowledge of prior conviction, known to increase the probability of conviction, is counteracted by juror knowledge of severe punishment for a minor current offense. Interviews with jurors in identified nullification cases may also help to understand the phenomenon.

It may be time to re-think judicial approaches to jury nullification. Current responses to the issue emphasize maintaining jury ignorance and suggest that juries are not to be trusted. Perhaps that response engenders the kind of haphazard pattern of nullification that all in the justice system find frustrating and many find inequitable. Jurors in some states already give sentencing recommendations. Providing the jury with all of the facts and a voice in sentencing may lead to greater consistency in application of the law. It may also provide for a greater sense that justice is being done.

References

Alegria, I. (1994). "California Judge Refuses to Enforce Three-Strikes Law." *National Public Radio.*

Applegate, B. K., Cullen, F. T., Turner, M. G., & Sundt, J. L. (1996). "Assessing Public Support for Three-Strikes-and-You're Out Laws: Global Versus Specific Attitudes." *Crime and Delinquency*, 42:517–534.

Blumstein, A., & Cohen, J. (1980). "Sentencing of Convicted Offenders: An Analysis of the Public's View." *Law and Society Review*, 14:223–261.

Borgida, E., & Park, R. (1988). "The Entrapment Defense: Juror Comprehension and Decision Making." *Law and Human Behavior*, 12:19–40.

Brody, D. C. (1995). "Sparf and Dougherty Revisited: Why the Court Should Instruct the Jury of Its Nullification Right." *American Criminal Law Review*, 33:88–122.

Clark, J. Austin, J., & Henry, D. A. (September 1997). "Three Strikes and You're Out: A Review of State Legislation." *National Institute of Justice*.

Cox, G. D. (29 May 1996). "Jurors Rise Up Over Principle and Their Perks." *National Law Journal*, A1.

Doob, A., & Kirshenbaum, H. (1972). "Some Empirical Evidence on the Effect of S. 12 of the Canada Evidence Act Upon the Accused." *Criminal Law Quarterly*, 15:88–96.

Dorfman, D. N., & Iijima, C. K. (1995). "Fictions, Fault, and Forgiveness: Jury Nullification in a New Context." *University of Michigan Journal of Law Reform*, 28:861–877.

Gonzales, E. (1995). "Simpson Case Focuses Attention on Jury Nullification." *National Public Radio*.

Gormlie, G. F. (1996). "Jury Nullification: History, Practice, and Prospects." *National Lawyers Guild Practitioner*, 53:49–70.

Greene, E., & Dodge, M. (1995). "The Influence of Prior Record Evidence on Juror Decision Making." *Law and Human Behavior*, 19:67–78.

Hans, V., & Doob, A. (1976). "Section 12 of the Canada Evidence Act and the Deliberations of Simulated Juries." *Criminal Law Quarterly*, 18:235–253.

Horowitz, I. A. (1985). "The Effect of Jury Nullification Instruction on Verdicts and Jury Functioning in Criminal Trials." *Law and Human Behavior*, 9:25–36.

Horowitz, I. A. (1988). "Jury Nullification: The Impact of Judicial Instructions, Arguments, and Challenges on Jury Decision Making." *Law and Human Behavior*, 12:439–453.

Jones v. Hennessey (1995). US Dist. LEXIS 19540 1, 3–6 (N D Cal).

King, N. J. (1998). "Silencing Nullification Advocacy Inside the Jury Room and Outside the Courtroom." *University of Chicago Law Review*, 65:433–500.

Krikorian, G., O'Neill, A. W., Corwin, M., Boyer, E. J., & Abrahamson, A. (1 July 1996). "Front-Line Fights Over 3 Strikes." *Los Angeles Times*.

Legislative Analyst's office (14 October 1997). "The Three Strikes and You're Out Law: An Update." Available: http://192.234.213.2/ho101497-3-strikes-update.html.

Levine, J. P. (1997). "Review Essay—Jury Wisdom." *Criminal Justice Ethics*, 49–56.

Lynch, R., & Cekola, A. (20 February 1995). "3 Strikes Law Causes Juror Unease in OC." *Los Angeles Times*.

Medley v. Commonwealth (1985). 704 SW2d 190, 191 (Ky).

Miller, J. L., Rossi, P. H., & Simpson, J. E. (1991). "Felony Punishments: A Factorial Survey of Perceived Justice in Criminal Sentencing." *Journal of Criminal Law and Criminology*, 82:396–422.

Morvillo, R. (7 June 1994). "Jury Nullification." *New York Law Journal*, 211, p. 3.

People v. Baca (1996). Cal. App. LEXIS 838.

People v. Cline (1998) E019186 (Super.Ct.No. FSB09681), Fourth Dist., Div. 2.

People v. Superior Court Romero (1996).

Reed, J. T. (1996). "Penn, Zenger, and O. J.: Jury Nullification Justice or the 'Wacko Fringe's' Attempt to Further its Antigovernment Agenda?" *Duquesne University Law Review,* 1125, 11602.

Samuel, W., & Moulds, E. (1986). "The Effect of Crime Severity on Perceptions of Fair Punishment: A California Case Study." *Journal of Criminal Law and Criminology,* 77:931–948.

Sherwood, B. (12 February 1995). "Deciding Guilt in a Three-Strikes Case." *Los Angeles Times.*

Shichor, D., & Sechrest, D. K. (1996). *Three Strikes and You're Out: Vengeance as Public Policy.* Thousand Oaks, CA: Sage.

United States v. Calhoun (1995). 49 F3d 231, 236 (6th Cir).

United States v. Manning (1996). 79 F3d 212, 219 (1st Cir) .

United States v. Thomas (1977). 116 F3d 606, 617 (2d Cir) .

United States v. Patrick (1974). 494 F2d 1150, 1153 (D.C. Cir).

Wissler, R. L., & Saks, M. J. (1985). "On the Inefficacy of Limiting Instructions: When Jurors Use Conviction Evidence to Decide on Guilt." *Law and Human Behavior,* 9:37–48.

20

Stripped Down like a Runner or Enriched by Experience?
Bias and Impartiality of Judges and Jurors

MARTHA MINOW

In phase one of the Senate Judiciary Committee hearings on the nomination of Clarence Thomas to serve as Associate Justice of the United States Supreme Court, Thomas testified that as a judge, "'You want to be stripped down like a runner," and "shed the baggage of ideology.'"[1] One observer commented that Thomas "painted a vivid image of a man methodically ridding himself not only of old ideas and even the desire to form new ones, but also of traits and attitudes that have formed the essence of his adult personality."[2] At the same time, his supporters argued that a man "who has experienced and overcome poverty and racial discrimination in his own life brings an important and perhaps irreplaceable perspective to the court."[3] Beginning with his opening presentation, Thomas presented himself as someone unburdened by a political perspective, yet enriched by his experiences of poverty and racial discrimination and therefore attentive to the concerns of disadvantaged people.[4]

After the second phase of committee hearings following the leak of Anita Hill's charges that Thomas sexually harassed her—the portion that

Reprinted by permission of the *William & Mary Law Review* from vol. 33, no. 4 (winter, 1991).

Thomas called a "high-tech lynching"[5]—the tension over perspective and impartiality only became compounded. Thomas explained that he had come to better and personally understand the need for rights for the accused.[6] He emphasized his own right to privacy and demonstrated deep concern about the operation of racial stereotypes.[7] Yet he also attacked liberal interest groups and the press, as well as the Senate itself, for staging the high-tech lynching. He conveyed his disrespect for everyone responsible for the process.

Do these experiences render him less, or more, qualified for the position he now serves on the United States Supreme Court? Will he be able to strip himself of his anger toward the Senate when he reviews questions of congressional intent? Will he be able to assure litigants of his impartiality in sexual harassment cases, in cases involving freedom of the press, or in cases addressing senatorial decisions?

These questions expose intense confusion about bias, impartiality, knowledge, and experience. This confusion permeates contemporary American legal thought, especially concerning the selection of judges and juries. The confusion is particularly pronounced because the ultimate goal of fairness in our society includes notions of representation as well as ideas of neutrality. The jury is to reflect a fair cross-section of the community.[8] Yet the very existence of peremptory challenges, which give litigants the power to strike a certain number of participants from the jury without having to state any reason,[9] creates tension with the goal of a cross-section in the very process of permitting the parties some modicum of control over what they perceive to be fair or advantageous at trial. The Supreme Court has ruled that peremptory challenges affecting the composition of both civil and criminal juries must not intentionally exclude participants on the basis of race or gender so as to undermine the goal of a fair cross-section of the community.[10]

My goal in this article is to consider three contrasting views of bias and their relationships to the ideal of fair representation in the selection of juries and judges. As a nation, we seem to want those who sit in judgment to have no axes to grind, no prejudgments about the people or issues they confront. We also want them to have the ability to empathize with others, to evaluate credibility, to know what is fair *in this world*, not in a laboratory. And we want jurors and judges to have, and to remember, experiences that enable their empathy and evaluative judgments. This ambivalence, I will suggest, reflects a misunderstanding of the preconditions for impartiality and of the role of fair representation in producing impartial jurors and panels of judges. Common sense, case law, fiction, and even movies illuminate these questions.

I. Do We Know Bias When We See It?

First, let me ask whether we know bias when we see it. Consider the cartoon depicting a judge with a large nose and mustache, looking down from the bench at a defendant with the same nose and mustache. The judge declares: "Obviously, not guilty." [11] This cartoon illustrates the usual meaning of bias. It refers to an inclination, a predilection, that interferes with impartiality. A potential juror poses the danger of bias when he or she is too close to the parties or the issue at hand. By knowing the people involved, by having a direct stake in the proceeding, or by having had a very similar kind of experience as the one under scrutiny, the potential juror may lack or appear to lack the distance necessary to judge fairly.

Normally, we think that a person is or appears to be biased toward friends, family members, or business associates. This view reflects a sharp departure from the early conception of a jury as a group of people from a community who knew the parties and who could serve as witnesses to give evidence about the dispute. [12] It is one of those curious historical transformations—much like the transformation of the term "jury of one's peers" from a reference to nobles to a reference to random cross-sections of society. The jury for Oliver North excluded anyone who had followed or even heard about his testimony in the congressional Iran-Contra hearings. [13] The jury included thus only members of that odd group of people who were able to sequester themselves from a major topic of broad public interest and discussion.

To be fair, this notion of removal reflects the desire to guard against prejudice—to avoid those who prejudge the issues at hand. A juror who has been exposed to pretrial publicity might have or seem to have a view about the merits of the case or the virtues and vices of one or more parties. The question remains, however: how is bias to be tested? A majority of the Supreme Court has recently ruled that the issue of bias in the face of pretrial publicity is avoided when the jurors report to the court that *they* think they can be fair. [14] The jurors' subjective reflections may be one component of any proper impartiality inquiry, but I wonder whether this is sufficient. A juror may not fully understand either the meaning or the demands of impartiality; the juror may miscalculate his or her ability to put aside knowledge that could prejudice judgment. In addition, the simple appearance of bias may damage the basic commitment to a fair trial process.

Variations on such questions of evidence and proof abound. For example, who has the burden of showing that a prospective juror is actually prejudiced? In a homicide case, one juror attended church with the mother of the decedent but was nonetheless allowed to serve on the jury. [15] A Supreme Court majority refused to grant certiorari in the case despite Justice Marshall's dissenting view that the defendant ought not to bear the burden of showing actual prejudice when the probability of bias was so great.[16]

Aside from such questions of proof, the first notion of bias begins to emerge with some clarity. A juror may be or may seem biased because of personal experience with the parties or exposure to publicity about their conduct. That juror seems too close to the matter at hand to render a fair and objective judgment.

Does this mean that no bias arises if the juror is in the opposite situation? What if the juror is extremely far from the matter at hand in either personal experience or knowledge? Professor Lon Fuller once discussed the danger that jurors called to judge a sailor charged with threatening another with bodily harm would not understand the mores of the waterfront and would attribute too much to testimony that the defendant had said in the past that he would "'stick a knife in [someone's] guts and turn it around three times.'"[17] Is it possible to risk actual bias, or its appearance, by having a total absence of experience or knowledge of the issue or evidence at hand? To be able to evaluate statements of witnesses, a jury needs sufficient knowledge of the witnesses' worlds to place their statements in context. Moreover, to be able to render judgment, jurors need sufficient knowledge of the life experiences of those before them to make sense of testimony and motivations. Even when women were excluded from jury service, for example, Anglo-American tradition provided for the use of midwife juries on occasions in which knowledge of pregnancy or childbirth would be critical to a reliable judgment.[18] Perhaps that practice also reflected some delicacy of feeling about whose ears should hear such intimate female matters; perhaps the practice embodied a notion of expertise rather than impartiality.[19]

Certainly arguments for the inclusion of women and African-Americans on juries have long encompassed the view that female and African-American litigants deserved the chance to be evaluated by those with shared experiences.[20] Some commonality is necessary to know enough to judge. Admittedly, this argument blends into the notion of a fair cross-section of the community regarded as an independently important concern about the jury. Both the appearance of fairness and the fact of equality in the jury selection process matter even apart from issues about what knowledge is necessary to judge fairly. But the Supreme Court has acknowledged that impartiality is served by juries that represent a fair cross-section of the larger society.[21] Although the distribution of knowledge and experience may not be equal, the collective deliberation process by a jury that is a fair cross-section will temper the dangers of ignorance.[22]

A confluence of the goals of fair representation and impartiality thus exists. Both include a basic idea about the distribution of experiences necessary to render fair judgments. The Clarence Thomas of September who sought to establish his impartiality, therefore, announced that he would retain his experiences of poverty and racial discrimination and his "'underlying concerns and feelings about people being left out, about our society not addressing all the problems of people.'"[23] Only a year earlier, David Souter had felt the need to convey to the Senate and to the watching public that despite a life as a bachelor and loner, he had women friends[24] and that once as a college adviser he had even counseled a young woman who contemplated an abortion.[25] Experience and familiarity with human emotions bring a judge or juror within the circle of people entitled and equipped to judge others. More particularly, both Thomas and Souter sought to establish that they had experiences with points of view not well represented at the high court. This reflects an admission that the Court's impartiality is threatened if it appears, because of its own narrow membership, to lack an understanding of the broad range of people who come before it.

A third kind of bias remains. It is perhaps the most elusive to state, and it also may be controversial to discuss. I want to explore it because I myself am suspicious of dualities. I am troubled by the suggestion that bias may arise when one is too close to but not when one is too far from a problem; but I am equally troubled by the idea that these two are the only dimensions that matter. Let us consider another dimension. Although someone may seem unbiased and removed from a matter, he or she may be implicated and seem not to be because of unexamined assumptions about the baseline used to judge neutrality and impartiality.

Consider a case involving a charge of sex discrimination against a law firm. In one such case, the defendant law firm asked Judge Constance Baker Motley to recuse herself from the case because she, as a black woman who had once represented plaintiffs in discrimination cases, would identify with those who suffer race or sex discrimination.[26] The defendant invoked the notion that the judge would be too close to the case. The defendant assumed that Judge Motley's personal identity and her past legal work deprived her of impartiality. Judge Motley declined to recuse herself and explained:

> [I]f background or sex or race of each judge were, by definition, sufficient grounds for removal, no judge on this court could hear this case, or many others, by virtue of the fact that all of them were attorneys, of a sex, often with distinguished law firm or public service backgrounds.[27]

Similarly, Judge Leon Higginbotham once was asked to remove himself from a race discrimination case because he is an African-American.[28] In declining, he noted that "black lawyers have litigated in the federal courts almost exclusively before white judges, yet they have not urged that white judges should be disqualified on matters of race relations."[29]

Judge Motley and Judge Higginbotham may be understood to suggest that they are no more too close to the matter than judges of a different race or sex might be too far from it. Yet they both advance a different view of bias and impartiality. They mean to expose the assumption that the neutral baseline against which to evaluate bias is the vantage point of a white male. They mean to show that even whites and males have a vantage point that can and should be evaluated for bias. Departure from a white male perspective, however, does not necessarily mean bias. Judge Motley and Judge Higginbotham mean to demand a more particularized showing of bias than an assertion of sex or race, and also to remind any who need reminding that men as well as women have a sex, and whites as well as blacks have a race. These categories implicate us all. If being implicated means bias, then everyone is biased, and perhaps then no one can judge. That result is unacceptable, but it helps suggest a norm of inclusion to govern who may serve as judge or jury. It points out the danger of considering an initial appearance of bias without probing how others may be similarly but more subtly implicated in the issue of bias.

Consider a problem chosen not at random—a case arising from a charge of sexual harassment. If brought before a woman judge or before women jurors some might worry about biased decisionmakers. If the decisionmaker herself were a victim of sexual harassment, some might worry that she would be unduly inclined to believe and favor the complainant. As polls conducted during Clarence Thomas's Senate hearings demonstrate, women who have been harassed may instead be skeptical of another woman's claims.[30] Perhaps the complainant did not respond the way the adjudicator did or would have; perhaps the complainant appears disloyal or otherwise blameworthy in the eyes of the adjudicator. These alternatives simply point to the multiple directions that bias may take, but not to its absence. Would restricting decisionmaking to a man or group of men be any better? Some people worried that Anita Hill's charges were not taken seriously enough by the Senate Judiciary Committee in part because the Committee was composed entirely of men who seemed not to comprehend the seriousness of the problem.[31] Some argue that the presence of even just one woman Senator would have made a difference on this score.[32] This is an asserted connection between notions of fair representation or cross-section and the impartiality necessary to judge the significance of a charge.

But a different line of criticism can be applied to a panel of male adjudicators of sexual harassment claims. Those adjudicators might identify with the accused and might worry about being accused themselves. They might worry about false accusations and the difficulty of rebutting them. They might worry about true accusations, yet not believe them serious enough to warrant public sanction. They also might worry about true accusations and seek to show their ability to overcome any appearance of bias by coming down hard on the accused.

I do not mean to suggest that everyone is equally or identically biased. I do mean to suggest that commonplace notions of being too close or too far from the parties or the problem at hand inadequately capture the issue of bias. Instead, people's multiple perspectives on a problem may diverge in different ways from the ideal of impartiality. For that very reason, a collaborative decisionmaking process involving people reflecting those multiple perspectives exhibits the special virtue of a jury or multijudge panel compared with a single judge. The value of consultation is enhanced not merely by the presence of more than one mind but also by the presence of more than one vantage point.[33] This is another way of saying that fair representation and impartiality converge.

II. Criticizing the Supreme Court

The Supreme Court's decision last Term in *Hernandez v. New York*[34] provides an occasion to test these comments and in turn, to test the Supreme Court. In *Hernandez*, the prosecution tried a case against a Latino criminal defendant and used its peremptory challenges to exclude jurors who failed to assure the prosecutor adequately that they could defer to the official English translation of any Spanish-language testimony.[35] The defendant claimed that the resulting jury violated equal protection guarantees because it effectively excluded all Spanish-proficient jurors.[36]

The case sharply divided the Supreme Court.[37] Four Justices signed the plurality opinion in which Justice Kennedy reasoned that the prosecutor offered explanations for his challenges, explanations sufficiently unrelated to race, and that thus no intentional discrimination occurred.[38] These Justices did not rely on the view that ethnicity or language proficiency are unrelated to race. They could have relied on the fact that many people who speak Spanish are not Latinos and that many Latinos do not speak Spanish, but they did not.[39] Indeed, Justice Kennedy's opinion includes a rather remarkable statement about the close relationships between language and identity and between language and ethnicity, close enough at times to justify equal protection scrutiny on the basis of language proficiency.[40] To reject the defendant's claim, therefore, Justice Kennedy's opinion had to reason that a prima facie showing of an equal protection violation had been rebutted by the absence of proof that the prosecutor intended to exclude based on race.[41]

The plurality argued more specifically that the prosecutor had offered a neutral explanation for the peremptory challenges: the Latino jurors raised doubts for the prosecutor when they hesitated before they answered that they would try to defer to the official English translation of Spanish testimony at the trial.[42] This doubt, the plurality claimed, was unrelated to race or ethnicity. Some Latinos would give no such grounds for doubt, and some non-Latinos would. Thus, the plurality found that the exclusions were not based on race.[43]

But let us examine the exclusions more closely. Why would it be legitimate to worry about a juror who could not ignore testimony given by witnesses, and not therefore need to defer solely to a court translator's version? Two linked reasons might be at stake. This Spanish-proficient juror might base judgment on information unavailable to other jurors and this juror might claim special knowledge and authority in the course of the jury deliberations. Why are these worrisome instead of desirable traits for a juror? These worries arise only if one supposes:

(1) that the normal juror would not know Spanish;

(2) that only the official English translation of Spanish testimony should be used in the jury's deliberations;

(3) that people who do not speak Spanish adequately can fairly judge people who do; and

(4) that the exclusion of Latinos from the jury leaves a jury that can be perceived as fair and impartial in a case involving a Latino defendant (and, in this case, Latino victims as well).

Underscoring these suppositions is Justice Kennedy's endorsement of the trial court's conclusion that, because Latino jurors might be sympathetic to both the Latino defendant and to the Latino victims and witnesses, it is not discriminatory to exclude Latino jurors; the sympathies wash out.[44] This view neglects not only Latinos in the community who view trial participation as a civic right but also ignores all those troubled by the omission of an entire perspective and knowledge base from the jury. Moreover, it also wrongly implies that only Latinos have sympathies in cases involving Latinos.

Treating only Spanish-speaking Latinos as a problem, the plurality cited a case "which illustrates the sort of problems that may arise where a juror fails to accept the official translation of foreign-language testimony."[45] In *United States v. Perez*,[46] a juror asked the judge if it would be possible to ask the translator about the meaning of a particular term. The translator had interpreted the word to mean a public bar although the juror thought it meant a restroom. The judge indicated that questions could be put only to the judge, not to the interpreter. The interpreter nonetheless volunteered that jurors "are not to listen to the Spanish but to the English. I am a certified court interpreter."[47] At this point, the transcript produced by the court reporter indicated that the juror called the translator an "idiot."[48] The juror later explained, however, that she had said, "It's an idiom."[49] (We have several layers of interpretation problems here!) The juror was dismissed from the jury.[50]

This episode, offered by Justice Kennedy as evidence of the sort of problems that may arise when a juror fails to accept the official translation of foreign-language testimony, may also indicate the sorts of problems that arise when the trial process fails to accommodate people who are bilingual. The juror's question was treated as an intrusion rather than as an effort to get at the truth; the witness's testimony, she suggested, would make more sense if it referred to a restroom rather than a bar. The court interpreter reacted defensively, and the judge responded by banishing the inquiring juror from the trial.

This story contrasts sharply with a case in which a man got into a fight in a bar with another man and killed him.[51] Both men were Mexican-Americans. The offender argued that his victim had given him "*el ojo*," meaning, "the eye."[52] At that time, no Mexican-Americans were eligible to serve on juries in Texas, where the incident occurred."[53] The defendant was convicted of murder. As one observer noted about the case:

> Anglos have a big thing about eye contact being something positive. You can take a man's measure by making contact. . . . Hell, in the Mexican community eye contact can kill you. It sends the other guy a message that says what the hell are you lookin' at, and if you don't like it, do something about it. In a bar that can lead to a killing. But if you don't know that you can't relate to what it means. And unless jurors understand the difference between *el ojo* and eye contact, the defendant is not being tried by a jury of his peers.[54]

The Supreme Court of the United States essentially agreed. In 1954, the Supreme Court—the same Court that decided *Brown v. Board of Education*[55]—reversed the conviction.[56] The Court was composed of Justices quite different from those serving on the present Court. The present Court has moved away from recognizing language, ethnic, and racial differences as important dimensions of American life and dimensions to be integrated throughout our institutions. Instead, the Court seems to fear differences and to desire to exclude those people it fears. Because Spanish-speakers soon will probably become a majority in parts of California and Texas,[57] these exclusions would be carried out in the name of a minority mistaken about the actual norm.

What if the Supreme Court instead exposed for discussion the assumption that English-speaking and not bilingual jurors are the norm? Even in last year's case, a majority of the Justices, in separate opinions, considered ways to change the jury to accommodate bilingual jurors.

Six of the nine Justices proposed that jurors proficient in a language used by witnesses be given an opportunity to indicate to the judge any problems they detect with the translations.[58] The plurality acknowledged the "harsh paradox that one may become proficient enough in English to participate in trial," given the English-language ability requirements for federal jury service, "only to encounter disqualification because he knows a second language as well."[59] Nevertheless, for these Justices, the treatment of bilingual jurors remained a marginal concern, largely relegated to footnotes. The assumption that the non-Spanish speaking juror is the impartial decisionmaker contributed to this failure. The problem of bias for juries and for judges arises not only when they are too close to or too far from those they judge but also when they fail to identify an entrenched and biased assumption about whose perspective is the norm.

The arguments for a jury that is a fair cross-section of the community only strengthen this critique.[60] To be perceived as fair by the entire community, to accord all citizens a chance to serve as jurors, and to grant parties the opportunity to be heard by their peers, the jury should reflect a fair cross-section of the community. Such a cross-section is more likely to bring to bear knowledge critical to evaluating evidence, credibility, and justice in a given case.

III. Prejudice vs. Prior Knowledge

In case I seem to have implied that bias and prejudice are not problems for juries and judges, let me turn to a distinction between prejudice and prior knowledge. I believe that an important distinction does exist. Prejudice interferes with impartiality. Prior knowledge may assist impartiality, however, if coupled with a willingness to be surprised, rather than always confirmed. Let me offer into evidence a short story by James Baldwin, entitled "Sonny's Blues."[61]

It is a story of two brothers, both African-American. One brother, the narrator, served in the Army and then became a high school math teacher, a husband, and a father. His younger brother, Sonny, became a heroin addict, a convicted felon, and a jazz pianist.[62] The school teacher ignored Sonny during the initial period of Sonny's incarceration. But when the teacher's daughter dies of polio, Sonny writes him a heartfelt letter.[63] They then stay in touch, and when Sonny is released, they reunite. But the teacher is wary, concerned that Sonny will continue to use drugs. He simultaneously feels guilty and worries that he is not fulfilling his mother's last wish that he watch out for his brother.[64] Sonny tells his brother he knows that he may start using drugs again.[65]

Reluctantly, the teacher accepts Sonny's invitation to join him at a nightclub. For the first time, he hears Sonny play the piano.[66] It is Sonny's first return to the instrument since his time in prison. The teacher-narrator notes: "All I know about music is that not many people ever really hear it. And even then, on the rare occasions when something opens within, and the music enters, what we mainly hear, or hear corroborated, are personal, private, vanishing evocations" different from what is evoked for the person making the music.[67] Drenched with his prior knowledge and suspicion of Sonny, and with feelings of guilt, the narrator still tries to discern what Sonny feels as he plays. He begins to recognize the dialogue between Sonny and the musician playing the bass fiddle. The bass player "wanted Sonny to leave the shoreline and strike out for the deep water. He was Sonny's witness that deep water and drowning were not the same thing—he had been there, and he knew."[68] The narrator watches his brother move from absence to real presence with the other musicians and then join them in finding new ways to make the audience listen to the not-new story of human suffering.[69] The narrator is brought to his own memories but also to a new respect for his brother, a man who chose not the norms of middle-class respectability, but expression of human experience through the blues.

The narrator is not asked to judge Sonny, although he does so. Nonetheless, the story suggests the difference between prejudging a matter, even when prejudice is based on actual knowledge, and the use of prior knowledge as part of a process of opening up to the possibility of surprise. The story suggests the difference between mulling over personal, private evocations and attending to the situation of another person. The story also suggests that, initially, the shared past and experiences of the two brothers stand as a barrier to mutual understanding. Later, however, the narrator is able to integrate his memories of his parents and his brother into a new understanding and respect for the path Sonny takes. It may be too much to suggest that we are all brothers and sisters in this way, although such an attitude need not interfere with impartiality if we try to use what we know to remain open to surprises about one another. I have used this story in teaching judges[70] and often asked these questions: "If you were asked to sentence Sonny in a new drug charge, would you want to know about the piano playing? Would you want to hear it? Would you want to include as judges and juries people who know Sonny's world or only people with no knowledge of it? Is there anyone who is not implicated in it?"

Let me contrast this story with the recent movie Thelma & Louise.[71] Two women plan a weekend away from the men in their lives, but they quickly find trouble at a honky-tonk. A man starts dancing with Thelma, then makes sexual advances toward her. When she resists, he violently starts to rape her. Louise appears with a gun, the man stops, but he shows no remorse, and Louise kills him. The rest of the movie follows their journey as outlaws, trying to escape legal repercussions. The movie includes their encounter with a truck driver who repeatedly makes gross sexual advances toward them and their fantasy revenge against him. The movie concludes with their suicide in a world aiming to capture and punish them, a world they do not believe could understand them.

The film triggered considerable press. In Boston, the *Globe* ran side-by-side columns: A woman's review was entitled, "She Loves It";[72] a man's review: "He Hates It."[73] The *Boston Globe* has its own problems of perspective. A common prediction about that paper is that if a nuclear bomb fell on New York, the headline in the *Boston Globe* would read: "Hub Man Injured in Explosion."[74] But the issue of perspective is unusually pronounced in evaluations of the movie *Thelma & Louise*. Some charge the movie with stereotyping men and giving bad role models for women. Others cheer its depiction of women fighting back in a world they find unsafe and inhospitable. Perhaps only a law professor would like best a particular line in the movie. It is uttered as the two women discuss how police and prosecutors would not understand how a woman who danced with a man could establish his sexual advances were unwanted. Thelma says, "Law is some tricky shit."[75] That statement summarizes the conviction that the male-dominated legal system will not understand how a woman could charge rape after she flirted with a man or how a woman could be excused or forgiven for killing a man after he had stopped raping a woman. Perhaps the polarized reviews confirm their doubt. In a way, Anita Hill's experience could be described as "Thelma and Louise Meet the Supreme Court Nomination Process—and Discover How Unsafe and Inhospitable the Senate is from a Woman's Point of View."

I put the film forward here for a different reason. I wonder whether the film, like the story, "Sonny's Blues," asks us to use what we know but to suspend our conclusions long enough to be surprised, to learn. One of the actresses who starred in *Thelma & Louise* said that people who find that the film mistreats men are identifying with the wrong characters.[76] She invites all viewers to identify with the journey of self-discovery and self-criticism undertaken by Thelma and Louise. They know they have done something wrong, and the film does not excuse them. But it invites understanding and wagers that gender is no obstacle to that. None of us can know anything except by building upon, challenging, responding to what we already have known, what we see from where we stand. But we can insist on seeing what we are used to seeing, or else we can try to see something new and fresh. The latter is the open mind we hope for from those who judge, but not the mind as a sieve without prior reference points and commitments. We want judges and juries to be objective about the facts and the questions of guilt and innocence but committed to building upon what they already know about the world, human beings, and each person's own implication in the lives of others. Pretending not to know risks leaving unexamined the very assumptions that deserve reconsideration.

IV. Prejudice, Prior Knowledge, and the Supreme Court

This prompts me, once more, to consider the situation of Justice Clarence Thomas, both as judge and as someone to be judged. Three versions of what has happened to him have emerged:

(1) The Republican story, put most cogently by the nominee himself, of a high-tech lynching, a process spun out of control through the manipulations of liberal interest groups, Senate staff members, and ambitious press people who conspired to produce a charge of sexual harassment, delay its evaluation, leak it at the eleventh hour, and prompt a circus-like hearing besmirching Thomas's good name.

(2) The Democratic story of a terrible process, but one with no better alternative, because the Constitution calls upon the Senate to advise and consent to presidential nominations, because the complainant's demand for confidentiality delayed consideration of the charge of harassment, and because an unfortunate leak to the press brought to public attention this serious charge and required public resolution.

(3) The baptism-by-fire theory, according to which we have witnessed a process of intensive job training, with the result that Clarence Thomas may end up emphatically defending privacy, and the rights of the accused. He criticized racial stereotypes and concluded that his own integrity mattered more than ambition—in contrast to positions he had taken previously.

I want to believe the third story, and Thomas himself has testified to it.[77] But he has also indicated his fury at the Senate, his disdain for liberal interest groups and, it seems, apparent disrespect for many Democrats and press people.[78] To some observers, he seems untrustworthy on questions of sexual harassment, perhaps even a lying perpetrator.

Will Thomas now recuse himself from cases of sexual harassment? From cases involving liberal interests groups or Democratic Senators? These matters will remain with his conscience. To be fair, we should not use our metaphoric peremptory challenges against him. But to earn the respect of the public, he must indicate how he will draw on the parts of his past that he claimed taught him about people left out, disadvantaged, and misunderstood. It would help if he worked to prompt other Justices to make explicit the assumptions they take for granted about whose perspective is neutral and whose is biased. It would help if he does not strip himself down like a runner, but instead acknowledges his own situation as a brother[79] implicated in the lives of others and able to be surprised while he builds upon what he already knows.

Endnotes

[1] Linda Greenhouse, "The Thomas Hearings: In Trying to Clarify What He Is Not, Thomas Opens Question of What He Is," *N.Y. Times*, Sept. 13, 1991, at A19 (quoting Judge Clarence Thomas). At another point, responding to a question from Senator Dennis DeConcini, Thomas said,

> I think it's important for judges not to have . . . baggage. I think . . . it is important for us . . . to eliminate agendas, to eliminate ideologies. And when one becomes a judge . . . you start putting the speeches away. You start putting the policy statements away. You begin to decline forming opinions in important areas that could come before your court because you want to be stripped down like a runner.

David Broder, "Thomas Backs Democrats into a Corner," *Chi. Trib.*, Sept. 15, 1991, at 3.

[2] Greenhouse, supra note 1, at A19.

[3] Broder, supra note 1, at 3.

[4] Greenhouse, supra note 1, at A19.

[5] 137 *Cong. Rec.* S14, 632 (daily ed. Oct. 15, 1991) (statement of Sen. Byrd).

[6] See Richard L. Berke, "The Thomas Nominations: Thomas Backers Attack Hill," *N.Y. Times*, Oct. 13. 1991, at 1.

[7] Id.

[8] See *Taylor v. Louisiana*, 419 U.S. 522, 526 (1975) (noting that the American concept of jury trial contemplates jury drawn from cross-section of community); *Hernandez v. Texas*, 347 U.S. 475, 482 (1954) (holding that conviction by unrepresentative jury violates equal protection). Even judicial elections, as the Supreme Court ruled last year, are governed by the Voting Rights Act. *Chisom v. Roemer*, 111 S. Ct. 2354 (1991).

[9] *Swain v. Alabama*, 380 U.S. 202, 220 (1965).

[10] See, e.g., *Holland v. Illinois*, 493 U.S. 474 (1990); *Batson v. Kentucky*, 476 U.S. 79 (1986). Challenges for cause more directly address the issue of bias. I focus here on the use of peremptory challenges rather than challenges for cause in the shaping of juries.

[11] Charles Barsotti, *New Yorker*, Nov. 21, 1988, at 55.

[12] Valerie P. Hans & Neil Vidmar, *Judging the Jury* 23–24 (1986).

[13] "North Jury Selection Bogs Down: Public Familiarity with Him Poses Problem, Judge Says," *L.A. Times*, Jan. 31, 1989, at 1.

> Thomas felt compelled to state that he had never discussed *Roe v. Wade*, 410 U.S. 113 (1973), with anyone. See "The Thomas Hearings: Excerpts from Senate's Hearings on the Thomas Nomination," *N.Y. Times*, Sept. 12, 1991, at A20.

[14] *Mu'Min v. Virginia*, 111 S. Ct. 1899, 1908 (1991).

[15] *Porter v. Illinois*, 479 U.S. 898 (1986).

[16] Id. at 901 (Marshall, J., dissenting from denial of certiorari).

[17] Lon L. Fuller, "The Forms and Limits of Adjudication," 92 *Harv. Law Rev.* 353, 391 (1978).

[18] See Lloyd E. Moore, *The Jury: Tool of Kings, Palladium of Liberty* 128–29 (2d ed. 1988).

[19] Cf. Judith Resnik, "On the Bias: Feminist Reconsiderations of the Aspirations for Our Judges," 61 *S. Cal. L. Rev.* 1877, 1912 n. 121 (1988) (proffering differences between male and female judgments as explanation of exclusion and inclusion of women on juries).

20 See Douglas Colbert, "Challenging the Challenge: Thirteenth Amendment as a Prohibition Against the Racial Use of Peremptory Challenges," 76 *Cornell L. Rev.* 1, 6 (1990); Carol Weisbrod, "Images of the Woman Juror," 9 *Harv. Women's L.J.* 59, 80 (1986).

21 See *Holland v. Illinois*, 493 U.S. 474, 480-81 (1990). But see id. at 495 (Marshall, J., dissenting) (arguing that the fair cross-section requirement serves purposes different from impartiality).

22 This goal may be jeopardized by extremely long trials, because a cross-section of the population is unlikely to be able to disengage from other commitments to serve on a jury for such a trial. For this reason, among others, some have proposed breaking long trials into smaller parts that can be heard by different panels, as Judge Robert Keeton has suggested to me in conversation.

23 Greenhouse, supra note 1, at A19 (quoting Judge Clarence Thomas).

24 See, e.g., Alan McConagha, "Souter's First Love: His Work," *Wash. Times*, July 26, 1990, at A6.

25 Ruth Marcus & Michael Isikoff, "Souter Declines Comment on Abortion: Nominee Moves to Dispel Image as Judge Lacking Compassion," *Wash. Post*, Sept. 14, 1990, at A1.

26 *Blank v. Sullivan & Cromwell*, 418 F. Supp. 1, 4-5 (S.D.N.Y. 1975).

27 Id. at 4.

28 *Pennsylvania v. Local Union 542, Int'l Union of Operating Eng'rs*, 388 F. Supp. 155, 156-57 (E.D. Pa. 1974).

29 Id. at 177.

30 Felicity Barringer, "The Thomas Confirmation: Hill's Case Is Divisive to Women," *N.Y. Times*, Oct. 18, 1991, at A10.

31 See, e.g., Carol Kleiman, "After Senate's Thomas-Hill Debate, Two Women Seek Entry to Men's Club," *Chi. Trib.*, Feb. 24, 1992, at 5.

32 See id. The confidence with which this point is uttered is challenged somewhat by the position of Senator Nancy Kassebaum, who voted in favor of confirming Clarence Thomas when the question reached the full Senate. Nevertheless, unlike some of her male colleagues, Senator Kassebaum also refused to be "a party to an intellectual witch hunt against Professor Hill." "The Thomas Confirmation: Women in Senate Have Their Say Before the Vote Confirming Thomas," *N.Y. Times*, Oct. 16, 1991, at A18.

33 A single judge can try to engage in an imaginative dialogue with people with different vantage points on the problem at hand. Cf. Hannah Arendt, *Between Past and Future: Six Exercises in Political Thought* 220-21 (1961) (suggesting that judgment derives its validity from agreement of individuals with various perspectives).

34 111 S. Ct. 1859 (1991) (plurality opinion).

35 Id. at 1864-65. The prosecution also used its peremptory challenges to exclude jurors with family members who had been convicted of crimes. Id. at 1864.

36 Id. at 1866-67.

37 Four members of the Court signed Justice Kennedy's plurality opinion, id. at 1864, two members signed another opinion authored by Justice O'Connor, id. at 1873, Justice Stevens wrote a dissent joined by Justice Marshall, id. at 1875, and Justice Blackmun dissented separately while indicating agreement with one part of Justice Stevens's dissent, id. at 1875.

38 Id. at 1866-67.

39 The plurality opinion did reject the defendant's claim that a close correlation between Spanish proficiency and Latino identity would be sufficient to treat exclusion of Spanish-proficient jurors as exclusions of Latinos. Yet the plurality acknowledged that, at least in this case, the exclusion of Spanish-proficient jurors had the effect of excluding virtually all Latinos. Id. at 1867.

40 Id. at 1868.

41 Id. at 1868–69.

42 Id. at 1864–65.

43 Id. at 1867.

44 Id. at 1871–72 (deferring to the trial court's finding).

45 Id. at 1867 n. 3 (citing *United States v. Perez*, 658 F.2d 654 (9th Cir. 1981)).

46 658 F.2d 654.

47 Id. at 662.

48 *Hernandez*, 111 S. Ct. at 1867.

49 Id.

50 Id.

51 See *Hernandez v. State*, 251 S.W.2d 531 (Tex. Crim. App. 1952), rev'd sub nom. *Hernandez v. Texas*, 347 U.S. 475 (1954).

52 Thomas Weyr, *Hispanic U.S.A.: Breaking the Melting Pot* 83 (1988).

53 *Hernandez*, 251 S.W.2d at 533.

54 Weyr, supra note 52, at 83 (quoting Gilbert Pompa).

55 347 U.S. 483 (1954).

56 *Hernandez v. Texas*, 347 U.S. 475 (1954).

57 See e.g., Lily Eng & Bob Schwartz, "City's Latinos on the Grow," *L.A. Times*, Feb. 26, 1991, at B1; cf. "Product Development Needed for Growing Hispanic Population, UPI, July 21, 1988 (noting that one in four Texans will be Hispanic by the year 2000), available in LEXIS, Nexis Library, UPI File.

58 *Hernandez v. New York*, 111 S. Ct. 1859, 1868 (1991) (plurality opinion); id. at 1877 (Stevens, J., dissenting).

59 Id. at 1872.

60 Those arguments include the rights of the parties to be evaluated by a jury of their peers, the rights of potential jurors to serve, and the prerequisites for public confidence in the process of trial. See *Holland v. Illinois*, 493 U.S. 474, 495 (1990) (Marshall, J., dissenting).

61 James Baldwin, "Sonny's Blues," in *How We Live: Contemporary Life in Contemporary Fiction* 747 (Penney Chapin Hills & L. Rust Hills eds., 1968).

62 Id. at 748–50, 761–62.

63 Id. at 751.

64 His mother had said, "'It ain't only the bad ones, nor yet the dumb ones that gets sucked under,'" id. at 756, and then she told him about his uncle who had been lynched, id. at 757. She said, "'You got to hold on to your brother . . . and don't let him fall, no matter what it looks like is happening to him and no matter how evil you gets with him.'" Id. at 757–58. She added, "'You may not be able to stop nothing from happening. But you got to let him know you's *there*.'" Id. at 758.

65 Id. at 768.

66 Id. at 769.

67 Id. at 770.

68 Id.

69 Id. at 771.

70 See Martha Minow, "Words and the Door to the Land of Change: Law, Language, and Family Violence," 43 *Vand. L. Rev.* 1665, 1689–95 (1990).

71 *Thelma & Louise* (MGM-Pathe 1991).

72 Diane White, "She Loves It," *Boston Globe*, June 14, 1991, at 29.

73 John Robinson, "He Hates It," *Boston Globe*, June 14, 1991, at 29.

74 "Hub" is the *Globe*'s abbreviation for Boston as the hub of the universe. See "Ask the Globe," *Boston Globe*, Sept. 8, 1990, at 60.

75 *Thelma & Louise*, supra note 71.

[76] See Judith Michaelson, "Downright Serious: With 'Thelma & Louise,' Geena Davis Is Forging a New Image, Closer to Her Own Reality of a Woman Who Takes Care of Her Life," *L.A. Times*, May 12, 1991, at 5 (quoting Geena Davis).

[77] See Neil A. Lewis, "The Thomas Swearing-In: After Ordeal of Senate Confirmation, Views on Thomas's Court Opinions," *N.Y. Times*, Oct. 19, 1991, at 8.

[78] See Peter G. Gosselin, "Thomas Says He'll Fight to the End," *Boston Globe*, Oct. 13, 1991, at 1.

[79] Thomas's treatment of his sister in a speech commenting on her dependency on Aid to Families with Dependent Children gave some critics another ground for attack, because he seemed to register callous disregard for her difficult times, ignorance about the gender difference that had contributed to their contrasting life stories, and recklessness with the truth. See Joel F. Handler, "The Judge and His Sister: Growing up Black," *N.Y. Times*, July 23, 1991, at A20 (letter to the Editor).

Questions to Consider

1. When an appellate court reverses a lower court's decision in a criminal matter, this new decision usually means that some ruling made against a defendant has been changed to favor the defendant. In approximately one-half of these cases, the prosecution still ends up obtaining some type of conviction against the defendant. Was this your understanding of how court reversals worked? If this was not your understanding, how did you arrive at your original opinion?

2. What type of attorney would you wish to represent you if you were charged with a crime? Does this answer depend on how much money you have? How does this affect your opinion about what type of attorney should be provided for others?

3. As you watch one of the many sensational jury trials on TV, you may see efforts to pick jury members who have heard or seen nothing about major political events. Do you think one has to be substantially ignorant about an issue in order to be unbiased? What would such a group of jurors be like? Would they really represent us? What do we potentially lose by selecting such a jury? Can there be bias not only when one is too close to an issue but also when one is too far from an issue?

4. Martha Minow argues that collaborative decision making works well to integrate our needs for representation and neutrality. Many judicial systems in Europe utilize multiple judges, both lawyers and non-lawyers, to decide cases. What does such a system offer that our system does not?

5. If depending on the multiplicity of a jury seems to be a better way to achieve justice than simply relying on one individual, what has been happening as the power of the jury to make decisions has been slowly eroded over the years?

6. In Minow's essay, she describes the Supreme Court case of *Hernandez v. New York* (1991). Do you believe those who speak Spanish should be excluded from a jury in a trial where Spanish will be translated? How do the twin goals of representation and neutrality affect your decision?

Section VI
Specialized Courts
Shopping the Boutique

One ongoing debate with courts, as with many other functions of government and the professions, is whether judges should cover a range of issues or specialize. Long ago we developed a separation between law and equity courts and earlier in this century developed juvenile or children's courts. Often courts of "general jurisdiction," with the luxury of numerous judges, will administratively separate civil from criminal cases or designate specific judges to deal primarily with such areas as domestic relations or traffic. A large set of specialized courts little understood by many are the tribal courts that dot the American landscape. They are of particular interest to students of courts because they operate as social laboratories, experimenting with alternative methods of dealing with such issues as compensation, restitution, and punishment. Judge Carey Vicenti of the Jicarilla Apache tribe explores alternative concepts such as shame, remorse, and dialogue between family and friends as methods of prevention and reintegration.

In stark contrast with such efforts at reintegration are current United States and Canadian efforts to prevent juveniles from being adjudicated by juvenile courts. Ruddell, Mays, and Giever track recent efforts to prevent juvenile courts from dealing with their historical purview over juveniles. In an effort to increase sanctions, we have limited who can be treated as a juvenile by juvenile courts, transferring these juveniles instead to adult courts. If we create specialized courts because we believe that specialized knowledge can impart an increasingly just response, why remove juveniles from an arena where judges are particularly able to deal with them? And if we remove them, who gets to make this decision: legislatures who mandate certain transfers, prosecutors who focus on the crime committed, or juvenile judges themselves? Alternatively, could juvenile judges be given more powers rather than transferring the juvenile to adult court?

Another salient issue involving specialized courts is whether such courts are mere bandages that cover up larger social problems and/or inadequacies in current policy. For example, are the drug courts described by McNeese and his colleagues a diversion from a drug war policy that focuses far too much on punishment, or is it the best we can do given the larger intractable realities of our current policy on drugs? McNeese makes a strong case that incarceration does little if anything to break the cycle of drug abuse and that treatment has been demonstrably effective. If we are to follow this "disease model" of prevention, we certainly need to know the difficulties of involving necessary players such as prosecutors, defense attorneys and judges, and McNeese does that well. The challenge of any such specialized court is to reconcile a treatment approach, which necessarily allows for "relapse," and a legal model, which simply focuses on use or nonuse. Thus, we are still left with the question of why courts rather than public health officials should be involved in the first place.

Similar issues are raised in Slate's description of specialized courts for mentally ill offenders. Numerous studies have documented the inappropriate relegation of the mentally ill to a criminal justice system often unable to professionally care for their needs. If our courts are to deal with the mentally ill, then Slate makes a strong argument that they need to recognize that law functions as a therapeutic agent, bringing about therapeutic or nontherapeutic consequences. The question here is whether courts really provide justice for the mentally ill or whether they actually make things worse. Certainly specialized courts for the mentally ill would be a step in the direction of caring for their needs, although if someone is truly mentally ill, then the situation again begs the question of whether criminal courts rather than health officials should be involved.

21

The Reemergence of Tribal Society and Traditional Justice Systems

CAREY N. VICENTI

For many years now, I have been very close in friendship to my medicine man. When we see each other on the streets we will often wave. On occasion he has come to me for my advice. During one of our cordial discussions, he complemented me on my wisdom, my patience, and my perseverance. He then pointed out to me that our roles within our society were very much the same, except that he dealt with the good side and I dealt with the bad side.

What I did, as a judge within our tribal court system, was never characterized to me in that manner. And for several days, I had to sort through my metaphysics in order to live—in a good way—with his esteemed observation. I am sure that, to him, there is a kinship regarding our stature within our tribal society; as well, he must have noticed that both of us perform functions of ceremony, consultation, and curing. And because of my knowledge of the man, I am without doubt that his observation was not intended as a criticism, nor to vex me with some existential curse.

The medicine man was making a simple observation as to how we Jicarilla Apache people are. He described his role. Then he described my role. One might say that he made a karmic observation.

Whenever a person makes reference to good and bad in American society, one assumes a basic dichotomy or conflict. This was not what my medicine man intended. The medicine man merely pointed out that I

Reprinted with permission from *Judicature*, Vol. 79, No. 3 (Nov.–Dec. 1995), pp. 134–141.

have been charged by my destiny to perform those ceremonies, consulta-tions, and cures in order to overcome the bad side of people's lives. It is my place in Jicarilla Apache society. And, as is often the case, I then send the individual to the medicine man in order for the medicine man to bless or baptize the individual towards complete cure of the calamity which has befallen him. We work together. For us, the rectification—or, if you prefer, the adjudication—of a problem spans a broad continuum from bad to good, and as good is accomplished, so too is the full restoration of the individual. While, on occasion, during the handling of problems within a court setting, the court may embark upon a determination of the mens rea of an individual, such a determination has limited usefulness and we must then return to our concern for the fate of the individual and the res-toration of his spirit.

When Americans and Indians talk about "culture," they mean two dif-ferent things. To the Native American, culture is pervasive, encircling, all-inclusive. To the mainstream American, culture consists of an elective identity added to the essential American character.

It is not surprising, therefore, that in American society the question of justice is relegated to one institution, and all other things are left to a mar-ketplace of religion and culture that prospers or fails depending upon how individuals choose to exercise the liberty given to them under Amer-ican law. By stark contrast, the Indian concept of the human being is one in which all aspects of the person and his or her society are integrated. Every action in daily life is read to have meaning and implication to the individual and guides how he or she interacts with tribal society or fulfills obligations imposed by society, law, and religion.

This helps explain why tribal courts do and should differ substantially from courts of the non-Indian world. Mainstream Americans do not con-sider that the very viability of the systems of tribal governance depend on the degree to which such governments are allowed to develop their institutions free from any outside interference. They assume that culture is a modular element to be merely added to one's life at one's election. Americans do not seem to understand that their system of government, that the institution of the courts and the workings of an adversarial sys-tem of justice, all amount to a large portion of American culture. Thus, America, in its attempts to correct what it perceives as a rampant injustice in Indian America, creates a greater injustice by forcing its culture upon Indian peoples.

Against the large tide of American culture that sweeps across Indian America with daily relentlessness, tribal cultures must struggle. Indian tribal culture is in crisis. We no longer possess the cultural objects that may stimulate our collective memory to recall many lost customs, tradi-tions, and values. And yet, every reservation is experiencing the return of educated Indian people who are capable of discerning the invasion of non-Indian values into the Indian world. These new Indians, who have equal footing in both the Indian and the non-Indian world, are capable of articulating the effects America has had on the development of tribal society. Over the past two decades they have been successful in litigating and in gaining passage of federal legislation ultimately to create a wide enough path for the distinct culture in Indian society to reemerge. For the tribal courts, this means the restoration of traditional forms of adjudication.

The reader will notice that the parts to the rest of this essay appear to have been placed in reverse chronological order, going from "Death" to "Birth." But it could not have been written any other way. It was specifically organized so as to illustrate that not every American presumption has implicit validity. Some peoples have a different frame of reference. I will always be an Apache man advancing the beliefs of my grandfather and his father, and all our predecessors. I am not unlike most other Indians, whether educated or not. I am willing to challenge the ineluctable death of our culture and bring it to a new life. With this essay I hope to take care of one portion of the bad side and I leave to my medicine man his blessing for the good side.

Death and Burial

The tribal court is a relatively new phenomenon in Indian country. It emerged originally out of the need, as perceived by the non-Indian occupants of Indian territory, to prosecute the "bad" Indian. In the early decades, therefore, the institution was inquisitional and was not intended to provide the constitutional safeguards that are now deemed indispensable. In 1934, Congress passed the Indian Reorganization Act,[1] which was intended to loosen the authoritarian grip the federal government exercised over the management of the internal affairs of Indian reservations. The act allowed a tribe to organize under two vastly different forms of government. Under section 16 of the act a tribe could adopt a constitution that governed the newly organized tribe. Under section 17, a tribe could organize a business committee to manage the tribe's affairs. It is important to recognize that many tribes did not take advantage of either section, choosing blindly to accept what the federal law would allow them to do in the future.

After 1934, much of the inquisitional nature of the tribal court was shed, due primarily to the fact that the constitutions adopted by the various tribes provided sufficient guidance to Indian people regarding the administration of law in Indian country. That is not to say that federal control over the internal affairs of tribes had disappeared altogether. Rather, more elusive mechanisms were employed by federal officials to maintain the degree of control they deemed necessary. It should also be admitted that in many Indian communities the newly appointed judges were incapable of fulfilling the colonial role that existed prior to 1934, so non-Indian officials were occasionally invited in to "advise." By the mid-1960s, however, the influence of the federal government in the internal affairs of tribes had waned substantially.

As Indians gained greater control over their internal affairs, corruption also crept in. Tribal courts were occasionally manipulated by politically elected leadership. It having been determined that the federal constitution was not applicable to Indian tribes,[2] the tribes freely adjudicated cases without concern for the emerging civil rights expectations of Indian people.

In the mid-1960s Congress recognized that federal Indian law did not require constitutional rights to be afforded to people subject to the powers of tribal government. In an era when civil rights were prominently in the foreground of American politics, such omission was considered to be irreconcilable with the mood of the times. Therefore, in 1968 Congress passed the Indian Civil Rights Act.[3] Under its terms, a list of civil rights, roughly reflecting the Bill of Rights, was imposed upon every tribal government.

Passage of the Indian Civil Rights Act was accomplished over the opposition of many Indian tribes. The relationship between the individual and his or her society was considered by many tribes to be their exclusive prerogative. By legislating civil rights upon Indian country, Congress inserted a portion American culture into Indian society and attempted to supplant tribal culture, imposing a new order within tribal society that elevated the interests of the individual well above that of family, the clan, the band, or the entire tribe. For many this signaled certain death to tribal society.

But tribal culture received a reprieve in 1978. In *Santa Clara v. Martinez*[4] the Supreme Court made it clear that although Congress had the prerogative through its plenary powers to impose a system of civil rights protection upon Indian country, it was nonetheless left to the Indian tribes themselves, through their judicial tribunals, to interpret how these concepts should be applied. The very narrow holding of *Martinez* was that the federal court was without jurisdiction to hear an alleged civil rights violation given that the only statutory relief into the federal forum was by a writ of habeas corpus. A claimant must therefore be in custody—suggesting that review within the federal court system was available only in criminal cases.

The *Martinez* decision was sufficient to place a makeshift wall between American culture and the cultures of the various tribes. The intrusion of civil rights philosophy into Indian society, and the commensurate elevation of the status of the individual, were postponed. Many Indian tribes took this opening as an opportunity to return to practices that had evolved since the initial establishment of the inquisitional form of court in the late 1800s. Other tribes took the opportunity to reinstate traditional practices of problem solving. This renaissance of traditional adjudication practices was reinforced by the growing dissatisfaction with Western legal process as a whole. American courts have been experimenting with alternate dispute resolution in its many Western forms, thus validating, in part, the restoration of traditional Indian practice.

In the early 1990s many tribal judges and tribal leaders sought additional funding from Congress. After 2½ years, Congress passed the Indian Tribal Justice Act, which was signed into law on December 3, 1993.[5] Although it authorized up to $58 million to reinforce the functioning of tribal courts, to this day the act remains unimplemented and unfunded.

Preparation for Death

The brief history outlined above does not fully explain the evolving tribal court. It is hard for many Indian people to believe that the Indian Civil Rights Act did not bring the demise of traditional values and practice. American society did not realize the genuine sadness felt by traditional Indian people as their way of life became slowly dismantled.

Over the past two decades tribes have made sporadic efforts to preserve tribal culture. Most have focused on the preservation of native languages. But rapidly those languages are disappearing. Many tribes have undergone initiatives to restore the various tribal arts. On many reservations the practices of basketry, pottery, beadworking, woodcarving, sculpture, quillwork, and many other native arts have been restored and have become part of daily life. However, the mere restoration of the Indian arts plays all too well into a modular notion of cultural pluralism. In part, these attempts to renew these traditional practices succeeded because they cater efficiently to the non-Indian concept of culture: a bit of culture one can buy at the market.

The real battle for the preservation of traditional ways of life will be fought for the bold promontory of guiding human values. It is in that battle that tribal courts will become indispensable. It is in the tribal court that the competing concepts regarding social order, and the place of the individual within the family, the clan, the band, and the tribe, will be decided. It has been clear to tribal court judges for the past several decades that the expectations of the litigants in the tribal forum have not wholeheartedly favored an open adoption of American justice values. But in order to fulfill the expectations of the tribal litigant, the courts have found it absolutely necessary to consult tribal custom and traditions and incorporate these values into American-style legal systems.

In the past 50 years, since the passage of the Indian Reorganization Act, Indian country has greatly diversified. Perhaps it would have been possible 200 years ago to give a finite number to all the various settled forms of justice systems existing in North America. Today we can point to more than 535 federally recognized Indian tribes. This does not necessarily mean there are that many different legal systems. Rather, there are more than 535 potentially identifiable discreet systems of adjudication, each of which must account for cultures in their midst that are in volatile transition.

Many contemporary popular movements now operate in Indian country, affecting the development of the tribal courts. For instance, many tribal societies are being affected by the forces of evangelical Christianity. Other communities have seized upon the Archaeological Resources Protection Act,[6] the Native American Graves Protection and Repatriation Act,[7] and the American Indian Religious Freedom Act[8] to assist in the assertion of traditional cultural rights. Those within Indian country are becoming vastly diversified compared to what may have been a more homogenous population 50 years ago. To a lesser degree, but not entirely absent as influences upon Indian society, are the global changes involving the fine tuning of human rights and the global trend toward regional and ethnic independence. Indian people also aspire to greater independence in spite of their long history as Americans.

Given the forces affecting tribal societies, the question must arise as to whether tribal courts can find stability within their own systems of governance, and, if so, to what extent Western notions of justice or traditional Indian notions of justice will become prevalent.

Maturity

Before contact with non-Indians ever occurred, every tribe had its own institution for resolving problems. A "court," in many cases, never really existed. But among Indian peoples murders did occur, property was stolen, adultery was committed, and other transgressions against the social order occurred. We Apaches had a context against which the transgression could be read, interpreted, and resolved. We did not centralize all of our remedial powers into one institution. Rather, we would involve different elements of our society—the chief, the warrior societies, the families, the clan, the medicine man, and so on—in the resolution of the problem. Laws were not made by an institution such as a legislative body but by the normative power of the entire society. Each individual knew what was prohibited, where the prohibition came from, who would be empowered to decide corrective action, who would administer corrective action, and what the corrective action would be.

Expectations of justice were entirely different. For instance, among the Apaches the telling of truth is extremely important. It was not because truthfulness had achieved such a high virtue in our society. Instead, we view our reputations as being the most important of personal possessions. Thus, if a person told a lie, the person would fall into disrepute as a liar. The implications of such values in current legal process have been that few criminal cases are contested. A person who has committed a wrong freely confesses it. To a certain degree, the requirement that government prove guilt beyond a reasonable doubt legitimizes deception. Therefore, a defendant's rights are not necessarily perceived by Indian culture as something good.

Apaches rarely seek compensation for injuries. This is because we come to view injuries as defining moments. A person who loses an eye loses an eye for a reason—in some way to define himself. It is a teleological view of human experience. For the most part, this view disposes of all injuries that occur by mere and gross negligence. Traditionally, if an intentional harm occurred, the offender would "own up" to the offense and make a restitutional gesture to the victim. An individual who confessed to having committed an offense could thus protect his or her good reputation.

In American society, restitution constitutes a very admirable traditional Indian practice. But our Apache restitutional gesture has little to do with economic value. The item or items used to provide restitution are symbolic of the remorse shown by the perpetrator. In the act of offering restitution, there is a transfer of power from the perpetrator to the victim. In offering restitution the perpetrator demonstrates the degree of remorse for having committed the intentional harm. The victim, after witnessing the gesture, has the power to determine whether the remorse was genuine. That determination depends on the degree to which the item or items involved in the restitutional gesture constitute a harm or loss to the perpetrator. If the offered restitution is without remorse, the victim can reject the restitution, and, thereafter, the perpetrator is disreputed until he or she comes forward with true remorse.

For certain problems there were certain known institutions that resolved those problems. One would not take a problem of one character to an institution that was not charged by tradition to solve those kinds of problems. And because we Apaches had placed such a high value upon our reputations, truthfulness was not a problem. Therefore, our institutions were not designed, as in American society, to discover the truth. Our institutions focused more upon determining the manner in which a transgression against social order would be remediated. As a result, in the development of the contemporary Apache courts, we have had a great deal of trouble developing a fine-tuned sense of legal process and a philosophy regarding evidence and burdens of proof and production. But our powers of remediation appear to go well beyond those employed by the Western world.

In our traditional society capital punishment consisted of exile. I know of no instances where death was ordered. "Shame" was our principal instrument of punishment (although "punishment" may not be an appropriate designation for the principle behind the corrective action). For the offense of adultery, a person had his or her nose sliced. (Adultery was considered an offense from which no person could recover and whose disrepute could show obviously on the perpetrator's face.) In the Apache concept of transgression, we do not necessarily assign to a person a degree of intent, be it mere negligence, gross negligence, spur of the moment intent, or intention backed by planning. Each individual may take actions resulting in the transgression of tribal norms or mores because of badness that is operating within his or her life. That badness can be, and often is, a badness of heart—what Westerners might call sociopathic behavior—but the badness also may be explained by religious or spiritual reasons that have caused the state of heart, or by medical reasons that have caused momentary or periodic changes of behavior. So, in fashioning a remedy, much more attention has been placed upon determining facts about the individual that can illuminate the metaphysical exploration of the individual undertaken by traditional participants.

The Apache remediator knows quite well that part of the remedy is in performing the exploration. Family members and friends may be brought in to discuss the changing world of the individual. We may explore everything from what he or she eats to which direction he or she faces when going to sleep at night. We recognize that many of the proscriptions that have been handed down from generation to generation, although potentially obsolete or dogmatic, may have their justifications in older times. We cannot altogether abandon those inherited cautions simply because we have acculturated to the English language and an American way of life and cannot fully understand or appreciate the wisdom of our predecessors.

Although restitution, consisting of equivalent economic value, may be an appropriate remedy under some circumstances, in traditional Apache society we recognize that dialogue about the transgression may also be the best remedy as we restore the individual's reputation. Depending on the nature of the transgression, we may require the restitutional gesture to involve more than merely a victim but a victim's family, and even the entire society. We value remorse as a state of mind to be accomplished by a perpetrator. An act of contrition is often considered necessary to give an open demonstration to the sense of remorse felt by the perpetrator. But we consider it essential that the internal and external life of any perpetrator be examined to determine whether the individual is healthy or whole. And ultimately, we desire to reintegrate the individual back into tribal society.

What I have described in very simple fashion are the salient points of a philosophy I consider important to this world. In our society, we see the importance of accomplishing a state of remorse, in order to humble the perpetrator, but also to cure the victim. In American society, there is no remorse. Remorse appears to be left to the victims and their families. A civil judgment is paid and business goes on, a punishment is meted and the remorseless criminal ferments his hatred in prison for years. How the remorselessness and the victimization collectively affect America is something worthy of exploration.

Youth

In the preceding text I gave what I hoped was sufficient guidance as to the dynamics which might cause a vast diversification of legal systems throughout Indian country. Certainly, by force of federal law, many tribes have had to import non-Indian values into Indian society. Indian people are influenced on a daily basis to accept Western values and to expect legal process as it is portrayed on television and in the media. At the same time, many people perceive the early signs of cultural extinction and are fighting furiously to preserve what little we have of the past.

Over the past two decades we have sent young tribal members off to schools and colleges to become educated and gain expertise about the Western world. After the return of the first waves of educated Indians, we experienced a brief era of acculturation during which time we accepted the apparent necessity of adopting written laws and refining our Western-style institutions of adjudication. But, in our growing sophistication, and as a new wave of educated tribal members returned home questioning the values which we had previously uncritically imported, we now perceive our rights to culture as being part of a larger global more.

As a result of a series of federal laws passed in the last century, and reflecting the shifting sentiments of America toward Indian people, we also have further grounds for unique adaptation. Federal law has treated Oklahoma uniquely, thereby placing the tribes of Oklahoma largely without territory over which to govern, nonetheless distributing Indian people throughout the state. Public Law 280 deprived Indian tribes in the States of California, Minnesota, Nebraska, Oregon, and Wisconsin of all criminal jurisdiction except within the Red Lake, Warm Springs, and Menominee reservations.[9] As a result of other provisions of Public Law 280, the States of Arizona, Iowa, Idaho, Montana, North Dakota, South Dakota and Washington assumed a portion of jurisdiction away from Indian tribes. Finally the Alaska Native Claims Settlement Act (ANCSA) established a corporate form of governance for the various regions of Alaska. This system now confuses the efforts of the Alaska natives and the Alaska tribes to organize their own systems of adjudication.

Native American tradition still flourishes in Arizona, New Mexico, Alaska, the Rocky Mountain States and the States of the Northern Plains. This is not to say that there are not communities throughout the United States that maintain a strong tie to the past. The tribes of the Iroquois Confederacy, for instance, have maintained a virtual unbroken tie with the vast complex of values held by their ancestors.

Over the past few years several conferences have brought together many tribes to discuss the emerging movement toward restoration of traditional justice practices. These conferences have also brought in representatives from the Native Hawaiians.[10] In addition, many tribal people have engaged in dialogue within indigenous groups from Central and South America, Polynesia, Papua-New Guinea, and other distant places. Thus, hybridization of tribal justice systems is not only influenced by traditional tribal and American culture, but also by the experiences of other tribes and other indigenous populations.

Among the tribes of the United States, there appear to be five general categories that describe the various developing tribal courts: the American model, the American-traditional hybrid model, the dual model, the traditional model, and the explorative or non-existent model.

The American model essentially follows the lead set by American jurisprudence. These courts generally appear within those tribal governments that have been organized under the Indian Reorganization Act. Under these systems there are distinct separations of powers, and mirror-image adoption of American legal process and jurisprudence. These courts refer to federal and state court decisions in order to formulate and justify the development of their own jurisprudence. Generally, these types of courts serve populations that are largely assimilated or acculturated to an American style of living with a more modular recognition of tribal culture and tradition. Often the courts have evolved in this manner due to the early influence of non-Indians. Either the Indian community found itself in close proximity to populations of non-Indians, individual federal officials exerted a great deal of authority and influence over the development of tribal systems, non-Indian attorneys hired by tribes were given greater freedom to influence the development of tribal legal systems, or Indian tribes employed non-Indians to serve in a judicial capacity during the formative years of the tribal court's development.

The hybrid American-traditional model far outnumbers all others. These courts fall in two general categories as well: those in proactive development, and those in reactive development. This hybrid group has developed in large part because of the indecision of populations to go with one or another expectation of justice. On the one hand, many tribal populations insist on importing and advancing traditional cultural values into the process of adjudication and urging a greater degree of flexibility and informality within court procedure. But many of the people are also taken by the allure of civil rights and legal process. These hybrid courts serve populations that have a fairly equal mix of traditional, native-language-speaking people and non-traditional, non-native-language-speaking people.

The proactive hybrid court is in the minority. Its proactive nature highlights the fact that it is often a well-developed, mature court. The maturity is evidenced by the court's ability to command substantial attention during the tribal funding process (to gain sufficient annual funding), by having experimented with the use of form orders and petitions, by having experimented with the use of computers (in order to organize dockets and generate necessary court documents), and by consciously examining the incorporation of tradition and custom into the jurisprudence of the tribe. To a degree, the Jicarilla Apache tribal courts fit into this category. The courts of the Jicarilla Apache tribe, however, have only recently emerged from the reactive category.

The larger portion of hybridized courts is reactive. The designation "reactive" actually portrays the court as reacting to the circumstances around it as it evolves into a hybrid type of institution. Those forces include interference from elected leadership, lack of funding, public expectations, human resources limitations (most notably education and training), and so on. This category easily encompasses a majority of the courts in the Northern Plains, Oregon, Washington, Idaho, and Arizona. Many of these courts are conscious of the option to select and incorporate traditional justice practices into the jurisprudence of the tribe, but there is an absence of meaningful communication with the executive or legislative bodies to enable the court to justify or gain approval for such incorporation. Many of these tribes are postured to emerge from a reactive to a proactive state. In large part, funding stands as the single greatest obstacle toward change.

It is useful to examine parenthetically the effects of funding on the development of tribal courts. Although the number of law-trained Native

Americans has increased substantially since the early 1970s, few Indian attorneys look to careers in the judiciary. In part, this has much to do with the fact that the educational process in law school, particularly in the field of federal Indian law, tends to encourage lawyers to aspire to careers in litigation. (The recent successful history of litigation of Indian issues tends to support that predilection.) Indian lawyers who fail to make it into the larger law firms generally look to Indian Legal Services or to solo practice. Recently, the Department of Justice has begun hiring many Native American attorneys in order to offset a deficit in its ranks. Still, the tribal courts are last in line to be considered for career development. Tribal courts have had to bear a reputation for providing little in the way of salary, and being particularly vulnerable to political forces, they tend to offer only short tenures on the bench. The inadequacy of funding also often means that courts do not have sufficient buildings, staffing, equipment, and supplies to do their work. This would not be a problem if there were other courts to resort to, but in many cases the tribal court has exclusive jurisdiction. Furthermore, tribal courts tend to take on other cases such as election disputes and constitutional challenges that test the validity and stability of tribal government.

In the absence of a viable court system, tribal government stands consistently at risk of shutdown or failure. In the absence of funding the courts can never quite attain the personnel who are competent to adequately justify the place and purpose of the court within the democratic structure of tribal government. This, in turn, undermines the remainder of tribal government. Legislative and executive efforts to reinforce their regulatory initiatives, such as resource development, environmental protection, and fire protection, or to stimulate economic development, always fall short by virtue of this fundamental defect.

The dual model exists where a tribe has chosen to employ a traditional and an American justice system model, but by keeping a clear separation between the two and diverting cases based upon subject matter to the different courts. Predictably, the Western-style court tends to be hybridized. The most notable of this class is the Navajo Nation Court. A brief examination of Navajo case law indicates a regular and methodic reference by the justices of the Navajo Nation Supreme Court to tribal traditions and customs in rendering their decisions. Navajo Nation has what appears to be an American model court, but the jurisprudence relies heavily on Navajo tradition and custom. Many domestic relations type of cases are funneled to the Peacemaker Court, which incorporates Navajo religion into the problem-solving process. Increasingly, business related cases are being submitted to the Peacemaker Court for solutions. The Peacemaker Court best represents traditional adjudication—healing practice. Nonetheless, it was pushed aside by federal authorities in favor of the American model. Eventually, under proactive judicial leadership the Peacemaker Court was re-established (although it was never truly gone). Many Pueblo courts have two court systems as well. The Pueblos have been highly successful at preserving traditional practice, but, nonetheless, they have found it necessary to create an American model court to handle an increasing number of commercial claims.

The traditional model court has become rare. Several Pueblos adjudicate transgressions and solve problems in accordance with age-old practices. Many do not allow non-Indian practitioners to participate in the deliberative process. This restriction has brought much criticism and very little sympathy.

Of the last category, the explorative and the non-existent, there are several important observations. A majority of the Indian tribes and Alaskan Native villages do not have formal recognized systems of justice. This is not to suggest that these different communities do not have some means of adjudicating transgressions or of problem-solving. Rather, these adjudicative institutions generally are not recognized by the organic or positive laws of the tribes. With the passage of the Indian Tribal Justice Act in 1993, many of these tribes were encouraged to explore creation of a court system. Irrespective of the jurisdictional limitations placed upon any of the tribes by either Public Law 280 or the Alaskan Native Claims Settlement Act,[11] it is clear that the tribes have inherent authority to adjudicate matters touching upon the organization of the family and tribal society. Therefore, the issues involving domestic relations and political organization are within their jurisdictional reach.

By this brief and rather rough generalization, it should be clear that most tribal courts are somewhat between formative and youthful stages of development. Few tribes have reached a level of maturity where they can meaningfully make choices between traditional practice and American legal process. We should all admit, though, that the development of the tribal courts has been significant in light of the fact that most of these courts began earnestly under Indian control in the 1950s and 1960s. American jurisprudence, by contrast, has had more than 200 years to develop.

Birth

Whether tribes adopt traditional cultural practices in the long run is not without impact upon the rest of America. Because tribes are exploring variations on American jurisprudence, they are potentially small laboratories that can test new directions for American jurisprudence. On a more tangible level, because the Supreme Court in the 1980s took up the cases of *National Farmers Union Insurance Companies v. Crow Tribe*,[12] and *Iowa Mutual Insurance v. LaPlante*,[13] federal courts (and to some extent state courts) may be forced to examine the workings of the tribal courts. These two cases, though not confirming the civil jurisdiction of tribal courts over non-Indians, nonetheless require federal courts to stay their hands until non-Indian litigants have exhausted their remedies within the tribal court system. If traditional practice is incorporated into the tribal system to such an extent that it does affect commercial transactions with non-Indians or domestic relations concerning non-Indians, the federal courts may be in a position to place tribal courts under a microscope.

Previously these types of cases may have resulted in one form of balancing test or other, which may have sorted out the legitimate governmental interests of the tribe as compared to those interests and rights possessed by the individual. But this type of cross-cultural scrutiny gives abundant opportunity to the federal judge to engage in a dangerous exercise of ethnocentrism, ignoring the history surrounding the development of the particular court, the cultural forces that have shaped the jurisprudence of the tribe, the stage of development the court may be in, the resource deficit the tribal court may have suffered in its development, and the effects the rights of a non-Indian individual may have upon the human rights possessed by a collective of individuals who have lived here for centuries.

The Iowa Mutual case made reference to the principle of comity.[14] When comity is brought forth as a measure between sovereigns, the courts abandon inquiries into jurisdiction or authority. The courts determine whether good relations between the sovereigns may outweigh any other interests. An enlightened federal court will surely perceive that with every Indian case appealed into the federal district court through the avenues created by National Farmers Union and Iowa Mutual, the notion of comity can be further refined. In the alternative, federal judges are likely to be faced with a difficult question as to what weight they must give to a tribe's need and desire to remain independent and unique. Federal courts will have to determine whether or not they are justified to criticize a tribal system where the tribe chooses consciously to avoid written laws, a written record, and other legal positivistic notions. Federal courts will have to develop a standard by which they can cross-culturally measure the validity of tribal process and of Indian expectations of justice. The challenge is whether or not federal and state courts, the American public, and Congress are willing to allow for the birth of a new respect between Indians and non-Indians.

Endnotes

1 Also known as the Wheeler-Howard Act, Ch. 576, 48 Stat. 894, codified at 25 U.S.C. §§461-479.

2 See *Talton v. Mayes*, 163 U.S. 376 (1896).

3 Pub. L. No. 90-284, 82 Stat. 77, codified at 25 U.S.C. §§1301-1303.

4 436 U.S. 49 (1978).

5 Pub. L. No. 103-176.

6 Pub. L. 96-96, codified at 16 U.S.C. §§470aa-470mm (1979).

7 Pub. L. No. 101-601 (Nov. 16, 1990).

8 Pub. L. No. 95-341, 92 Stat. 469, codified at 42 U.S.C.§1996 (1978).

9 Act of Aug. 15, 1953, Ch. 505, 67 Stat. 588-90. Alaska was added to the list of Public Law 280 states by the Act of Aug. 8, 1958, Pub. L. No. 85-615, 72 Stat. 545, as it was admitted to the Union.

10 The Native Hawaiians have been consistently omitted from the operation of federal laws which pertain to Native Americans. Native Hawaiians are Native Americans but, like Alaska Natives, have been pigeonholed into a separate category as suits federal, state, and private interests.

Native Hawaiians have been successful in creating a diversion from state prosecution into the traditional process of *Ho'oponopono*.

11 Act of Dec. 18, 1971, Pub. L. No. 92-203.

12 471 U.S. 845 (1985).

13 480 U.S. 9 (1987).

14 Iowa Mutual interpreting National Farmers Union said that "considerations of comity" underlie the rule of exhaustion of tribal remedies. 480 U.S. 15. The deference prescribed in Iowa Mutual suggests that comity considers the extent to which Federal Court action would "[impair] the [tribe's] authority over reservation affairs" 480 U.S. 16, or "[infringe] upon tribal lawmaking authority."

22

Transferring Juveniles to Adult Courts
Recent Trends and Issues in Canada and the United States

RICK RUDDELL, G. LARRY MAYS, and DENNIS M. GIEVER

This research focuses on the practice of transferring juvenile offenders to adult courts in the United States and Canada. The questions we ask are whether American juvenile justice systems are more punitive than their Canadian counterparts, and what are the consequences of the policies pursued by both nations. We will examine the numbers of youngsters transferred to adult courts in both nations, the offenses that precipitated the transfers, and the legislative mechanisms by which these youths are transferred to adult courts. Also we are concerned with the variables affecting transfers in Canada and the United States from 1986 to 1994, and with the juvenile justice legislation in both nations. Because federal Canadian juvenile legislation was first implemented in 1985, the research represents a nine-year summary of Canadian transfers to adult court.[1] The transfer of juveniles to adult, or general jurisdiction criminal, court is not a new phenomenon: since the juvenile court was created, legal provisions have authorized removal of the most serious delinquents from juvenile court jurisdiction for prosecution as adults (Forst, 1995; Osbun and Rode, 1984; Whitebread and Batey, 1981). In the past two decades,

Reprinted by permission from the *Juvenile and Family Court Journal*, Vol. 49, No. 3 (Summer, 1998) pp. 1–16. Copyright © 1998 by the National Council of Juvenile and Family Court Judges, 1041 North Virginia Street, Third Floor, Reno, NV 89557. All right reserved.

however, widespread legislative changes have facilitated these transfers and increased the number of youths transferred to criminal court (Feld, 1987; Fritsch and Hemmens, 1995; Torbet et al., 1996).

The transfer of youths to criminal courts—also defined as waiver, certification, or remand—represents the cornerstone of a contemporary get-tough movement directed at juvenile offenders. Transferring a youth to a criminal court typically puts the youngster at higher risk of more serious legal sanctions, including the death penalty in some American states (Federle, 1996; Forst, 1995). Currently, the research on whether transferred youths actually receive tougher sanctions is mixed (Fagan and Deschenes, 1990; Fritsch, Caeti and Hemmons, 1996; Houghtalin and Mays, 1991; Poulos and Orchowsky, 1994). The findings vary across jurisdictions and depend on the nature of the offense(s) with which the youth is charged, the youth's prior criminal record, and extra-legal factors such as the youth's age, organizational factors within the juvenile justice system, politics, and the influence of the media.

While considerable research studies youngsters transferred to criminal courts in the United States, there has been relatively little international comparative analysis of juvenile justice legislation; much of the literature is merely descriptive in nature (see, for example, Feld, 1994; Hessle, 1992; Kashti, 1992). By learning from the experiences of other nations, we can maximize research efforts, improve policy development, and create opportunities for legislative change. Perhaps, more important, by studying others we can learn more about ourselves.

The Canadian and U.S. juvenile justice systems share legal traditions in British common law (Parsloe, 1978; West, 1991). As a result, even though the United States and Canada have differing political, economic, cultural and legal histories, many of the juvenile justice strategies their respective legislators have initiated to address delinquent behavior have been quite similar. For example, the first juvenile court based on the *parens patriae* doctrine was established in Cook County, Illinois in 1899 (Bernard, 1992). Canada adopted this social welfare orientation in 1908, when it enacted the Juvenile Delinquents Act (Caputo, 1993; West, 1991).

A cornerstone of the social welfare oriented juvenile justice policies was the belief that youngsters could be deterred from further delinquency if they received appropriate treatment or rehabilitation. Accordingly, both Canadian and American juvenile justice systems traditionally were characterized by informal, confidential, and nonadversarial courts. Because youths ostensibly were being rehabilitated and not punished, there was little perceived need for due process protections. The focus was on the offender, not on the offense.

A growth in youth crime during the 1970s and 1980s and a concern over a lack of due process rights for juveniles created considerable dissatisfaction with the juvenile court (Greenwood, 1995; Schwartz, 1989). In the United States a series of Supreme Court decisions beginning in the mid-1960s effectively minimized *parens patriae* in favor of due process rights for juveniles (see especially, Feld, 1987). The 1974 enactment of the federal Juvenile Justice and Delinquency Prevention Act (18 U.S.C. Section 5031) also mandated significant changes in juvenile justice. At the same time, states enacted increasingly tougher legislation for juvenile offenders despite federal policies suggesting restraint.

By contrast, Canada also enacted federal juvenile justice legislation, the Young Offenders Act of 1984, after almost twenty years of debate. The YOA attempts to balance the rehabilitative needs of youngsters in conflict with the law against the need for community protection. In many ways, the YOA represents a compromise between the child welfare and the adult criminal justice approaches. Some believe that the YOA has been undermined by lack of adequate facilities, resources and programs to deal with juvenile offenders (Bala and Kirvan, 1991). Consequently, the YOA has been amended on several occasions during its 14 years of existence. Many of these amendments have made sanctions for convicted youths more serious.

A Brief Comparison of Canadian and U.S. Justice Systems

The present research provides an opportunity to learn about juvenile justice systems from a cross-national perspective. The Canadian and American juvenile justice systems have many similarities, but also important differences. By learning how different nations attempt to control crime and delinquency, we ultimately learn more about our own mechanisms for controlling crime.

As one-time English colonies both Canada and the United States developed legal systems based on common law principles. However, the two nations have differences in law because of their different legal histories. On the one hand, U.S. law evolved after a revolution with England. On the other hand, the Canadian structure and practice of law developed in relationship with England both as a colony until 1867, and still as a constitutional monarchy and member of the British Commonwealth of Nations.

Current American criminal justice systems have been critically described as being loosely coupled, highly politicized and racist (Hagan, 1989). Interagency coordination is hampered by the existence of some 20,000 law enforcement agencies (Reichel, 1994). Many of these interagency relationships are characterized by a lack of cooperation and, on occasion, by competition for resources. Additionally, criminal law is legislated by both the states and the federal government, resulting in more than 51 different legal codes for juveniles, since the Virgin Islands, Guam, Puerto Rico, and other U.S. possessions have their own. A further difference is the political nature of American criminal justice practice, with the election of judges, prosecuting attorneys, and county sheriffs in most jurisdictions. Corrado and Turnbull (1992) observe that public opinion often compels modifications of state and federal law due to political pressures.

Canadian criminal justice systems, by contrast, are influenced by a strong federal history, with national criminal code legislation, the presence of a strong national police force, and prosecutors appointed under the auspices of the ruling monarch, and who prosecute all criminal code offenses on her behalf.

American Juvenile Transfer Legislation

The transfer of juveniles to adult criminal courts is neither a recent nor a rare phenomenon in the United States. Legal provisions have always existed to remove the most serious delinquents from the jurisdiction of the juvenile court and prosecute them as adults in the criminal courts (Fagan, 1990; Feld, 1987; Forst, 1995; Snyder and Sickmund, 1995). Today transferring youths to adult courts is a common practice: in 1992 an estimated 11,700 juvenile delinquency cases were transferred to adult courts (Sickmund, 1994). Research has been mixed on whether youngsters actually receive more severe sanctions in adult courts (see, e.g., Fagan and Deschenes, 1990; Fritsch et al., 1996; Gillespie and Norman, 1984; Houghtalin and Mays, 1991; Kinder et al., 1995; Poulos and Orchowsky, 1994). However, transfer facilitates a range of more serious sanctions, including the death penalty in some American states.

The legal mechanisms that facilitate transfers are the judicial waiver, legislative waiver (sometimes called legislative exclusion or automatic waiver), prosecutorial waiver, and self-certification or demand waiver.[2] Judicial waiver is the most common transfer mechanism, and all states but Connecticut, Nebraska, New Mexico, and New York have provisions for judicial waivers.

While the different mechanisms states use to transfer youths to adult courts are fairly clear, the goals that underlie transfer decisions often lack clarity (Bortner, 1986; Cintron, 1996). Any sentencing decision is based on competing principles of retribution, isolation, incapacitation, rehabilitation, and deterrence. When we intentionally expose a youngster to more severe sanctions through transfer to adult court, it is apparent that the principles of retribution, isolation, and deterrence are elevated above rehabilitation.

Canadian Juvenile Transfer Legislation

Under Section Nine of the Juvenile Delinquents Act (1908) provisions for judicial transfers authorized judges to transfer to adult courts juveniles over 14 who had committed indictable offenses. Indictable offenses are the Canadian equivalent to an American felony. Because many provinces defined the onset of adulthood under the JDA at age 16, a transfer to regular criminal court was a relatively rare occurrence. Most serious offenses tend to be committed by the older teenagers.

The Young Offenders Act of 1984 changed the contrasting definitions of youth and adulthood by instituting a uniform maximum age. The YOA provides a national standard for the administration of juvenile justice across all ten provinces and two territories. The Act prescribes a judicial waiver mechanism. where the youth court judge makes the transfer decision (Besta and Wintemute, 1988; Manfredi, 1991). Such transfers are requested by the crown prosecutor. In the most recent amendment to the Act, youths 14 or older may be transferred to adult court, if they are alleged to have committed first degree murder, second degree murder, attempted murder, manslaughter, or aggravated sexual assault.

Youngsters 16 or 17 when they commit the offense appear in youth court, and they must demonstrate why they should remain within the youth court's jurisdiction. These presumptive transfer provisions represent the latest (December 7, 1995) amendment to the YOA. Prior to this, the conditions by which a youth could be transferred were more difficult to establish, since the crown prosecutor had to convince the youth court judge that a transfer was appropriate. The recency of some of these changes limits the availability of data for this research. However, placing the burden on youngsters to demonstrate why they should remain within the youth court likely will result in increasing numbers of transfers.

The transfer process is adversarial. According to the 1996 version of the YOA, the parameters of the transfer decision include the seriousness of the offense; the young person's age, maturity, character, and background; previous convictions; the availability of treatment or correctional resources; and any other factors the court considers relevant.

Like *Kent v. U.S.*,[3] Canadian Supreme and Appellate Court decisions have given some direction to lawyers and judges. Some western provinces, such as Alberta, British Columbia, and Manitoba, frequently have exercised a more punitive orientation than the rest of the nation. These provinces place youngsters in custody or transfer them to adult courts at a higher rate than the other provinces.

Doob and Sprott (1996:441) examined this interprovincial variation in the use of custodial sanctions and suggest that this is "less likely to be caused by differential behavior of youth than it is to the behavior of criminal justice personnel." Despite the existence of a punitive orientation in some jurisdictions, the transfer of a youngster to criminal court is a rare occurrence. However, since 1992 two legislative amendments to the YOA have eased the transfer process, and we suspect that the numbers of youngsters transferred will increase over time.

Like American juvenile justice systems, transfers to adult courts under the YOA represent the last resort on the continuum of sanctions (Emerson, 1981). Every year a significant number of American juveniles, and a lesser number of Canadian youngsters, are tried as adults. This is an extremely complex issue, which has polarized opinion from both liberal and conservative crime control perspectives. As a result, it is a potentially fruitful area for investigation.

Research Methods

This research explores legislative trends and examines juvenile codes in the United States and Canada. We seek to determine the types of changes the juvenile justice codes have undergone that make sanctions on youths more severe. This information is interpreted in terms of juvenile code changes over a four-year period, through the end of 1995. Information from the Office of Juvenile Justice and Delinquency Prevention was used to compile the American legislative data. These data were current at the end of the 1995 legislative sessions for all 51 jurisdictions in the United States.

Information about legislative changes in Canada was collected through a review of legislation within the YOA, located in the Criminal Code of Canada, from 1992 through the 1996 edition. This research uses the December 7, 1995 amendments to the YOA as the last legislative change. As the YOA was amended too late in the legislative year to be included in the 1995 Criminal Code, the 1996 edition of the Criminal Code of Canada is used as a reference for the latest amendments.

We analyzed the national juvenile transfer trends in Canada and the United States from April 1, 1986 to March 31, 1994. These national trends are examined from a comparative perspective, with emphasis on two issues: the stability over time of the populations of youths transferred from juvenile to adult courts; and the nature of the offense that precipitated transfer.

Data about juvenile transfers for Canada were obtained from the Canadian Centre for Justice Statistics (CCJS), Statistics Canada in Ottawa, Ontario. Data about national trends for the United States were obtained from the National Center for Juvenile Justice (NCJJ) in Pittsburgh, Pennsylvania.

The national juvenile justice data in both nations suffer from limitations. U.S. juvenile court statistics are based on estimates. Additionally, the data identify only juveniles transferred to adult court through the judicial waiver mechanism. Youths who enter the adult system through statutory conditions or through prosecutorial discretion are not counted in this total, and there are no current estimates for the youth population affected by these practices. During the period of analysis, the United States transferred about 85,000 juveniles to adult courts.

Canadian data suffer from similar limitations. While the YOA was originally enacted in 1984, the federal government gave the provinces until April, 1985 to implement it. The transition from the Juvenile Delinquency Act to the Young Offenders Act was not smooth, and one of the consequences is a lack of data pertaining to transfers for the first 18 months of the new legislation. A further limitation of the data was the non-participation of the province of Ontario from April 1, 1986 to March 31, 1991, and of the Northwest Territories from April 1, 1988 to March 31, 1990. The exclusion of Ontario, Canada's most heavily populated province, is more significant than the exclusion of the Northwest Territories, Canada's least populated territory.[4]

A further weakness with the Canadian data is the limited information provided by the Youth Court Statistics. The only data available from CCJS are the numbers of offenders, their ages and offenses, and the province which transferred the youth. These data lack more specific information about the offender's prior criminal history, educational level, or race. In total, 521 Canadian youths were transferred to adult court during the period examined.

In addition to the criminal justice statistics from both nations, we also make reference to the number of youths at risk. This refers to the number of adolescents who potentially could fall within the jurisdiction of the juvenile court. For U.S. data, information from the NCJJ was used. The 1995 population projections for the United States were obtained from Census Bureau statistics. Canadian data were obtained from Statistics Canada's Annual Demographic Statistics. These estimates are based on the 1991 Canadian Census. As only youngsters 14 and over may be transferred to adult court, youths at-risk were compiled by adding all of the estimated populations of 14- to 17-year-old youths from 1986 to 1994. The reader should note that all statistics calculated in this research are rounded. As a result some tables may be subject to rounding error.

Data and Analysis

Data collection for this research was guided by four propositions. In this section we will present these propositions (or working hypotheses) and the evidence we gathered to test these propositions.

Proposition 1: A majority of youths transferred to adult courts in the United States from 1986 to 1994 committed non-violent offenses

Table 1 outlines the categories of offenses that precipitated transfer to adult court in the United States from 1986 to 1994. The National Center for Juvenile Justice, which provided this information, defines violent offenses as criminal homicide, forcible rape, robbery, aggravated assault, simple assault, sex offenses and other personal offenses. Table 1 also outlines the total population of youths at-risk in the U.S., the total number of youngsters appearing before juvenile courts, as well as the numbers of transfers.

A review of Table 1 indicates that over the nine years examined, the total number of youths at-risk in the U.S. decreased by 228,000. However, during this period the number of youngsters appearing before juvenile courts increased by 35%. Transfers to adult courts ranged from a low of 7,000 youths in 1987 and 1988 to a high of 12,300 in 1994. This represents an increase in transfers of 76%.

The number of youths transferred to adult courts for violent offenses ranged from a low of 2,000 in 1987 and 1988 to a high of 5,400 in 1994, an increase of 170% over this time period. Clearly, Table 1 illustrates that over time the number of transfers is increasing, as is the percentage of youths transferred for committing violent crimes. Nevertheless, despite the recent increase of youngsters being transferred for violent offenses, Proposition 1 seems supported: a majority of youths transferred to adult court in the United States between 1986 and 1994 were charged with committing non-violent offenses.

Proposition 2: A majority of the youths transferred to adult courts in Canada from 1986 to 1994 committed violent offenses

Table 2 illustrates the numbers of Canadian youths transferred to adult courts from 1986 to 1994. The Canadian Centre for Justice Statistics defines a violent offense as murder, manslaughter, attempted murder, sexual assault, sexual assault with a weapon, indecent assault, aggra-

Table I
American Youths Transferred to Adult Courts: 1986 to 1994

Year	Total Youths At-Risk	Youths Appearing*	Gross Transfers	Violent Offenses
1986	12,960,000	1,151,000	7,500	2,400
1987	12,608,000	1,154,600	7,000	2,000
1988	12,139,000	1,170,500	7,000	2,000
1989	11,797,000	1,211,900	8,300	2,300
1990	11,677,000	1,299,200	8,700	2,800
1991	11,810,000	1,406,500	11,100	3,600
1992	12,023,000	1,482,300	11,500	4,800
1993	12,296,000	1,482,300	11,600	5,000
1994	12,732,000	1,555,200	12,300	5,400
Totals	*110,042,000*	*11,913,500*	*85,000*	*30,300*
Nine Year				
Average:	*12,226,888*	*1,323,722*	*9,444*	*3,366*

*Total of all cases appearing before the Juvenile Court

vated assault, assault with a weapon, causing bodily harm, minor assault, assault on a police officer, robbery, dangerous use of a weapon, possession of a weapon, kidnapping/hostage taking, and criminal negligence. For the most part, these categories are consistent with the definitions used in the U.S. by the National Center for Juvenile Justice.

A review of Table 2's data demonstrates that from 1986 to 1994, the total number of Canadian youths at-risk remained almost constant. The number of youngsters appearing before youth courts, by contrast, increased substantially. It is important to note that the non-participation of the province of Ontario from April 1,1986 to March 31, 1991 and of the Northwest Territories from April 1, 1988 to March 31, 1990 in the collection of youth court statistics does affect the totals.

The numbers of juveniles transferred to adult courts during this era ranged from a low of 33 in 1989 to a high of 85 in 1994. This represents a variance of 158%. Of particular importance, the greatest numbers of transfers occurred in 1986 and 1994, the start and end dates of this inquiry.

The numbers of Canadian youths transferred to adult court for committing violent offenses also show some variation. However, it is especially important to note that in 1986, 1987, 1988, and 1990 the numbers of offenders transferred for non-violent offenses exceeded those transferred for violent offenses. For the entire period, 521 youths were trans-

Table 2
Canadian Youths Transferred to Adult Courts: 1986 to 1994

Year**	Total Youths At-Risk	Youths Appearing*	Gross Transfers	Violent Offenses
1986	1,554,800	35,252	79	37
1987	1,535,000	36,097	68	25
1988	1,507,400	36,050	50	20
1989	1,498,700	37,597	33	21
1990	1,511,700	37,975	41	20
1991	1,527,100	73,527	59	33
1992	1,538,300	70,235	42	30
1993	1,551,100	70,406	64	39
1994	1,565,500	67,490	85	67
Totals	*13,789,600*	*464,629*	*521*	*292*
Nine Year Average:	1,532,177	51,625	57.8	32.4

*Total of all cases appearing before the Juvenile Court
**Note: Table does not include youths appearing, or transfers, for Ontario from
   1986 to 1991 or the Northwest Territories from 1988 to 1990

ferred to adult courts, and 292 (56%) were for violent offenses. Although this lends support to Proposition 2, it provides a surprisingly marginal difference.

One advantage the Canadian youth court statistics provided was comprehensive information on the breakdown of violent versus non-violent offenses that precipitated transfer, and the provinces from which youths were transferred. This information is presented in Tables 3 and 4. Although there are no similar U.S. data to compare with these Canadian figures, these tables do provide a more comprehensive understanding about Canadian youths transferred to adult court.

Table 3 provides some important insight into the offenses that precipitated transfer to adult courts. In terms of violent offenses, youngsters are more likely to be transferred to adult court for their participation in a robbery (12% of the youths transferred) than for a homicide (11% of the youths transferred). Other serious offenses that tend to instigate transfers are assault with a weapon, attempted murder, and sexual assaults. It is interesting to note that minor assaults are a very small proportion of all offenses precipitating transfer (with only 3% of the total violent offenses), even though common assault is the most frequent violent crime committed by young offenders.

Table 3
**Offenses Precipitating Transfer to Adult Courts: Canada,
1986 to 1994**

Violent Offenses	Number of Youths Transferred	
Total	292	*(56%)*
Robbery	61	(12%)
Murder	57	(11%)
Assault with weapon	35	(7%)
Attempted Murder	28	(5%)
Sexual Assault	28	(5%)
Minor Assault	17	(3%)
Rape/Sexual Assault	16	(3%)
Aggravated Assault	9	(9%)
All other Violent	39	(7%)
Non-Violent Offenses	**Number of Youths Transferred**	
Total	229	*(44%)*
Break-and-Enter	116	(22%)
Theft Over $1000	18	(3%)
Escape Custody	18	(3%)
Young Offenders Act	17	(3%)
Possession of Stolen Property	14	(3%)
Fail to AppearAll Other	10	(2%)
Theft Under $1000	8	(2%)
All Other	28	(5%)

The data on non-violent offenses are also enlightening. From 1986 to 1994, 116 Canadian youngsters were transferred to adult courts for participating in break-and-enter offenses. This number represents over one-half of all non-violent offenders transferred, and 22% of all offenders transferred. In fact, it represents the largest single category of offenders tried as adults. By contrast, during this same period, 57 youths were transferred for murder. This finding seems to suggest that Canadian youth courts are placing a greater emphasis on punitive sanctions for property offenses than violent offenses. However, we should keep in mind that break-and-enter is a very common juvenile offense, and the numbers reported here represent the total number of transfers and not the rate of transfer. Furthermore, the CCJS statistics do not indicate whether youths transferred for such offenses are persistent offenders.

Additional data regarding Canadian transfers are found in Table 4. This table outlines the provincial and regional nature of transfers in Canada. It demonstrates that some jurisdictions, such as Alberta and Manitoba, transfer youngsters to adult court at a higher rate than other provinces.

Table 4
Canadian Youths by Province and Region, 1986 to 1994

Jurisdiction	Percentage of Canadian Pop.*	Total Transfers=521	
Alberta	9.3%	105	(20%)
British Columbia	12.9%	43	(8%)
Manitoba	3.8%	132	(25%)
New Brunswick	2.5%	6	(1%)
Newfoundland	1.9%	9	(2%)
N.W.T	.2%	9	(2%)
Nova Scotia	3.1%	15	(3%)
Ontario	37.6%	60	(12%)
P.E.I.	.5%	1	(0.2%)
Quebec	24.6%	130	(25%)
Saskatchewan	3.4%	9	(2%)
Yukon	.1%	2	(0.2%)
Western Canada:			
(B.C., Alta., Sask., Man.)	29.45%	289	(55%)
Eastern Canada:			
(Nfld, N.E., P.E.I.)	70.21%	221	(42%)
Territories:			
(Yukon, N.W.T.)	.33%	11	(2%)

NOTE: Ontario did not participate from 1986 to 1990
     N.W.T did not participate from 1986 to 1990
*Source of Demographic Statistics: Statistics Canada, October, 1996 Population
  estimates

Also, the provinces that form Western Canada transfer a higher number of youths than would be expected by their population. This means that while as a nation Canada does not transfer as many youngsters as the United States, some jurisdictions within Canada clearly seem more punitive than others.

The data presented in Tables 1 and 2 indicate that during the nine years examined, juveniles in the U.S. were more likely to be transferred to adult court for committing non-violent offenses. In Canada, we found that youths were more likely to be transferred for committing violent offenses. The overall percentage of youths transferred for violent offenses (56%), however, gives only marginal confirmation to Proposition 2. By breaking these data into specific offenses, we can see from Table 3 how the offense that precipitates most Canadian transfers is break-and-enter.

Proposition 3: The number of youths transferred to adult courts in the United States from 1986 to 1994 increased significantly

This proposition examines whether transfers are being used at an increasing rate over time. If more juveniles are being transferred to adult courts, then one might argue that juvenile justice systems are becoming more punitive. If juvenile justice systems become more punitive, are they also becoming obsolete? In other words, are we abandoning the principles of juvenile courts?

Table 5 shows how expansive the use of transfers has been in the United States, ranging from a low of 7,000 in 1987 and 1988 to a high of 12,300 in 1994. It is important to observe that the number of juveniles transferred from 1986 to 1990 was fairly consistent: between 7,000 and 8,700. This represents an increase of only 24% over the four years. By 1991 there was an explosive growth in the number of youngsters transferred, an increase of 28% in one year. Once again we add a word of caution: such a sudden, significant jump may be partially attributable to changes such as reporting practices occurring during this period.

One trend evident in Table 5 is the growth in the percentage of violent offenses precipitating transfers. During the first six years in this study, the percentage of violent offenders transferred ranged from 28% to 32%. This contrasts with the final three years when the percentage of violent offenders increased to 44% of all transfers.

These data clearly show that number of youths transferred in the U.S. has grown steadily from 1988 to 1994. Because the numbers have increased by 76%, Proposition 3 seems substantiated.

Proposition 4: The number of youths transferred to adult courts in Canada from 1986 to 1994 has remained relatively stable

Trends for Canadian youths being transferred to adult courts are outlined in Table 6: the range is from 33 to 85 youngsters. An interesting aspect of this variance is that after introduction of the YOA in 1986, relatively high numbers of youths were transferred. These numbers declined over three years, then stabilized for three years. This stabilization was followed by another increase in transfers.

The range in the numbers of youths transferred—from 33 to 85 cases—represents a variance of 158% over the period examined. This range is double that found in U.S. statistics: during the same period the American rate of transfer increased 76%. As a result, Proposition 4 is not supported; Canadian rates of transfer have fluctuated over time. However, we must

Table 5
Stability of Transfers in the United States: 1896 to 1994

Year	Gross Transfers	Violent Transfers		Non-Violent Transfers	
1986	7,500	2,400	(32%)	5,100	(68%)
1987	7,000	2,000	(29%)	5,000	(71%)
1988	7,000	2,000	(29%)	5,000	(71%)
1989	8,300	2,300	(28%)	6,000	(72%)
1990	8,700	2,800	(32%)	5,900	(68%)
1991	11,100	3,600	(32%)	7,500	(68%)
1992	11,500	4,800	(32%)	6,700	(58%)
1993	11,500	5,000	(43%)	6,600	(57%)
1994	12,300	5,400	(44%)	6,900	(56%)
Totals	*85,000*	*30,300*	*(35%)*	*54,700*	*(64%)*

Table 6
Stability of Transfers in Canada: 1896 to 1994

Year	Gross Transfers	Violent Transfers		Non-Violent Transfers	
1986	79	37	(47%)	42	(53%)
1987	68	25	(37%)	43	(63%)
1988	50	20	(40%)	30	(60%)
1989	33	21	(64%)	12	(36%)
1990	41	20	(49%)	21	(51%)
1991	59	33	(56%)	26	(44%)
1992	42	30	(71%)	12	(29%)
1993	64	39	(61%)	25	(39%)
1994	85	67	(79%)	18	(21%)
Totals	*521*	*292*	*(56%)*	*229*	*(44%)*

NOTE: Table does not include statistics on transfers for Ontario from 1986 to 1991 or the Northwest Territories from 1988 to 1990.

issue a very important caveat: the relatively small youth population transferred, and the missing data previously mentioned, certainly affect the Canadian numbers.

To summarize, the data gathered from Canada and the United States indicate that in 1994 the likelihood of a Canadian youth's being transferred to an adult court was one of every 18,417 youths at-risk. By contrast, the likelihood of an American youth's being transferred to an adult court during the same year was one of every 1,035 youths at-risk. Thus, we can say that a youth in the U.S. is 18 times more likely to be transferred to an adult court as a Canadian youth. Perhaps this figure most clearly affirms the notion that juvenile justice systems in the United States are more punitive than their Canadian counterparts.

Conclusions

A quick review of legislation in Canada and the United States reveals that both nations have very similar transfer provisions in their respective juvenile justice codes. It is also apparent that these codes are not static, but dynamic: legislators are frequently changing and modifying juvenile codes in many jurisdictions. For instance, from 1992 to 1995 Canada and 48 American jurisdictions changed their juvenile justice legislation to make sanctions more severe for youngsters appearing before the courts.[5] These sanctions made dispositions more severe, reduced confidentiality levels for offenders, involved victims more in the justice process, eased transfer processes, and made correctional programming more punitive.

One major difference between the two nations is that U.S. jurisdictions are more likely to transfer youngsters who commit non-violent offenses, while Canadian courts are more likely to transfer youths who commit violent offenses. Over the nine years examined in this research, only 36% of American juveniles transferred to adult courts committed violent offenses. During the same period, 56% of Canadian young offenders were transferred for violent offenses. However, in four of the nine years examined, Canada also transferred more youths for property offenses than for violent offenses.

The relatively low numbers of violent offenders transferred in the U.S. might be due to youths who bypassed the juvenile court altogether as a result of prosecutorial discretion, lowered age limits for adult court jurisdiction, and statutory exclusion of many violent offenses. If we were able to include these youths in our data, the American percentages of violent versus non-violent youths transferred might be more consistent with the Canadian data. Unfortunately, the information about juveniles in the U.S. sent directly to adult courts is not available.

One unexpected Canadian finding occurred after the offenses that precipitated transfer were classified as the actual crimes instead of the broad categories of violent and non-violent offenses. Of the 521 Canadian youngsters transferred to adult courts from 1986 to 1994, 116 were transferred for the offense of break-and-enter. This contrasts with 57 youths transferred for homicide.[6] Another Canadian finding involves provincial and regional variations in transfers. Provinces such as Alberta and Manitoba transfer youngsters to adult courts at a higher rate per capita than other provinces or territories. In addition, the provinces that form Western Canada transfer a higher rate of youths per capita than Eastern Canada or the Territories.

In terms of youths transferred to adult courts, both the U.S. and Canadian data demonstrate a significant increase over the years: 76% for the U.S. and 158% for Canada. The lack of stability for the Canadian data might be attributable to problems occurring after implementation of the YOA (for example, no suitable custodial facilities for older young offenders who already had served dispositions in adult facilities). This could have created a higher initial rate of transfer than in subsequent years. Another factor that might have affected the lack of stability over time is the lack of uniform reporting by the provinces.

The numbers of youths transferred certainly vary between the two countries: in 1994 one of every 1,035 youths at-risk was transferred to adult courts in the United States. By contrast, Canada transferred one of every 18,417 youths at-risk during the same year. Nevertheless, the clear trend was for both nations to transfer increasing numbers of youngsters to adult courts from 1986 to 1994.

Does this research indicate that U.S. juvenile justice systems are more punitive than their Canadian counterparts? Unfortunately, there is a lack of information on dispositional and custodial histories of youths transferred to adult courts, and research to date has been contradictory about whether the formal sanctions youths actually receive are more severe (Barnes and Franz, 1989; Bortner, 1986; Fagan et al., 1987; Fritsch et al., 1996; Gillespie and Norman, 1984; Hamparian et al., 1982; Houghtalin and Mays, 1991). One reason why juvenile offenders in the U.S. receive less severe sanctions in adult courts is an apparent punishment gap where transferred youths receive the leniency typically given to any first-time adult offender (see, for example, Feld, 1987).

From this research, one could make a case that the juvenile justice systems in Canada and the United States are on parallel paths. Based on legislation they are very similar: the Canadian YOA closely resembles the juvenile justice codes in most U.S. jurisdictions. Additionally, recent Canadian Supreme Court decisions and legislative changes have reduced the formal barriers to transferring youngsters. However, while Canada has in many ways prepared to transfer large numbers of offenders to adult courts, there seems to be a reluctance to do so. The transfer trends from 1986 to 1994 indicate that the juvenile justice systems in the United States still remain more punitive than their Canadian counterparts.

Endnotes

[1] The research presented here contains the latest available comparable data on juveniles transferred to adult courts from the National Center for Juvenile Justice and the Canadian Centre for Justice Statistics. At the time revisions were being made to this article, current U.S. data had not been added to the National Center for Juvenile Justice's website, and the Canadian data for 1995 and 1996 will not be available until after this article goes to press.

[2] These processes are described in detail in Champion and Mays (1991).

[3] 383 U.S. 541 (1966).

[4] Ms. Dorothy Gonzales-Singh, a Case Analyst with the Ontario Ministry of Justice, was consulted about information on Ontario's transfers for the missing years. She was able to provide some raw data about the number of offenses transferred in some Ontario jurisdictions. This information was not used as it reflected only a few of the districts, and it focused on criminal charges, not individual offenders. As a result CCJS data solely are used for purposes of this research.

[5] For a complete review of the U.S. legislative changes see Fritsch and Hemmens (1995) and Torbet et al. (1996).

[6] As we noted previously, this represents the gross number and does not account for the rate of youngsters transferred.

References

Bala, Nicholas and Mary-Anne Kirvan (1991). The Statute: Its Principles and Provisions and Their Interpretation by the Courts. In *The Young Offenders Act: A Revolution in Canadian Juvenile Justice*, eds. Alan W. Leschied, Peter G. Jaffe, and Wayne Willis. Toronto: University of Toronto Press.

Barnes, Carole Wolff and Randal S. Franz (1989). Questionably Adult: Determinants and Effects of the Juvenile Waiver Decision. *Justice Quarterly* 6(1): 117–135.

Bernard, Thomas J. (1992). *The Cycle of Juvenile Justice*. New York: Oxford University Press.

Besta, Randall W. and Paul J. Wintemute (1988). Young Offenders in Adult Court: Are We Moving in the Right Direction? *Criminal Law Quarterly* 30(4): 476–491.

Bortner, M. A. (1986). Traditional Rhetoric, Organizational Realities: Remand of Juveniles to Adult Court. *Crime and Delinquency* 32(1): 53–73.

Caputo, Tullio (1993). The Young Offenders Act: Children's Rights, Children's Wrongs. In *Youth Injustice: Canadian Perspectives*, eds. Thomas O'Reilly-Fleming and Barry Clark. Toronto: Canadian Scholars' Press.

Champion, Dean J. and G. Larry Mays (1991). *Transferring Juveniles to Criminal Courts: Trends and Implications for Criminal Justice*. New York: Praeger.

Cintron, Lisa A. (1996). Rehabilitating the Juvenile Court System: Limiting Juvenile Transfers to Adult Court. *Northwest University Law Review* 90(3): 1254–1282.

Corrado, Raymond R. and Susan D. Turnbull (1992). A Comparative Examination of the Modified Justice Model in the United Kingdom and the United States. In *Juvenile Justice in Canada: A Theoretical and Analytical Assessment*. Toronto: Butterworths.

Doob, Anthony N. and Jane B. Sprott (1996). Interprovincial Variation in the Use of the Youth Court. *Canadian Journal of Criminology* October: 401–412.

Emerson, Robert M. (1981). On Last Resorts. *American Journal of Sociology* 87(1): 1–22.

Fagan, Jeffrey (1990). Social and Legal Policy Dimensions of Violent Juvenile Crime. *Criminal Justice and Behavior* 17(1): 93–133.

Fagan, Jeffrey and Elizabeth Piper Deschenes (1990). Determinants of Judicial Waiver Decisions for Violent Juvenile Offenders. *The Journal of Criminal Law and Criminology* 81(2): 314–347.

Fagan, Jeffrey, Martin Forst, and T. Scott Vivona. (1987). Racial Determinants of the Judicial Transfer Decision: Prosecuting Violent Youth in Criminal Court. *Crime and Delinquency* 33(2): 259–286.

Federle, Katherine Hunt (1996). Emancipation and Execution: Transferring Children to Criminal Court in Capital Cases. *Wisconsin Law Review* 3: 447–494.

Feld, Barry C. (1987). The Juvenile Court Meets the Principle of the Offense: Legislative Changes in Juvenile Waiver Statutes. *The Journal of Criminal Law and Criminology* 78(3): 471–533.

Feld, Barry C. (1994). Juvenile Justice Swedish Style: A Rose by Another Name? *Justice Quarterly 11* (4): 625–650.

Forst, Martin L. (1995). *The New Juvenile Justice.* Chicago: Nelson-Hall Publishers.

Fritsch, Eric J., Tory J. Caeti, and Craig Hemmens (1996). Spare the Needle but Not the Punishment: The Incarceration of Waived Youth in Texas Prisons. *Crime and Delinquency* 42(2): 593–609.

Fritsch, Eric and Craig Hemmens (1995). Juvenile Waiver in the United States 1979–1995: A Comparison and Analysis of State Waiver Statutes. *Juvenile & Family Court Journal* 46(3): 17–35.

Gillespie, L. Kay and Michael D. Norman (1984). Does Certification Mean Prison? Some Preliminary Findings from Utah. *Juvenile & Family Court Journal* Fall: 23–34.

Greenwood, Peter W. (1995). Juvenile Crime and Juvenile Justice. In *Crime*, eds. James Q. Wilson and Joan Petersilia. San Francisco: ICS Press.

Hagan, John (1989). Why is There So Little Criminal Justice Theory? Neglected Macro- and Micro-Level Links Between Organization and Power. *Journal of Research in Crime and Delinquency* 26(2):116–135.

Hamparian, Donna M., Linda K. Estep, Susan M. Muntean, Ramon R. Priestino, Robert G. Swisher, Paul L. Wallace, and Joseph L. White (1982). *Major Issues in Juvenile Justice Information and Training—Youth in Adult Courts: Between Two Worlds.* Columbus, OH: Academy for Contemporary Problems.

Hessle, Sven (1992). Welfare in Sweden: The Family and Problematic Adolescents. In *Problem Adolescents: An International View*, ed. Roger Bullock. London: Whiting and Birch.

Houghtalin, Marilyn and G. Larry Mays (1991). Criminal Dispositions of New Mexico Juveniles Transferred to Adult Court. *Crime and Delinquency* 37(3): 393–407.

Kashti, Yitzak (1992). The Education of Problem Adolescents in Israel. In *Problem Adolescents: An International View*, ed. Roger Bullock. London: Whiting and Birch.

Kinder, Kristine, Carol Veneziano, Michael Fichter, and Henry Azuma (1995). A Comparison of the Dispositions of Juvenile Offenders Certified as Adults with Juvenile Offenders Not Certified. *Juvenile & Family Court Journal* Summer: 37–42.

Mamfredi, Christopher P. (1991). The Young Offenders Act and Juvenile Justice in the United States: Perspectives on Recent Reform Proposals. *Canadian Journal of Law and Society* 6: 45–63.

Osbun, Lee Ann and Peter A. Rode (1984). Prosecuting Juveniles As Adults: The Quest for Objective Decisions. *Criminology* 22(2): 187–202.

Parsloe, Phyllida (1978). *Juvenile Justice in Britain and the United States: The Balance of Needs and Rights.* Boston: Routledge and Kegan Paul.

Poulos, Tammy Meredith and Stan Orchowsky (1994). Serious Juvenile Offenders: Predicting the Probability of Transfer to Criminal Court. *Crime and Delinquency* 40(1): 3–17.

Reichel, Philip L. (1994). *Comparative Criminal Justice Systems: A Topical Approach.* Englewood Cliffs, NJ: Prentice Hall.

Schwartz, Ira (1989). *(In)Justice for Juveniles: Rethinking the Best Interests of the Child.* Lexington, MA: Lexington Books.

Sickmund, Melissa (1994). How *Juveniles Get to Adult Court.* Washington, DC: U.S. Department of Justice.

Snyder, Howard N. and Melissa Sickmund (1995). *Juvenile Offenders and Victims: A Focus on Violence.* Pittsburgh: National Center for Juvenile Justice.

Torbet, Patricia, Richard Gable, Hunter Hurst IV, Imogene Montgomery, Linda Szymanski, and Thomas Douglas (1996). *State Responses to Serious and Violent Juvenile Crime.* Pittsburgh: National Center for Juvenile Justice.

West, Gordon (1991). Towards a More Socially Informed Understanding of Canadian Delinquency Legislation. In *The Young Offenders Act: A Revolution in Canadian Juvenile Justice,* eds. Alan W. Leschied, Peter G. Jaffe, and Wayne Willis. Toronto: University of Toronto Press.

Whitebread, Charles H. and Robert Batey (1981). The Role of Waiver in the Juvenile Court: Questions of Philosophy and Function. In *Major Issues in Juvenile Justice Information and Training: Readings in Public Policy,* eds. John C. Hall, Donna M. Hamparian, John M. Pettibone, and Joseph L. White. Columbus, OH: Academy for Contemporary Problems.

23

Evaluating Drug Courts
An Alternative to Incarceration

ELIZABETH MAYFIELD ARNOLD, PAMELA V. VALENTINE, MARGUERITE McINNIS, and C. AARON McNEECE

Substance abuse has been a long-standing problem throughout the United States, where thirty-eight billion dollars are spent annually on cocaine consumption alone. Three-quarters of the funds for intervention are earmarked for domestic enforcement, while only 7 percent is dedicated to treatment (RAND, 1994). The criminal justice system has been radically transformed by the impact of the substance abuse problem as the number of offenders arrested on drug-related charges has increased. Since the early 1980s, state and federal prisons have become inundated with drug offenders.

The federal response to the drug problem was to declare a "War on Drugs" and to establish mandatory sentencing requirements as a condition of financial assistance to the states' criminal justice agencies. These tactics had at least three repercussions: (1) an escalation in the number of persons incarcerated for drug-related offenses; (2) overcrowded prisons; and (3) increases in the number of early releases from prison. Florida, for example, has traditionally ranked near the top of the nation in rates of incarceration. In recent years, the Florida prison system has also ranked near the top in early releases in response to a federal mandate to decrease overcrowding in state prisons. The magnitude of these trends is astounding. In the 1980s, Florida's prison admissions increased by 332 percent; prison releases increased by 399 percent; and the prison population grew by 108 percent (National Council on Crime and Delinquency

Written especially for *Courts and Justice*, 2nd ed.

[NCCD], 1991). In summary, the number of felony drug arrests has increased; court dockets have burgeoned, and available resources for addressing the problem are severely limited. From the conundrum associated with the "War on Drugs," at least three points have become increasingly clear: (1) incarceration in and of itself does little to break the cycle of illegal drug use and crime; (2) offenders sentenced to incarceration for substance-related offenses exhibit a high rate of recidivism once they are released; and (3) drug abuse treatment has been demonstrably effective in reducing both drug abuse and drug-related crime (Drug Court Clearinghouse and Technical Assistance project [DCCTAP], 1996, p. 8).

Since treatment for substance abuse addiction is seen as a key component in preventing re-offenses, the need for alternative programs is evident. More than one million people who need drug treatment are in custody or under community supervision; yet only one in ten is receiving the needed services (Gerstein & Harwood, 1990). In an attempt to combat substance abuse at the community level, several alternatives to incarceration have been tried in recent years. A new, promising and innovative approach to the growing substance abuse problem is the establishment of diversionary programs known as drug courts. Two main types of drug courts exist: those organized simply to speed up the processing of drug offenders and those which exist to provide treatment to offenders. Our focus in this paper is on treatment-oriented drug courts.

In 1989, the first treatment-focused drug court was established by Janet Reno, the sitting State's Attorney for the eleventh Judicial Circuit (Miami, FL). The Miami Drug Court has served as a model for the development of many other courts throughout the nation. The mission of drug courts is to eliminate substance abuse and the resulting criminal behavior through a "team effort that focuses on sobriety and accountability as the primary goals" (National Association of Drug Court Professionals [NADCP], 1997, p. 8). The team of professionals generally includes the state's attorney, public defender, pre-trial intervention or probation staff, treatment providers, and the judge, who is considered to be the central figure on the team.

Because the common goal among the drug court professionals is the recovery of clients from substance abuse, not proving the merits of legal charges against those persons, drug courts tend to be non-adversarial (Goldkamp, in press). Drug court professionals collaborate to provide a structured, ordered, and predictable environment in which offenders can begin and maintain recovery from substance abuse.

While sharing the common belief that incarcerating substance-abusing offenders is not the ultimate solution to the overwhelming problem of substance abuse in this country, drug court officials differ in several respects in their paradigms for viewing addiction. The three competing ideologies historically have been addiction as an illness (the disease model), addiction as behavioral choice affected by psychological and environmental factors (the free-will model), and addiction as the result of low morality standards and bad character (the moralistic model) (Schaler, 1994).

The notion that drug addiction is an illness has been popularized by twelve-step programs such as Alcoholics Anonymous (AA), founded in 1935 by a stockbroker and a physician (Miller, 1995). Inherent in the AA philosophy is the notion that recovery is not a linear process without obstacles to sobriety. Total abstinence from day one of the recovery process is not expected. The AA philosophy is not to chastise those who have a slip or lapse but to be sympathetic and direct in giving guidance about how to handle the situation next time (Nowinski & Baker, 1992). The relapse prevention model of treatment, a cognitive-behavioral technique for the treatment of substance abuse, also reflects the philosophy that a lapse in abstinence is not a sign of failure but a learning opportunity that should be viewed in an optimistic manner (Marlatt & Barrett, 1994). Some believe that relapse is "an unfortunate characteristic of addiction" that should be viewed as an opportunity to evaluate the client's treatment and recovery plan rather than as a sign of treatment failure (Miller, 1995, p. 269).

Drug courts differ from regular criminal courts in their philosophy about substance abuse. In drug courts the disease model is generally accepted, and offenders are offered treatment in lieu of traditional sanctions such as incarceration or probation. While participation is generally voluntary (except in some juvenile drug courts), offenders must adhere to program requirements in order to successfully complete the program. In addition to receiving treatment at no or little cost to them, offenders also may be inclined to participate in drug court programs because many programs offer possible expungement of the offenders' criminal records upon successful completion of the program. For some offenders, the opportunity to have one's record expunged is a strong incentive to participate. However, as this evaluation revealed, the extent to which expungement is actually accomplished in such cases is unclear.

Methodology

The purpose of this study was to evaluate a series of drug court programs throughout the State of Florida; therefore the general method utilized will be described as a program evaluation. The definition of program evaluation used at the Southern Regional Conference on Mental Health Strategies guided the collection and analysis of data. This definition states that the purpose of program evaluation is "determining the degree to which a program is meeting its objectives, the problems it is encountering and the side effects it is creating" (NIMH, 1973, p. 75). Our approach takes note of the distinction between evaluation (making judgments of worth) and evaluative research (involving scientific methods and techniques). This research is strictly evaluative and does not attempt to simply critique the inherent worth of such programs, but to rigorously evaluate their structure and operation.

This evaluation study examined the population of drug court professionals throughout the state of Florida who are: (1) involved in a juvenile or adult drug court, and (2) receive federal Byrne grant monies (Public Law 90-351) for their drug court programs. The judicial circuits that received these funds were identified by the Florida Department of Community Affairs, the statewide funding agency for Byrne fund programs and for this evaluation. All of the judicial districts who participated in this study applied for and were granted federal funds to support one or more aspects of their drug court operations. Their functions and numbers of key professionals varied by judicial circuit, depending on the organization of the court. Twelve counties representing eleven judicial districts in the state of Florida participated in this study. The counties that were included in the evaluation were: Alachua, Bay, Brevard, Duval, Escambia, Hillsborough, Leon, Martin, Monroe, Okaloosa, Pinellas, and Polk.

Interview Procedures

The research team members contacted the program administrators listed in each circuit's grant application who identified the key professionals in their particular drug court program. The key professionals were then contacted by phone and interviewed regarding their involvement in the operations of drug court, thus refining the original list of names. The final sample reflected this process of refinement, resulting in the exclusion of a small number of professionals from the original list who were not currently participating in the functions of drug court in their circuit.

Site visits were scheduled for each judicial circuit over a five-month period, during which interviews with key professionals were conducted by the evaluation team. With permission from all informants, interviews were audiotaped in order to ensure uniformity and consistency among interviewers. Length of the interviews ranged from 20 minutes to two hours. The majority of interviews were one-on-one, but due to time and scheduling constraints group interviews were conducted in some situations.

Guiding Questions

Open-ended, semi-structured questions addressed the following areas: initial drug court experience, history of drug court in that judicial district, definition of drug court in their judicial circuit, court processes, client processes, and treatment component. Following the discussion of these topics, the subject was given the opportunity to elaborate on any concerns, issues, or recommended changes for their drug court.

Role and Theoretical Orientation of the Researchers

Five individuals composed the research team for this study: three Ph.D.-level researchers, one doctoral student, and one masters-level student. All are social workers and have had extensive training and experience in qualitative research and program evaluation. The aim of the research team was not to maintain an objective perspective but rather to glean that information which was meaningful to the participants. This perspective is congruent with ethnoscience theory (Goodenough, 1957), which influenced the orientation of the researchers. This perspective assumes that one can describe what the participants think and believe about a particular issue by listening to what they say. By using linguistically driven techniques, the researcher creates categories that reflect the participants' worldview (Fetterman, 1989). Understanding the subjective beliefs and experiences of the participants was the primary goal of the interview process.

Survey Results

In addition to the qualitative part of this evaluation, measurement instruments were developed for each drug court role for each professional to complete. The measures addressed the responsibilities and functions associated with each position, as well as the resources needed to perform their job duties. As no appropriate standardized measures on this topic existed, the need to develop a new series of measures was evident. The measures were judged to have face validity as determined by two drug court professionals from outside of Florida who were not involved in this evaluation.

Program Similarities and Differences

Since drug courts are relatively new phenomena that can encompass many different aspects of treatment and are organized in a variety of ways, part of the goal of this study was to compare and contrast the similarities and differences of the drug court programs throughout the state. For the most part, drug courts in the state began as diversionary programs targeting first-time, nonviolent, felony drug offenders. Those charged or suspected of selling drugs are generally excluded from participation. However, one change that has occurred in some counties is that offenders with previous arrests or convictions (for nonviolent offenses) are allowed to participate, as well as those with a history of less serious violent offenses.

Beyond the similarities noted above, each drug court is organized and operates somewhat differently. Offenders arrested on drug charges may be referred to drug court in a variety of ways. Offenders may learn of the program through the judge, the state's attorney, the public defender, or the pretrial release staff—depending on the program. In all programs except one offenders must volunteer for participation, The exception is Pinellas County, where juveniles may be mandated by a judge to participate in juvenile drug court. All other programs allow offenders to decline participation in lieu of traditional criminal court proceedings. Some offenders choose this option, as sentencing for a first-time felony drug offense in the state tends to be probation. Those not desirous of treatment may elect to go to a regular criminal court for processing to avoid what they perceive to be a less intrusive sentence.

The twelve courts evaluated also have several other important differences. First, the manner in which sanctions are delivered varies dramatically, depending on the district and the presiding judge. When an offender is not compliant with the terms of the program, some courts have specific or progressive sanctions in place, while others sanction offenders on an individual basis. The use of sanctions also appears to be related to the attitude of the drug court team—specifically, the judge—toward relapse. In courts where relapse is not expected or tolerated, sanctions tend to be more stringent, thus affecting the overall number of offenders who are able to successfully complete the program.

Second, the drug courts evaluated differ in their method of communication among team members. The majority of the courts have team meetings or pre-conference meetings prior to court to discuss the status of cases and make recommendations for offenders. By contrast, some courts appear to have little formal communication between the drug court team members outside of the courtroom. These courts tend to rely on written notes in an offender's chart or direct communication during the drug court proceedings.

Third, the courts differ in the type of treatment services provided. Two of the twelve courts provide in-house treatment, while the remainder contract with outside treatment providers for substance abuse services. In all but one drug court, outpatient treatment services are provided to program participants at no charge. However, clients who need residential or inpatient treatment must generally pay for the treatment themselves or wait for such services to be available through a county-funded facility. The majority of the courts require a substance abuse assessment, outpatient individual counseling, group counseling, and attendance at twelve-step meeting such as Alcoholics Anonymous or Narcotics Anonymous. Three of the twelve counties offer acupuncture as part of the drug court program,

Finally, the manner in which urinalysis is conducted and handled varies dramatically by judicial district. All but one program (Martin County, a juvenile drug court) require offenders to submit to urinalysis to test for the presence of drugs. However, the manner in which the urine specimens are collected varies, with some using sophisticated methods for randomizing and others requiring that specimens be provided at set times or appointments. The number and types of drugs for which the offender is screened also differs. As mentioned above, the manner in which a positive analysis is treated varies by program. Some judges uniformly sanction offenders who test positive for a drug, some require that the offender start the program again from the beginning, and others tolerate occasional relapses as long as the offender is perceived to be making a legitimate effort.

Issues

The diversity of the drug courts throughout the state allows for an evaluation of the perceived weakness of the present structure and operation of these programs. The first and foremost issue is the need for ongoing funding to support the basic operation of the courts and for other needed ancillary services such as residential treatment. Numerous program staff reported uncertainty about future funding and the desire to provide additional services if monies so allowed.

Second, drug court professionals acknowledged a lack of publicity or the inability to promote their programs. Fear of public disapproval of these programs appears to inhibit some from disseminating information within their communities about their availability and/or benefits. In some cases, one or more key individuals may informally mandate that no attention be drawn to the existence of the program.

Third, the lack of uniformity in which professionals in the legal system participate in the program may be cause for further examination of this issue. Those key players in some judicial districts may play a minor role; they may not be involved in any aspect of drug court in other districts. Of particular concern is the absence of participation by the public defender in many programs and the absence of a significant role by the state's attorney in several programs. The primary issue is whether individuals who participate in the drug court program have access to legal counsel to adequately advise them of their legal rights or of other options available to them besides drug court (e.g., pleading guilty in a regular criminal court and most likely receiving probation).

Fourth, several programs reported that offenders do not receive explicit information about expungement of their records. Additionally, some drug court professionals were unable to recall who on their drug court team was responsible for letting the offender know how to go about this process. Offenders may be assuming that this is an automatic process, when expungement generally requires that an offender file a motion and pay a fee. Evidence suggests that many offenders may never hear about expungement.

Findings

Each drug court professional completed a measure for his or her specific role. The results were analyzed, and the key findings are described below.

Among states' attorneys there is disagreement about whether it should be a role of the state's attorney to meet with key members of drug court. However, all states' attorneys agreed that it was and should be their responsibility to collaborate with the drug court team. The majority, though, do meet with members of the drug court team on a regular basis, even though some do not believe pre-court meetings are necessary. Most states' attorneys believed that it is and should be their responsibility that clients know that they will bear the consequences if they violate their drug court contract. Approximately two-thirds of the state attorneys believed it was and should be their responsibility to recommend termination of treatment for a noncompliant offender. Disagreement existed among the states' attorneys about whether it was or should be their responsibility to help draw up prescribed sanctions.

Among public defenders, two-thirds strongly agreed or agreed that they should regularly attend drug court team meetings, but only half do so. The majority of public defenders believed that it should be their responsibility to make recommendations to the court regarding sentencing offenders, but only half do this as well. There is disagreement as to whether it should be the public defender's responsibility to educate offenders about drug court. However, the majority do so. Disagreement exists regarding whether there should be an explicated protocol for the first encounter with the client. All public defenders agree or strongly agree that they should explain to the offender the advantages and disadvantages of participating in drug court; however, this is not done consistently in practice. Additionally, there is disagreement among the public defenders as to whether it should be their responsibility to sanction the offender for failure to comply with drug court; the majority do not sanction offenders.

Adult treatment providers were asked questions about their roles as drug court professionals, and overall there was agreement regarding the roles and responsibilities of adult treatment providers. All agree that they should assess treatment progress at status review hearings, and this is done 75 percent of the time by treatment providers. Treatment providers all agree or strongly agree that they should review a client's treatment plan once a month. All but one treatment provider believe that it is their responsibility to maintain correspondence with drug court personnel, but only 50 percent do this in all cases. Agreement exists among treatment providers that they should submit progress reports on a timely basis, and all do this most or all of the time. Regarding treatment, all agree that they should provide relapse interventions, and this is done most or all of the time.

For pretrial release and probation officers, all strongly agree that they should communicate with key drug court professionals, and this is done most or all of the time. The majority of probation officers believe that they should request sanctions for offenders when appropriate, and this is done by the majority of the probation officers most or all of the time. Only one pretrial officer strongly disagreed that it was his or her responsibility to request sanctions for the offender; this is never done by 25 percent of the pretrial officers. One probation officer did not believe that it was his or her responsibility to check with offenders on a regular basis, but three-fourths of pretrial release officers strongly agree or agree that it is their responsibility to check with offenders on a regular basis. All probation and pre-trial officers strongly agree or agree that it is their responsibility to meet with the drug court team on a regular basis; four-fifths of probation officers and pre-trial officers do this all of the time. Disagreement exists about whether the probation officer should conduct an initial drug court orientation with the offender, but four-fifths do this all of the time.

Among program directors, agreement exists that they should maintain communication among the team of drug court professionals. All also agree that they should be responsible for coordinating drug court team meetings, and this is done by the program director all or most of the time.

Disagreement exists among program directors as to whether they should be responsible for generating reports on the offender, and considerable variation exists as to whether they do so. They also disagree as to whether the program director should attend drug court, but 60 percent do so all of the time.

For judges, all believe that they should meet regularly with the team of drug court professionals. Only one reported never doing this, and one reported doing this only half of the time. The rest did this most of the time. All believe that it is the role of the judge to ensure that sanctions are carried out, and judges do this most or all of the time. Half of the judges agree or strongly agree that it is the judge's role to impose sanctions uniformly on all noncompliant offenders, yet only 30 percent do this all of the time. Additionally, half of the judges believe that it is their responsibility to educate offenders regarding substance abuse, but only 20 percent do this most or all of the time. All judges believe that it is their responsibility to educate the offender regarding the consequences of continued drug use, and all do this at least half of the time.

Recommendations

Based on the previous discussion, a number of recommendations are suggested to enhance the effectiveness and efficiency of the drug courts that receive Byrne Grant funding. First, the minimal level of participation by the state's attorney and public defender is cause for concern. It is recommended that a representative from both offices be required to attend all drug court hearings. With some counties not utilizing the public defender, offenders may not have access to legal counsel when issues arise. It is also recommended that no drug courts be able to require an offender to waive the right to legal counsel as a requirement for program participation.

Second, the lack of clarity and information provided to the offender about expungement needs to be addressed. It is recommended that: (1) each drug court appoint an individual to be responsible for informing the offender about expungement; (2) the public defender associated with each drug court program assist the offender in filing a motion for expungement; and (3) the drug court programs absorb or subsidize the cost of expungement for offenders who successfully complete the program.

Third, it is recommended that each drug court program be required to have some type of pre-court staffing meeting to discuss cases. Having such a meeting appears to enhance communication among drug court staff and allows for better organization and planning.

Finally, the lack of uniformity of sanctions needs to be addressed. While there appears to be no way to establish uniform standards across drug courts, it is recommended that each drug court program establish standards regarding sanctions for specific violations of the drug court contract. Due to the higher graduation rates among drug court programs that view relapse as an integral part of recovery, it is also recommended that programs have some provision for relapse and do not summarily dismiss offenders from the program who have only one or two positive urine samples.

Implications for Drug Treatment and Policy

Drug treatment professionals were identified as key professionals involved in the direct provision of services in all drug courts evaluated. These individuals played an important role in the operation of drug courts as part of a systemic response to substance abuse in a criminal setting. Drug treatment professionals were employed as direct practitioners providing assessment and treatment, as administrators, or as staff members of agencies providing ancillary services to drug court clients. The increasing popularity of drug court programs nationwide has had a potentially significant impact on the need for drug treatment professionals in criminal justice settings. The voluntary nature of drug court programs will allow treatment professionals the opportunity to provide assessment, treatment, and case management services for clients who are not involuntarily mandated for treatment. The provision of services to mandated clients is not a new issue for drug treatment professionals but presents numerous challenges (Rooney, 1992).

The development of drug court programs that provide much needed treatment in lieu of traditional punitive methods such as incarceration and probation provides numerous opportunities for drug treatment professionals to serve as advocates. The need for advocacy at a macro level is demonstrated by the lack of publicity attributed to these programs and reflects the long-standing problem in criminal justice settings that new programs may be resisted because they challenge previous norms and procedures (Treger, 1997). The use of treatment as an alternative to more adversarial methods of handling criminal offenses also allows a broader definition of treatment. Traditionally, criminal justice settings have adhered to a narrow definition of treatment but must continually re-evaluate what constitutes "real treatment" and use effective methods that are appropriate and meet client needs (Cunningham, 1997). Additionally, drug treatment professionals can serve as advocates for offenders seeking expungement and as brokers by providing the necessary resources and information needed to initiate the expungement process.

From a policy perspective, drug courts offer an opportunity for a new focus on the needs of offenders with substance abuse problems in the criminal justice system. Although diversity of opinion exists about how to best handle first-time drug offenders, drug courts that provide treatment provide one of the few feasible alternatives to incarceration. These efforts show promise in preventing these individuals from coming back into the legal system, which traditionally viewed them as criminals primarily and as individuals in need of treatment secondarily or not at all. To ignore the substance-abuse treatment needs of first-time offenders does nothing but ensure that they will most likely reappear on court dockets in the future with the same or more severe treatment needs. In order to ensure that these types of programs meet the long-term needs of participants, further evaluation and longitudinal studies of successful program graduates are needed.

Conclusion

The use of drug court programs to provide treatment to offenders with substance abuse problems is an encouraging alternative to incarcerating offenders who may not otherwise receive the services needed to live drug-free lives. Such programs provide the incentive and opportunity for offenders to pursue help for their addiction, when they may otherwise lack the motivation or financial resources to do so. In most cases, the offender must pay some fees to participate, but the program generally provides treatment at minimal cost. Drug court programs appear to be a feasible alternative to traditional criminal proceedings that may prove more effective in combatting the nationwide drug problem. Although there is some room for improvement, drug court programs have numerous advantages over sentencing drug-addicted offenders to probation or incarceration. Since traditional approaches have not stopped the use of drugs among criminal offenders, new innovative programs such as drug courts deserve a closer look as a potential step in the right direction.

References

Cunningham, G. (1997), Social work and criminal justice: Historical dimensions in practice. In A. R. Roberts (Ed.), *Social work in juvenile and criminal justice settings* (pp. 295–308). Springfield, IL: Charles C Thomas.

Definitions and Classifications Committee, National Institute of Mental Health (1973). Definition of terms in mental health, alcohol abuse, drug abuse, and mental retardation. Mental Health Statistics Series, #8.

Drug Court Clearinghouse and Technical Assistance Project. (1996, May). *Fact sheet* (Tech. Rep). Washington, DC: American University.

Fetterman, D. M. (1989). *Ethnography step by step*. Newbury Park, CA: Sage Publications.

Franklin, J. L. & Thrasher, J. H. (1976). *An introduction to program evaluation*. New York: John Wiley & Sons.

Gerstein, D. R. & Harwood, H. J., Eds. (1990). *Treating drug problems* (Vol. 1). Washington, DC: National Academy Press.

Goldkamp, J. S. (in press). Challenges for research and innovation: When is a drug court not a drug court? In C. Terry (Ed.), *Judicial change and drug treatment courts: Case studies in innovation*.

Goodenough, W. H. (1957). Componential analysis and the study of meaning. *Lan-*

guage 38, 195–216.

Marlatt, G. A., & Barrett, K. (1994). Relapse prevention. In M. Galanter & H. D. Kleber (Eds.), *The American psychiatric press textbook of substance abuse treatment* (pp. 285–299). Washington, DC: American Psychiatric Press, Inc.

Miller, N. S. (1995). *Addiction psychiatry: Current diagnosis and treatment.* New York: John Wiley & Sons.

National Association of Drug Court Professionals. (1997, January). *Defining drug courts: Key components.* Washington, DC: Drug Court Standards Committee, NADCP.

National Council on Crime and Delinquency (1991). *Evaluation of the Florida Community Control Program.* Madison, WI: NCCD.

National Institute of Mental Health. (1973). Definitions and Classifications Committee. *Definition of terms in mental health, alcohol, drug abuse, and mental retardation.* Mental Health Statistics Series No. 8. Washington, DC: Author.

Nowinski, J., & Baker, S. (1992). *The twelve-step facilitation handbook: A systematic approach to early recovery from alcoholism and addiction.* New York: Lexington Books.

RAND (1994). *Projecting future cocaine use and evaluating control strategies* (RB6002). Santa Monica, CA: RAND.

Rooney, R. H. (1992). *Strategies for working with involuntary clients.* New York: Columbia University Press.

Schaler, J. A. (1994). Alcoholism is not a disease. In B. Leone (Ed.), *Alcoholism* (pp. 34–44). San Diego, CA: Greenhaven Press, Inc.

Treger, H. (1997). Guideposts for community work in police-social work diversion. In A. R. Roberts (Ed.), *Social work in juvenile and criminal justice settings* (pp. 116–125). Springfield, IL: Charles C Thomas.

24

Courts for Mentally Ill Offenders
Necessity or Abdication of Responsibility?

RISDON N. SLATE

The treatment of the mentally ill who come in contact with the criminal justice system may vary from jurisdiction to jurisdiction and from criminal justice practitioner to criminal justice practitioner. The following vignettes are illustrative of how haphazard this process can be.

Scenario #1

An individual encounters a man in a hotel bar whom he envisions to be his deadbeat dad, and an argument ensues. The hotel manager asks both individuals to leave the premises. After the alleged father vacates the hotel property, the other individual returns only to be picked up by the police. At the police station this individual repeatedly refuses to answer any questions unless Detective Bobby Simone comes forth and interrogates him; the suspect is in the throes of a manic episode and believes that he is on the set for filming of an episode of "NYPD Blue."

Scenario #2

An individual is released from the psychiatric section of a local hospital. Upon release said individual stands in the doorway of the hospital waiting for his ride. Hospital security asks the subject to leave, and a call is made to the police. When approached by police, the individual states that he is waiting for Cher, who is coming to pick him up in a white stretch limousine to take him to New York, where the two of them would be married. He also advises that he is the world's most prominent scientist and

Written especially for *Courts and Justice*, 2nd ed.

that a call to the Central Intelligence Agency would confirm his status as a totally protected individual who cannot be ordered to do anything.

Scenario #3

A high school geometry teacher leaves city X with his wife to attend a high school reunion in another state. Approximately two months prior to his trip a psychiatrist new to his case changes the medication that the teacher has been taking for ten years. He has been on this medication since having had what is couched in layman's terms as a nervous breakdown. However, the psychiatrist's diagnosis concludes that what the teacher suffered some ten years ago was a brief reactive psychosis to a precipitating stressful event, and the geometry teacher is not afflicted with bipolar disorder. Upon arrival at a friend's condominium complex, the usually mild-mannered teacher is in the grips of a full fledged psychotic episode and goes off uncontrollably for a naked swim in the pool at the complex. Although there are no residents by the pool, the police are called. Confronted by the police, the teacher advises them that he is the victim of a conspiracy initiated by the Attorney General of the United States as well as several federal judges, who are in collusion to persecute him. He informs the officers that he is seeking asylum and asks the officers to take him into protective custody. His wife advises the two officers on the scene of her husband's history of mental illness and informs them that he is currently following a psychiatrist's instructions. She even produces plainly labeled vials containing the prescription drug lithium previously taken by her husband.

Scenario #4

An individual who has suffered brain damage from a traumatic head injury as the result of a motorcycle accident is hearing voices inside a department store. In an attempt to get away from the voices, he bolts through the doors of the store only to run into an elderly woman outside, knocking her purchases from her arms and her to the ground. He tries to put her merchandise back in the bag and hand her pocketbook back to her. The police are called, and the woman ultimately dies from injuries sustained in her fall.

The four scenarios posited actually occurred, although minor modifications not detracting from the factual basis have been made to protect the innocent. The term innocent is utilized here because an essential element of a crime is intent (mens rea). If one is not rational, criminal intent is not readily formed. Immediately following are the actual official responses by the legal authorities.

In scenario # 1, one of the officers recognized there was a problem that might fall outside regular criminal jurisdiction upon the continued insistence by the subject that only Detective Simone do the questioning, and fortunately the individual was taken to the hospital for treatment and processing outside of the criminal justice system. In scenario #2, however, the individual awaiting Cher's arrival was arrested for trespassing at the hospital. Upon his arrival in court, his outbursts so offended the presiding judge that he was given 179 days in jail for contempt of court. Upon appeal, subject was ultimately referred to the process that evolved as a result of the impact of scenario #4, which will be discussed shortly.

In scenario #3 the officers arrested the geometry teacher. He was taken to jail and placed in a holding cell with approximately 15 other inmates. While in custody he began to tell other detainees about the conspiracy against him. Irritated by this irrational rambling, another inmate assaulted the geometry teacher. Perhaps unknowingly contributing to his survival, the teacher began a ritualistic chant and dance that might be likened to that of an Indian medicine man, replete with feces smeared on like war paint. Although the rather unpleasant result of this action served to prevent the teacher from further bodily harm, unfortunately this was no act. However, it was just another day at work for his jailers, and despite repeated demands to see President Clinton so this injustice could be halted, the geometry teacher had his initial appearance before a judicial authority. The detached neutral authority was apprized of the situation and was unamused by the teacher's demands that Johnny Cochran, Jr. be appointed as his legal representative. The magistrate set bail at $500. However, the teacher had thrown his wallet, containing his credit cards and money, away as he had readied himself for skinny dipping. It would take time to have money wired, and, if released, how would his family be able to handle a psychotic individual on no medication in a distant city? Thus, he was returned to jail and ultimately moved to solitary confinement in a strip cell. Finally, an old high school friend who happened to be a probation officer in the area learned of the geometry teacher's predicament. Under no authority whatsoever, the probation officer marched into the jail and demanded release of his old friend to his custody. The release was granted, and the probation officer drove the teacher directly to the emergency room of a local hospital where he was transferred to a private treatment facility.

The geometry teacher was ultimately stabilized and returned to work. Thoughts of suing the psychiatrist as well as the jail were entertained. However, consultation with attorneys revealed that one needs damages to prevail in such a lawsuit. The teacher was advised that damages need to be expressed in monetary amounts. The psychiatrist who took the geometry teacher off his medication understood the money issue. It seems the teacher had failed to pay for his last two visits prior to being jailed. Although the teacher had been jailed on Sunday and his doctor did not bother to return calls until Tuesday, the doctor did have his office call the teacher upon his return home regarding payment due for the two earlier visits to the doctor's office. Needless to say, the doctor was not paid and no longer has the teacher as a patient.

In scenario #4, in which the mentally disordered subject knocked down the elderly woman outside a department store, the individual was initially charged with first-degree murder. However, the grand jury ultimately indicted him for manslaughter. Simultaneously, public defenders astutely maintained that if the grand jury was going to come forth with an indictment against their client, then the mental health system, which had repeatedly failed their client prior to the incident in question, should also be indicted. The grand jury in turn launched an investigation that culminated in a 153-page report, which lambasted both the mental health and criminal justice systems (Broward County Grand Jury, 1994). In turn, the nation's first mental health court in Broward County, Florida (Baker, 1998; Miller, 1998) emanated from the impetus provided by the grand jury's recommendations.[1]

The Need for Intervention

As stated by Stone (1997:286), "[t]here is no more complicated or intractable a problem within criminal justice than that posed by the needs of persons with severe mental disorders, and . . . the failure to rationally respond to the issues raised by the incarceration of persons with severe mental disorders results in the unfair and disproportionate criminalization of persons with severe mental disorders." Jails have replaced state mental hospitals as the primary custodians of the mentally ill (Wax, 1987). Jails in San Diego, Seattle, and Miami are among those that are the chief mental health providers in their respective counties, and the Los Angeles County jail system is in effect the nation's largest mental institution (Torrey, 1995). In fact, "[b]etween 1955 and 1985, the annual national state hospital population fell from 634,000 to 221,400 while the number of persons with mental illness in jails rose from 185,780 to 481,393" (Walsh and Bricourt, 1997:421). Approximately half of all mentally ill individuals are arrested at least once, usually for minor offenses (Walsh and Bricourt, 1997; Solomon and Draine, 1995a). Seriously mentally ill individuals who exhibit signs of their illness to the police are more likely to be arrested and tend to spend longer stints in jail than those persons who are not mentally ill (Solomon and Draine, 1995b). This remains the case, although an extensive study has concluded that "[t]he 'criminalization of mental illness' . . . makes no more sense than punishing persons with Alzheimer's disease or brain tumors for the behavioral problems caused by their disease" (Sargeant, 1992:97).

While state laws vary as to whether an individual can be held in jail without formal charges being filed, Sargeant (1992) reports that in practice, regardless of legal dictates, some individuals are detained for months. Torrey (1995) found that approximately one-third of jail administrators surveyed acknowledge locking up the mentally ill without criminal charges being filed. Furthermore, most jails do not have the capability of separating the mentally ill from the general inmate population.

Depending on the study and the facility surveyed, "estimates of the percentage of those who are seriously mentally ill . . . range from 6% to 15% of the total population of those incarcerated in jails and prisons (Torrey, 1995:1612). Even if an estimate of 8% is accurate, Torrey (1995) equates that to roughly 163,000 seriously mentally ill persons incarcerated, which is two times the number in state mental hospitals. Likewise, Stone (1997) reports a higher prevalence of severe mental disorders among those confined in prisons and jails than in the general, non-inmate population. Torrey (1995:1612) adds that the number of seriously mentally ill currently incarcerated "is also greater than the entire population of the cities of Chattanooga, Fort Lauderdale, Hartford, New Haven, Providence, Reno, or Salt Lake City."

The Criminalization of the Mentally Ill

The deinstitutionalization movement is blamed for the quandary resulting in the criminalization of the mentally ill, as individuals were released from state hospitals with the idea that community treatment programs would fill the void (Winfree and Wooldredge, 1991; Kalinich, Embert and Senese, 1991). For various reasons, including a lack of funding, local programs generally never emerged (Jerrell and Komisaruk, 1991; Sargeant, 1992; Torrey, 1995). Further exacerbating the situation, private psychiatric hospitals and care providers have tended to reject treating the indigent mentally ill, and psychiatrists face the dilemma of losing their jobs or being slapped with malpractice lawsuits because of inadequate treatment as a result of managed-care penalties for excessive referrals (Miller, 1997).[2] Thus, the only chance for treatment for the impoverished mentally ill is often through arrest, and that mechanism typically opens the door to a system that is wholly inept at providing adequate treatment (Butterfield, 1998). As noted by Stone (1997:343), improvements in mental health insurance coverage would reduce the number of those in jail, as "there is a causal connection between insurance coverage restrictions and serious mental illness morbidity." While several states, including Maryland, California, New Hampshire, and Texas, have enacted anti-discrimination laws insisting upon parity coverage whereby mental illnesses are accorded the same preference for treatment as physical illnesses (Stone, 1997), the majority of states have no such laws on the books.

Before the civil rights reforms of the 1960s and early 1970s psychotropic medications were administered, with little or no say, to those psychiatric patients who had been involuntarily admitted. However, procedural justice extremists have intervened and advocated fairness of processes over results, contributing to an increasing demand for more restrictive civil commitment laws (Miller, 1997). This end result has been the criminalization of the mentally ill (Stone, 1997; Miller, 1997; Cornwell, 1998). Because of the mental health system's refusal to accept responsibility for this problem, the police often resort to jail as a means of removing the mentally ill from society (Miller, 1997). Due to a lack of community alternatives and/or a lack of awareness of the existence of such alternatives, some law enforcement officers acknowledge using "mercy bookings" to provide safety, food and medical treatment for those such as the homeless (Sargeant, 1992:97).

Unfortunately, sensationalism—the aberrant exception rather than the rule—often drives criminal justice policy (Walker, 1994; Perlin, 1997; Geis, 1996). Thus, while most mentally ill offenders are involved in relatively minor law violations (Torrey, 1995; Walsh and Bricourt, 1997; Sargeant, 1992), it is the crazed killer on the evening news that ultimately influences laws and regulations. Tragic events oftentimes occur before action is taken to attempt to remedy an existing problem in the criminal justice system (Miller, 1998).[3]

The fact is that jails often do not provide the care and treatment needed and are not very safe places for the mentally ill. Minimum training standards vary from state to state. In some states police officers are not adequately trained to deal with the mentally ill, although a few jurisdictions are attempting to overcome this problem.[4] Furthermore, training for correctional officers in jails across the country is inadequate, with 36% of 1,330 jails surveyed offering no training to officers in how to deal with the mentally ill and 84% of the jails providing either no training at all or less than three hours of instruction (Kerle, 1998). More than 20% of jails have been found to offer no formal access to mental health treatment (Walsh and Bricourt, 1997), and Kerte (1998) has determined that only 35 jails nationwide have been touted as being worthy of being models for the design of mental health treatment programs—out of more than 3,000 jails across the country. As one researcher put it, "[t]he bad and the mad don't mix" very well (Torrey, 1995:1612). The seriously mentally ill are prone to assaults from both detainees and officers and have been found to comprise around half of jail suicides (Torrey, 1995; Sargeant, 1992).

The Right to Treatment

The aforementioned statistics continue to mount, even though it has been determined that the mentally ill in jails have a constitutional right to both emergency and routine mental health services while incarcerated (Teptin, Abram and McClelland, 1997; Kalinich, Embert and Senese, 1991; Steadman and Veysey, 1997; Miller, 1997). The standard established in *Estelle v. Gamble* (1976) for the medical care of those incarcerated has been extended to include mental health services as well in *Bowring v. Godwin* (1977) and *Hoptowit v. Ray* (1982). Thus, as held in *Estelle*, deliberate indifference on the part of the authorities in providing treatment can result in a violation of the cruel and unusual punishment prohibition of the Eighth Amendment. Also, as noted by Kerle (1998), gross negligence on the part of authorities in not providing adequate supervision and training can prove detrimental to agencies and taxpayers in terms of lawsuit settlements and judgments in the area of mental health treatment.

In the law, duty follows knowledge (del Carmen, 1998; *City of Canton v. Harris*, 1989). It is imperative that communication commence and continue between law enforcement, judicial, correctional and mental health personnel to solidify workable solutions to this dilemma in the handling and treatment of the mentally ill.

Involuntary commitment authority falls within the legitimate interests of the state under its parens patriae power (for those with emotional disorders unable to care for themselves) and police power (for those who are dangerous) (Miller, 1997; Cornwell, 1998).[5] The standard for involuntary commitment generally requires clear and convincing evidence (Cornwell, 1998),[6] and, as established in *Foucha v. Louisiana* (1992), the focus on dangerousness refers to physical safety rather than to safety of property. Further, as established in *Humphrey v. Cady* (1972), potential harm to self or others is a sufficient criterion to assess dangerousness and impinge on one's liberty interest. The U.S. Supreme Court in *Washington v. Harper* (1990) determined that in the prison setting psychiatric medications can be forced on prisoners provided that the intrusion is authorized by a physician and is warranted for security needs or for the inmate's own medical interests and welfare. In *Riggins v. Nevada* (1992), the Court established that before pretrial detainees could be forcibly medicated such treatment should be "medically appropriate and, considering less intrusive alternatives, essential for [one's] own safety or the safety of others" (p. 127).

As noted by Stone (1997), with the majority of those jailed for noncriminal reasons or incarcerated on minor offenses, the use of jails is unlikely to diminish mental illness and in fact can have deleterious effects on mental illness. In similar fashion to the language used by the U.S. Supreme Court in *Wolff v. McDonnell* (1974), Stone (1997) urges that the Americans with Disabilities Act should penetrate jail and prison walls, ensuring access to adequate programs and treatment.

Abdication of Responsibility

With few alternatives available for intervention, without adequate community placement and insurance compensation, the health of the mentally ill continues to deteriorate as a result of confinement within the criminal justice system (Stone, 1997). Unfortunately, having the right to treatment and receiving effective treatment are not necessarily the same thing. The criminal justice system is said to be antitherapeutic, as the criminal defense model is not conducive to addressing the needs of the mentally ill. Attorneys are typically in tune with the wishes of their clients while engulfed in the adversarial process (Miller, 1997), and they tend to ignore the consequences of their actions both on those they represent and on society. Further, punishment seems to have been the rule of late in the United States, and a problem with punishment is that the focus looks backward—finding fault and assessing blame. The future of the offender, as well as the impact on society, is often ignored in the process.

For example, discharge planning for jails is generally weak in nature, typically with no follow-up regarding treatment status once someone is released (Steadman and Veysey, 1997). Lack of follow-up ensures failure (Stone, 1997), and a major problem in trying to divert the mentally ill from jails is finding a suitable place to send them—as community treatment may be inadequate or simply not accessible (Miller, 1997). According to Haney (1997:504), it is imperative that "crimogenic, situational and contextual factors . . . after release" be addressed to prevent the revolving door of incarceration: "Because commitment offense and sentence length now largely determine classification levels (and perforce, housing assignments), tens of thousands of developmentally disabled and mentally ill persons are confined in jails and prisons across the country, undifferentiated from the rest of the inmate population" (Haney, 1997:548). As noted by Haney (1997:500; 501),

> [t]he profession of psychology bears a degree of responsibility for the current crisis in American prison policy . . . [, and t]he challenge now is to move beyond harm [, adverse consequences,] as the organizing

principle of corrections. . . . It is time for the discipline of psychology both to assume responsibility for its historical connection to the shape and direction of past correctional policies and to play a more significant role in developing pathways out of the current crisis.

Cooperative Therapeutic Jurisprudence

Miller (1997:1213) has maintained that "[a] combination of the concepts of procedural justice and therapeutic jurisprudence would seem to provide the best hope of stimulating the interdisciplinary and cross-system collaboration which is essential" to balancing the best interests of society and the mentally ill. A cooperative, team approach of the major inter-system players is recommended for handling the problems faced by the mentally ill who come in contact with the criminal justice system (Miller, 1997; Steadman and Veysey, 1997). Challeen (1986) has recommended a commonsense approach to resolving many of the dilemmas faced within the criminal justice system, and the impetus for the nation's first mental health court was actually established by mere laypersons—members of a grand jury.[7]

Professor David Wexler has been identified as the founder of "therapeutic jurisprudence" (Finkelman and Grisso, 1994), which has been defined as the study of how "substantive rules, legal procedures and the roles of lawyers and judges produce therapeutic or antitherapeutic consequences" (Wexler and Winick, 1991:981). Traditionally, consequences of a legal decision have not mattered (Finkelman and Grisso, 1994). However, as noted by Winick (1997:187), "Therapeutic jurisprudence seeks to apply social science to examine law's impact on the mental and physical health of the people it affects. It recognizes that, whether we realize it or not, law functions as a therapeutic agent, bringing about therapeutic or nontherapeutic consequences."

With consequences in mind, if no interventions are undertaken, recommendations have been posited for the establishment of programs to divert the mentally ill from the criminal justice system. Although these recommendations have been offered, a national study has recently concluded that only fifteen diversion programs exist for the mentally ill in association with jails that house 50 or more inmates (Kerle, 1998). Diversion programs generally fall into one of two categories; police driven (prebooking) or jail or court initiated (postbooking) (Steadman, Morris and Dennis, 1995). An example of prebooking is seen in a sheriff's policy in Wyoming that requires all mentally ill misdemeanants, unless under court order, to be transported to the hospital emergency room instead of to the jail (O'Reilly, 1995). A postbooking diversion program will be discussed shortly in the form of Broward County's mental health court.

It has been recommended that these programs for diverting the mentally ill from the criminal justice system do the following: (1) incorporate interagency communication and cooperation between the criminal justice and mental health systems, with regular meetings of the pivotal actors (police, correctional personnel, judges, district attorneys, public defenders and mental health personnel); (2) include someone to oversee, coordinate and facilitate interagency contacts—a strong leader with a keen awareness of the capabilities of the program and the available alternatives is required; (3) recognize that early identification and intervention is essential; and (4) acknowledge that case management and follow-up of those individuals diverted from the system is crucial (Steadman, Morris and Dennis, 1995).[8] Even so, as noted by Haddad (1995) in a national study of jails by the National Alliance of the Mentally Ill, almost half of the jail administrators surveyed reported that they were not aware of whether those inmates who were seriously mentally ill had received any follow-up treatment after their release.

Mental Health Court

Via administrative order, the Chief Circuit Judge established the mental health court within the County Court Criminal Division of Broward County (Ross, 1997). The court is responsible for processing mentally ill misdemeanants, as long as they are not facing domestic violence, driving under the influence, or charged with assault (unless their victim voluntarily consents for the case to be handled in mental health court).

Figure 1 outlines the flow of cases through mental health court. Formal referrals to the court, as specified in the administrative order establishing the court, can come from sources such as other judges, assistant district attorneys and defense attorneys, and the court will determine if the accused meets the requisite criteria. Others, including family members, the police and jail personnel, can informally initiate referrals.

All arrested individuals within the state of Florida are required to have a probable cause affidavit filled out by the police upon arrest, and Broward County has modified the form so officers can check whether they noticed any sign of mental illness during the arrest process. If transported to jail, attention is called at booking to such notifications, and proper handling is to follow. Also at booking, pertinent information on each arrestee is logged into a computer system and then cross-referenced with mental health care providers in the area in an attempt to determine if an individual in custody has a history of mental illness. Furthermore, the process

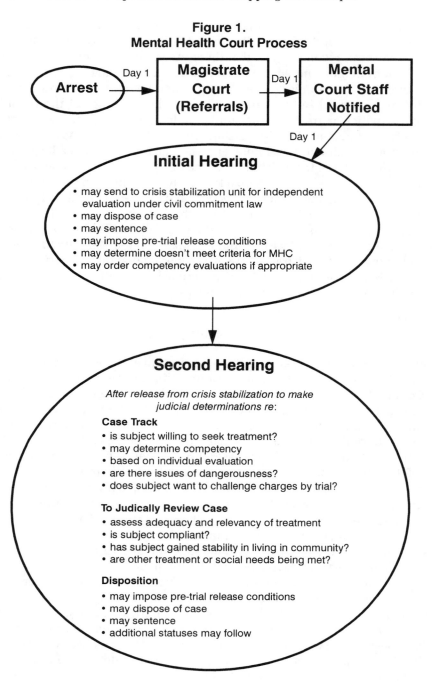

Figure 1.
Mental Health Court Process

for civilly committing individuals has often been time consuming, keeping law enforcement officers tied up for hours and away from what they may perceive as more pressing crimefighting duties. Thus, it has often been much simpler and to the benefit of police officers to drop the mentally ill off at jail, as opposed to becoming involved in the commitment process. To combat this problem, Broward County has implemented the utilization of mobile crisis stabilization units. The police who encounter a mentally disoriented subject on the street can merely call the mobile unit, staffed with clinicians specially trained in the transportation and treatment of the mentally ill who will respond to the designated location and ensure the subject is transported to an appropriate receiving facility and receives treatment, thereby freeing the police to return to their normal duties.[9]

Assisting the judge in making assessments within the courtroom and in follow-up are contractual employees—a court monitor from a local private mental health center and a court clinician, who is a licensed clinical social worker, from the State Department of Children and Families. The court clinician offers clinical expertise to the Court in assessing treatment needs, and the court monitor keeps the court apprized of the treatment status and compliance of participants.

The purpose of the mental health court is to balance the dignified treatment of the mentally ill with the protection of society. The goals include cooperation between the criminal justice and mental health systems, identification of the most effective and least restrictive treatment interventions, ensuring effective legal advocacy for the mentally ill, the monitoring of mental health service delivery and receipt of services, involvement of consumers and family members in the court process, and diversion to community mental health treatment programs (Cowart, 1997). As noted by Finkelstein and Brawley (1997), the aim of mental health court is to become part of the solution instead of remaining part of the problem by countering the cyclical process that spins the mentally ill in and out of jails with much longer stays than those experienced by similarly situated non-mentally ill defendants.

According to Stone (1997), with no adequate community health placements available and lack of insurance coverage, an individual's mental health deteriorates—resulting in incarceration. However, most jails, even those operating diversion programs, do not have follow-up programs to oversee offenders' therapeutic progress once they return to the community and therefore, as currently configured, are inept at halting this cyclical process (Steadman, Morris, and Dennis, 1995; Walsh and Bricourt, 1997). The courts are the ideal entity to spearhead this task, as Mays and Thompson (1991) have referred to the courts as the gatekeepers of America's jails—having the ability to directly impact jail populations.

Judge Lerner-Wren (1997) reports that she practices the previously discussed therapeutic jurisprudence in the mental health court, in an attempt to balance public safety first and foremost, and then the treatment needs and constitutional rights of those appearing before the court. Even the prosecutor's office is supportive of this concept, acknowledging that the court's ability to monitor long-term treatment plans guards public safety and helps to keep defendants closely monitored and functioning in the community instead of being caught in the revolving door of the criminal justice system (Raybon, 1997).[10] In similar fashion to the drug court process, which originated in South Florida (see Goldkamp, 1994; Curriden, 1994), mental health court operates to ensure that the nonviolent, misdemeanant mentally ill have the option of treatment as a diversion from jail (Lerner-Wren and Finkelstein, 1997).

As noted by Miller (1997:1213), "A combination of the concepts of procedural justice and therapeutic jurisprudence would seem to provide the best hope of stimulating the interdisciplinary and cross-system collaboration which is essential if meaningful answers" are to be uncovered. The mental health court employs such an approach in almost textbook fashion (see Steadman, Morris, and Dennis, 1995). Utilizing a team approach that has been highly recommended by advocates for change (Steadman and Veysey, 1997; Miller, 1997), the Mental Health Court Task Force includes members from the judiciary, the public defender's office, the state's attorney's office, mental health care providers, and law enforcement/corrections representatives; outsiders are invited and welcomed to attend meetings (Finkelstein and Brawley, 1997).

During the first year of operation, almost 400 cases were processed by the mental health court, with the judge presiding over mental health cases on her lunch hour and on Thursday afternoons, unless a special hearing is required, while maintaining a regular criminal court caseload.[11] What remains to be seen is the impact of the court upon recidivism rates of the mentally ill who have been diverted from the criminal justice system into some type of community treatment.[12]

Conclusion

Critics may question whether the mental health court results in a net-widening effect within the criminal justice system and whether the court is appropriately cognizant of due process rights. As for the net-widening effect, the clientele that the court finds itself processing would otherwise be in jail, and it does not require the added burden of making its existence appear necessary to justify a full-time docket, as the court operates on a part-time basis. In terms of due process rights, "the observation of legal rights does not need to interfere with the provision of clinical rights. . . . [T]he two can work together as long as each side considers the broader systemic issues. . . . It is only when extremists on either side ignore [the big picture] that problems occur" (Miller, 1997:1213). Thus, contrary to the sensationalized view that crazed killers with the aid of unscrupulous attorneys feign mental illness to avoid responsibility for their actions (Perlin, 1997), the mental health court provides a reasoned, balanced approach for diverting the nonviolent, misdemeanant defendant from jail—thereby providing a responsible alternative due to the inherent problems caused by the abdication of responsibility by both the mental health and criminal justice systems.

Additionally, some may argue that there may be a stigma attached to those processed through mental health courts. However, negatively labeling someone for a biochemical imbalance would be the equivalent of blaming a person for being diagnosed with diabetes. Perhaps what is needed is education of a largely ignorant public, beginning with criminal justice system personnel, instead of thwarting the access to possible treatment and recovery for individuals provided through mental health court. This could ultimately result in a beneficial outcome for all concerned parties. Jailing individuals for actions for which they are not responsible, with little to no treatment and virtually no follow-up upon release is unconscionable. The possibility of avoiding a conviction on one's criminal record and obtaining treatment to ward off future violations via mental health court processing is much less stigmatizing, more promising and more humane than the alternatives currently in place.

George Bernard Shaw once said, "If you are to punish a man you must injure him. If you are to reform a man you must improve him, and men are not improved by injuries" (Kittrie, 1978:1–2). In essence, it seems our current means of processing the mentally ill who come in contact with the criminal justice system is often analogous to a crap shoot and does more harm than good, exacerbating mental health problems and creating a costly revolving door for jails and society. While other attempts at diversion have been made, the mental health court, with a collaborative task force and a judge with legitimate authority to get things done within both the mental health and criminal justice systems, may be a reasonable solution to a system that is unreasonable and deleterious to mental health. While the verdict is still out, mental health court seems to be a logical step in the right direction for balancing the commingled interests of therapeutic jurisprudence. How many more tragedies must occur before something is done? While it may be costly up front to implement intervention strategies, it is the right thing to do, and cost savings should be realized in the long run for all concerned parties.

Endnotes

1 In a personal interview on June 25, 1998, Chief Broward County Assistant Public Defender Howard Finkelstein delineated the impact of the grand jury's investigation into the events that precipitated and surrounded the previously discussed scenario #4. While several years have passed with the client in private treatment and no disposition in his case, there is optimism the charge will be dismissed as a multimillion-dollar judgment on the client's behalf was recently rendered against the state's mental health system, according to Finkelstein in a subsequent telephone interview on November 6, 1998.

2 Judge Ginger Lerner-Wren, who presides over Broward County's Mental Health Court, sees managed health care's increasing control over the delivery of mental health services as a potential impediment to judicially mandated treatment for the mentally ill—similar to the pitfalls that have been experienced by drug court administrators with managed care providers (*Mental Health Weekly*, 7(33):6). Also, during this writer's visit to Broward County's mental health court, one employee indicated that he/she was aware of actual monetary bonuses being paid by managed care providers to health care providers who would turn the mentally ill away from expensive hospital stays and treatment.

3 Tony Rolon, a trainer for the St. Petersburg, Florida Police Department, calls the mentally ill contact with the criminal justice system a high liability area in the law and indicated, on November 18, 1998, during a training session observed by this writer, that his department implemented an eight-hour training sequence for all sworn law enforcement officers on how to appropriately deal with the mentally ill. According to Rolon, this training program was initiated after a tragic shooting incident of a mentally ill suspect. Although the police happened not to be at fault at the time of the shooting, it was felt that proper training was necessary to provide guidance for future situations. Likewise, Lieutenant Sam Cochran of the Memphis Police Department explained on December 4, 1998, at a Decriminalizing Mental Illness Conference in Orlando, Florida, that his department began 40-hour specially training of selected officers to comprise crisis intervention teams (CIT) and to better deal with the mentally ill they encounter. Cochran acknowledged that the Memphis CIT training was initiated on the heels of a police officer having shot and killed a mentally ill person.

4 See endnote 3 above. Also, while some departments are exceeding state minimum requirements in training their officers to deal with the mentally ill, most are not. For example, Craig Rockenstein (Regional Legal Advisor for the Florida Department of Law Enforcement) stated on November 19, 1997, that only one hour of training on how to deal with mentally ill persons has been required for law enforcement and correctional personnel to meet the state minimum training standards. Furthermore, Tony Rolon (St. Petersburg Police Department) indicated on November 18, 1998 that with the shift in latitude to the regional training academies in the state of Florida there is now wide-ranging discretion in curriculum; therefore, officers may not even be getting the one hour of training previously required.

5 "Gravely disabled" has been defined to include individuals who "manifest severe deterioration in routine functioning evidenced by repeated and escalating loss of cognitive or volitional control . . . and [who] are not receiving such care as is essential for their health or safety. . . . Under [such] standards individuals would no longer remain free to deteriorate in the community until becoming actively dangerous" (Cornwell, 1998:386).

6 Judge Ginger Lerner-Wren informed this writer on December 3, 1998 that clear and convincing evidence is the standard that she utilizes.

7 In a personal interview with Chief Broward County Assistant Public Defender Howard Finkelstein on June 25, 1998, he informed this writer that he essentially told the grand jury that if they were going to indict his client (as depicted in scenario #4) for murder,

they should also indict the mental health system for having allowed this travesty to have occurred. This ultimately resulted in a 153-page document, delineating the inadequacies of the mental health and criminal justice systems with recommendations for change, produced by the grand jury investigation.

8 Broward County's mental health court fulfills each of these requirements.

9 This writer witnessed the mobile crisis stabilization unit being summoned to the Judge's courtroom to remove a debilitated, jailed individual for civil commitment processing during my period of observation.

10 In a telephonic interview on June 29, 1998, Assistant State Attorney Lee Cohen indicated that traditionally, prosecutors are generally viewed as punitive in their orientation. However, we should punish when punishment is deserved, but when someone does not possess the mental capacity to form the intent to commit a criminal offense then they should not be punished. The goal is to ensure public safety and bring justice by prosecuting and/or restoring competency. Restoring competency with an aim toward prevention of future deviant acts and reoccurrences of mental aberrations can serve to bring justice. Assistant State Attorney Cohen also added that the Mental Health Court allows for more time and more information in rendering decisions and ensures more efficiency by having all the knowledge and resources managed within one courtroom.

11 Judge Ginger Lerner-Wren not only possesses the requisite legal requirements for being a judge, she also has extensive experience in mental health law and working with persons with disabilities, including supervision of the Office of Public Guardian and monitoring a Federal Class Action settlement impacting a state hospital.

12 In a personal interview with Judge Lerner-Wren on December 3, 1998, she estimated that approximately 70 percent of the cases are disposed of by the mental health court. However, the court is in its infancy (having been established by administrative order on May 22, 1997) for assessing its effectiveness, but at least, thus far, the publicity has been positive—with jurisdictions from Seattle to New Jersey having observed the court and met with key employees for possible implementation of similar programs in their respective jurisdictions. In fact, District Court Judge James Cayce, of the King County Court in Seattle, Washington, in a telephonic interview on January 25, 1999, confirmed that the opening of their mental health court is imminent. Judge Cayce also reported that while the court he will oversee is modeled after Broward County's mental health court, it is not an exact replica. For instance, the King County mental health court does not exclude any misdemeanor offenses committed by mentally ill individuals from consideration, and Judge Cayce expressed hope that one day the court's jurisdiction could be extended to felony offenses. Also, Judge Cayce stated that to his knowledge the King County court system is the second court in the nation to implement a mental health court, although he has received inquiries from a number of jurisdictions in California that have the finances and are interested in beginning the operation of such courts.

References

Baker, D. (1998). "Special Treatment." *ABA Journal* (June), 20–22.

Broward County Circuit Court. (1997). *Administrative Order: Creation of a Mental Health Court Subdivision within the County Criminal Division.* Issued by D. Ross, Chief Judge, Seventeenth Judicial Circuit, Broward County, Florida.

Broward County Grand Jury. (1994). *Interim Report of the Broward County Grand Jury: Mental Health Investigation.* Circuit Court of the Seventeenth Judicial District, Broward County, Florida.

Butterfield, F. (1998). "Prisons Replace Hospitals for the Nation's Mentally Ill." The *New York Times*, Mar. 5, pp. 1A; A18.

Challeen, D. A. (1986). *Making It Right: A Common Sense Approach to Criminal Justice*. Aberdeen, SD: Melius and Peterson.

Cornwell, J. K. (1998). "Special Theme: Sex Offenders: Scientific, Legal, and Policy Perspective: Legal Theory and Sex Offenders: *Kansas v. Hendricks* and Its Implications for Civil Commitment: Understanding the Role of the Police and Parens Patriae Powers in Involuntary Civil Commitment Before and After Hendricks." *Psychology, Public Policy and Law* 4:377–413.

Cowart G. R. (1997). "Mission Statement." *Mental Health Court News* I(1): 3.

Curriden, M. (1994). "Drug Courts Gain Popularity." *ABA Journal* 80 (May): 16–18.

del Carmen, R. V. (1998). *Criminal Procedure: Law and Practice*, 4th ed. Belmont, CA: Wadsworth Publishing Company.

Finkelman, D., and Grisso, T. (1994). "Therapeutic Jurisprudence: From Idea to Application." *New England Journal on Criminal and Civil Confinement* 20:243–257.

Finkelstein, H., and Brawley, D. (1997). "The Mission of the Mental Health Court is to Address the Unique Needs of the Mentally Ill in Our Criminal Justice System." *Mental Health Court News* I(1): 1–2.

Geis, G. (1996). "*People v. Simpson*: Some (Ir)Relevant Variables, Research, and the Future." In G. Barak, ed., *Representing O. J.: Murder, Criminal Justice and Mass Culture*, pp. 9–21. Guilderland, NY: Harrow and Heston.

Goldkamp, J. S. (1994). "Miami's Treatment Drug Court for Felony Defendants: Some Implications of Assessment Findings." *Prison Journal* 74(2): 110–166.

Haddad, J. (1995). "Jails Must Accommodate the Mentally Ill." In W. Barbour, ed., *Mental Illness: Opposing Viewpoints*, pp. 218–223. San Diego, CA: Greenhaven Press.

Haney, C. (1997). "Psychology and the Limits to Prison Pain: Confronting the Coming Crisis in Eighth Amendment Law." *Psychology, Public Policy and Law* 3:499–588.

Jerrell, J. M., and Komisaruk, R. (1991). "Public Policy Issues in the Delivery of Mental Health Services in a Jail Setting." In J. A. Thompson and G. L. Mays, eds., *American Jails: Public Policy Issues*, pp. 100–115. Chicago: Nelson-Hall.

Kalinich, D., Embert, P., and Senese, J. (1991). "Mental Health Services for Jail Inmates: Imprecise Standards, Traditional Philosophies, and the Need for Change." In J. A. Thompson and G. L. Mays, eds., *American Jails: Public Policy Issues*, pp. 79–99. Chicago: Nelson-Hall.

Kerle, K. E. (1998). *American Jails: Looking to the Future*. Boston, MA: Butterworth-Heinemann.

Kittrie, N. N. (1978). *The Right to Be Different*, 5th ed. Baltimore, MD: The Johns Hopkins University Press.

Lerner-Wren, G. (1997). "Message From the Judge." *Mental Health Court News* I(1): 2.

Lerner-Wren, G., and Finkelstein, H. (1997). "Florida County Diverts Offenders in Nation's First Speciality Mental Health Court." *Mental Health Weekly* 7(33): 1; 6.

Mays, G. L., and Thompson, J. A. (1991). "The Political and Organizational Context of American Jails." In J. A. Thompson and G. L. Mays, eds., *American Jails:*

Public Policy Issues, pp. 3–21. Chicago: Nelson-Hall.

Miller, R. D. (1997). "Symposium on Coercion: An Interdisciplinary Examination of Coercion, Exploitation, and the Law: III. Coerced Confinement and Treatment: The Continuum of Coercion: Constitutional and Clinical Considerations in the Treatment of Mentally Disordered Persons." *Denver University Law Review* 74:1169–1214.

Miller, S. L. (1998). "Mentally Ill Getting Respect in Court: Broward System First in Nation." The *Miami Herald*, Feb. 22, pp. 1A; 10A.

O'Reilly, C. (1995). "The Mentally Ill Should Not Be Jailed." In W. Barbour, ed., *Mental Illness: Opposing Viewpoints*, pp. 213–217. San Diego: Greenhaven Press.

Perlin, M. L. (1997). "'The Borderline which Separated You From Me': The Insanity Defense, the Authoritarian Spirit, the Fear of Faking, and the Culture of Punishment." *Iowa Law Review* 82:1375–1426.

Raybon, K. (1997). "State Attorney Perspective." *Mental Health Court News* I(1): 2–3.

Sargeant, G. (1992). "Back to Bedlam: Mentally Ill Often Jailed without Charges." *Trial* (Dec.), 96–98.

Solomon, P., and Draine, J. (1995a). "Issues in Serving the Forensic Client." *Social Work* 40(1): 25–33.

———. (1995b). "Jail Recidivism in a Forensic Case Management Program." *Health and Social Work* 20(3): 167–173.

Steadman, H. J., Morris, S. M., and Dennis, D. L. (1995). "The Diversion of Mentally Ill Persons from Jails to Community-Based Services: A Profile of Programs." *American Journal of Public Health* 85(12): 1630–1635.

Steadman, H. J., and Veysey, B. M. (1997). "Providing Services for Jail Inmates with Mental Disorders." *American Jails* (May–June): 11–23.

Stone, T. H. (1997). "Therapeutic Implications of Incarceration for Persons with Severe Mental Disorders: Searching for Rational Health Policy." *American Journal of Criminal Law* 24:283–358.

Teplin, L. A., Abram, K. M., and McClelland, G. M. (1997). "Mentally Disordered Women in Jail: Who Receives Services?" *American Journal of Public Health* 87(4): 604–609.

Torrey, E. F. (1995). "Jails and Prisons—America's New Mental Hospitals." *American Journal of Public Health* 85(12):1611–1613.

Walker, S. (1994). *Sense and Nonsense about Crime and Drugs: A Policy Guide*, 3rd ed. Chicago: Nelson-Hall.

Walsh, J., and Bricourt, J. (1997). "Services for Persons With Mental Illness in Jail: Implications for Family Involvement." *Families in Society: The Journal of Contemporary Human Services* (Jul.–Aug.): 420–428.

Wax, J. (1987). "Criminal Treatment: The Jails Become Holding Tanks for the Mentally Ill." *The Progressive* (Oct.): 26–27.

Wexler, D. B., and Winick, B. J. (1991). "Therapeutic Jurisprudence as a New Approach to Mental Health Law Policy Analysis and Research." *University of Miami Law Review* 45:979–1004.

Winfree, L. T., and Wooldredge, J. D. (1991). "Exploring Suicides and Deaths by Natural Causes in America's Large Jails: A Panel Study of Institutional Change, 1978 and 1983." In J. A. Thompson and G. L. Mays, eds., *American Jails: Public Policy Issues*, pp. 63–78. Chicago: Nelson-Hall.

Winick, B. J. (1997). "The Jurisprudence of Therapeutic Jurisprudence." *Psychology, Public Policy and Law* 3:184–206.

Cases Cited

Bowring v. Gamble, 551 F.2d 44 (1977).
City of Canton v. Harris, 489 U.S. 378 (1989).
Estelle v. Gamble, 429 U.S. 97 (1976).
Foucha v. Louisiana, 504 U.S. 71 (1992).
Hoptowit v. Ray, 682 F.2d 1237 (1982).
Humphrey v. Cady, 405 U.S. 504 (1972).
Riggins v. Nevada, 504 U.S. 127 (1992).
Washington v. Harper, 494 U.S. 210 (1990).
Wolff v. McDonnell, 418 U.S. 539 (1974).

Questions to Consider

1. If you were brought before a court for a minor infraction, which elements of tribal adjudication described by Vicenti would you like to see incorporated in the process? Why do you believe this would be important in your case?

2. If a person commits a crime, why not simply use courts of general jurisdiction that determine whether that person has committed the crime? (Special facts such as the person's age could then be taken into consideration at sentencing.) What is lost by such a process?

3. If we expect that specialized courts will have increased knowledge of special circumstances that will allow the judge to make more just responses, why take that ability to make just responses away from juvenile judges and give the decision to legislatures or prosecutors? Why are we more punitive than Canada? Are our juveniles worse off?

4. Law models focus on whether a person committed a crime, and repeated crimes are more severely punished. Drug abuse rehabilitation is seldom this simple, with the vast majority of addicts experiencing some level of "relapse" on the way to a cure. What conflicts do you see when legal models are married to therapeutic models?

5. What responsibilities do judges have to understand those they are sentencing? If someone is mentally ill, how can judges "do justice" if they know little about mental illness or whether their actions would actually make the person more mentally ill?

Section VII
The Future of Courts
Thinking Outside the Lines

Now that we have some idea of the range of challenges facing our court system, where do we go from here? In an effort to sample possibilities, this final section can be divided into three areas. First we look at two seemingly good ideas, day fines and court access, which appear to be going nowhere fast. We have some answers to the question of why court access appears to be at a standstill but must speculate regarding day fines. Clearly, merely proposing good ideas is not enough. Second, we look at one recent trend, that of court secrecy, and ask why it is catching on and where it is taking us. Third, we explore a range of options for reforming the criminal trial, using examples from other countries as possible alternatives.

First we look at a recent European import that has the potential for increasing justice, the day fine. Winterfield and Hillsman remind us how traditional fixed fines are often unfair, as they punish the poor more heavily than they do the rich. Day fines, like fixed fines, are related to the severity of the offense but differ in that the final amount is based on each offender's income. Early results in the United States indicated that such a reform may be quite successful. Not only were the results fairer, but more money was collected at a higher rate, with fewer warrants issued for failure to pay. Given this success, why has this reform not been adopted by more jurisdictions? What cultural assumptions or social interests have kept this policy from being implemented?

Another problem that many face when having to deal with courts is access. Access usually requires sufficient money to pay for the services of an intermediary—a lawyer who knows the language, routines, and politics of the local court. Unfortunately, many people with legal claims cannot access our courts because they do not have the money to hire a lawyer. Mark Kessler looks at one reform that was designed to extend court access by providing legal services to the poor living in rural areas. He outlines why this justice reform was resisted by local lawyers who felt economically and politically threatened. The local legal professional culture substantially limited the expansion of court access and in effect "captured" the rural programs that were created by national reform efforts. Clearly, with any attempts at reform, we must ask what interests will be threatened and what we must do to meet the resulting challenge.

We currently have secret federal wiretap courts and recently have allowed secret reasons for the deportation of resident aliens. John Gibeaut documents an increasingly pervasive secret justice system that allows litigants to use public courts, but to hide the process and outcome from public scrutiny. While there are several reasons given by the advocates of secrecy, we also present for reflection Michael Pahl's article on recent events in Colombia. Colombia instituted "needed" secret courts to address drugs and terrorism, two of the major concerns now challenging us as well. The goal was to provide protection for judges and witnesses and to increase the conviction efficiency of courts. Unfortunately, while the conviction rate went up, creating secret courts also enabled the government to punish the political opposition with impunity.

Craig Bradley sees lack of efficiency as the problem of American courts. He makes numerous suggestions for changes in criminal procedure, such as banning plea bargaining, eliminating voir dire, and limiting lawyer trial arguments. Are such reforms plausible while maintaining the goal of justice? To answer this question we first use Zoran Milovanovich's article on European prosecutors. Among court professionals, American prosecutors have by far the most discretion and, many say, the most power. Judges have seen their discretion substantially limited by recent legislative sentencing schemes, with much of their power being transferred to prosecutors. Now we have complaints of prosecutorial abuse of power and ongoing concerns about plea bargaining abuses. Milovanovich argues that professionalizing prosecutors in a civil law model may produce more rational and uniform decision making. He also gives some possibilities for eliminating charge bargaining, which is the most susceptible to abuse.

Finally, we turn to Richard Andrias, who provides a roller-coaster ride through recent changes in Russian courts. While contending with the problems of social change and lack of resources, they are developing innovative models of court procedure in which defendants, victims, and juries actively participate in the court process. Can the traditional Russian quest for justice, married to our Western due process models, provide possibilities that we can incorporate in turn?

25

The Staten Island Day-Fine Project

LAURA A. WINTERFIELD and SALLY T. HILLSMAN

Day fines, so called because the amount of the fine is tied to an offender's daily earnings, are common in some European and South American countries; not so in the United States, where fines have traditionally been based on the individual crime rather than on the individual offender's ability to pay.

But as American jurisprudence seeks alternatives in sentencing, day fines have been proposed as one promising area of experimentation. This *Research in Brief* describes the first day-fine experiment in American courts, a National Institute of Justice (NIJ) project planned and implemented between 1987 and 1989 in the Criminal Court of Richmond County (Staten Island), New York.[1] This joint project of NIJ, the court, and the Vera Institute of Justice was also supported by the German Marshall Fund of the United States and New York City's Office of the Deputy Mayor for Public Safety.

An NIJ evaluation of this successful implementation demonstrated that:

- The day-fine concept could be implemented in a typical American limited-jurisdiction court.

Reprinted from the *National Institute of Justice, Research in Brief,* January, 1993. Washington, DC: U.S. Department of Justice.

- Day fines could substitute for fixed fines.
- Fine amounts were higher for affluent offenders under the day-fine system.
- Overall revenues increased.
- High rates of collection could be sustained (and possibly improved) despite the higher average day-fine amounts.

Evolution of Day Fines

Fines are an ancient and widely used penal measure, and noncustodial sanctions are not new in American sentencing. What is new is an increased enthusiasm for the systematic incorporation of "intermediate sanctions"[2] into sentencing systems, primarily in response to pressing justice and fiscal concerns. The financial implications of getting tough on crime have spurred interest in creating a graduated progression of intermediate penalties.

Until recently, the fine was not a prominent intermediate penalty in the United States because of deep skepticism among American criminal justice professionals. Skeptics doubted the ability of judges to set fines in amounts large enough to punish and deter while making the fines fair to offenders with vastly different economic circumstances. Doubters also questioned the courts' ability to enforce and collect such fines.[3]

The skepticism is beginning to dissipate, however, as more American courts explore fining systems that systematically vary fine amounts in relation to the means of the offender as well as the severity of the offense—systems with which some European courts have long experience.

The variable fine systems used in Europe are typically called "day fines" because some portion of an offender's daily income is used to calculate the fine amount. This differs greatly from the typical fixed flat-fine system used in American courts (see "How Day Fines Work"). In setting fine amounts. American judges generally apply "going rates" or "tariffs" based upon understandings (usually informal) that the same or similar amounts are imposed on all defendants convicted of similar offenses.

Such tariff systems have limited the usefulness of the fine as an intermediate sanction in the United States because tariffs tend to be set to reflect the lowest common economic denominator of offenders coming before the court. This practice depresses fine amounts, diminishes the punitive weight of fines for better-off offenders, and constricts the range of offenses for which judges view a fine as an appropriate sole sanction.

How Day Fines Work

The general concept is simple: determining the amount of punishment to be administered to an offender is separated from a consideration of how much money that offender must pay. Judges determine how much punishment an offender deserves; this is then denominated in some unit other than money. These *punishment units* are translated into monetary terms based on how much money the offender makes per day.

Practically speaking, the day fine approach consists of a simple, two-step process. First, the court uses a "unit scale" or "benchmark" to sentence the offender to a certain number of day-fine units (for example, 15, 60, or 120 units) according to the gravity of the offense and without regard to income. To guide the court's choices, benchmarks or unit scales are typically developed by a planning group of judges, prosecuting attorneys, and defense counselors familiar with disposition patterns in a court.

The value of each unit is then set at a percentage of the offender's daily income, and the total fine amount is determined by simple multiplication.

Day fines, on the other hand, ensure the routine imposition of fines that are proportionally punitive—based on the seriousness of the offense—and equitable for offenders with differing means.[4]

Implementation of the Day-Fine Experiment

In evaluating the implementation of the day-fine system in Staten Island, NIJ's researchers concluded that the program was successfully initiated.[5] Judges were able to obtain the offender income information they needed to set the fine amount promptly without disrupting the rapid flow of cases. Once trained to use the day-fine workbook they had helped develop, judges found the mechanics of computing a day-fine sentence simple. No practical or ideological opposition to the principle was voiced by either prosecutors or defense attorneys.

The sole implementation problem encountered was one the planners had anticipated: Statutory fine maximums in New York State are very low and have not increased since 1965. In a significant number of cases, the day-fine amounts calculated by judges for more affluent offenders convicted of more serious violations exceeded the statutory limit.

In these instances, the judge sentenced the defendant to the statutory maximum but recorded the day fine as calculated. This established a record for later use in the legislative process, where more widespread use of day fines in New York State hinges on statutory changes to increase the existing fine limits.

Goals of the Evaluation

The evaluation tested the impact of day fines on the court's sentencing patterns and sought to determine:

- Whether the theoretical complexity of the day fine or the burden of its two-stage procedure decreased the use of fines.
- Whether the use of fines shifted from one type of offense to another.
- Whether, on average, day-fine amounts were higher than the previous fixed fines and, if so, whether this had any negative effect on the existing high collection rate.
- Whether the day fine alone or in concert with new collection techniques had any impact on collection outcomes.

In addition, the research developed a model in an attempt to predict the sentences offenders would have received if there had not been a day-fine option. Analysis of this kind can provide a basis for gauging the extent to which introducing day fines displaces other types of sentences or replaces existing fixed fines.[6]

Evaluation Design

The design chosen for this evaluation was a before-and-after comparison of penal-law felony and misdemeanor attests disposed of in the Staten Island Criminal Court both before the introduction of day fines and during the day-fine project's pilot year. The sample from before the experiment consisted of all penal-law cases disposed of before the start of the day-fine pilot, from April 1, 1987, through March 31, 1988; there were 4,461 cases in this sample.[7] The pilot-year sample consisted of all cases disposed of during the pilot year, from September 1, 1988, through August 31, 1989: there were 4,883 cases in this sample.[8]

During the pilot year, researchers also tested the impact of new collection procedures introduced as part of the day-fine program. Part of the Staten Island pilot project was a new collection and suspension component that developed individualized collection schedules and stressed prompt notification of payments due and missed. This was in contrast to the conventional method of collection, in which cases not fully paid at sentencing were continued on the court calendar, with subsequent hearings set infrequently and arrest warrants issued if offenders failed to appear.

To compare the effects of day fines *without* the new collection techniques, the fixed-fine system *with* the new collection techniques, and the new day fines *in combination* with the new collection techniques,[9] day-fine cases were randomly assigned to two groups after sentencing: The "experimentals" were those day-fine cases processed according to the experimental collection procedures; the "controls" were day-fine cases handled using the collection process routinely administered by the court.

Comparisons of collections between the day-fine experimentals and the pre-day-fine cases measured the effect of introducing new day-fines along with new collection techniques. Comparisons between the "controls" and cases from the year prior to the experiment measured the independent effect of introducing day-fine sentences without the new collection procedures. Comparing collection outcomes for the "experimentals" with the "controls" measured the effect of the new collection procedures alone.

A variety of analyses were performed. prior to any before-and-after comparisons being made, the 2 years' samples were compared with regard to arraignment charge; the two samples were found to be statistically equivalent given the mix of cases coming into the court.

Impact on Sentencing

Day fines were successfully introduced into routine sentencing in the Staten Island court during the pilot year.

The mechanics of imposing a day fine consist of establishing the number of day-fine units based upon the offense and estimating the offender's net daily income and number of dependents to calculate the monetary value of each unit. This process was neither too complex nor too time-consuming to be applied routinely in a relatively fast-paced criminal court. Two-thirds of the fixed fines in penal law cases were replaced by day fines during the pilot year.

Those fixed fines assessed during the pilot year were imposed by non-Staten Island judges sitting temporarily as replacements for vacationing or sick colleagues; these judges had not been trained to use day fines and, therefore, used the traditional tariff system in setting fine amounts.

The introduction of day fines did not appreciably affect judges' sentencing decisions during the pilot year.

When prior conviction records and arraignment charges were controlled, overall sentencing patterns remained steady during the year in which day fines were applied. The only noticeable change in sentencing patterns was a small increase in jail sentences for some drug cases, a change that occurred during the height of the crack cocaine epidemic in New York City. Therefore, it appears safe to surmise that the introduction of day fines did not create this shift in sentencing.

After introduction of the day fine, average fines imposed for penal law offenses rose 25 percent.

Fines rose from $205.66 before the experiment to $257.85 during the year in which the day fines were introduced. However, if day fines had not been restrained by statutory maximum fine limitations, the average fine during the pilot period would have been $440.83—more than twice the average fixed fine amount ($205.66). Even if these uncapped day fines were combined with fixed fines imposed during the pilot year, the overall average fine amount would have risen 84 percent in the experimental year (table 1).

The total amount of the fines imposed by the court in penal law cases increased by 14 percent during the pilot year (from $82,060 to $93,856).

The impact of the day-fine system on total fine revenue would have been even more dramatic if day fines had not been constrained by statutory maximums. In the absence of the caps, the total amount of fines in the experimental year would have been almost 50 percent higher than the total amount actually ordered (rising from $93,856 to $137,660). This would have represented a 67 percent increase over the total fine amount ordered the year before the experiment (table 1). Using day fines could potentially raise revenues, provided that the higher rates did not inhibit collection of the fines.

As expected, there was more variation among individual fine amounts when they were calculated using the day-fine system.

The judges relied substantially less on traditional tariffs and calculated day fines with more gradations, many of which fell above the statutory fine maximums. Furthermore, as seen in table 1, during the pilot year the fines that fell between the tariff points were, for the most part, day fines.

Changes in Collection Rates and Patterns

The Staten Island pilot study demonstrated that by taking into account an offender's ability to pay when the fine amount is set, the levied fine is collectible and proportionate to the severity of the offense.

Despite the substantial increase in average fine amounts, introduction of the day-fine system did not undermine the court's high collection rates.

Table 1. Comparison of Fine Amounts Levied in Pilot Year, Capped by Statutory Maximums and Uncapped

| | | Capped | | | | | Uncapped | | | | |
| | Pre-day-fines pilot | | Day fines and flat fines | | Day fines only | | | Day fines and flat fines | | Day fines only | | |
	n	%	n	%	n	%	% of total*	n	%	n	%	% of total*
$1–24	1	0.3	1	0.3	1	0.4	100.0	1	0.3	1	0.4	100.0
$25	33	8.3	4	1.1	3	1.3	75.0	4	1.1	3	1.3	75.0
$26–49	—	—	4	1.1	4	1.7	100.0	4	1.1	4	1.7	100.0
$50	69	17.3	29	8.0	12	5.0	41.4	29	8.0	12	5.0	41.4
$51–74	2	0.5	6	1.6	4	1.7	66.7	6	1.6	4	1.7	66.7
$75	34	8.5	15	4.1	10	4.2	66.7	15	4.1	10	4.2	66.7
$76–99	—	—	9	2.5	8	3.3	88.9	9	2.5	8	3.3	88.9
$100	78	19.5	38	10.4	22	9.2	57.9	38	10.4	22	9.2	57.9
$101–149	1	0.3	15	4.1	14	5.8	93.3	15	4.1	14	5.8	93.3
$150	14	3.5	18	4.9	11	4.6	61.1	18	4.9	11	4.6	61.1

Fine amount	No.	%	No.	%	No.	%	%*	No.	%	No.	%	%*
$151–199	3	0.8	11	3.0	10	4.2	90.9	11	3.0	10	4.2	90.9
$200	22	5.5	18	4.9	11	4.6	61.1	18	4.9	11	4.6	61.1
$201–249	8	2.0	9	2.5	6	2.5	66.7	9	2.5	6	2.5	66.7
$250	79	19.8	124	34.0	84	35.0	67.7	56	15.4	16	6.7	28.6
$251–499	8	2.0	12	3.3	8	3.3	66.7	37	10.2	33	13.8	89.2
$500	22	5.5	22	6.0	12	5.0	54.5	17	4.7	7	2.9	41.2
$501–999	4	1.0	7	1.9	6	2.5	85.7	37	10.2	36	15.0	97.3
$1,000	21	5.3	22	6.0	14	5.8	63.6	16	4.4	8	3.3	50.0
$1,001+	—	—	—	—	—	0.0	—	24	6.6	24	10.0	100.0
Total	399	100.0	364	100.0	240	100.0	65.9	364	100.0	240	100.0	65.9
Total fines ordered	$82,060.55		$93,856.00		$61,994.00			$137,660.00		$105,798.00		
Average	$205.66		$257.85		$258.31			$378.19		$440.83		

*This percentage was calculated, for each fine amount, by dividing the number of day fines of that amount by the total number of fines of that amount, to determine what percentage were day fines.

Introducing day fines into the Staten Island court did not significantly alter collection rates, despite substantially higher average fines (table 2). In 85 percent of the day-fine experimental cases (those subject to the new collection strategy and the day fine) and in 71 percent of the day-fine control cases (those disposed of using the collection process routinely administered by the court), the offender eventually paid in full, compared to 76 percent of the fine cases from the year before the experiment. These differences are not statistically significant.

However, when a comparison is made of cases in which fined offenders paid nothing, it is apparent that the new collection procedures significantly improved collection outcomes: Only 6 percent of day-fine experimental cases resulted in no payment at all, compared to 22 percent of cases prior to the experiment and 26 percent of day-fine control cases. And when full payment was not made, some payment was much more likely in the day-fine experimental cases than in the cases from before the experiment or in the day-fine control cases.

These data suggest that the higher average fine amounts levied in the day-fine cases did not make collection more difficult for the court and that the new enforcement procedures independently improved collection rates.

While the introduction of day fines did not diminish the court's success in collecting fines, day fines did take longer to collect than fixed fines prior to the experiment.

Day fines, both with and without the new collection techniques, took longer to collect than the earlier tariff-only fines (table 2). This pattern was closely related to the higher average day-fine amounts. The mean number of days to full payment was significantly fewer for fines before the experiment (55 days) than for either the day-fine experimentals (114 days) or controls (119 days). The longer collection period for day fines is not surprising in light of the substantially higher average fine amounts imposed.

Despite these higher fine amounts and longer periods before payment, the use of day fines, when coupled with the new collection techniques, did not increase the number of postsentence court appearances during the enforcement period. As intended, the new collection techniques kept fined cases off the court calendar until the end of collection and enforcement activities. While fines before the experiment had required an average of 1.96 postsentence appearances, the day-fine experimentals required 1.76 such appearances. However, in day-fine cases in which the court's conventional collection procedures were used, the higher average fine amounts did require more court appearances (2.66). Thus, without the more individualized collection techniques used in the pilot program's experimental cases, day-fine offenders were brought back to

Table 2. **Summary of Collection Rates, Collection Patterns, and Enforcement Outcomes**

	Fixed fines[b]	Day-fine experimentals[c]	Day-fine controls[d]
Percent paid in full at sentencing	16%	8%	17%
Amount paid as percent of amount due:			
Percent paid nothing	22%	6%*	26%*
Percent partial payment	2%	9%*	3%*
Percent ever paid in full	76%	85%	71%
Mean number of days to full payment	55	114*	119*
Mean number of total appearances[a]	1.96	1.76	2.66*
Mean number of warrants ordered[a]	.55	.26*	.83*
Percent paid in full at 9 months[a]	72%	37%*	49%*
Enforcement outcomes:			
Percent paid in full	76%	85%	71%
Percent absconded	11%	6%	14%
Resentenced or jailed	10%	6%	14%
Unresolved	3%	3%	1%

[a]These variables reflect information as of 9 months after sentence, thus controlling for the followup time period. The other variables did not need to be so constructed because they reflect information about the final case outcome. Thus, to have equal followup periods for each year, 7-month subsets of each year were created, allowing for 17 to 23 months of followup.

[b]Fixed-fine cases were taken from the year before the pilot year.

[c]Experimentals are those cases that were subject to new collection procedures as well as day fines.

[d]Controls are those cases subject to standard collection procedures as well as day fines.

*Indicates comparisons, whether of fixed-fine cases vs. experimentals, fixed-fine vs. controls, or experimentals vs. controls, in which $p < .05$.

court for nonpayment more frequently than either the fine cases before the experiment or the day-fine experimentals.

The day-fine program significantly reduced the number of arrest warrants issued for failure to appear at postsentence hearings.
The court issued fewer arrest warrants for nonpaying day-fine experimentals who failed to appear for scheduled court hearings. The day-fine experimental cases averaged 0.26 warrants, in comparison to the cases sentenced before the experiment (0.55 warrants) and day-fine controls (0.83), as shown in table 2. These data suggest that when the old collection techniques were used in conjunction with day fines, which were higher on average than the fixed fines, the court did have to rely more heavily on warrants to collect the fines.

Despite significantly higher average fine amounts and longer collection periods, day fines were collected at rates as high as those for the smaller fixed fines. For those offenders who did not pay in full, significantly more day-fined offenders paid something as opposed to nothing. Thus, jurisdictions that implement a day-fine system can expect to successfully collect the additional revenue associated with a day-fine system.

Further, the new collection techniques piloted in Staten Island could compensate for the decreased collection and enforcement some jurisdictions might expect from raising fine amounts. The individualized collection strategy had the following advantages over the court's routine collection procedures:

- More extended terms for payment of the larger day fines.
- Fewer costly court appearances.
- Fewer warrants for nonappearance at postsentence hearings.

Jurisdictions whose existing collection systems are similar to Staten Island's can expect collection rates to remain stable after introducing a day-fine system of similar design. However, if jurisdictions experience additional court appearances and warrants as a result of the average higher fines generated by a day-fine system, they might need to devote more resources to collection efforts. Thus, shifting to individualized collection systems when introducing day fines (a shift that ought to be financially feasible because day fines are likely to generate higher total fine revenues) would probably be the best approach for other American courts wishing to implement the day-fine concept.

The Relationship between Income and Fine Amount

Under the day-fine system, individual income plays a greater role in determining the fine amount, even when other factors are controlled.

As expected, various factors influence fine amounts. These factors include the severity of the arraignment charge, the offender's income, and whether the penalty was a fixed fine or a day fine. Fine amounts increased for more severe charges, for higher individual income, and for day fines as compared to fixed fines.

Further, income has more effect on fine amount when the severity of the arraignment charge is controlled and the statutory maximums are set aside. But because the effect of income level can be seen in fixed-fine cases as well as in day-fine cases, it appears that implementing the day-fine pilot standardized and made explicit the decisionmaking principles that were already in place. Under the day-fine system, this "calculus" was explicit and systematic, resulting in more uniform sentencing.

Low-income offenders were no better or worse at complying with day-fine sentences than with tariff-fine sentences.

Similarly, offenders sentenced to high or low day fines generally did as well paying the fines as those who received the lower fixed fines before the experiment. Although the average day-fine amounts were higher, they were no more likely to exceed any group of offenders' ability to pay and did not disproportionately increase the burdens on low-income offenders. However, the numbers were too small for significant testing, and this finding needs to be confirmed through additional research.

Conclusion

Through the introduction of day fines, it is quite possible that judges have become more comfortable with the imposition of monetary penalties when the amounts can be adjusted to individual cases and circumstances.

With a means-based method for setting fines, fairer punishments were meted out without making the process of imposing fines too difficult or time-consuming for judges. Further, average fine amounts were higher under the day-fine system without undermining the court's collection rates.

The day-fine approach has the potential added benefit of raising total collected fine revenues. Using a two-step procedure to set fine amounts so that they systematically reflect the gravity of offenses and offenders' means eliminates most of the objections usually raised about use of monetary penal sanctions. The door may now be open to wider acceptance and use of monetary sanctions in the United States. Indeed, the results from Staten Island have encouraged adaptation of the day-fine concept in American jurisdictions outside New York.[10]

Endnotes

1 The Staten Island Criminal Court is a lower court—a trial court of limited jurisdiction.

2 Castle, M. N. 1991. "Alternative Sentencing: Selling It to the Public," NIJ *Research in Action*; MacKenzie, Doris L., and James M. Shaw, "Inmate Adjustment and Change During Shock Incarceration: the Impact of Correctional Boot Camp Programs," *Justice Quarterly*, 7, 1 (March 1990): 125–150; Morris, Norval, and Michael Tonry, 1990. *Between Prison and Probation—Intermediate Punishments in a Rational Sentencing System*, New York, Oxford University Press; Joan Petersilia, and Susan Turner, 1990. *Intensive Supervision for High-Risk Probationers: Findings From Three California Experiments*, Santa Monica, RAND Corporation; Dennis Wagner, and Christopher Baird, "Evaluation of Florida Community Control Program," NIJ *Research in Brief* (forthcoming).

3 Hillsman, S. T. 1990. "Fines and Dayfines," In M. Tonry and N. Morris (eds.), vol. 12, *Crime and Justice: A Review of Research*. Chicago, University of Chicago Press.

4 Greene, J. *The Day-Fine System: A Tool for Improving the Use of Economic Sanctions*, New York, Vera Institute of Justice, March 1992.

5 For more on implementation of the Staten Island day-fine experiment, see Judith Greene, "The Staten Island Day-Fine Experiment," Part II of *Day Fines in American Courts: The Staten Island and Milwaukee Experiments*, ed. Douglas C. McDonald, Washington, D.C., NIJ *Issues and Practices*, April 1992.

6 Project planners focused on demonstrating whether the day fine could be implemented and substituted for fixed fines but did not, in this first test of the idea, encourage the court to displace other sentences with day fines.

7 Because imposition of statutory fine minimums is required for the serious traffic cases heard in this court (for example, driving while intoxicated [DWI]), they were eliminated from the research. Although theoretically possible, it is more complicated to calculate day fines for cases in which judges are required to set a specific fixed amount. In this first implementation attempt, it was not feasible to address this more complex issue. This was a necessary but unfortunate limitation of the pilot because it is likely that a significant number of DWI offenders would be fined more than the statutory minimum (the typical tariff rate) under a day-fine system.

8 This research sample differs by several weeks from the sample of cases followed by program operators/planners during the pilot year and discussed by Judith Greene in *Day Fines in American Courts*, n. 5 above.

9 Because the new fining technique and the new collection method were introduced simultaneously, it was important to separate the effects of each reform on collection outcomes.

10 Over the past several years, seven jurisdictions began to implement day-fine systems. Maricopa County in Arizona was the first: the other six—four sites in Oregon and one each in Iowa and Connecticut—are taking part in a Bureau of Justice Assistance project through which technical assistance is provided to sites implementing day fines.

26

Expanding Legal Services Programs to Rural America
A Case Study of Program Creation and Operations

MARK KESSLER

For most of their relatively short history, federally-funded legal assistance programs for the poor have been immersed in political controversy.[1] To insulate the programs from political pressure and interference at the national level, Congress established the Legal Services Corporation in 1974. The corporation replaced an earlier program, the Office of Economic Opportunity (OEO) Legal Services Program, removing administrative authority for it from the executive branch and placing it in an independent agency.[2]

Soon after its creation, the LSC's national governing board sought to remedy a significant problem with the OEO program, the disproportionate allocation of resources to local programs serving the urban poor. Based on the findings of an influential study conducted by the Bureau of Social Science Research,[3] the LSC announced its commitment to expand legal assistance into areas previously unserved or dramatically underserved. Chief among these areas were nonmetropolitan counties throughout the United States. As part of its stated goal to provide the

Reprinted by permission of the American Judicature Society and the author from *Judicature*, vol. 73, no. 5 (Feb./March, 1990), pp. 273–280.

poor with "minimum access" to attorneys, the LSC in the late 1970s encouraged local legal organizations in rural areas to submit proposals for funding. It reserved a portion of its total budget exclusively for expanding services into nonmetropolitan areas and developed a formula for allocating financial resources among existing programs based on the number of eligible clients residing in the service area.[4] This formula, at least in the short-term, would benefit newly created programs.[5] From 1976 to 1980, the LSC successfully opened numerous offices serving the rural poor and, in 1980, announced that it had met its short-term goal of providing two attorneys for every 10,000 eligible clients throughout the country.[6]

The impetus for expanding staffed legal services programs into rural areas came not only from the recognition that such areas had not received their share of federal funds from the OEO, but also from a number of empirical studies on the legal needs of the rural poor and the quality of representation provided to them by private attorneys.[7] In general, these studies showed that the incidence of poverty in rural America was as great or greater than in urban areas, that the rural poor had as many or more problems that could be characterized as "legal" as the urban poor, and that private attorneys in rural areas met only a small portion of the poor's legal needs. Further, these studies suggested that rural private practitioners were so intimately linked to those with power and wealth in the local community that they refused to handle cases that challenged the political and economic status quo.

Even though funding for the LSC has been cut since the election of Ronald Reagan in 1980, most of the local programs established and funded during the period of expansion continue to operate. However, no published research examines the establishment and operations of rural legal services programs. This article examines the establishment and operations of one such program created in the late 1970s to serve a rural county. The case study seeks to answer a few important questions about rural legal services programs. What problems were experienced by the LSC in expanding services to rural America? What reception did rural programs receive from important local interests? Have rural programs provided the type of aggressive advocacy on behalf of the poor that was lacking in the representation provided by private attorneys? How does the policy goal of providing aggressive advocacy mesh with the conservative political climate found in many rural areas?

The description and analysis presented here are drawn from two major sources: semi-structured interviews in the winter of 1982 with all four lawyers and one paralegal in a rural legal services program and interviews with 15 individuals representing organizations that interact with the program—two judges, six members of the program's governing board of directors, two private attorneys who were not members of the governing board, two leaders of community organizations dealing with the poor and issues of poverty, and one national, one regional, and one state legal services official involved in or knowledgeable about the establishment of the program under study.[8]

Setting

The program studied is located in a nonmetropolitan county approximately 100 miles from the closest large city.[9] Nearly 50 percent of its 100,000 residents live in a small city, with the remaining population scattered among smaller towns and farming communities. Farms of varying size dot the county's landscape, covering over one-fourth of the county's land area.

The vast majority of the county's population are white and identify with a variety of Protestant religious denominations. A small Catholic and Jewish population resides in the small city along with most of the county's tiny minority population (less than 1 percent of the county's population are black). One striking feature of the county's population mix is its large number of elderly residents. Indeed, 13 percent of its population is over 65 years of age, placing it well over the statewide average. The county's per capita income of $3800 ranked it as one of the poorest counties in the state. Nine percent of its families earned incomes below the poverty line and 4 percent received Aid to Families with Dependent Children (AFDC) benefits.

The county's political climate is very conservative, with nearly 60 percent of its registered voters Republican and an even larger percentage of actual voters in 1980 and 1984 casting their ballot for Ronald Reagan in the general election. All of its state and national legislators are Republicans and nearly all political candidates running for office advocate low taxes, balanced budgets, and limited government involvement in the lives of citizens.

The county's legal community is quite small, composed of less than 100 members. Due to its size, each member of the bar handles cases quite frequently with and against most other lawyers in the county. A few identifiable groups of lawyers socialize together and group members often are allied politically, sharing political values and supporting the same candidates for public office. Norms of cooperation, trust, and courtesy are shared by most lawyers in the bar and encourage a method of case processing which relies heavily on informal negotiations. One local lawyer described the county's legal community as follows:

> I think the county's changing slowly, but we've always had a close
> knit bar. There are certain cliques of lawyers that hang around

> together and view things, politically and otherwise, in similar ways.
> We call each other up on cases and discuss things. We're able to
> settle many cases that in other places would go to trial. Here
> everything doesn't have to be in writing.

The norms of cooperation, trust and courtesy shared by members of
the local bar apply exclusively to attorneys with strong local roots. In
general, the legal community is unreceptive to lawyers from outside the
county using their local court. Further, members of the local legal
community are suspicious of, if not openly hostile to, lawyers born and
raised outside the county opening a practice within the county. The
attitudes of the legal community to outsiders are illustrated in the
comments of one veteran local attorney:

> If you're part of the community, practicing law here can be great.
> But it's not particularly pleasant for out of county people. There's
> a very tight knit organization over here that doesn't particularly care
> for the outsider.

The frequent interaction among local lawyers also led to the establishment of informal norms regarding appropriate attitudes and demeanor.
Lawyers seeking acceptance into the legal community are expected to
express conservative political views and dress appropriately. A story
told by one local lawyer illustrates quite well the effectiveness of the
socialization process:

> In this county, the bar has their own way of viewing things. And
> there's a subtle pressure to conform to that view. These views are
> political, but also relate to such things as lifestyle and dress. When
> I started practicing law here, I rode a motorcycle and wore a beard.
> Now there are not too many lawyers here who did these things. And
> other lawyers made it clear that that's the case. So you feel that to
> get along here you need to conform. There's a requirement of
> conformity in this county if you want to really be part of things.

The county's poverty community is relatively unorganized and
passive. A few low-income organizations exist, but typically they do
not engage in political activity. Instead, these organizations serve two
functions, providing information on social service programs to the poor
and a place to socialize. The county's low income groups never
employed direct action tactics on behalf of their constituents. The
handful of groups interested to some extent in political issues perceived
demonstrations and other forms of direct action as ineffective in a county
so conservative and some feared repercussions for participants. A
community organizer commented:

> If you demonstrate here, your cause would be lost. They're so
> conservative here that demonstrations are for black people in big

cities . . . And I think a lot of it is because they're scared to death that if they would mount some kind of campaign, they might get a rough time in public housing.

Establishing the Program

Prior to the introduction of government funded legal services in the county studied, the bar association operated a volunteer legal aid program. A secretary was stationed in the courthouse to assign members of the private bar to indigents needing civil legal assistance. A pool of attorneys, consisting of those most recently admitted to the county's bar, were required by the program to offer services at no cost or reduced fees.

A government sponsored program was not instituted in the county until 1975. This was not due to lack of funds for such a project, for state monies had been available since 1968. Rather, the failure to establish a legal services agency is explained by the county bar association's opposition.

During the mid-1970s, the state and national legal services organizations began to encourage rural counties to develop legal services agencies based on the full-time, staff attorney model employed by the OEO Legal Services Program and its successor, the Legal Services Corporation. Believing that the local bar association would not pursue government funding and that a large number of the poor were not receiving adequate legal assistance, the county's Community Action Agency applied for state and national funds. At this time, both the state legal services office and the Legal Services Corporation expressed its intention of funding a program to the county's bar association. Further, the state bar association began to pressure the county bar to support the establishment of such a program in the county.

The dramatic difference between the state and county bar associations' support for government funded legal services is explained by the varying backgrounds and legal practices of members of their governing committees. State bar committees were controlled disproportionately by attorneys from large corporate firms in the state's urban jurisdictions. The rural bar association, in contrast, was governed by solo practitioners and small firm lawyers with more of a financial stake in the provision of legal services to low income clients. Consequently, the local bar was much more concerned with the economic impact of a legal services program on their membership. The opposing positions taken by the local and state bar organizations in this case are reminiscent of splits between local bar associations and the American Bar Association over the establishment of the OEO Legal Services Program in the 1960s.[10]

In response to these events, the county's bar association filed an application for funding with the state legal services office. However, the program proposed in the application was not based on the staff attorney model, but rather sought to involve private attorneys in a "judicare" program, whereby local attorneys service indigents and receive fees from a state grant or directly from the national LSC. Modeled after the medicare program, indigents would receive a "judicare card" and present it to any participating attorney for service.[11]

After a short period of intense lobbying by prominent members of the county's bar association, the state legal services office rejected the judicare proposal. Two related events then convinced the county bar association to change their position and apply for funds to be used to establish a staff attorney agency. First, the state legal services office along with the national LSC informed the bar of its intention to fund a staff attorney program with or without its cooperation. Many in the local bar believed that their refusal to cooperate at the agency's origin could ultimately result in an inability to influence its operations once established. One prominent member of the bar remembered:

> We really got a runaround in our efforts to fund a judicare program and it became obvious to us that the state office didn't want to fund a judicare program. They wanted a different type of program and they were going to make it as difficult for us to get it as possible. So, the local community action group got tired of waiting for a legal services program to develop and they were going to start a corporation . . . So at that point we were put between a rock and a hard place. Although we very much wanted a judicare program, we thought we had better get on board or we would have little to say about this program.

The county bar also believed that if they did not cooperate in the establishment of a staff attorney agency, the state legal services office and the LSC would control the new program and staff it with attorneys from outside the county. Indeed, several local lawyers remarked in interviews that just prior to the bar's decision to cooperate, the state legal services office sent a few lawyers from outside the county to rent an office within the county. It was significant to members of the county bar that the outsiders differed in appearance from county lawyers and many believed that they had come from the largest city in the state, a situation which evoked images in their minds of radical lawyers who would refuse to play by the county's informal rules. The comments of two local attorneys illustrate the fear of a legal services agency controlled and staffed by outsiders:

> R1. We could not get judicare. They wouldn't fund it. We either founded our own legal service corporation and manned it with people we hired or we were gonna get the outsiders coming in and setting up a store front operation. And as a matter of fact, they came here

and looked over the situation. They were looking for a store front at the time.

Q Is that right?

R1. Oh, yea. They were here. They came and looked over the lay of the land, three guys with beards. I never had any hesitation in my mind when we found that the judicare program was shot down that we had better be an active participant in founding a legal services operation that would get funded.

R2. There was a definite concern that we were gonna have a lot of outside lawyers coming in here. All of a sudden these lawyers are gonna come in, set up their magic office, and be something different and tell us how to do things. We thought that some of these lawyers from _____ [the largest city in the state] were here looking around. And this stuff can have an effect. As soon as one lawyer starts playing these games, filing all kinds of cases and motions and whatnot, the other lawyers may respond to that in kind. So I think there was a feeling that there might be a bad effect on the whole bar.

Ultimately, the state legal services office and the LSC accepted the county bar's application for a legal services agency. However, the struggles between the bar and state and national funding sources created tremendous animosity for the new program among members of the local legal community.[12] The general reception of the program by the local bar is shown in the comments that follow of a program attorney and a prominent member of the county bar:

We have dealt with opposition here from day one. We were not a planned for child. We were found on the doorstep by the bar association. So, sometimes I feel like I have to deal with Cinderella's step-sisters, you know. They're not enthusiastic about our being here and it shows in our relations.

The bar association had to be dragged, kicking and screaming, before there was a legal service corporation established here. And as a result these lawyers haven't been embraced as perhaps other members of the bar are. There has been some tension and a certain degree of animosity which is understandable given its history.

The County Bar and the Board

After the program's establishment, the local legal community moved quickly to gain control of it. Its chief source of control was the program's governing board of directors, a board required by LSC regulations to be composed of a majority of attorneys.[13] Provisions in the program's charter, drafted by members of the county bar association, permitted the organized bar to select its representatives for the board. And further, any future vacancies on the board of directors could only be filled by persons receiving the approval of a majority of sitting members of the board.

One consequence of the procedures established by the bar for placing people on the board is that from its establishment to the time of my field research, the program's board was composed primarily of attorney members who zealously monitored and attempted to shape the program's growth, direction and operations. At the program's inception, the attorney members of the board were those with the greatest concerns and fears about the new agency. These members typically volunteered for board membership in order to monitor the program's operations as closely as possible. Specifically, most were concerned with the economic impact of a legal services office on the private bar, as illustrated in the comments of two board members:

> I originally joined the board for self-preservation . . . When I originally got into it, I said, wait a minute. I've got a wife and three kids. I gotta put these kids through college. I want to make sure there's some salary there, still some clients left to come see me. The public defender's office does 75 percent of the criminal work in the county. If legal services had an open pocketbook, they'd do the majority of the civil work . . . So, originally when I got involved, it was on the basis of I wanted to know where they were going and what they were doing.

> I suppose, to be quite honest, my concern was more perhaps toward the interest of my profession and a concern that there was some involvement by legal services as a bureaucracy in the private practice of law. My motivating force was largely out of a sense of duty to the profession, not any strong commitment toward legal services as an entity.

Control of Program Operations

The program's governing board of directors played a large role in program operations. In particular, the board closely scrutinized budgetary and other financial matters. It did not defer to the judgments and decisions of program administrators, but rather exerted an independent influence, often differing with the positions taken by the program director and formulating alternatives. Some of the flavor of the board's role in budgetary matters is shown in the comments that follow of one veteran board member:

> We have what I believe to be some lawyers on the board who are very conscientious. We get into budget sessions and they last for

hours and there's a lot of screaming and shouting and all that. Sometimes the director will tell us, "we've got this much money left over so we have to spend it or we're not gonna get as much next year." That meets with some resistance from the taxpaying members of the board. I think it's basically a situation where we're not willing to sit back and say, "Well, go ahead and do whatever you want to do and where do you want me to sign my name." I think that's been a thorn in the side of the legal services corporation here.

One frequent source of conflict between the board and the program's executive director over budgetary allocations came in the area of staff salaries.[14] The board carefully examined and, on several occasions, opposed requests for funds to cover staff salary increases. The youngest and least financially secure lawyers on the board were most resistant to salary requests, arguing that poverty lawyers should not enjoy an income comparable to their own. But even prominent members of established firms expressed concern about granting increases because news of such action traveled swiftly through the bar and they feared that junior members of their firms and secretaries would request comparable increases.[15] The conflict between the board and program director over salaries and some of the reasons for it are shown in the following comments of two board members:

> The fights that come about at budget time and things like that come about as a result of younger attorneys who are not getting paid much. They don't want to see legal services attorneys getting paid much either. And some attorneys don't want legal services secretaries getting paid more than their own, because it's only a matter of time before their secretaries say, "hey, what about me. You gave the legal services people more money."

> You have members on the board who have in the past been resentful of the fact that legal services lawyers were making more money, as much money, or not enough less money than they themselves were. And some were concerned that some of the younger members in their firm would follow the program's example and ask for more money. I can think of several members of the board since I've been on it who seemed to be motivated a great deal when it came to salary and fringe benefit considerations.

In addition to determining the salaries of program staff, the board sought to restrict the program's growth. For example, in the late 1970s the program applied for a small LSC grant to improve its library and phone system. The LSC funded this request and offered the program an additional $40,000 to hire a paralegal, an additional lawyer, a secretary, and make additional improvements in the program's facilities. To receive the funding, the program was required to formulate a new proposal with the approval of its board. The board initially refused and only after several meetings and an extremely close vote did they accept. The program's director remembered these events as follows:

> When we received expansion funds from the LSC, we had to put together a new budget, a new proposal, and sign some grant papers. At our next meeting, we went over to tell the board that we had received $40,000 from the LSC. We would now be able to add a lawyer, a secretary, and a paralegal. The board voted at this point not to accept the money. If the money came we were to send it back, I guess. They just were not going to accept the expansion of the program from two lawyers to three lawyers, from one paralegal to two, and add a secretary. It caught me completely by surprise. So we had another meeting in ten days. We brought in a regional director of the Legal Services Corporation. LSC sent a number of observers. And we brought in some supportive people from county agencies, like the Office of Aging . . . And by one vote, the resolution was passed to accept the money. The vote was taken after an enormous debate and great outpouring by opponents of legal services that we were growing too large, that we were becoming an octopus.

Another example of the board's concern with the program's growth occurred in the late 1970s when the program's director requested funds to open an office in an outlying area of the county. The board flatly refused, with several attorney members arguing that the poor in this area were able to transport themselves some 40 miles to the existing office. As one board member put it:

> No one could show us the need to expand. In other words, was it cost effective to locate an office in _____? If you could show me that there were people there that couldn't get to the office, then yea let's look at it. But if you're telling us that somebody is just too lazy or doesn't want to make the trip . . . and I find that.

The board jealously guarded the influence it obtained from its scrutiny of budgetary and expansion issues. On several occasions, it refused to accept nominations for membership to the board of private attorneys perceived to be less interested than they in closely monitoring the program's operations. Significantly, several of the failed nominees received the support of the program's executive director. Thus, because of the self-perpetuating nature of the board and its interest in controlling program growth and operations, it was impossible for the program to achieve any significant degree of autonomy. The comments of two board members show how the board rejected lawyers who did not share their interest in playing a "watchdog" role:

> The bar members know the basic attitude of other members of the bar. And I think we have rejected those that have an attitude of

outright liberalism or outright I don't care. You know, we don't want lawyers with the attitude of if that's what the executive director wants, then go ahead and do it. So we don't really want a liberal or someone who will simply rubber stamp anything the program wants.

I would say that there are efforts, largely by the executive director, to secure several members of the bar who I know are perceived to be more congenial to his particular direction. And believe me, I don't fault him for that. This is an extremely conservative bar in a conservative area. And his efforts to secure members of this bar were rebuffed on more than one occasion. So there has been a great deal of success I think from the standpoint of more reactionary members of the board in keeping out those whom they see to be more aligned with the executive director.

The program's executive director expressed his frustration in placing sympathetic private attorneys on the board as follows:

There aren't that many people who have been supporters of legal services or at least want to vocalize that support publicly. Maybe a year ago we had a process in which our nominating committee acquired as a candidate a female attorney in the county . . . I pushed her nomination to the board. She was interested in serving. It was well known that she felt that legal services was a worthwhile adjunct to the judicial system here. The board at that time was flabbergasted that she would be nominated. They tabled the nomination and at the next meeting nominated someone else from the floor and elected him. None of the lawyers voted for my nominee. All of the client members voted for her, so she lost 8–5.

The Board and Legal Representation

As the discussion above indicates, the county bar association and its representatives on the program's board of directors were concerned from the time of program creation with the economic impact of a legal services agency on the private practitioner. Therefore, the board's attorney members sought to limit the number of clients and case categories handled by program staff. To guard against a substantial loss of income and clients, the board employed its control over the budget to restrict the number of lawyers hired by the program and the number of offices operated throughout the county. By restricting the size of the program as much as possible, the board hoped to limit the number of cases handled and guarantee that private attorneys would not lose much of their low-income clientele. One program attorney commented:

The majority of the board, the attorney members, obviously would prefer that we maintain a very small scope of influence and a small clientele within the community . . . They've attempted to limit the growth of the program so that we would not have enough lawyers to service more clients. Remember, they wanted judicare. They've never wanted us to have too much of an effect here. And from that standpoint, they've been fairly successful.

The program's board of directors also promulgated policies that prohibited program attorneys from handling certain case types perceived as potentially lucrative for lawyers in private practice. Interpreting the Legal Services Corporation Act's prohibition against handling fee generating cases quite broadly, the board proscribed program staff from handling cases involving social security disability claims, unemployment compensation, and workmen's compensation, areas that other legal services agencies routinely handle. The program's director explained:

> The board has been quite interested in what cases we handle. They still believe we are taking business from the private practitioner. At one point the board delineated what were fee generating cases and excluded a number of cases that traditionally are handled by legal services. They excluded Title II social security disability cases where the claimant has paid into his account, workmen's comp and unemployment compensation. I had a hard time with all of these.

The program's board of directors also sought to influence the type of legal strategies employed by program staff. Early in the program's history, the board's attorney members clearly expressed their opposition to the use of legal strategies and cases that sought major reforms of laws and institutions perceived as biased against the poor.[16] In general, the board viewed the proper role of the legal services lawyer as representing individual clients and resolving individual problems and disputes. The majority of the board perceived law reform as beyond the scope of the agency's mandate, as shown in the comments of one veteran member:

> In the beginning, there might have been some thought over there about starting some class actions, both locally and at the federal level. The board found that repugnant, very repugnant. The lawyers who were members of the board were all members of the bar in this county, where the spirit of the practitioner that was passed on to each of us as we came to this bar was you are here to do a job for your client. You are not a crusader.

To ensure that program attorneys did not bring cases that challenged existing laws and institutional practices, the board passed a resolution requiring the program's executive director to receive the board's approval before filing class action lawsuits or any other potentially "controversial" case. A board member explained:

> We said, ''don't you ever start a class action without first bringing
> it to the board for approval.'' Because we don't look favorably upon
> class actions or test cases. We aren't here to test laws. We're here
> because somebody is being thrown out of their house. We're here
> because somebody's car is being taken away. We're here because
> this lady's husband beats her once a night and she can't afford a
> divorce. We're not here as a social commentary. We're not here to
> deal with all the social problems in the world. Your clients may
> encounter some of those social problems, but we'll deal on the basis
> of what we're doing for that client, not the whole group. So very
> early on it was very well established, very clearly stated, ''don't mess
> with class actions and test cases.''

The board supported its opposition to reform litigation with explicit
threats to the program's executive director. The board warned the
director that reform cases brought by program staff would result in his
termination as director. While all of the board members and program
staff I interviewed reported that the board did not interfere in cases
involving individual client representation, most believed that such
nonintervention would not apply to proposed reform cases. The pressure
exerted by the board on the program's executive director is illustrated
in the comments of one board member:

> I don't think that _____ [the director] ever had a question in
> his mind that if in fact he flagrantly went in opposition to the
> expressed policy of the board, he'd be fired. I don't think there ever
> was a doubt in his mind. It was very clearly stated by me and I know
> by others that we would never tell him how to handle a case . . .
> But don't get into the class action business . . . I don't think there
> was ever a doubt in his mind that if we really had a showdown on
> something like that, he'd be looking for a job.

Faced with such clear opposition to reform litigation by the board of
directors, the program's director discouraged class action suits and test
case development by communicating informally to staff his belief that
generating controversy threatened the program's continued survival. In
an interview, the director discussed his informal policy:

> I've certainly told my staff on occasion to be careful not to stir the
> waters. Sometimes it does more harm than good. I've always had
> the attitude that there's no sense going in with the idea of stirring
> up the water. You don't just go in and make waves. There's no sense
> in doing that because you'll create animosity, especially in a real
> conservative type place like this. There's no sense in you allowing
> yourself to put your head on the chopping block for no damn good
> reason. When you lose a controversial case, that hurts every other
> case and every other client. So if you win one, fine, but is it worth
> it really?

Program staff heeded the director's recommendation that they avoid controversial cases and focus on more routine service for individual clients. Indeed, even though each of the program attorneys interviewed believed that the program should be doing more reform oriented work, they had never filed a class action lawsuit, had not developed test cases, and had never brought a case generating controversy in the county. The vast majority of cases handled by program attorneys dealt with domestic relations, especially routine divorce actions. In all of their cases, program staff sought to informally negotiate agreements with the opposing party. One important reason for the conciliatory posture of the program was the recognition by program staff that a more aggressive, reform-oriented program faced serious opposition from the board and that such activity likely would be accompanied by negative political repercussions. The comments of one program lawyer are typical of the staff's views:

> A major reason why you don't see any class action suits from us is just the flack that the program would get from the board. They have a great deal of influence here and it's felt in this area particularly. They control salary, hiring and firing, how much money we'll ask for, and how much we'll accept. And for those reasons, you don't want them disturbed.

Conclusion

In some important respects, the finding from this research on the creation and operations of one rural legal services program parallel those from older studies of programs in more urbanized settings funded by the OEO's Legal Services Program.[17] For example, Stumpf, Schroerluke, and Dill; Champagne; and Johnson, document the serious opposition to program creation that some local agencies faced from the local legal community.[18] In addition, Stumpf and, more recently, Meeker, Dombrink and Song show that local bar organizations often have expressed opposition to legal reform activity engaged in by federally funded poverty attorneys.[19]

Some evidence from the extant research suggests that the preferences of local attorneys and bar groups may have affected the activities actually engaged in by some of the agencies studied.[20] However, even in the face of such opposition, some urban programs have been able to overcome it and pursue aggressive, reform-oriented legal work.[21] Elsewhere I have argued that differences among legal services programs in law reform activity are explained by variations in the organizational environments of local programs. In a larger study of five local programs from which the case discussed in this article is taken, one urban program was found to engage in a substantial amount of law reform work, even though many established groups and individuals opposed such activity. This program was able to do so because it shielded itself from pressures from conservative local organizations by allying itself with low-income community groups supportive of law reform. Low-income groups, several of whom had become significant political forces in the city, assisted poverty attorneys in identifying policy problems experienced by the poor and, as important, provided crucial political support when the agency became the target of criticisms and political pressures from conservative local organizations and political officials.[22]

The case study presented here, along with the handful of studies that have been conducted on the general operating characteristics of rural legal systems, suggest that the lack of politically powerful, advocacy-oriented low-income organizations combined with the generally conservative political climate and local legal culture found in rural areas present serious obstacles for programs and attorneys in nonmetropolitan areas who seek to provide reform-oriented legal representation to the poor.[23] In perhaps the most systematic study of rural legal culture and its influence on the legal community, Landon found that attorneys he interviewed in rural Missouri avoided handling certain types of controversial cases, such as medical malpractice, sexual abuse, and especially those involving civil rights.[24] Because community residents and prominent local attorneys opposed legal and political action that challenged traditional community standards and practices, individual practitioners typically were wary of taking such cases, fearing adverse effects on their professional aspirations. Further, rural lawyers generally assumed a conciliatory posture in their legal work, seeking to informally resolve disputes rather than litigate in courts. These general operating features of the rural legal process are consistent with studies of rural political processes which find that political disputes typically are settled outside of formal institutions.[25]

The decentralized structure of the Legal Services Corporation, which places decisionmaking authority in the hands of a variety of local interests, may be crucial for generating and maintaining local and federal political support and insuring the program's continued survival. However, this administrative scheme further compounds the problem for local legal services programs that wish to provide aggressive, reform-oriented legal representation, virtually guaranteeing that those who hold dominant values and norms will control the program's board of directors and will exert influence over program activity and operations. Indeed, the decentralized structure of federally funded legal services for the poor renders it more likely that rural programs will be captured by dominant interests than programs in other social settings. Studies of community political power suggest that power tends to be more concentrated in small communities and dispersed in larger ones.[26] Because dominant interests in rural areas do not have to contend with countervailing sources of power they are able to effectively control and exercise influence over most, if not all, organizations in the local community. Thus, although in part local participation in legal services decisionmaking was required initially to provide the poor and their representatives with a voice in the governance of programs,[27] the power structure in rural America facilitates program control by established interests.

In the program discussed in this article, the county bar association seized control by writing the program's charter, a charter ensuring that a majority of the program's board would share values and norms with prominent members of the bar. The board then exercised its control of the program to restrict its growth, determine the types of cases program attorneys could handle, and influence the types of legal strategies employed. No organized groups in the county provided alternative and countervailing sources of support for the legal aid program, permitting it to gain at least some degree of autonomy from the county bar association.[28]

In some important respects, the findings discussed here are consistent with those reported in Selznick's seminal study of the Tennessee Valley Authority.[29] The TVA was established in the late 1930s to produce power, control flooding, build dams, and accomplish other economic goals. At the same time, it was to assist poor farmers, develop recreation areas, and preserve forests. Selznick shows how the TVA's policy of encouraging grassroots involvement in decisionmaking led to the co-optation of the program by local political and business leaders and the subverting of its goals. For example, poor farmers did not receive adequate aid or services. Some recreation areas were handed over to private business which diminished their natural beauty. And rather than preserve forests, many were virtually destroyed by the lumber industry. Much like the Legal Services Corporation, the TVA sought to forestall opposition and attacks on its programs at the national level by involving local interests in decisionmaking. However, these environmental contingencies create the conditions under which the achievement of original goals becomes difficult, if not impossible.

Providing attorneys to assist the rural poor with their routine legal problems is a significant step in ensuring some measure of equality in the civil justice system. Between 1974 and 1980, the Legal Services Corporation created more programs in rural areas and allocated more funds to them than any previous federal effort.

The program discussed in this article performed a valuable function in protecting and furthering its clients' legal rights, a function that in many cases was not performed adequately prior to the creation of the program. For example, attorneys interviewed reported that private practitioners filed few bankruptcy actions prior to the establishment of the legal services office. Private lawyers with close ties to local business establishments and banks protected creditors' interests by negotiating payment schedules for debts. The private bar also was reluctant to file actions under the state's statute providing women protection from spousal abuse, for fear of upsetting local judges unsympathetic to their plight. Therefore, in simply requiring the local legal system and decisionmakers to apply established laws, poverty attorneys provided important benefits to their clients.

However, while this office played a crucial role in forcing the implementation of established rules, it was unable to provide the same scope of legal services as attorneys for more affluent clients. The program guaranteed the poor equal access to courts in certain substantive areas, but it did not provide the diversity of representation and the full range of advocacy that wealthier clients enjoy.

In sum, this case study suggests that providing attorneys to the rural poor does not necessarily result in aggressive, reform-oriented legal advocacy. Federal programs which encourage local control of program operations can expect the activities of local grantees to reflect prevailing values and norms, which in turn reflect prevailing distributions of power.

Endnotes

[1] Sullivan, "Law Reform and the Legal Service Crisis," 59 *Calif. L. Rev.* 1–28 (1971); Falk and Pollack, "Political Interference with Public Lawyers: The CRLA Controversy and the Future of Legal Services," 24 *Hastings L. J.* 599–646 (1979); Stumpf, *Community Politics and Legal Services* (Beverly Hills: Sage, 1974); Hannon, "From Politics to Reality: An Historical Perspective of the Legal Services Corporation," 25 *Emory L. J.* 639–654 (1976); Johnson, *Justice and Reform: The Formative Years of the American Legal Services Program* (New Brunswick, NJ: Transaction Books, 1978); Champagne, "Legal Services: A Program in Need of Assistance," in Champagne and Harpham, eds., *The Attack on the Welfare State* (Prospect Heights, IL: Waveland Press, 1984).

[2] George, "Development of the Legal Service's Corporation," 61 *Cornell Law Rev.* 681–730 (1976); Champagne, supra n. 1.

[3] Goodman and Walker, *The Legal Services Program: Resource Distribution and the Low Income Population* (Washington, DC: Bureau of Social Science Research, 1975).

[4] For example, the LSC reserved $14 million in 1977 and $27 million in 1978 for expanding its services into unserved areas. See Legal Services Corporation, *Annual Report* (Washington, DC: LSC, 1978).

[5] Legal Services Corporation, *Annual Report* (Washington, DC: LSC, 1977, 1978, 1979, 1980). Legal Services Corporation, *Background* (Washington, DC: LSC, 1980).

[6] Legal Services Corporation, *Background*, id.

[7] See, "The Legal Problems of the Rural Poor," 1969 *Duke L. J.* 495–620 (1969); "Rural Poverty and the Law in Southern Colorado," 47 *Den. L. J.* 82–176 (1970); Widiss,

"Legal Assistance for the Rural Poor: An Iowa Study," 56 *Iowa L. Rev.* 100–138 (1970).

[8] Data reported in this article are drawn from a larger research project which examines the operations of several legal services programs in diverse social settings. See Kessler, *Legal Services for the Poor: A Comparative and Contemporary Analysis of Interorganizational Politics* (Westport, CT: Greenwood Press, 1987). Interviews conducted with lawyers and paralegals were lengthy, lasting from one to three hours. Topics covered included personal backgrounds, political attitudes, program characteristics (e.g., structure, policies, operations, environment), and legal strategy. Interviews with representatives of organizations that interact with the program ranged from 45 minutes to two hours in length. Topics covered included their organization's relationship with the legal aid program, their general assessment of its quality, and avenues available to express criticism or praise. All interviews were tape recorded and transcribed. I also had access to numerous written documents, such as the program's charter and minutes of board meetings.

[9] Participants in the study were assured that their identities and the location of the program would not be revealed in reports of this research. This guarantee was essential to gain the cooperation of legal services lawyers at a time when the Reagan Administration had announced its intention to eliminate funding for the LSC.

[10] See Johnson, *Justice and Reform*, supra n. 1.

[11] For a discussion of judicare programs, see Brakel, *Judicare: Public Funds, Private Lawyers, and Poor People* (Chicago: American Bar Foundation, 1974).

[12] Opposition to local legal services programs by local bar groups also accompanied the establishment of several urban programs by the OEO. See Hannon, "Law Reform Enforcement at the Local Level: A Legal Services Case Study," 19 *J. of Pub. L.* 23–48 (1970); Stumpf, *Community Politics and Legal Services*, supra n. 1; Johnson, *Justice and Reform*, supra n. 1.

[13] The LSC required that 60 percent of the local governing board be composed of local attorneys. The remaining 40 percent are to be eligible clients and representatives of other community groups. In the program studied, 9 of 15 members were attorneys. Like all of the programs studied in the larger project from which this case is drawn, the remaining seats were difficult to fill with members who regularly attended meetings. Client nonparticipation on legal services governing boards appears to be quite typical. Abel argues that client representatives that do attend meetings are quickly discouraged because they are outnumbered and dominated by attorney members who are more articulate, better educated, and of higher social status. See Abel, "Law Without Politics: Legal Aid Under Advanced Capitalism," 32 *UCLA L. Rev.* 523 (1985).

[14] The entry level salary for staff attorneys at the time of my field research was $14,000. The program's executive director reported that salary increases failed consistently to keep pace with inflation.

[15] Unfortunately, I do not have data on the income of private practitioners in this county. Such data would permit an assessment of the validity of attorney concerns. However, Landon's comparative study of urban and rural lawyers in Missouri suggests that, on average, the incomes of rural attorneys are comparable to their urban counterparts. Indeed, his sample of rural attorneys earned $36,250 per year on average compared to an average of $34,100 earned by a sample of attorneys in Springfield. See Table 14 in Landon, "Lawyers and Localities: The Interaction of Community Context and Professionalism," 1982 *Am. B. Found. Res. J.* 473 (1982); and Table 7 in Landon, "LaSalle Street and Main Street: The Role of Context in Structuring Law Practice," 22 *Law & Soc'y Rev.* 233 (1988). Of course, rural attorneys fall short of the incomes earned by corporate attorneys in urban settings (as do most urban lawyers). For data on incomes for corporate attorneys, see chapter 5 in Nelson, *Partners With Power:*

Social Transformation of the Large Law Firm (Berkeley: University of California Press, 1988).

[16] Local bar opposition to law reform has been reported in a number of previous studies. See, for example, Stumpf, *Community Politics and Legal Services*, supra n. 1; and Meeker, Dombrink, and Song, "Perceptions About the Poor, Their Legal Needs, and Legal Services," 9 *Law & Pol'y* 143–169 (1987).

[17] An important difference of note between the OEO program and the LSC is that the OEO program was much more centralized. To encourage local programs to engage in reform activity, national OEO officials allocated funding to local programs based on the amount of law reform pursued. See Johnson, *Justice and Reform*, supra n. 1. In contrast, the LSC avoided stating explicit program goals and allocates funds to local grantees based on the number of people in the program's service area with incomes below the OMB's poverty line. Thus, while national OEO officials may have exerted influence on local programs through its method of funding, LSC officials have been unable to do so.

[18] Stumpf, Schroerluke, and Dill, "The Legal Profession and Legal Services: Explorations in Local Bar Politics," 6 *Law & Soc'y Rev.* 47–67 (1971); Champagne, "Lawyers and Government Funded Legal Services," 21 *Villanova L. Rev.* 860–875 (1976); Johnson, *Justice and Reform*, supra n. 1.

[19] Stumpf, *Community Politics and Legal Services*, supra n. 1; Meeker, Dombrink, and Song, "Perceptions About the Poor, Their Legal Needs, and Legal Services," supra n. 16.

[20] Finman, "OEO Legal Services Programs and the Pursuit of Social Change: The Relationship Between Program Ideology and Program Performance," 1971 *Wis. L. Rev.* 1001–1084 (1971); Stumpf, *Community Politics and Legal Services*, supra n. 1.

[21] Katz, *Poor People's Lawyers in Transition* (New Brunswick, NJ: Rutgers University Press, 1982); Kessler, *Legal Services for the Poor*, supra n. 8.

[22] Kessler, "Legal Services Agencies and Low Income Community Groups," in Nagel, ed., *Research in Law and Policy Studies: Volume I* (Greenwich, CT: JAI Press, 1987), and Kessler, *Legal Services for the Poor*, supra n. 8.

[23] For a good review of the literature before 1982 on rural legal systems, see Eisenstein, "Research on Rural Criminal Justice: A Summary," in Cronk, ed., *Criminal Justice in Rural America* (Washington, DC: National Institute of Justice, 1982). This article summarizes much of the extant research on rural politics, legal culture, and the operations of legal institutions.

[24] Landon, "Clients, Colleagues, and Community: The Shaping of Zealous Advocacy in Country Law Practice," 1985 *Am. B. Found. Res. J.* 81–111 (1985).

[25] For example, see Vidich and Bensman, *Small Town in Mass Society: Class, Power, and Religion in a Rural Community*, Rev. ed. (Princeton: Princeton University Press, 1968); Gilbert, *Community Power Structure: Propositional Inventory, Tests, and Theory* (Gainesville: University of Florida Press, 1977); Swanson, Cohen, and Swanson, *Small Towns and Small Towners*, (Beverly Hills: Sage, 1979).

[26] Dahl and Tufte, *Size and Democracy* (Stanford: Stanford University Press, 1979); Gilbert, *Community Power Structure*, supra n. 25; Swanson, Cohen, and Swanson, *Small Towns and Small Towners*, supra n. 25.

[27] Johnson, *Justice and Reform*, supra n. 1.

[28] Program staff on several occasions sought to help build welfare and tenants groups, but each time had failed.

[29] Selznick, *TVA and the Grassroots* (New York: Harper & Row, 1966).

27

Secret Justice

JOHN GIBEAUT

It cost plenty for reporter Kirsten B. Mitchell and her newspaper to tell readers about a $36 million secret settlement of an environmental lawsuit between Conoco Inc. and residents of a mobile home park in Wrightsboro, N.C.

U.S. District Judge W. Earl Britt found Mitchell and the Wilmington, N.C., *Morning Star* in civil contempt and ordered them to pay the oil company $500,000. Then, Britt fined Mitchell another $1,000 in late February for criminal contempt.

Her offense: Obtaining the settlement figure from a sealed file inadvertently handed her by a court clerk.

"I've never seen a case like this, where you're held in contempt for looking at a document the government gives you," says George Freeman, assistant general counsel for the newspaper's parent corporation, The New York Times Co.

Media lawyers say Mitchell is a casualty of an increasingly pervasive secret justice system that allows well-heeled or famous litigants to make private use of the public courts while the travails of ordinary citizens are revealed for all to see.

"That's an example of how bizarre things can get," says lawyer Jane E. Kirtley, executive director of the Reporters Committee for Freedom of the Press in Arlington, Va. "I would say it's reaching epidemic proportions."

But while Mitchell and the *Morning Star* may pay a high price, the cost of secret justice to the public ultimately may be even higher. Whether judges seal files, close courtrooms or allow anonymous jurors to hear

Reprinted with permission from the *ABA Journal* (April, 1998), Vol. 84, pp. 50–55.

cases, critics complain such practices erode public oversight and confidence in the system, and reduce accountability for some protected wrongdoers.

"People who can afford to buy secret justice do, and that's just not what our system's about," says lawyer Kelli L. Sager, who represents media interests in Los Angeles.

In the long run, critics say, such secrecy creates a two-tiered justice system, one for the rich and famous, and a second one for everyone else. And sometimes, as in the Conoco case and others, major public safety and consumer concerns are swept under the rug.

"There's this concern that public figures get to clean their laundry in a private or semiprivate cubicle while everyone else has to use the Laundromat," says St. Paul, Minn., lawyer Paul R. Hannah, who concentrates on media and entertainment law. "If, in fact, justice is the great leveler, you no longer see a system that protects the weaker against the strong."

Concerns about secrecy are not just from nosy reporters and cranky editors trying to mind everyone's business but their own. New York lawyer Eugene R. Anderson recently filed an amicus brief on behalf of United Policy Holders, a public interest group that wanted to know what's contained in voluminous sealed files in litigation between the 3M Co. and its insurers over coverage for the company's potential liability for silicone-gel breast implants. "I don't [care] about the media," Anderson says. "We represent policyholders. The insurance industry is the most secret industry in the world."

Still, media lawyers primarily form the front line. Although no figures are available, media lawyers across the country report increased problems in obtaining access to criminal and civil court proceedings and documents. Judges, often unaware of serious constitutional and other legal requirements, frequently close the system to public scrutiny, often simply because the parties to a case want it that way.

Sometimes celebrities don't even have to ask a court for help. Los Angeles prosecutors listed Steven Spielberg as "John Doe" in a case against a man accused of stalking the filmmaker, although Sager says there was no indication Spielberg requested anonymity.

Also in Los Angeles, a state judge partly closed a 1996 civil trial in which actress Sondra Locke accused her former lover Clint Eastwood of fraud. "Neither Eastwood nor Sondra Locke requested that the trial be closed," says Sager, who represents the *Los Angeles Times* and *California Community News* in an ongoing appeal on the access issue to the California Supreme Court.

As for Locke and Eastwood, they settled for—you guessed it—an undisclosed amount of money as jurors deliberated.

Notorious criminal defendants, too, can get some of the same advantages as celebrities when courts decide their fair trial rights are special enough to trump First Amendment rights. Convicted Oklahoma City bomber Timothy McVeigh and co-defendant Terry Nichols were able to hide from view chunks of documents that routinely would have become public in other cases.

Money Talks

Perhaps the most troubling aspect of the latest wave of secrecy springs from cases involving large corporations that want to control costs and maintain solid public images while taking advantage of the finality of res judicata that only a public court can offer.

"I'm seeing this a lot," says Minneapolis lawyer Mark R. Anfinson. "I think it's becoming standard operating procedure, especially in complex commercial litigation."

While the U.S. Supreme Court has long held that the public has a nearly unqualified First Amendment right to attend all phases of criminal proceedings, it has issued no specific pronouncement regarding court files themselves or civil trials.

Thus, lower courts are all over the map when it comes to files and civil matters, with some finding varying degrees of First Amendment rights in individual areas, more limited common-law rights in others, and, in still others, no rights at all.

The California Supreme Court, however, is expected to decide this year whether a specific First Amendment right exists to attend civil trials in the Locke-Eastwood case. *KNBC-TC v. Superior Court*, No. S056924.

But the Minnesota Supreme Court in early March refused to hear arguments to unseal the 3M case. *State Insurance Co. v. Minnesota Mining and Manufacturing Co.*, Nos. C0 97-2257, C4 97-1872. Media lawyers were uncertain what they would do next in the case.

"If they rule there is no First Amendment right, we'll continue in a helluva mess until we get a definitive statement from the U.S. Supreme Court," says lawyer Richard M. Schmidt Jr. of Washington, D.C., counsel for the American Society of Newspaper Editors.

Observers and participants say the California case is especially important because the government, which is supposed to ensure openness, is pressing for secrecy instead of the parties. And the sheer scope of the Minnesota case starkly illustrates its public interest, they say.

"It's just astounding," says Anfinson, who represents the Minneapolis *Star Tribune* in the case against St. Paul-based 3M and the insurance companies. "It's far and away the most astonishing example of secret justice

I've ever seen. It's truly mind-boggling. This is big-time litigation with lots of consequences for lots of people."

Different Drummer

Lawyers seeking closure for corporate clients pack a different agenda. Although legal arguments for closure typically center on the need for secrecy as an incentive to settle and courts' traditional deference to the parties' wishes, money lurks at the bottom.

In the Conoco case, 178 mobile home residents claimed leaks from one of the company's gas stations had polluted their drinking water. The deal in the case was struck last summer after a public trial that lasted more than a month and after the jury had found Conoco liable for the pollution. Jurors were considering punitive damages when the settlement came. Conoco lawyer Jonathan D. Sasser of Raleigh, N.C., says the *Morning Star*'s disclosure of the settlement amount will cost the Houston-based company a pile because it's involved in about 50 similar cases.

"It increases the expectations of other plaintiffs and other plaintiffs lawyers," Sasser says. "We were harmed to the tune of millions of dollars. It will raise the value of settlements in the future and raise the costs of defending these cases."

The judge declined other requests by Conoco to find *Morning Star* reporter Cory Reiss in contempt and force him to identify two confidential sources who gave him the same information on the settlement figure. But it was the publication of Mitchell's information citing court documents that really stung, Sasser says. "That adds a degree of credibility to it." Although Judge Britt wrote in his Jan. 21 civil contempt order that "this matter is not about the freedom of the press, but about the respect that any citizen, individual or corporate, should have for an order of the court," he also echoed Conoco's complaints. *Ashcraft v. Conoco, Inc.*, No. 7:95-CV-187-BR(3) (E.D.N.C.).

Although irrelevant to the contempt proceeding, newspaper lawyer Freeman says Conoco overlooks one significant factor: "None of this would have happened if the settlement hadn't been sealed in the first place."

Freeman, co-chair of the ABA Litigation Section's First Amendment and media committee, says Mitchell had no reason to believe the settlement wasn't public because the clerk had pulled a different sealed document from the file before handing it to her.

Minneapolis lawyer Dale Larson, who represents 3M in the insurance case, tells of concerns similar to Conoco's. The 3M court file has to remain sealed, he says, because it contains privileged attorney work-product information, including strategy and defense costs in the separate breast-implant litigation. The insurers have a right to that information, but the plaintiffs in the underlying case do not, Larson says.

"If the insurance case was open while your suit was pending, the other party would have all your privileged and confidential information," Larson says.

He's especially steamed that one of those seeking access is Mealey Publications Inc., a suburban Philadelphia newsletter publisher that distributes dozens of titles dealing mostly with the insurance industry and litigation. As part of its service, Mealey sells copies of court documents to its readers. Some of those readers include plaintiffs lawyers, who Larson says aren't entitled to know 3M's secrets.

Give me a break, says Mealey's lawyer, Lee Levine of Washington, D.C. "The fact that readers of Mealey Publications include plaintiffs lawyers, who 3M assumes are evildoers, is basically irrelevant," Levine says. "They have no less right to information than anyone else."

Even accepting that 3M must surrender and keep secret some privileged materials, *Star Tribune* lawyer Anfinson wonders why it had to file them with the court in the first place. He has an even harder time swallowing the idea that the voluminous file is so rife with legitimately confidential stuff that it can't be weeded out.

Moreover, he says, the case also deals with the court's refusal to release transcripts of some hearings. Although the court maintains that those hearings were public, the docket scheduling them was not.

"That's one of the Alice-in-Wonderland aspects of this whole thing," Anfinson says.

Blame for the Bench

Still, critics don't blame secrecy all that much on lawyers seeking closure. For example, they say, a criminal defense lawyer runs a risk—albeit remote—of giving ineffective assistance by failing to ask for protective orders and other measures to guard his or her client's Sixth Amendment rights.

Judicial ignorance probably plays the most crucial role in expanding secrecy, critics say. They place much of the blame directly on judges who often agree to requests to seal off the system without even acknowledging the competing and, indeed, sometimes conflicting public interest in openness.

Closure orders typically arise out of stipulations reached by the parties and presented to unsuspecting judges who may not know any better, lawyers say.

That criticism is just too brutal, says Judge Michael G. Harrison, chair of the National Conference of State Trial Judges.

"Why is it so difficult to believe that a judge isn't familiar with something?" asks Harrison, a circuit judge from Lansing, Mich., who says he only rarely orders closure himself. "There are thousands of issues that come up. You can't expect a judge to know about them all."

The system's pressure on judges to keep the docket moving and speed civil cases toward settlement also is key, says St. Paul lawyer Hannah, who waged an unsuccessful battle for newspapers and television stations in the Twin Cities area trying to lay their hands on a lawsuit involving the personal life of Minnesota Vikings coach Dennis Green.

"I hear more and more judges mumble that these are two private parties," Hannah says. "The feeling I get is that judges tend to look upon individual lawsuits as a dispute resolution process and not as an exercise of the power of the court."

Obtaining access is even harder these days because courts commonly close the system first without public notice and only entertain questions later. Although the bulk of First Amendment jurisprudence presumes an open system and places the burden on the party seeking closure, the presumption and the burden often are flipped once a courtroom is closed or a document sealed. Making things even more difficult, lawyers trying to pry open cases often don't know exactly what they expect to find. "Rarely do we know what we are looking for," Hannah says. "Our arguments are very general, and the response is much more specific."

"In the Dennis Green case, I felt I was tilting at windmills." All the same, some news outlets are venturing into uncharted territory.

In Southern California, a coalition of influential media entities is trying to use an unusual feature in state law to unseal grand jury transcripts of an aborted criminal investigation of Merrill Lynch & Co. in connection with the 1994 Orange County bankruptcy.

In upstate New York, the 35,000-circulation Glens Falls *Post-Star* is appealing a federal judge's refusal to release documents from settlement discussions in an environmental case involving a town government and General Electric Co.

The New York case concerns allegations that GE dumped 452 tons of hazardous waste from 1958 to '68 at a disposal site in the town of Moreau, just north of Albany, and contaminated the town's drinking water. The newspaper tried to learn more last year when it heard a settlement may be near. But the parties, including town officials, already had agreed to keep both negotiations and draft settlement documents secret, although they had publicly discussed the talks. That was enough for U.S. District Judge Lawrence E. Kahn to keep the paper out of settlement conferences and from getting hold of the documents, which were given to the court clerk's office but not filed. Settlement negotiations and documents traditionally have been private affairs, and few cases ever would settle if the parties had to deal publicly, Kahn wrote last September in *United States v. Town of Moreau*, 979 F. Supp. 129 (N.D.N.Y.).

Despite the inherent secrecy of settlement talks, a significant First Amendment card comes into play when they involve elected officials, says the paper's lawyer, Thomas F. Gleason of Albany. The case is pending before the 2nd U.S. Circuit Court of Appeals in New York City.

"The reason we thought it was important is because the settlements that were being bandied about, like million-dollar payments and a new water supply, have long-term implications for the town," Gleason says. "An essential tenet of our argument is that it was public officials acting."

In Orange County, news organizations are trying to use a provision of California law that allows release of grand jury transcripts once an indictment is issued.

The local district attorney began a criminal investigation after the 1994 bankruptcy, which cost cities, schools and county agencies $1.64 billion. As one of the county's financial advisers, Merrill Lynch was a target of the probe.

Sealed Settlement

But as a grand jury considered the case, Merrill Lynch and the district attorney reached a $30 million settlement in June 1997 that included a multimillion-dollar payment for costs to the prosecutor's office. The investigation ended and the grand jury records were sealed, until a trial judge ordered them opened in September.

The state supreme court spurned Merrill Lynch's protest and shipped the case to an intermediate appellate court, where it remained in late February. *In re Request for Transcripts of Phase Three Grand Jury Proceedings*, No. G022076 (Cal.Ct.App. 4th Dist.).

Although California normally does not release grand jury materials in cases that don't result in indictments, the Merrill Lynch case is different because of the settlement with the state, says media lawyer Sager.

"Here, the grand jury didn't get a chance to decide whether to issue an indictment," Sager says. "And here, Merrill Lynch paid millions of dollars, which suggests something was wrong. And the district attorney's office cut them a deal."

Meanwhile, the Wilmington *Morning Star* and the New York Times Co. are taking the *Conoco* contempt case to the 4th U.S. Circuit Court of Appeals in Richmond, VA.

As for Reporter Mitchell, she carried a copy of the novel *Midnight in the Garden of Good and Evil* to her sentencing, perhaps in anticipation of hard time ahead.

But, besides the hefty fine, she got little else for her trouble. Her information accounted for only a tiny portion of the published story. She didn't even get a byline.

28

Concealing Justices or Concealing Justice?
Colombia's Secret Courts

MICHAEL R. PAHL

I. Introduction

The recent escape of Pablo Escobar, head of the Medellin drug cartel, from his luxury "maximum security" jail represents another sad chapter in the long history of a criminal justice system in crisis. For decades, judges have been threatened or bribed into compliance with the demands of criminals from both left and right. Further, Colombia's antiquated criminal justice system, with little emphasis placed on criminal investigation, has produced one of the highest impunity rates in the world.[1]

Colombia desperately needs to reform its criminal justice system. The existing judicial crisis is an abdication of the state's fundamental and primordial function—to protect its citizens from a Hobbesian state of war.[2] Without an adequate criminal justice system, Colombia will remain one of the world's most violent democracies, unable to achieve what Alexis de Tocqueville called in *Democracy in America* the "great aim of justice . . . to substitute laws for the idea of violence."

Fortunately, Colombia is a country ripe for reform. In 1991, Colombia ratified a new constitution, affecting numerous areas of Colombian

Reprinted by permission of the *Denver Journal of International Law and Policy* from vol. 21, no. 2 (1993), pp. 431–440.

political life. The rights of indigenous peoples have been recognized, and important human rights reforms have been adopted.[3] Equally important, the new constitution promotes pluralistic participation in political life by eliminating the power-sharing agreement between the two main political parties. This agreement was adopted in the mid-1950s in order to end the decade-long civil war known as "la violencia" in which an estimated 200,000 Colombians were killed.[4] As a result, former leftist guerrillas and other traditionally marginalized and powerless groups[5]—workers, peasants, and indigenous peoples—have played an active role in the new government. The 1991 constitution is thus seen by many as a political social revolution, a commendable exercise in the recreation of constitutional democracy in a country long bled and drained by civil strife.[6]

In 1991, Colombia enacted important changes in its criminal justice system. One of the most interesting changes was the creation of a secret court system for drug and terrorism cases. The hope is that judges who are granted anonymity by having their identities concealed will be protected from threats or assassination, enabling the judges to bring criminals to justice. The crucial question, however, is whether these secret courts can achieve the twin goals of protecting the judiciary and increasing the conviction rate, without sacrificing the rights of criminal defendants which are guaranteed in the new constitution.

The short answer is that these rights are sacrificed. Although the secret court system has increased the conviction rate and provided some protection to the judiciary, it has done so at the cost of basic rights of the criminal defendant. Moreover, the secret court system has been used for political ends, punishing legitimate political protesters as "terrorists." As such, the secret court system should be abandoned, as the pursuit of justice is too precious a jewel to be bought with authoritarian coin.

II. Blood on the Robe: Colombia's Embattled Judiciary

Violence against the Colombian judiciary has been pervasive, persistent, and deadly. According to a recent study[7] by the Andean Commission of Jurists, a human rights group in Bogotá, an average of twenty-five judges and lawyers have been assassinated or have been attacked each year since 1979. In all, 515 cases of violence against judges and lawyers have been reported between 1979 and 1991, 329 of which have been murders or attempts to murder.[8] And, of the approximately 4,500 Colombian judges, roughly 1,600 have received threats to themselves or their families.[9]

Although Colombia is popularly perceived as a country besieged by drug-related violence (narcoterrorism), it is important to note that judicial intimidation has been neither exclusively nor primarily linked to drug trafficking.[10] According to the Andean Commission study, of the 240 cases of violence against the judiciary with a known author or cause, eighty have been linked to paramilitary groups, fifty-eight to drug traffickers, forty-eight to state agents (including the military and the police), thirty-two to guerrillas, and twenty-two to other factors.[11] Corruption and violence, like blood, runs thick in Colombia, and few have kept their hands clean.

Violence to the judiciary is as widespread as it is deadly. No sector of the judicial hierarchy has been untouched. While criminal trial court judges are the most affected, Justice Ministers and Supreme Court justices have been threatened or killed as well. Perhaps the most graphic and poignant illustration of Colombia's embattled judiciary occurred in November of 1985, when M-19, a leftist group, stormed the Palace of Justice, taking twenty-four Supreme Court justices hostage. The government refused to negotiate, choosing a military option instead. In the ensuing raid, involving over twenty-eight hours of intense fighting and the bombing of the Palace of Justice by the government, thirty-five members of M-19, several dozen hostages, a dozen soldiers, and eleven Supreme Court justices were killed.[12]

What has happened to those who kill members of the judiciary? Virtually nothing. According to the Andean Commission study, in over 80 percent of the cases reported, there is no evidence of criminal action being carried out.[13] As a result, criminal sentences have been imposed in only 2.1 percent of cases.[14] The inability of the justice system to investigate and prosecute the crimes committed against it reflects the dire situation of Colombia's judiciary: how can the judiciary protect others if it cannot protect itself?

III. Jueces sin Rostro: Faceless Judges

In response to this drastic situation, Colombia has created a special jurisdiction of secret courts with *jueces sin rostro*, or faceless judges, to protect the judiciary. These courts are known as Courts of Public Order, dealing with crimes disproportionately affecting the public order, such as drug trafficking, terrorism, kidnapping, and the illegal transportation of arms.

These special courts were established in 1984 for drug cases and were expanded in 1987 to include "political crimes"—rebellion, sedition, and other acts of violence committed with criminal intent.[15] In November of 1991, the current President Cesar Gaviria unified both systems under the Statute for the Defense of Justice. These courts were originally implemented under the state of siege legislation and considered "exceptional," as a scaffolding to be used only until a solid structure of criminal justice could be constructed. However, with the passage of the New Code of Criminal Procedure on November 30, 1991, they became a permanent fixture in Colombia's criminal justice infrastructure.[16]

Eighty-two judges (of which forty-nine are trial judges and thirty-three are investigative judges) currently sit in these secret courts. All communication is done either through two-way mirrors using Darth Vadaresque voice distorters, or in writing. Witness statements are authenticated by a complex system of fingerprints in lieu of signatures. Opinions are unsigned, with only a judicial number affixed to the decision. The identity of police agents and informants may be kept secret as well.[17] As a final protection, a chief of security is assigned to each court to coordinate threat assessments, and the judges are provided with arms escorts to and from work.

The Colombian secret court system, with no known analogue in the world, has received accolades from the international law enforcement community, who finally see Colombia cracking down on drugs.[18] Indeed, in terms of effective law enforcement, the secret court system is to be commended. After all, the conviction rate is estimated to have jumped from approximately 10 percent in ordinary courts to 70 percent in the secret courts.[19] And, according to the Andean Commission study, threats against judges have dropped dramatically, by 80 percent. But at what cost?

IV. Procedural Nightmares in Colombia's Secret Courts

The high conviction rate in these special courts should come as no surprise, given the absence of basic constitutionally-protected procedural rights that criminal defendants in the United States take for granted. If one were to red-line the U.S. Bill of Rights and drastically reduce or eliminate many protections for criminal defendants, the result would be similar to the situation facing the accused in Colombia's secret courts.

For example, the criminal defendant in the Colombian secret court system has no 8th Amendment right to a bail hearing.[20] Under U.S. law, by contrast, pre-trial detention through the denial of bail is considered the exception rather than the rule. The Framers of the U.S. Constitution prohibited the imposition of excessive bail in the Bill of Rights to prevent the recurrence of the harsh treatment suffered by colonists in British jails during the Colonial Period.[21] From this constitutional basis, U.S. law has developed to the point that in the federal system, pre-trial detention is only available if the government can demonstrate by clear and convincing evidence that the defendant is likely to flee the jurisdiction, or that no release conditions "will reasonably assure . . . the safety of any other person and the community."[22]

In Colombia's secret courts, by contrast, the accused must suffer the indignity of incarceration, separated from family and friends, with absolutely no burden on the government to justify this deprivation of liberty. More importantly, the absence of 8th Amendment protection may seriously prejudice the criminal defendant in the preparation of his defense. Stuck in jail with no hope of release, the criminal defendant may find it difficult to contact and prepare witnesses for his defense, or confer with his lawyer at his leisure.

At the trial stage the treatment of the accused turns from bad to worse. Secret proceedings eliminate the 6th Amendment right to a public trial,[23] ensuring that violations of constitutional rights are concealed from public scrutiny.[24] On the political level, secret courts also militate against the openness in government reflected in the new Colombian constitution. Through public trials, citizens may learn about the machinery of their government, acquiring confidence that the judicial process is not being used for abusive ends.[25] Further, as a practical matter, public trials make the proceedings known to possible witnesses who otherwise might be unknown to the parties.[26]

The system of secret witnesses, violates the 6th Amendment right to confront witnesses, one of the most valuable defense tools. In these courts, defense lawyers may neither question witnesses before trial nor cross-examine them at trial. This prevents the defense from calling a witness' demeanor, credibility, or bias into question (although a conviction cannot be based on a single secret testimony). As a result, a central principle of the U.S. trial system—that truth is best revealed through an adversarial process in which both parties present their case, with witnesses subject to cross-examination and evidence subject to contradiction—is severely curtailed.

Colombians may be familiar with the adversary system in action through the popular television show "*Las Leyes de Los Angeles*," or "L.A. Law." But the adversary system's utility extends far beyond making exciting television episodes. Rather, on the philosophical level, the adversary system attempts to check what Weber called the modern state's monopoly on force[27]—its power to investigate, prosecute, and punish—through giving the defense the opportunity to put into question the government's evidence and witnesses. Regrettably, in Colombia's secret courts, there is little to control the Leviathan. The danger is that the judge will consider only the evidence and uncontroverted testimony proffered by the government; tipping the scales of justice in their favor.

The criminal defendant is further prejudiced by the massive system of protection provided for government informants. The cornucopia of benefits provided those who collaborate with the authorities by testimony against the accused include pecuniary compensation, a new identity, exit from the country, immediate conditional release, and exemption from punishment.[28] While the Federal Witness Protection Program[29] in the U.S. provides similar benefits and protections,[30] there is a crucial difference.

In the U.S. system, the witness must still be present at trial. This subjects the witness to the moral constraint of lying in front of the accused, and, more importantly, to the cross-examination of an aggressive defense attorney.[31] Further, having the witness present at trial tends to assure testimonial trustworthiness by inducing fear that any false testimony will be detected.[32] The danger in Colombia is that the government, in its zealous pursuit of convictions, may play the role of the serpent in the Garden of Eden—tempting witnesses and informants to lie with the fruit of governmental goodies—unchecked by the power of a probing and thorough cross-examination.

In short, the Colombian secret court system amounts to a criminal defendant's nightmare. Colombia has its Gabriel Garcia Marquez to describe the *realismo fantastico* of Colombian life; what it lacks is a Franz Kafka to describe the judicial absurdity its many Joseph K's face in the secret court system. Criminal defendants are being convicted by unknown witnesses paid by the state, absent from the trial, and immune from cross-examination. Further, if the judge decides the evidence must be kept secret, the "judicial decision" may be a mere piece of paper, containing only the judge's number. The concept of feeling guilty without knowing why may make for interesting existential novels, but it has no place in criminal law—especially when one is being punished for crimes that carry penalties of up to thirty years in jail. A system that cripples a solid criminal defense, and leaves judicial decisions unexplained, reflects a process of judgment more reminiscent of the Medieval Inquisition than of modern standards of criminal justice.[33] The "miracle" of the Colombian secret court system is not that 70 percent of those accused are convicted, but that 30 percent go free.

V. Casting the Criminal Net:
Political Abuse of Colombia's Secret Courts

The lack of procedural rights in the secret court system are problematic; however, its potential for political abuse is even more concerning. Latin America is notorious for its *caudillos* or dictators of both left and right, from Castro to Pinochet, who have abused power to strengthen their regimes while violating basic human rights. Accordingly, any increase in the state's power, particularly the removal from the public eye of the state's power to discipline and punish, must be subject to the strictest scrutiny.

The Colombian government has claimed that the purpose of the secret court system is two-fold and inter-related: to protect judges and to combat terrorism. While fighting terrorism is a valid and essential goal, a wide criminal net can be cast over that rubric. The danger is that the Colombian government, seeking a surcease of the violence that has made Colombia one of the world's most violent democracies, will use an overexpansive definition of "terrorist" to mask prosecutions against political dissidents or to cover daily arbitrary violations of human rights.[34]

The problem of interpretation is essentially one of language. As Anglo-American legal theorists from H.L.A. Hart to Albert Saks have noted, restricting legal terms to one fixed literal meaning is difficult, for words are inherently ambiguous. Continental deconstructionists such as Michel Foucault or Jacques Derrida would go even further, claiming that the meaning of the written word eludes even the author herself, and must be interpreted in a sociological and contextual framework.

While this presents problems for a judge seeking the "literal" meaning of a statute, it can have grave consequences when applied to a slippery term such as "terrorist" or as manipulable a phrase as "acts of rebellion or sedition." For, as Montesquieu sagely noted, ". . . not defining what is meant by treason is enough for the government to become despotic."

Who has been caught in Colombia's terrorist net? Human rights advocates report that student protestors, peasants, and others critical of the present regime have been convicted in these secret courts for legitimate acts of social protest.[35] Indeed, the irony is that a liberal interpretation of the phrase "acts of rebellion or sedition" could be applied to the very grass-roots student movement which led to the important constitutional reforms of 1991. An over-broad net has been cast in the fight against narcoterrorism as well, dragging in both major drug traffickers such as Pablo Escobar, with millions to spend in his defense, and mere consumers too poor to afford their own lawyer.[36]

By punishing acts of political protest, the Colombian government is frustrating the purpose of the new constitution, which seeks dialogue for the resolution of social conflict. Voices muted in the past by a *de jure* power-sharing arrangement between the two main political parties and *de facto* class stratification, will remain silent if the government continues to abuse the secret courts for political ends. Further, expanding the criminal net in this manner violates a time-honored and internationally-respected principle of criminal law, *nulla poena sin lege* ("no punishment without a crime"). According to this doctrine, criminal statutes are to be narrowly construed as a check on the government's power, to protect citizens from arbitrary and unanticipated incarceration. No one should be judged and punished without conforming to the preexisting law for which he is punished.[37] Regrettably, such is the situation facing these erstwhile political protestors turned "terrorists" by the secret court system.

VI. Conclusion

The Colombian secret court system has been a moderate success. Supporters of the system point to the degree of security it provides to a beleaguered judiciary, helping to remove the death sentence under which many judicial officials worked in the past. They note as well that criminal convictions have risen dramatically, helping to lower the high impunity rate plaguing the country.

Supporters of the system fail to recognize two critical points, however. The first is the limited efficacy of the protection the system provides. The second is the tremendous cost to personal liberty and political participation of the secret court system.

The argument that the secret court system provides greater protection for judges is specious in several aspects. First of all, security is limited to a minority of judges—*jueces sin rostro* and Supreme Court justices— while the great majority of judicial functionaries go unprotected. Even the protected judicial elite is only safe from 9 to 5. Further, it appears that the efficacy of the secret court system will be of limited duration. As recently as September 19, 1992, a *jueza sin rostro* and her three bodyguards were assassinated in front of her home by *sicarios* in Medellin.[38] As critics had predicted, the veil of secrecy has been irreparably torn. Finally, the decrease in violence to the judiciary should not be too quickly accredited to the secret court system. The ban on extradition of Colombian nationals and the inclusion of leftist groups in the new constitution have played an equally important role in the recent cessation of attacks on the judiciary.

The second argument in favor of the secret court system, that it has increased the conviction rate, is equally troubling. High conviction rates can always be achieved by clipping the rights of criminal defendants. Furthermore, troublesome political "enemies" can always be more easily dealt with through the long arm of the law rather than through the long and arduous process of negotiation and dialogue which democracy demands. Colombia is a country seeking to create itself anew, to secure a respite from the violence which has plagued the country for years on end. The 1991 constitution, promoting pluralistic participation in political life and the laying down of arms, is a step in the right direction. The secret court system, with its clipping of procedural rights and criminalization of dissent—is not. Justice, like the beautiful emeralds for which Colombia is renowned, is too precious a jewel to be bought with authoritarian coin.

Endnotes

[1] See Gabriel Gutierrez Tovar, "Reflexiones sobre la Impunidad," in *Justicia, Derechos Humanos e Impunidad* 225 (Hector Peña Diaz, ed., 1991).

[2] See Armanda Borrero, "Constitucion y Orden Publico," 13 *Revista Foro* 34 (1990).

[3] See generally *Const. Colom.* arts. 11–94.

[4] "In Colombia, Killings Just Go On and On," *Wall St. J.*, Nov. 17, 1987, at 10.

[5] See Hernando Valencia Villa, *The Grammar of War* 1–2 (1986).

[6] For a less sanguine view, see William C. Banks & Edgar Alvarez, "The New Colombian Constitution: Democratic Victory or Popular Surrender?," 23 *U. of Miami Inter-Am L. Rev.* 39, 85–86 (Fall 1991) ("It is unclear whether the invocation of popular sovereignty to legitimate the reform process in Bogotá reflects a genuine public demand for a new set of societal rules and institutions. Instead, it could simply be another episode of constitutional reform serving as a shield to protect the less populist and shorter term political goals of those in power. Legally, it makes no difference. The Colombian electorate indicated by plebiscite that they wanted a chance to vote for a constitutional assembly, and did just that by conferring their primary sovereignty upon a popularly elected body").

[7] For a thorough description and in-depth analysis of the violence facing Colombia's judiciary, see Guido Bonilla & Alejandro Valancia Villa, *Justice for Justice: Violence Against Judges and Lawyers in Colombia: 1979–1991* (1992) (on file at the Andean Commission of Jurists: Colombian Section, Bogotá, Colombia).

[8] Colombian Section, Andean Commission of Jurists, *Justicia para la Justicia: Violencia Contra Jueces y Abrogados en Colombia: 1979–1991* (1992) [hereinafter *Justicia*].

[9] "Colombia Struggles to Seal Its Judges' Armor," *N.Y. Times*, Oct. 13, 1991, at 10.

[10] *Justicia*, supra note 8.

[11] Id.

[12] Federal Research Division, Library of Congress, *Colombia: A Country Study* 298 (Dennis M. Hanratty & Sandra W. Meditz eds., 1990).

[13] *Justicia*, supra note 8.

[14] Id.

[15] Americas Watch, *Political Murder & Reform in Colombia: The Violence Continues* 98 (1992).

[16] Id.

[17] Colombian Section, Andean Commission of Jurists, *Una Justicia Amenzadas Commentarios al Estatuto para la Defensa de la Justicia* 2 (1991).

[18] See Steven Flanders & Ana Maria Salazar, "Colombia's Purgatory," *N.Y.L.J.* 2 (Jan. 21, 1992).

[19] "Colombia Struggles to Seal Its Judges' Armor," supra note 9.

[20] See Colombian Section, Andean Commission of Jurists, *Sistema Judicial y Derechos Humanos en Colombia* 43 (1990).

[21] Ironically, the "bail clause [adopted by the Framers] was lifted with slight changes from the English Bill of Rights Act." See *Carlson v. Landon*, 342 U.S. 524, 545 (1952), reh. den., 343 U.S. 988. The right to a bail hearing, however, has not been extended to state prosecutions. See *Collins v. Johnston*, 237 U.S. 502, 59 L.Ed. 1071, 35 S.Ct. 649 (1915).

[22] See *United States v. Salerno*, 481 U.S. 739, 95 L.Ed.2d 697, 107 S.Ct. 2095 (1987) ("In our society liberty is the norm, and detention prior to trial or without trial is the carefully limited exception."). Expressed in a different vein, the Federal Bail Reform Act, codified in 18 U.S.C.S § 3142(f), requires that a judge inclined in the first instance towards the release of an accused on his own recognizance or upon unsecured bond.

[23] The Sixth Amendment right to a public trial has been made applicable to the States through the Fourteenth Amendment. In re *Oliver*, 333 U.S. 257, 68 S.Ct. 499, 92 L.Ed. 682 (1948). Exceptions to a right to the public trial have been held permissible in certain exceptional circumstances. As stated by the Supreme Court, "the party seeking to close the hearing must advance an overriding interest that is likely to be prejudiced, the closure must be no broader than necessary to protect that interest, the trial court must consider reasonable alternatives to closing the proceeding, and it must make findings adequate to support the closure." *Waller v. Georgia*, 467 U.S. 39, 104 S.Ct. 2210, 81 L.Ed.2d 31 (1984). As an illustration, see *United States v. Hernandez*, 608 F.2d 741 (9th Cir. 1979) (exclusion of spectators allowed when witness had been subjected to pretrial threats); United States ex rel. *Bruno v. Herold*, 408 F.2d 125 (2d Cir. 1969) (exclusion of spectators who threatened witness at trial); United States ex rel. *Lloyd v. Vincent*, 520 F.2d 1272 (2d Cir. 1975), cert. denied, 423 U.S. 937, 96 S.Ct. 296, 46 L.Ed.2d 269 (exclusion of spectators during the testimony of an undercover agent engaged in ongoing investigations proper); United States ex rel. *Orlando v. Fay*, 350 F.2d 967 (2d Cir. 1965) (exclusion of spectators permissible when necessary to preserve order in the courtroom).

[24] See In re *Oliver*, supra note 23 ("The traditional Anglo-American distrust for trials has been variously ascribed to the notorious use of this practice by the Spanish Inquisition, to the excesses of the English Court of Star Chamber, and to the French Monarchy's abuse of the *lettre de cachet* . . . [W]hatever other benefits the guarantee to the accused that his trial be conducted in public may confer upon our society, the guarantee has always been recognized as a safeguard against any attempt to employ our courts as instruments of persecution").

[25] See *Ravinsky v. McKaskle*, 772 F.2d 197 (5th Cir. 1984).

[26] See 6 J. Wigmore, *Evidence* § 1834 (Chadbourn rev. 1976).

[27] For a discussion of the moral justification of the modern state's monopoly on force, see Robert Nozick, *Anarchy, State and Utopia* 89–119 (1974).

[28] Id.

[29] The Federal Witness Protection Program, established by Congress in 1984, authorizes the Attorney General to take such action as he deems "necessary to protect the person involved from bodily injury and otherwise to assure the health, safety, and welfare of that person [or an immediate family member or close associate], including the psychological well-being and social adjustment of that person, for as long as, in the judgment of the Attorney General, the danger to that person exists." 18 U.S.C. § 3521(b)(1).

[30] Among these include new identification documents, housing, moving expenses, employment assistance, and "a payment to meet basic living expenses." 18 U.S.C. § 3521(b)(1)(A)-(H).

[31] For a sample of an effective cross-examination, see Frank Rubino's cross-examination of Federal Witness Protection Program participant Danny Martinez in "Dealing with the Devil (and Lesser Imps)," 20 *Crim. Prac. Man.* (BNA) 464 (Sept. 30, 1992); see also "Expert Can Show How Sweet Cooperating Witness's Deal Is," 5 *Crim. Prac. Man.* (BNA) 465 (Oct. 2, 1991).

[32] See Wigmore, supra note 26.

[33] See Alejandro David Aponte, "Como Matar a la Justicia en la Tarea de Defenderla: 'Estatuto para la Defensa de la Justicia,'" 11 *Analisis Politico* 77 (1990).

34 See Fernando Velasquez V., "El Estatuto para la Defensa de la Justicia: Un Retorno a la Inquisition!," 51 *Nuevo Foro Penal* 4 (1991).

35 Interview with Alejandro David Aponte, Professor of Law, Universidad de Los Andes, at the Andean Commission of Jurists, Bogotá, Colombia, Aug. 18, 1992.

36 Id.; see also Aponte, supra note 33, at 79.

37 In the United States, constitutional due process requires that the statute which defines a substantive crime must "give a person of ordinary intelligence fair notice that his contemplated conduct is forbidden." *Papachristou v. City of Jacksonville*, 405 U.S. 156, 162, 92 S.Ct. 839, 843, 31 L.Ed.2d 110 (1972).

38 "Asesinada una Jueza sin Rostro," *El Tiempo*, Sept. 19, 1992, at 1A; see also "Narcos Amenazan a Jueces sin Rostro," *El Tiempo*, June 6, 1992, at 1A.

29

Reforming the Criminal Trial

CRAIG M. BRADLEY

As a prosecutor in Washington, D.C., trying numerous cases before a jury over a three-and-a-half-year period, I was often struck by how needlessly inefficient the jury trial frequently was. A small percentage of the time expended at a typical felony trial was devoted to presenting the testimony of the victim and the other witnesses. A much larger amount of time was used to pick the jury, argue to the jury, hold conferences out of the presence of the jury, instruct the jury, and wait for the jury to reach a verdict. At a time when criminal courts everywhere are overwhelmed with cases,[1] it is appropriate to examine whether this system can be streamlined.

In 1982, and again in 1992, I lived in Germany and studied the operation of the criminal justice system there. The German system has two features of interest to Americans.[2] First, cases are tried before a mixed panel of judges and laymen (three judges and two laymen in the most serious cases—a four-to-one vote is required for conviction). There is no "picking" of this panel by the lawyers. They simply show up and the trial begins. The panel is already familiar with the dossier of the case so that extended arguments are neither necessary nor allowed. A typical felony case is tried in two to three hours.

The second aspect of the German system is that plea bargaining, while no longer prohibited, is done much less frequently—about twenty to thirty percent of the time—and only rarely in cases "involving violent

Reprinted by permission of the author from the *Indiana Law Journal*, vol. 68 (1993), pp. 659–664.

and other very serious crimes.''[3] Even if a bargain has been reached, and the defendant confesses during preliminary examination at the beginning of the trial, the prosecutor must be ready to offer such witnesses as the court deems necessary to support a finding of guilt. Thus, as Professor Hermann observes, in Germany "a confession does not replace a trial but rather causes a shorter trial."[4] This fact, plus section 153a of the German Code of Criminal procedure, which allows the prosecutor to terminate the proceedings only when the defendant's guilt is "minor,"[5] keeps plea bargaining to a minimum in felony cases.[6] It is most commonly used in cases where the penalty is "a fine or no criminal sanction at all."[7]

One might well argue that the first aspect of the German system is not a satisfactory safeguard for civil liberties and lacks the democratic virtues of a jury trial.[8] However, the first aspect must be considered in concert with the second. In many American jurisdictions, as many as ninety percent of all cases are plea bargained.[9] Plea bargaining (as opposed to a plea to the indictment when the government's case is extremely strong) is a bad arrangement for both the state and the defendant. It forces the defendant to give up his rights to trial by jury, to object to illegal searches, to confront witnesses, and so on. It forces the state to convict the defendant on a charge that is less than the charge he deserves. The Katzenbach Commission declared in 1967 that "few practices in the system of criminal justice create a greater sense of unease and suspicion than the negotiated plea of guilty."[10] This sentiment was echoed recently in the American Bar Association report *Criminal Justice in Crisis*.[11]

The U.S. Supreme Court's approval of plea bargaining in the 1971 case of *Santobello v. New York*[12] was based largely on the pragmatic concern that the criminal justice system could not afford to accord every defendant his constitutional rights, rather than on a claim that such a practice was inherently desirable. By constructing a more efficient trial system, the Germans have been able to require a trial for every defendant who is charged. Even if one concedes (as I do not) that the German trial is, say, only eighty percent as "good" as the full-fledged American jury trial, it could be utilized by three times as many defendants if it only takes one-third as long as an American trial, and would thus seem to be a better system.

It is not necessary, however, to abandon the traditional jury in order to improve and speed up the American criminal trial substantially. The rest of this essay is devoted to proposing ways in which the jury trial, as it is practiced in most states, could be modified, consistently with constitutional proscriptions, to render it more efficient. In turn, this would allow other states to follow Alaska's lead in forbidding plea bargaining,[13] or perhaps in limiting guilty pleas, as the Germans have done.

Frequently, the most tedious part of a case is choosing the jury. Lawyers correctly believe that one can begin the persuasion process during the voir dire, and perhaps use the voir dire to ascertain which jurors are likely to be favorable and which unfavorable to the case, though this latter exercise is fraught with obvious peril. It is not unusual for an entire day to be lost in choosing the jury, and the process can drag on for weeks as the William Kennedy Smith trial recently illustrated.[14] Lawyer-conducted voir dire and peremptory challenges should be eliminated. If the parties are required to go to trial with the jury that shows up, subject only to a few, brief inquiries by the trial judge as to possible sources of bias, justice will be as well served as it is now, and much more swiftly.

Rule 24(a) of the Federal Rules of Criminal Procedure provides that the court may conduct the voir dire.[15] This should be made mandatory. In the run-of-the-mill case, two questions would suffice: "Do any of you have personal knowledge of the participants or events of this case?" and "Is there any reason why any of you cannot render a fair and impartial verdict in this case?" Of course, the judge, at the attorneys' suggestion, could ask further questions as necessitated by a particular case, and certain types of cases, such as death penalty cases, would always require a more searching inquiry. Preliminary screening of the jurors could even be performed by the jury commissioner before the jurors reach the courtroom.

In the 1988 case of *Ross v. Oklahoma*,[16] the Supreme Court made it clear that "peremptory challenges are not of constitutional dimension."[17] Peremptory challenges are largely a matter of wild guesses about how jurors will decide the case based upon their answers to one or two questions in the voir dire. Studies have shown that these guesses are as likely to be wrong as they are to be right.[18] To the extent that they are not wild guesses, they are worse: an exercise in "cooking" the jury to be more favorable to the view of the attorney exercising the challenge.

In *Batson v. Kentucky*,[19] the Supreme Court struck down the prosecutor's use of peremptory challenges to strike members of the defendant's race from the jury. Obviously, the prosecutor was doing this in order to end up with a jury that might be less sympathetic to the defendant. Prosecutors routinely challenge anyone with a word like "social" in their job title, such as social workers or sociologists.[20] The theory is that such jurors are more likely to feel that people who commit crimes are not really to blame for them—the blame is society's. In the same way, defense attorneys are likely to strike people who are themselves, or who have close relatives, involved with law enforcement. Even if peremptory challenges served their apparent function of eliminating people on the far ends of the political spectrum from the jury, it does not seem that this is a necessary or desirable goal, and it tends to interfere with the "fair cross-section" requirement as defined by the Supreme Court.[21] The elimination of jurors at the far ends of the political spectrum is especially unnecessary if, as discussed below, non-unanimous verdicts are allowed.

Peremptory challenges can give the prosecutor a particularly unfair advantage where, as is common, the same jury venire staffs all of the petit juries for an extended period of time. Toward the end of that period, the prosecutor's office begins to develop a "track record" of conviction- or acquittal-prone jurors. The prosecutor will then use this information either to strike the latter, or to strike "neutrals" in order to impanel the former.[22] Since all defendants are not represented by a single office, it is impossible for defense attorneys to develop a similar "jury book." In *Batson*, Justice Marshall urged that peremptory challenges be banned.[23] Since they are sometimes exercised unfairly, and, even when they are not, they are a waste of time, I agree.

The next big time-waster is attorney arguments. Most attorneys seem to believe that "longer is better." While everyone else in the courtroom nods off, attorneys ramble through every aspect of the case and the judge's instructions. Whatever else *L.A. Law* may have done for the legal profession, it has illustrated what I have believed for years: that the essence of the argument to the jury in most cases can be captured in a very few minutes. Limiting opening statements to five minutes and closing to ten is more than enough in the simplest cases, such as a one- or two-witness armed robbery of a convenience store, and would allow the jury to convene to decide the case while the evidence was still fresh in their minds.[24] Given the attention span of the average juror, shorter arguments would likely be more effective than long ones.[25]

By the same token, many jury instructions are unnecessary and incomprehensible to the average juror. In most cases, little more is required beyond listing the elements of each offense, stressing that the prosecution must prove each element beyond a reasonable doubt, making some attempt at explaining what "reasonable doubt" is, and enjoining the jury to decide the case on the law and facts as adduced in court.

Finally, trial judges should require attorneys, particularly prosecutors, to justify the calling of each witness, since it is not uncommon, though not always good strategy, for attorneys to call multiple witnesses to testify to the same thing. Since the typical defense case is brief, and since the defendant has a right to compulsory process and ought not to be left with the feeling that he has not been allowed a full defense, limitations on the calling of defense witnesses should be undertaken with care. Limiting each side's case to a set time period, such as two hours in the simplest cases, and leaving it to the attorneys to decide which witnesses to call is another possible approach.

Jury deliberations can be accelerated by allowing non-unanimous verdicts and juries of less than twelve members. Both of these devices have been approved by the Supreme Court.[26] While the Court has never declared what the "bottom line" is in this regard, it has upheld a nine-to-three verdict,[27] but indicated that a guilty verdict by a bare majority would probably not be sufficient.[28] A five-to-one verdict has also been struck down,[29] but a unanimous verdict by a six member jury has been upheld.[30] A consideration of all of the cases leads me to the conclusion that a six-to-two vote is the minimum combination of smaller size and non-unanimity that the Court's cases would allow. While this reform would be less important than the others, because the judge and lawyers can move on to other business while the jury deliberates, it would nonetheless yield three significant advantages. First, reducing the size of juries and the time each juror spends per case would reduce juror costs to the system and the time required to empanel the jury. More importantly, smaller, non-unanimous juries would be much less likely to hang—a very wasteful result since it means that a trial that may have lasted for weeks must be done over. Finally, as noted above, allowing non-unanimous verdicts makes a detailed voir dire less necessary.[31]

All of these suggestions are offered in the name of efficiency—it is better to provide a more efficient trial to more defendants, even if that proceeding might not develop all issues as fully as the traditional trial. However, in my view, following these suggestions would also improve the *quality* of trials. Given the realities of short juror attention spans that shorten even more as a long trial drones on, a trial that moves swiftly from voir dire to verdict would be a marked improvement in both fairness and efficiency over the current, tedious system. If shorter trials would mean that plea bargaining could be eliminated or reduced (because more court time would be available for trials), the net gain to the system of justice would be even greater.

Endnotes

[1] See, e.g., "Special Comm. on Criminal Justice in a Free Society," Am. Bar Ass'n, *Criminal Justice in Crisis* 40 (1988) [hereinafter *Criminal Justice in Crisis*] (referring to a "tidal wave of [criminal] cases that have flooded all agencies in the criminal justice system") (quoting Nat'l Inst. of Justice, U. S. Dep't of Justice, *Assessing Criminal Justice Needs* (1984)).

[2] For a detailed discussion of the German system, see John H. Langebein, "Mixed Court and Jury Court: Could the Continental Alternative Fill the American Need?"1981 *Am. B. Found. Res. J.* 195. See also Thomas Weigand, "Continental Cures for American Ailments: European Criminal Procedure as a Model for Law Reform," in 2 *Crime and*

Justice: An Annual Review of Research 381 (Norval Morris & Michael Tonry eds., 1980) (discussing the advantages of simplified procedures practiced in Europe); Richard S. Frase & Thomas Weigend, "How the Germans Do It—Comparisons with American Criminal Justice" (1992) (unpublished manuscript on file with author).

3   Joachim Herrmann, "Bargaining Justice—A Bargain for German Criminal Justice?", 53 *U. Pitt. L. Rev.* 755 (1992).

4   Id. at 763. "[I]n simple cases, [however], an extensive and credible confession can make it unnecessary to hear additional witnesses." Frase & Weigend, supra note 2, at 37 n. 169 and cases cited therein.

5   Strafprozeβordnung § 153a. For an English translation, see *The German Code of Criminal Procedure* 88 (American Series of Foreign Penal Codes No. 10) (Horst Niebler trans., 1965).

6   However, even in felony cases, plea bargaining is not unknown, at least where a fine is the appropriate penalty. Herrmann, supra note 3, at 758.

7   Id. at 756.

8   The Germans do not think so. They adopted a jury trial requirement in 1877 and abandoned it in 1924. Langbein, supra note 2, at 198.

9   Yale Kamisar, et al., *Modern Criminal Procedure* 17 (7th ed. 1990).

10   *Criminal Justice in Crisis*, supra note 1, at 67 n. 78 (citing "President's Commission on Law Enforcement and Administration of Justice, The Task Force on the Administration of Justice, Task Force Report: The Courts" 9 (1967)).

11   Id. at 40–41.

12   404 U.S. 257 (1971).

13   Michael J. Rubenstein & Theresa J. White, "Plea Bargaining: Can Alaska Live Without It?," 62 *Judicature* 266 (1979).

14   See Christine Stapleton, "Smith Jury Pick a Game of Chance," *Atlanta Const.*, Oct. 27, 1991, at A3.

15   *Fed. R. Crim. P.* 24(a).

16   487 U.S. 81 (1988).

17   Id. at 88.

18   E.g., Hans Zeisel & Shari Seidman-Diamond, "The Effect of Peremptory Challenges on Jury and Verdict: An Experiment in a Federal District Court," 30 *Stan. L. Rev.* 491, 528 (1978) ("[V]oire dire . . . did not provide sufficient information for attorneys to identify prejudiced jurors.").

19   476 U.S. 79 (1986).

20   At least this was the practice of prosecutors in Washington, D.C., when I was an assistant United States attorney.

21   See *Taylor v. Louisiana*, 419 U.S. 522, 530 (1975).

22   See *Hamer v. United States*, 259 F.2d 274 (9th Cir. 1958) (discussing use of the "jury book" and rejecting defense attorney's request for access to it); see also Kamisar, et al., supra note 9, at 1299–1332.

23   *Batson*, 476 U.S. at 107 (Marshall, J., concurring).

24   The Supreme Court approved, in dictum, time limits on closing arguments in *Herring v. New York*, 422 U.S. 853, 862–63 (1975) (holding that closing argument by defendant's attorney may not be forbidden altogether). See also Michael R. Flaherty, Annotation, "Propriety of Trial Court Order Limiting Time for Opening or Closing Argument in Criminal Cases—States Cases," 71 *A.L.R.* 4th 200, 209 (1989) (discussing various time limits on attorney arguments and noting that "it is generally recognized that courts may limit the time consumed by counsel in final argument"). But see *Stockton v. Florida*, 544 So. 2d 1006 (Fla. 1989) (reversing conviction because 30-minute time limit on closing arguments in a murder case with 15 witnesses was unreasonable).

[25] See. e.g., Daniel G. Linz & Steven Penrod, "Increasing Attorney Persuasiveness in the Courtroom," 8 *Law & Psychol. Rev.* 1, 28–29 (1984) (finding longer, more complex arguments less persuasive).

[26] *Williams v. Florida*, 399 U.S. 78 (1970) (upholding a six member jury); *Apodaca v. Oregon*, 406 U.S. 404 (1972) (upholding a non-unanimous verdict).

[27] *Johnson v. Louisiana*, 406 U.S. 356 (1972).

[28] In *Johnson*, the Court indicated that a "substantial majority" of the vote was required for conviction. Id. at 362.

[29] *Burch v. Louisiana*, 441 U.S. 130 (1979).

[30] *Williams*, 399 U.S. 78.

[31] For "[a]rguments pro and con on the effectiveness of a jury of six compared to a jury of twelve," see *Colgrove v. Batin*, 413 U.S. 149, 159 n.15 (1973) (concluding that a jury of six was adequate). But see Michael J. Saks, "Ignorance of Science Is No Excuse," *Trial*, Nov.-Dec. 1974, at 18 (criticizing the *Colgrove* Court's conclusion).

30

Prosecutorial Discretion
A Comparative Perspective

ZORAN MILOVANOVICH

Comparative criminal procedure has become an area of considerable interest among legal scholars because the study of diverse systems of criminal procedure offers scholars and students a way of getting outside their own legal tradition so as to gain valuable perspectives on their own system. Exposure to a completely different criminal justice tradition might enable those exposed to see more clearly the important elements of their own system and tradition.

For American scholars, the study of the civil law tradition as embodied in the legal systems of European countries has been particularly rewarding. These systems, especially the German and the French, seem to be fairly efficient and reliable while appearing to treat those who come into contact with the system, such as defendants and victims, with respect. Because the United States shares many societal values in common with these nations, the discovery that they have such radically different systems of criminal procedure makes civil law models excellent subjects for comparative study.

This article primarily focuses on the comparison between the American prosecutor, armed with broad discretion, and prosecutors in the civil law tradition, who have much less discretion and are subject to close judicial supervision (Davis, 1980; Herrmann, 1974; Vouin, 1970; Weigend, 1980). It emphasizes that the role of the prosecutor is different because, among other things, certain fundamental elements of political system

Written especially for *Courts and Justice*, 2nd ed.

differ between the two systems: distinct procedural models and roles that these models assign to main actors. Comparative in nature, this article is neither a defense of nor an attack on the American prosecutor. It is written from a point of view that is respectful of both legal traditions and accepts the fact that the institution of prosecution and role of the prosecutor in different legal systems have evolved in dramatically different directions.

Role of the Prosecutor

Civil law systems have primarily sought to define the role of the prosecutor within relatively narrow legislative boundaries. The law specifically enumerates the functions of the prosecutor, and if he does something beyond the scope of his responsibilities his actions are most likely to be considered illegal. The prosecutor is a career civil servant who works in a hierarchically organized system in which promotions up the career ladder are merit based and in which the prosecutor is mostly isolated from political pressures (Langbein, 1977; Frase, 1990; West, 1992). The main function of the prosecutor in the system is to control the investigation of any reported crime, to assemble a complete and balanced file or "dossier" of a case, and to file appropriate criminal charges if the evidence shows that a crime has been committed (Langbein, 1974; West, 1992).

Distinctive features of the public prosecutor's office in civil law systems include organization in a single national hierarchy, a nationwide entrance examination and training program, and a tradition that views the position of prosecutor as a career rather than a stepping stone to other careers. Prosecutors serve in a bureaucratic hierarchy headed by the Department of Justice. Although individual prosecutors are theoretically free to speak their own minds in court, in their written submissions they must observe and follow directions of their superiors. Failure to do that may result in disciplinary action, including dismissal. Within each chief prosecutor's office all individual decisions are subject to review and correction by superiors, and prosecution policies can be enforced uniformly within those offices and, to some extent, nationwide (Merle & Vitu, 1979; Vincent, Montagnier, & Varinard, 1985; West, 1992). Responsibility for prosecution policy is thus centralized at higher levels.

Nationwide hierarchical structure is, of course, incompatible with American federal system. As for state and local prosecutors, some states have already adopted a unified prosecution hierarchy under the state attorney general,[1] thus achieving—or at least clearing the way for—benefits the civil law systems might provide. In other states, the county attorney (and sometimes also the city attorney) is an elected official. This implies that he or she is not subject to supervision by the state attorney general and could not be made so without a state constitutional amendment. Nevertheless, in many states the attorney general enjoys concurrent statutory authority to prosecute some or all criminal offenses, which provides at least the possibility of a parallel check on local decisions not to prosecute (National Association of Attorneys General, 1977, 104–107). Moreover, it would not necessarily be inconsistent with the status of local prosecutors as elected officials to adopt statewide standards for hiring and evaluation of assistant prosecutors and perhaps even statewide charging standards for all state criminal laws.[2]

Another major difference between prosecutors in civil law jurisdictions and in the United States is that civil law prosecutors appear to be better trained for their roles. France, Germany and other civil law countries, including Japan, have instituted nationwide recruitment and training programs for both prosecutors and judges. For example, in France, the normal path of entry into either profession is by completion of a twenty-four-month training program (Vincent, Montagnier, & Varinard, 1991). The few positions in this program are open primarily to law graduates who have completed three years of study (Pugh, 1962) and who are selected on the basis of a nationwide competitive entrance exam.[3] The first seven months of the program are spent in classes at the National Magistrates' School, followed by three periods of internship: (1) thirteen months in one of the provincial courts of appeal; (2) two months with a judge or prosecutor in Paris; and (3) two months in the office selected by the candidate for his or her first post (Applebaum, 1986). During the entire twenty-four-month period, candidates receive a salary and are subject to most of the requirements applicable to magistrates, including an oath of office, no outside employment, and no right to strike. Candidates must also agree at the outset to remain in the magistracy for at least ten years (Vincent, Montagnier, & Varinard, 1991). During the first four years after their installation, all new magistrates are required to complete four months of additional, specialized training in sessions of at least two weeks each.

Although the role of the prosecutor is at least as important in the United States as it is in civil law countries, the procedures for training American prosecutors are rudimentary at best. Chief prosecutors are typically elected or appointed after limited criminal practice experience, and assistant prosecutors are often hired right out of law school where any clinical or trial practice training is likely to have involved only criminal defense or civil procedure (Jacoby, 1979). In recent years, many new prosecutors have attended in-service training programs, but there is a lot to be learned from civil law systems in this area.

While the average tenure of prosecutors in the United States is relatively short (Jacoby, 1979), the prosecution function in civil law jurisdictions is a long-term career choice. For example, in Japan, prosecutors usually remain in their positions for life (West, 1992). Only in the rarest of circumstances does a prosecutor use the position as a stepping stone to becoming a politician, a judge, or a private attorney. Vested with a kind of tenure, prosecutors do not have to worry about job security. They may be dismissed only for gross misconduct (West, 1992).

Prosecutorial Discretion

Charging Discretion

The aspect of criminal procedure in civil law systems that first attracted the attention of American reform-oriented scholars is the limitation on the civil law prosecutor's decision whether to file charges (Davis, 1980; Herrmann, 1974; Langbein, 1974). Decisions not to charge are particularly controversial in the United States because they are less likely to be successfully challenged by courts or by interested parties.

The American prosecutor has broad discretion over both initial decisions to decline to file charges, and postfiling decisions to decline to file or drop additional counts of charges ("horizontal" charging discretion).[4] The American prosecutor's ability to "change his mind" at virtually any point prior to trial causes American declination decisions to occur either too early or too late. They may occur too early and too hurriedly when prosecution is declined at the initial case-screening stage, which is usually shortly after arrest but before the detained suspect first appears in court (Miller, 1969). On the other hand, declination decisions may occur too late when the original decision to file a complaint was made simply to retain the option of prosecution or to extend investigatory detention. In such cases, declinations are often delayed until shortly before trial, as part of the plea bargaining process.

American prosecutors can also exercise broad pre- and postfiling discretion over the level of charge severity ("vertical" charging discretion). They may reduce severity of already filed charges by moving to amend the complaint or information or by filing a nolle prosequi and refiling with less serious charges (Goldstein, 1981). The availability of such reductions almost inevitably leads to initial overcharging because it eliminates any need to screen cases carefully at the outset. American prosecutors actually have an incentive to exaggerate initial charges so as to leave more room for later plea bargaining concessions. This practice frequently results in distorted arrest and pretrial detention decisions and adds to caseload pressures in those courts handling the most serious criminal offenses. At the same time, postfiling charge reductions also raise a risk of eventual undercharging, if initially correct and provable charges are routinely reduced in return for a guilty plea.

The civil law prosecutor's discretion with respect to the decision whether or not to file criminal charges is significantly more limited in comparison to American prosecutors.[5] The prosecution today is an outgrowth of the civil law tradition of "compulsory prosecution,"[6] which demands that a prosecutor file criminal charges whenever the evidence is strong enough to support such charges. While the doctrine of compulsory prosecution has softened with the passage of time, it is still accurate to say that a prosecutor's charging discretion in felony cases remains limited.[7] In the first place, the tradition of compulsory prosecution encourages prosecutors to "play it safe" in close cases and file criminal charges. Secondly, a decision not to prosecute someone with a crime is subject to review by superiors who tend to be conservative in matters of discretion not to prosecute (Damaska, 1981; West, 1992).

If a prosecutor decides not to file criminal charges because he believes that the evidence in the case is insufficient to support the prosecution, civil law systems usually afford victims the right to challenge such decisions unless the crime involved is rather minor (Herrmann, 1974; Frase, 1990). Sometimes this challenge is administrative in the form of a complaint about the prosecutor's actions (Langbein, 1974), but sometimes the victim's challenge can be brought directly in court seeking reversal of the decision not to prosecute or even through a form of private prosecution (Langbein, 1974; Frase, 1990). If review of the prosecutor's decision reveals a violation of the duty of compulsory prosecution, this would be entered in the prosecutor's file and could have a negative impact on the speed with which the prosecutor advances up the hierarchical career path typical of civil law systems (Herrmann, 1974).

The restrained position of the civil law prosecutor is even more obvious in making postfiling decisions. He has no formal nolle prosequi power to drop charges once the matter has been sent to a trial court or examining magistrate. The lack of formal power to dismiss the filed charges means that civil law prosecutors also lack formal power to dismiss selected counts or charges. Sole discretion to decide whether the charges fit the facts alleged by the prosecutor or disclosed by further investigation is given to the court (Merle & Vitu, 1979; Stefani, Levasseur, & Bouloc, 1984). Finally, civil law prosecutors have much less vertical charging discretion. They have no formal power to reduce already filed charges nor do they appear to exercise any such power in practice, at least not in cases initially filed as felonies (Merle & Vitu, 1979).

To understand correctly the prosecutor's charging discretion, one should note that the prosecutor in civil law systems is much less focused on the trial than his American counterpart. The prosecutor's main task is to make sure that the investigative file of the case, the dossier, is complete in the sense that it contains all relevant evidence and all relevant information on the background of the defendant. But the trial itself is the responsibility of the trial judge (or judges), not the prosecutor (Langbein, 1979). It is the judge who decides whether to summon witnesses and in what order the witnesses will be heard. Also, it is the judge who conducts the bulk of the questioning in an effort to determine whether the defendant committed the crime (Langbein, 1974). Most of the prosecutor's work is normally completed before the trial takes place, and he plays a relatively minor role at trial. Adversary pressure that calls for caution in filing charges when the evidence is not strong is, if not entirely absent, far less important in the thinking of a civil law prosecutor. As long as there is sufficient evidence to support the prosecution, the stigma attached to "losing a case" is not present in the civil law system (Damaska, 1981).

Operating in an adversarial environment, American prosecutors are forced to think about cases quite differently than are prosecutors in civil law systems. Trials in the United States are personalized to a very great extent. Prosecutors and defense attorneys talk about the cases they've "won" and those they've "lost." When a prosecutor obtains a conviction, he will be congratulated by others in the office for the "victory" and when he "loses" a case, he will often spend some time wondering what he might have done differently to have changed the outcome and to have convinced the jury to convict (Weinreb, 1977). As a result of the widely held belief that the outcome of a trial may be a reflection of the quality of the advocacy, the adversary system imposes a strong feeling of responsibility on the part of the prosecutor for winning a case.

Because jury trials require considerable preparation and are often rather demanding, prosecutors generally do not want to file charges against a defendant unless the chances of conviction are very good.[8] This will be especially true of the type of routine, rather minor criminal cases that are the bread and butter of most prosecutors' offices. Thus, the adversary system serves as a screen to discourage prosecutors from pursuing weak cases.

While it is true that prosecutorial zeal is tempered by the ethical duty not to prosecute without probable cause, it is also true that once a prosecutor decides there is sufficient evidence to convict, that goal is pursued with commitment close to, and on occasion even exceeding (Felkenes, 1975), that of the defense attorney.[9] Cases of prosecutorial over-reaching in the effort to obtain a conviction, often amounting to prejudicial misconduct, abound in the United States (*Brown v. Borg*, 1991; *U.S. v. Roberts*,

1980, *U.S. v. Vargas*, 1978; *U.S. v. Corona*, 1977). Furthermore, the prosecutor occasionally pursues the conviction of one whose guilt is highly questionable. After having studied the case file, having convinced reluctant witnesses to testify, and having developed a trial strategy, the prosecutor often has a considerable investment in a case and may feel a powerful commitment to try the case and obtain a conviction. In this context, the aim of achieving justice can easily translate into a desire to convict regardless of the facts, particularly if the prosecutor rationalizes that the defendant is a "bad guy" who deserves imprisonment for having committed other crimes for which he was never convicted.

There are several reasons to hypothesize that the civil law approach to charging discretion is superior and that decisions are more rational and uniform than in most American jurisdictions. The hierarchical, career-oriented nature of the civil law prosecution system suggests that screening decisions are likely to be made in a more consistent manner, based on established prosecution policies and subject to internal, supervisory review (West, 1992). Second, the multi-stage screening process appears to give a civil law prosecutor more time for careful selection or rejection of charges, without unduly prolonging detention of suspects. Third, the crime victim in many civil law jurisdictions plays a role that serves as a useful check on actual or perceived abuses of the discretion to decline prosecution.

Decision to Prosecute

Although decisions to forego or drop charges have been especially difficult to regulate in the United States (Davis, 1980; Frase, 1990), decisions to go forward with prosecution also raise important problems. If weak or baseless charges are not promptly reviewed and dismissed, defendants may face unnecessary hardship and embarrassment, and everyone involved—witnesses, parties, and public officials—is subjected to needless expense. Insufficient screening and intentional overcharging also aggravate the problems of plea bargaining: Extra cases and counts add to the court congestion traditionally seen as necessitating plea bargaining. Additional charges (even weak ones) increase the pressure on defendants to bargain rather than to risk potentially far greater punishment by going to trial on the original charges.

In civil law systems, the decision to prosecute on felony charges is strictly regulated. Decisions by civil law prosecutors to file felony charges are subject to close judicial review by both the examining magistrate and the indicting chamber (Tomlinson, 1983; West, 1992). The examining magistrate may decide that the evidence does not support any charges or only supports charges of lesser offense. Consequently, he may order dismissal or transfer for trial in courts of limited jurisdiction. If the examining magistrate finds that the evidence supports the felony charge, the entire file is then sent for review to the indicting chamber.

The indicting chamber is a panel of judges with supervisory power to order a dismissal or a trial on lesser charges. Asking an American judge to play a similarly aggressive role with respect to charging decisions would raise both practical difficulties and serious separation-of-powers problems. It would run contrary to the adversary tradition in which judges are assigned a neutral and passive role with respect to charging decisions and the development of evidence at trial. Put bluntly, except in the narrow band of cases where a prosecutor's actions violate the Constitution, an American judge has no power to reduce or reshape criminal charges to fit the evidence or the equities of a particular case.[10]

If the prosecutor in civil law systems decides to file only charges for a minor criminal offense, the matter is usually sent directly to the court of limited jurisdiction with no judicial screening whatsoever. Since felony trials constitute a relatively small portion of the judicial caseload, and all other decisions to prosecute are unreviewed prior to trial, a question arises: How do the civil law countries avoid the problems of insufficient screening and intentional overcharging? Again, the answer lies in the combination of structural safeguards—hierarchy and a multi-stage screening process—and in the absence of explicit nolle prosequi and plea bargaining practices. The hierarchical structure of the office of the public prosecutor makes possible degrees of training, supervision, specialization, and accountability likely to produce a high level of screening efficiency. Because decisions to prosecute are often made weeks, rather than days, after the police identify the suspect, these decisions are more likely to be based on a complete investigation that may have revealed weaknesses in testimony and new evidence. Perhaps most importantly, the lack of formal nolle prosequi powers gives prosecutors maximum incentive to screen cases carefully before filing, and the absence of explicit plea bargaining removes a major incentive for prosecutors to overcharge when they do file.

Plea Bargaining

The issue that has received a great deal of attention in the reform-oriented comparative criminal procedure literature of the past twenty years is the extent to which civil law systems depend on practices analogous to American plea bargaining. This focus is not surprising: Being central to the American system of criminal justice, plea bargaining has been widely criticized by both liberals and conservatives. At times it has been accused of involving unfair coercion, prosecutorial overcharging, imposition of penalties for asserting constitutional trial rights, increased risk of convicting the innocent, or unjustified charge and sentence disparities (Alschuler, 1983; LaFave & Israel, 1985).

At a certain point, American reformers began to look to foreign systems in the hopes of finding ways to cut back or to eliminate dependence on plea bargaining. Some scholars, notably Professors John Langbein and Albert Alschuler, concluded that the continental countries had indeed avoided the overt form of this practice—explicit trading of charge or sentence concessions for the defendant's guilty plea (Alschuler, 1983; Langbein, 1979). Professor Langbein concluded that Germany has avoided both overt forms and implicit or tacit analogues of plea bargaining by simplifying and streamlining trial procedures, thus reducing the sheer economic necessity of negotiating with defendants to waive their trial rights, and by sharply curtailing prosecutorial control over charging decisions (Langbein, 1979).

Other scholars, however, claimed to have found both explicit and implicit forms of plea bargaining in these continental systems (Goldstein & Marcus, 1977). The truth is that there is no equivalent of plea bargaining in civil law countries because there are no "pleas." Even in Italy, the only civil law country that has adopted a mild form of plea bargaining in its new Code of Criminal Procedure (1989), there is no actual plea of guilty given in exchange for prosecutorial and judicial concessions.

Charge and Sentence Bargaining

To legal commentators dissatisfied with the abuses of American plea bargaining, one of the clearest examples of the superiority of criminal procedure in civil law systems is the absence of most forms of charge bargaining. All forms of plea bargaining may raise serious problems (LaFave & Israel, 1985; Alschuler, 1983), but charge bargaining—especially "nonevidentiary" charge bargaining (the dropping of provable charges in return for a plea)—is particularly susceptible to abuse. Charge bargains tend to understate the true severity or frequency of the defendant's crimes and distort his or her criminal history record. Furthermore, these bargains allow prosecutors to exercise sentencing power directly—an authority exclusively belonging to the court—often without benefit of any detailed, independent, presentence investigation. Finally, charge bargaining effectively undercuts sentencing and parole reforms linked to specific conviction offenses (Alschuler, 1978; Frase, 1985).

Also, charge bargaining is more difficult for judges to control than sentence bargaining. Sentencing decisions have traditionally been relegated to judges, who must take primary responsibility for those decisions, whereas charging decisions have traditionally been considered a matter of prosecutorial discretion (Goldstein, 1981; LaFave & Israel, 1985). More-over, even if judges wanted to place limits on nonevidentiary charge bar-gains, it is difficult for them to identify those bargains. Given the limited means available to courts to assess the strength of charges that the pros-ecutor wishes to drop, often a judge's easiest course is to presume that the charges were not provable and thus defer to the prosecutor's request.

As already pointed out, the central reason for the absence of charge bargaining in Europe is that continental prosecutors lack the common law prosecutor's nolle prosequi power to drop pending charges. Moreover, in several countries, notably in Germany, prosecutorial discretion is also tightly controlled prior to the filing of charges in court (Goldstein & Mar-cus, 1977). In France, Italy and Japan, however, prosecutors enjoy a cer-tain amount of informal vertical charging discretion (Merle & Vitu, 1979; Stefani, Levasseur, & Bouloc, 1984; West, 1992), which may sometimes produce similar effects to charge bargaining—namely, the defendant may receive a charge reduction in return for his or her "cooperation." How-ever, this similarity fades away when viewed within the broader concept of the criminal justice process. The charge reductions may not be "bar-gained" for (Pizzi & Marafioti, 1992). Rather, they are made unilaterally and usually occur before the defendant has an attorney (Langbein & Wein-reb, 1978; Weigend, 1980). They are not conditioned either on the defen-dant's confession (which can be withdrawn later anyway) or on his or her cooperation (Merle & Vitu, 1979). Most importantly, those defendants who fully confess to a crime receive a trial like those who did not confess. The trial is a mandatory stage of the criminal justice process and cannot be replaced by interparty arrangements. At the trial, the defendant can fully contest the charges.

While the exercise of charging discretion in the prefiling context may take a disguise of vertical charge bargaining, horizontal charge bargaining in civil law jurisdictions is essentially a conceptual impossibility. Although the civil law prosecutor has the power to drop all or some charges, this power cannot be used to offer concessions and to reward defendants who confess or otherwise cooperate at trial. The concept of the criminal process as an ongoing official inquiry does not relieve the civil law judge of his duty to conduct trial in the usual manner.

As with charge bargaining, prosecutors in the United States may either explicitly or implicitly exercise a considerable discretion in sentence bar-gaining. They may directly recommend or choose not to oppose a lenient sentence or sentence "cap," or jointly, with defense, recommend sentence (usually with the understanding that the defendant may withdraw his or her plea if the court refuses to be bound by the agreed-upon sentence). Implicit or tacit sentence bargains involve expectations that the defen-dant's cooperation will be rewarded with a more lenient sentence. Such leniency is extended for the same reasons that prosecutors explicitly offer lenient treatment to defendants who cooperate: the perception that such defendants deserve less punishment, that lesser punishment is necessary to induce an acceptable number of guilty pleas, or for both these reasons (A.B.A., 1986).

In civil law jurisdictions, with the exception of Italy, prosecutors have no means of directly influencing the sentencing decision. Sentencing is firmly in hands of the trial judge. The prosecutor may try to generate a certain influence on the judge's decision by including a sentencing recommendation in the charging document. However, this recommendation is unilateral and has no binding effect on the judge, who may choose to completely disregard it.

To some extent, the situation is different in Italy. The 1988 Code of Criminal Procedure has adopted a mild form of sentence bargaining.[11] This entirely new (for a civil law country) institution is called "the application of punishment upon the request of the parties." Under this procedure, before the trial begins the public prosecutor and the defense attorney may agree on a sentence to be imposed and ask the judge to impose it (Pizzi & Marafloti, 1992). The normal sentence can be reduced by as much as one-third, so long as the final negotiated sentence is not more than two years. Prosecutors can bargain to defer the sentence, since any sentence up to two years can be deferred.[12]

Although Italian-style sentence bargaining may appear similar to U.S. plea bargaining, certain limitations differentiate it from what occurs in U.S. courts. First, in the Italian system the public prosecutor and the defendant do not bargain over the nature of the crime to which the defendant will plead guilty. Second, the fixed maximum reduction of one-third of the normal sentence, coupled with the restriction that the final sentence may not exceed two years, considerably limits the range of cases in which the Italian prosecutor may exercise this discretionary power. Third, the defense may ask the judge for the one-third reduction in sentencing under the statute even if the prosecutor refuses to join in such a request.[13] In such cases, the prosecutor must state his reasons for refusing the proposed disposition.[14] The intent of the Italian Code is to make sentence reduction available to all defendants who wish to plea bargain, whether or not the prosecutor agrees. This arrangement reflects the traditional civil law distrust of prosecutorial discretion and commitment to uniform treatment of defendants—that defendants would receive different sentences simply because of a prosecutor's whim is anathema to civil law (Damaska, 1973; Langbein, 1977).

Prosecutorial Discretion at Trial

At trial, American prosecutorial power is enhanced and stands as a counterweight to aggressive defense advocacy. This is evident in both the examination of witnesses and the final arguments. To balance aggressive defense cross-examination, the American prosecutor is afforded great control over the presentation and examination of witnesses. It is the prosecutor, rather than the judge, who decides whom to call and in what order. Also, in restrictive discovery jurisdictions, the defense is neither provided the names of the witnesses before trial nor given the statements of witnesses until after they have testified on direct. The prosecutor can control the elicitation of testimony and present a one-sided account of the facts through "guiding," though generally not "leading," questions. Finally, in jurisdictions following the common law, the defense may use inconsistent statements only for the purpose of impeaching or contradicting the witness.

In contrast, the judge in the civil law model calls and questions the witnesses, who may first respond in narrative, in which there is no limit on the use of inconsistent statements. Of course, American defense lawyers have similar control over their witnesses. Nonetheless, as a practical matter, American prosecutors have the advantage of proceeding first, and in virtually all cases it is the prosecutor who calls the greatest number of witnesses.

The American prosecutor enjoys even greater advantages at the end of a trial. All American criminal trial lawyers are fully aware of the great significance of the prosecutor's opportunity both to open and to close argument to the jury, but few are aware that in civil law systems, as well as in England, the prosecutor generally does not have the final word. In most nonadversary systems, the closing argument is a privilege of the defense attorney. Moreover, the defendant personally is allowed to address the court at the end of trial (Damaska, 1975b; Langbein, 1977). In England, the prosecutor cannot answer the final argument of a defendant's barrister, and if a defendant represented by counsel rests without presenting any evidence, the prosecutor's argument powers are further restricted.[15]

While both on the Continent and in England the defense has the last word, judicial intervention provides a counterweight to defense advocacy in the form of summation and comment on the evidence. In civil law systems professional judges are part of the mixed tribunal, and the presiding judge often summarizes the evidence at the commencement of deliberations. The strong comment and summation powers of English judges are used to balance the defense barrister's opportunity to give the closing argument, to which the prosecution cannot respond. In this country, with American toleration of unrestrained advocacy on the part of the lawyers, the accused has little protection against the aggressive and emotional prosecutor during the final and unanswerable argument.

Conclusion

This paper has tried to compare the conceptual differences of prosecutorial discretion between the American criminal justice system and civil law systems. In both legal environments prosecutorial discretion stems from a convergence of many forces including political and legal traditions, procedural design and a system of pretrial and trial procedures, and the concept of adjudicating bodies. It is quite evident that that prosecutorial discretion occupies center stage of the American criminal justice process. If Americans wish to reduce prosecutorial discretion, they need to look at the entire system and determine why it has moved so far away from adjudication and why they have to rely more and more on compromise and negotiation.

There is a great deal of skepticism that Americans can improve the system of criminal justice by borrowing important procedural controls from civil law systems. In the first place, pieces from one system cannot be easily separated from the rest of that system and isolated for incorporation in a different legal system. In this case, the concept of an American prosecutor is tightly intertwined with the fundamental principles of the political system in this country. The American legal system, as any other legal system in the world, is much more than a set of procedures for determining guilt and sentencing defendants. It is tied to important cultural, historical, and political values, making it unlikely that any reform incorporated from a system that does not share those values will be adopted or, even if adopted, will ever accomplish what it was intended to do.

Endnotes

[1] In the state of Alaska, for example, the attorney general has supervisory authority over all district attorneys and assistant district attorneys in the state because they are members of the State Department of Law, of which the Attorney General is chief executive officer. Alaska Stat. §§ 44.23.010–.020 (1989). It was apparently this unusual authority which permitted the Alaska Attorney General in 1975 to abolish at least the most visible forms of prosecutorial plea bargaining throughout the state (Rubinstein & White, 1978).

[2] American Bar Association Standards for Criminal Justice, Standard 3–2.2(c) (suggesting that states should assure "maximum practicable uniformity" in criminal law enforcement throughout state); Standard 3–2.2(e) (recommending "central pool of supporting resources and manpower").

[3] Although students are eligible to enter the magistrate training program after three years, many do not do so until after four or five years of law school. Admission to the bar requires the maitrise (fourth-year) degree (Vincent, Montagnier, & Varinard, 1991).

[4] Some states retain the common law nolle prosequi power, giving the prosecutor complete discretion to drop charges at any time before trial (LaFave & Israel, 1985). Other states and the federal system nominally require leave of the court to dismiss serious charges (Federal Rules of Criminal Procedure, 48(a) (dismissal of indictment, information, or complaint requires leave of court); Minnesota Rules of Criminal Procedure, 30 (dismissal of indictment requires leave of court), but permission is rarely denied (Goldstein, 1981).

[5] For example, German prosecutors have no discretion to decline prosecution of felony charges "in cases where adequate incriminating evidence is at hand" and may decline provable misdemeanors only if the accused's guilt is "minor" and "there is no public interest in prosecuting" (Langbein, 1974).

[6] The principle of compulsory prosecution in Germany is contained in section 152(2) of the German Code of Criminal Procedure, which Professor Langbein (1974) translates as follows: "[The public prosecutor] is required . . . to take action against all judicially punishable . . . acts, to the extent that there is a sufficient factual basis" (p. 443). In Italy, the principle of compulsory prosecution is enshrined in the Italian Constitution (Constituzione della Republica Italiana, 1947), art. 112 (Pizzi & Marafioti, 1992).

[7] Over the years, this doctrine has, in the words of one German scholar, become "encrusted with exceptions" (Weigend, 1980, p. 401). Professor Frase reports similar developments in France: French prosecutors have considerable discretion to adjust or drop charges, but at the same time, their discretion "is significantly more restrained . . . than in the United States" (Frase, 1990, p. 611).

[8] "As a practical matter, the prosecutor is likely to require admissible evidence showing a high probability of guilt, that is, sufficient evidence to justify confidence in obtaining a conviction" (LaFave & Israel, 1985, § 13.1, p. 157).

[9] Judge Frankel stated that "most criminal defense counsel are not at all bent upon full disclosure of the truth" and suggested that "[t]o a lesser degree" neither are prosecutors (Frankel, 1975, p. 1038). Recognizing the mixed enthusiasm of prosecutors for the principle that they must seek justice, not merely convictions, Frankel concluded that "it is the rare case in which either side yearns to have the witnesses, or anyone, give the whole truth" (p. 1038).

[10] The United States Court of Appeals for the D.C. Circuit has made the following observations on the limited role of the judiciary in reviewing prosecutorial discretion:

> Few subjects are less adapted to judicial review than the exercise by the Executive of his discretion in deciding when and whether to institute criminal proceedings, or what precise charge shall be made, or whether to dismiss a proceeding once brought. . . . No court has any jurisdiction to inquire into or review his decision. . . . While this discretion is subject to abuse or misuse just as is judicial discretion, deviations from his duty as an agent of the Executive are to be dealt with by his superiors. . . . It is not the function of the judiciary to review the exercise of executive discretion whether it be that of the President himself or those to whom he has delegated certain of his powers (*Newman v. United States*, 382 F.2d 479, 480–82 (D.C.Cir.1967); *Oyler v. Boles*, 368 U.S. 448 [1962]).

[11] Codice di Procedura Penale, arts. 444–448.

[12] Id. art. 444.

[13] Id. arts. 444, 446.

[14] Id. arts. 446, 448.

[15] *Regina v. Bryant* 2 All E. R. 689 (1978); 67 Cr. Ap. R. 157, C.A. (When a defendant represented by counsel does not testify and calls no witnesses, the prosecution's right to make a closing speech should be spartanly exercised and, on rare occasions when the right is exercised, should be brief).

References

A.B.A. (1974 & Supp. 1986). *Standards for Criminal Justice,* Washington DC: American Bar Association.

Abrams, N. (1975). Prosecutorial Charge Decision Systems, *University of California Law Review,* 23:1.

Alschuler, A. (1978). Sentencing Reform and Prosecutorial Power: A Critique of Recent Proposals for "Fixed" and "Presumptive" Sentencing, *University of Pennsylvania Law Review,* 126:550.

_____ (1983). Implementing the Criminal Defendant's Right to Trial: Alternatives to the Plea Bargaining System, *University of Chicago Law Review,* 50:931–1050.

Amodio, E. & Selvaggi, E. (1989). An Accusatorial System in a Civil Law Country: The 1988 Italian Code of Criminal Procedure, *Temple Law Quarterly,* 62:1211–1224.

Applebaum, D. (1986). Congestion and Beyond: Change and Continuity in Modern French Legal Education—A Design for U.S. Law Schools, *Nova Law Journal,* 10:297–318.

Arenella, P. (1983). Rethinking the Functions of Criminal Procedure: The Warren and Burger Court's Competing Ideologies, *Georgetown Law Journal,* 72:185–248.

Bradley, C. (1993). The Emerging International Consensus as to Criminal Procedure Rule, *Michigan Journal of International Law,* 14:171–211.

Damaska, M. (1986). *The Faces of Justice and State Authority: A Comparative Approach to the Legal Process,* New Haven: Yale University Press.

_____ (1981). The Reality of Prosecutorial Discretion: Comments on a German Monograph, *American Journal of Comparative Law,* 29:119.

_____ (1973). Evidentiary Barriers to Conviction and Two Models of Criminal Procedure: A Comparative Study, *University of Pennsylvania Law Review* 121:506–589.

_____ (1975a). Structures of Authority and Comparative Criminal Procedure, *Yale Law Journal,* 84:480.

_____ (1975b). Presentation of Evidence and Factfinding Precision, *University of Pennsylvania Law Review,* 123:1083.

Davis, K. (1980). *Discretionary Justice: A Preliminary Inquiry,* Westport, CT: Greenwood Press.

Felkenes, G. (1975). The Prosecutor: A Look at Reality, *Southwestern University Law Review,* 7:98.

Frankel, M. (1975). The Search for Truth: An Umpireal View, *University of Pennsylvania Law Review,* 123:1031.

Frase, R. (1985). Defining the Limits of Crime Control and Due Process, *California Law Review,* 73:212–251.

_____ 1990). Comparative Criminal Justice as a Guide to American Law Reform: How Do French Do It, How Can We Find Out, and Why We Should Care? *California Law Review,* 78:539–683.

Frassler, L. (1991). The Italian Penal Procedure Code: An Adversarial System of Criminal Procedure in Continental Europe, *Columbia Journal of Transnational Law,* 29:245–278.

Freccero, S. (1994). An Introduction to the New Italian Criminal Procedure, *American Journal of Criminal Law*, 21:345–383.

Fuller, J. (1961). The Adversary System. In Harold Joseph Berman (ed.), *Talks on American Law*, New York: Vintage Books, pp. 30–43.

Goldstein, A. (1981). *The Passive Judiciary: Prosecutorial Discretion and the Guilty Plea*, Baton Rouge: Louisiana State University Press.

Goldstein, A. & Marcus, M. (1977). The Myth of Judicial Supervision in Three "Inquisitorial" Systems: France, Italy, and Germany, *Yale Law Journal*, 87:240.

Herrmann, J. (1974). The Rule of Compulsory Prosecution and the Scope of Prosecutorial Discretion in Germany, *University of Chicago Law Review*, 41:468.

Jacoby, Joan E. (1979). *The American Prosecutor: A Search for Identity*, Lexington, MA: Lexington Books.

Jescheck, H. H. (1970). Principles of German Criminal Procedure in Comparison with American Law, *Virginia Law Review* 56:239–253.

LaFave, W. & Israel, J. (1985). *Criminal Procedure*, St. Paul, MN: West Publishing Company.

Langbein, J. (1974). Controlling Prosecutorial Discretion in Germany, *University of Chicago Law Review*, 41:439.

_____ (1977). *Comparative Criminal Procedure: Germany*, St. Paul, MN: West Publishing Company.

_____(1979) Land Without Plea Bargaining: How the Germans Do It, *Michigan Law Review*, 78:204.

Langbein, J. & Weinreb, L. (1978). Continental Criminal Procedure: Myth and Reality, *Yale Law Journal*, 87:1549–1569.

Merle, R. & Vitu, A. (1979). *Traite de Droit Criminel Procedure Penale*, Paris: Editions Cujas.

Miller, F. (1969). *Prosecution: The Decision to Charge a Suspect with a Crime*, Boston: Little Brown.

National Association of Attorneys General. (1977). Powers, Duties and Operations of State Attorneys General, Raleigh, NC: The Committee.

Pizzi, W. (1993). Reforming the Role of the American Prosecutor, *New Law Journal*, 143:1160–1201.

Pizzi, W. & Marafioti, L. (1992). The New Italian Code of Criminal Procedure: The Difficulties of Building an Adversarial Trial System on a Civil Law Foundation, *The Yale Journal of International Law*, 17:1–40.

Pugh, G. W. (1962). Administration of Criminal Justice in France: An Introductory Analysis, *Louisiana Law Review*, 23:1.

Rubinstein, M. L. & White, T. J., (1978). *Alaska's Ban on Plea Bargaining*, Anchorage: Alaska Judicial Council.

Schlessinger, R. et al. (1988). *Comparative Law: Cases, Text Materials* (5th ed.), Mineola, NY: Foundation Press.

Stefani, G., Levasseur, G., & Bouloc, B. (1984). *Procedure Penale*, Paris: Dolloz.

Tomlinson, E. (1983). Nonadversarial Justice: The French Experience, *Maryland Law Review*, 42:131–195.

Vincent, J., Montagnier, G., & Varinard, A. (1991). *La Justice et ses Institutions*, Paris: Dalloz.

Volkmann-Schluck, T. (1981). Continental European Criminal Procedures: True or

Illusive Model? *American Journal of Criminal Law*, 9:1–32.

Vorenberg, J. (1981). Decent Restraint of Prosecutorial Power, *Harvard Law Review*, 94:1521.

Vouin, R. (1970). The Role of the Prosecutor in French Criminal Trials, *American Journal of Comparative Law*, 18:483.

Weigend, T. (1980). Continental Cases for American Ailments: European Criminal Procedure as a Model for Law Reform. In M. Tonry & N. Morris (eds.), *Crime and Justice*, 2:381.

Weinreb, L. (1977). *Denial of Justice: Criminal Process in the United States*, New York: Free Press.

West, M. (1992). Prosecution Review Commissions: Japan's Answer to the Problem of Prosecutorial Discretion, *Columbia Law Review*, 92:684–723.

31

Jury Trials, Russian-Style
An American Jurist Reports on a Country's First Steps Toward a New Method of Justice

RICHARD T. ANDRIAS

It began like any other day. Up and out before 7 A.M., a light breakfast, and off to court by 8 A.M. In the courthouse lobby, knots of lawyers and clients briefly paused to nod good morning. After a conference with colleagues, I entered the courtroom.

There the routine ended. It would not be like any other day or any other week. I was not going to be *on* the bench, as I had been almost every weekday for more than a decade, I would be in the audience on the other side of the rail, observing another judge preside over his courtroom, 5,000 miles from my home in New York.

Under the auspices of the ABA's Central and East European Law Initiative (CEELI), I was in Saratov, Russia, with two American law professors to conduct trial advocacy training.

Nestled on the western bank of the fabled Volga River, 350 miles southeast of Moscow, the city of Saratov is the capital of the region by the same name, which has an overall population of two-and-a-half million. The birthplace of Yuri Gagarin, the first man in space, Saratov was closed to foreigners during the Soviet era because of its strategic heavy industry.

Although I taught Russian lawyers last summer during a 10-day CEELI

Reprinted by permission from *Criminal Justice*, Vol. 11, No. 2 (Summer, 1996), pp. 14–27. Copyright © ABA Publishing.

program in Springfield, Massachusetts, this would be my first opportunity to observe a Russian jury trial. No doubt it would also be the first jury trial witnessed by the somewhat dazed-looking citizens waiting to be ushered into Judge Druzin's courtroom. Czarist legal reforms of 1864 introduced the jury for serious crimes, but the last such trials in Russia were conducted in 1917 and were abolished by the October Revolution.

In the waning days of the Soviet Union, legislation was passed that allowed member states to provide for trial by jury in death penalty cases or those where the sentence could be 10 years or more. As with many other "rights" in Russia, however, this right required further legislative authorization and an executive decree for financing. It was two years after the 1991 dissolution of the Soviet Union, in July 1993, that enabling legislation was finally passed to provide for jury trials in Russia itself.

Saratov was one of the nine areas selected to initiate jury trials. Four additional regions were to begin jury trials by 1996. Nizhny Novgorod, the second city our American training team visited in early December 1995, was scheduled to begin jury trials in January, but for a number of reasons it did not. This "phased-in" approach has created a number of anomalies. For example, the region surrounding the capital city of Moscow has jury trials, but the city itself does not.

Coming in from the Saratov airport on a Sunday night, the city appeared grim. Street lights were strung low across the avenues, illuminating only the bottom half of shuttered buildings. While there were fewer potholes than in Moscow, the streets and buildings were dirty from the sand applied after each snowfall. Men in dark overcoats clustered about the ever-present sidewalk kiosks, having a vodka nightcap and catching up on the weekend gossip.

The drive to court Monday morning, however, presented a startling contrast. Sunlight revealed a well laid-out city of tree-lined boulevards, stately buildings, London-style squares, and an elegant main street crowded with pedestrians walking to work.

As we drove to the imposing courthouse, I asked our unofficial host, a prominent defense lawyer, if I could get a city map in order to extend my early morning walks. "Your Honor," he replied, "in Saratov, only the militia [police] have maps." It was a cheerless joke and no one spoke. He didn't have to add that here the police don't carry Miranda cards and that pretrial release is rarely granted to arrestees. The somber mood was dispelled somewhat as we walked up the courthouse steps: "Do you like our fine building? When the Communists were thrown out here in Saratov, we took over their headquarters for our *oblast* [regional] court."

In the courtroom, the morning light streamed through the floor-to-ceiling windows, revealing at first glance a scene not unlike thousands scattered throughout the county seats and urban centers of America. The raised judge's bench, dominating the room from the front, looked out over a number of tables for counsel and court personnel. A waist-high rail separated the bar from the public. Six to eight rows of pew-like benches provided seating for 100 members of the public. A red, white, and blue flag hung behind the bench. Along the right wall stood a standard jury box with 14 seats.

Once seated, a more leisurely inspection of the courtroom presented a number of features totally alien to an American practitioner. Along the left wall, situated as far from the jury box as possible, stood a steel cage guarded by an armed member of the militia [police]. Within the cage, a sullen-looking young man conversed with his lawyer, who stood just outside the bars. Not 10 feet from the defendant's cage, just inside the rail, was a table where two young women were seated, the victim and her representative, in this case, her sister.

"All rise."

The judge, robes flowing, entered the room and acknowledged his official staff, the prosecutor, the defense lawyer, and the visitors in the audience. After a brief bench conference, the lawyers stepped back and the prosecutor announced the charge: rape.

The judge then addressed the lawyers: "If we are not empowered to hear this case, you must speak up now. [There was a silence.] Since there is no objection, let us proceed."

Addressing the defendant directly, the judge said: "Mr. Yurchuk, I will now explain to you your procedural rights. You have a right to defend yourself and to be represented by counsel. You may defend yourself by all means not contrary to the Criminal Code. You may present the court-written questions to be asked on your behalf. You may ask to have jurors dismissed if they are relatives, friends, or acquaintances, or are otherwise related to the case. You may also dismiss two jurors without giving any reason. You may also, after the jury has been formed, ask the court to dismiss the entire jury if you believe it cannot fairly try your case. You have a right to testify, but also a right to remain silent. You may choose when you want to speak. You can present motions and evidence. You can participate in examining witnesses and make objections to any evidence if you feel it violates the Code. You can object to the court's presiding over your trial if you feel that I am not being fair or if I failed to inform you of your rights. If you are convicted, you have three days to review the record. Do you understand? Yes. Good."

The judge then turned to the victim and her sister, saying: "Ms. Levina, you have a right to participate in this trial. You are considered to be one of the parties. You can present written questions to the court. You can be involved in selecting the jury. You can exempt anyone who is a relative, friend, or is related to the case in any way. When the jury is formed, you can ask to have the entire panel excused if you believe the jury cannot be fair. You can present evidence and make motions. You can ask questions during the investigative proceedings or question evidence that is being introduced at trial. You can ask that any matter be excluded. If you change your mind at any point, you can ask the trial to stop. If the prosecutor wants to stop the trial, you can insist on its continuation. If my charge to the jury at the conclusion of the case is not fair, you can ask that the jury be excused, and we will start over. Do you understand your rights? Any questions? No. Then let us proceed."

The judge then asked the parties if there were any further motions. There were none. He then inquired as to whether there were any additional witnesses not on the list. The defense lawyer indicated there were some from the same village where the incident occurred. The judge signed three subpoenas and presented them to the lawyer.

"Can we start the jury selection? Yes. There are no objections? None. Let us proceed."

As the prospective jurors filed in, I asked one of my hosts the source of the jury lists and whether they had any trouble getting jurors to show up. Apparently, as a legacy of former times, the voter lists are derived from housing lists that, because of general housing shortages, are very comprehensive. Also, jurors are relatively well paid; they receive no less than their regular pay or an amount equal to one-half of the judge's salary. Finally, it is now a crime to fail to show up for jury duty. While compliance is good in Saratov, we learned during a later legal conference that juror attendance is a major concern in other regions.

The 48 prospective jurors filled the front rows of the courtroom. The parties must select 12 jurors and two alternates. Each side has two peremptory challenges, so the judge's objective is to end up with at least 18 qualified jurors.

The judge addressed the jurors directly: "Jurors, the charge of rape is merely an accusation by the authorities. The defendant is presumed innocent until proven guilty in the privacy of your deliberation room. You must hear all of the evidence before you decide the question of whether the accusation is right or not. You will use your life experience, your sense of justice. You must be unbiased, impartial, fair, and just. The parties will select 12 jurors and two alternates. Do not be angry if you are asked to step down. Your expenses will be reimbursed.

"Your obligations are to answer the court's questions truthfully, to obey the court's directives, to be orderly and calm in the courtroom, and never to leave without the court's permission. If there are violations, you may be fined—or worse. Any questions? We will have no problems, I'm sure.

"My name is Judge Druzin. My secretary and the protocol clerk are here to assist you. Ms. Zubkova is the prosecutor. Seated across the courtroom is the victim, Ms. Levina, and a member of her family, her sister. [They stand.] The defendant is Mr. Yurchuk. [He stands in the cage.] He is being defended by his lawyer, Ms. Sokolova."

The judge then proceeded to collectively question the 48 jurors seated in the audience. According to Russian law, a juror must be a citizen of the Russian Federation, have full mental capacity, be of appropriate age, and have no criminal convictions. The judge queried:

"Is there anyone who knows any of the parties or anyone connected with the case? [Silence.] "Who does not know the Russian language? [Silence.] "Who is mute, blind, or an invalid? [Silence.] "Who is over 70 years of age or under 25 years of age? [Silence.] "Who heads an administrative agency? [Silence.] "Who is a judge, lawyer, notary, or involved in law enforcement or a legal body? [Silence.] "Who is a member of the clergy? [Silence.] I see no such people."

"Jurors, I may also excuse at your request those over 60, women with children under three years, those with critical jobs, and anyone else with a valid excuse."

A number of prospective jurors were ushered through the bar and up to the bench, where hushed bench conferences ensued. Several were excused and departed; the others returned to their seats.

"Do the parties have any questions they want to put to the jurors?" The prosecutor handed up a list of questions. The defense counsel offered none.

"I will be asking you some additional questions, jurors. Does anyone know of this case from the press or media? Are there among you friends or acquaintances of the prosecutor, defense counsel, defendant, or victim? Is anyone related to criminal justice or law enforcement personnel?"

A woman in the audience stood up and said, "My son is in the militia."

"Will that influence you here?" asked the judge.

"I can be unbiased," she declared.

"Prosecutor? I hear no objection. Defense counsel? I hear no objection. So you remain."

"Are any of you People's Jurors [lay assessors]?"

Four prospective jurors volunteered that they had been lay assessors. (Under the Soviet system, two citizens sat with a professional judge and decided serious cases by a majority vote.)

"Any objections? None. You stay."

A juror stood and declared, "I was a juror in a jury trial in October 1994." The judge informed him that the law provides that he can be a juror 10 days per year and that he must stay.

"Has anyone been a party to a lawsuit?" [Silence.]

In a perfunctory manner, the judge asked whether anyone had any special feelings about the crime of rape or biases against the defendant himself. [Silence.]

"Are there any of you who are not satisfied with law enforcement? Have you had a friend or family member who has not been dealt with fairly by the militia?" [Silence.]

"Are there any of you that work with children or juveniles?"

A middle-aged woman stood and said she worked as a teacher. "Are there any juvenile delinquents in your classes? No. Then You may remain. Let us proceed."

Addressing the prosecutor and the defense counsel, the judge asked whether they sought to "exempt" any jurors—challenge them for cause. Neither had any challenges for cause, nor did the victim or her representative.

As a result of the judge's questioning, half of the 48 prospective jurors had been excused for various personal reasons. The names of the remaining 24 jurors were placed in a box on the judge's bench, from which he withdrew six. He then presented the remaining 18 cards to the prosecutor, who then used both of her two peremptory challenges. The judge turned directly to the defendant. "Mr. Yurchuk, you may exempt two jurors without giving a reason."

"My lawyer will act for me," he replied. The defense lawyer examined the cards, her notes, and removed two names. leaving 14.

The judge asked the lawyers, the defendant, and the victim whether they had any objections to the results of the selection process. There were none. "Ladies and gentlemen, we have a complete set of jurors and two alternates."

The entire jury selection process took no more than 40 minutes. The lawyers were not allowed to question jurors individually or collectively, and if they presented the judge with any questions directed at a particular juror, it was not evident. Throughout our two-week visit, the main complaint from practicing lawyers and legal scholars alike was that there is no individualized questioning by the judge and no opportunity for the lawyers to question jurors individually or even as a group. Furthermore, no alternative methods, such as a questionnaire, were available to develop useful information on which they could intelligently exercise a challenge. The official cards used in the selection process contained only the prospective juror's name, profession, and date of birth.

The judge called out the names of the 14 jurors who had been selected and, with profuse thanks, excused those remaining in the audience. Addressing the selected jurors, he stated, "Your first duty is to go into the privacy of the jury room and by majority vote select a foreman. The foreman's duties are to address jurors' questions to the judge or the judge's secretary, to preside over deliberations, to read the questions to be answered by the jury when deliberations begin, and to announce the verdict."

The jury returned after a brief recess led by a distinguished-looking middle-aged man who had been elected the foreman.

"Do you swear to carry out your duties as jurors, to decide the case only on the evidence as free citizens and just persons?" As each person's name was read, he or she answered "I swear."

Lawyers are not permitted to make opening statements in the American sense. However, the prosecutor outlined the charge of rape and summarized the results of the investigation by reading at some length from the file/dossier. The defense was not allowed to address the jury at this stage.

The judge then proceeded to instruct the jury on its duties and trial procedure.

"What you have just heard are merely charges. They must be proven. The defense counsel will be allowed to prove the defendant not guilty or to explain the circumstances surrounding the crime. Remember, the prosecutor and the defense counsel are equals. The defendant and the state are equals. Evidence presented by the defense and the state is to be considered in a similar fashion. This also applies to evidence by the defendant himself or by the victim herself. The defendant and the victim are citizens, not professionals, so keep this in mind. They may appear awkward.

"The defendant may speak, but he has no obligation to testify. If he declines to testify, you should not hold it against him. If he does testify; you must consider it and weigh it just like any other evidence.

"As the judge, I preside and make all the legal decisions. You are not to consider the legal aspects of the case. I will tell you what not to consider. Most of all, you will consider the testimony from the perspective of justice."

While the new procedures reflect the common-law distinction between issues of law to be determined by the judge and questions of fact to be decided by the jury, the Russian jury does not render a verdict of guilty or not guilty. The judge instructs the members of the jury, at the end of the case, that they will be asked to answer three basic questions:

1. Did the prosecution prove that the incident alleged took place?

2. If the event took place, was this defendant involved?

3. If so, was he legally responsible?

The jury is also instructed to consider any mitigating circumstances and whether to recommend leniency.

In the past, the judge and lay assessors determined the law, the facts, and the ultimate verdict by majority vote. Under jury procedures, a defendant is guilty if each of the three basic questions is answered affirmatively. The required standard of proof is that guilt should be convincingly proven: the jurors should be "sure." If no unanimous vote can be achieved after three hours, then a simple majority vote is sufficient. An acquittal occurs if six jurors answer at least one question in the negative. While the jury can recommend leniency, or special leniency, it plays no formal role in sentencing, with one exception: the court must follow a jury's recommendation of clemency when the death penalty is involved. As with the selection of the foreman, deliberations are conducted in secret.

"Jurors, please concentrate on the evidence. As I stated, I will decide if a question is legally permissible. You may ask questions by passing them to the secretary, who will refer them to the court. If your question is not allowed, do not take it personally. Either a legal impediment is involved or the question will be addressed later.

"You have a right to take personal, private notes. However, please listen attentively and do not be distracted by your note-taking.

"At the end of the trial, the parties will be given an opportunity to present their views to you. Their statements are not the final truth; they are for your convenience. Your own recollection controls.

"My concluding instruction to you is, in effect, a warning. If anyone approaches you on the subject of the trial, you must avoid them. You cannot discuss the case with anyone, even your relatives or friends. Also, if the case is covered by the media, you must avoid reading or viewing those reports. If there is something that is not clear to you, you must direct your questions to me and me alone."

His instructions completed, Judge Druzin ordered a break in the proceedings, urging the jury to relax in their deliberating room. Together with his chief judge, he took the opportunity to meet with the foreign visitors in his chambers. Judge Druzin had handled the jury with confidence and skill. He was equally at ease with Americans—a combination of natural poise and his experience working with other American delegations that have participated in the reintroduction of jury trials in Saratov. As our group left his cramped but orderly quarters, he pulled me, the only foreign jurist, aside and proudly displayed a frayed but current edition of the California Code of Criminal Procedure, apparently a gift of one of my predecessors.

The vast majority of civil and criminal cases in Russia today are handled in the city and rural district courts. The regional or provincial (oblast) courts, such as the Saratov court we visited, handle appeals from the district courts and also have original jurisdiction over a very limited category of the most serious crimes. Even in the oblast courts, most trials are still conducted by one of the two traditional methods: (1) by a professional presiding judge and two lay judges called "people's jurors" or (2) by a single judge. There is also a new method of a panel of three professional judges. However, since the reintroduction of the jury in late 1993, an increasing number of defendants request a jury in the most serious cases. According to the Ministry of Justice, during the first half of 1995, 376 jury trials occurred in Russia.

Under the Soviet regime, almost everyone was convicted at trial. The acquittal rates in jury trials are substantially higher than those in other forms of trial. The overall acquittal rate in Russia remains at .0046 percent. In jury trials, however, the rate is 21 percent, and it is as high as 30 percent in some regions. One recent study suggests that this rate would be even higher but for a uniquely Russian form of jury compromise. Eighteen percent of jurors questioned said they voted to recommend special leniency (i.e., a lesser sentence) even where they felt the charge had *not* been proven and an acquittal would have been the appropriate result. The practice of submitting the question of sentencing mitigation along with the three basic questions regarding guilt undoubtedly accounts for this phenomenon.

We did not get to watch the testimony in *The case of Yurchuk* because our advocacy program was scheduled to begin that afternoon, and, in any event, sexual assault trials and cases involving juveniles are closed to the public. Although there was no mistaking the peculiarly Russian nature of the law and procedure in Judge Druzin's instructions and jury selection process, the references to familiar concepts of presumption of innocence, burden of proof, right to counsel, a neutral judge, equal adversaries, and the right to silence could give the impression that the Russian system is evolving toward the Anglo-American mold.

Nothing could be more misleading. While the reintroduction of the jury has resulted in profound procedural changes and necessitated a more adversarial approach, their system remains radically different from our own and is firmly rooted in unique aspects of Russian culture and tradition. In this regard, one of CEELI's guiding principles is to look to the host country's concerns and priorities rather than proselytize that American methods will provide solutions to their problems.

Under the old system, the judge was seen as an extension of the prosecutor and the government bureaucracy. The two lay assessors often were employees whose supervisors could spare them as the least productive workers at the social factory or collective. The professional judge was a reliable party appointee who dominated the panel and all too often received a telephone call from his political superior dictating the verdict in any significant case. Consistent with the inquisitional goal of determining all of the facts and the truth, the professional judge approvingly read the charges, conducted the bulk of the questioning, and generally dominated the proceedings. To save a weak prosecution case, the judge could send the case back to the investigator at any point for further inquiry without a motion from either party.

Under jury procedures, the judge still dominates the proceedings and the questioning, but the prosecutor reads the charge to the jury, and the judge informs the jury that the parties are equal and that he or she will rule only on the law and that the jurors will determine if the charge is proven. The case can no longer be sent back for further investigation without the application of one of the parties.

During our two weeks in Russia, I spoke to numerous judges. The legacy of the past includes decaying facilities, poor conditions, inadequate pay, low prestige, and low morale. A number of prominent judges have left the bench to become advocates, a far more financially rewarding career under Russia's evolving economic system. However, with the reintroduction of the jury trial and its principles of adversariness and theoretically neutral, objective, and impartial judges, the judiciary has been presented with a way to emerge from its dubious past. Many judges are vigorous proponents of change, yet a surprising number are fiercely resistant to the concept of jury trials or any other reform. Their reluctance to embrace the jury system was premised on a number of factors: untrained lawyers, a lack of resources, and the likelihood that "unsophisticated" jurors would not understand the law or reach the "proper" verdict. No judge overtly mentioned loss of control over verdicts, but that often seemed to be the unstated theme in many of our conversations.

Law enforcement functions are the responsibility of the powerful Procurator General's Office (*procuratura*), which has subordinate agencies in the various cities and provinces. While the Ministry of Internal Affairs has administrative control over the militia, the procurator's office supervises the legality of the activities of all law enforcement agencies and investigates and prosecutes all serious criminal cases in the courts.

After an arrest, the defendant is invariably held in jail awaiting the outcome of the investigation. This inquiry is conducted by an investigator who is a police officer supervised by a prosecutor. Sometimes the inquiry is handled by an actual prosecutor, but not necessarily the prosecutor who will try the case. In theory, the investigation should be completed in three months, but in practice this period is often extended repeatedly.

Given the extensive periods of pretrial detention, virtually all cases involve one or more admissions of guilt that often form the core of the prosecution's case. Almost everyone agrees that one of the byproducts of reintroducing the jury system should be improved investigations and better prepared prosecutions because the prosecutor will no longer be able to assume that the fact finder—a skeptical jury—will automatically accept a presentation based on a "confession" resulting from the pressures of pretrial incarceration.

Under the old system, the judge read the charge, giving it official standing. Now the prosecutor merely reads a summary to the jury without the judge's imprimatur. In theory, the prosecutor and the defense lawyers are equal, but it is the prosecutor, as the arm of a very powerful state, who remains the more significant party in the proceedings. Defense lawyers see the jury as their vehicle for achieving some semblance of true equality in the trial process.

While there are a growing number of Western-style law firms primarily representing private businesses, most Russian lawyers in private practice are members of colleges of advocates called *collegia*, which are coextensive with Russian territorial subdivisions such as cities, regions, republics, or autonomous entities. Collegia members are the primary advocates in civil and criminal litigation and receive substantial tax benefits in return for taking on indigent defense in criminal matters.

While defendants have no access to lawyers upon their arrest and detention, they are supposed to be seen by the investigator within three days. The investigator must immediately inform the defendant of his or her right to a lawyer. I was told, however, that investigators routinely inform defendants that they do not need a lawyer and the lawyer will only get in the way.

At the conclusion of the investigation, there is a preliminary inquiry. If there has been a decision to indict, the defendant and his lawyer are given an opportunity to review and copy the investigator's entire file. A major complaint of some defense lawyers is that neither time nor facilities are provided to meet with their clients to prepare the case and thus no meaningful relationship is allowed to develop. In other regions, however, lawyers indicated that they had full access to clients.

The dominant roles that the prosecutor and the judge had in the past all too often limited the advocate's role in the trial to arguing mitigating circumstances. Furthermore, in Russian practice, lawyers are limited to *presenting* evidence to the court. The introduction of the jury has sparked an ethical debate as to whether—and to what extent—advocates can independently *gather* evidence for the defense. Although they are precluded from making opening statements and are uncharacteristically weak in cross-examination, Russian lawyers are renowned for their oratorical flair in closing arguments. The introduction of the jury will require them to further broaden their considerable skills.

Although held before trial for an indeterminate period in reportedly horrendous conditions and actually caged in the courtroom, a defendant in a Russian trial nevertheless has some extraordinary rights not present in American practice. The defendant, while not obligated to testify, may choose precisely when to present evidence during the trial if he or she decides to testify. Furthermore, the defendant traditionally has the last word in a Russian trial and may make a final statement in the trial, even after the close of evidence and after the lawyer's closing arguments. Many of the defendant's rights to participate and ask questions are personal to the defendant, although defendants may designate their lawyers to act on their behalf. These personal rights have been continued in the jury trial context where, for example, the defendant himself or herself has the right to exercise two peremptory challenges, to ask questions of witnesses, and to make a final appeal.

The aggrieved party—the victim or a close family member—has the right to be present at the preliminary hearing and the trial and to participate actively in the proceedings. While this is consistent with the Russian sense of justice, my limited observations revealed it to be a vehicle for the admission of damaging, prejudicial material that would otherwise be inadmissible. Furthermore, when a motion to dismiss a case would otherwise be granted, the victim can object and insist that the case proceed. Another unusual practice with respect to victims is that the aggrieved party has a right to seek civil damages within the criminal trial itself, and the court may make a monetary award based on the trial evidence.

Lack of Certainty, Finality

In addition to the practice of sending a case back for further investigation at any point during the proceedings, either side can appeal a jury verdict. First, the trial court has to sustain or approve a verdict, whether for conviction or acquittal, in a formal decision. It is this decision that can be appealed to a higher, intermediate court, and eventually to the Supreme Court of Russia. the formal appellate procedure regarding the legality of the trial court's decision is called "cassational review"; however, convicted defendants themselves, or citizens on their behalf, also can bring appeals even after the time for a formal cassational review has expired.

In addition to the uncertainty resulting from the availability of an appeal to either side and the procedure for stopping the trial and sending the case back for further investigation, it is difficult to predict the outcome of a case or ruling because, unlike countries with a common-law tradition, the decisions of a Russian court usually do not have precedential value. Thus, the lawyers and judge often make endless references to provisions of the Code of Criminal Procedure but rarely to a case interpreting it. There is little judge-made law as we know it, such as *Miranda*,

Mapp, and *Wade*. While statutes and regulations must theoretically conform to the Russian constitution, a court of general jurisdiction cannot nullify a statute by holding it unconstitutional. Judges will, however, refer directly to the constitution itself when they decide that the constitution and a statute are in conflict.

Preliminary Hearings

Once the investigator has completed the inquiry and recommended an indictment, the defendant must petition for a jury trial. If the defendant fails to apply at this stage, he or she has waived this right. When there has been an application for a jury trial, a preliminary hearing is held where the parties, including the victim, are present in court. The judge reviews the decision to indict and hears other procedural applications.

Article 69 of the Russian Code of Criminal Procedure provides that evidence obtained "in violation of the law" cannot be used at trial. Thus, the American practice of suppressing evidence is of particular interest to Russian lawyers. Because no case law precedents exist, the issues of exclusion of evidence are decided on a case-by-case basis. Thus, while inflammatory pictures and the contents of the dossier may not be admitted at trial, there is little real guidance as to whether other evidence should be excluded. It is an all or nothing proposition because the practice of admitting evidence with a cautionary instruction to the jury is not common. As noted above, impermissible references to a defendant's criminal past often come in through the victim's testimony or questioning.

Given the lack of precedent, the arguments over evidence are often hypertechnical. For example, the police are required to have two civilians present when they seize and voucher any item of physical evidence or search a premises. Defense lawyers repeatedly question where people were standing and what they observed in an effort to demonstrate police impropriety.

With respect to identification procedures, the police are required to conduct a lineup if the defendant is not a fugitive. Finally, given the prevalence of admissions and confessions, invariably the advocates argue coercion before the judge at the preliminary hearing and, when unsuccessful, again to the jury.

While the prosecutor has the burden of proving the charge to the jury, no formal order of a trial exists as with our practice: prosecution case, defense case, if any, and rebuttal. Instead, with the court's permission, the prosecution may put on a witness or the victim in an arbitrary sequence, or the defendant might be the first witness. Further complicating matters is the form of questioning. All witnesses are court witnesses. Thus, instead of the direct examination and cross-examination sequence that we are accustomed to, the witness takes the stand (or the defendant stands in the cage) and, after the judge asks some preliminary questions, the witness is asked to explain what happened. The question-and-answer format of Anglo-American practice is absent. Often the witness's narrative contains irrelevant and prejudicial material that is presented in such a manner that it is difficult to object to or to rectify.

A Russian Jury Trial

In our nation's capital the White House, the Capitol, and the Supreme Court stand out as distinctive symbols of the three coequal branches of government. Notwithstanding dramatic changes in the American landscape, in almost every region of the country the venerable county courthouse retains its place as a source of order and stability.

In Russia, the dominant role of the executive branch is reflected in every aspect of daily life. The legislative branch is just now struggling to be heard. The judicial branch ranks a very distant third in their political and cultural universe. Finding a courthouse in Moscow is a major challenge for native and visitor alike. Courthouses are not on the map and any inquiry as to the location of the district court (oblast) is met with a shrug.

The Moscow Regional Court, serving the area surrounding the city, is actually located within the city limits. It is wedged in between the zoo, an equipment storage yard, a parking lot, and a major subway station. It is a squat, four-story, off-yellow brick building with dark, damp halls, and public spaces. The entry way, hardly noticeable from the walkway it abuts, appears more like an alley or service entrance.

None of the people we met, however, were deterred by the shabby surroundings. Our hosts at the oblast court, Elena Lvova and Svetlana Dobrovolskaya, are leading proponents of the jury system and prominent scholars on Russian law and procedure. They also practice with the Moscow Regional Collegium. We had met them previously in Nizhny, where they were the most succinct and informative of the lecturers at a legal conference.

After a brief tour of the building and a crowded lawyer's suite that contained computers and other modern office equipment, we were ushered into the chambers of Chief Judge Svetlana Viktorovna Marsanova. Her office was not large by American standards but was well appointed and bright, in stark contrast to the rest of the building. Judge Marsanova and her deputy, Alexander Baitsurov, who also presides over trials, provided us with an overview of the court's operation and an update of their experience with jury trials.

The Moscow Regional Court was one of the first to begin jury trials in November 1993. To date, the judges have conducted the most jury trials in the entire country. Presently 50 percent of the eligible cases involve a defense motion for a jury, particularly when murder, manslaughter, or kidnapping is charged. As administrators, the main problems the judges encounter are insufficient funds to pay jurors, little legislative guidance regarding the mechanics of jury trials, and insufficient training for everyone concerned. As we left to observe a murder trial, the chief judge sheepishly confided to me her most pressing problem: "The lawyers are late or not available."

"If that's your major problem," I told her, "a fact-finding trip to America won't help."

The door to Judge Elena Vladimirovna Snegiryova's courtroom was locked and guarded by a machine-gun toting member of the militia. Once we were settled inside, however, the drab, institutional surroundings were quickly eclipsed by the animated proceedings. The four defendants sat on backless benches inside a steel cage to the extreme left. The jury sat against the right wall in a makeshift box, and in the area in front of the bench were tables for the victim's family, the prosecutor, the clerk, and the four defense lawyers. the room was rectangular, but the long axis ran left to right, resulting in the spectators being closer to the judge than the defendants were to the jury.

The four defendants had been charged with various crimes surrounding the death of police detective Alexander Alekseevich Shalimov. Defendant Stogov was charged with the first-degree murder of a policeman on duty and the theft of a policeman's identification; defendant Levin with not informing officials about a crime; defendant Zamanin with withholding information about a murder; and defendant Onisko with resisting arrest and fighting with a policeman on duty.

The judge's reputation as a fair-minded, intelligent, and sharp-tongued jurist was well deserved. The lawyers were knowledgeable and articulate, although seemingly at a loss as to how to relate to the jury. The incident that formed the basis for the prosecution was, I was told, a classic Russian tale: too much time, too much alcohol, too little common sense.

While the trial was a visiting clinician's dream, it was a nightmare by American due process standards. Each defendant had his own lawyer; however, a severance is highly unusual, even where defendants are charged with crimes of vastly different levels of culpability. The defendants had been incarcerated for months prior to trial, and they looked and sounded that way: their clothes were filthy and faces unshaven, and their hacking, tubercular coughing constantly interrupted the proceedings.

The judge began the formal proceeding by asking each defendant directly if he was guilty. The main defendant, Stogov, stated, "No, I'm only partly guilty. I only made three stabs." Then he added, "I'm absolutely not guilty."

"Will you testify?"

"Yes!"

"Now or later?"

"After a few witnesses."

Levin and Samanin pled not guilty and were equivocal about testifying. Onisko stated he was partly guilty.

The prosecutor proposed that the order of trial be the victim's representative, the defendants, and then prosecution witnesses. No one objected.

The victim's widow, Mrs. Shalimov, was called to testify. The judge warned her of the consequences of false testimony and admonished her not to speak of the victim's personal characteristics. The witness was told that the lawyers could question her and that the jury might also hand the court questions.

The prosecutor asked Mrs. Shalimov to tell all she knew about the incident.

"My husband was a detective. He was on duty that day. The shop where the incident took place was close to our home." She interjected that the defendants all had prior criminal records, but there were no objections or court reaction to her remarks. She stated that she had been called to the hospital, where she learned that her husband was gravely injured with knife wounds. To her knowledge, he had just received his monthly salary and he had been dressed in civilian clothes and had his briefcase with him. "I never received his police identification papers back."

The court invited questions by the defense counsel. The first lawyer asked, "How is it that you remember the day?"

"Well, it was Friday; we were going to our dacha the next day."

The next lawyer queried, "Please repeat how he was dressed?"

"A light shirt."

"When did you learn of his death?"

"Saturday morning."

"Were you told where he was found?"

"No, just that he was seriously wounded."

The third lawyer asked, "Did your husband drink only on weekends?"

"Usually!"

The victim's aunt, who was seated in the audience, stood up and shouted at the lawyers. The judge reminded her that her conduct was inappropriate and that there would be no questions or comments from the audience.

The judge then asked the defendants if they had any questions of the witness. All four responded in the negative.

Mrs. Shalimov asked the court if she could be excused from the remainder of the trial. "My child has been left without a father. I have been left without a husband! My child tells his friends his 'Daddy' is away. I must be home with my child, and also my mother is sick, I must care for her." In open court, in front of the jury, there was an argument as to whether an aunt could be the deceased victim's legal representative under section 130 of the Code, which specifies a "close relation" must be the legal representative. "His father and mother live in the Ukraine and they can't be here," Mrs. Shalimov added.

The judge ruled that the aunt could be the representative and that the widow could leave. The judge asked the widow if she was seeking damages for "moral reimbursement."

"Yes, and I'll return for the verdict."

"You're excused. If you can't return, you'll be informed of the result, and you'll have seven days to file any objection to the verdict."

Defendant Onisko stood up in the cage and was questioned by the prosecutor. He related that at about 1 A.M. he and the other three defendants needed to get money to buy vodka. They had been drinking earlier at Stogov's brother's place. He had not known Stogov or either of the other two defendants before that night. There were three girls there, too, one who was Stogov's sister Tatiana.

"Who suggested you should get money?"

"I don't recall. We went to the commercial kiosk but didn't ask them for money or vodka. They wouldn't have given us any!"

"Did people give you money?"

"I can't recall. [Pause.] Yes, people did, and we bought alcohol."

"You're healthy [i.e., capable of getting a job]. Didn't people question you as to why you were begging for money?"

"Not really. We received money from a man, and Stogov and I drank vodka behind the kiosk."

"A young man of 35 gave you money?"

"Yes. The man approached us himself."

"Did you fight with this man?"

"No, a fight started."

"Who started the fight?"

"I did."

"Did he insult you?"

"No. He said, 'I'm taking you to the sector [militia precinct],' so I hit him. He didn't look like a policeman."

"Did others participate in the fight?"

[No answer.]

"Did you have a knife?"

"No, I didn't have a knife."

"Did Stogov have a knife?"

"No."

"Did Levin or Zamanin have knives?"

"No."

"Did you use a knife?"

"No."

"Did you see Stogov strike the policeman with a knife?"

"No, but I was told by Stogov's sister that Stogov told her he stabbed the victim three times with a knife. I myself just rolled into the bushes and fell asleep. I didn't hear any further cries, noises, or signs of a fight. I was sleeping in the bushes three or four buildings away."

"You do admit you hit him?"

"Yes, but I only hit him with two punches with my hand. He was still standing after I hit him."

"Did you or Stogov kick him?"

"No."

"Did you learn that Stogov took the policeman's identification?"

"No."

"What were you wearing?"

"A brown coat and sneakers."

Onisko's own lawyer then asked him two questions. "Did the police officer tell you why you should go with him to the sector, and did the police officer show you his identification?" The answer to both questions was "No."

The prosecutor rose and asked the judge to read from the defendant's deposition in the investigator's file. It became evident that there were numerous contradictions between the defendant's testimony at his trial and his prior statements.

The judge proceeded to question the defendant. "You testified here today that the man gave you money. In your prior statement, you say that you asked numerous people, one by one, to give you money, and several people gave you money?"

"Well, earlier, people gave us money, and we bought vodka."

"Did you approach the victim, as your statement indicates, or did he approach you?"

[Silence.]

"Did you see him buy vodka?"

"No, we drank from our own bottle."

"Did he ask you to come to the station right away?"

"Yes."

"In the past, you stated that he asked you to come in the next day and ask at the desk for him. Today you tell us that after you punched him, the detective remained standing! Your statement indicates the policeman punched you and jumped on top of you on the ground!"

[Silence.]

The victim's widow, who had not left and who had quietly remained in the audience with the victim's aunt, shouted from her seat, "My husband is a small man; you are a large man. he could not have knocked you to the ground!"

"Well, it's true that he had me on the ground and was on top of me."

The judge instructed the defendant, who had been looking at the floor, to look directly at her when he answered.

"Did you see Stogov and the victim talking?"

"Yes; nearby, in front of an apartment house. They were arguing, just talking. Defendant Zamanin was close by them."

"Did you see the victim with a briefcase?"

"No."

"A man approached you with vodka, and you argued, and you never saw his briefcase?"

[Silence.]

"When you were on the ground, where was the bottle?"

"I went three blocks away and fell asleep in the bushes. At 5 A.M. I awoke and went home to my place."

"You testified that Stogov's sister told you that Stogov had struck a man three times with a knife?"

"I went home, not to Stogov's place."

"When you *later* spoke with his sister, was Stogov present?"

"Yes, at that point, we were at his apartment, and he was on the couch."

"Any further questions, lawyers?"

"Yes," the prosecutor said. "Mr. Onisko, could you see what the detective purchased at the kiosk?"

"No, I couldn't."

During the lunch break, advocate Svetlana Dobrovolskaya and the judge answered questions about Russian trial practice; and the judge allowed us to review the voluminous investigator file. They agreed that tactically the defendants should have waited until after the prosecutor had put her witnesses on the stand, but they felt that given the defendants' extensive pretrial admissions, it might not matter because their statements would come into the case one way or another. I inquired whether the Russian system had a rule like our *Bruton v. United States* to protect a defendant from being implicated by a nontestifying defendant's statements. They have no such severance procedure, but we were informed most defendants will testify anyway. We suggested that the defense lawyers appeared to be very passive, which was hardly consistent with what we had come to expect. The judge and our host assured us that these were very experienced and aggressive lawyers, but they were trying to "get a read" on the jury and had also been waiting until the widow left so as not to antagonize the jury.

When I asked why the prosecutor was allowed to question a defendant first, the judge explained that all witnesses are court witnesses.

The official file containing the chronological "protocols" [statements] of all witnesses concerned with the case was several inches thick. the defendants each receive their own copy of the indictment and are allowed to review and take notes of the contents of the file. In theory, however, the contents of the investigative file are not supposed to be mentioned to the jury by either side.

Given the extensive pretrial investigation and the admissions extracted during that period, the judge indicated that most defendants plead guilty, and often the only issue at trial is mitigation. Those who do not plead guilty inevitably change their testimony after the investigation to sway the jury and thus at trial there is endless examination of defendants regarding the consistency of their trial testimony.

I asked the judge why there were no sidebar conferences when the lawyers had legal arguments. She agreed that it was not a good practice to have lawyers argue in front of the jury, but it was a carry-over from the days of three-judge trials. She added, however, that what I had seen was tame compared to the yelling and screaming that often took place before a jury when she concluded her final charge to the jury. In the most belligerent manner, the lawyers would attack her charge as unfair and insist that the defendants were being framed. The jury, she lamented, was often influenced by this spectacle.

An equally disturbing problem, she felt, was the Russian procedure of submitting the issue of mitigation along with the three basic culpability questions. The jury is, or is supposed to be, unaware of a defendant's prior criminal record at this stage, and therefore, all too often, it votes for mitigation. One of the reforms she and her colleagues would like to see implemented is to have the mitigation issue taken up separately by the jury and, obviously, only after the defendant has been found guilty.

When the trial resumed, the main defendant, Vyachesav Nikolevich Stogov, rose to testify.

According to him, he and some friends had been drinking near the kiosk. Onisko got into a dispute with a man and the two fell to the ground. Stogov testified that he had attempted to separate the man from Onisko, and while trying to aid his friend, he slipped and fell. Gesturing, Stogov admitted having a knife in the sleeve of his coat.

The prosecutor rose to cross-examine the witness. "Why did you carry such a knife?"

"Well, it was only a kitchen knife."

"Were there any threats to your life?"

"Well, I pulled away from the struggle when the man said he would shoot Onisko. The man reached in his pocket."

"Where was your knife?"

"Here," he said, pointing to his left sleeve. "I was trying to throw it away so as not to cut myself. I threw it away and struggled with the man on the ground."

"Where was Onisko?"

"He was beating him, too."

"Why did you wrestle with him?"

"Well, by that time I was trying to get away. I was suffocating. I hit him once. He did not react. I hit a second time, and he did not react, so I hit him a third time."

"Did you strike him with a knife?"

"Yes I must have hit him with the knife. He screamed after the third hit. He ran toward a nine-story apartment house, and we didn't follow him. I ran home to Tatiana's house."

"Did the victim have a briefcase?"

"Yes, but I did not take his ID or his money, although I saw he had money when he bought his vodka."

"When you were all fighting, did the victim call for help?"

"The victim tried to get away from us and into the kiosk, but they threw him out. I tried to calm the man down when he was having the dispute with Onisko. I was not successful."

"Mr. Stogov, did you hear Onisko tell the court that in your presence Tatiana told him you stabbed the policeman?"

"I never told Tatiana what happened. I told no one."

"Well, was it your codefendant Onisko who told Tatiana what happened?"

"How could she know? I never told anybody what happened."

"Did you take the victim's police ID?"

"No. I never had his ID. I saw it the next morning lying on the table in Tatiana's apartment."

"Did you give it to someone?"

"No, I do not know where it went. I asked Tatiana where she got it."

"Did she tell you she picked it up at the scene?"

"I don't remember."

"One last time, did you ever tell Tatiana or Onisko that you stabbed the police officer with a knife?"

"No, no. I told no one that."

"Mr. Stogov, can you tell us why it is that you gave different testimony during the investigation?"

"Well, it was imposed on me!"

"The investigator was not at the scene, was he? How could he know the details, such as when Onisko cut and beat the policeman?"

"Well, it was Onisko who told the investigator that; I didn't. In fact, the investigator let him go under a promise of leniency, let him go and hide in another city, when Onisko told him I was guilty."

"Mr. Stogov, you testified here at trial that you hit Detective Shalimov with a knife?"

"Yes."

"But now you claim they beat you, but you did *not* confess. Why should they beat you and not have you confess?"

The defendant yelled to the jury, "I have been in detention for a year, but they let Onisko go. The investigators made me talk to them. I wasn't allowed to speak to any family. They didn't know my fate [whereabouts]."

"Mr. Stogov, you never made a complaint about being beaten by the investigator, did you?"

"No, no, I did not. How could I? It's the master's territory."

The judge interjected, "Answer the question!"

"My mother was told I wasn't alive. Investigator Gustov told my mother that I was dead."

"Mr. Stogov," the judge lectured, "You learned of these falsehoods that the police told your family from Onisko, not from Investigator Gustov or your mother! You know our law prohibits contact with family prior to trial."

Stogov was then questioned by his own lawyer. "Did you see Detective Shalimov buy any alcohol?"

"Yes, he purchased liquor. He bragged, 'I'll have liquor.'" He said to us, 'You have beer or vodka,' passing vodka around."

"Mr. Stogov, when you were punched, you threw the knife away?"

"I don't remember the details of the fight."

"What was your intent when you pulled the knife?"

"I had none. My head wasn't clear; I couldn't control myself. I didn't think about it. I needed to put an end to it. To get him off me."

The questioning of defendant Stogov and the remaining defendants continued for the next two days. If the testimony and the questioning sound confusing, it is because they were. The defendants changed their stories in midsentence and constantly contradicted previous trial testimony and their statements to the investigators. If the charge had not been so serious, the pathetic, rambling narratives would almost have been comical.

The remaining witnesses all testified for the prosecution. A colleague of the victim testified that he and Shalimov had stopped at the kiosk late in the evening after work and had a beer and a bottle of vodka. Detective Shalimov remained and bought another bottle of vodka, but his colleague testified that he had left and saw nothing of the altercation. A salesperson at the kiosk also testified. She recalled both policemen buying vodka. Shalimov was later approached by a man asking for money. Shalimov seemed friendly with him. Fifteen minutes later, at about 11 P.M., she heard the sounds of a fight. The salesperson at the neighboring kiosk testified that at about 11 P.M. a man who claimed to be a policeman, and who was very drunk, was hanging around. The salesperson asked him to leave, and 15 to 20 minutes later, he heard the sounds of a fight.

During the break on the first day of the trial, the judge had informed me that her intended charge to the jury would take approximately 90 minutes. Her practice was to summarize the evidence briefly, without giving an opinion or evaluation. She would also briefly review the positions of the parties. She would remind the jury of the presumption of innocence, instruct them to decide the case only on the evidence, and inform them about the process of deliberations and how to answer the three questions that would be put to them.

At the end of the testimony in *the Case Stogov et al.*, however, there were no closing arguments or charge to the jury. One of the defense lawyers asked that because of the numerous contradictions in the testimony of the defendants, all of their testimony should be excluded. The prosecutor asked that the case be resubmitted for further investigation, and the advocates agreed. The case was removed from the jury and sent back for further investigation. Of the 529,055 criminal cases handled in Russia in the first six months of 1995, 47,413, approximately 9 percent, were remanded in this fashion for additional investigation.

Conclusion

Obviously, four or five weeks with Russian lawyers and a few days observing Russian jury trials hardly makes one an expert on Russian criminal procedures. Yet the impression left by our trip is that Russian society—and the Russian legal system in particular—desperately needs to develop stable, independent institutions. The jury trial, whether based on the Russian nineteenth-century version or adapted from our Western due process model, can provide one such pillar.

Questions to Consider

1. How do day fines work? Could this form of punishment be expanded to include some crimes for which we have traditionally imprisoned people? Can this form of punishment provide more compensation for victims? Explain.

2. Given the apparent success of the day fine system in early American experiments, why do you believe this system has not been more widely adopted? What interests may be resistant to adopting it?

3. Access to our legal system is usually dependent on having sufficient money to purchase the gate-keeper services of lawyers. How might lawyers have a vested interest in limiting changes to our current system of access?

4. First Amendment freedom of the press is in effect the ability for us to know what is going on in public life. What aspects, if any, of public courts should be kept secret? Explain. What are the dangers of creating more secrecy?

5. Craig Bradley argues that changes designed to promote efficiency would improve the quality of criminal procedures. Which of his suggestions do you believe are the best and which of his reforms has the most danger of lowering quality as efficiency increases?

6. Which of the civil law rules regarding prosecutors do you believe would be worth trying in the United States? Which improvements would you have to see?

7. Russian courts are experimenting with numerous ways defendants, victims, and juries can become more involved in the court process. Which of these possibilities do you believe are worth trying here and why? Can you think of any other changes that would be worth trying?

Index